MILITARY AFFAIRS
IN
NORTH AMERICA
1748–1765

MILITARY AFFAIRS IN NORTH AMERICA
1748-1765

SELECTED DOCUMENTS
FROM THE CUMBERLAND PAPERS
IN WINDSOR CASTLE

EDITED BY

STANLEY PARGELLIS

ARCHON BOOKS
1969

SBN: 208 00797 0
LIBRARY OF CONGRESS CATALOG CARD NUMBER: 69-19219
PRINTED IN THE UNITED STATES OF AMERICA

ACKNOWLEDGMENTS

It is with the gracious permission of His Late Majesty King George V that I print these selected documents and reproduce these original maps from the rich collection of Cumberland Papers and Maps in the Royal Archives. To Mr. O. Morshead, Librarian of the Royal Archives, I am deeply indebted for his many kindnesses to me, and I am under especial obligations to Miss M. Mackenzie of the Division of Manuscripts and her staff. Her patience with me for several years past has been no less extraordinary than the care with which she has supervised the transcribing of documents. For their helpful suggestions and aid I should like to thank Dr. J. C. Webster of Canada, Miss Norma Cuthbert of the Huntington Library, Professor Leonard W. Labaree, and Professor Roy F. Nichols, chairman of the Beveridge Fund Committee of the American Historical Association. I owe much to the former chairman of that committee, Professor Ulrich B. Phillips, who will not see the book he encouraged me to compile. Finally I should express my gratitude to those friends of the late Senator Albert J. Beveridge who, by establishing the Beveridge Fund in his memory, made possible this publication.

New Haven, Conn.   S. P.

CONTENTS

INTRODUCTION

WILLIAM AUGUSTUS, Duke of Cumberland (1721–1765), the second son of George II, from whose private papers the documents in this book are selected, was captain general of the British army from 1745 to 1757. Highest ranking officer in the military hierarchy, his business dealt with everything which concerned the running of the army as an effective military unit, with the selection and promotions of its officers, with its discipline and drill, with the coördination of the various departments and boards which equipped, supplied, clothed, transported, mustered, paid, and quartered it. His connection with America, therefore, was with those units of the army which served there. A shadowy and incompetent figure he has appeared to most writers on the war in the colonies; these documents give the range of his interests and the extent of his influence.

Cumberland's involved position in the administration and government of his day needs to be understood before even his American papers can be rightly read. His tenure of his office marks one of the more interesting stages in the working-out in Great Britain of the constitutional adjustments between civil and military, which are for any state complicated, delicate, and important. While clearly to be decided in favor of the civil, especially after the administrative changes of 1855 and 1870, the issue was not finally settled until the army reforms of 1904. Throughout the eighteenth century the primary question involved was intensified by the nature of the constitution and by Parliament's exaggerated fear of a standing army. In Cumberland's time it was well understood that, to be efficient and fit to meet Continental troops, an army needed a unified, professional command, with a control over choice and promotion of officers completely free from the demands of political patronage. But Parliament refused to assign such authority to any one but the King, who, bound as he was by constitutional restrictions, seemed the only safe head. The army, therefore, became the King's especial concern. But in practice the King found it impossible to divorce his functions as head of the army and as head of the executive. His ministers depended upon every shred of patronage at his disposal to maintain his majority in Parliament. So after Ormonde's impeachment, when the post of captain general lapsed, inevitably military appointments came more and more to be dictated by the secretary of state. When the Jacobite rebellion and the war on the Continent made necessary the reëstablishment of a supreme command, Cumberland's appointment seemed to assure both the maintenance of the Hanoverian line and the military efficiency demanded by the war. Continued after the peace of 1748, his office became an immediate target for the same kind of attack as before. Pelham had to defend it against violent parliamentary criticism in 1751. He called it a post of dignity and not of power. He meant that with regard to promotion and employment of officers Cumberland possessed only the privilege of recommending, either directly to the King or through his ministers, and that with regard to the administration of the army, as distinct from its command, responsible civil ministers continued control. In the hands of the secretary at war, a civil minister with access to the King, were all matters concerning the financing of the army and the relations between the army and the civil population, such as recruiting, quartering, and marching of troops. The judge advocate general reviewed courts-martial; the Ordnance Board, a civil department, had charge of munitions. In theory, then, and such was Pelham's defense, enough limitations were imposed upon the captain general to keep him powerless under constitutional control.

But in the arena of practical politics many circumstances combined to force Cumberland into a position which seemed to men like Hardwicke and Pitt to challenge the adjustments of the constitution. He had unusual ability. Of the impression his incisive mind left on those he met, it is enough to recall Horace Walpole's remark that Cumberland was one of five great men he had known. He was the King's trusted son, and his father tended to give him a confidence enjoyed by no minister since Sir Robert Walpole. And because his rank was royal, he became in spite of himself the nucleus around which a parliamentary faction might grow. That faction, over a ten-year period, became formidable. It included men as vigorous as Bedford, Halifax, and Henry Fox, as well as Marlborough, Richmond, and Sandwich. After the break-up of the Prince of Wales's group in 1751 it offered the most dangerous challenge which the Old Guard had to meet. For Cumberland's faction tried to rely not only on the parliamentary interest its adherents had, but on the votes of army officers who had seats in Parliament and knew the value of Cumberland's favor. Moreover, Henry Fox, after Bedford the leader of the faction, held for ten years the post of secretary at war, which he administered in close conjunction with the captain general. The adjutant general, an officer in charge of drill and discipline under the secretary at war, became, log-

ically enough under these conditions, Cumberland's military secretary. Then in 1754, because the Duke alone could persuade the King to
send troops to America, the Newcastle ministry asked his opinion and
aid. Thenceforth he sat in cabinets when American policy was discussed, and from exercising the command over the army itself he came
to have more weight than any other individual in determining where
and how the army was to function abroad. Well might other men see
a threat both to their political aspirations and to the balance of the
constitution in such a situation as this one seemed to be: a military
bloc, led by able men, relying upon the King's unwavering confidence
in a royal personage at the head of the army, who, standing outside the
constitution, nevertheless appeared to dominate the civil ministers who
served it. There was a weak link, however, in that apparently irresistible
offensive. Once the King's good will was withheld, and a civil minister
possessing abilities equal to Cumberland's headed the government,
the captain general was bound to lose. One cannot understand the circumstances of Pitt's rise to power without realizing that Cumberland
was the great rival whom he had to destroy.

Whether the peculiar nature of Cumberland's power furnished any
real danger to the constitution is questionable. Regarded institution-
ally, it was probably more than is desirable in a civil government. But
Cumberland was not the man to use it unjustly. His latest biographer,
the Honorable Evan Charteris, makes clear that his ambitions were
not unscrupulous. That he had ambitions is obvious; he was willing to
utilize his parliamentary strength in passing an act to make him
Regent. But in reading of his decisions one is struck again and again by
the grounds on which he made them. He guided himself by the principle of loyalty to the throne and by his professional outlook, and in his
mind there could be no conflict between them. The army reforms for
which he was responsible improved the quality of officers and the
discipline of the rank and file. His opinions on policy, if not flawless,
were as statesmanlike as those of his successors. His ruthlessness in
Scotland in "The Forty-five" was born neither of cruelty nor of abstract justice, but of calculated expediency. And it is difficult to read
his correspondence or follow his career without accepting a contemporary judgment that, in a selfish age when political honor was low,
Cumberland held his personal honor the higher—so high indeed that it
seemed out of place, and inspired by an ancient and mysterious sym-
bol, the honor of a king.

Likewise to American affairs Cumberland applied his own criteria,
not always the same as those of the faction which used his name. His

parliamentary group identified itself more completely than any other with a vigorous anti-French policy in America. Ever since the capture of Louisbourg in 1745 a strong section of public opinion, backed by merchants with interests in the colonies, had been demanding that the ministry turn its attention westward. Some were definitely moved by the possibilities of trade expansion; some wanted only to protect the existing colonies from French attack; some saw that the capture of French territory in the New World would markedly decrease the trade, and therefore the power, of France. To Bedford and Fox alliance with such opinion may have seemed the most convenient means for embarrassing the Pelham-Newcastle ministry and for gaining cabinet rank. Certainly Bedford's colonial ventures after 1745, Halifax's spirited leadership of the Board of Trade and his parading the question of French encroachments in Parliament, and Fox's warlike orders in the autumn of 1754 are all open to that interpretation. But Cumberland supported the settlement of Nova Scotia, not for the public favor it would win, not even for the sake of trade and colonial security, but because it would contribute to the stability of Scotland and to the welfare of those soldiers left unemployed at the peace of Aix-la-Chapelle. Nor did the winning of an empire in the New World, not even for the effect it would have on French mercantile strength, appeal to him; Loudoun's assumptions that Canada, if conquered, would be returned to France at the peace (pp. 279–280) can be interpreted only as a subordinate's repetition of some one's statements. Pitt carried to even greater extremes a warlike policy in America, and his reinforcement of the army there, after he was firmly fixed in power in July, 1757, met with Cumberland's strong disapproval. To Cumberland, as a point of policy and not merely because he commanded in Germany, the war on the Continent came first, and when he had to choose between following the program to which his faction had apparently been committed and the interests of the royal family, he did not hesitate. In all such matters, as clearly as in the question of his personal ambition, Cumberland's principles remained constant: loyalty to the throne, and loyalty to the profession of arms.

The Cumberland papers bear out such an interpretation of his attitude toward American affairs. About 400 documents in the collection deal with American matters. Yet they leave an impression of having been accidentally amassed and carelessly kept. Some original letters have certainly disappeared, loaned or given by Cumberland to men who could use them. Those that remain show the character of the information upon which he acted, but seldom his actions. He gave his orders and made his suggestions by word of mouth, or through the adjutant general, whose original letters, with one exception, are not among his papers. Some hint of his conception of a captain general's authority can be got from his correspondence with Barrington and Holderness in the summer of 1757 (pp. 380–398, *passim;* 475–476), when he was in Germany, while the part he played in the determination of policy is suggested by the outlines of campaign plans and public documents which exist in a memorandum form with space for corrections and additions.

The American papers fall into five categories:

(1) Copies of letters and documents from public offices relating to questions upon which Cumberland's military opinion was asked.

(2) Copies of private letters to public officials or to private individuals passed on to Cumberland because they contained information of possible military significance.

(3) Original letters from army officers to whom had been granted the privilege of correspondence with Cumberland, either direct or through the adjutant general, Robert Napier. In practice this meant either commanding officers or engineers under the Ordnance Board. Cumberland paid especial attention to the engineering branch. St. Clair, as a deputy quartermaster general sent to Virginia before Braddock, and Prevost, a foreign colonel in the British service, were exceptions to the closely followed regulation that inferior officers could communicate with the heads of the army only through their superiors.

(4) Unsolicited original letters from officers and civilians with complaints or suggestions to make.

(5) Cumberland's own scanty private correspondence.

Of these 400 documents less than 100 have been printed elsewhere. About 100 would seem to be unique. More than 100 are unprinted letters and enclosures sent by Loudoun, available also in the Huntington Library and often in the Public Record Office. The remainder are either enclosures in other letters or copies from public offices.

A collection of this nature, amassed accidentally, some parts out of proportion to others, does not deserve to be printed *in toto.* The chief reason for printing any part of it is its comparative inaccessibility to scholars. Those documents have been selected which seemed valuable, the editor realizing, as all selective editors must do, that *value* is nearly as undefinable a term for the historian as for the economist or the philosopher. Some have been included because they concern the vexed question of colonial currency (pp. 3, 41, 244, 245), illustrate what some mercantilists thought of the colonies (pp. 68, 257), or state the proprietor's side of the Pennsylvania dispute (pp. 367, 368, 384) or an engineer's understanding of Western problems after the peace (pp. 455–471). But most of them possess a greater intrinsic unity than such a statement suggests. They deal with the primary problem of the military historian: Was the strategy followed in successive campaigns of the war best adapted to achieve its ends? Was the execution faulty or capable? Nothing of importance has been omitted, to the best of the editor's knowledge, which bears on the forming or the carrying-out of plans.

The reader who wishes to see these documents in their proper unity must have a clear notion of the two different kinds of military problems which the American war arena in the mid-eighteenth century presented. It is not adequate to consider them both as adjuncts to problems of naval strategy, after the fashion, admirable and final in its way, of Sir Julian Corbett. The war in the interior must be sharply distinguished from that on the coasts.

In the Canada which the French occupied, the nerve-centers were Montreal and Quebec, the only artery of supply from home was the St. Lawrence River, and the only means of access from the British colonies were two waterways: one by Lake Champlain and Richelieu River; the other by the upper Ohio, Lake Ontario, and the upper St. Lawrence. Those two waterways they could control by a series of forts, which strategically must be considered as outposts of Canada itself, and each fort was in easy and direct communication with the center. For defense Canada was superbly equipped. The only unimpeded access by water lay up the St. Lawrence itself, but for its protection the French relied upon Louisbourg, which only a daredevil would leave unstormed in his rear; upon the hazards of river navigation, which they exaggerated; and upon the impregnability of Quebec. For offense, on the other hand, Canada possessed no advantages. The French had but one stronghold, Fort Beauséjour, which directly threatened but one British province, Nova Scotia, and its lines of communication with the center were long and included an overland carry. To make a continuous attack in any other part of America the French would have been forced to change their military dispositions, to turn their outposts into bases, and to find other means of transport than bateaux. Such alterations in military methods were beyond French resources in the New World. They were condemned by their position to fighting a defensive war, and the only two captures of British forts which they made—Oswego and Fort William Henry, both stationed on their own waterways—must be regarded as moves wholly defensive. Under Montcalm the

French admirably adapted their strategy to their position, hoping to defer the conquest of Canada until the issue had been fought out in Europe and the diplomats had saved the day. Every move they made was a move for time.

If, then, there was to be war in America, the British had to wage it. Theirs was the strategy of offense, the conducting of the siege of Canada. Once Canada is considered as a single vast fortification, it becomes a simple matter to understand the problems confronting the British. (1) They had to roll up one or both of the interior approaches to Canada, proceeding fort by fort until they reached the center. (2) They had to make a direct attack on the nerve-centers themselves, up the St. Lawrence. As corollaries of these two main problems, they had (1) to prevent the whole of Canada's force being concentrated at a single point by setting on foot at least two expeditions each campaign, though not necessarily of equal strength, and (2) to lessen Canadian powers of resistance by cutting off the influx of supplies and troops from France. Surprise, as an element of strategy, the British could rarely use, for knowledge of every expedition reached the French either through colonials who traded with their enemies or through London offices. Their success depended upon sheer massing of strength at obvious points.

The character of that strength was no less important than the points where it was to be applied. Wherever the British attacked in the interior, they were separated by a watershed from their objectives, though they could make some use of water carriage on both sides. For the opening of their own lines of communication, and for maintaining them when opened, they needed boats for the rivers and men to handle them, wagons or sledges for land carriages, ships or armed scows on Lake Ontario and Lake George to transport artillery and keep the mastery, and men to serve as supply guards and scouts. Since their objectives were in every case fortified posts defended by European soldiers, they needed artillery, preferably large mortars, for no frontier fort could withstand thirteen-inch shells. For the technical side artillerymen and especially engineers were wanted. Lastly, they needed a small mobile force of trained officers and men, with enough reserves to garrison captured posts and maintain a lengthening line of communication. In brief, the British needed a small, highly trained army of experts, some of whom could be found only in the colonies.

These are the considerations which apply to any study of the war in the interior.

Attack against Louisbourg or up the St. Lawrence, on the other hand, was of a different nature. It involved a larger force and joint land-and-sea coöperation. In its simplest form, it meant nothing more than the employment of European methods. There was no difference either in tactical problems or in equipment between an attack on Louisbourg and one on Gibraltar or Rochefort.

There was a third area, Nova Scotia, which cannot be considered as falling within these two strategical categories. The problem there was as unique for the British as for the French. The British were on the defensive in Nova Scotia, and the capture of Fort Beauséjour achieved for them the same military purpose as did the capture of Oswego and Fort William Henry for the French. The British could not use the captured forts on the isthmus as a base for penetrating to the center any more easily than the French could make Oswego or the lower end of Lake George a base for invading New York. The tactical problems involved in the siege of Fort Beauséjour were comparatively simple and more European than American in nature: the British had the advantage of water transport to Fort Lawrence on the Missaguash River, where their landing could not be disputed, could cut the French communications with the north by encamping on Cumberland ridge above the fort, and could be assured of success the moment their heavy mortars were in place (p. 147). The operations on Chignecto Isthmus, therefore, furnish for both French and British an exception to the general strategy demanded of them.

Such are the factors, of geography, of technical equipment, and of personnel, which determine what the strategy of this particular American war should have been and provide the only feasible yardstick for evaluating the conduct of it in its several campaigns. It is notorious that Great Britain undertook an offensive war for which she was utterly unprepared and which she did not understand. It is equally notorious that it took an unusually long time to win it. By such criteria as these can perhaps be discovered where and how her military brains were numb. For military history differs from other history in this: that its objectives are limited, are definable, and can be judged in accordance with universally acceptable, scientific rules.

The diplomatic situation in 1755 required that the plans for the American campaign (pp. 45–48) be framed to avoid the appearance of aggression. War had not been declared, and the only excuse that can be made for these plans is that they represented a gesture against all four of the chief French encroachments on territory deemed British. For though they were sound enough on paper—the fall of the three interior forts would have begun the process of rolling up the approaches to

Canada—the details of their execution were the product of colossal con-
ceit and ignorance. Braddock should have been sent to New York, as
the anonymous author of the "Considerations" (pp. 36–39) argued
pointedly, if too tardily to be effective; and there he should have concentrated his principal efforts on Crown Point, even if it meant the
dispersal of the New England forces under Johnson. The taking of
neither Fort Duquesne nor Niagara, in spite of the effect the latter's
fall would have had on the Indians, was worth the labor and expense.
Improvement of communications to Oswego, strengthening of the forts
there, and construction of ships on Lake Ontario should have been the
sole objects of attention in the West. Not one of these expeditions, except Monckton's, was properly equipped, supplied, or manned. Johnson was helpless without supplies, transport, or boats (pp. 142, 150);
Shirley could find neither supplies nor an engineer. Braddock's expedition, except for the deficiency in wagons which Franklin could only
partially supply, was best fitted for success, but its excellent equipment
was vitiated by the commanding officer's failure to obey elementary
rules of European warfare (*Amer. Hist. Rev.*, XLI, 253–269). In general, however, it is scarcely just to blame either British or colonials for
the ill results of their first venture in the extraordinary technical problems posed by the American war.

Of the plans for 1756, with the conquest of Canada the unhampered
objective, Cumberland's rightly stressed the importance of New York
as the strategical center and emphasized the prime need of the supply,
transport, and naval services (pp. 133–136). But Shirley's plans, prepared from experience, were superior strategically in making Fort
Frontenac, and not Niagara, the point of attack in the West. One can
even sympathize with Shirley's fondness for his Kennebec River project, which offered both an unimpeded overland approach to Quebec
and an incentive to Massachusetts' participation (pp. 22, 314). But
that route only multiplied the obstacles present in New York and was
not feasible in this war. Shirley's attachment to it betrays his great
weakness, his failure to appreciate the difficulties of execution. Winslow's expedition of 1754 up the Kennebec did not even reach the point
where the stiffest natural obstacles began (pp. 54–58), while Mackellar's journal (pp. 187–218) and Vickers's report (pp. 286–290) picture
the pitiful state to which Shirley's technical incapacities reduced the
Oswego forts.

In the annals of this war the years 1756 and 1757, usually regarded as
a complete waste, saw the development of the only sensible procedure
the British could follow: preparation to cope with American conditions.

Whatever faults Loudoun had, and his own letters show them better than any comment, he came in the course of time to learn some of the essentials a successful army would need. He unified the command, so that an ill-equipped provincial army could no longer monopolize the most direct road to Canada (pp. 171–173). He set up a crown-owned transport system; he encouraged the formation of companies for special services; he improved the supply system up the Hudson River; he saw to it that his regulars learned to march with safety in the woods. He insisted upon more and better engineers and adequate artillery for colonial sieges. Amusing as his detailed plans for a winter expedition sound (pp. 399–402), it was the only expedition of the sort undertaken by a British general in this war, and it shows how far along the road one commander, at least, had come. Loudoun in time saw more clearly than Cumberland, who would have been the first to admit it, that American conditions demanded experts, not numbers. He did what his predecessors should have done, and when he was superseded England lost the ablest administrator, in matters of detail, that the war produced.

By 1757 the British were in a position to have ended the war within one or two years. It dragged on for four. The reasons can, perhaps, be reduced to this: until 1760 men with authority, both in England and America, failed to distinguish between the opposing tactical problems presented by attack by sea and attack overland, while men who did so distinguish were without authority. It is to Pitt's great credit that he understood the right use of a fleet; Sir Julian Corbett has written the final word on Pitt's system. For the first time there appears in the Cumberland papers in 1757 a set of "Considerations" (pp. 294–298) which outline it, and, by whatever hand written, they show a great sea power coming into its own. They are worth careful reading, as much for their fallacious assumptions about the war in the interior as for their appreciation of the tactical strength of joint operations. But Pitt never learned the real lessons hidden in the letters from New York. He could lift to command European soldiers, Amherst and Wolfe, but he never recognized the two geniuses the American war produced, Bradstreet and George Scott of the 40th regiment. Each was a superb leader of irregulars, and each, unlike Rogers, the ranger, knew how to use artillery against a frontier fort. They were men to employ for diversions while the main force concentrated elsewhere. The lack of appreciation shown Scott is one of the many tragedies of this war.

The strategy for 1757, begun by Loudoun and developed by Pitt, was seriously at fault. Intent upon winning the war by a single blow, Loudoun neglected to use the services he was training. He should have led an attack himself on Ticonderoga and have left the Louisbourg or Quebec expedition in the hands of men sent from Europe. His plans were those of a gambler: to attack Quebec directly, disregarding all else but the main objective. It was gambling with too great odds against him, and the plan did not deserve success. But in Loudoun's plans for 1758 no such flaw can be found; their strength sprang from experience, and little can be added to Robertson's comments on them, as far as interior operations are concerned (pp. 429–432). In the actual plans followed—those of Pitt—Abercromby was stupidly handicapped. Instead of the small mobile army of experts which it had taken three campaigns to develop, Abercromby could scarcely move without stepping on provincials who were not fitted for their job. And nothing can excuse the short-sightedness which stripped him of engineers (pp. 420–422). As for the attack on Fort Duquesne, it cannot even be considered a diversion, but rather a defensive move to protect the Pennsylvania frontier. It was necessary, as Loudoun saw, but not significant enough to deserve an independent command, and lacking in any of the strategical advantages gained by Bradstreet's expedition against Fort Frontenac. The weakness in Loudoun's plans was the soldier's inability to see, as Pitt saw, what a fleet could be made to do. The combination for a speedy victory had at last, by the end of 1757, been developed, Pitt with his system, his fleets, and his European-trained armies, Loudoun with his American services. Failure to use the combination prolonged the war. Cumberland's resignation as captain general (see p. 410) gave a free hand to Pitt, whose first use of his unrestricted power was to supplant Cumberland's appointee. Once more a civilian controlled British armies; the constitution had again been preserved.

There are no documents in this book bearing on the interior operations in 1759 or 1760. But one comment is necessary. It is questionable whether Amherst in 1759, for all his laudable military qualities, realized how to accomplish the task set him or grasped the objectives at which he ought to aim. He knew nothing previously of New York conditions, and a European soldier needed either youth or time to adapt his ideas to them. More slowly even than Abercromby, Amherst moved against Ticonderoga, hampered by similar clogs upon his freedom of movement. With nothing in readiness for immediate construction of boats to carry the necessary forces against Isle-aux-Noix, he settled down instead to build a fort. His diversion was launched not up the St. Lawrence but against Niagara, a post which would have fallen in due course had vessels been built to control the lake. His partial success derived from the fact that Wolfe, in the only operation in this war which

the British won with the odds against them, confined Montcalm to
Quebec. Amherst's ideas and actions would have been admirable ones
in 1756, but not when a British expedition had penetrated into Canada
with a chance of success. At it was, he left Wolfe's army, after its victory, with all communications cut and a near prey to Lévis's superiority (pp. 439–446).

It took Amherst as long to learn his lesson as it had taken Loudoun.
In strategy and execution his 1760 campaign was without flaw. Advancing by the three approaches to Montreal, with enough skilled
troops to open communications and enough reserves to defend them,
the British overwhelmed the remnants of French resistance. It was
done so smoothly that one is apt to forget the services which made it
possible, or the peculiar training which British regulars had got. To
move 10,000 men from Albany to Montreal by way of Lake Ontario
required a highly specialized supply and transport system and depend-
able rangers. Six years it took to teach each of a succession of British
generals that basic truth. If Amherst had been recalled at the end of
1759, by that rule which seemed to state that a general should be
superseded as soon as he had learned the lessons of one complete campaign in America, his successor would not have won the war until 1761.
And perhaps it would have gone on and on, each successive general
fighting himself, until the French died through sheer starvation. For of
the twelve great French fortresses in America toward which British
strategy was directed, eight fell with scarcely a shot fired as soon as
the British managed to reach them. That is not a very sporting record,
and neither is it war. If Wolfe's exploits at Louisbourg and Quebec
are excluded, the conquest of Canada sheds but faint glory on British
arms.

Responsibility for a string of failures is difficult to assess. England in
all her great wars has done some swapping of horses in mid-stream, but
seldom with the completeness of the change which replaced Cumberland with Pitt. Ideally, they should have worked together, each the
complement of the other. For Cumberland's way was to send over an
able soldier, let him learn from experience the special requirements of
the American terrain, fulfil his demands as far as possible, and give him
his head. Cumberland's letters to Loudoun leave no doubt of that
(pp. 255, 263, 325–326). But Cumberland's appreciation of sea power
was elementary; to him the navy was a convoy service, and its sole use in
operations the blocking of the St. Lawrence, as one ran a line of forts
across Flanders to keep out the French. And Cumberland had no power
to stir into action sluggish London departments. Pitt's strength lay

where Cumberland was weak. But neither Pitt's clear grasp of naval strategy nor his energy should excuse his defects. Knowing nothing of American warfare, sensing only that something was amiss, he tried to direct military operations in New York from London. After 1757 he made the plans; he decided the number, character, and distribution of troops; he arranged for their equipment. There is a strange inconsistency between Pitt's treatment of the navy and of the army. He let the navy alone; he never told Admiral Boscawen how many sailors a ship of the line ought to carry. He should have let his American generals alone, too, and believed them when they told him that one heavy mortar was worth a dozen twelves, and one company of ship's carpenters or boatmen or light infantry or rangers a whole untrained regiment. The years required to win Canada stand in ratio to the slowness with which Pitt grasped, if indeed he ever did grasp, a commonplace of war.

LIST OF DOCUMENTS

LIST OF MAPS

MILITARY AFFAIRS
IN
NORTH AMERICA
1748–1765

Some Observations on the Payment of the Troops in the West Indies, 1741/2 [1]

(COPY)

Species	Sterling Value	Passes in Currency in Jamaica for	Which for every £100 sterlg is at the Rate of	And every £100. Sterlg Carried to Jamaica in	and deliver'd there in Currency for Bills at 125 p Ct produces Sterlg in London — or	a Gross Profit Sterlg p Cent of
A Guinea	£1. 1. –	£1. 8. 9	£136. 18. –	Guineas	£109. 10. 4⅘	£9. 10. 4⅘
A Port Ps of	1. 16. –	2. 10 –	138. 17. 9	Ports	111. 1. 7½	11. 1. 7½
A Pistole	– 16. 8.	1. 3. 9	142. 10. –	Pistoles	114. –. –	14. –. –
A Moider	1. 7 –	1. 18. 9	143. 10. 4	Moiders	114. 16. –	14. 16. –
The medium of these Four different Species is			£140. 9. –	and delivered in Jamaica as above produces	£112. 7. 2 or	£12. 7. 2
of Ports Pistoles and Moiders			141. 12. 8.	....	113. 5. 7.	13. 5. 7
of Pistoles and Moiders			143. –. 2.	....	114. 8. –.	14. 8. –
of Ports and Moiders			141. 4. ¼	....	112. 9. 2¼	12. 9. 2¼
And if Moiders only are Sent			143. 10. 4.	....	114. 16. –.	14. 16. –
Or if Bills are drawn from thence Suppose at 140 p Cent			140. –. –.	....	112. –. –.	12. –. –

The Charge to the Contractors, if they send Specie from England, may be Reckon'd Viz^t.

Freight .... 1½ or say 2 p Ct
Insurance 3½ 4
Commission 2½ 3
other Charges .... ¾ 1
Interest 6 Months. 2 2
10¼ or 12 p Ct

So that their Profit or Loss must be in proportion to the Species they send, which hitherto have Chiefly been Ports & Moiders, the Medium whereof is £141.4.—Producing £ 12.9.2¼ sterlg p Cent.

But if their Agents in Jamaica take up Money there & draw on them here, suppose, at 140 p Cent which is the Price of good bills in Currency, then their Charge would stand Nearby thus Viz^t.

---

[1] This document would seem to have found its way into Cumberland's possession in connection with the 1754 discussions about the money contract and the payment of troops on colonial service. See pp. 41–43. The negotiations between the Treasury and Peter Burrell and John Bristow, the money contractors for Cathcart's expedition, can be followed in *Calendar of Treasury Books and Papers, 1739–1741*, pp. 287, 326, 482, 512, 561; *1741–1745*, pp. 6–8, 12, 31.

Commission in Jamaica .... 2½ or 3 pCt   ⎫ And the profit on 140 Ja-
Commission & other Charges here ... 2   2½   ⎬ maica Currency redeliver'd
                            4½   5½ pCt ⎭ for Bills at 125 pCt £12. —. —
                                           Charge .... 5.10. —
                                           Net Profit   £6.10. —

But as 140 p Cent was not Certain, suppose they had drawn at 135 p Cent, the Medium betwixt 140 & 130 p Cent, which too is nearly Equal to the present Rate of Silver there, and redeliver'd the same at 125 p Cent the Difference then would have been   8. —. —

                                       Charge .... 5.10. —

                                 Net Profit .. £2.10 p Cent

And thus their gain would have been greater as the Exchg. might happen to be from 135 to 140 p Cent.

Now the Supposition is that the Government might have sent out Specie as above, or having sent part to supply Immediate Wants have ordered the Deputy PayMasters to draw for more as they most Conveniently Could do it, by which the Troops in the West Indies could have been paid their Subsce. [subsistence] at more than 120 p C^t, the Rate first Agreed with the Contractors, & even at better than 125 p C^t, the present rate of payment there, if Ports & Moiders had been the Specie sent. for as the Charge to the Government would have been less than to the Contractors, Viz^t.

    Freight .... O p Cent, being in His Majestys Ships
    Insurance, if Needfull 3½ or 4 "
    other Charges .... 1 .. 1½
    Deputys Clerks &c   1 .. 2 ... or at fix'd Salaries which pos-
      their Salaries about   sibly would not have amounted
                                           to so much as 1 or 2 p C^t on
                                           the whole.

             5½ or 7½ p Cent, there would have been a saving at 125 p Cent even on Guineas the lowest Denomination; and this Saving would have been greater in Proportion as the other Species increase in Value in Currency. And if the Deputy Pay-Masters had drawn from 140 to 135 p Cent the Government could not have Lost by paying the Troops at 125 or 126 p Cent.

A Calculation likewise has been Made of the Profits arising to the Contractors for supplying the Army with Money; and as this has been done on the footing of the first Agreement with them Viz^t 120 p Cent, and on Moiders only which are at the rate of £ 143. 10s. 4d. Jam^a Curr^y for £100. Sterlg. which Sum deliver'd there at 120 Curr^y p C^t produces in London 19.11.8 p C^t Sterlg Profit; and this Computed for the

Whole of the Troops employed there, as if Each Regiment had been Constantly Compleat, whereby the Gain from the Contract is Raised to a very large Sum, and consequently the loss to the Troops much Magnified, it will not be Improper to set this Matter in a truer light, & to observe in the first place, That these Troops were paid at 120 p Cent for about Two Musters only and that in Ports as well as Moiders, the Medium whereof is £141.4.—Jam^a Curr^y; & secondly, That no more money was to be Received by Contract than what was Necessary to pay the Effectives in each Regim^t whose Numbers lessen'd daily; so that the Gain arising from it, considering the Charge, cannot amount to the Sum it is given out to be.

But in order to Lighten the Loss and to Redress any hardship that might be thought to Arise to the Army from this Contract, & as the Agents, named by the Contractors in Jamaica, declined the Transacting of their business there, & that the Deputy Pay Masters were obliged to draw on their Principals, the Pay Master General of His Majesty's Forces immediately ordered them to Pay the Troops there at 125 p Ct. and to Reserve the difference betwixt what they drew at, & what they paid at till further orders; and this has been the Rate ever since the 25th April 1741.

A Certain Rate must be fixd for the payment of Troops serving abroad; nor must it be allow'd to Vary, to prevent Mutiny & Complaints among Men who Know little of the Nature of Exchanges; and this fixd Rate must be such as the difference betwixt it & the Current Exchange of the Place at a Medium,* will answer the Charge of supplying them with Specie for their Subsistence, whither the same be done by Contractors or by the Government, unless there was to be an Allowance by Parliament, for defraying such Charge, over and above what is Granted according to the Estimates for the full Pay of Troops so Employed.

Besides the Rate now fix'd, Viz^t 125 p Ct is agreeable to an order of Council in the Reign of Queen Anne which Regulated the Par with our Colonies in America at 125 p Ct, Valuing the Ounce of Silver here at 5/4, and there at 6/8, which is Exactly 1/4 more than Sterlg and what is Call'd Currency. and tho this Regulation has greatly Varied since that time in the different Colonies, and consequently their respective Rates of Exchange; yet in Virginia, even at this day, the Ex-

---

* That is; Suppose the Exchange from Jamaica to London to Vary from 140 to 130 p Ct. the Medium of that is 135, and the Rate of Payment now fix'd being 125 p Cent the Difference betwixt them is 10., which at 125 p Cent gives £8.—.— Sterling for the Charges, but if taken at 135 gives only £7.8.1 for the Charges.

change is from 125 to 120 which is under that Par; and in Barbadoes it did not rise for a long time above 128 p Ct. 'tis true the present Value of the Ounce of Silver in Jamaica, possibly Occasion'd by a former Want of good Bills, is 7/2 Currency which may be said to have Constituted a new Par with that Island at about 134⅜ p Ct and this Price of Silver raised the Value of Bills from 135 to 140 p Ct and upwards, and probably Bills will Continue at this Value till Silver Falls there, because Merchants who Remitt, chuse Rather to take good Bills than to send Bullion home, while the difference of the Price of Bills does not Exceed that of Bullion above the Freight & Insurance attending a Remittance in the last. for Instance Silver to the Value of £100

Sterlg cost's in Jamaica at 7/2 Curr^y p Ounce   £134. 7. 6

Freight home at 2½ p Ct   3. 7. 2¼
Insurance at 4 p Cent ..   5. 7. 6

£143. 2. 2¼

So that a Bill of £100 Sterlg bought in Jamaica for 140 Currency is a Cheaper and more Convenient Remittance by £3.2.2 Curr^y but should the price of Silver happen to fall, which it may do being a Commodity, the Exchange must follow; and as this holds in all Exchanges and that the same Vary and Fluctuate from time to time, a Certain rate for the Payment of Troops whether they serve in America or Europe, must be fix'd; and it must be such as abovemention'd; for none but Merchants who understand Exchanges can Deal in them, or Attend to their Daily Variations; and Payments following those Variations are Altogether unfit for Armies, who Knowing but very little of the Matter would be apt to Mutiny on a falling Exchange.

BEDFORD [1] TO CUMBERLAND
(A.L.S.)

London. Oct: 11th 1748.

private

S^r

I received of the 9th instant, the Letter your Royal Highness was pleased to honour me with, and shall according to your directions, turn

---

[1] John Russell, Fourth Duke of Bedford (1710–1771), opposed Walpole in the 1730s, identified himself in the 1740s with Sandwich and Halifax, and somewhat less closely with Gower, Chesterfield, Cobham, and Pitt. First lord of the Admiralty in the Pelham coalition ministry of 1744, he supported the New England expedition against Louisbourg, and in 1746 forced upon his colleagues a scheme for the conquest of Canada. Secretary of state from 1748 to 1751, he had much to do with the settlement of the town of Halifax. He lent his strong parliamentary influence during these years to the group formed about Cumberland. He was forced out of office by Newcastle in 1751, and served as lord lieutenant of Ireland in Pitt's first two administrations.

in my thoughts, what encouragements, it might be proper to grant to any part of Lord Loudon's Regiment, or other Highlanders, his Majesty may not think proper to continue in his Service in Europe, to induce them to settle in, and people the Colony of Nova Scotia.

When I first had the honour to mention this to your Royal Highness, it was only designed by me, to suggest to Y.R.H.ˢ consideration, a Plan which (if it could be put in execution) might render these People usefull to his Majesty in North America, when their Service should be no longer required in Europe; and I was the more confirmed in opinion of the utility of some Plan of this Sort, for disposing of, in a proper manner those Highlanders, who were to be disbanded out of the Highland Regiments, as I feared many of them would take on in foreign Services, and the remainder might be judged not proper to settle again in their own native Country, under their Chiefs, of whom the loyalty of some might be under just cause of suspicion, especially as these Men by having continued so long in his Majesties Service, must have acquired a thorough knowledge of their Arms, and been accustomed to, the discipline of the Army. As no Plan for the sending these people to Nova Scotia, can be put in execution without incurring an additional publick expence, I believe it will be necessary, before I digest anything to be submitted to Y. R. H.ˢ determination, to consult with Mʳ Pelham, how far the present exigencies of affairs, will permit an expence of such a nature to be undertaken at present, and as I hope it will not be long, before I have the honour of paying my duty personally to your Royal Highness in England, I fear it will be impossible for me to prepare any thing for Y. R. H.ˢ consideration before that time.[2]

Permit me, Sʳ, to congratulate your Royal Highness, upon the pleasing prospect of our Affairs at Aix la Chapelle, and to assure you that I am with the highest respect and duty, Sʳ, Your Royal Highness's most faithfull, and most obedient humble Servant

BEDFORD

[Endorsed] Lond. The 11ᵗʰ Octʳ 1748 The Duke of Bedford Recᵈ the 26ᵗʰ N S. Answᵈ the 29ᵗʰ

---

2 Cumberland's letter to Bedford of October 4/11, Bedford's report on October 28 of his conversation with Pelham, and Cumberland's final reply of November 12, are printed in *Correspondence of John, Fourth Duke of Bedford*, edited by Lord John Russell, I (1842), 563–564, 572–574, 578–579. Bedford originated the proposal to settle Loudoun's regiment in Nova Scotia. Cumberland acceded partly for the sake of the soldiers, partly from the same reasons advanced by Bedford in the above letter, and partly because he was unwilling to land a regiment of Highlanders in England. The project was laid aside on grounds of expense, the ministry being unwilling to send to Nova Scotia a regiment still on the establishment.

Colonel Edward Cornwallis [1] to Robert Napier [2]

(L.S.)

Sir

Upon considering the State of this Province, I am obliged to represent to His Grace The Duke of Bedford & The Lords of Trade that there is an absolute necessity for greater Force In order to secure & effectualy settle it. I know my letters will be laid before His Royal Highness, yet when Troops are demanded I think it my Duty to acquaint him with it & give my reasons for so doing.

One Regiment, Six Companys of Gen. Philips's, one Company of Rangers are all the Force here at present. With these I have to guard & protect an Extent of 200 miles to reckon only the Peninsula, within which there is a number of Indians a declared Enemy, waiting Opportunitys to do all the mischief they can—the greatest part of the Inhabitants, The Accadians certainly more Friends to the French than us. The French excite & support both the Indians & Inhabitants & will stick at nothing to hurt the Settlement. They will probably prevail on the Indians of Canada & St. Johns River to join those of this Province.

The Governor of Canada is making Incroachments in the most unwarrantable manner. On pretence of hindering us to make Settlements before the limits are settled he has sent Detachments to three different Places near the Entrance of the Peninsula, so as to pour in the Savages upon us & succour them as he pleases.

For some time Halifax alone, already a town of great extent will require one Regiment to secure it. Annapolis Royal cannot have less than 200 men. There must be 100 men at least at Minas & as many at

---

[1] For Edward Cornwallis (1713–1776), who acted as governor of Nova Scotia and became colonel of Phillips's foot on March 30, 1750, see sketch by James S. Macdonald, "Hon. Edward Cornwallis, Founder of Halifax," in Nova Scotia Hist. Soc. *Coll.*, XII (1905), 1–17.

[2] Robert Napier was adjutant general, with the rank of colonel, and Cumberland's secretary for military affairs. He was therefore the normal channel of intercourse between army officers and the captain general. Napier entered the army in 1722 as an ensign in Pearce's 5th foot, became a lieutenant in 1723, and quartermaster of the regiment in 1725. On January 21, 1738, he was appointed captain in Kirke's 2d regiment of foot. He served on the staff at Ghent, 1742–1743, as deputy quartermaster general (though *Notes and Queries*, Vol. 155, p. 64, names a William Napier in that post, his name is not in the Army List of 1740), after Fontenoy was promoted to be lieutenant colonel and deputy quartermaster general to the army in the Netherlands, and in 1746 was made adjutant general of South Britain. He became colonel of the 51st regiment in 1755; major general in 1756; colonel of the 12th foot in 1757; and lieutenant general in 1759. He died in November, 1766. Richard Cannon, *Hist. Record of the Twelfth Regiment of Foot* (1848), p. 99.

the Fort upon the Bay. So that I have no Troops at all to send upon any Emergency, or to spare for the protection of other Settlements that may be proposed.

I am firmly of Opinion that the Province cannot be Secure without a good Strength at the Isthmus, both against the French in case of War & The Indians at all times. This without a whole Regiment be sent there cannot be undertaken, as nothing will more exasperate both French & Indians.

The Settlement is advanced beyond expectation. I hope you got the plans sent you. I am very truely yours etc

ED: CORNWALLIS

Halifax Dec^br 6th 1749

COLONEL ALEXANDER DUROURE [1] TO ROBERT NAPIER

(A.L.S.)

Sir

Since my landing here with our late Governor Mr Mathew, my time has been imployed in getting the best Information I was able of the State of this Regim^t. Indeed I have Soon been convinced that it labours under many hardships that all other Regiments in His Majesty's Service are happily free from.

As these hardships mostly arrise from the Scanty provision made by the Island for the lodging of it as a body of regular troops, Considering the Climate and our Numbers, as likewise from the trifling addition of pay when compared to the Excessive prices given for all necessaries of life, I have colected from the Knowledge of the Eldest Officers here, and my own observation, such facts as plainly evince how much both Officers & Men suffer, as likewise the tendancy it must have to prevent that Discipline being carried on, which alone can make this body of any Military Service to the Island.

These facts I had prepared to lay before the Legislature of this Island, by the means of our late Governor, but his Ill State of health, and ensuing Death prevented Me, since which I have adressed this plain State of the Case, to the Council & Assembly of the Island. A

---

[1] Alexander Duroure (1692–1765), younger son of Francis Duroure, a refugee French officer in Ireland, entered the army in 1714, became a captain in 1722, major of Douglass's Marines (with whom he served on the Cartagena expedition) in 1739, lieutenant colonel of Wentworth's 24th foot in 1741, and colonel of the 38th foot, stationed in the West Indies, in 1751. He was an elder brother of Scipio Duroure, Napier's predecessor as adjutant general. He became colonel of the King's Own Regiment of Horse in 1756, and lieutenant general in 1760. He died at Toulouse. Charles Dalton, *George the First's Army, 1714–1727* (1910), I, 219, n. 26.

Coppy of which I take the liberty to send you, as such an appeal to the publick here, may be less suspected of partiality to the Corps, than any representation I could do my self the honnour to transmit to you for the Information of His Majesty or His Royal Highness.

I have confined my self barely to facts as a very ample Discusion of most of them already lies before Lord Holderness, and some of a late date I believe before Lord Halifax, through the Channel of Mr Sharp, who is Solicitor to the Island. All which, as they are prior to my time I may not be a Sufficient Judge of. Tho' from what I have seen, & hear'd, since I am here, I am inclined to believe, nothing but strict truth was aimed at by those who upon several occasions have represented in behalf of the Regiment.

You will perceive Sir in this adress to the Publick that I acquaint them I am about to Discharge a Number of Men who for a considerable time past have been incapable of Service through distempers and ailings Contracted in this Island and Incurable here.

As the Island have obliged themselves to be at the Expence of removing to England a Number of such not exceeding ten in a year; I have by this opportunity sent such as will I hope be thought objects deserving His Majestys bounty at Chelsea; Ten more of the same Kind the Island will provide for in some of their small Forts, and the like number tho utterly unfitt for Soldiers can find a maintenance amongst the Inhabitants. Indeed there are still more I could wish to be rid of, so fatal is the Havock that has long attended this Regiment, from the nature of the Climate, and the miserable Situation it has always been in.

This reform would in part have been atempted sooner, by the Officer Commanding in my absence but the low Numbers the Regim^t was reduced to when I was appointed to the Command of it, would not admit of a greater diminution untill Recruits were sent out. And from the best Judgement I can make, the Numbers that dye yearly, and those that must be descharged as Incurables, will render it absolutely impossible to keep up to a Number of Effective Men fitt for Service in any proportion equal to what other Regiments may do in temperate Climates, and where a better provision is made for their Subsistance.

However as it is my Duty I shall have the strictest attention that the Noneffective fund be appropriated soley to keeping up the fullest Numbers that may be.

I can hardly Sir find expressions strong enough to point out the wretched condition of the Subaltern Officers, and private Men. Permit me therefore to become an Advocate for the former, that through your

Intercession with His Majesty they may be paid the Arrears due to them since December 1746.

For what ever cause of Suspicion may lye against those who could profit from regular Returns not being sent to your Office during some time, as from all other Regiments; As the Subalterns could reap no benefit from such an Omission, you will I believe think their case full hard, and perhaps unpresidented, should they suffer so essentially through the fault of others: For as they were not conscious any neglect of their duty had subjected them to such a loss, they have as their necessities drove them borrowed on the Strength of that fund, and in consequence are daily exposed to the severe effects of their Creditors Impatient for want of payment.

I shall not at present trouble you with a farther detail of the Regiment, as no representation at this distance could point out to you as I could wish its true State in every particular: Permit me therefore to hope that through your Protection I may live in hopes ere long to sett before you personally several things in a clear light. I have unfortunately more reason to press your Interest in this Instance than I wish I had. The excessive heat of this place affects me so much more than it did formerly, that I am apprehensive any continuance here must shorten my days, and this I assure you does not proceed from the *Helvetick Malady,* which forty five years Service in various Climes must long ago have cured me of. So that could my residence here further the good of His Majestys Service in the case of this Regiment, my attachment to my duty would make me runn any hasard with great chearfulness. But as I flatter my self my character stands unsuspected of the least tardiness in point of duty, strickt truth Warants me to say that my abiding here can no way conduce to that end, while the Regiment stands Circumstanced as it must do in this Island.

I was just going to conclude this Letter to you Sir when your Commands of the 29th June relating to Lieu^t Colonel Talbot have been deliver'd to me, which I shall be sure to comply with.

As the Legislature of this Island have desired a longer time to give in an Answer to my representation to them, I must wait their leasure to transmit it to you, and in the mean while, beg leave to subscribe My self with great truth and Respect,

Your Most Obliged and Most Obedient humble Servant

DUROURE

St. John's In the Island of Antigua Sep^{tr} 21st 1752

[*Endorsed*] Col^l Duroure Antigua Sep^{tr} 21st rec^d Novr 14. 1752.

An Account of the Forts in Louisiana and Canada [1]
(copy)

La Balise Isle, à l'Entrée du Mississipi.

Fort de Terre; Soldats 200, Canons 24.

Au Detour à L'Anglois.

Deux Forts de Terre: L'un sur un des Bords et l'autre sur l'autre; Soldats dans les Deux Forts 150, Canons 30, Maisons d'Habitants 40. Il y a beaucoup de Nègres pour faire l'Indigo.

La Nouvelle Orleans Capitale du Païs.

Il'y vient Journellement des Vaisseaux frettés pour le Roi chargés de soldats, et de Provisions et pour l'utilite de la Colonie ces Vaisseaux s'en retournent chargés d'Indigo de Boisure et de Mats pour les Vaisseaux. Les Vaisseaux Espagnols ÿ viennent avec beaucoup de Vin et d'olives. Et l'on y fait beaucoup d'Indigo, du Ris et du Maiz. Il ÿ a deux beaux Corps de Casernes; il y a 5000 Soldats environ 8000 Habitants et au moins 12000 Nègres.

Chez les Oumas.

Petit Fort de Bois dans un petit Village Sauvage; soldats 50, Canons 6, et quelques Habitants.

Au Village de Alleman.

Fort de Bois; soldats 50, Canons 4, environ 600 Habitants et 2000 Nègres, pour travaller à l'Indigo, au Ris et au Maiz.

à La Pointe coupée.

Village, Fort de Bois; soldats 50, Canons 8, environ 800 Habitants et 3000 Negres pour faire de la Charpente de Maison, que les Vaisseaux emmenent dans les Isles de l'Amerique.

Chez les Natchitoches.

Fort de Bois; soldats 100, Canons 4, situé sur la Riviere Rouge à 4 Miles des Espagnols. Habitants environ 300 et 500 Negres. L'on n'ÿ fait que du Maiz.

Chez les Natches.

Fort de Terre; soldats 100, Canons 12, il'ÿ a deux Habitants et une 100ne de Négres pour faire du Tabac: le Fort est situè sur une Montagne assez élévéé.

Chez les Arquantchas ou Akansas.

Fort de Bois; soldats 200, Canons 4. Habitants environ 200, et une 100ne de Negres pour faire du Tabac et du Maiz.

---

[1] The first part of this document to the final paragraph on p. 13 has been re-punctuated by the editor.

Le Grand Oviat.

Fort de Bois; soldats 200, Canons 8, Habitants environ 500, et Negres 300, pour faire du Maiz et quelque peu de Bléd.

Le Petit Oviat.

Fort de Bois; soldats 100, Canons 4, Habitants environ 100 et Negres 100 pour faire du Tabac et du Maiz.

chez les Illinois sur le Mississippi.

Fort de Bois; soldats 600, Canons 12, il y a 5 Villages Francois dont il y en a Deux où il y a des soldats, Caszasiat et l'Etablissement. Les Autres sont gardes par les Habitants Eux-mêmes. Il y a Une Saline, une Mine d'Argent et Une Mine de Plomb à 20 Milles des Villages; de l'autre Coté de la Riviere, il y a dans les 5 Villages environ 6000 Habitants et 5000 Negres. On y fait beaucoup de Bled et du Maiz. Les sauvages Ennemis viennent souvent donner des Allarmes à ces Villages.

Les Cachot.

Fort de Bois; soldats 50, Cans 4, Habitants point.

Les Missouris.

Fort de Bois; soldats 50, Cans 4, Habitants point.

Les Cant ou Cansas.

Fort de Bois; soldats 50, Cans 4, Habitants point.

La Mobile situé au Bord de la Mer.

Fort de Brique; soldats 3000, Canons 25. Habitants environ 3000, et Negres 5000, pour faire de l'Indigo, du Goudron beaucoup de Mâts pour les Vasseaux du Ris et du Maiz.

Chez les Alibamous.

Fort de Bois; soldats 50, Canons 4. Habitants point.

Les Tonbebec, ou Tombêche.

Fort de Bois; soldats 50, Cans 2, Habitants point.

Le Grand Baicoux.

Fort de Terre; soldats 50. Canons 8, Habitants environ 200 et Negres 300 pour faire du Ris du Maiz et de l'Indigo.

Quand nous avons deserté il y avoit dans le Pais 12000 soldats, la Desertion y est forte; il y en a beaucoup qui vont aux Espagnols. Nous avons deserté des Illinois le 16 Mars 1752 au Nombre de Vingt et trois, il y en a eu un de noié et un de perdu dans le Bois. Nous sommes arrivés au Nombre de Vingt et un, Aux Chaovanons Le 26 May 1752.

ETAT DE LA NOUVELLE FRANCE

	Soldats,	Canons	Maisons Habitants
La Balise			
Fort de Terre situe sur le Bord de la Mer .	200	24	
Detour à L'Anglois			
2 Forts de Terre aux Bords du Mississipi			
L'Un d'un Coté et l'Autre de l'Autre ..	150	30	
Sur l'un des Bords			50
La Nouvelle Orleans			
Capitale du Pais	5000	40	600
Les Oumas			
Fort de Bois	50	6	
Village d'Alleman			
Fort de Bois	50	4	20
La pointe coupée			
Fort de Bois	50	4	250
Les Natchitoches			
Fort de Bois	100	4	100
le Village est situé sur le Bord de la Riviere Rouge à 4 Miles des Espagnols.			
Les Tonicas			
Fort de Bois	50	2	
Les Natches			
Fort de Terre	100	12	
Les Acansas			
Fort de Bois	200	12	100
Les Illinois			
Fort de Bois	600	12	260
Misere petit Village			
Fort de Bois sans Garnison			
La Prairie des Roches			
Village sans Fort			100
L'Etablissement			
Fort de Bois	200	8	150
Petits Villages			
Fort de Bois sans Garnison			100
Les Cachots			
Fort de Bois........................	50	4	

	Soldats	Canons	Maisons Habitants
Les Missouris			
Fort de Bois	100	4	
Les Canses			
Fort de Bois	50	4	
Le Grand Oviat			
Fort de Bois	200	8	200
Le Petit Oviat			
Fort de Bois	100	4	60
La Mobile			
Fort de Briques	3000	24	400
Tonbebec ou Tombeche			
Fort de Bois	50	2	
Alibamous ou Albama			
Fort de Bois	50	4	
Le Grand Bacoux			
Fort de Terre	50	8	40

Total
Soldats   10,400
Canons   220
Maisons   2,610

Besides the Several Forts and Garrisons in Louisianna they have the following ones in what they call there Government in Canada, which begins at the Mouth of the River Illinois.

1º Pimiteoui a Fort on the Lake of the Illinois where the French have been settled ever since the Year 1682 and have all the Natives of the Country entirely at their disposal.

2º Le Rocher a very impregnable Fort on the Top of a Rock in the Country of the Illinois and surrounded by a Village of the Miamis.

3ᵈ Mascoutins a small Fort & Mission among the Indians of that name.

4ᵗʰ Missilimakinac.

5 Sᵗ Marie, which two places the French have been in possession of ever since those parts were known and have always maintained a small Fort & Garrison at each of them in order to protect their Indian Allies and those that carry on a Trade with them from their Enemies; but We cannot suppose that those places or their Forts & Garrisons at them are any way considerable as there is no occasion that they should be altho they are sufficient to take possession and are made strong enough

to serve when occasion requires, which may be said of all the other little Forts & Settlements that they have in those Inland parts of America or indeed in any other places which we have hitherto so much despised.

These are all the settlements the French have in those parts of America to which they can Justly lay any Claim; all the rest above Montreal are in the Territories of the Six Nations and within the Dominions of Great Britain.

6 Fort S[t] Joseph on the River of that Name where they have long had the most considerable place & Fortress of any in those remote Parts of America.

7[ly] S[t] Ignace a small Fort opposite to Missilimakiac to which they have lately removed their Garrisons from that Place & S[t] Maries.

8[ly] Le Detroit

9[ly] Fort of the Miamis

10 Sandoski

11 Niagara

12 Fort Toronto a small Fort that they have lately erected on the Borders of the Lake Ontario opposite to Oswego in order to aw[e] the Indians of the Six Nations on the North side of that Lake and to Intercept the Northern Indians as they go to Oswego.

13 Cataracoui

14 Chambli

15 Fort Sorrel

16 Crown Point

The Account of the French Forts &c in Louisiana was given to M[r] Dinwiddie, Governor of Virginia, by a Deserter, who offered to take his Oath of the truth of it; It is certain from all Authoritys, that the French have actually the Number of Forts stated in this Paper; but it is to be doubted, whether they have so large a Military Force in Louisiana.

[Endorsed] An Account of the *Forts* & Number of Men in Garrison in *Louisiana,* given to Gov[r]: *Dinwiddie* by a French Deserter in *1752* and transmitted by him to the Board of Trade, *175..* with some Account of the French Forts in *Canada;* taken from the French Authors & other Informat[n].[2]

[2] The Board received Dinwiddie's list on March 8, 1753. *Board of Trade Journal,* 1749/50–1753, p. 401.

REPRESENTATION OF THE BOARD OF TRADE RELATING TO THE FRENCH AT THE RIVER ST. JOHNS

(COPY)

Whitehall, December 7: 1753.

To the King's most Excellent Majesty.

May it please Your Majesty,

Having lately received a Letter from Peregrine Thomas Hopson Esqr, Your Majesty's Governor of the Province of Nova Scotia, dated the 18th of October last, in which he acquaints Us with the Intelligence he had received of the Strength and Proceedings of the French at the River St Johns within that Province; We think it our Duty to lay before Your Majesty the annexed Extract of Mr Hopson's Letter, and at the same time humbly to represent to Your Majesty,

That We have had great Reason to believe, from the Accounts, which We have from time to time received from Your Majesty's Governor of Nova Scotia, and more particularly from the manner in which the Indians of the River St John's soon afterwards departed from that Treaty of Peace into which they entered with Your Majesty's Subjects upon the Arrival of the Settlers, that the French have always intended to fortify themselves at this River, although the Possession the French have gained of the Isthmus & their Ascendance over the Inhabitants of that District have till now prevented our receiving any positive and certain Intelligence of it.

Uncertain however as our Accounts were, We thought it our Duty from time to time as We received them to lay them before Your Majesty's Secretary of State; and in a letter to His Grace the Duke of Bedford, dated the 16th of January 1750/1, We represented to His Grace the fatal consequences which would inevitably follow from the French being suffered to take possession of this part of Your Majesty's Territories, to which Your Majesty's Right has been so clearly & incontestably proved.

Some of the Evils pointed out in that Letter have already taken place, and others of a more extensive Nature will necessarily follow from this Settlement of the French, unless timely prevented, which We humbly beg Leave to submit to Your Majesty's Consideration.

Should the French continue in possession of any Settlement on the River St Johns, the direct Communication between Your Majesty's other American Colonies and Nova Scotia will be intercepted and broken, and that Province, instead of being a Barrier to the rest of Your Majesty's Dominion on the Continent of America, will be itself a separate Colony, exposed to the French encompassing it on every side; the force of Canada and Cape Breton will be united, and a Chain of Possession and Territory formed from Cape Breton thro' the Country north of the Peninsular to the Post now erected at St Johns River, which may hereafter be formidable to Your Majesty's Colonies and Interest in America; the extensive and very beneficial Trade to those parts for Lumber and Furrs, now chiefly carried on by Your Majesty's Subjects, in the continuance of which Your Majesty's Sugar Islands have so very immediate and important an Interest, will be left open to the French; France will directly secure to herself a Port in the Atlantic Ocean, than which nothing can be more advantageous to her, as it will remove from her Trade in America the many very heavy Inconveniences now arising from the tedious, dangerous and sometimes impracticable Navigation of the River St Lawrence; and in one word several of those great commercial Advantages and national Views, for the Attainment & Security of which so large Sums have from time to time been chearfully expended by this Nation in the settling Nova Scotia, will be not only lost to Great Britain, but transferred to the Power of France.

All which is most humbly submitted.

DUNK HALIFAX.
J. PITT.
J. GRENVILLE.
DUPPLIN.
FRAN. FANE.
CHA^s TOWNSHEND.
ANDREW STONE.

CADWALLADER COLDEN [1] TO HALIFAX [2]

(COPY)

New York August the 3^d 1754.

My Lord.

Since the news-papers have informed us that Monsr Galissoniere, lately Governor of Canada, is appointed Commander of the French Squadron fitting out in the Mediterranean, it has given the same ap-

[1] Cadwallader Colden (1688–1776), since 1721 a member of the Council of New York, was a strong opponent of James DeLancey, the lieutenant governor. He became lieutenant governor himself in 1760, and as such defended the rights of the crown in successive administrations until 1775.

[2] George Montagu Dunk, Second Earl of Halifax (1716–1771), was president of the Board of Trade from 1748 to 1761. He was attached, though not as intimately as some other members of the group, to the Cumberland-Bedford faction. This letter,

prehensions here, which I find some have in England of the destination of that Squadron; but as such designs cannot escape the Vigilance of His Majesty's Ministers, and we have no directions to be on our guard, I am confident there can be no foundation for such fears. However since the amity between the two crowns seems not firm, while acts of hostility continue both in America and the East Indies, I think it my duty to inform your Lordship of what I know of the present state of New York. We have a great number of fine large Cannon, above a hundred large, and, if I mistake not, above 150 of all sorts; but as I think, notwithstanding of this, that the place is in no condition of making any defence against the least force, which can be imagined will be sent against it, the great number of large cannon may be rather of prejudice, than of advantage, by the Enemy's easily possessing themselves of them. Our Fortifications at best never could make a good defence. The Engineers Armstrong and Eyers [Eyre], who have been in New York lately, can inform your Lordship we have not one Engineer, nor one Gunner, nor any kind of Artillery men, nor any Magazine of Powder, and the fortifications such as they are now ruinous. I know not that we have one man in the Country, Except a Lieutenant or two of the Independant Companies, who ever were present at any military service. Two of the Companies are now removed to Virginia, and I believe your Lordship is informed what may be expected from them which remain. Our Militia is under no kind of discipline, nor do I think it possible to bring them under any, without being intermixt with regular Troops. I had convincing proof of this in the year 1746 at Albany, when the forces of the Colonies designed against Canada were there. The Officers themselves could not be brought to observe discipline, notwithstanding of their suffering shamefully by want of it, on several occasions. The Inhabitants of the Northern Colonies are all so nearly on a level, and a licentiousness, under the notion of liberty, so generally prevails, that they are impatient under all kind of superiority and authority. The French in America seem to have a most daring opinion of their superiority in conduct, and contempt of ours, as has appeared in several Instances.

It appears from Charlevoix's History of New-France, that the French at several times formed designs of possessing themselves of New-York.[3]

---

and other letters in the following pages from Shirley, Lawrence, and Hardy (pp. 22, 26, 149, 154, 170), are private letters to him, and are not in the Board of Trade correspondence, the C.O. 5 series, in the Public Record Office. References to this letter are in the *Cadwallader Colden Papers*, IV, New York Historical Society *Collections*, 1920, pp. 463, 469, 474.

[3] De Charlevoix, in *Histoire et Description Generale de la Nouvelle France* (1744), II, 392–410, discussed the plans of de Callieres and de Dénonville in 1689.

Indeed no place on the Continent can be of such use to them, as thereby they would open a more safe and speedy communication with Canada than any they now have, and with the great Lakes thro' which they carry on their commerce with the inland Nations, and by the resources they may have from Canada in supporting themselves in the possession of it. All these advantages plainly appear from the French Maps; the English have none good. Monsr Galissoniere was Governor of Canada at the conclusion of the last war. He has the character of having great acquired as well as natural abilities, and of having been indefatigable in acquiring the knowledge of every thing, which can be of advantage to the French. He sent many Officers to New-York after the conclusion of the Peace, under pretence of regulating the Exchange of Prisoners, where it could not be difficult for them to learn every thing they wanted to know, and I am afraid they are too well apprised of all our weaknesses, which may make them attempt what otherwise they would not. If the French have any designs on new York, it cannot be secured with less than a regiment of regular Troops; in conjunction with such a number of Regulars, the Militia of the country may be of great service, and I am afraid they will otherwise be of little use in its defence against regular Troops. I know not the number of regular Troops in Canada, but I am told that the number is considerably increased since the peace.

The Crown of Great Britain has an undoubted right to the navigation of Lake Ontario or Cadarackui Lake, as it is entirely surrounded by the Countries belonging to the Five Cantons of Indians, and we have a fortified trading House with a small Garrison at the mouth of a River, which falls into that Lake, but we have made no use of the Navigation. The French have two small vessels on it. I am convinced with submission of opinion that one large armed Vessel with two or three smaller on that Lake would more effectually and with less expence defeat the designs of the French on the inland parts of the Continent, and their ingrossing the Trade with the Indian Nations than any other method, which can be thought of: At the same time it would be a security to the Southern Colonies; for every thing from Canada to the westward and southward must pass thro' that Lake. But the method of putting this in execution ought to be previously better concerted than our Enterprises in America have usually been.

The Southern Colonies, who formerly thought themselves little concerned in the enterprises of the French on the Northern Colonies, now see the necessity of uniting for the common safety. Their Commissioners, when they came to New York in their way to Albany to meet the Indians there, and found that my state of health did not permit me to go to the congress at Albany, communicated to me a scheme which they had formed for uniting all the Colonies in their mutual defence, and in their return informed me of what had been done, and likewise of a joint representation formed there of the state of the colonies in respect to the French and Indians, which your Lordship will find nearly agrees with what on several occasions I have formerly represented. Tho' the Commissioners did agree to the plan, as formed at Albany, to be laid before their several Assemblies, they were not all equally satisfied with it; but they thought it better to agree in any one, than in none. The general purport of it is to constitute a President and grand Council for the General Government of the Colonies, and command of their united military Force, and for the entire management of all Affairs with the Indians. The President to be appointed and supported by the Crown, and the Council to be chosen by the several Assemblies, and supported by their Constituents. The General Expence to be provided for by a General Duty, by Act of Parliament, on some kinds of merchandise imported into the Colonies. In place of reasoning, I think it better, with most humble submission, to tell your Lordship my own opinion of what I think may be the most easy and effectual method for uniting the Colonies for their mutual defence or annoyance of an Enemy. It is this, that the civil Government of the several Colonies remain as it is, but that all military affairs, and the command of the Militia in all the Colonies be put under one Captain General or General Officer, to act with the advice of a Council, either nominated by the crown, or elected, or partly nominated, and partly elected. That this General Officer have the sole management of all affairs with the Indians, and of regulating the trade with them, with the Consent of the Council. But I believe, that no Gentleman, who knows the present state of the Colonies, will accept of this great trust, without having some regular troops under his command. Our Mother Country must for some time bear a considerable part of the charge, till the Colonies are more inured to bear the necessary expence of Government. An easy Duty on Wine, Rum, or other Spirits, Molossus and Sugar, to extend equally thro' all the Colonies, would bring in a considerable sum, more than I believe is imagined, could it be fairly collected. The Merchants in America are so accustomed to despise all Laws of Trade, that if the duty be made high it will produce less than a small duty will.

Your Lordship can be at no loss to discover the reasons why the People of America are fond of elective Officers, tho' they be swayed severally by different motives. However I have seen a King's Governor, by the esteem which he had universally obtain'd, carry the Authority of a Governor to all the length that a wise man would desire, and I have seen others brought to the lowest degree of contempt. Then your Lordship may believe, that I think the success in Government depends more on the choice which His Majesty's Ministers make of the Persons to govern us, than on any thing else.

I have great reason to dread that I have presumed much too far; If the Subject does not excuse me, nothing else can. I trust to your Lordship's candour, that you'll perceive it done with a good intention, and that it cannot be with any personal or private view; and for this reason only I expect pardon for so bold an Intrusion on your Lordship's patience.

I am with absolute Submission Yr Ldship's most obedt & most humble Servant

CADWALLADER COLDEN.

GOVERNOR WILLIAM SHIRLEY [1] TO HALIFAX
(COPY)

Falmouth in Casco Bay, Augst 20th 1754

My Lord,

Your Lordship will perceive by my frequent Letters how desirous I am of obeying the commands, which your Lordship was pleas'd to honour me with, of writing to you often.

My Public Letter to the Board, which I transmit by the same Ship with this, will discover to your Lordship at large the Service, that brought me to this place.

The principal Object I have in view in it, is finally to get a Fort erected at or near the head of the River Kennebeck, of sufficient Strength to withstand any sudden Attack from Quebeck, (which is about 100 Miles distant from it) and capable of receiving such a number of Men, as might be able to pay the French a visit upon occasion within a few days at that place, or at least to destroy all their Settlements on this side the River St. Laurence.

I have it much at heart, My Lord, to compass this point, as it seems to me very clear, that the maintenance of such a Fort there would, in conjunction with one of the same strength, built on the eminence

---

[1] William Shirley (1694–1771) was governor of Massachusetts from 1741 to 1756 and temporary commander in chief in America from August, 1755, to June, 1756. He deserves a full-length biography, which has not yet been written. For to the awakening of imperialist sentiment in England probably no man, not even Pitt, contributed as much as this American governor. So high came to be the opinion in which the ministry held him that cabinets, for a brief period in 1754, made his recommendations and suggestions their own. His misfortune was to be thrown into a command which only a professional soldier of extraordinary adaptabilities could successfully handle.

which I have in a former Letter mention'd to your Lᵈship, near the French Fort at Crown point, (which place is computed to be within 120 miles distance of Montreal) put it in our power to make sudden descents upon Quebec and Montreal at one and the same time, with a superior force of Militia to that, which they could raise in Canada to resist us.

The immediate good Effects of building these two Forts would be, that the latter of them would effectually command Fort St. Frederic, and fix such at least of the Castles of the five Nations, as are not gone over already to the French Interest, in a close Attachment to the English; and both these Forts together by continually hanging over Canada, like two Thunder-Clouds, keep the French and their Indians in a proper Respect and awe of the English Colonies in that Quarter, and restrain them within their due limits, better than a thousand Treaties; and I can't but think, it would have a great tendency to prevent the French from pushing on their Encroachments further upon his Majesty's Western Colonies on this Continent.

In preparing the way for erecting the propos'd fort at the head of Kennebeck River, I hope, my Lord, I shall have made a considerable progress before I leave this place.

It was impracticable at the first step to have erected and supported the propos'd Fort, as high up the River as it's head, which is computed to be about 110 Miles distant from any English Settlement; the country on each side, as well as the Navigation of the river for the last 70 miles is very little known to the English, and it could not be supported at so remote a distance against a sudden attack from Quebec, without first building some intermediate Forts for securing stores in their transportation to it, and fortifying the other parts of the River.

The River is not navigable for Sloops, or other small vessels higher than a place called Cushenoe, which is but 43 miles from the mouth, so that it is necessary to have one fort or defensible Magazine there; and at another place called Taconnett, which is but 20 miles above that, are falls 17 foot high; near which there is a small Portage or Carrying Place between the river Kennebeck and Sebastoocook; thro' the latter of which the Penobscot Indians have a communication with the Norridgewalks, so that it is necessary to have another Fort there, as well for lodging the Stores designed for the Supply of the Fort at the head of the River (which must be landed at the Falls in their way thither) as for cutting off the the communication of the Penobscotts with the Norridgewalks, and Kennebeck River, thro' which lies the shortest and most commodious passage for the Penobscotts to Canada.

At the first of these places a fort is already erected, and at the latter another is building, and will I hope be so far advanced as to have the cannon soon mounted, and I expect, when the Body of troops, which are now upon their march on each side of the river with Battoes for carrying their provisions up the river, and who have orders to survey the country with the course and navigation of Kennebeck up to the head of it, as well as to remove any French settlements, which they may find there, shall be return'd, that we shall then have knowledge enough of the river and country to judge which will be the most proper place for setting the Capital Fort at, and whether it will be necessary to build another fort between that and Taconnett.

In the mean time this Fort at Taconnett will be impregnable by any Force the Indians can bring, and defensible even against the French themselves, unless they should attempt to transport cannon or Mortars thro' the woods on the back of it; which will be difficult for them to do: And besides the advantages I have before mention'd, it will cut off the Norridgewalk Indians from a very great Salmon fishery upon Taconnett falls, and other Subsistence on this river, in case of a rupture between Us and them, as also from making descents thro' it upon our eastern Settlements, which was the common rout of their Inroads into the Province in time of war: and it will moreover, by cutting off the Penobscotts from their communication with the River Kennebeck, render their going to Canada, and drawing support from thence very inconvenient and difficult, so that it will keep that Tribe, as well as the Norridgewalks, in a much greater dependance upon us than they have ever yet been.

Before I came to this place I desir'd Col. Lawrence to assist me, in case I should find that the French had erected any Fort upon the river Kennebeck, or on the carrying place near the head of it, which might require the force of cannon or mortars to dislodge them, with such a small Train of Artillery, as might be requisite for that purpose, from Halifax (distant about 70 leagues from Kennebeck) which he promis'd to do upon 12 hours notice of my having occasion for them.

I have the pleasure of a very cordial correspondence with that Gentleman, and to have receiv'd promising accounts of the new settlements he is engaged in; which there seems to be great reason, from his disposition for the public Service, and activity in it, to hope will succeed.

I find by his Letters, that from the experience, he hath had of the behavior and spirit of the Accadians in general, he is of sentiment with me, that the refusal of the revolted Inhabitants of Chicgnecto to comply with the terms, upon which they had permission given to return to their former possessions there, is happy for the country, and even thinks it would be fortunate, if a favorable opportunity should offer for ridding His Majesty's Government there of the French Inhabitants of the two districts of Minas and Annapolis River: And if the present conjuncture, when the French have their hands full of business upon the Ohio, and have given us such high provocations should be thought a proper time to dislodge them from their Forts upon the Isthmus and St. John's river, I cant but think the work would prosper well in his hands. That, my Lord, would indeed be a day of Jubile for His Majesty's northern Colonies; the Era from whence their deliverance from the danger of French Incroachments might be dated; and I need not repeat to y^r L^{d}ship, how ready I am to contribute every thing in my power towards hastening this happy event: I took the liberty to mention to yr L^{d}ship at Horton, that if it should not be accomplish'd before an open rupture happens between the two crowns, an attempt might then be too late; and as my fears are easily alarm'd upon this occasion, I confess that the appointment of Monsr. La Galissoniere to command the Toulon Squadron, makes me think it possible that the destination of some part of the armament may be for an attempt upon Nova Scotia; He being the most proper Officer which France could employ upon such an enterprise.

The open and avowed breaches of public faith already made by France in violent seizures of great part of that Province, and her instigations of the Indians to ravage the remaining part, and commit a most unparell'd murder under the sanction of a flag of truce, as I look upon that of Captain Howe [2] to have been, will I hope excuse me in this case, if my apprehensions should be ill-grounded.

The Commissioners for this Province at the late Congress at Albany for holding an interview with the Indians of the five Nations are returned from that service, since my being here, and the Principal of them hath sent me a copy of his Journal of the Proceedings there: The Appearance of Commissioners from so many of the English Governments had I understand a very good effect upon the Indians; But their appearance was thinner I hear than was ever known upon such an occasion: To what causes that is to be ascribed, as also of the late wavering disposition of those Tribes, and falling off of some of them from the English Interest, it is necessary for His Majesty's Service that your Lordship should be fully apprised of; I am not furnish'd with the proper papers for that purpose here, but will take the first Opportunity of doing it after my return to Boston.

The Accounts we have had of the defeats of the Virginian Forces

[2] A brief sketch of Edward Howe, a member of the council of Nova Scotia who was killed in October, 1750, appears in J. C. Webster, *The Forts of Chignecto* (1930), p. 91.

are very mortifying: Those rich western Colonies, which are so nearly concerned in the late Encroachments made by the French on the Ohio, have been double the time in raising about 800 men to oppose a great force of the French, who they were certain had made a considerable progress in building Forts within their territories, than this single Government hath been in raising the like number of Men, and building two Forts, upon an uncertain Intelligence only that the French had made Settlements within the Limits of the Province; and for want of timely assembling even that force in one body, have been oblig'd to surrender the greatest part of them to the enemy.

I have this day had the honor of your Lordship's Letter dated the 14th of March by Mr. Yorke, and shall to the utmost of my power with great pleasure execute y^r L^{d}ship's commands for serving his Interest, which I have given him an assurance of.

I am, with the highest respect, My Lord, Y^r L^{d}ship's most oblig'd and most devoted Servant.

W. Shirley.

Lieutenant-Colonel Charles Lawrence [1] to Halifax
(copy)

Halifax Augst 23rd 1754.

My Lord,

I was honour'd with the receipt of y^r L^{d}ship's Letter of May the 29th by Captn Rous; the Approbation you are pleased to express of my conduct, and the permission I am indulg'd with of communicating my private thoughts to y^r L^{d}ship, are favours that will ever make the deepest impression upon my memory. I have by this Opportunity in my letter to the Board described at large the present Situation of our Affairs, and I should have been glad to have transmitted to their Lordships as exact an Account of what is going forward at Beau Sejour and St. John's River, but the Person, whom I sent to obtain intelligence, is not yet return'd, tho' every day expected.

The Plan, that has hitherto been pursued, of making our Settlements under the protection of the Troops, has succeeded as well as

---

[1] Charles Lawrence (1709–1760), third son of Lieutenant General John Lawrence of Portsmouth, entered the army in 1727 as ensign in Montague's foot, and in the ten years from 1741 to 1750 rose in the 45th regiment from captain lieutenant to lieutenant colonel. His regiment was sent to Louisbourg in 1747, and to Nova Scotia after the peace. A member of the council in 1749, he became lieutenant governor of Nova Scotia in 1754 and governor in 1756. In 1757 he was given Jefferey's 3d battalion in the Royal American Regiment, and in 1758 the local rank of brigadier general in America. There is a sketch of him by James S. Macdonald in Nova Scotia Hist. Soc. *Coll.*, XII (1905), 19–58.

could be expected, and I believe in a few years will so far answer the intention, as to enable us to Supply ourselves with the provisions we consume; but this Situation of Affairs, tho' it may make us appear in a more florishing condition to Strangers, has in reality this inconvenience, that our Troops are so much divided, and of consequence our military Strength so much impair'd, that We are in no condition to assert His Majesty's just rights, in the manner I could wish, against those unwarrantable Encroachm^{ts} the French have made on the North Side of the Bay of Fundy, where they are every day doing all in their power to inhance the difficulty of removing them, and from whence (particularly from Beau Sejour) they have made all their incursions upon us, and committed every kind of outrage: As this is a growing Evil, and the greatest Obstacle that can be imagined to your Lordship's design of establishing this Province, I should esteem myself most happy in having the least hint from y^r L^{d}ship how far any attempt I should make to dispossess them would be well received at home: If such a Step should be approved of, I flatter myself I could with Mr. Shirley's assistance raise a Body of Men in New-England, which joined to the few troops we could muster on so good an occasion would I believe make a pretty successful Campaigne.

If Yr L^{d}ship should approve of this for our next Summer's Employment, I believe it would be necessary to postpone the Settlement at Chibnaccadee I have now propos'd to the Board, till we are more at leisure, but it will be most useful to have a fort there at any rate, as it will command all the Settlements, where the French Inhabitants are, prevent in a great degree the incursions of the Indians, and put us in (almost) secure possession of the most fertile pleasant Country we have yet discover'd.

Immediately on the receipt of the Letter I had the honor to receive from the Board of March the 4th,[2] I set about clearing the land for the battery their L^{d}ships have order'd Mr. Brewse to build, and have done every thing in my power to make the necessary preparations for that work, against Mr. Brewses Arrival, tho' I cannot in duty to Y^r L^{d}ship omit acquainting you that I greatly fear this Battery, and the Works on George's Island will not altogether answer the end of keeping Ships out of the harbour, as the passage is full wide for the Shot to do much execution upon Ships, that are coming in with a fair Wind, and when they have passed, we are intirely defenceless for want of those Batteries, that were formerly projected in the front of the Town.

[2] The reference is apparently to the Board of Ordnance, under whose orders John Brewse served as engineer, and not to the Board of Trade letter of that date, printed in part in Thomas B. Akins, ed., *Selections from the Public Documents of the Province of Nova Scotia* (1849), I, 207.

I thought myself the more bound in duty to lay before your L^dship my opinion of the insufficiency of the new Battery, as it is probable, if we should attempt driving the French from that important Post of Beau Sejour, the Ships of War that are every Year at Louisbourg, which are generally at least a Sixty four, a thirty Six, and an eighteen Gun Ship, would make some Attempt upon this place, unless we had more naval Force for our protection.

I hope by the Fall of the Year to give Yr L^dship a perfect Account of the Situation of the French in the Bay of Fundy, As the Person I have sent will bring me information of their Numbers, and the Forts and Settlements they have made and Captain Rous is just now setting out upon a cruise to discover whether they have done any thing towards the Water.

It has long been the Object of my Attention to take some Step that might contribute to ease that heavy and important Article of Provisions for the Troops; I am afraid if we depend upon the gradual progress, that is made by the Settlers in clearing the land, it will be a long time before it can be brought to bear. If indeed the French were driven from the Bay of Fundy, Chicgnecto (as it is already a fine cleared Country) would soon become a florishing Settlement, and the same expectations might be had from Annapolis Royal, Piziquid and Minas, when the Inhabitants were brought under proper Submission to His Majesty's Government; but still at Halifax, and the neighbouring Posts, where the greatest part of the Troops must generally reside, Provisions would be very dear, as the Inhabitants do not find that immediate profit in clearing Land they expect from other kinds of Labor; To remedy this Inconvenience, as well as many others that arise from the neglect of Agriculture, a Sum of £4000 or £5000 over and above the usual Grant, to be disposed of, with the Advice and consent of the Council here, in Bounties upon bringing Land under actual Improvement, would not fail of a good Effect; And such an Encouragement I am persuaded would contribute greatly to bring many considerable Settlers here from the Continent; As this, tho' so apparently useful, might seem a glaring Article in the Estimate, I have not presumed to insert it, but have taken the liberty humbly to submit it to y^r L^dship's consideration.

The late Ill-Success of our Arms upon the Continent under Col. Washington, together with the disunion of the Colonies, and the discord which subsists in general between the Provinces and their Governors on account of the necessary Subsidies, will I fear contribute so much to strengthen the French in their Encroachments to the Southward, that they will soon begin as heretofore to give us all the Trouble they are able; While the Opportunity yet remains I would willingly endeavour to put it out of their power, and that effectually: The first and indeed the only important Step, as I before acquainted y^r L^{d}ship, would be the Demolition of Beau Sejour; And when that is done the French Inhabitants on that side must either be removed to this, or driven totally away by Fire and Sword; for if all the villages beyond Beau-Sejour are not destroyed, and some of the Dykes cut, The French (who will easily know that the Force we had collected was but occasional) would immediately return to take possession of their habitations, and rebuild their Forts.

I fear it would be vain to move for another Regiment to be sent to Us, tho' it would be indisputably of the greatest Use (Especially now that the Troops are so divided, and the duty severe) towards both obtaining and preserving His Majesty's just Rights: Could that once be performed, it might be well expected that our natural Strength would increase so fast, that we should soon be able to defend and support ourselves with very little Expence to England: On the other hand, if it cannot, that is, if the French Fort is to Stand, either on account of the Expence necessary for destroying it, or for any other reasons, that I cannot judge of, in that case I fear our Progress will prove very slow; and I would with all submission entreat y^r L^{d}ships Leave to erect the Fort, proposed to be rais'd on Chebunaccadie River, as the next best expedient for securing the interior Parts of the Province.

If any thing I have now the honor to propose should be approved of, and thought proper to be carried into execution, I need not represent to Y^r Ldship how necessary it would be that I should know it as early as possible, as the Success of such an undertaking depends very much thereon; Not only as I must apply to Mr. Shirley, before I can begin, but if it could be carried thro' before the Ships of War from France arrive at Louisbourg, we shall be in a better capacity to repel any Attempt they may form to revenge or reinstate themselves.

After being honour'd with Y^r L^{d}ship's permission to write without reserve on Provincial Affairs, I humbly hope the uncommon length of this Letter will not be look'd upon by your L^{d}ship as exceeding my duty, and I flatter myself it's imperfections will be overlook'd thro' y^r L^{d}ship's extreme Goodness, which I have already so largely and so happily experienced.

I beg leave to Subscribe myself with the greatest gratitude and respect, My Lord, Y^r L^{d}ship's most obedient and most humble Servant.

CHA^s LAWRENCE.

Postscript Aug^st 26th

Yesterday, My Lord, arrived the Ship Cornwallis with Mr. Brewse on board, and the Tools for erecting the Battery on the Eastern Shore, which work I shall make the cheif Object of my Attention, and use my utmost endeavours, that it be carried on with all possible Expedition.

The Person I sent to St. John's River is also returned, and I have related his Account at large in my letter to Y^r L^dship's Board; the most material Circumstance being that the French have there only an Officer and sixteen Men in the old Earth Fort, which is in a ruinous Condition, has three bad Guns in it, and that they have not raised (as was reported) any other Fort whatever on that River.

He also adds that the French are every day strengthening the Fort at Beau Sejour, but by his account of it's bigness, and the manner in which the necessary Barracks and Buildings are crowded into it, I am of opinion a Couple of Mortars would fire it about their Ears in half an hour. I am, Y^r L^dships most dutiful Humb^le Servant.

CHA^s LAWRENCE.

ACCOUNT OF THE FRENCH FORTS IN CANADA AND UPON THE LAKES [1] [OCTOBER, 1754]

(COPY)

FORT St VINCENT upon Miamis River at the West end of Lake Erie.
a Logg Fort, no Guns, 16 Regulars, and 2 Officers.
SANDOSKI upon the south side of Lake Erie.
A Logg Fort, no Guns, 8 Regulars, and one Officer.
Le DETROIT a Logg Fort, no Guns only a few Chambers, 35 Regulars, 200 Militia, can collect about 300 Indians.
NIAGARA two Forts; one small wooden one 9 Miles above the head of the Falls, no Guns, 6 Men; another 9 Miles below the falls at the Place where the River empty's itself into the Lakes, built of stone, 2 Bastions, 40 Men, 4 Officers, Eight Guns—6 Pounders.
Imagined it may be taken without Cannon; a few Shells would infallibly destroy it.
TORONTO a Square Fort of Wood, no Guns, 20 Regulars, 2 Officers.
CADARAQUI Stone Fort, Strength and Number of Men the same as Niagara.

---

[1] This list has been punctuated by the editor.

N.B. The French have 2 Barks upon the Lakes 60 Ton each, no Guns, about 7 Men.

LA GARRETTE Thirty Leagues down St Lawrence River. Block Fort, no Guns, 15 or 20 Men and an Officer.

FORT St MARIE further down the River. a Wooden Fort, no Guns, 15 or 20 Men.

IROQUOIS FORT Three Leagues further down the River. Wooden Fort, 15 or 20 Men, no Guns.

MONTREAL, 4 Company's. Town consists of 4 Streets surrounded with a Stone Wall, no Ditch capable of mounting any Cannon but only few mounted for Salutes.

QUEBEC, 6 Companys of Regulars.

NB The foregoing account was given to Lord Halifax the 14th of October 1754 by John Defievre late a Matross in Captain John Chalmers Company was discharged at the time of the Reduction, went to America and was a servant to an Indian Trader upon the Ohio, was taken Prisoner by the French in 1749 and carried through their several Settlements to Quebec from whence he was sent to Louisburg and made his Escape to Rhode Island.

John Defievre has now a Pension from the Ordnance.

DIFFERENT ROUTES IN NORTH AMERICA [1754]
(COPY)

Route from Williamsburg to the French Fort upon Lake Erie near the Ohio by Land.

From Williamsburg to Fredericksburg across two Ferries, one over Pamunkey River, the other over Mattapony River at the Places marked in the Map. 100 Miles.

From Fredericksburg to Winchester 90 Miles, i.e., 70 to the Mountains and 20 beyond them.

From Winchester to Wills's Creek. 50 Miles.

Thus far the Road is very good, and passable with all sorts of Carriages.

From Wills's Creek to Gist's Plantation on the Monongehela 70 Miles.

From Gist's Plantation to the Forks 50 Miles. Here the Fort built by Us and taken by the French is situated.

From the Forks to Loggs Town. 20 Miles.

From Logg's Town to Venango 60 Miles. Here the French are supposed to have another Fort. The Form and Strength of it and the Number of Men in Garrison unknown.

From Venango to the head of Riviere aux Bœuffs 70 Miles. Here is a Fort built by the French in the Year 1753, situated on the South Side of the River near the Water; and is almost surrounded by the Creek, and a small Branch of it which forms a kind of Island; Four Houses compose the Sides; the Bastions are made of Piles driven into the ground, standing more than 12 feet above it, and sharp at top, with Port-holes cut for Cannon, and Loop-holes for the small Arms; there are eight six Pound Pieces mounted in each Bastion, and one Piece of four Pound before the Gate. In the Bastions are a Guard-House, Chapel, Doctor's Lodgings, and the Commander's private Store, round which are Plat-forms for the Cannon and Men to stand upon; there are several Barracks without the Fort for the Soldiers dwelling, covered some with Bark and some with Boards made chiefly of Logs.

N.B. From Wills's Creek to this Place there is no Road but what the Indians and Traders have made thro' the Woods.

From Riviere aux Bœuffs to Presque Isle upon Lake Erie is 20 Miles. Here is another Fort built by the French in 1753; it is about 120 feet square, and built of Chesnut Logs squared and lapt over each other to the height of 15 feet; a Log-House at each Angle, and two Gates one to the Southward and another to the Northward.

From Riviere aux Bœuffs to this Place there is a Waggon Road made by the French.

N.B. The French have now upon the Ohio & in their different Forts about 1500 Regulars, & are said to have been joined by 500 or 600 Ottoway Indians.

Route to the Ohio by Water.

From the Mouth of Potomack River to the Great Falls is 170 Miles, navigable for Vessels of 200 or 300 Tons.

From Alexandria at the lower part of the Falls to where the River is again navigable, a Land Carriage of 30 Miles good Road.

From hence to next Falls thro' the blue Ridge 60 Miles, navigable for Canoes carrying about 1000 W^t.

Land Carriage of 3 or 4 Miles to where the River is again navigable.

From hence to Wills's Creek 200 Miles, navigable for small Boats, which will carry about 1000 Weight.

From Wills's Creek a Waggon Road to the Head of Yaughyaughgani River 80 Miles.

From the Head of Yaughyaughgani River to the Forks, distance unknown, navigable for Boats carrying about 1000 Weight.

From the Forks up the Ohio to Venango, distance unknown, the Current not rapid.

From Venango to the head of Riviere aux Bœuffs the Navigation impracticable.

N.B. There is said to be a nearer Way to the head of Yaughyaughgani River than that from the Mouth of Wills's Creek, which is to go up Wills's Creek, some times called the Northern Branch of the Potomack, navigable for small Boats, near the head of which is a Gap through the Mountains to the head of Yaughyaughgani River at the distance of not more than 20 Miles.

Route from Winchester to New York.

From Winchester to Lancaster 100 Miles.
From Lancaster to Philadelphia 68 Miles.
From Philadelphia to Trenton 30 Miles.
From Trenton to New York 66 Miles.
N.B. A Good Waggon Road passable for all sorts of Carriages.

Route from New York to Niagara.

From New York to Albany 140 Miles up Hudson's River.

From Albany to Schenectady by Land 16 Miles, good Road.

From Schenectady to the head of Mohawks River about 90 Miles.

From the head of Mohawks River to Oneyda River Land Carriage about 4 Miles.

From Oneyda River to Oneyda Lake about 30 Miles.

From Oneyda Lake to Oswego 60 Miles.

From Oswego to Niagara along the Lake about 100 Miles.

Niagara Fort before the Year 1749 was only built of Logs palisaded, but since that time has been made a strong & regular Fortification of Stone.

SKETCH OF REGULATIONS & ORDERS PROPOSED RELATING
TO AFFAIRS OF NORTH AMERICA. NOVEMBER, 1754
AND QUÆRIES RELATING TO THE SAME [1]

(COPY)

That Sir Peter Halket's, & Colonel Dunbar's Regiments of Foot be
sent from Corke to Virginia; consisting of 30. Serjeants, 30. Corporals,
20. Drummers, & 500. private Men, each Regiment; To be augmented
to 700., Rank & File, each Regiment, in Virginia, N⁰ Carolina, S⁰
Carolina, Maryland, & Pennsylvania.

That Directions be sent to the Governors of those Colonies, respectively, to make the proper Dispositions for the said Augmentation.

That Cloathing be provided here; And

That the Board of Ordnance furnish compleat Arms, & Tents for the
Two said Regiments.

That the Admiralty do provide Transport Vessels, with Victualling,
& Bedding, for the said 1000. private Men, their Officers, & respective
Attendants, &cᵃ, &cᵃ, &cᵃ. And also, Two Ships of the Line, & Two
Frigates, for the said Service.

That 1000. Barrels of Beef, & 10. Tons of Butter, be provided in
Ireland, & put on Board with the said Troops, for their immediate Use
upon their Arrival; &, in case They have no Occasion for Them, That
the said Provisions be turned over to the Navy.

That Mʳ Pitcher be appointed Commissary of the Musters of all
His Majᵗʸˢ Forces, That are, or shall be, employed, in His Majᵗʸˢ
Colonies, & Provinces, in N⁰ America; & the Governors, & Command-
ing Officers, respectively, be directed to give Him all Assistance, in the
Execution of that Duty.

That Sir John Sinclair be appointed Deputy Quarter Master General. And

That They be Both dispatched to America, forthwith.

That Directions be given to the Governors in N⁰ America, to provide fresh Victuals, for the said Troops, against their Arrival, at the
Expence of their respective Governments.

That Directions be, likewise, sent to the Governors, To provide all

---

[1] Another copy of this document, headed "Memoranda with regard to the intended
embarcation for North America. Oct. 22, 1754. Rec'd from Sir Thomas Robinson." is
in the Hardwicke Papers, Add. MSS. 35,909, f. 196. A note in the hand of the second
Lord Hardwicke reads: "N.B. This plan was probably formed by Cumberland, Mr
Pitt early declared that it did not go far enough." The document is in memorandum
form, written on the right-hand side of the page only.

Officers, who may have Occasion to go, from Place to Place, with all Necessaries for Travelling by Land, in case there are no Means of going by Sea: And, in general,

That the Commander's Orders be obeyed, every where, for Quartering Troops, and Impressing Carriages, & providing all Necessaries for such Troops, as may arrive, or be raised, in their respective Governments.

NB. That Duplicates of these Letters to the Governors, for this purpose, be sent by Lieut Colo Ellison, & Lieut Colo Mercer.

That Two New Regiments be raised in No America, at 1000. private Men Each Regiment, under the Command of Govr Shirley, & Sir William Pepperell.

That a certain Number of Half Pay Officers be sent from England for the said Two Regiments.[2]

That Blank Commissions be sent, for the Rest, to be appointed, in America, by the said Two Colonels.

That the said Two Colonels do appoint their own Agents.

That the Cloathing of the said Two Regiments be sent from England.

That Governor Shirley's Regiment do rendezvous at Boston; And Sir William Pepperell's, at New York, & Philadelphia.

Q. 1mo. As to the Commencement of the Establishment of the said Regiments?

Q. 2do. As to the Manner of providing the Levy Money for the said Two Regiments; & for Compleating the Two Irish Regiments, from 500., to 700. Men, Each?

Q. 3tio. As to the General Regulation of the Subsistence of the King's Troops, whilst in America?

That Majr Gen1 Braddock be appointed to command in Chief all His Majty's Forces in No America, & be sent thither, as soon as conveniently can be, with all the Authorities, and Instructions, proper for this Service.

Colonel Johnson.

That Two proper Persons be sent, The One to the Southern, the Other, to the *Northern*, Indians, to engage Them to take part with, & join His Majty's Forces, in their several Operations.

That the Board of Ordnance do furnish, for this Expedition,

Six light Six pounders.

Four light Twelve pounders.

Four Hautbitz.

with a full proportion of Stores. And, also, Compleat Arms, & Tents,

[2] This statement is queried in the Hardwicke copy.

for the Two Regiments, to be raised in Nº America, abovementioned.

That the said Board do provide a proper Number of Vessels for this Service.

That One principal Engineer, & Four Inferior Engineers, be appointed, together with about 100. Persons, to attend the Train, who are to be furnished with Victuals, on Board their own Store Ships, by the Commissioners of His Maj^{ty's} Victualling.

That the Provincial Officers, in America, shall have their Rank ascertained, in the following manner; vizt. That their General, & Field Officers, shall not roll with the King's Regular Forces, but only have the Inspection, & Direction, of their Provincial Corps.—That, If any of these Provincial Troops should be employed with Detachments of the King's Regular Troops, Their Captains shall be Junior to all Captains, who have the King's Commission: In like manner, Their Lieutenants to be Junior to all the Lieutenants; And their Ensigns to be Junior to all the Ensigns, who bear the King's Commission:— For which purpose, a Regulation shall be issued, by Order of Council; & printed Copies thereof shall be dispersed in Nº America.[3]

CONSIDERATIONS RELATING TO MEASURES TO BE TAKEN WITH REGARD TO AFFAIRS IN NORTH AMERICA.[1]
NOVEMBER 1754
(COPY)

There seem to be three Methods of disappointing the present Incroachment and preventing the like for the future,

1st. That of dispossessing the French from their present Establishment by bringing a sufficient Body of Forces together in that part, European, Provincial and Indian, with a proper Quantity of Artillery and Stores, to attack and drive them out from the three or four Forts which they have already built, and in other Places to remain upon the Defensive;

2^d. To carry on other Attacks in different Places at the same time in order to produce a Diversion of their Forces;

3^d. To make the principal Attack in other Places, (if such shall be found more proper for that purpose,) whereby their present intended

[3] This statement is queried in the Hardwicke copy.
[1] The author of these "Considerations" was well acquainted with New York problems. The argument for building a fort at Tierondoquat (the Senecas' landing-place between Oswego and Niagara) had long been advanced by New York governors. He knew also the two points upon which the ministry were determined: to commit no overt act of aggression on French territory; and to save expense. Lord Halifax best fits these qualifications.

Project may, by such Diversion, be either abandoned, or so weakened, as that it may be broke up by a very small Force.

These three Methods are equally just, as the French Establishments at Niagara and Crown Point within the New York Frontier, or where they possibly may attempt one further down upon the Ohio on the Frontier of Carolina, are Incroachments upon the British Rights equally unjustifiable with that of their present one upon the Head of the Ohio. The Preference therefore to either of these three Measures is to be determined upon from Circumstances of Conveniency only, i.e., by which of them Great Britain may be enabled to bring the *greatest Force* to operate most effectually and with the *least Charge*.

With respect to the first, there seem to be the following Objections to it,

1st. The Strength of the French by their Forts already built, furnished with Artillery, Stores & Provisions, and the Number of Forces collected in and about them upon a digested Plan to a certain point of view.

2d. The established Communication by water, not only betwixt that Place and Canada, but their Settlements among the Western Indians, whereby all Convoys of Stores, Provisions and auxiliary Forces may be brought to them with the utmost Facility, as they are secured by a Chain of Forts.

3th. All the Indians in that part seem to be in a great measure gained to the French Interest.

4th. The Western and Far Indians must remain and continue in their Interest from the same Causes.

5th. The Difficulty on the part of the English of bringing any proper Force to attack these Forts with a probability of Success, while this Communication is suffered to remain as it is, from which Circumstance and the Nature of the Ground, it seems probable, that 1200 French in and about the Forts already built, with their Indian Auxiliaries, may be able to defend them at least against four times their Number, which could not be brought to act without a very great Expence and very great Difficulty from the back Settlements of Virginia 150 Miles distant from these Forts; and as all Convoys of Provision for their Subsistence, as well as the Artillery, must be brought the same length of Way thro' a Country full of Woods, it is sufficiently obvious how liable they would be to be intercepted.

6th. The great Improbability of any Indian auxiliary Force, if the Design is confined to the single Attempt of dispossessing the French from their present Establishment on the Ohio; For the Indians in that part are already lost and intimidated, and the five Nations upon the back of New York will, it is feared, hardly be brought to act at such a distance from their own Residence, while the Forts Niagara, Frontenac and Crown Point are left to *subsist* upon their Backs: fear would prevent them, whatever their Interest or Affection might otherwise lead them to; and from the Manners of those People it is hardly to be presumed, that they would have any great Confidence in a Scheme for dislodging the French from an Incroachment upon the Territory of Virginia, while such manifest ones as those of New York, and in which they themselves were so strongly interested were suffered to subsist.

7th. Because even the other Colonies will hardly be brought to act to a proper Extent either of Force, Money or Authority, while the Project is confined to Virginia.

These Objections make it probable, that the first of these Methods is not the most eligible.

As to the second, the different Attacks upon different Places seem to be the most effectual Means of harrassing and distressing the Enemy; yet as unsuccessfull Attempts of this kind are attended with manifest Inconveniences, and to make them all with a probable Expectation of Success, would require a very large Expence, it will be found perhaps necessary, that, tho' Preparation should be made for various Attacks in order to distract the Forces of the Enemy, yet that one principal one should be chiefly intended, for which such Preparation should be made, and such Measures laid down as to leave little human Probability of a Disappointment.

It is therefore necessary the third Proposition should be examined, viz. If there are not to be found some more convenient Places, where the French may be dispossessed of Incroachments upon the back of New York with greater Facility than from this on the Ohio, and which in their Consequences might even make this more easy and at a less Charge of Force and Expence.

And there seem to be the following Reasons for thinking, that this is the Case both with respect to the French Forts of Niagara and Crown Point.

1st. The Communication from Albany to Oswego is already easy, and from thence no great Difficulty of carrying any Force or Artillery to drive the French from Niagara, and to build a Fort at Terondoquat, which is assured to be the best Harbour upon the Lake Ontario, where armed Vessels may be built and an Establishment made with good Effect.

2^d. By these Measures the five Nations would be absolutely detached from the French, & secured in the Interest of Great Britain.

3^d. The whole of this Indian auxiliary Force would be brought to operate in the most effectual Manner by intercepting all Communication between the French upon the Ohio and Canada by the Lake Ontario; it would open a way for those Indians to attack the French Western Indians and their Settlements in those Parts, to the Defence of which they would probably be obliged to recall a great part of their Force, French as well as Indian, now employed upon the Ohio; it would open a Way for attacking the French upon the Ohio from a different Quarter than that from the Back of Virginia; and would probably have a very great Influence in recovering the Ohio Indians from their present Dependence upon the French, by the Authority and Influence of the five Nations.

4th. It would insensibly and infallibly engage the Province of New York in Measures of Hostility, which it is feared will hardly be accomplished, if an Establishment upon the Ohio and the Interest of Virginia appear to be the only Object of them.

5th. This Link of the Chain betwixt Canada and the Ohio being once broke would probably make the French abandon their present Undertaking, or at least reduce them to the employing so small a Force upon it as would put it in the power of the Virginia, Pennsylvania and Maryland Governments to break it up.

6th. An Attack upon Crown Point might probably be made with Success, tho' it would not be attended with all the Advantages that would result from the taking of Niagara.

The New York, Massachusets and New Hampshire Governments would probably be brought to relish this Undertaking, and its Vicinity to them would probably render it easy in its Execution; but it plainly would not have such good Effect in cutting off the Communication betwixt Canada and the Ohio, nor so great an Influence upon our Indian Auxiliaries; but if a proper Spirit be exerted in the Colonies, and, in consequence of His Majesty's Orders, a considerable Body of Men be raised, the French might be dispossessed of their Incroachments both at Crown Point and Niagara, which would be the greatest Service that could be done the British Cause in America, and the greatest and most effectual Check that could be given the ambitious Designs of France.

REMARKS ON THE PASS OF NIAGARA. NOV. 1754 [1]
(COPY)

To Denonville or Niagara Fort by way of the Ohio is 600 MILES and Upwards, but from SUSQUEHANNA River at the head of CHESAPEAK bay, or from the head of DELAWARE River, the greatest Distance does not exceed 250 Miles, so that besides the Vast difference in the March, the following Advantages it is humbly Apprehended will attend going first to NIAGARA.

Taking it for granted that the Regular Forces now intended for the OHIO, with what Aids they will receive from our AMERICAN Colonies, will be able to drive the French from every post they now hold in that Quarter, And to demolish their little Insignificant Temporary Forts there, in a very short time; if this should happen, the French will retire from place to place untill they arrive at NIAGARA, where they have several Stone Forts comparatively speaking very Strong, & if ever they are able, or determin'd to make a Stand in any part of NORTH AMERICAN Disputed Territories it will be there, because it is the only Communication they have from CANADA to the Rivers OHIO or MISSISSIPPI, or that they can ever acquire so as to enable them to Transport a great Number of Men, Artillery, Stores Provisions &c. that way, because the Lake ONTARIO is the only one of the five great Lakes that has a Communication with the River St LAWRENCE, or the French Metropolis QUEBECK, and likewise with the Lake ERIE by the River NIAGARA, near which are the heads of the OHIO, St JEROMES &c., So that by the loss of Niagara the French on the OHIO will be obliged to Retire or Starve in a few Months, which will answer the same End as if they were beat off.

If our Army should be finally obliged to go to the OHIO it is Still humbly thought, that the best scheme is to reduce NIAGARA first, for from that to the Ohio is all Water Carriage but about 20 or 30 Miles and with the Stream mostly, And the French there can receive no Supplys from CANADA, if we are possess'd of NIAGARA, whereas by going first to the Ohio that Communication remains Uninterrupted both to and from Canada, the Consequence of which will be, that whatever Numbers or Supplys that Country Can afford will be immediately Sent to Niagara, which with the French Suppos'd to retire before us from the Ohio, will make a much greater Force than we should meet with

---

[1] These "Remarks" can be tentatively ascribed to a London merchant concerned with the colonies, perhaps to Sir John Barnard, whose plan of operations was discussed at a cabinet on November 10, Add. MSS. 32,995, f. 342.

in any one place were we to Attack Niagara first, while the French expect us on the Ohio. If to secure possession of the Ohio it is thought Necessary to Build Forts on it, there must in that Event be three at least, & these at a vast Distance from one another, Supported at a great Expence in very remote & Unsettled Countries, Whereas the pass of Niagara may be easily fortify'd & defended & may at all times be well Supply'd, as it lys nearly centrical to all our Colonies, And not above 150 Miles from Crown point; this pass being yet the only Communication the Canada French have with the Ohio, their being depriv'd of it will render any Forts there unnecessary, for the French at the Mouth of the Mississippie having 1000 Miles & more to the Mouths of the OHIO will not probably attempt comming there, when they find their Communication with Canada cut of, And if they should, one Strong Fort at the Mouth of St Jeromes River where it joins the Ohio, will intirely prevent them.

Memorial and State of the Exchange with the British Colonies in North America

(copy)

? 1754

WHAT is calld the Par of Exchange in our American Colonies, is the price fix'd on Dollars by the Several Legislatures, or the Sum of the Respective Currencies which by the same Authority is made the Stated Equivalent for £100 Ster[1]. But as Bills of Exchange are a Merchandise, they often rise & fall Considerably, According as it [is] easie or difficult to get them, or the Demand for them greater or less.

The Purchasers of Bills are commonly such Merchants as want to make Remittances to Europe, the West Indies or any of the other Colonies, and the Ballance of Trade being mostly against our Colonies in favour of Britain, they are obliged to make a great part of their Remittances in Money or Bills, and the Exchange or price they give for these Bills, is a good deal Regulated by the price of Silver in London of which they have Advice by every Ship. And when Silver is so dear in London as to bear the charge of Freight, Insurance, Commission &c., Exchange falls in America or the Specie is remitted, but as that is not allwise the Case, they generally chuse good Bills & give the full Value for them rather than be at the trouble of Remitting the Cash; but if at any time there should be a greater Demand for money than for Bills in America, (which might often happen if a Number of Troops

A State of the Exchange in the British North American Colonys Showing the Value of a Dollar & the Equivalent for £100 Sterling in each Province Currency as Stated by Act of Assembly, and likewise the Number of Dollars One Hundred pounds Sterling Bill will purchase when Exchange is at Par. N.B. Exchange often Varies. A Spanish Mill Dollar or piece of Eight Value in London from 4s 6d to 4s 8d According to the price of Silver. [1754?].

Provinces	Value of a Dollar in each Province's Currency (£ s d)	No of Dollars for £100 — Dollars	No of Dollars for £100 — Currency (shs · Pence)	Par of Exchange by Acts of the Assemblys	Exchange: often under,	seldom over,	or at Par
Boston New England Specie very scarce in general	— 6 —	444	2 · 8	133 · 6 · 8			
New York & East Jersey	— 8 —	437½	" · "	175 · " · "	from 174	to 186	for 100 st[1]
West Jersey & Philadelphia	— 7 · 6	453⅓	" · "	170 · " · "	169	186	D⁰
MaryLand	— 6 —	444	2 · 8	133 · 6 · 8	136	142	D⁰
Virginia, Paper currency in all the Colonys but this.	— 5 · 7½	444	2 · 6	125 · " · "	120	135	D⁰
South Carolina	1 · 11 · 6	444	14 · "	700 · " · "	600	800	D⁰
New Hampshire Connecttut & Rode Island	} Dollars at no fixt price, paper Currency alwise Fluctuating from				1000 to	1300	D⁰

Provinces that have a Silver Medium.

North Carolina little Transactions in Exchange & mostly Governed by Virginia & South Carolina

Georgia, Nova Scotia & Newfoundland (being mostly Supported by Parliamentary Grants) Transactions are in Nominal Sterling in Nova Scotia a Dollar passes for 5s Sterling which is from 4 pence to Six pence more than its Value in London.

The Charge of sending Specie to any of the Colonys from London, is Freight £1 or £1.10 p Ct Insurance £2.10 p Ct were amongst them) then the Merchants, ever Mindfull of their own Interest, would not fail to take the Advantage, and in such Event the Proprietors or Sellers of Bills must lose from £5 to 15p Cent, from which it is Obvious, that Regular Forces sent to America should never be totally without a Resource of ready Money within themselves to prevent their being under a Necessity of Selling Bills at so great a loss. Suppose therefore that Six Months Subsistence should be sent with the Troops intended for America, for themselves & those to be levied there, it would Render them Independent of the Merchants, who in that Event would Court their Favour, and the Principal of them would probably offer to Contract at the most reasonable Rate for what Money might be Afterwards wanted; this ready Cash however not to be expended but in part, & only at times & places where Bills cannot be Sold for their full Value.

The Principal, if not the only, places where Bills need be Negotiat, are Boston in New England, New York, Philadelphia, Maryland & Virginia, and if the Par of Exchange can be got in these Several places, it amounts to near the same Sum as if all the Bills were Negotiat in one only, for tho their Currencies differ nominally they are to a triffle the same in real Value, & there is further this Advantage in Selling Bills in different places, it prevents their being a Drug at any one Market. In the four Provinces of New England Specie is extreamly Scarce, & often not to be had at any Exchange, which makes it more Advantagious to Negotiat Bills in the Southern Colonies where they have generally Plenty of Money.

Sketch of an Order about the Rank &Cᴬ of the Provincial Troops in North America [1]

(COPY)

WHEREAS some doubts have arisen with regard to the Rank and Command, which Officers and Troops raised by the Governors of Our

[1] The same as the sign-manual order of November 12, 1754, printed in *New Jersey Arch.*, 1st ser. VIII, pt. 2, p. 29, with changes as indicated below. Precedents for this order are in the "Proposed Regulations relating to the East Indies, February, 1754" (also in the Cumberland Papers), which read in part:

"13. In order to avoid all Disputes or Misunderstandings between the Troops in His Majestys service, and those in the service of the Company His Majesty is pleased to order that the Former shall always take Rank of those of the Company: That, Officers of the same Degree shall roll together upon Guards, Parties or Courts Martial: but that the Officers in His Majesty's Service shall always take Rank or Precedence of those in the Company's: that, in Garrison, the Governor, if a Military Person, shall have the Honours directed by His Majesty's Regulation and the confirming of Sen-

Provinces in North America, should have when joyned or serving together with Our Independent Companies of Foot doing Duty in Our said Provinces; In order to fix the same and to prevent for the future all Disputes on that Account, We are hereby pleased to declare,[2] It is Our Will & Pleasure, that all Troops serving by Commissions signed by Us, or by Our General Comanding in Chief in North America,[3] shall take Rank before all Troops which may serve by Commission from any of the Governors or Councils [4] of Our Provinces in North America: And It is Our further Pleasure, that the Generals [5] and Field Officers of the Provincial Troops shall have no Rank with the Generals [5] & Field Officers who serve by Commissions from Us: But that all Captains & other inferior Officers of Our Forces, who are or may be employed in North America, are on all Detachments, Courts Martial or other Duty, wherein they may be joyned with Officers serving by Commissions from the Governors or Councils [4] of the said Provinces, to command and take Post of the said Provincial Officers of the like Rank, though the Commissions of the said Provincial Officers of the like Rank, should be of elder Dates.

We are further pleased to declare, that the Troops which may serve by Commissions from the Governors or Councils of the Provinces aforesaid, are, whenever they shall be joyned, or serve with Our Regular Forces, to be under the same Rules & Articles of War with them, and are to be liable to the like Pains & Penalties.[6]

---

tences of Courts Martial. But if no military officer, the Discipline of the Troops and the confirming of Sentences of Courts Martial shall be in the Hands of the Commanding Officer of the Troops.

"14. That all Courts Martial be held, and Sentences thereof put in Execution, agreeable to His Majestys Rules and Articles of War."

[2] Sign-manual order inserts "That."

[3] This clause is inserted in the margin, the document being in a memorandum form.

[4] Sign-manual order reads: "Governors, Lieutenant or Deputy Governors, or President for the time being."

[5] Sign-manual order reads: "General."

[6] This paragraph was omitted in the sign-manual order, as needing parliamentary authority. A clause was inserted in the Mutiny Act, in committee, December 11; the act received royal assent December 19.

Sketch for the Operations in North America.
Nov^R 16: 1754 [1]
(COPY)

1.

His Majesty's Intentions in sending the Forces to *North America* being to *recover* the Territories belonging to His Colonies there & to His subjects & allies the Indians, which the French have (most unjustly & contrary to Solemn Treaties subsisting between the two Crowns of Great Britain & France) invaded, & possessed themselves of, & raised Fortifications upon: the most speedy & most effectual Means should be taken to drive them therefrom; to destroy their strong Holds, & to secure, for the future, His Majesty's subjects & allies in the just Possession of their respective Lands & Territories.

2.

The French will, in all Probability, endeavour to reinforce the several Posts they now have on the River *Ohio;* & on the Lakes to the Westward of it, by sending Troops up the River *Mississipi:* as the season will allow the King's Troops to take the Field much sooner in those southern Parts than in any other Part of the Colonies; the operations should begin there as soon as the Weather will permit. The Troops should therefore be carried up the *Potomach* River, as high as *Will's Creek,* where Covering is ordered to be erected for them by Deputy Quarter Master general Sir John St Clair; as also Magazines & a Park for the amunition & artillery, which may be necessary upon this first Part of the Expedition: the Quarter Master general having likewise orders to prepare conveniencies for the gen[l] Hospital at *Hampton,* & for a flying one at the *Creek* before mentioned.

3.

When the French shall be drove from their Posts upon the *Ohio;* a good Fort should be erected on the most convenient Pass upon that River; & a strong Garrison of the three independant companies now

---

[1] This document is in memorandum form. A copy is in the Newcastle Papers, Add. MSS. 33,029, f. 144. This sketch formed the basis for Braddock's secret instructions (E. B. O'Callahan, ed., *Documents Relative to the Colonial History of the State of New York* [hereafter cited as *N. Y. Col. Docs.*], VI (1855), 920–922). Cumberland discussed them orally with Braddock and added details in a letter from Napier to Braddock, November 25, 1754, printed in J. B. Moreau, *A Memorial containing a summary View of Facts . . .* (1757), pp. 114–117.

in *Virginia,* sustained by such a *Part,* or the *Whole* of the Provincial Troops, be left to defend it, & to protect the Indians in those Parts, as well as the Brittish Settlements lately broken up.

4.

The next service & which is of the greatest importance, therefore demands the utmost Care & attention, is, the dislodging the French from the Forts they now have at the Falls & Passes of *Niagara;* & the erecting such a Fort there as shall, for the future, make His Majesty's subjects masters of the Lake *Ontario,* by that Means cutting off the Communication between the French Forces on the *Mississipi* & those on River St *Lawrence:* and, if, for this Purpose, the General should think it necessary to have ships upon the said Lake *Ontario,* he should have Power & orders for constructing such Vessels as shall be deemed most proper for that service.

5.

By that time that the service on the *Ohio* is finished, it is hoped that the Regiments of Shirley & Pepperel will be raised: if then he should find it necessary (as he probably will) to march his whole Force to make himself master of the Posts before mentioned at *Niagara;* he should take the most prudent & effectual Means of joyning his said Forces with the two Brittish Battalions, to effect this most necessary & essential service: and when he has performed it, he will leave the remaining independant companies, & such other Reinforcement of Troops as he shall judge to be a sufficient Garrison for the Fort or Forts he shall erect there.

6.

If the General should find that the two British Regiments will be sufficient for performing the service at *Niagara,* the two American Regiments may, at the same time be employed in dispossessing the French from their Post at *Crown Point* on the Lake *Chamblois,* which is the next Point to be gained. But, no positive Instructions can be given him on this Head, as he only can, hereafter, be judge whether such a separate operation can be undertaken at the same time that he is to make himself Master of that most material one at *Niagara.* However, after being possessed of the *Niagara* Forts, and a secure comunication opened betwixt that & *Oswego,* which will not only secure the back Settlements, but likewise bring back those Indians who may have fallen off from His Majesty's interest, & joyned the French, the next service is

7.

The reducing the Fort at *Crown Point,* & erecting an other upon the Lake *Chamblois,* in such Part as shall be found most effectual for bridling the French Indians in those Parts, and for securing & protecting our Neighbouring Colonies.

8.

The last & material service to be performed is the destroying the French Fort of *Beausejour,* & by that means recovering His Majesty's Province of *Nova Scotia.* But, on this, no positive instructions can be given to the General; only, that he should correspond constantly with Lieut Colonel Lawrence who commands *H:M:'s* Forces in that Province; and, if, whilst the service of *Niagara,* or *Crown Point* is going on (which must necessarily divide the French Forces) Cqⁱ Lawrence can, with a moral Certainty, undertake the reducing that Fort with the King's Forces which are now there; or, by an addition of *4:* or *500:* of the Provincial Forces, & that the General could spare such Numbers; it would be gaining much time in finishing the operations. But, if it should be found adviseable for Coⁱ Lawrence, to undertake that service in the manner before mentioned, but that it should require a greater Force: the General should be directed after his having finished the Reduction of *Crown Point* & fixing a proper Fort there, to proceed with such, or all of his Forces to *Nova Scotia;* & there to make himself thoroughly master of *Beausejour;* & by that means, of the whole Province.

9.

The two Companies of Artillery in *Newfoundland* & *Nova Scotia* will afford a sufficient supply of artillery officers & Gunners for any of the services before mentioned: and His Majesty's ships of war should have orders to give all the Assistance possible in their way.

10.

The General should cultivate the best Friendship & Harmony possible with the Governours of the Provinces, & the Chiefs of the Indian Tribes; & should transmit, by every opportunity, particular Accounts of his Transactions and situation, to His Majesty's Secretary of State.

Quære, Prisoners.

Quære, next Winter Quarters.

INSTRUCTIONS FROM THE LORDS OF THE ADMIRALTY TO ADMIRAL KEPPEL [1]

(COPY)

By the Commissioners for executing the Office of Lord High Admiral of Great Britain and Ireland &c

Instructions for the Honble Augustus Keppel, Comamnder in Chief of His Majesty's Ships and Vessels employed and to be employed on the Coast of North America.

WHEREAS His Majesty hath been pleased to direct, That two of His Ships of the Line, and Two Frigats, should be got ready to be employed in North America for the Protection of His Colonies, and that a sufficient Number of Transport Ships should be provided and Victualled, for carrying from Cork in Ireland to Virginia in North America Sir Peter Halket's & Colonel Dunbar's Regiments of Foot, each consisting of 644 Persons, together with 74 Commission Officers their Servants and Baggage; and 354 Tuns of Arms, Accoutrements &c[a] for Col[o] Shirley's and Sir William Pepperel's Regiments to be raised in New England; likewise for the Director of an Hospital, with a Number of Officers, Servants & Stores amounting in the whole to about 100 Tuns; also, for taking on board one thousand Barrels of Beef, and Ten Tuns of Butter, for the Use of the said Forces; to proceed under Convoy of the Two aforementioned Frigats; And Thirteen Transport Ships being provided for this purpose (as in the List hereunto annexed, wherein is the Disposition of Officers, Soldiers, and Stores for each) [2] and Victualled for the Numbers of Persons they are to carry, with Four Months Proportion of Beef and Pork, and Three Months of all other Species, at Whole Allowance, altho' the Persons on board are to be Victualled at Two Thirds, as usual; the said

---

[1] This document is in memorandum form, half the page having been left blank for corrections and additions.

[2] On these thirteen transports, with a total tonnage of 3,525, was space for 150 officers, 1,620 men, and 354 tons of baggage. This is the usual mathematical proportion of two tons a man, which to prevent crowding and sickness was seldom followed on trans-Atlantic voyages.

Thirteen Ships, with Three others laden with Ordnance Stores in the Service of that Office, are ordered to proceed directly from Cork to Virginia, under Convoy of His Majesty's Ships the Seahorse and Nightingale, commanded by Captains Pallisser and Digges.

And whereas we did, on the 9th of last Month, appoint you Commander in Chief of His Majestys Ships and Vessels employed and to be employed on the Coast of North America, empowering you to hoist a broad Pendant on board such of them wherein you may be, and to have a Captain under you; And we having ordered His Majesty's Ship the Centurion, now in her Passage to Spithead, to be fitted for your Reception, You are hereby required and directed to repair on board and take her under your Command, as also the Norwich (which Ship We have appointed to receive Major General Braddock, with his Attendants, Servants, and Baggage,) and proceed with them to Virginia; but if the General should be embarked, & the Centurion not arrived, You are to permit the Captain of the Norwich to proceed agreeable to the Orders he hath received from Us, and to follow in the Centurion without calling at any Place whatever in your Passage.

When you arrive at Virginia, in the Centurion, you will probably find there the Three other aforementioned Men of War, with the Transports; and also the Ships named in the Margin, which are Stationed in North America, and ordered to rendezvous at Virginia; All which you are to take under your Command, if you find them at that place, or as they shall arrive there.

Syren.
Guarland.
Portmahon.
Mermaid.
Jamaica.
Baltimore. } Sloops.

And His Majesty having appointed Major General Braddock to be Commander of His Forces that are or shall be raised in North America, We do hereby require & direct you to cultivate a good Understanding & Correspondence with the said General, during your Continuance upon the Service with which you are now entrusted, the said General having received Directions of a like Nature, with regard to his Conduct & Correspondence with you.

Whenever the General, or Commander in Chief of the Forces shall find it necessary to call to his Assistance a Council of War, by the Advice of whom all Operations to be performed by the said Forces under his Command are to be determined, as well as all other important Points relating thereto, you are to assist thereat, if the same be held at a convenient Distance.

If on your arrival at Virginia, you find the Transports with the Forces there, and not disembarked; or, when they arrive within the Capes of Virginia, You are to Consult with the General, and the Governor, where it may be most convenient they should debark, and if it shall be judged necessary to send them up any of the Rivers in that Province, you are to direct the Transports, with such of His Majesty's Ships as may be fit for that purpose, to proceed accordingly as far up as the Pilots will take Charge of them, and to give all necessary Assistance from the Ships in landing the Forces, Artillery, Stores &c^a, and in Case a proper Quantity of Provisions shall not be provided in the Country for the Subsistance of the Forces, You are to cause the General to be supplyed (if he desires it) with the Thousand Barrels of Beef and Ten Tuns of Butter beforementioned, and as much more of those Species of Provisions, or any other, as may be remaining on board the Transports after the Forces are landed, taking Care that proper Receipts be given for what shall be supplied.

And whereas there are now dispersed on board the Transports 74 Commission Officers, with their Servants, and also 354 Tuns of Arms, Accoutrements &c^a belonging to Colonel Shirley's and Sir Willm Pepperel's Regim^ts to be raised in New England, You are to cause them forthwith to be put together on board such of those Ships as shall be found most convenient, with a proper Quantity of Provisions, and order them to proceed to Boston in New England, under the Convoy of one of His Majesty's Ships, or a Sloop, the first Opportunity that offers; and having landed the Officers, Arms &c^a, the Masters of the Transports are forthwith to return the Remains of the Kings Provisions, Cask &c^a which the Commander of the Convoy, after taking so much on board the Ship under his Command as she can conveniently stow, is to get secured in a proper Place till there may be an Opportunity of bringing the same to you in one of His Majesty's Ships, and the said Commander is also to give the Masters of the Transports Receipts for what they so return, together with Certificates of their being discharged the Service; which done, he is to permit them to proceed where-ever they please, and then he is to return to you with the Ship or Sloop under your Command. But if you find, there is more probability of a Passage being gained to Boston by Ships of War, than by the Transports, You are to appoint One, or more, of the Ships of your Squadron, if the same can be spared, to carry the said Officers, Servants, Arms, and Accoutrements &c thither.

You are to Order Lieu^t William Shackerly, who is appointed to Act as Agent for the Transports, to clear them, immediately after the Debarkment of the Forces, of their Provisions & Stores, to prevent the Charge of Demurrage, which commences within Twenty Days after their arrival within the Capes of Virginia, and to distribute amongst

the Ships under your Command such Part of the Provisions as they
may want, and to provide Store-room for the Remainder, with the
Stores, either at Hampton, or whatever place you shall find most convenient, and immediately to discharge the Transports, unless, upon
advising with the General, and Governor, it shall be found expedient
to keep part of them in the Service, which in that Case you are at
liberty to do, but to have regard to the Contracts made with the Navy
Board for those Ships, in some of which it is expressly stipulated they
shall be discharged upon their Arrival at Virginia.

You are to employ His Majesty's Ships under your Command in
such manner as shall be most conducive to the Protection of His
Colonies in North America, and to that end you are at liberty, when
it shall be judged for the Good of the King's Service, to land any
Number of Men that can be conveniently spared from the Ships, with
discreet Officers, to co-operate with the Land Forces, or act in such
manner as may be agreed on at a Council of War, where you have
been present and concurred.

Whereas we have thought it necessary, that Two Lieutenants of
His Majesty's Fleet should serve under You, in addition to the proper
Number of Lieutenants belonging to each Ship, to be employed in
attending the Land Forces in their Marches, in order to assist in making Floats for their passing the Rivers, Drafts of the Country through
which they pass, and on such other Services as you shall find necessary; And We having appointed Lieutenants William Shackerly and
Charles Spendelow to perform these Services, You are to employ them
accordingly, keeping one of them constantly with the Forces, particularly Lieut Spendelow, he being furnished with Instruments for
taking Observations, and making Drafts; and you are to direct him
to be very particular therein, and to transmit the same to Us, from
time to time, through your Hands.

And it having been represented to us that two or three small Armed
Vessels to be employed upon the Lake Ontario would Countenance the
Trade of His Majesty's Subjects in these Parts, and be a Security to
our Rights and Possessions, You are to consult with the General and
Governors of His Majesty's Provinces thereupon, and if it shall appear
to You and them to be of the Service represented, You are to cause
proper Vessels to be built and fitted upon the Boarders of the Lake
in the most frugal manner, We having directed the Navy Board to
put a sufficient Quantity of Iron Work, Cordage & Canvas on board
the Centurion for One of them (a particular Account whereof is annexed) and also to give you the Draught of an Armed Vessel of about

Sixty Tuns, which you will make Use of, or otherwise as upon further Enquiry in the Country You may find most proper, and you are to draw Bills upon the Navy Board for the Expence, and when these Vessels are properly fitted, You are to put on board them Ten Swivel Guns from the Ships & Sloops under your Command with a proportion of Ordnance Stores, and small Arms, causing them to be Mann'd with 25 or 30 Men, and to appoint Lieu[t] Spendelow to take the Command of One, who is not only to be Employed for the Purposes beforementioned, but to make an Accurate Survey of the Lake and adjacent Country, and to continue on this Service till further Order.

In case Major General Braddock shall apply for the Assistance of the Kings Ships to bring two Companies of Artillery or part of them from S[t] Johns in Newfoundland or Nova Scotia, You are to Order such of the Ships under your Command to perform this Service, as you shall judge proper.

It having been represented to His Majesty, that an Illegal Correspondence and Trade is frequently carried on, between the French and the King's Subjects in the several Colonies, You are to take all possible Measures to prevent the Continuance of such dangerous Practices, and more particularly to hinder the French being supplied, on any Account whatever, with Provisions, or Naval or Warlike Stores.

In Case the Whole, or any Part, of the aforementioned 1000 Barrels of Beef, Ten Tuns of Butter, and Remains of Provisions in the Transports at the Debarkment of the Forces, shall not be desired by the General, for the Use of the said Forces, you are to cause the same to be distributed and expended on board His Majesty's Ships under your Command.

You are to remain on this Service till you receive further Orders; but you are not to keep with you, longer than you shall find necessary, the Ships and Sloops stationed at the several Colonies, but to send them back to their Stations so soon as the Service will admit; and, in the mean time, to let them visit the Colonies they are Stationed at, as frequently as you can spare them long enough to do so, and you are not to take the Nova Scotia Ship and Sloop away from that Station, without an absolute Necessity for your so doing.

When you shall return to England, You are to take Care, that the Ships which shall be ordered home with you, have not more than Three Months Provisions on board for their Passage; nor are any of the Ships under your Command to have their Provisions at any time compleated to more than a Three Months Proportion, unless you shall find any particular Service you may employ them upon shall render more necessary; and You are to take Care, that timely Demands be made upon the Contractors, or their Agents, for what may be wanted.

For the better maintaining a proper and good Government and strict Discipline in the Squadron under your Command, We do hereby Authorize You to call and assemble Courts Martial in Foreign Parts, as often as there shall be Occasion.

And whereas Vacancies of Officers may happen in the said Squadron, We do empower You to fill up such as shall be occasioned by Death, or Dismission by a Court Martial; which are the only Cases in which we shall confirm Officers appointed by Commanders in Chief Abroad.

PRIVATE INSTRUCTIONS FOR MAJOR-GEN. BRADDOCK
(COPY)

GEORGE, R.   Private Instructions for our trusty & well-beloved *Edward Braddock,* Esqr Major General of our Forces, & whom we have appointed General & Commander of all and singular our Troops & Forces that are now in North America, & that shall be sent or raised there to vindicate our just Rights and Possessions in those Parts. Given at our Court at St James's the 25th Day of Novr *1754:* in the 28th Year of our Reign.

Whereas You are acquainted by the 6th & 7th Articles of our *General Instructions* [1] with the Dispositions that we have ordered to be made in our Colonies, for establishing a common Fund, to be employed provisionally for our Service in North America & particularly for the Charge of Levying Troops; You will be very diligent in informing yourself, upon your arrival what has been, or what is likely to be done for that Purpose; and, in case, you should find that the several Colonies do not contribute a sufficient sum to the said common Fund, to enable you to defray the Charge of raising the Troops intended, you will then, & in that Case, cause such an addition to be made thereto, out of the money deposited in the Hands of our Pay-Master in North America, as shall be sufficient to pay each private man, so raised, by way of Levy-money, a sum not exceeding £3: sterling p man. However, that our service may not be disappointed, or the intended Troops not be raised for want of the full Levy-money that may be re-

[1] Printed in *Pennsylvania Archives, 1748–1763,* p. 203, and in Winthrop Sargent, *The History of the Expedition against Fort Duquesne in 1755 under Major-General Braddock,* Appendix I, p. 393.

quisite, in case, the said £3: sterling p man shall not prove sufficient, we are hereby pleased to authorise & empower You, upon such Emergency only, to exceed the said sum of £3: sterling p man, as far as you shall find the same to be absolutely necessary & unavoidable.

G:R.

JOHN WINSLOW [1] TO CHARLES GOULD [2]

(L.S.)

Boston, New England.
Decr 30th 1754.

Good Sir,

My last to you was from the Camp at Bangs Island Casco Bay the latter end of June past if I remember right (My papers being all in the Country) wherein I inform'd you I was at the head of Eight hundred of my Country Men bound up the river of Kennebeck, shall for your Amusement without Ceremony give you a Short Narration of our proceedings hope you will excuse all Slips & Mistakes in Stile as you know I am no Scholar.   To Begin—

We Decampt from Bangs Island July 4th and Embarqued on Board our several Vessells in the Morning, and in the Evening Anchored in the Mouth of the river Kennebeck Distance about Ten Leagues on the 5th & 6th our whole Force got up as far as Richmond Fort a Number of Indians also Arriving at the same time, I ordered them to Incamp on the Opposite side of the river from the Fort, this is a Wood Fortification Built with hewen Timber, Mounts Ten Guns, and is used as a place of Trade with the Indians carryed on by this Government, and is Twenty five Miles up the river from its Entrance into the Sea, and stands on the West side. On the 7th orderd our Men under the Cover of our Guns to Incamp on shore & refresh themselves, and that Lieu^t Coll^o Preble with one hundred & Fifty Men reconnite the Country, and to assist the Carpenters to bring up Timber &c., which the Government before hand had procured in order for Building a

---

[1] John Winslow, a native of Plymouth, Massachusetts, had served as a captain of Massachusetts troops on the Cartagena expedition, had transferred into Phillips's regiment at Halifax, thence into Shirley's regiment formed in 1746. On British half pay in 1754, Shirley appointed him to the Kennebec River command.

[2] Charles Gould was a son of King Gould, agent for Nova Scotia until 1749 and army agent for the 40th regiment until about 1753, who died at Little Ealing in 1756. Charles Gould's answer of March 4, 1755, is printed in Winslow's journal in Nova Scotia Hist. Soc. Coll., IV (1884), 170.

Fort. On the 8th reimbarq'd, & came to sail, pass'd by Frank Fort, which is two Blockhouses well Picquetted in standing on the East side of the river, which was Built and is Maintain'd at the Cost of the Proprietors called the Plymouth Company, who have also near it divers Settlements on the same side of the river and is Distance from Fort richmond a Mile & Quarter and is the Uttermost English Settlement on the river Kennebeck, and that Evening arriv'd at a place call'd Cobesaconte Ten Miles above richmond on the Eighth proceeded up the river having a Captins Command Marching on each side thereof to prevent a Surprize from the Indians, and as this has been a Navigation disused by the English for Eighty years past, I proceeded with our Whale Boats & Masters of Vessells in their Boats to sound the river as we went, and for four Miles above Cobesaconte found a fine Twining Channel, at the end of which we were strangely Embarras'd with Rocks & Shoals at the Entrance whereof we Anchored. 9th 10th 11th Spent in Sounding the river, examining the Country to find a proper place to erect a Fort, and as the Tide & Weather would admit kept moving up the river with our Vessells on the 12th at a Council of War determind to Build our first Fort at a place called Cushenoc Near the Spot where one hundred years ago the late Plymouth Colony had a Garrison, and is Seventeen Miles above Richmond, and on the East side of the river, & is at the end of Navigation for Vessells of Burthen, as the Falls begin within a Mile of it, and even to this is Common Tides we carry but about eight foot of Water, and here we Incampt raisd our Blockhouse, Houses & Pallasaded them in, and put ourselves in a posture of Defence, cleard the Land all round to the Distance of two Musquett Shott, which employd all our Men except a party we sent to reconniter the River as far as the great Falls of Teconnett which is Eighteen Miles Distant from Cushnoe & took us till the 21th Day when we set forward with two Gundeloes, (Boats built some what like your West Country Barges, but draw less Water) with our heavy Stores and train of Artillery, Consisting of Eight Cannon, two Mortars, and some Swifells, ten Whale Boats, Twenty Battoes of our own Building, & some Canoes. And altho the party sent up the river returnd and gave us an Account that it was Impracticable to proceed with the Gundaloes, yet I was determined to attempt it, being sensible, that if those Boats could not be got up we must leave our Train of Artillery; being thus equipt for Sailing or rather Rowing & Towing we set forward with about Six hundred Men by Land & Water determind at events to gain our point and well it was we were so for it took us five days to March Row & Tow eighteen Miles, and was five days of the hardest Duty that

ever I saw any Troops employ'd on, we were Continually in the Water
from Morning till Night getting our Boats over Rocks, Sand & Falls
many places of which there was scarse half the Water they drew, and
as these were Difficulties that the Men thought unsurmountable, the
Officers were Obligd to exert themselves, and I assure you that I on
this Occasion was not Lacking, and dont Remember any of these Days,
but that I was some hours of each in the Water and once in a while
put to Swimming, but however at the last on the 25th Arrivd safe
without the Loss of a Man, within Cannon Shott of the Falls of Teconnett where on a Point made by the river Sebastacook emptying
itself into the River Kennebeck we Incampt, and on the 26th got up
our Cannon, & Fortified our Campt Landed our Stores &c, and also in
a Council of War determind where to set our Fort, and on the next
Day laid out the Ground began to clear it, seated our Guns & Mortars,
Hoisted the Kings Colours with the Beat of Drum, and sound of
Trumpet, and the Discharge of our whole Artillery, and small Arms
Drank his Majesty, and calld this place Fort Hallifax, as we before
that below had calld Fort Western, (and this by his Excellency Govr
Shirley's Direction) by which names I shall hereafter call them, in this
place we continued Imploying our people, as well Soldiers as Artificers
& Labourers in Cutting Timber and Picquets, and erecting them, saw-
ing Boards & Plank, Building Store Houses, getting Clapboards &
Shingles, procuring Stones out of the river, making Bricks, Burning
Coals &c. and by the Seventh of August got in a good posture of Defence, and on that Day at a Council of War determind to proceed as
high up the river as the Indian Carrying place, and from that to half
the Distance to the river of Shodier which falls into the river of St.
Lawrence near Quebeck and thro which the Indians go to Cannada,
and to examine that pass, and on the next day began to put that
projection in execution, setting out with five hundred Men for that
purpose Leav^g Two hundred Men at Fort Halifax & one hundred at
Fort Western besides Labourers, having with us fifteen Battoes for
Transporting Provissions which Boats & all we were Obligd to carry
over Land half a Mile on Mens shoulders round the Falls of Teconnett
and found great Difficulty afterwards in getting up the river, the Water
being low at that Season and at that time a great Drouth which ren-
derd them more so, however we kept on having a Surveyor & Chain
Men aserting the Distance of our March as well as the Course of the
river by Compass & Measure till the Ninth (Unhappy Day to me) when
after Marching very hard & being extream Hot, I came across a fine
Spring of Water, Drank plentifully, and Marching with the Advancd

party, and fatigued throw'd myself under a Tree to sleep till the rear came up, but was presently awak'd in an od Condition a Universal stagnation, Crampt and Convulst to the last Degree, My Surgeon being with me took from me Two pound of Blood, gave me Volatives by the help of which after laying about three hours I March on two Miles; which Brought us nine Miles Distance from Fort Hallifax where we Campt under the Bows of Trees, and provd a Rainey Night, the next Morning found my Self so Weak and faint, and my Nerves & Mussells so disordered as to render me unfit for Marching Duty, therefore on the tenth in the Morning sent for Coll° Prebble gave him the Command & orders to Compleat the March I had begun, Kept with me an Officer & fifteen Men & two Boats to return to the Garrison. This March Coll° Preble performd agreeable to the plan herewith sent and returnd to Fort Hallifax in fifteen Days having lost one Man only and of him they could give no Account, at the end of which the pond Mark'd we supose & are pretty certain by the Degrees of Lattitude to be within Fourteen Leaques of Quebeck the Capital of Cannada.[3] but to return to my Self got to Fort Hallifax in the Evening of the tenth; lay by the next day, found the Regiment 801 Effective, besides Artificers & Labourers. On the 12th set out for Casco, arriv'd at Fort Western, 13th View'd the Fort, gave the proper orders, continued my Route for Casco to wait on his Excellency the Governour arrivd on the 14th at Night continued there with his Excellency to settle a plan for our future Opperations till 20th, receivd directions relaiting to the Fortifications yet to be erected, set out for Fort Hallifax, arrivd there the 21th at Night Distance from Casco to Fort Hallifax 76 Miles. On the 22nd gave orders for Building the Fortifications, and Barracks, agreeable to the Plan. Kept all hands at Work, and Continued in it, till the 20th Septem[r] when we were Obliged by our Terms of Enlistment to Disband. On the 21st Embarqued for Boston and arrivd here the 30th. Thus I have Led you a Wild Goose Chase in a Wild Wilderness, & like the Moose & Bears the Native Inhabitants, and the more savage Aboriginals the Indians, Made Mother Earth our Bed, and the Canopy of Heaven our Covering, yet thro Gods goodness lost but three

[3] It was sixty-four miles from the place Preble left Winslow (near Hinckley) to the beginning of the carry above Carritunk. From there to Dead River was twelve miles, from Dead River to the Chain Ponds at the foot of the Height of Land about fifty-six miles, twenty-one miles across the Height of Land to Lake Megantic, and 137 miles more to Quebec. If Preble went at the same rate as Winslow had done the first day, nine to ten miles a day, and returned within fifteen days, he could not have got much further than the carry itself. The pond he reached was probably one of the three Carry Ponds. The best description of this route is in Kenneth Roberts, *Arundel* (rev. ed.).

Men only and not one of them fairly. By this I judge you are Tyred, and shall therefore Drop the Doctrimental part, and proceed to the Application. Vizt—That by Gov[r] Shirleys Unwearied Endeavours to serve this province, as well as the King of Great Britain whome he honours by being faithfull to his Trust and the Dilligence of me his Substitute a nearer way is found to Quebeck than has ever heretofore been thought of, and I am in no Doubt, but that all these things have been properly Laid before the people at Home [?] by the Governour yet notwithstanding, whenever you think proper you may Shew these things, and depend on it they are Facts. And should His Majesty want any Service done on this side the Water it may be rely'd on, I am both able & Willing to Obey & persuade my self can bring more effective Men into the Feild than any Man on the Continent, (my Gov[r] excepted) have Briefly Mentiond these Things to your Hon[d] Father, and also told him you would shew him this Epistle, and am persuaded that your joint Friendship, could carry any thing into Execution with the little pretentions I have and every thing will be acknowledg'd that is done for me, shall hear further from me soon, Service to all Freinds, and be assured I am—

Your Sincere Friend & humble Servant

JOHN WINSLOW

SIR JOHN ST. CLAIR [1] TO ROBERT NAPIER

(A.L.S.)

Williamsbourg Feb[ry] the 10th 1755.

Sir,

I know no better way of giving you an account of my proceedings in this Country than to transcribe two Letters which I wrote to General Braddock, the one of the 15th of Jan[ry] and the other of the 9th of Feb[ry]; which I hope will be satisfactory.

Sir,   Williamsbourg Jan[y] the 15th 1755.

"I was very sorry that I had it not in my power to receive your Commands before I embarked for America, least you may find any thing neglected on your Arrival. I landed at Hampton the 9th Ins[t] and

---

[1] Sir John's title was probably spurious (George E. Cockayne, ed., *Complete Baronetage* (1904), IV, 301). He was the son of Sir George St. Clair or Sinclair of Kinnaird, Fife. He served as deputy quartermaster general in North America from 1754 until his death in 1767, an efficient officer in that important post. He married an American girl, Betsy Moland. His will is in *New Jersey Arch.*, 1st ser. XXXIII, 370. A sketch of him by C. R. Hildeburn is in *Pennsylvania Magazine of History and Biography*, IX (1885), 1–14.

have ever since been endeavouring to comply with my orders: I shall here send you the Heads of them, and shall inform you what Steps I have taken in the Execution of them.

1st. To provide an Hospital at Hampton or Williamsbourg for 150 Sick.

2dly. To provide provisions against the landing of the Troops and during their stay at Wills's Creek.

3. Bass Horses to be provided for the Officers when they arrive.

4. To consult with the Governour the proper Measures for erecting Log Houses or Barns at Wills's Creek.

5. Floats or Batteaus for the transporting the Artillery and Bagage from the falls of the Pattomack to Wills's Creek.

6. To settle with the Governour the best and speediest manner to compleat the two Battalions with 200 good Men each. The 10th I went to Williamsbourg and delivered my Dispatches to the Govr. The next day I consulted with His Excellency the properest Methods for going to work on this urgent piece of Service. That Day one hundred Horses were contracted for, 40 of which were to be deliver'd the 1st week in Feb^{ry} and the remaining part the first day of March; each of these Horses are to carry 200 lb of Flower to Wills's Creek.

"The 12th I went with the Governour to Hampton in order to provide an Hospital & lodging for its proper Officers. Next day I went and examined the whole Town of Hampton but cou'd not find any one place Sufficient to contain any Number of Sick; all I cou'd get was two very small Ware Houses; But there are no Houses in Town which will be shut to us on this occasion: So how disagreeable it may be to the Surgeons to have their Sick separate, there is a necessity for it at present. There are Numbers of indigent people who will take the Sick into their Houses, and least Bedsteads may be wanting I have given Directions for 100 Cradles to be built. I have provided extreme good Lodgings at the Town Clerks House for two of the principal Officers of the Hospital, the others may lodge with those people who keep publick Houses untill Mr. Graham leaves his dwelling house which will be towards the End of Feb^{ry}. I shou'd not have hesitated one Moment in running up a large Hospital of Boards if I cou'd have got a Sufficient Quantity of Deal and Artificers, but both are wanting.

"I gave Directions to Mr. Hunter (who delivers you this) concerning a Stock of fire wood for the Hospitals, and to get as much fresh Provisions collected together for the Sick as possible; as likewise to throw on board of the Transports some Sheep and fresh Pork, and some Beefs if they are to be had.

"The Governour has been extremely active and diligent in gathering together all kind of Provisions for Wills's Creek, & to make a deposite at Fredericksbourg & Winchester to be near at hand. The Carriage to the Creek is immensely difficult at this Season on account of the Scarcity of Horses, and if we had them, Forage is scarce to [be] had. I am in Hopes we shall be able to collect 200 Horses. If we had more, how are they to be fed? I return'd to Williamsbourg the 13th in the Evening.

"Jan: 14th I saw some more Horses bought for the use of the Troops. I wrote Letters to the Governours of all the Provinces & sent my Dispatches to them.

"I must, Sir, refer you to the Governour with regard to compleating Sir Peter Halketts & Col: Dunbar's Regiments, all I shall say [is] that Men will not be wanting when you please to call for them.

"That part of my Instructions which regards the building of Batteaus or Floats on the Pattommack at the Falls of Alexandria, I am obliged to delay executing, as I am informed the doing of it wou'd be in vain, for that in Winter the Stream is so rapide that there is no rowing heavy Boats against the Current, and that in Summer there are many flatts and Shoals which will render the Navigation almost impracticable. On the whole I have acted to the best of my Capacity, and whatever Difficultys may arrise I shall do what I can to surmount them.

"I propose going to morrow morning from hence to Wills's Creek, I shall go the one Road and return the other; my Journey will take me at least twelve Days going and coming back, being 600 Miles with the same Horses; I shall stay there about Six Days which I hope will be Sufficient to see our Barracks in a fair way of being built. Shou'd you arrive with the Troops before my return I beg of you to send me your Orders by an Express that I may know how to conduct my Self.

"I have been talking to the Governour concerning the properest Method of landing the Troops; He is of opinion they shou'd proceed to Alexandria in their Transports, and march as soon as possible to Wills's Creek; For if they were to land at Hampton & be dispersed about the Country, they wou'd have a long march by land, that all the Horses & Carriages which will be wanted to carry Provisions to the Deposites, wou'd be wanted, to attend the Troops, on their march to Alexandria; and that if they were to march by land, they have Ferrys to cross, which might be attended with a long delay. After examining the situation of the Country, and the quick Dispatch that Affairs require, I am of the above opinion with the Governour, for we shall at least gain three Weeks by going up directly by Water.

"I am in hopes we shall not want Flower and Salt Pork, which is what is easiest to be had in this Country. The Governour has wrote to New England for a Cargoe of Salt Fish, and if you are of opinion that Rice will do for our Men, it may be easily had. We may get some Calavances of the Pea kind which I believe our People will be fond of. That you may be the better Judge of the Difficulty of carriage from Alexandria to Wills's Creek, the Govr pays 20 Shillings for the carriage of each Barrell of Beef, for the 900 [?] Men that have been building a Fort at that place & who continue at Work.

"I think if no unforseen accident happens to me that I shall return hither the 2^d Day of Feb^{ry} or sooner if I can do my business. I have the Honour of being with the greatest Respect Sir, Your most obedient and most humble Servant.

JOHN ST. CLAIR

"pS. If a large quantity of Iron is not brought out with the Artillery, it will be necessary that a Dozen of Quintal shoud be bought at Hampton to make portable Ovens.

"To Major General Braddock."

"Sir   Williamsbourg Feb^{ry} the 9th 1755.

"I did my self the Honour of writing a Letter to you of the 15th of January, giving you an account of my proceedings till that time, least you shou'd have arrived during my absence. I shall now let you know in what manner I have been employ'd since the Date of my last Letter, least my Duty shou'd call me from this place or from Hampton, which might deprive me of the pleasure of receiving your Commands untill my Return.

"The 16th of Jan: I set out for Fredericksbourg, and got to that place the 18th being 104 Miles of very good Road. I saw at that place 190 Men of the Companys raised in this Province. I was from the 19th to the 22^d in getting to Winchester which is 93 Miles of very bad Road, I saw a Detatchment of 70 Men of the same Troops. From the 23^d to the 26th I was on the Road to Wills's Creek, this is 85 Miles of the worst Road I ever travelled; and greatly lengthen'd by the Roads being in the Channells of the Rivers, when they might be shorten'd by cutting them along the Ridges of the Mountains: Which Lord Fairfax promised me shou'd be done about this time. This will shorten that

Road about 15 Miles, and avoid the bad Road by Patersons Creek.

"When I had got about two Miles on the other Side of the South branch, I had a full view of the Mountains on each side of the Pattomack above Wills's Creek, and from what I cou'd see, there is a Road easily to be made across the Country to the Mouth of Savage River which will be gaining 30 Miles: If I am not more deceived than I have been of late with regard to Ground, the Mouth of Savage River is the place where we ought to cross the Allegany Mountains. I have only been able to find one Woodsman who can give me any distinct Account of that Ground, which gives me great Satisfaction. I have wrote to Lord Fairfax to have the Road marked out to the mouth of Savage River.

"I cannot learn what cou'd induce People ever to think of making a fort or a Deposite for Provisions at Wills's Creek; It covers no Country, nor has it the Communication open behind it either by Land or Water; the River not navigable and by the least Rains that fall, the Rivers which one has to cross (some of them five times) were without Floats or Canoes, untill within these few Days that they have been set about to be built.

"I found the Governour of Maryland at Wills's Creek, who had been at that place but a few Days, not long enough to make any Considerable alteration nor to reconoitre the Country. He had with him at the Fort (or more properly a small piece of Ground inclosed with a Strong Palisade joined pretty close) three Independent Companys, the one of South Carolina, and the other two of New York: the latter seem to be draughted out of Chelsea. The Excuse they make for having so many old Men does very little Honour to those Companys that are left behind at New York; for they say that they are draughted from them. The Carolina Company is in much better order and Discipline. I likewise saw at Wills's Creek 80 Men of the Troops raised in Maryland, they are a good body of Men, and if the rest of the Troops raised in that province be as good (which the Govr has reason to expect) we may get 150 Men from that Province to enable us to complete the two British Regiments.

"Least it shou'd be still more adviseable to pass the Mountains at Wills's Creek, there are a Number of Trees cut down for erecting Loghouses, and I gave directions for Palisading a House near the Fort for a Powder Magazine.

"In my last letter to you, I acquainted you that Governor Dinwiddie told me that the Navigation of the Pattommack is impracticable, this I can now affirm from Experience, for Governour Sharp and I found it so for all other Vessells but Canoes cut out of a Single Tree; We attempted to go down the River in this Sort of Boat, but we were obliged to get on Shore and walk on foot especially at the Shannondeau Falls: So that the getting Batteaus or Floats made for the transport of the Artillery and the Bagage of the Regiments, cou'd serve for no other thing, but to throw away the Governments Money to no purpose, and loose a great deal of time.

"As Governour Sharp expected to have found you arrived, he came to this place by Alexandria and Fredericksbourg, at the latter I saw him review 80 Men of the Virginia Troops, which amount by this time to 700 or 800 Men: By what I saw of them, I am afraid the Officers who recruited them, have looked more to their Numbers than to the goodness of the Men. These 80 were the only ones which Govr Sharp has seen. I make no doubt, but that from the Report I made to Govr Dinwiddie of his new Leavies, that their Numbers will be diminished before you arrive.

"As the Nature of the Service we are going on, will require a great Number of Carpenters, a Company totally composed of these is now a forming of 100 Men, from whom we may expect great advantage. I wish we may be able to find people to form into two Companys of Rangers.

"Whatever Scheme, Sir, you may think proper out of your prudence to pursue; the first thing to be done at all Events is to have our Artillery, Bagage and Provisions carried up to Winchester from Alexandria; for which reason I have ordered all kinds of provender for Horses to be laid in at these two places, in as great quantity as the Country can afford, which is but small. I expect 100 Waggons with Flower from Pensilvania at Winchester by the 15th of March, which Waggons will serve for carrying the Amunition and Stores from Alexandria, least the Horses of this Country employ'd before that time shou'd fall off. On this depends the dispatch we shall be able to make, I hope to get as much Oats, Hay and Indian Corn Blades as will enable us to transport the whole to Winchester: But I am afraid we shall not be able to cross the Mountains till the latter End of April when the Grass begins to shoot.

"During the Transport of the Artillery to Winchester, there will be sufficient time to cut the Road to Savage River, and to reconoitre the Ground towards the head of the Youghangany, one branch of which seems to lock in with the former.

"As I have seen most of this Country, I shall more freely give my oppinion with regard to the Disposition of the Troops on their Arrival, both for the Security of our Magazines, Subsistance of the Troops, ease of the Inhabitants and that as few Countermarches may be made as possible.

"That the Transports which have on board one Regiment may stop in the River Pattommack as near Fredericksbourg as they can, that Regiment may be quartered in the following manner.

$3\frac{1}{2}$ Companys at Winchester 6 Days march from Fredericksbourg

  $\frac{1}{2}$ of a Company at Conogogee 8 Days by Winchester

6   Companys at Fredericksbourg & Falmouth, one march from their landing

    "The other Regiment

5 Companys at Alexandria with the Company of Artillery & Stores of all kind.

1 Company at Dumfries 2 Days march from Alexandria.

1 Comp^y at Upper Marlbro' 1 Days march ⎫

1 Company at Bladensbourg 1 Days March ⎬   in Maryland

2 Companys at Frederick 6 Days march ⎭

    "By this Disposition the Companys which are quartered at Winchester Conogogee and Frederick form the Chains, to cover our Magazines, and will be near at Hand to advance either to Wills's Creek or Savage River as you shall Judge most proper.

    "I have pressed the Governour of Pensilvania to have his Country reconoiter'd towards the head of the Youghangany and to have the Road leading to it marked out, ready to be cut; or if there is any nearer way to the french Forts, to have all these Roads marked out: For that when we cross the Mountains we must depend a great deal on the Supplys of Provisions from that Province. I am with the greatest Respect Sir, Your most obedient and most humble Servant

JOHN ST. CLAIR.

"To Major General Braddock."

    I am in Hopes Sir that this will give you some light into our present Situation, if I have not been full enough, great allowance is to be given to one coming into a Country where he is an intire Stranger, and I may say where the Inhabitants are totally ignorant of Military Affairs: Their Sloth & Ignorance is not to be discribed; I wish General Braddock may be able to make them shake it off. I shall undertake to talk to the Germans in the language they have been brought up under in Germany. There is no such thing as to perswade any of them to enlist in the Virginia Companys.

I have not had time to make my self Master of the Indian Affairs, so shall only say in General Terms that I am afraid the French have drawn most of them over to their Interest, especially the Six Nations. We may expect to see a great Number of them, but never to feel them. Since I came from Wills's Creek there are some Letters come to Governours Dinwiddie and Sharp of the 3ᵈ of Feb^{ry} which makes them apprehensive of being attacked, as the french are making great quantity of Indian Shoes at their fort, that the first Column of the Indians are arrived, and two more, on their March. The Commanding Officer at the Fort has orders to be on the defensive, but that is not necessary for two of his Companys have neither Legs to get upon the Heights nor to run away thro' the Valleys.

I am in great hopes that this advice is true, and that they will make their Attacks in different parts, if so they are already in a Pannick; but on the Contrary if they are lying quiet and relieving their out posts often and at irregular Hours, then their Attacks will follow, and may succeed. I shoud be pleased they were making Incursions in the Country, for the above reason, this is the only thing will awake the Sleepy headed Mortals of this and the Neighbouring Provinces.

I shall now acquaint you in what manner I am to be employ'd for some time to come, if General Braddock with the Troops do not arrive.

Governour Sharp goes to morrow for Maryland, being obliged to meet his Assembly the 20th. He takes his Road thro' Fredericksbourg and Alexandria: at the former he is to review the Virginia Detatchment, Discharge the bad Men (which are too numberous) and choose out those who are fit to fill up our Regiments: at the latter he is to form the Company of Carpenters to be ready on our Troops landing.

I shall carry this Letter to Hampton with my others on the 14 (as the 16th is fixed for Capt. Sprys sailing) and shall see the Hospitals and every thing in order for the Sick. I shall return to Williamsbourg the 16th and the 18th set out for Winchester where I shall execute the same thing that Govr Sharp does at Fredericksbourg on 600 of the Virginian Troops, and see that Forage is laid in; This may take me up some Days: Then I go to Alexandria either to wait General Braddocks Arrival or go where the Service requires me most. I wish I have not tired your patience with a long Letter, but if you find that I have been too particular, I am sorry for it; I thought it was erring in the safe Side. I am with great Sincerity Sir, Your most obedient and most obliged humble Servant

JOHN ST CLAIR

pS. In Jeffery'ss Map, Winchester is marked Frederick. Wills's Creek is marked Caicuctuck Creek. The Road to Savage River which I mention runs from a small River which runs from the West into the South Branch. I send you an Account of the Strength of the French which I look upon to be genuine, and an uncorrect Map of the Country on the other Side of the Allegany Mountains.

JOHN BARRELL [1] TO CUMBERLAND

(A.L.S.)

May it Please YOUR HIGHNESS

When the Borders of a Country are Attack'd, by an Enterprising Treacherous Enemy: I am Sensible a Treatise on the further Improvement of their PRODUCE, may at first View appear Premature. but May It Please Your Highness.

The Inclosed Plan for the Amendment of One, making another, and droping the third Act; is to be presumed to be pursued or delay'd agreeable to the Exigency of the State, especialy in Such Articles as are Imature.

But the Northern Colonies Abounding in the Articles of White Oak and Pine Timber; and their Consumption Immence in Great Britain; Ought immediatly to be Encouraged; because they are now purchased with money of Forreigners! Whereas in Justice and good Policy, they should be purchased of the Plantations (to the great Emolument of the BRITISH TRADE), who would gladly Barter their Deal &ᶜ for ENGLISH MANUFACTURES, could they do it without loss. But when with the Benifits to Trade it is Consider'd, the great addition the Supply of LUMBER FROM AMERICA would make to the ENGLISH NAVIGATION; and the VAST INCREASE OF SEAMEN for the BRITISH NAVY; with great humility is hoped will appear to YOUR ROYAL HIGHNESS at this CRISIS, as Necessary and as Interesting a Point, as any yet thought of; for the Utility & Security of

---

[1] This is probably John Barrell of Boston (b. 1707, *Report of Record Commissioners of Boston*, XXIV) who, with Joseph Gerrish, was a merchant there in the 1740s and early 1750s (*Acts and Resolves of Mass. Bay*, XIII, 287; XIV, 159, 499, 525, 664). There is a draft of an unimportant letter in the Cumberland Papers, Cumberland to Joseph Gerrish of Boston, January 25, 1749/50, acknowledging the receipt of a haunch of American venison. The partnership would seem to have broken up in 1753 or 1754, when Barrell went to London and Gerrish to Nova Scotia, where he became a member of the council and judge of the Court of Common Pleas (*New Eng. Hist. and Geneal. Reg.*, LXVII, 110). There is a John Barrell, merchant of London, in the list of bankrupts for 1768 (*Gentleman's Mag.*, XXXVIII, 495).

the BRITISH EMPIRE! and may be Effected without any Inconveniency to the GOVERNMENT; by Exchanging the BOUNTY ON TAR (brought TO MATURITY) for a BOUNTY ON DEALS &ᶜ.

Neither Can I think of a more prudential well timed Encouragement to the NORTHERN COLONIES; nor of any other Plan, (without an Additional Expence to the Nation) that would give Such a Spring to their Navigation, as a BOUNTY ON DEALS; and an Amendment of the WHALE FISHERY ACT. EXCEPT TAKING OFF THE DUTY ON FORREIGN MOLASSES, A CORDIAL that would Cheer the Drooping Spirits, revive the Sinking Trade and Diffuse Universal Joy to the NORTH AMERICANS. But when they Knew YOUR ROYAL HIGHNESS was their PATRON, it would Inspire that Loyal Brave People with more Courage and resolution; and prove of more Efficacy at this Juncture; then the Arrival of Ten Battalions of BRITISH TROOPS! Distinguish'd by the PRINCE Possess'd with Every Noble Passion for the Felicity of the BRITISH EMPIRE.—

The Prince whom non with Integrity of heart Approach In Vain; tho' wanting in Elegance of Stile or Accuracy of form; if the Supplication be rational and Conducive to the HONOR AND INTEREST OF THE ENGLISH NATION: the Supplicant has nothing to fear, and all to hope; from Their Friend & PATRON.

Such were my Sentiments, from the Amiable Aspect; when first I Saw YOUR ROYAL HIGHNESS. at STAINS; return'd from hunting, In the Dawn of life May 24ᵗʰ 1738! Then I was Struck with a longing desire, and Enthusiastick Faith. that I should one day have an oppertunity, to express my Pleasurable Ideas; of the PRINCE; Most Admirably disposed; for the true Interest of the BRITISH SUBJECT; & not only Admired and Beloved; by every honest Man under his Auspicious Influence but even those of the most restless Cast. are obliged to Confess the Greatest Merit, and Join the PUBLICK ACCLAMATIONS; of YOUR HIGHNESS: In the Imitation of YOUR ROYAL FATHER. who has ever Made, The WELFARE OF MANKIND his Care.—

Compel'd by these Striking Virtues of YOUR ROYAL HIGHNESS. and the Strongest Ties of DUTY, to MY KING & COUNTRY! I could not, I dared not longer Suppress my thoughts, of these Interesting Points. of the Most Natural, and Surest Tendency: to the TRUEST INTEREST AND WELFARE, OF THE BRITISH EMPIRE. with the Utmost Deference and Esteem; Submitted to Your PRINCELY CONSIDERATION. By May it Please YOUR ROYAL HIGHNESS. YOUR HIGHNESSES Most Obedient, And Most humble Servant

JOHN BARRELL

Forrest Coffe House, Charing Cross, March 6ᵗʰ 1755.

An Account of the Northern Colonies, by John Barrell

(A.D.)

THE NORTHERN COLONIES, being now become of the most Serious Concern; it is to be hoped, every one acquainted with their Situation and produce; will not be backward, but freely give his thoughts touching their further Improvement, as the best means to Secure and render them of the most Service to the BRITISH NATION.

And tho' under the Best of KINGS, the best System of GOVERNMENT, and in the Enjoyment of the most and best Advantages, of any Nation in the World (truths as evident as the Government, that is best Administred is best) yet they are neither So happy nor So Independent as they might be; were their Natural Advantages better known and pursued. especially in regard to their Plantations Abroad; that are Capable of producing many Valuable Staples, Very Essential to the Increase of the English Trade and Navigation; I had almost Said as Shamefully as they are Impoliticly neglected.

As every Man Concern'd in the American Trade, That has but an indefferent knowledge of the produce of these COLONIES must know they are not of so much Utility to GREAT BRITAIN, as they might be made; was their Country better Peopled & Improved.

As it ABOUNDS WITH IRON MINES, MASTS, SHIP TIMBER, DEALS, TAR, PITCH, TURPENTINE &c and employs great Numbers of Sea Men, in their Codd and Whale Fishery; their West India and other Trade, and Annually build Several hundred Ships; which they lade with their own produce; FOR SPAIN, PORTUGAL & ITALY: the West Indias, Virginia Carolina &c from whence they are freighted to GREAT BRITAIN with TOBACCO, SUGAR, RICE, NAVEL STORES, LOGWOOD &c in return for BRITISH MANUFACTURES.

A Consideration, one would think (without any other) Sufficient to Rouse our attention and Ingage us, to an Imitation of our Judicious Neighbours the DUTCH; our POLITICAL RIVALS the FRENCH; and other Wise Nations; that with true WISDOM; ESTEEM THE RICHES OF THEIR PLANTATIONS their Own; and do all they Can, to make them as Useful to their MOTHER COUNTRY; as their SITUATION and PRODUCE CAN ADMIT.

And Shall not Wise BRITONS, from a happy Experience of the great UTILITY of their COLONIES, Pursue the Same prudent Maxims of their Sagacious Neighbors, in regard to their AMERICAN SETTLEMENTS? that are not only, Admirably form'd for the Support of each other; but

for the Riches, and Security of OLD ENGLAND, and without the most
Criminal Neglect; must in the Course of a few years render the
BRITISH EMPIRE, INDEPENDENT.

These are truths we hope, that Can Never disgust our Friends, and
that ought to Silence Such as murmer at the Expense of SETTLING NOVA
SCOTIA. A SETTLEMENT of as much IMPORTANCE to the AMERICAN as
GIBRALTAR is to the MEDITERANIAN TRADE. And Infinitely more useful
from its SITUATION AND PRODUCE, being the most Convenient for the
COD FISHERY, that Important NURSERY OF SAILORS, that Consumes great
quantitys of WOOLENS and other BRITISH MANUFACTURS, besides many
other benefits Natural to that part of the WORLD: That when they have
the Same Plan of Government, with others of HIS MAJESTYS COLONIES;
there can be no doubt, but far from being burthensom to ENGLAND, as
they now Are; they will become a Vast addition to her STRENGTH,
TRADE, and NAVIGATION—

Which of Course leads, to the Consideration of other Advantages,
that will unavoidably Arrise to the MOTHER COUNTRY from the right
Improvement of her NORTHERN COLONIES; that have been too long
neglected, and Exposed to many discouragements Contrary to the General Maxims of good Policy; which with great deference I will endeavor to Illustrate by,

Showing wherein it is the true Interest of GREAT BRITAIN; to promote
and Encourage their AMERICAN SETTLEMENTS by *Bountys* and other
Methods, on SHIP TIMBER, MASTS, DEALS, HEMP, unwroght IRON, and
POT ASH; STAPLES, ENGLAND is in Absolute need of; and which they may
be Supply'd with from Their own PLANTATIONS, in Returns for BRITISH
MANUFACTURS instead of Purchasing them with MONEY, as they now do
from Forreigners.

THE WOOLEN MANUFACTURE, being the Grand Staple of England, the
Increase of it, has ever been the Grand Object of the BEST MINISTERS;
and as at the present day, we trust it ever will be the Care of Britons,
to promote Such Settlements; as shall best promote the GOLDEN FLEECE;
that is of more intrinsick Value, Ten Thousand times, then the Mines
of PERU & MEXICO. because it not only procures the PUBLICK WEALTH,
but it fills the NATION with INDUSTRIOUS *Subjects, the Greatest Wealth
of all;* Whereas while the SPANISH MINES, INRICH A FEW: they beggar
MILIONS through SLOTH AND IDLENESS.

I believe no Man will deny, that the AMERICAN COLONIES, would take
from England, more of their MANUFACTURES then they now take; if they
could find remittances for them.

Which proves their Country is not so fertile, as Some would make

us believe, or not so well Cultivated as it might be, Or, that the PEOPLE
ARE CRAMP'D, in Some Shape or other to their discouragement and
ENGLANDS REAL HURT.

THAT THE ENGLISH NORTH AMERICA, Abounds with IRON MINES; and
that they make as GOOD BAR IRON, for General and better for perticuler
Uses, then the SPANIARDS or SWEEDS is well known to many that have Imported it—

WHENCE then the Infatuation (for Such it must be) that a General
Importation of this VALUABLE STAPLE from our PLANTATIONS is not
permitted into all the Ports of this Island; is a mistery to all the World,
that hear of the Immense Sums of money paid every year to STRANGERS
for that Commodity.

The objection is as partial, as it is impolitic. if I am rightly Informed, it has been Strenuously argued; that the General Importation
of Iron from the Plantations; would prejudice the PROPRIETORS of the
BRITTISH IRON MINES; which cannot be the Case; until they can Import
more then England Consumes; with her own; and when that is the
Case; it will be time enough to put a check to it, for I would by no
means Indulge THE PLANTATIONS to the Manifest hurt of any MANU-
FACTURE IN ENGLAND. wherefore until the Plantations can Supply us: it
is to be wished, the GENERAL GOOD OF THE NATION may prevail, in the
General IMPORTATION of this Interesting STAPLE: and if thought necessary a higher duty may be laid on FORREIGN IRON. to facilitate So great
a benifit to our PLANTATIONS; who want the Incouragement as a return
for our *Woolens* & other BRITISH MANUFACTURES Consumed in AMERICA—

LUMBER is another very Valuable STAPLE in NORTH AMERICA, And
begins to Show it Self Very Interesting to GREAT BRITAIN.—

The Prohibition of Exporting it from Some part of the NORTHERN
COUNTRYS; has in Some Small degree, open'd to England, the Necessity
of giving an Incouragement to the Importation from her Own Plantations; which the more we Import, the more we Shall discover of its
Utility and Importance; and the Sooner a bounty is given on American,
or a *higher Duty;* laid on *Forreign Deal;* the Sooner *England* will enjoy the benifits that have been too long thrown Away! And the great
number of Forreign SHIPS EMPLOY'D IN THE DEAL TRADE; Sufficiently
proves the Vast Advantages; that would ACCRUE TO A NATION; whose
Security and Riches; depends on the Increase of their TRADE & NAVIGA-
TION.

And that Such a Country as NORTH AMERICA, Cover'd with the best
Woods in the World; and extreemly wanted in GREAT BRITAIN: Should
So long be without a proper Encouragement, that would Create a Vast

Number of Large Ships; and make a Vast Number of Sailors; is marvelous indeed! Especially when a bounty on the English, or a higher duty on forreign Deal; Sufficient to yield the Adventurer of *Ship & Lumber* his first Cost at the English Market would effect this *Necessary return* and not only Enable the Americans to pay for more BRITISH MANUFACTURES But it would prove Such a Saving of the ENGLISH OAK (now used for Merchant Ships) As Ought in good Policy, to be PRESERVED for the ROYAL NAVY.—

HEMP is another Valuable Article; for wch ENGLAND Annually Pays, *Severl hundred thousand pounds in Cash to Strangers!* that may be Saved in the NATION, by a Small *Bounty;* on that Commodity raised in America; For which the SOIL & CLIMATE; is well known, to be as Suitable as any in the World: and if it was once become *a Staple* of the Plantations; it would Introduce great Numbers of Industrious People Used to that Manufacture; who would gladly Exchange the *hardships* of their *Native Countrys;* for the Plentiful Country of America: where in the Course of forty or fifty years; they might raise HEMP enough for the BRITISH NAVIGATION, to which as in the Article of *Lumber;* it would Prove a Vast Addition—

POT ASH, another Valuable Commodity; and for making it, there is not on the Globe, a more Suitable Country then NORTH AMERICA; and, for it large sums in *Cash:* is paid every year by Great Britain to *Forreigners!* that might be paid for, with *English Manufactures,* was a Suitable Bounty given for making it in our *Own Plantations.*—

For IRON, DEAL, HEMP & POT ASH, if I am truely Informed, the BRITISH NATION pays to Strangers a MILLION Sterling one Year with Another; more, then the Nations that Import them, take of our Manufacturs; an Immense Sum Indeed! that might be saved in the NATION, and paid for with BRITISH MANUFACTURES to their Own Plantations; and to the Vast Increase of NAVIGATION, SAILORS and other USEFUL SUBJECTS; and the Cultivation, of one, of the Best Countrys in the World: tho' in a distant, yet *Important Corner* of the Earth to Great Britain! at this day Evidently the Aim, and Envy of the FRENCH NATION!

NAVAL STORES proves the Vast Utility of a BOUNTY On the PLANTATION produce; and Shows besides the Benifits Arrising from the Employment of many Ships; besides the advantages of Payment with BRITISH MANUFACTURES, and the Settling, Clearing, and fitting their Lands for Agriculture; TAR that was formerly purchased of the Sweeds with money at 60/ a barrell; has been Since Sold on a medium under 10/— and at this day don't Sell for 7/ p barrel: that together with the Bounty after freight Commisions and other charges are deducted; don't yield the

Importer his first Cost—and proves there is too much made and, that the Salutary purposes proposed by the Bounty is fully answered; in the Maturity of an Article now become a Staple; and So Natural to the Carolinians; that the advantage of clearing their Lands; will hereafter lead them to make a Sufficiency for the British Consumption; and turn to their greater Advantage; as they apply themselves to Cutting Deals, raising hemp, and making POT ASH: and of Course prevent the English Markets being over Stock'd. *and the present Bounty on Tar.* may be taken off without prejudice—and applied *as a Bounty on hemp Lumber &c* until those Articles are brought to Maturity.

But as these weighty matters lye before the British PARLIMENT The Spirit of the British Empire; and not only give Being to the Useful, but remove all impediments (that Appear) to the General Welfare of the Nation—Britons have every thing to hope for a Suitable Incouragement: by Bountys or otherwise, on these Valuable Staples, as their Expediency and Utility may appear; and they may Safely rely on the removal of the Grand Impediment to the General Utility of the British Whale Fishery—*the Compulsive Clause* of that Act Viz[t] that all *Ships built* and *fitted out in America Shall make their Oil in Some part of Great Britain*—which has hitherto prevented any Considerable Experiment from the Western Plantations; and Consequently rendred Abortive, one of the grand ends proposed by the Bounty. Viz[t] the Increase of Our Navigation; that will of Course follow, when this impediment is removed: As the American Whalers; when they have liberty to make their Oil at home: will, not only have the *benifit* of giving their *Ships* a full freight, But, they will be ready to Improve the Season of Killing Whales on their own Coast; without being Exposed to a European Voyage; which they dread from the Terrors of the Small Pox.

This Indulgence may be granted; the Utility of the Bounty Answer'd; and every Imposition prevented; by a Certificate from the Custom House, Swore to before the Governor & Collector, where the Whales were kill'd, and where the Oil; was made.—

And here we are led to the Consideration of the *Pernicious Duty on Forreign Molases* Imported into *North America*—That has for more than twenty years past, been a great hindrance to the Growth of those Colonies!—

MOLASES being an Article of the most use to the Inhabitants Who Cannot Cultivate their Lands, nor Carry on their Fishery without it—well known to many in England, that have felt the Extremitys of Heat and Cold in that Country: and Can Attest, to the husband Man in

Summer; it is Death to drink beer or Water in the field: And in the Winter, without the Mixture of Rum; it is impossible to endure the Cold. An Article So Useful and Necessary, Ought to be free; especially that tends So much to the well being of the Inhabitants Settled on that Continent; at least 1500 miles, from the Eastermost Settlement in New England; to the Westermost in South Carolina. and this is not all, for the Newfound Land Fishery, are great Sharers in the bad Consequences of the Molases duty; and every Individual that is Concern'd in the Articles of Tobacco, Rice, and all other North American produce, is greatly Injured by it; without any benifit at all, to any of His Majestys Subjects: but a few West India Merchants; that, have made great Fortunes by runing French Molasses and destilling it into Rum.

A Duty, of Such General prejudice is most humbly hoped, will be no longer Continued; that a few may Swell in State: and wallow in pleasure! and to the real hurt of our West India Islands! for if the Northern Colonies are not Supported, the English in the Southern Settlements Cannot Subsist: Wherefore if the Islanders understood their real Interest; they would agree, that all His Majestys Subjects in America: Should be on such an Establishment as that each Settlement; should be made to subserve to the Welfare of the other; and all to the General Good of their Mother Country; which can never be the Case, whilst any of them enjoy benifits to the prejudice of the other as some have done ever since the Molases Act 1733—from which time the Northern Colonies have had little or non at all of that Article from any of the English Islands but Jamaica.

And here I may Safely Assert; that the North Americans are So farr from barring their West India Brethren of their Natural right; that they would be pleased with a Prohibition of all Forreign destill'd Spirits. and if my Judgment Could Prevail. I would have a Prohibition of the Trade of the Northern Colonies to Cape Britton! Which is not only prejudicial to the Trade of Great Brittain in General! But the Colonies had better be without it—As they not only Supply the French with what they want on their own terms! but they take from them what they please to give us; and Molases; the only Article we Want; they will let us have but a little! and that at an Advanced price; and every one must know French rum. Brandy & Silks; our Colonies have no occasion for.

And another Injurious Supply of the English to the french is flower, at least 50 p C^t under what they could be Supplied from Old France; whereby the French Rival us in our Fishery (as their Men have not half the wages ours have) and Supply the Indians to Cutt our throats! These are matters of the Utmost Concern at this Critical Conjuncture; and if longer delay'd may prove of Fatal Consequence!—

The French, that restless Nation! not Satisfied with being the disturbers of Europe, are now become the Plague, and Pest of every Corner of the Globe! against Such Enemys None can be too much on their guard! and Surely England Cannot be too Speedy in preventing every Supply from her Plantations that tends to Strengthen the Common Enemy of Mankind.

Neither can they do a better thing then by making their useless members at home become useful abroad.

and the first object that presents in View, is the removal of the Crouds of troublesom Importers that throng the Streets of their Metropolis; Some through Idleness, and Some by their perverse obstinacy! Abuse the Most humane Charitable Citty in the World! by making themselves, but are not, the objects they appear to be.

Whilest another unhappy Sett of Men; that would, if they could; but Cannot releive themselves, because Confin'd to a Goal (by Merciless Creditors)! and that would gladly part with the last farthing, to obtain their liberty! and would Joyfully Imbrace the favour of a passage from the Goverment to America—

And the beggers Should be compell'd—and thereby be made useful; who are now a dead weight to the Nation.—thus would the Streets be Clear'd of a troublesom set of Beings; and the Prisons emptied of unfortunate Debtors; and both Settled on the Borders of our Colonies, would give a happy turn to the *Indians:* who by Nature Sagacious; when they Saw the *English Superiour in numbers to the French;* would gladly Court our Alliance.

Another unhappy Set of Men; that by their Attrocity have made themselves obnoxious, and by their Crimes, forfeited their lives to the Government: tho' by the *frequency of Executions, the Terrors of Death* are So farr lost; as not to Answer *the Ends* proposed by their *punishment!* Yet, they are not altogether unworthy of our thoughts! and if a Punishment more Dreadful then Death; Could be thought of! whereby the Publick may be Satisfied; and a total loss of those Abandon'd Wretches prevented! by Such a Mask of Infamy, as no Art Should Efface: and instead of hanging they Should be Sentensed for life to guard the Frontiers In America: and thereby made useful to the Publick; in the Ease and Security of the husband Men, Mart Men: and others exposed by Various Employments!—

For it is a Melancholly reflection! that Some Such Method as this, has not been thought of; for the Salvation of many lives, that have been lost; and others that will be lost: if Somewhat like this is not done to prevent them!—

And now, I am to guard my Self; against the Suspicion of Some Seeming improbabilitys; that attend the Propositions here advanced.

And altho' from my Soul I declare, that I have the General Security, and prosperity of the British Empire in View; Inseperably Connected with the Welfare of the American Colonies.

Yet I am aware, that my Sentiments are So Plain, and Natural; it will be difficult to reconcil them to the Conduct of their Rulers, that have been ever esteem'd: for their Sagacity.

That Such a People, for more then a Century; Should neglect Application, for a reasonable Encouragement, on Such Valuable, and Such necessary Staples; as IRON, DEALS, HEMP, AND POT ASH: Articles, as Natural to their Country, as they are Conducive to their Wealth: is hardly to be Credited!

Wherefore, to remove the Incredibility, of this Strange neglect: be it remembred, as Strange as it may Seem; IT IS TRUE! Sagacious as the Americans may be thought; or as they may think themselves! a Fatality has hitherto attended all Efforts that have been made for these Salutary purposes! and a Wretched Insensibility; especially in the Massachusets Province; has prevented their People in Power from being Rich: or in better words; their Imaginary Rich in Waste lands: from being really So in the Improvement of them! but they are obstinate; and to this Day (having purchased their lands for little or nothing) hold them at Such hard terms of Settlement: (for fear as Some have Said Strangers Should eat the bread of their Children) that the Industrious Man that would, dare not ingage to Settle them!.

Which has been, a great obstruction to the Peopling New England; and without the Interposition of the Brittish Parlament: is not likely to be removed.—

Tho' of the greatest importance; that Such Sensless *Proprieters* Should be *taxed* for their *Waste lands;* and the *Tax* applied as a *bounty,* to Such as should *Cultivate & Settle them—*

A Remedy this; not to be expected in that Goverment (tho' the dictates of Common Sense) whilest a Majority of the *Council, & house of Representatives;* are the Men, that will be *most affected by the Tax.*

Wherefore it is from the Parliment, the Guardians of the British Empire; who to their Greatest Honor, never touch *Private property;* but when it is absolutely necessary for the *Publick Utility,* a remedy is humbly hoped, against these *Monopolisers of Lands,* that have exposed that *Country* to the Necessity of Supplicating the Assistance of *the Crown* against The Present Incroachments of their Avow'd Enemy the *French*.

The Want of a Civil Government in NOVA SCOTIA, has been before hinted, as the Grand Bar; to the Increase of the Settlement; and too many people in Office, too many Lawyers, and too many Law Suits! will ever Cramp an Infant Plantation—and if not remedied, must break up HALIFAX; or Continue it a Burthen to the NATION.

And, of Some other of the American Settlements, it may be truely Said; there are too many Law Suits!

Tho', the Wish, and prayer of every FRIEND TO THE BRITISH EMPIRE.

That the Number of Lawyers may be limitted, in all the Plantations; as they were in England; in the Reign of Edward the 3ᵈ.

The Sallerys of Judges, as well as the Judges; equal to their Dignity and Importance!

And a time fixed for the Definitive Judgment of all Causes.—

These Salutary Establishments, would, not only Banish useless Members from the Colonies; or make them become Servisable; but, they would Introduce honest, Industreous Inhabitants: the best Security, and truest Riches any Country Can enjoy.

And who Can desire a greater Satisfaction, then being the Author of those Extensive Benefits to a NATION. Above all others: that may be truly Said: to be Satisfied with their Own Dominions: and to this Satisfaction Can add; THE GLORY OF BEING THE DEFENDERS; OF THE LIBERTYS OF EUROPE!

And yet, as there are different degrees of pleasure, they must be proportionate, to the benefits Confer'd; Therefore, the Man that is the best Benefactor, must enjoy the greatest felicity: And a greater; the most Ambitious, would not Aspire After! then being the promoters of Such an addition to the Trade, and Navigation of Great Britain; As the Invaluable Articles of IRON, HEMP, DEALS & POT ASH will be: when they become the Staples of NORTH AMERICA. For it is to that Quarter of the World, that Great Britain is obliged for the Figure they now make in the Commercial World, and for the Vast Increase of the ROYAL NAVY.

And this being the real State of these Interesting Staples &ᶜ to Great Britain; and the Salutary methods that leads to make them Such in AMERICA: if I may be indulged with a repetition of the Necessity of the Expulsion of that CLAUSE in the WHALE FISHERY ACT. that Obliges all SHIPS BUILT AND FITTED OUT IN AMERICA to make their Oil in Some part of Great Britain. I hope it will be granted there Can never be a better time for it then the present and that a more prudential Encouragement Cannot be given to the Americans at this Crisis. then the ENTIRE DEMOLITION OF THE DUTY ON FORREIGN MOLASES Imported into the NORTHERN COLONIES. which would Inspire that LOYAL BRAVE PEOPLE with more Courage and Resolution to repel and Extirpate the French out of America and prove of more Service then Ten Battalions of BRITISH TROOPS—who may be of more Service at home, and these Necessary measures pursued abroad, together with Money and SHIPS which would Answer every good purpose in the Security and Greatest Utility to the English American Settlements, and the GLORY AND PROSPERITY OF THE BRITISH EMPIRE.

[*Endorsed*] Mr Barrell's Account of the *Situation, Produce,* &^c of the *Northern Colonies.* London, March the *6th 1755.*

GENERAL EDWARD BRADDOCK [1] TO ROBERT NAPIER

(COPY)

Williamsburg March 17. 1755.

Sir,

By the Gibraltar which sail'd about a Fortnight ago I wrote to you to acquaint you with all I then knew; Every thing as I then told you was in the utmost confusion; We have with a good deal of difficulty put our Affairs in some sort of Method. The Transports are all arriv'd, except one, which is expected every hour. Without Mr. Keppel I should have been in great distress, the Embarkation having been made in great confusion, Arms, Men, Stores, Officers of different Regiments in one Ship, and as Sir John St. Clair foretold a thousand Difficulties rais'd in case I had gone up to Annapolis, as I had propos'd before the Transports came in, but with the Commodore's assistance, who by the by I think is an Officer of infinite Merit, we have pack'd them all up to Alexandria with very little grumbling, whither I propose to follow them the day after to morrow, and in all probability be there a day or two before them. There is not one sick Man among them, which is pretty extraordinary considering the length of the passage, in which one Man was wash'd overboard. As to the provisions they made a Rout about there were never known better deliver'd. I at first in-

---

1 Edward Braddock (1695–1755) was for forty-three years in the Coldstream Guards, becoming lieutenant colonel of the regiment in 1745. Colonel of the 14th regiment at Gibraltar in 1753, he became major general in 1754 and commander in chief in North America.

tended to have canton'd the Troops according to the Account sent you by Sir John St. Clair, but as the Winter seems to be now so far broke up as to admit of their encamping without any ill consequence, I have order'd those that first arriv'd, as I have the others since, to proceed up the River Potomack to Alexandria, there to disembark and encamp immediately, by which means they will have time to discipline their additionals which otherwise would be spent in marching backwards and forwards. The Levies of Virginia and Maryland are likewise to join me at Alexandria: After I have augmented the two English Regiments to 700 Men each with the best of 'em, I purpose to form the others to the following Establishm^t which has been agreed to by Govr Dinwiddie; vizt Two Companies of Carpenters, consisting each of a Captain, two Subalterns, three Serjeants, three Corporals, and fifty Men; Four Companies of Foot Rangers or six, if I can get them, upon the same Establishment; One Troop of Horse Rangers, consisting of one Captain, two Subalterns, two Serjeants and thirty Men: These Companies are to receive from the Province the same nominal pay in the Currency of the Country with the Establishment of his Majesty's Forces, the Difference of Exchange between which and Sterling is about 25 p Cent. I have also settled a Company of Guides, one Captain two Aids and ten Men. I have fix'd posts from the Head Quarters to Philadelphia, Annapolis and Williamsburg, to facilitate the Correspondence necessary for me with those several Governments. There are here Numbers of Mulattoes and free Negroes of whom I shall make Bat Men, whom the province are to furnish with pay and Frocks, being resolv'd to allow none out of the Troops.

I hear Governor Shirley's Regiment is near if not quite compleat; I have heard nothing of nor from Sir William Pepperell: Mr. Keppel has sent the Arms Cloathing, Officers and whatever else belongs to those two Regiments to the Northward in two transports under the Convoy of a Man of War.

As soon as I can assemble the Troops provide Forage provisions and other Necessaries for their March I shall proceed to attempt the Reduction of the French Forts upon the Ohio: It is doubtful whether there will be grass on the other side the Alliganey Mountains before the latter End of April, which is indeed as soon as it will probably be in my power to get there.

It is not in my power as yet to give you a certain Account of the Number and Strength of the Forces I shall have with me: If I am able to compleat the two English Regiments to 1400, and the provincial

Levies to the Establishment above mention'd, I dont find they can amount in the whole with the Independent Companies of New York and Carolina (which two first are good for nothing) to above 2300 or thereabouts. I had propos'd to send for a Detachment from the American Regiments, but as I have thought it necessary to have an Interview with Govr Shirley, and have accordingly sent him Orders to meet me at Annapolis in Maryland I have deferr'd giving Orders on that head till after I have seen him. At this Interview which I expect in about a Fortnight (and at which I have desir'd the Governors of New York and Pensilvania to be present if the Affairs of their Governments will admit of it), I propose to settle the Operations to the Northward: By the first opportunity after it I shall acquaint you with what has been determin'd.

It is likewise impossible for me to give you any certain Account of the French Force upon the River Ohio; If anything can be collected from the various Acco^ts of 'em it is that their Numbers exceed 3000, a considerable part of which are Indians. It is universally agreed that all the Tribes of the Iroquois except the Mohawks are gone over to their Interest; but as the present Attachment of these Nations, and such others of the Southern Indians as are in alliance with them, is attributed to the late Superiority of the French, it may be hop'd that the Appearance of our Army, or at least any Advantage gain'd, may make a great Alteration in their Dispositions.

Sir John St. Clair having inform'd me that we shall be oblig'd to break ground before the Fort upon the Ohio, and there having been only four twelve pounders sent out with the Train, I have applied to Commodore Keppel for four more from the Ships with a proper Quantity of Ammunition, and for many other Things that were necessary, all which he has supplied [with] the greatest expedition; and has upon every occasion shewn the utmost Readiness in concurring with me in all measures for promoting the Success of the present Service: He has likewise order'd thirty Sailors with proper Officers to attend the Army, who will be of the greatest use in assisting the Conveyance of the Artillery over the Mountains. I have settled the pay of these Men with Mr. Keppel at 3/6 p day for the Midshipmen, and /6 for the common Sailors, which I shall be oblig'd to charge to the Contingencies.

I am, Sir, Your most Humble and most Obedient Servant,

E. BRADDOCK.

MAJOR-GENERAL EDWARD BRADDOCK TO NEWCASTLE [1]

(COPY)

Williamsburgh March 20th 1755.

My Lord,

In Obedience to your Grace's Commands I take the earliest opportunity that has been in my power to acquaint You with my arrival here, as well as that of all the Transports with the Forces under my Command. My own Voyage was troublesome, but the Transports met with better Weather, and I have the pleasure to acquaint your Grace there has not been one Man sick on board them all.

What Effect His Majesty's Directions to His several Governors upon occasion of the present Expedition may have in the Colonies under their Command, I know not; I cannot say as yet they have shewn the Regard to 'em that might have been expected. I have used, & shall continue to use my Endeavours to excite in 'em a better Spirit, and to prevail upon 'em to bear such a Share of the Expence, which will attend the present Undertaking, as their Duty to His Majesty, and the Interest they have in the Event of it requires from 'em.—For this purpose, among others, I have sent Orders to M[r] *Shirley* to meet me at *Annapolis* in *Maryland,* and have desired the Governors of *New York* & *Pensilvania* to accompany him thither, if the Affairs of their Governments will admit of it.

I shall not trouble Your Grace with the Detail of Business under my Direction in the Service I am engaged in: As I have wrote fully to the Secretary of State by this Opportunity, I beg leave to refer You to my Letter to him for any Particulars you may have an Inclination to be informed of.

As I hear M[r] *Shirley's* Regim[t] is nearly or quite compleat, and am in hopes Sir William Pepperell may have made some progress in raising his, I shall, immediately after I have seen Gov[r] *Shirley*, give Orders for employing those Forces in such manner to the Northward, as may appear most conducive to the Service intended. I shall myself proceed with the Force I shall have with me to attempt the Reduction of the French Forts upon the *Ohio*, and hope to be on the further side of the *Alliganey* Mountains by the End of *April*.

I have receiv'd all possible Assistance from Commodore *Keppel*,

[1] This letter, translated into French and retranslated, is in Jacob Nicholas Moreau, *A Memorial containing a summary View of Facts, with their Authorities in answer to the Observations sent by the English Ministry to the Courts of Europe* (1757), 132. The general sense of the original was not altered by the double translation.

who is an Officer of great Capacity and Merit. I must likewise acquaint Your Grace, that I have met with the readiest Concurrence from the Governor of this Province in every measure I have proposed for the Service of the Expedition, & that the people under his Command seem now dispos'd to contribute largely & chearfully to the support of it, which is more than I can say of the other Governments.

As small coined Silver will be greatly wanted for the payment of the Troops, and as no considerable Quantity of it can be got in this Province; I must beg of your Grace to direct the Contractors, M[r] *Hanbury* & M[r] *Thomlinson,* to send over as soon as possible, if they have not already done it, four or five Thousand pounds, in *Piastrines* & Half *Piastrines:* which is the more necessary, as all the Money already brought over by the Regimental Paymasters is in Spanish Gold and Dollars.

I am &c[a]

E: BRADDOCK.

P.S.
I have heard nothing yet of the Deputy Paymaster Gen[l].[2]

[*Endorsed*] Williamsburgh—March *20th 1755.* Maj[r] Gen[l] *Braddock* To the D: of *Newcastle.* R/ May 29.

GENERAL EDWARD BRADDOCK TO ROBERT NAPIER

(COPY)

Sir,

I had the pleasure of writing to you from Williamsburg last March by a Vessel which was to sail in about a Weeks time, and have since sent the Duplicate by another. Mr. Shirley with the other Northern Governors met me at this place last Week, we then settled a plan for the Operations in these parts: Gov[r] Shirley lay'd before me the Measures concerted between him and Gov[r] Lawrence for repelling the French from their new Encroachments on the Bay of Fundi, which I approv'd of, and immediately sent orders to Lt. Colonel Monckton to take upon him that Command and carry it into execution. I also settled with the Governors present a plan for the Reduction of Crown Point, which is to be undertaken by provincial Troops alone, rais'd in the Northern Colonies to the Number of about four thousand four hundred to be commanded by Col. Johnson a person particularly qualify'd for it by his Knowledge of those parts, his great Influence

2 William Johnston.

over the Six Nations and the universal opinion they have of him in the Northern Colonies: I am to supply him with an Engineer. I propos'd of Colonel Shirley to go in person to attack the Fort at Niagara; He express'd the greatest Readiness to engage in it; I therefore order'd him to take his own Regiment which is compleat, and Sir William Pepperell's which will probably be so too by the time he wants them, and to proceed upon it as soon as possible with my Orders to reinforce the Garrison at Oswego with two Companies of Sir William Pepperell's and the Effectives of the two Independent Companies at New York, and to put the Works in such Repair as to preserve the Garrison and secure his Retreat and Convoys. Col. Shirley apply'd to me to put the two American Regiments upon the same footing as to their provisions with those to the Northward and Southward telling me that from the general Discontent of the Men he was apprehensive of a Mutiny, they being put under Stoppages for their provisions, when the others receive them as a Gratuity. I therefore directed him to give them the same Allowance as the other Regiments, as the Service requir'd their immediate Aid, and might suffer by this Discouragement, and indeed I must say that a Soldier here should have every Advantage as their Fatigue is very great and their pay not near sufficient in this dear and desolate Country. I shall set out to morrow for Frederick in my way to Fort Cumberland at Wills's Creek, where I shall join the two Columns which are now upon their March at about fifty Miles distance: This Disposition I was oblig'd to make for the Conveniency of Horses and Waggons, by which means I employ those of Maryland which would not be prevail'd upon to cross the Potomack. I have met with infinite Difficulties in providing Carriages &c for the Train nor am I as yet quite reliev'd from one, a great part still continuing here which has delay'd me for some time; I shall get them dispatch'd tomorrow or next day. I am impatient to begin my March over the Mountains, which in my last I told you were fifteen Miles over, tho' I now know them to be between sixty and seventy, about half way are those Meadows which are not very large, where the French attack'd our people that were under Washington. I am to expect Numberless Inconveniences and Obstructions from the total want of dry Forage from the being oblig'd to carry all our provisions with us which will make a vast Line of Baggage and which tho' I reduce as much as possible will nevertheless occasion great Trouble and retard me considerably. I have found it absolutely necessary to appoint eight Ensigns to the two Regiments to act without pay 'till Vacancies shall happen; The Nature of the Country made this Step unavoidable as I am oblig'd to make a Number of small Detachments with every one of which the Service requires an Officer, and without this Expedient the Regiments must have sometimes been left without a sufficient Number of Subalterns. As I have and shall find it often necessary to oblige the Men to take with them seven or eight days provisions, it being frequently impossible to supply them by the great distance from one Magazine to another, in order to enable them to carry any Additional Weight I have lighten'd them as much as possible, and have left in store their Swords and the greatest part of their heavy Accoutrements. I have also made a Regulation which I think will be of great Advantage in posting every Officer in time of Service to his own Company and ordering the oldest Battalion Company to act as Second Grenadier Company upon the left, by which means the eight Companies form so many Firings or sixteen platoons as I shall find necessary commanded by their respective Officers: I was induc'd to make this Regulation on account of the additional Recruits that the Officers and Men might know one another, which by Companies they might easily do, but by Battalion scarcely possible; and in case of Alarm the Men and Officers will know their respective posts sooner than by the usual Method. I have receiv'd His Majesty's orders for the Augmentation and immediately sent an Express to Govr Lawrence who is about seven hundred Miles off to acquaint him of it, and from the spirit and Military Turn of the Northern Colonies I don't doubt of his raising his Numbers, but I fear it will be long before I can compleat these two Regiments as I meet with but few Recruits and those very indifferent. I have not even yet quite compleated them to seven hundred: I have great promises, what the performances will be a little time will shew. The officers and Men of these two Regiments behave well and shew great Spirit and Zeal for the Service, which will be a good Example to the rest. I shall go against the Forts upon the Ohio with a smaller Number of Men than I at first intended because I would not weaken the Force destin'd for the Attack of Niagara, but I can't help flattering myself with Success as the plan which I have inclos'd to Mr. Fox, and which I presume you will see, takes in all the considerable Encroachments the French have made upon His Majesty's Dominions in America, in the most important parts in the attacking of which if we succeed it appears to me very evident that the Colonies will be effectually secur'd from all future Encroachments if they chuse it. I have been greatly disappointed by the neglect and supineness of the Assemblies of those provinces, with which I am concern'd; they promis'd great Matters and have done nothing whereby instead of forwarding they have obstructed the Service. When I get to Wills's Creek I will send you an exact account of my Numbers and exact Returns of the whole, it being impossible to do it regularly now we are so divided: Also whatever other Information or Intelligence I shall get there, it being impracticable to get any here, the people of this part of the Country laying it down for a Maxim, never to speak Truth upon any account. I beg my humblest Duty to His Royal Highness and believe me to be with the greatest sincerity, Your most Humble and most Obedient Servant,

E. BRADDOCK.

Alexandria April 19. 1755.

PS. I have appointed Captain Morris of Dunbar's my other Aid de Camp, and have given the Major of Brigade's Commission to Captain Halket, at Sir John St. Clair's Recommendation.

GENERAL EDWARD BRADDOCK TO ROBERT NAPIER

(L.S.)

Duplicate.

Sir,

I had the pleasure of writing to you from Frederick the latter End of April, when I gave you an Account of all I then knew. On the 10th of May I arriv'd here; the Train who have been very near a Month on their March, arriv'd the 17th; and the whole of the Forces are now assembled, making about two thousand Effectives, the greatest part Virginians, very indifferent Men, this Country affording no better; it has cost infinite pains and labour to bring them to any sort of Regularity and Discipline: Their Officers very little better, and all complaining of the ill Usage of the Country, who employ'd them last Year without pay or provisions. I am told they have made a pretty good hand of this year's recruiting Affair, tho' I can get no proof of it. This part of the Country is absolutely unknown to the Inhabitants of the lower parts of Virginia and Maryland, their Account of the Roads and provisions utterly false. From Winchester to this place which is Seventy Miles is almost uninhabited, but by a parcel of Banditti who call themselves Indian Traders, and no Road passable but what we were oblig'd to make ourselves with infinite Labour. It would take up too much of your Time were I to tell you particularly the Difficulties and Disappointments I have met with from the want of Honesty and Inclination to forward the Service in all Orders of people in these Colonies, which have occasion'd the great Delays in getting hither, as well as my being detain'd here a Month longer than I intended. I was assur'd at Williamsburg that two hundred Waggons and two thousand five hundred Horses would be here by the 10th of May, as also great Quantities of Forage at proper distances upon the Road, where the Artillery and Waggons were to pass, and that proper persons and such as could be depended upon were employ'd for that purpose; but I soon found that there was hardly any Forage in the Country and that the promises of the people of Virginia and Maryland were not to be depended upon: If we press'd Waggons, as we were oblig'd to let the Horses go into the Woods to feed, they went off directly, the pack Horses the same, for which reason I determin'd before I left Frederick to desire Mr. Franklin of Pensilvania (a province whose people tho' they will contribute very little to the Expedition are exact in their Dealings, and much more industrious than the others) to contract in my name for an hundred and fifty Waggons and a Number of pack Horses to be sent to this place with all expedition. It was well I took this precaution, for the Number of Horses and Waggons procur'd in these Colonies do not amount to the tenth part of what I was promis'd: Mr. Franklin undertook and perform'd his Engagements with the greatest readiness and punctuality. By this means I hope to leave this place to morrow with a less Quantity of provisions than I propos'd from the Disappointment of the Waggons and Weakness of the Horses. To remedy as much as possible this Inconvenience I have sent forward a strong Detachment with a large Convoy of provisions to be lodg'd upon the most advantagious spot of the Alliganey Mountains with directions for the Waggons to return with a proper Escort. My being oblig'd to draw my Supplies from distant provinces lays me under a Necessity of employing a Number of Assistant Commissaries, none of which will serve without exorbitant pay and am forc'd to make more Contracts than I otherwise should, to guard against the failure of some of them, in which Contracts the people take what Advantage they can of our Necessity. Nothing can well be worse [?] than the Road I have already pass'd and I have an hundred and ten Miles to march thro' an uninhabited Wilderness over steep rocky Mountains and almost impassable Morasses. From this Description, which is not exaggerated you conceive the difficulty of getting good Intelligence, all I have is from Indians, whose veracity is no more to be depended upon [than] that of the Borderers here; their Accounts are that the Number of French at the Fort at present is but

(continued on page 92)

Corps, & Companies	Officers Present										
	Commission						Staff				
	Colonel	Lieut Colonel	Major	Captains	Lieutenants	2d Lieuts or Ensigns	Chaplain	Adjutant	Qr Master	Surgeon	Mate
The 44th Regiment of Foot	1	1	1	7	13	10	1	1	1	1	1
The 48th Regiment of Foot	1	1	1	8	14	9	1	1	1	1	1
Capt John Rutherford's Independt Compy N: York	.	.	.	1	3	.	.	.	.	1	.
Capt Horatio Gates's Independt Compy N: York	.	.	.	1	2	1	.	.	.	1	.
The Detachment from South Carolina ..... Commanded by Capt Paul Demeré	.	.	.	1	2	1	.	.	.	.	.
Total	2	2	2	18	34	21	2	2	2	4	2

Absent Officers

Capt William Eyres, Of the 44th Regt of Foot. gone to New York, to assist Col: Johnson, as Engineer.

Non Comission		Effectives Rank, & File				Wanting to compleat to the Establishmt		Since last Return			
Serjeants	Drummers	Fit for Duty	Sick Present	Sick in Hospitals	Total	Serjeants	Rank, & File	Recruited	Dead	Discharged	Deserted
30	20	685	66	19	770	10	270	258	3	14	1
30	20	645	19	20	684	10	356	174	2	8	9
3	2	82	9	.	91	.	.	.	.	.	.
3	2	84	7	.	91	.	.	.	.	.	.
4	2	96	4	.	100	.	.	.	.	.	.
70	46	1592	105	39	1736	20	626	432	5	22	10

A Return Of the Detachment of Sea-men
Commanded by Lieut Spendelowe.

	Lieutenant	Mid-ship Men	Boatswains Mates	Sea-Men
Total	1	3	2	30

[*Signed*] E BRADDOCK

Troop, Or Companies.			Officers Present					
			Commission			Staff		
			Captains	Lieutenants	2ᵈ Lieuᵗˢ Ensigns, or Cornetts	Adjutant	Qʳ Master	Surgeon
Capᵗ Robᵗ Stewarts Troop of Light Horse			1	1	1	.	.	.
Capᵗ George Mercer ⎫ Artificers			1	1	1	.	.	.
Capᵗ Willᵐ Polson ⎭			1	1	1	.	.	.
Captain Adam Stevens ⎫	Virginia		1	1	1	1	1	1
Captain Peter Hogg			1	1	1	.	.	.
Captain Thoˢ Waggoner			1	1	1	.	.	.
Captain Thoˢ Cocke ⎬ Rangers			1	1	1	.	.	.
Capᵗ Wᵐ Perronée ⎭			1	1	1	.	.	.
Capᵗ John Dagworthy	Mary-Land		1	1	1	.	.	1
Capᵗ Ed: Brice Dobbs ⎭	North Carolina		1	2	1	.	.	1
		Total	10	11	10	1	1	3

TROOPS, ENCAMP'D AT WILL'S CREEK—JUNE THE 8th 1755:

Non Comission		Effectives Rank, & File				Wanting to compleat to the Establishmt		Since last Return			
Serjeants	Drummers	Fit for Duty	Sick Present	Sick in Hospitals	Total	Serjeants	Rank & File	Recruited	Dead	Dischargd	Deserted
2	.	28	5	.	33	.	.	.	.	.	.
3	1	27	.	15	42	.	11	.	.	1	2
3	1	49	.	1	50	.	3	.	1	.	.
3	1	51	.	2	53	.	.	1	1	.	.
3	1	36	4	2	42	.	11	.	1	.	.
3	1	42	9	2	53	.	.	.	.	.	.
3	1	46	1	.	47	.	6	.	.	.	1
3	1	47	.	5	52	.	1	.	.	.	.
3	1	51	2	.	53	.	.	.	.	.	.
3	1	72	.	.	72	.	28	.	.	.	.
29	9	449	21	27	497	.	60	1	3	1	3

[Signed] E BRADDOCK

A Return Of The Detachment of the Royal Reg^t of

Commanding Officer Capt Robt Hind	Military Branch										
	Captain	Lieutenants	Lieu^t & Adjutant	Lieu^t & Q^r Master	Surgeon	Serjeants	Corp^{ls} & Bombardiers	Gunners	Matrosses	Drummer	Total
Fit for Duty	1	3	1	1	1	2	8	15	26	1	59
Sick in Hospitals	.	.	.	.	.	.	2	3	6	.	11
Total	1	3	1	1	1	2	10	18	32	1	70

ARTILLERY, ENCAMPED ATT WILL'S CREEK: JUNE 8TH 1755.

Civil Branch							Abstract Of the Artillery			
Waggon Master	Master of Horse	Commissary	Comissary Assistant	Conductors	Artificers	Total	Nature of Guns		N⁰ of Guns	N⁰ of Carriages

Waggon Master	Master of Horse	Commissary	Comissary Assistant	Conductors	Artificers	Total	Nature of Guns		N⁰ of Guns	N⁰ of Carriages
							12	Pounders	4	
							6	Pounders	6	
							8	Inch Howitzers	4	
								Cohorn Mortars	15	
								Waggons	.....	...16
1	1	1	1	5	12	21		Powder Carts ..	.....	... 8
.	.	.	.	1	.	1		Tumbrils for Intrench⁵ Tools	.....	... 2
								Spare Carriages for Guns	.....	... 2
1	1	1	1	6	12	22		Forge	.....	... 1
								Money Tumbril	.....	... 1
								Total	29	30

[Signed] E BRADDOCK

small, but pretend to expect a great Reinforcement; this I do not entirely credit, as I am very well persuaded they will want their Forces to the Northward. As soon as I have join'd the Detachment, who have been seven days making a Road of twenty four Miles, I shall send people for Intelligence, who I have reason to beleive I can confide in. I have order'd a Road of Communication to be cut from Philadelphia to the Crossing of the Yanghyanghain, which is the Road we ought to have taken, being nearer, and thro' an inhabited and well cultivated Country, and a Road as good as from Harwich to London, to some Miles beyond where they are now opening the new Road. I am inform'd the long expected Arms for the New England Forces bound to Nova Scotia are arriv'd and that they are sail'd. Boats and Floats are preparing for the Troops destin'd to Niagara and Crown point, the province of New York have been dilatory in regard to that Service of which I presume you will have a particular Account from Governor Shirley, who is upon the Spot and which he may convey to you as soon as to myself untill the Communication can be open'd. Inclos'd I send you the Return of the Forces I propose to proceed with, had I more it would be out of my power to subsist them. With these I flatter myself to be able to drive the French from the Ohio, and to open a Communication with the rest of His Majesty's Forces in the other provinces. Captain Bromley of Sir Peter Halket's is dead, I have dispos'd of the Commissions in the Regiment according to Seniority. Mr. Hervey has the Ensigney. I receiv'd a Letter from Sir William Pepperel complaining of his ill State of Health from his sufferings at Louisbourg, and to let me know his Regiment is near compleat; as it is some time since, I presume they are so by this time. Shirley's has been so long since. I have wrote to them both to send their Returns to England by the first opportunity.

I am, dear Sir, Your Most Humble and Most Obedient Servant

E. BRADDOCK.

Fort Cumberland Wills's Creek
    June 8th 1755.

I receiv'd this Morning a Letter from Sr Wm Pepperel who tells me his Regim^t is not half compleat, occasion'd by the great Numbers that have enlisted for Nova Scotia and Crown point.

Sir John St. Clair to Robert Napier

(A.L.S.)

Camp of the Van Guard of the Army at
the little Meadows, June 13th 1755.

Sir,

Since General Braddocks arrival about the 20th of Feb[ry] I have not wrote to you, I delayed it from time to time expecting to be able to give you a full account of our Situation: I certainly shou'd have wrote to you on the arrival of all our Troops at Wills's Creek, but I was so employed about cutting the Roads, that I had not one Moment to spare.

In my last letter to you I acquainted you that I was to review the Independent Companys and to form the Provincial Troops of Virginia and Maryland in which Service I was employd till the 24th of March, they being scattered all about the Country. On my coming that day to Alexandria I found the British Troops disembarked and beginning to land their Stores. The 26th General Braddock and Governour Dinwiddie arrived. I left Alexandria the 2[d] of April, in order to forward the Transport of our Artillery & Stores to Wills's Creek, but did not get to the fort till the 16th being obliged to repair old Roads and cut new ones, in which I made very great progress considering that we had Snow in the Mountains till the 15th of April. The Roads leading to the Fort were not cleared till the 1st of May; the next Day the first Division of our Troops arrived and the 10th the last Division; the first Division of the Artillery the 16th of May & the last the Day following: from that Day till the End of the Month, things were preparing for the march of the whole.

The Situation I am in at present puts it out of my power to give you a full discription of this Country; I shall content myself with telling you that from Winchester to this place is one continued track of Mountains, and like to continue so for fifty Miles further. Tho our Motions may appear to you to have been slow, yet I may venture to assure you that not an Hour has been lost; considering that no Magistrate in Virginia or I believe in Maryland gave themselves the least trouble to assist in collecting the Country People to work upon the Roads, and to provide us with Carriages: But on the Contrary every body laid themselves out to put what money they cou'd in their Pocketts, without forwarding our Expedition. In this Situation we never cou'd have subsisted our little Army at Wills's Creek, far less carried on our Expedition had not General Braddock contracted with the People in Pensylvania for a Number of Waggons, which they have fullfilled; by their Assistance we are in motion, but must move slowly untill we get over the Mountains. I cou'd very easily forsee the difficultys we were to labour under from having the Communication open only to Virginia, which made me Anxious of having a Road cut from Pennsylvania to the Yaugheaugany; I wrote to Govr Morris the 14th of Feb^{ry} on this Head, notwithstanding of which, that Road has not been set about till very lately. The last Report that I had of it, was, that it wou'd be finished in three Weeks hence; the two Communications will join about forty Miles from hence, but it is not fixed on which side of the Yaugheogany.

The little knowledge that our People at home have of carrying on War in a Mountaneous Country will make the Expence of our Carriages appear very great to them, that one Article will amount near to £40,000 Stir.

Thus far I do affirm that no time has been lost in pursuing the Scheme laid down in England for our Expedition; had it been undertaken at the beginning from Pensylvania it might have been carried on with greater Dispatch and less expence: I am not at all surprized that we are ignorant of the Situation of this Country in England, when no one except a few Hunters knows it on the Spot; and their Knowledge extends no further than in following their Game. It is certain that the ground is not easy to be reconoitered for one may go twenty Miles without seeing before him ten yards.

The Commanding General pursues his Schemes with a great deal of vigour and Vivacity; the Dispositions he makes will be subject to be changed in this vast tract of Mountains, I mean instead of marching the whole together (the Van Guard excepted) in one Body, he will be obliged to march in three Divisions over the Mountains and join about the great Meadows, fifty two Miles from the fort. The General is bent on marching directly to Fort du Quesne, he is certainly in the right in making his Dispositions for it: But it is my opinion he will be obliged to make a Halt on the Monagahela or Yaughangany untill he gets up a Second Convoy, and untill the Road is open from Pensylvania, which the Inhabitants will not finish unless they are covered by our Troops.

The insert opposite is a reproduction of the whole of the original drawing, measuring twenty-six and a half by eighteen and three-quarters inches, among the Cumberland Maps in the Royal Library at Windsor Castle. It is unsigned, but is perhaps the "sketch" to which Harry Gordon refers in his letter of July 23, 1755 (p. 108).

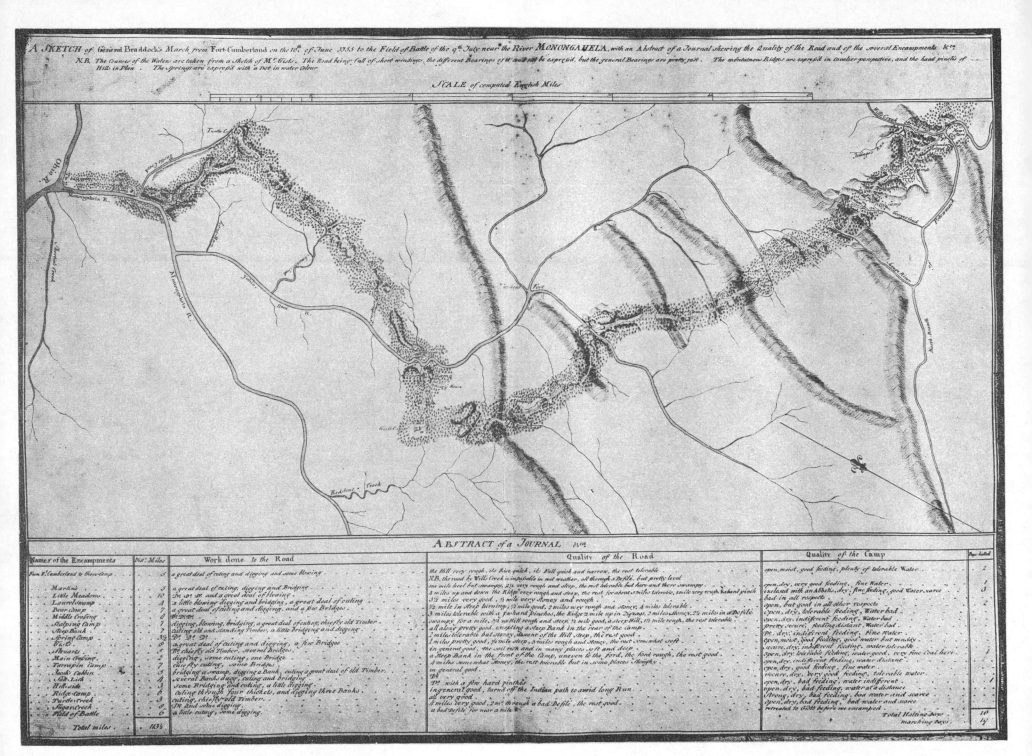

A SKETCH of General Braddock's March from Fort-Cumberland on the 10th. of June 1755 to the Field of Battle of the 9th. July near the River MONONGAHELA, with an Abstract of a Journal shewing the Quality of the Road and of the several Encampments &c.

N.B. The Courses of the Waters are taken from a Sketch of Mr. Gists. The Road being full of short windings, the different Bearings of it could not be express'd, but the general Bearings are pretty just. The montainous Ridges are express'd in cavalier perspective, and the hard pinches of Hills in Plan. The Springs are express'd with a Dot in water Colour

SCALE of computed English Miles

ABSTRACT of a JOURNAL &c.

Names of the Encampments	Dist. Miles	Work done to the Road	Quality of the Road	Quality of the Camp	Days halted
From Ft. Cumberland to Grove Camp	5	a great deal of cuting and digging and some blowing	the Hill very rough, its Rise quick, its Bull quick and narrow, the rest tolerable	open, moist, good feeding, plenty of tolerable Water	2
			N.B. the road by Wills Creek is impassable in wet weather, all through a Defile, but pretty level		
Martins	5	a great deal of cuting, digging and Bridging	one mile level but swampy, 2½ very rough and steep, the rest tolerable but here and there swampy	open, dry, very good feeding, fine Water	3
Little Meadows	10	Do. Do. Do. and a great deal of blowing	4 miles up and down the Ridge very rough and steep, the rest for about 5 miles tolerable, 1mile very rough & a hard pinch	inclosed with an Abbatis, dry, fine feeding, good Water scarce	3
Laurel swamp	4	a little blowing digging and bridging, a great deal of cuting	3½ miles very good, ½ mile very stoney and rough	bad in all respects	
Bear camp	7	a great deal of cuting and digging, and a few Bridges	½ mile in steep turning, ½ mile good, 2 miles very rough and stoney, 4 miles tolerable	open, but good in all other respects	2
Middle Crossing	6	Do. Do.	3 miles tolerable with a ½ hard pinches, the Ridge ½ mile up in 2 & ½ swap, 2 miles stoney, 2½ miles in a Defile	open, dry, tolerable feeding, Water bad	
Scalping Camp	7	digging, blowing, bridging, a great deal of cuting, chiefly old Timber	swampy for a mile, ½ up Hill rough and steep, ½ mile good, a steep Hill, 1½ mile rough, the rest tolerable	open, dry, indifferent feeding, Water bad	
Steep Bank	7	cuting old and standing Timber, a little bridging and digging	all along pretty good, excepting a steep Bank in the rear of the Camp	pretty secure, feeding distant, Water bad	
Spring Camp	3½	Do. Do. Do.	2 miles tolerable but stoney, descent of the Hill steep, the rest good	Do. dry, indifferent feeding, fine Water	
G. C.	8	a great deal of cuting and digging, a few Bridges	2 miles pretty good, ½ mile steep, 3 miles rough and stoney, the rest somewhat soft	open, moist, good feeding, good water but muddy	
Steuarts	6	Do. chiefly old Timber, several Bridges	in general good, the soil rich and in many places soft and deep	secure, dry, indifferent feeding, water tolerable	1
Main Crossing	2	digging, some cuting, one Bridge	a steep Bank in the front of the Camp, uneven to the ford, the ford rough, the rest good	open, dry, tolerable feeding, water good, very fine coal here	
Terrapin Camp	7	chiefly cuting, some Bridges	4 miles somewhat stoney, the rest tolerable but in some places sloughy	open, dry, indifferent feeding, water distant	
Jacobs Cabbin	5	bridging a swamp, digging a Bank, cuting a great deal of old Timber	in general good	open, dry, good feeding, fine water	
Salt Lick	4	several Banks dugg, cuting and bridging	Do.	secure, dry, very good feeding, tolerable water	1
Hill-side	4	some Bridging and cuting, a little digging	Do. with a few hard pinches	open, dry, bad feeding, water indifferent	
Ridge Camp	3	cuting through four thickets, and digging three Banks	in general good, turn'd off the Indian path to avoid long Run	open, dry, bad feeding, water at a distance	
Turtle Creek	6	cuting, chiefly old Timber	all very good	strong, dry, bad feeding, but water and scarce	
Sugar Creek	6	Do. and some digging	4 miles very good, 2mi. through a bad Defile, the rest good	open, dry, bad feeding, bad water and scarce	
Field of Battle	6	a little cuting, some digging	a bad Defile for near a mile	retreated to Gists before we encamped	
Total miles	113½			Total Halting Days	10
				marching Days	14

I have not as yet talked to the General of this, nor shall I, untill we get over the Mountains, for then things may appear in another light, and I am unwilling to propose any thing which might look like starting Difficultys. The marching to the french fort is certainly practicable with this present Convoy; but in what light must we appear if we are obliged to abandon our Conquests for want of Sustenance. What was looked on at home as easy is our most difficult point to surmount, I mean the passage of this vast tract of Mountains; Had we a Country we coud subsist in after we get over them, the thing wou'd be easy.

I am at this place with 400 Men as a Van Guard, and to cut the Roads, I was not able to reach this Ground till the 8th Day, 'tho only 20 Miles from Wills's Creek, it is certain I might have made more dispatch but I was charged with a Convoy of 50 Waggons. The Roads are either Rocky or full of Boggs, we are obliged to blow the Rocks and lay Bridges every Day; What an happiness it is to have wood at hand for the latter!

One of our Indians who left the french Fort the 8th Inst, tells me that there are only 100 french & 70 Indians at that place; that they were preparing to set out the Day after to dispute the passage of the Mountains. I have seen nothing of them as yet, nor do I expect th[at] they will come so far from home. They have lately received Six 4 pounders which they were busy mounting when the Indian came away. I shoud be glad to have a Visit from them at this Camp, it is a very good one Surrounded with an Abattis.

I expect the General with the Army will be at this Camp the 15th and that I shall receive his Orders to move on the same Day. I shall take care to let you know every thing that happens amongst us which I dare say will be to your Satisfaction. I am with the greatest Regard, Sir, Your most obedient and most humble Servant,

JOHN ST. CLAIR.

[*Endorsed*] 1755 Journal from Sir Jn. St. Clair. June 13. Rec^d Aug^st 29th.

SIR THOMAS ROBINSON [1] TO EDWARD BRADDOCK

(COPY)

Whitehall 19th June 1755.

Sir,

I have been favoured with your Letter of the 18th March, & am in

[1] Sir Thomas Robinson (1695–1770), ambassador at Vienna from 1730 to 1748, one of the British plenipotentiaries at Aix-la-Chapelle, was secretary of state for the southern department in 1754–1755.

daily Expectation of receiving from you an Account of what passed at the Meeting which You mention in your said Letter was intended to be held at Annapolis, but which I find by a Letter from Commodore Keppel of the 30th April, was held at Alexandria.

The Lords Justices having been pleased to direct, that the several Governors of His Majesty's Colonies should apply to you, or to the Commander in chief of His Majesty's Forces for the time being, in North America, & to no other Person, for such Sums of Money as shall be necessary to discharge the Expences that have been or may be incurred by Services or Operations performed by them, or under their Direction; I inclose to You a Copy of my Circular Letter to the Governors upon this Subject; & I am to acquaint You, that as all Bills drawn by You, or such Commander in Chief upon the Pay Master General of His Majesty's Forces, or his Deputy, & all Warrants issued by You in Consequence thereof, will be duly & regularly answered, You shouuld be particularly carefull to be fully informed, that every such Application is well founded, so that His Majesty's Service may be carried on in the most frugal Manner. I am &c^a

T: ROBINSON

RETURN OF ORDNANCE BY THOMAS ORD [1]
AND JAMES FURNIS [2]

(D.S.)

Little Bear Camp 18th July 1755.

RETURN OF BRASS ORDNANCE howitzers & Cohorn Mortars &c^a sent from England, Lost in the Action Near Fort Du Quesne and Distroy'd at the Camp 6 Miles from the Great Meadows by order of General Braddock with the Remain in North America.

[1] Thomas Ord was a first lieutenant in the Royal Regiment of Artillery in 1741. As a captain lieutenant he fought at Fontenoy, and became a captain on March 1, 1746. He commanded the artillery detachment with Braddock. He became major and lieutenant colonel in 1759, when he served with Amherst. In 1762 he commanded the artillery company at the siege of Martinique. He was in North America again in 1776, became colonel commandant on January 1, 1777, and four months later died at Bath. W. H. Askwith, *List of Officers of the Royal Regt. of Artillery* (1900).

[2] James Furnis, Commissary of Stores for the Ordnance Board in Braddock's expedition. Some of the difficulty in settling the accounts with the waggoners for which Franklin had contracted arose from Furnis's refusal to advance money to them until he could be certain how many wagons were reserved for the use of the artillery. Minutes of the Ordnance Board, W. O. 47: 47, p. 17.

SPECIES OF STORES		Proportion sent from England	Expended & Lost in the Action near Fort Du Quesne	Distroy'd by order of Genl Braddock	Remain
Light Brass Ordnance Mounted on Travelling Carriages Compleat with Limbers Ammunition Boxes & Elevatg Screws	12 pounders	4	4	....	....
	6 pounders	6	2	....	4
Brass Howitzers with Carriages and Limbers Compleat	8 Inch	4	4	....	....
Brass Cohorn Mortars Mounted on their Beds with Lashing Ropes Compleat	4⅖ Inch	15	3	8	4
Round Shott with Wooden Bottoms	12 pounders	100	100	....	....
	6 pounders	450	102	....	348
Tin Cases fill'd with Iron Shot and fix'd with Wooden Bottoms	12 pounders	400	24	176	200
	6 pounders	1200	148	148	904
Spare Round Shott ..	12 pounders	1200	150	1050	....
	6 pounders	1200	....	100	1100
Empty Shells for Howitzers of 7¾ Inch		400	200	200	....
Ditto for Cohorns..of 4⅖ Inch		1500	200	1300	....
Corn'd powder Copper hoop'd for the Guns, Howitzers & Small Arms	Whole Barrells	Expended 75		162	300
		571	34		

THOMAS ORD   JAMES FURNIS

N.B. A particular Account of the Small Stores & Atterail will be sent as
    soon as the Remain can be taken—

CAPTAIN ROBERT ORME [1] TO ROBERT NAPIER

(L.S.)

Fort Cumberland July 18th 1755.

Sir

As I am perswaded the General woud have taken the most early opportunity of informing you of every remarkable event, I take the liberty of transmitting to you by the first express an account of the unhappy affair which happen'd on the 9th of this Month near the Banks of the *Monongahela* within seven miles of *Fort Du Quesne*.

After Marching ab^t *twenty* Miles from this place to a Camp calld the *little Meadows,* the General finding the delay so great from the extreme line of Baggage and also that it was impossible from the small number of Troops he had to make his line of March secure, he determined to proceed himself with *twelve hundred Men, ten* pieces of *Ordinance, Amm^n* and *Provisions* proportion'd to the undertaking, and left *eight hundred* Men with the body of the Convoy under the Command of Col^o *Dunbar* with orders to move forward as fast as the Nature of the Service woud admit; with this Command His Excellency marchd with great expedition and safety, and Encamp'd on the *8th* of this Instant within *ten miles* of the *French Fort*. Here the Guides were all summons'd and question'd as to the first part of the next days March His Excellency having been informd of a very *bad* and *dangerous* Defileé called the *narrows;* upon their report it was judg'd most expedient to pass the Monongahela twice at two different Fords which were neither of them knee deep, by which measure the *narrows* were to be avoided and a very bad passage of the *Turtle Creek*. To secure the two passages of the River the General order'd the two Grenadier's

---

[1] Robert Orme, after serving a brief time as ensign in the 34th regiment, became in 1745 ensign in the Coldstream Guards, of which regiment Braddock was a field officer, and in 1751 lieutenant with the rank of captain. Braddock took him to Virginia as an aide-de-camp in 1755. Orme resigned from the army in October, 1756, probably in disgrace (*Amer. Hist. Rev.,* XLI, 267). Soon after he married Etheldreda (Audrey), daughter of Charles, third Viscount Townshend (Clutterbuck, *Hist. of Hertfordshire,* II, 316), without the family's consent, says Walpole (*Letters,* ed. Toynbee, III, 336, 337n). She died at Hertford in February, 1781, and he is probably the Robert Orme of Hertford who died June 17, 1790, at Mr. Bourchier's house in Mayfair (*Gents. Mag.,* LX [1790], pt. 1, 577). If so, he was the father of Audrey Orme, who died in Hertford in January, 1791 (*Gents. Mag.,* LXI [1791], pt. 1, 92); of Frances Orme, who married Benjamin Cherry, son of a Hertford alderman, in 1791 (*Gents. Mag.,* LXI [1791], pt. 1, 381); and of the Reverend Robert Orme, who was successively Rector of Layston, Vicar of All-Saints, Hertford, and from 1790 to 1843 Rector of Essenden (Clutterbuck, II, 134, 157; Cussans, *Hist. of Hertfordshire,* II, 158). This Robert Orme, at the time of his admission to Trinity College, Cambridge, in 1778, described his father as resident in Bergham, Brabant, the Netherlands (*Admissions,* Trinity Coll., Cambridge).

Companys as a part of a Detachment which was to be compleated to *300:* Men with *two Six pounders* under the Command of Lieut. Col⁰ *Gage* with proper Guides to March before break of Day making the two crossings of the *Monongahela,* of which the first was a mile distance, and to take an advantageous Post at the last, Sir *John St. Clair* with a working party of *200:* Men was to follow at Day break, and the whole was to March at *Six.* this Plan was exactly and punctually executed, and the *Artillery, Ammunition, Provisions, Baggage* and all the Troops had passd the river the *second* time at *one o'clock;* as soon as the whole was over the *General* order'd the two Detachments to advance, and *Sir John St. Clair* to proceed in making the Road as usual; about half a Mile after the Junction of the two Roads Viz^t the *narrows* and the *River,* a heavy and quick Firing was heard in the Front; The General beleiving a party of *French* and *Indians* had taken post, ordered Col⁰ *Burton* with his Van Guard to reinforce them, and at the same time dispos'd the Column in such a manner as to defend it from any attack and to disengage more men for action. The *French* and *Indians* as we found after had possessed the *sides* and *Brow* of a Hill in a kind of Semicircular form, from the extremes of which, some of them fired upon one of our advanced Flank Parties, this immediately brought on a *general Pannick,* the Men coud never be perswaded to form regularly, and in great confusion fell back upon the Party which Sir *John St. Clair* commanded, as did Sir *John St. Clair's* upon Col⁰ *Burton's,* every exhortation entreaty and perswation was used by the General and Officers to make them advance or fall back into the line of March, examples of all kinds were likewise given by the Genl. and the Officers, but the Pannock was so universal and the Firing so executive and uncommon that no order coud ever be restor'd, after *three hours* of irregularity, and the *waste* of all the ammunition, during which time allmost all the Officer's were killed or Wounded by advancing sometimes in bodys and sometimes separately in order to encourage the Men, they left the Field and crossd the River with great precepitation, abandoning the *Artillery, Ammunition, Provision,* and *Baggage,* to the Enemy, and their Terror was so great that many of them *threw away* their *Arms* and *accoutrements,* nor coud they be stopt till they had run *forty* Miles notwithstanding the Enemy pursued no further than the *River;* The General had *five* Horses shot under him and receiv'd a mortal wound in his Lungs, and in this unhappy state was very near being left in the Enemys power being deserted by the Men and brought off by the assistance of a few Officers who were determined not to forsake him; *he died* of his wound the *13th* Instant. An Express was immediately sent off to Col° *Dunbar* with orders to send to us *Ammunition, Provisions,* and *Waggons* for the Wounded, we were then sensible of the good effects of this disposition, for an additional number of Men cou'd have been of no advantage the Pannick being so prevalent, and the want of Provision must have thrown us into the hands of the Enemy.

The Men have by no means recover'd their fright & are so little to be confided in, that Col° *Dunbar* is mov⁸ to this place where I and some other wounded Officer's arrivd from ~~Col° Dunbar~~ [*sic*] the 17th Inst. under an Escort. I have Inclosed you Sir the most perfect List that coud be got and I know it may be much depended upon.

I am Sir, Yʳ most Hᵇˡᵉ & most Obedᵗ Servᵗ

ROBT. ORME.

I woud have wrote in my own hand but am render'd incapable by the wound in my Thigh.

CAPTAIN ROBERT ORME TO HENRY FOX [1]

(COPY)

[undated] [1755]

Sir,

The General the Day before his Death Order'd Me as soon as I was Able to transmitt to Yoù, Sir, An Account of the Unhappy Action near the Monongahela about Seven Miles Distance from Fort Duquesne on the Ninth of this Month.

Our Encampment on the Eighth was about ten Miles from the Fort and upon Calling all the Guides the General from the Intelligence he Could Collect determine[d] to pass the Monongahela twice in Order to Avoid a very bad and Dangerous Defilee called the Narrows. to Secure Our passage Lieut. Coll. Gage was Order'd about an hour before break of Day to March with a Detachment of three Hundred Men to make the two Crossings and to take post upon Advantageous Ground After the last Crossing. Sʳ John St. Clair with a working party of two

---

1 Henry Fox (1705–1774) was secretary at war from 1746 to November, 1755, an office he filled in close connection with Cumberland, to whom he was intimately attached politically. He became secretary of state for the southern department in November, 1755, went out when Pitt came in in the following year, and became paymaster general in the Newcastle-Pitt coalition of July, 1757.

Hundred follow'd at Day Break and the whole March'd at Six oClock
—Lieut. Coll: Gage and Sr John St. Clairs Detachment having made the
two passages the General past with the Column of Artillery Ammunition provision and Baggage and the main Body of the Troops about
One oClock when the whole had Marched about half a Mile the
Advanced party found Some French and Indians posted on a very
advantageous Hight some of whom fired upon one of their Flank
parties which immediately Alarm'd the whole and brought On a very
Severe fireing without any Order or Execution. The General immediately sent forward his Van Guard Under the Command of Lieut.
Coll. Burton to Sustain the two Detachments and instantly formed
the Column in Such a Manner as to Secure it and to be Able to bring
more Men to Act in Case of Necessity.

The two Advanced parties gave way and fell Back Upon Our Van
which very much disconcerted the Men and that Added to the Manner of fighting they were quite Unacquainted with struck them with
such a pannick that all the Intreaties perswasions and Examples of the
General and Officers could Avail nothing nor could Order ever be
regain'd after fireing away All their Ammunition they gave Ground
and left the Artillery Baggage &c in the Hands of the Enemy.

The General was with great Difficulty brought out of the Field
he had five Horses shott under him and was at last Mortally Wounded
of which he died the thirteenth.

I had the Generals Orders to Inform You, Sir, that the Behaviour
of the Officers deserved the very Highest Commendation.

Mr. Morris the Other Aid De Camp and Myself being very danger-
ously wounded and the Secretary Kill'd all the papers are lost.

[*Endorsed*] 1755 A Coppy of the Acc^t sent to Mr. Fox by Capt [1] Orme. Rec^d
Oct 3.

---

[1] Other accounts of the battle by Orme, similar to this one and less full than in
the letter to Napier, are printed in *Correspondence of William Shirley*, edited by
C. H. Lincoln, II, 207–209; American Antiquarian Society *Transactions*, XI (1909),
174–175; Massachusetts Historical Society *Collections*, 2d. ser., VIII, 153–157; *Historical Magazine*, VIII, 353–354; *Archives of Maryland*, VI, 252–254; *Pennsylvania
Colonial Records*, VI, 487–492.

SIR JOHN ST. CLAIR TO ROBERT NAPIER

(L.S.)

Fort at Wills's Creek 22ᵈ July 1755.

Sir,

I wrote to you a letter of the 12th of June, which I hope you have received by this time, that letter gave you an Account of the obstructions we was like to meet with on our march on account of Carridges; a few days after writeing that letter, General Braddock with the Army arrived at the little meadows; about the 17th of June General Braddock sent for me and told me, he laid down a Scheme of his own for marching on, which before that time, had been given to the Brigade Major in orders. The Scheme was, that a detachment should be form'd of those of the British Battalions, which Came from Ireland and that those should march with the artillery together with three Companys of the Virginia forces, under the Command of General Braddock, the remaining part of the Army under the Command of Colonel Dunbar, was to follow with the Great Convoy, this Step I look'd upon to be a prelude to marching in divisions, which was the only way we Could have brought up our Convoy.

This strong detachment march'd on and arrived at the Strong Camp of the Great-Lick which is Twenty one miles on the other side of Yanehagane and Eighty miles from this fort. The Great advantages of this strong Ground made me propose to the General, to halt with his detachment and bring up Colonel Dunbar with his Convoy; this proposal, was rejected with great indignation; we march'd on 'till the seventh of July Twenty three miles further, I then objected to our marching any longer in that order of march with a Convoy, and proposed, since this small body must march to the french fort, that we should march part of our small numbers and take post before the Fort leaving our Convoy to Come up I urged strongly that no General had hitherto march'd up at midday to the Gates of the Town he was to beseige leading his Convoy and if Genl. Braddock attempted it, he must look to the Consequences.

Tewsday the 8th we march'd to a riseing ground within three quarters of a mile of the Monaganhela and Encamp'd there.

Wensday the 9th Colonel Gage with about 300 men march'd at

daylight, past and repast the Monaganhela where he took post, the Workmen and Cover'ers immediately follow'd and then the rest of the detachment—so that the whole had past by half an hour after Twelve o'Clock, being three miles; The reason of passing the Monaganhela twice was to avoid the Narrows, which is a road on the bank of the River, Commanded by a high hill, which would have taken a days work to have made passable. After Colonel Gage and I had pass'd the river, we received orders from Cap: Morris Aid du Camp to March on; the underwood Continued very thick for about one quarter of a mile beyond the Monaganhela then we Came into an open wood free from underwood with some gradual riseings, this wood was so open that Carridges Could have been drove in any part of it; about a mile on the other side of the last Crossing, we began to feel the Enemys fire and to hear their Shouts; those who were under my Command immediately form'd. On those in my front falling back upon me, I ran to the front to see what the matter was, when I received a Shot through the body. I then return'd to my own people, posted Cap: Polsons Company of Artificers and Cap: Periwees Company of Rangers to Cover my two Cannon. I then went up to General Braddock who was then at the head of his own Guns and beg'd of him for God-Sake to gain the riseing ground on our Right to prevent our being Totally Surrounded. I know no further of this unlucky affair to my knowledge being afterwards insensible. It will be needless for me to give you any account by hear-say. Our affairs are as bad here as bad Can make them, with regard to my self in particular, I was fully resolved, if we had met with Success to desire leave to have been recalld, finding I could be of little use being never listen'd to: but as our affairs stand at present it is a thing I shall not think of and should be glad of haveing another opportunity of makeing use of the knowledge I have of the Country and its inhabitants; by the time I shall have your answer, I hope to be in a Condition of doing my duty therefore should be glad you would point it out to me whether its to be here or in New England under General Shirrly.

I am with the greatest respect Sir, your most obedient and most obliged humble Servant.

JOHN ST CLAIR.

[*Endorsed*] 1755 Sr John St. Clair July 22. Rec^d Oct 3^d.

JOURNAL OF PROCEEDINGS FROM WILLES'S CREEK TO
THE MONONGAHELA: HARRY GORDON [1] TO ?

(L.S.)

Wills's Creek, 23rd of July 1755

Sir,

I have not troubl'd you hitherto with any Letters, altho' when I took
my Leave at London I Receiv'd your Commands to write you the most
Remarkable Occurrences of our Expedition.

I shall now trouble you with a short Journal of our March & proceedings, from this place to Beyond the Last Crossing of the Monan-
gahela, where we were unfortunately Defeated.

On the 11th of June we March'd from this fort with such a train
of provision & Amunition Waggons, that the first days March Convinc'd us that it was impossible to Get on with so many Carriages so
heavily Loaded. The General Diminish'd the Carriadges By putting
the greatest part of the provisions on Pack horses, & sending Back two
of the 6 pounders with their Amunition; in this Reformation we
March'd as far as the Little Meadows, which are only Distant 15 miles

---

[1] Harry Gordon, son of George Gordon of Knockespock, Clatt, Aberdeenshire,
joined the Royal Engineers in 1742, served in Flanders in 1745 and again in 1747
and 1748 under Cumberland. In 1754 Cumberland particularly recommended him
to Braddock as a good man for laying out and supervising road construction (*Scottish Notes & Queries*, 3d ser., XI, 67). Gordon served throughout the war, attaining
the rank of captain, with a company in the 6oth regiment, and distinguishing himself at the siege of Havana in 1762. He was sent out to North America again in
1764 and explored the West (his journal is printed in Alvord and Carter, *The New
Régime*, p. 290). From 1767 to 1773 he was chief engineer in the ceded islands, as
well as proprietor of an estate in Grenada which came into his possession on his
brother Peter's (Patrick's?) death in 1768. During the campaign of 1776 he served
as chief engineer in Canada, but resigned over a question of rank. In 1783 he went
out to the Leeward Islands as chief engineer. On his way home, in 1787, he died at
Eastbourne. He married Hannah Meredith of Philadelphia, and had four sons. (C.
O. Skelton and J. M. Bulloch, *Gordons under Arms*, pp. 136–138, being Volume III
of the House of Gordon in the New Spaulding Club *Publications; Scottish Notes &
Queries*, 3d ser., III, 209–210.)

Archer Butler Hulbert, in *Braddock's Road and Three Relative Papers*, Volume
IV of *Historic Highways of America* (1903), Chapter IV, printed the original version
of the "Seaman's Journal" which in an expanded form is printed in Sargent, *History
of the Expedition against Fort Duquesne*. Hulbert argues that the latter version was
written by Harry Gordon from the original. The author of the original was certainly that midshipman who went into the hospital at Wills Creek on June 9 and
did not rejoin the expedition. It is possible that Gordon may have copied and expanded the original; it is more probable that he furnished some of the entries found
in both. But only up to the time that the midshipman was taken ill; the narrative
of the battle in both versions needs only to be compared with this vivid letter of
Gordon's to show that it was not the account of an eye-witness, but was pieced together from various accounts, including perhaps that of Gordon himself, after the
army's return to Wills Creek.

from our first Camp, yet took us five Days to Get up all our Carriages, the Roads Being steep & the horses very weak.

At the Little Meadows the General order'd another Reform, which Reduc'd us to a Pick'd Body of Eleven hundred men & officers; our Carriadges consisted of two 6 pounders, four 12 pounders, four Howits's, 3 Cowhorns, & 75 Rounds of Amunition, 3 or 4 provision Waggons, which made our whole train of Carriadges three or four & thirty. We Left the Little Meadows the 19th of June with a Resolution of pushing on Directly to fort Du Quesne, & to leave Coll: Dunbar with the rest of our Army & Carriadges to Get up in the Best Manner he cou'd. We Came on Extreamly well, Considering the Difficulty of making the roads, which was so Great, that Altho' Every one us'd their Utmost Endeavor & only halted four Days on the Road, it was the 8th of July Before we Cou'd Get within 10 miles of the french fort.

on the 8th we Cross'd the Long Run which was a small Rivulet that runs in to the Monongahela about 12 miles frcm the F: fort. We were Oblig'd to Cross it many times in the Space of two Miles, in which Distance we came along a Narrow Valley At the widest a Quarter of a Mile, very much Commanded on Both Sides By Steep hills. In this March Every proper precaution was taken to secure us, By Detaching all the men that cou'd Be Spar'd from the Advancd party, that day Commanded By C: Burton on our flank the General Likewise orderd 350 men to take possession of the heights on Each Side; & the Grenadier Company of Sir P: H[alket's] Reg^t, the Advance of the Advanc'd party, to Gain the Rising Ground, which Shut up the Valley in our front. No Enemy appear'd, & we Encamp'd on the last Mention'd Rising Ground, which Brought us within a Small Mile of the River Monongahela.

in our Next Days March we must Either Go along the Narrows, a very Difficult pass, on the Right Side Entirely Commanded By high ground & on the Left hemm'd in By the Monongahela; A Small Consultation was held, & it was carryied to Cross the Monongahela at the Nearer End of the Narrows, to keep along the South Side, & to Cross it again Below where turtle Creek runs in, & without the Narrows; As there was Danger Imagin'd, the 2 Comp^{ys} of Grenadiers with 150 men of the two Reg^{ts} Commanded By Coll: Gage were Order's to March By 2 o'Clock of the Morning of the 9th to take possession of the Banks of the second Crossing of the River; two of the light 6 pounders were sent along with this party; the rest of our Little Army March'd at four, Cross'd peaceably, & Came up with Coll: Gage about Eleven o'Clock in peaceable possession of the furthest Banks of the

Last Crossing. Every one who saw these Banks, Being Above 12 feet perpendicularly high Above the Shore, & the Course of the River 300 yards Broad, hugg'd themselves with joy at our Good Luck in having surmounted our greatest Difficultys, & too hastily Concluded the Enemy never wou'd dare to Oppose us.

In an hour which Brought the time about Noon, the Bank was slop'd & passable for Artillery & Carriadges; Coll: Gage with the same Advanc'd party was ordered to [sic] forward; the covering party of the Carpenters & Pioneers followed immediately in his Rear, after them then came two 6 pounders, their Amunition Waggon, & a Guard in their Rear, after them follow'd the Main Body in their Usual Order of March with a strengthen'd Rear Guard of 100 men. this Order of March was in My Opinion the [sic]

The flank partys of the Advance & Main Body were No Stronger than Usual & Coll: Gage's party march'd By files four Deep our front had not Got above half a Mile from the Banks of the River, when the Guides which were all the Scouts we had, & who were Before only about 200 yards Came Back, & told a Considerable Body of the Enemy, Mostly Indians were at hand, I was then just rode up in Search of these Guides, had Got Before the Grenadiers, had an Opportunity of viewing the Enemy, & was Confirm'd By the Report of the Guides & what I saw myself that their whole Numbers did Not Exceed 300.

As soon as the Enemys Indians perceiv'd our Grenadiers, they Divided themselves & Run along our right & Left flanks. The Advanc'd party Coll: Gage order'd to form, which Most of them Did with the front Rank upon the Ground & Begun firing, which they continued for several Minutes, Altho' the Indians very soon Dispers'd Before their front & fell upon the flank partys, which only consisted of an officer & 20 men, who were very soon Cut off. The Indians Making their Appearance upon the Rising Ground, on our Right, occasion'd an Order for Retiring the Advanc'd Body 50 or 60 paces, there they confusedly form'd again, & a Good many of their Officers were kill'd & wounded By the Indians, who had got possession of the Rising Ground on the Right. There was an Alarum at this time that the Enemy were attacking the Baggage in the Rear, which Occasion'd a second Retreat of the Advanc'd party; they had not Retir'd But a few paces when they were join'd By the rest of the troops, Coming up in the greatest Confusion, & Nothing afterwards was to Be Seen Amongst the Men But Confusion & Panick. They form'd Altogether, the Advanced & Main Body in Most places from 12 to 20 Deep; the Ground on which they then were, was 300 yards Behind where the Grenadiers

& Advanc'd party first form'd. The General Order'd the officers to Endeavor to tell off 150 men, & Advance up the hill to Dispossess the Enemy, & another party to Advance on the Left to support the two 12 pounders & Artillery people, who were in great Danger of Being Drove away By the Enemy, at that time in possession of the 2 field pieces of the Advanc'd party. This was the Generals Last Order; he had had Before this time 4 horses killed under him, & now Receiv'd his Mortal wound. All the Officers us'd their Utmost Endeavors to Get the men to Advance up the hill, & to Advance on the left to support the Cannon. But the Enemy's fire at that time very much Encreasing, & a Number of officers who were Rushing on in the front to Encourage the men Being killed & wounded, there was Nothing to Be seen But the Utmost panick & Confusion amongst the Men; yet those officers who had Been wounded having Return'd, & those that were not Wounded, By Exhorting & threatning had influence to keep a Body about 200 an hour Longer in the field, but cou'd not perswade them Either to Attempt the hill again, or Advance far Enough to support the Cannon, whose officers & men were Mostly kill'd & wounded. The Cannon silenc'd, & the Indian's shouts upon the Right Advancing, the whole Body gave way, & Cross'd the Monongahela where we had pass'd in the Morning. with great Difficulty the General & his Aid de Camps who were Both wounded were taken out of a Waggon, & hurryed along across the River; Coll: Burton tho' very much Wounded attempted to Rally on the Other Side, & made a Speach to the Men to Beg them to get into some Order, But Nothing would Do, & we found that Every man wou'd Desert us; therefore we were oblig'd to go along; we march'd all night, & never halted till we Came to Guests's which was near 60 Miles from the place of the Action, we halted that night there, & next Day join'd Coll: Dunbar's party which was 6 miles further.

Thus Sir I have sent you an Account of those transactions Entirely consisting with my own Certain knowledge. I never was a Critick, therefore leaves it to you to make what Remarks you see proper, As you are a Much Better Judge in these Matters than I shall Ever pretend to Be. only One thing cannot Escape me, which is, that had our March Been Executed in the same manner the 9th as it was the 8th, I shou'd have stood a fair Chance of writing from fort Du Quesne, instead of Being in the hospital at Wills's Creek.

I am a Good Deal hurt in the Right Arm, having Receiv'd a Shot which went thro', & shatter'd the Bone, half way Between the Elbow & the wrist; this I had Early, & altho' I felt a Good deal of pain, yet I was too Anxious to allow myself to Quit the field; at the last my horse having Receiv'd three shots, I had hardly time to shift the Sadle on another without the Bridle, when the whole gave way. The passage that was made thro the Bank in the Morning, I found Choack'd up; I was oblig'd to tumble over the high Bank, which Luckily Being of Sand, part of it fell along with me, which kept my horse upon his feet, & I fortunately kept his Back. Before I had got 40 yards in the River, I turn'd about on hearing the Indians Yell, & Saw them Tomohocking some of our women & wounded people, others of them fir'd very Briskly on those that were then Crossing, at which time I Receiv'd Another Shot thro' the Right Shoulder. But the horse I Rode Escaping, I got across the River, & soon came up with the General, Coll: Burton, & the rest of the officers & men that were along with them, & Continued along with them in the Utmost pain, my wounds not having Been Dress'd untill I came to Guests's.

On the Road I propos'd fortifying a Camp at Licking Creek 10 miles to the Westward of the Crossing of the Yohiogany, a very advantagious Situation, & which Cover'd the Richest part of the Country which Lyes Betwixt Guest's & that, or at least I imagin'd we might have Been join'd By Coll: Dunbar's party at Guest's, where a Good Camp might Easily Been had, which fortified with two or three Redoubts in front cou'd have Been defended By our Numbers (above 1000 fitt for Duty) against any force our Enemys cou'd Bring against us.

Instead of all this Nothing wou'd Do, But Retiring, & Destroying immense Quantitys of Amunition & Stores, with which Last all our Instruments & Stationary wares shar'd the fate.

Here we are at present, But the talk is of going into Pensilvania, & No talk of putting this fort or the frontiers of this Country in any posture of Defence; as it is at present, 3 pieces of 6 pound Cannon, with the Advantage the Ground wou'd Naturally give them, cou'd knock the fort to pieces, & nothing after we are gone cou'd hinder 150 french Indians from Ravaging to Alexandria.

I have tir'd My Secretary, & I'm afraid you'll think me too prolix, But I cou'd not help it, & indeed it was my intention, to Lay Before you our Proceedings, & the Situation of Affairs in this Country. Had I had the Use of my Drawing hand, I woud have sent you a Sketch of the field of Action, & some other Principal Crossings of the Rivers on our March. I hope soon to Be Able to Lay these things Before you, & will take the opportunity of Describing the Country which we pass'd at the same time; This is all hopes, as Nothing certain is determin'd with Regard to the Lower wound of my Arm, at present I conclude with my best wishes for your health, & always shall Be with the greatest Respect, Sir, your most obligd & obed^t Humble Servt

HARRY GORDON.

A left hand Subscription

Wills's Creek
23^d of July 1755

P.S. I shoud Be Extreamly oblig'd to you if you woud Be kind Enough to Remind H:R:H of my former petition for a Commission in some Reg^{tt}. I have Reason to Believe that had General Braddock Liv'd I shou'd have Been provided for in some of the Reg^{ts} here.
to Be Copied for Coll: Napier.

[*Endorsed*] 1755 Mr. Gordon, Engineer. (Sent by his Brother,^{2} Oct. 3^d.

COLONEL THOMAS DUNBAR ^{1} TO ROBERT NAPIER

(L.S.)

Fort Cumberland July the 24th 1755.

Sir,

The Army under General Braddock proceeding to Fort Duquesne halted at the little Meadows, on the 17th of June there was Orders for a Detachment of About twelve hundred of the best Troops to March, part Under Coll: Gage to March the 18th and the rest the 19th. the Officers for this Detachment were All Named. this was the first Sr Peter Halkett or I knew of this design, the Generall March'd with them leaving Me with the remains of the Army to bring Up About One hundred And fifty Waggons and near three hundred Horse load of bread flower and Bacon, telling Me he never would be more than a days March before Me, so that in Case of Necessity we might joyn in two or three hours, that this was then his Intention is plain for his Orders to Me was to fire A Gun (a Six pounder) if I wanted his Assistance and if he wanted Mine he was to do the Same but if he fired two or More I was to Join him with all the force I had and leave the Convoy.

---

^{2} Probably James Gordon of Argyll Street.

^{1} Thomas Dunbar, after thirty years in the army, most of them in the 18th (Royal Irish) regiment of which he became lieutenant colonel, was made colonel of the 48th in 1752. After his misguided retreat following Braddock's disaster, he was recalled, resigned his regiment, and became lieutenant governor of Gibraltar. He became major general in 1758 and lieutenant general in 1760 and died in 1767.

As soon As he Marched I sent for the Waggon Masters and Commissarys to lett Me know the Number of Horses could be furnish'd with Waggons and back loads, and the Quantity of provisions to be taken As Also the Number of Carriages the Artillery would want, when these returns were brought I was told the General had Ordered Six of the Best Horses to be put to each of the Carriages that went with him and many Spare Horses in Case of Accidents As Also the Ablest Horses for back loads, and what remain'd would Only furnish two thirds of the Waggons with four each and for back loads there remained of very bad as many as would take About One half of the provissions.

As soon As I knew this I wrote to the General leting him know the Condition I was in to Execute his Orders, his Answer Express'd Anger saying I knew he could not help Me but that Expedients must be Used to bring All Away.

I March'd according to his Orders and took with Me all I could and On My Arrival where I was to halt that night I Ordered All the Horses back to bring Up what was left behind under the Care of a party. the rear division of Waggons did not Arrive untill very late the next Evening the Horses being very bad and Weak, the next day I was Advised to halt for the Horses were So Work'd they would Not be Able to travile, in this Manner I was Obliged to proceed sometimes 6 or 7 Miles in three days and sometimes four.

I again and Again Sett forth My Scituation to him he Once told Me he sent Me a Waggon and Eleven Horses the first I saw and such as could be of little Service, Again he wrote Me he sent me forty Horses tho' unloaded there was but Sixteen could Come they were so wore down, in One Letter I told him it was Impossible I could gett Up with him Unless his Goodness would halt and send Me his Horses to help Me but he did not but proceeded, Some time before the Action He called a Council of Warr when it was proposed takeing possession of some strong Camp and halting untill I Joyn'd but it was rejected and He Continued Marching untill the Ninth Instant when they fell into the Unhappy Trap at which time I was About fifty Miles from them the next Morning by five o'Clock I had the Account by a follower of the Army that was in the Engagement and in a few hours Another Arrived and About One o'Clock Sr John St. Clair who saw the whole, the next day in the Evening the General Arrived the Eleventh the 12th We remained in the same Ground which time was Imployed in destroying provisions Ordnance Ammunition &c. by the Generals Orders, by this Evening great Numbers of Wounded Officers and Soldiers Arrived and many More that were not. On the 13th We March'd and that day he resign'd the Command to Me After we had gott About a Mile from Our Ground, soon After we gott into our ground for that Evening where he died and I proceeded to this as was his intention and brought all the Wounded With Me. here wee have fixed a General Hospital and I purpose leaving some of the Independants and provincial Troops to protect them and proceed with the remains of the two Regiments to philadelphia for Winter Quarters which Capt. Orme tells Me they were all lost, so that I am left to do as I think best, And hope I shall Act as Will be agreeable to All I am Accountable to I have wrote to General Shirly and desired his instructions for My future Conduct.

As I was not in the Action I can Only send You such An Account as I could gett and believe what I send which I had from Capt. Orme is the same Sent before I could dispatch One.

The Officers by All Accounts behaved As Well as Men could and the Soldiers dont seem to think they deserve all that is Said. that they fought an invisible Enemy is by All Accounts Certain for I have heard many say both Officers and Soldiers they did not see One of the Enemy the whole day tho A Warm Constant fire in the front and on both flanks Colo Gage who was in the front and first Attacked declares he does not know he saw One of the Enemy the whole time this Manner of fighting confounded the people; they saw and heard fireing and the fatal consequences but few saw an Enemy, that for the Number better could not be found. Many of them had been often tryed and proved themselves so; I am perswaded there is many Accounts of this Affair sent home and that All will not Agree.

This Climate by no means Agrees with My time of Life and bad Constitution, I was willing to try and hoped I should be Able to go through all that came in My Way, but find it otherwise, therefore beg Your Interest to gett Me leave to go home; was I as Able as I am Willing I Assure You I would Gladly Stay.

I have dispatch'd an Indian with a Letter desiring to know what Officers of Ours are prisoners untill I have an Answer to that, Cannot be Certain who is Kill'd, I am, Dear Sir, Your most humble and Obedient Servant,

THO DUNBAR.

[Endorsed] 1755 Col Dunbar F. Cumberland July 24 Recd Oct 3d.

ANONYMOUS LETTER ON BRADDOCK'S CAMPAIGN [1]

(A.L.)

Wills's Creek 25th July 1755.

Sir,

When every body's expectation was rased to the highest pitch, Concerning the expidition under the Command of General Braddock in America, those who were under his Command, and gave attention to his proceeding, forsaw, what must happen (if any opposition should be made by the Enemy) from the measures taken, and was sorry, so good natured a man should be so much misled by a favourite, or two, who, realy had not much experience and were very ignorant of the detail of an Army, how much depend on the Oeconemy [Economy] and Just regulation of every Branch; therefore I presume to lay before you the following remarks, as well as facts, which Can be attested by many, in doing which, I have endeavour'd to advance nothing but what Consists with my own knowledge, or that of the best Authority; neither have I attempted to give any reason for our bad Success to any other person in Europe, as it would not only be great presumption, but likewise improper; notwithstanding, I shall always think it my Duty to lay before you every Truth, Consisting with my own knowledge, especially things of so much importance to his Majesty and to the Publick, therefore shall make no other Apology for this long narration which I beg your patience to read as something may be mention'd which is overlook'd in other accounts; I know pains have been taken by some (who were deeply Concern'd) to dress up an Account to excuse their own folly, presumption and manifest ill Conduct: but in Spite of every Gloss *Truth* will remain and the more the operation of this Expedition is inquired into and the Conduct from the time of devideing the Army to the fatal 9th of July and for three days after things will appear the worse and most deserveing the severest Censure.

About the 18th of June General Braddock march'd from the Little Meadows with a detachmen[t] of above 1200 men besides officers as will appear by the inclosed return exclusive of Bat-men Waggoners

---

[1] There is no endorsement or hint of the authorship of this violent letter, an example of the backbiting that was practised in the British army before Cumberland became captain general. The handwriting is the same as the scribe's who wrote St. Clair's letter (p. 102). The author was obviously an officer of sufficient rank to learn Dunbar's and Halkett's secrets, provided his comments are taken at face value; he is exact when mentioning provisions, transport, and such matters as fall within a quartermaster's province. It is possible that he may have been Captain Gabriel Christie, who assisted St. Clair on this expedition and had his strong support. Christie became deputy quartermaster general, a general in the army, and proprietor of Isle aux Noix in the Richelieu River.

and other followers of an Army—he took with him the best part of the Artillery tho' the Amunition was not more than make one days fireing if there had been occasion again[st] a fort. Also fifty Waggons loaded with different things, to each of which he had six of the best horses— and 400 more horses with back loads of flower &c. and about 100 spare horses—after which he had a supply sent him of one hundred loads of flow'r—upwards of 100 fine fat Oxen and a number of sheep which all joind the day before the action, Consequently fell into the hands of the french.

After all this was fix'd he left Colonel Dunbar with the remainder of the Army to bring 357 Waggons after him, besides 200 back loads and horses only for 100; the Weakest and worst of the horses were left with C. Dunbar and the proportion run to be Just Three Waggons to one sett of bad horses—partly oweing to the number of spare ones the General had taken as before mention'd—so you may Judge of the slowness of Col. Dunbars motions marching a little way one day with one sett, then sending Back for another sett &c. therefore every days march (as to distance) took up three days dureing which time neither man nor beast had any rest and the latter no meat but the leaves of Trees—this way of going on together with the Gen[ls] hurry from the little Meadows brought Colonel Dunbar to be near fifty miles in the Gen[ls], rear on the day of action. To give you an acco[t] of which that will intirely agree with every other, is almost impossible, as most officers, as well as men, differ, in Triffleing Circumstances and even in a few material ones —however the Conducting of the Whole from the beginning might have been retrieved had not a final Issue been put to all by what happen'd last.

On the 9th of July Lt Col. Gage Commanded two Companys of Grs [Grenadiers] which was by way of an advance Guard[2] to the main body under the General as well as for Covering a working party then Cuting the Road under S[r] Jo: St. Clair's dirrection about two o'Clock that day, after Crossing the River Call'd Monanganhely where a Plantation of one fraser had been and within six or seven miles of the french fort Call'd du Queesny (or Kane) and within 3 quarters of mile of the Crossing at frasers house—on the Fort Side of Turtle-Creek —The advance Party was attack'd rather from a riseing ground by a party of Indians and french in Indian dress. The Number of the Enemy by those who makes the largest allowance did not appear to be above

2 The advance party was larger than this. It had 300 men, including the grenadier company, a detachment from the 44th regiment, and half of Horatio Gates's New York independent company.

The two maps on the following pages are photographic reproductions of the essential portions of one set of the originals, signed by Patrick Mackellar, the engineer en second on Braddock's expedition, in the collection of Cumberland Maps in the Royal Library at Windsor Castle. There is a similar set in the Public Record Office. The originals measure 14 by 7 inches, on a scale of 300 yards to an inch. The reproductions are reduced to a scale of 375 yards to an inch.

No. 1

A Sketch of the Field of Battle of the 9th July upon the Monongahela, seven miles from Fort du Quesne, between the British Troops commanded by General Braddock and the French & French Indians commanded by Monsr de St Pierre, shewing the Disposition of the Troops when the Action began.

Explanation

⊞ British Troops, the long Lines express the Number of Files. ◇ French and Indians. ⊹ Cannon. ⊹⊹ Howitzers. ⌂ Waggons, Carts and Tumbrils. ⊦ Provision and Baggage Horses.

a, { French and Indians upon their march to attack the British, when first discover'd by the Guides

b, Guides and six light Horse

c, Van-Guard of the advanced Party

d, Advanced Party commanded by Col Gage

e, Working Party commanded by Sr Jn St Clair D.Q.M.G.

f, Two six pounder Field Pieces

g, Carts & Waggons wt Ammunition & Tools

h, Rear Guard of the Advanced Party

i, Light Horse

k, Sailors and Pioneers

l, Three 12 pounder Field Pieces

m, General's Guard, Foot & Horse

n, { Main Body in Divisions upon the Flanks of the Convoy, wt the Cattle, Provision & Baggage Horse between them & the Flank-Guards

o, a 12 pounder Field Ps in the rear of the Convoy

p, Rear-Guard

q, Flank-Guards

r, a Hollow Way

s, { a Hill which the Indians took possession of soon after the beginning of the Action

t, Frazer's House

Engaged		in the Field	kill'd	wounded
Genl Braddock	Officers Staff included	96	26	36
	Sergeants Corporals & private Men }	1373	430	484
	Total	1469	456	520
Monsr de St Pierre	French	200	8	
	Indians	600	20	
	Total	800	28	

N B The Number of the French & Indians is not yet certain

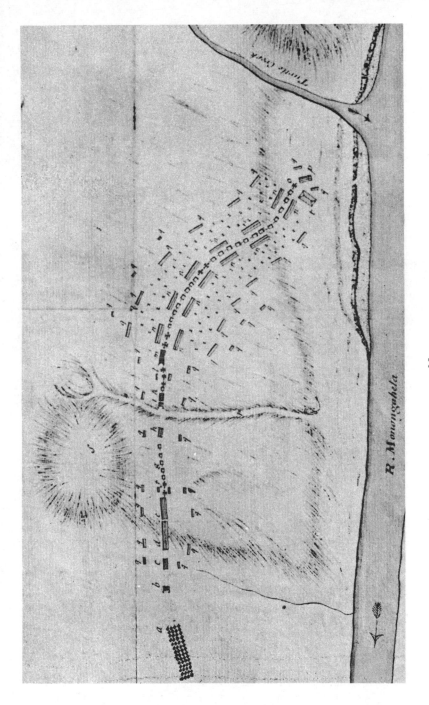

R. Monongahela

No. 1

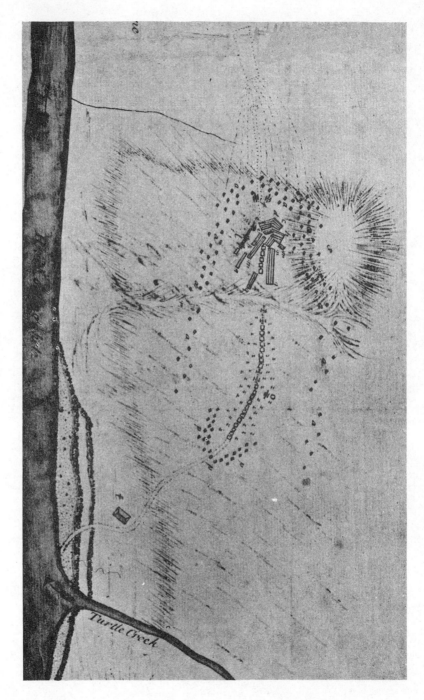

No. 2

Turtle Creek

Three hundred and others dont scruple to say did not exceed one hundred. The first fire of the Enemy was on the left of the advance Guard which Gradualy Came to the front and extended to their Right something like a half moon, which kill'd about 10 or Twelve Grenadeers—this alarm'd them a little and they return'd the fire, notwithstanding they did not see the Enemy—which was return'd tho not in a regular manner, but like Poping shots, with little explosion, only a kind of Whiszing noise; (which is a proof the Enemys Arms were riffle Barrels) this kind of fire was attended with Considerable execution, which soon put the Grenadeers in some disorder and on the Continuance of the Enemys fire the advance Guard was repuls'd but were suported by the Working party in their Rear, which afterwards Joind in the disorder; dureing which time, General Braddock was with the main body about a Quarter of a mile in their Rear—upon the alarm of the advance fire, the General immediately rode to the front and his aid-du-camps after him, some officers after them, and more men without any form or order but that of a parcell of school boys Coming out of s[c]hool—and in an instant, Blue, buff and yellow were inter-

---

No. 2

A Sketch of the Field of Battle &c, shewing the Disposition of the Troops about 2 a Clock when the whole of the main Body had joined the advanced and Working Partys, then beat back from the Ground they occupied as in Plan No 1.

Explanation

a, The French and Indians skulking behind Trees round the Brittish

f, The two Field Pieces of the advanced Party now abandoned

c, d, e, h, i, k, m, n, q, The whole Body of the British joined, with little or
    no order, but endeavouring to make Fronts towards the Enemys Fire

l, the three 12 pounder Field Pieces of the main Body

o, The rear Field Piece. 12 pounder

p, { The Rear Guard divided (round the rear of the Convoy, now closed up)
    { behind Trees having been attacked by a few Indians

N.B. The Disposition on both sides, continued about two hours nearly as here represented, the British endeavouring to recover the Guns (f) and to gain the Hill (s) to no purpose. It was proposed to take possession of this Hill before the Indians did, but unhappily it was neglected. The British were at length beat from the Guns (l). The General was wounded soon after. They were lastly beat back accross the Hollow way (r) and made no farther Stand. All the Artillery, Ammunition, Provision & Baggage were left in the Enemys Hands, and the General was with difficulty carryed off. The whole Action continued about three hours and a half. The Retreat was full of Confusion, but after a few Miles, there was a Body got to rally.

mix'd. Soon after an order was given to the main body to move on
(that is, those who keep'd at their post) without any form or order, but
that of the line of march which is four deep faced to the Right or left
as occasion might be, with an intention to separate on each side of the
road to march Two deep according to his original plan of march a
Copey of which *I send you inclosed* (before I proceed I have only one
obvious observation to make on the line of march—which as I before
said is 4 deep, instead of three the Usual way—which marches by files
—only divides on each side of the line of Waggons, baggage &c. in the
Center. Consequently their is a file of two deep on each side of the
Waggons on the march but what I'm going to observe, is, that when
the Battalion is Compleated (always four deep) the officers are all
posted to the front half files (if I may be allow'd the expression) at
their respective posts where they were order'd to remain—therefore
when the Battalion is faced to the right by files 4 deep—the officers are
all on the left flank—if to the left the Contrary—Consequently they're
always upon one side—therefore when ever you Come to devide on the
Center on each side of the Waggons and have occasion to form the
line—the officers are every one *to one Wing*—without a single officer
to the other. this was a Constant practise with us notwithstanding of
the most evident absurdity) but to proceed—one officer, indeed says, he
had orders from an aid du camp to double his front, instead of four,
to march eight in front, as if one was going to attack a breach—however I beleive it was meant only to keep the line of march, in which
order the main body moved, without the least dirrection to officer or
man but *"March on my lads and keep up your fire*["] when he Came
up with the repuls'd party after passing with difficulty the line of Waggons, Baggage, Cattle &c. in their front together with the Artillery, all
which occupy'd the space between the main body And the advance or
van Guard [1] or Party whos[e] Confusion had some effect on them and
occasion'd their throwing away their fire without seeing the Enemy,
which was return'd by them in the manner before describ'd with some
execution: but our own fire did much more, however both together
Contributed not a little to a general disorder; after which, The General would have Changed his disposition (or more properly made one)
but the Men were then turn'd stupid and insensible and would not
obey their officers in makeing the intended movements which were
unhappily too late attempted. The officers behaved extremely well as
possibly Could be, which fact is strengthen'd by the number of kill'd

---

[1] "There were no other van Guard to the Army but Co. Gage's party tho the
contrary has been said in some Accots. sent home." [Marginal note.]

and Wounded—tho' I'm sorry to say the men are accused of misbehaviour, notwithstanding of the number of kill'd and wounded among
them, which is Great, Considering the number of Effectives in the
field: but I Can't help thinking their misbehaviour is exaggerated, in
order to palliate the Blunders made by those in the dirrection, as they
make no allowance for regular Troops being surprised, as was manifestly the Case here, and no manner of disposition made—but one of
Certain destruction—in these Circumstances it has generaly I beleive
been the Case—misbehaviour. its the general opinion more were kill'd
by our own Troops than by the Enemy particularly C. Tatton—by the
Grenadiers. The Rear Guard (tho' only a Caps. Command) did more
execution than the whole, among the Enemy, as the officer had time to
recolect himself Consequently made a dispossition and extended his
Guard in advantageous posts behind trees by which he both repuls'd
and kill'd a great number. The Ground was extraordinary good when
Compared to the rest of the Country. The Trees were high very open
and little or no underwood—nor Can any reason be given why they
allow'd us to Cross the Monanganhela ¾ of a mile from the Attack—
where the banks were vastly high and the most advantageous post for
them they possibly Could have, except it was, to lull us in Security,
that we had no Enemy, which was too generaly beleived, on the whole
march, and that the Fort would be found abandon'd; there was nothing of Entrenchments—Swivvel-Guns &c. &c. as some officers and several
men affirm—which from the best information has no foundation but
in their own Brain. Scarce an officer or soldier Can say they ever saw
at one time six of the Enemy and the greatest part never saw a Single
man of the Enemy.—Col. Gage who Commanded the advance party and
distinguish'd himself by Encouraging the men as much as he Could
and after they were broke, in rallying them, says, were he put to his
oath he Could not say he saw above *one* french or Indian dureing the
action—he had several narrow escapes by shots through both hat &
Coat and one which Grased on his belly but did not break the skin,
there were a few french and some Indians the french mostly in the
Indian dress notwithstand[ing] several were seen in the french uniform
—particularly by some who were left in the field of Battle and Crawl'd
off afterwards, saw the french take possession of our Guns and over
sett some from the Carridges, likewise over turn some of the Waggons,
which they scarce would have done had they expected to keep the
field; another Circumstance to prove they were not strong of Indians
and that they doubted likewise of Success, is, that they never begin
scalping, if sure of victory 'till all is over; on the other hand, if the

affair is doubtful or if they're sure of being beat they begin scalping when ever opportunity offers, as soon as they've kill'd their Man—in this late affair, they scalp'd some very early. I dont apprehend they knew the General was there with the main body, at first—besides they knew very well Col. Dunbar with a strong body was behind him, but they never beleived so much as fifty miles—which even few or none of our own officers knew or imagin'd except the General himself and his people, as he had made several remonstrances to the former of his situation to no manner of purpose—the above reasons I give for the Enemys hurry and why they did not pursue, Cross the River, which only a few Indians attempted, but retired agen; it was very natural to imagine, there was a reserve there and that Regular Troops would rally again and return to the field and retake what they lost which I believe might eassily have been done; I dont pretend to be a Judge, but submit my Opinion, if it was not a great error in the General to march his whole body without a dispossition to support an advance Party and without leaveing himself a Reserve? whereas, when he found the Advance Guard attack'd had he *halted* and spoke to the Officers and Men—told them what they might expect and what they were to do, at the same time detach'd some men to support those attack'd but what was more matterial to [*sic*] made a dispossition and form'd his own *line* likewise detach'd 100 men on each flank where the attack was to have march'd round the Enemy, which he had time enough to have done, but none of these Steps nor any other but those before mention'd were taken, which occasion'd a Total defeat. The Gen[1] and the rest with him, retreated about 43 miles before ever they thought of sending any acco[t] to C. Dunbar at last they did from Guests Settlement within seven miles where Col. Dunbars Camp was at that time—for him to send up some fresh Troops, for a rear Guard, likewise some flower—Amunition &c. and some Empty Waggons for the Sick and Wounded which was accordingly done the 11th the same day all Join'd Col. Dunbar. The General in the Action received a Shot in the Arm which went through & penetrated his body and tho' I am, and every other person perswaided he was in no Condition to be spoke to or to give orders—notwithstanding, in the Generals name, was orders given to destroy every thing in Colonel Dunbar's Camp Provisions of all kinds—upwards of 150 Waggons all the Artillery Stores of every kind and even some officers Baggage &c. &c. &c. The Confusion, hurry and Conflagration attending all this, Cannot be describ'd, but I Can assure you it affected every body who had the least sense of the Honour of His Majesty or the Glory of England at heart, in the deepest manner.

Scandlous as the action was, more Scandlous was the base and hurried Retreat, with the immense destruction and expense to the Nation —what was lost in the Action with what was destroy'd afterwards by our selves, amounted upon a moderate Calculation to near Three hundred Thoussand pounds value besides the loss of Blood &c. We Carried with the sweat of our Brows, a pritty Train of Artillery up to the ffrench, which they never Could have obtain'd otherwise. The other part, and the *Greatest,* which we destroy'd our selves might have been saved perhaps, if things had been left to the management of Col. Dunbar, who for private animosity's &c. never was Consulted—but the most absurd orders given in his Camp under the Gen¹ˢ sanction tho' as I before said from good reasons was thought Could not be Consulted—how far the adviser's or dirrectors Can answer to God their Country or their own Conscience I shall not determine. I shall Conclude this Account by telling you the grossest mismanagement has been in this expedition from our landing to our Defeat as every officer except (perhaps) a few, must own on inquiry—happy for our Troops they were not pursued or not a single soul Could have been Saved.

In the time of the Action, The General behaved with a great deal of Personal Courage, which every body must allow—but thats all that Can be said—he was a Man of Sense and good natur'd too tho' Warm and a little uncooth in his manner—and Peevish—with all very indolent and seem'd glad for any body to take bussiness off his hands, which may be one reason why he was so grossly imposed upon, by his favourite —who realy Dirrected every thing and may Justly be said to've Commanded the Expedition and the Army.

On the 13th after the before mention'd destruction we all March'd —I mean Join'd the Gen¹ in his Retreat—before we had moved far (with Waggons only for the Sick and Wounded) it was discover'd The Train had reserved a Waggon with Powder and *Seven Cohorns* on which a halt was order'd and Cap: Dobson of Col. Dunbars Regt. who was an acting under aid du camp from the time C. Orme was Wounded—order'd the Pioneers to be got together—and a hole to be Dug—a little off the road—in sight of the Army—Waggoners—Indian Traders &c &c—where the Cohorns were burried— Who gave him such orders I Cant say but they were accordingly Comply'd with, without any order in Writeing, at this time the Genl was within a few hours of his Death. This Gentlemans activity in the intrest of C. Orme recommended him so strongley that he was to have been Lt. Colonel to a Regt. form'd from the Independent Companys of which its said Lt. Col. Burton was to be the Colonel—but since the Generals Death

Dobson ask'd leave of Col. Dunbar to sell his Commission for £1500 to a Lieut.—how far he'll succeed at home is another question. on Sunday the 13 we Came to an encampment within a few miles of the Great Crossing of the Yauchnaganey at which place Genl. Braddock still Continued to give orders 'till he expired at nine o Clock same night, and was burried next morning on the high road, that the Army might march over, to deface any marks of a Grave, after which Col. Dunbar took upon him the Command and try'd every method to stop a Licentious Spirit in the Troops—and nothing but the want of powers prevents him makeing examples of some—no person Could Come to a Command under more disadvantages—as he knows nothing of His Majestys intentions nor of Genl. Braddocks instructions—as every paper was lost at the Action, neither Can he obtain any particular information from C. Orme.

When Genl. Braddock landed in America, affairs were by no means in readiness for him, as he expected; Virginia was a bad place, to be supplied in—Pensilvania was infinitely better, but we never had recourse there, 'till repeated dissapointments obliged us—a vast deal of time, was spent to little purpose, waiting for Carridges, horses &c, & in laying up a Magazine at Wills's Creek of salt provisions flower &c. more than possibly we Could have occasion for—between 7 and Ten Thoussand bushells of Oats were laid in, tho' none Issued out, to Enable the horses to go on, in their march (which Oats since the Generals Death, C. Orme gave orders to Sell agen as they were the Generals property—but Col. Dunbar has interposed and will not permit it, as he says they are the Publicks). there were about 300 Waggons hyred at 13[sh][?] Currency or 10[sh] English money a day, with 4 horses to each Waggon with the value of horses and Waggons ascertain'd if not return'd to the owners—600 back load horses at two shillings a day each —Waggons and horses immensly loaded and little food on the Ground but leaves of Trees—more followers and attendants on this little Army than would have serv'd an Army of 20,000 Men in flanders; a Licentiousness which prevail'd among the Troops, in Consequence of being told, Genl. Braddock was sure of there good behaviour in the day of action, therefore would dispense with the Ceremonial part of Duty— it's impossible to express the bad effects of this hint—those who were inclin'd to be more exact were not more in favour on that acc[t] never one Deserter punish'd—The Army never seen by the Genl. but once Comeing along the line as Com[r] in Cheif; add to all this, The Pride, Insolence and overbearing Spirit of the first aid du camp C. Orme— despersing all former military orders ordinances and Customs of an

Army in flanders or any where else either in old, or latter times, Commanding and dictateing to every Branch from the lowest to the highest and no bounds of Resentment Again[st] those who would not *Bow to Dagon* and who had resolution enough to tell him the bad Consequences attending such measures which (to our misfortune) he had always influence enough, to obtain The Generals sanction to.

The heads of both military and Civil Branches with us were despised as ignorant &c and if ever their opinions were ask'd (which was rarely) after a Sneer at them—the Contrary was sure to be follow'd. Poor Sᵣ Peter Halket who behaved in the late action with the greatest bravery and Coolness—divided his men and fired some platoons by his own Dirrection, before he was kill'd; at the very time, he was approveing of the fire his Men had made before, and biding them do the same again—he was shot through the body. This Gentlemen who had before, given proofs of his abilitys as a Soldier and Confirm'd it by his Death, yet was publickly told—"he was a fool, he wanted leading strings" of which facts there are many Evidences—for some time before he died, he was in Disgrace—and the reasons he gave himself for it was, for his adviseing to train some people to the Great Guns as we had so few who understood that branch, likewise dissaproveing of the Line of March and proposeing to build block houses or stockades at proper passes for Magazines both for places of security as well as to encumber our March the less with Carridges—for giveing this advice he was told it was foolish and too much presumption—this fact I had from Sᵣ Peters own mouth—and the same he mention'd to several others—after which he neither was Consulted nor did he ever go near the Genl. but once when he was sent for about some storrie that had been Carried to the Genl. that he and some others were liveing well when their officers wanted, at which time Sᵣ Peter only had the King's salt provisions and Could get no other—notwithstanding he was threaten'd with his Regt. and advised to take Care of himself—to which he answer'd he did not depend on it for a livelyhood—and had not his honour been Concern'd he never would have Come on the Expedition.

Col. Dunbar one day, giveing his Opinion (when ask'd) with a good deal of reason and instanceing the practise of Great Genls. he had served under &c. was told in presence of Genl. Braddock, by Cap: Orme that it was *Stuff,* and that he might as well talk of his *Grand-Mother* to which C. Dunbar reply'd with some Warmth Sᵣ "if she was alive, she would have more sense, more good manners, and know as much of military matters as you do—on which the General interposed and said, Gentlemen you are both Warm—to which Dunbar answer'd—"General, you See the Provocation I got—so it ended then—but his opinion was never ask'd for the future. I forgot to mention, at Will's Creek, The Genl. desired Orme to be admited into the Council of War—which was accordingly done, but Sr Peter finding how every thing went, as he dir- rected he desired every body might afterwards sign their opinion—this gave great offence, so they had no more Councils—Sr Peter declared if ever he Came to ye Command he would dismiss C. Orme next day from the Army and regreted much that the General had such a man about him who's advice would both be the ruin of the General & the Expe- dition.

As to what is before mention'd about C. Dunbar he repeated it when it happen'd and has often mention'd it since. Soon after this the make- ing of the Detachment and devideing the Army was plan'd and beleived by everybody—it was done with a Design to vex C. Dunbar, who realy was very much embarrass'd with such a number of Carridges &c and many other Difficultys—but haveing no orders how to act he sent for instructions but Could obtain no other—but that he must do the best, and to be on his Guard, as he might expect to be made answerable for his Conduct &c. with several other threatning expressions and ordering him not to tease the General with Complaints which sometimes Came at unseasonable hours, dureing the Seperation, every method was taken to embarrass (to appearance) Col. Dunbar—by sending orders to for- ward to the Genl. every thing that Could be thought of. C. Dunbars Complaints at last became so well grounded that the General order'd 40 horses to be sent back to him but such methods were taken that only the useless and those near their end were sent—so that only 16, of the 40 was able to Join Dunbar. The General at parting told Col. Dunbar, he would always keep within three hours march of him—at last when he advanced a Considerable distance, he was heard to say he beleived he would be obliged to bring to—till C. Dunbar Join'd him—but that was opposed by C. Orme and orders were then sent to Col. Dunbar to Join the General, the best way he Could with the Convoy at Fort du Queesny (or Kane), which at the rate he was obliged to go on at Could not have been before Septem^r. They say the principle Councellor with *Orme* was Lt Col. Burton who was privy to every thing, but this, I Can't affirm, from authority sufficient for you to depend on. When the General sep- arated with his detachment both Reg^ts were pick'd and Cull'd without the knowledge either of Sr Peter Halket or Col. Dunbar and the officers names mention'd in publick orders without regard either to tour of Duty—health—fitness or anything else but Just as the projectors pleased (which C. Orme Call'd a new Scheme proper for the Army to follow)

after the separation, it then—I mean the part of Col. Dunbars Regt.—
lost its name, and was Call'd *Col. Burtons detachment*, which in short
began to do wonders, and all in a few days, which it seems was intirely
oweing to Col. Burton—but unluckily in praiseing one so much they
depress'd the other and took every opportunity to find fault with
Sr Peters detachment in order to sett off the other—matters run high,
from a dryness among the officers to an indifference and Jelous'y which
at last reach'd the men and where it would have ended, if it had more
time to Operate in, is hard to tell, but the general Calamity put an end
to that; and the remaining part of the Two Regiments heartily agree,
in the neglect of Duty, dissobedience of orders, mutinous dispossitions,
worse than any Militia I ever saw, Cowardly principles, frighten'd now
almost at their own shaddows, or the name of an Indian, partly perhaps
from the hurry we were in by a general destruction of every thing, as
well as from their own inclinations; Plunder was the word at the Battle,
as well as afterwards, but it was plundering ourselves—this is a bad picture of Soldiers and such I'm tyred of, which nothing but the stricktest
discipline and greatest severity Can possibly reclaim and I beleive
they're now in very good hands, I mean in Col. Dunbars if he knew
his power which Cap. Orme has taken Care to keep him in the Dark
about, and took every method from the beginning to ruin him and make
him uneassy, and even since the Generals Death seems equally determin'd to frustrate C. Dunbars designs at least as far as is in his power
to do.

In Nine days from the time we Retreated after the Junction of the
Genl. we arrived at Wills' Creek where we now are—but Col. Dunbar
soon proposes to move to Philidelphia with the Kings Troops 'till he
receives orders from England. Pity it was that the Genl. (even after
his Retreat) when he Join'd C. Dunbar—instead of destroying the value-
able stores & provisions & makeing a shameful flight—notwithstanding
their was not one Indian or french man in pursute—did not determine
on building a stockade at Guests or the Great Crossing where their was
fine Ground—in which Case it would have Secured the Fronteers—and
been a Cheque on the Enemy our being so far advanced in the Country;
we destroy'd provision enough, which, without any supply would have
lasted us all, these six months.

Which way all the Accots and Contracts will be settled here is hard
to tell but their is an immense sum due for Contracts of one kind and
other. I dare say not far short of £100000. The General in some of his
Trunks the day of action had Two thousand five hundred pounds all
which, with much more money and private effects fell into the Enemys

hands—a supply they much Wanted and an ample one it was—from *Guests* their was a bag of flower left here and thereon the road, least any Soldiers should have been in need of it. Several stragglers have Join'd us since who says they should have starv'd but for Provisions they found on the road—but report, the road was full of Dead and people dieing who with fatigue or Wounds Could move on no further; but lay down to die—this melancholy Acco^t Convinces, what use our Staying, would been of, to save the life of many a poor fellow.

What we have seen, Convinces us that such an immense number of Waggons and horses will never do to be under the Care of so small a body of Troops. Col. Dunbar affirms that to avoid the Carridges he Could have had live Cattle drove—and flow'r Carried on their backs with out the least trouble to the Army, except to give a Guard to the Conductors—in which Case they would have found one pound of fflower and one pound of fresh meat to each man; for within Eight pence Currency a day, where, as the Case stood, each Soldier stands for his Salt provisions and flow'r Three shillings a day & upwards upon the nearest Calculation—this is oweing to the expence of Carridge &c. The Ground was so mountainous from Wills's Creek upwards, that we were all Work'd and sweated both man and beast to get the Waggons up the hills which the horses never Could have done without the men, and be assured notwithstanding it has turn'd out to so little purpose, yet it has been a most fatigueing Campaign, in a Wilderness where nothing is to be seen but wood. We have yet a pretty little march to take to Philidelphia of about 250 miles—we have brought few horses of all we had, here, with us, they being either kill'd or Dead—and vast numbers stole off by the Waggoners and Drivers. This is the Conclusion of the American expedition under General Braddock which was more amply provided for by the Government than any expedition of so small a number ever had been before. The truth of this is very well known to you. I'm heartily sorry I have it not in my power to give a more favourable account which might have been shorten'd if I had avoided some Circumstances—but I thought it best to be particular as they might not Come to your hand so soon—but I'm sure you'll hear all I have advanced and much more—as soon as you have opportunity of seeing any impartial person on this expedition, which will be Ninety-nine out of a hundred.

A Return of the Troops Encamp'd at Wills's Creek, distingushing the Fit for Duty, Sick and Wounded, July 25th 1755

Corps	Fit for duty																
							Staff										
	Colonel	Lieut. Cols	Majors	Captains	Lieutenants	Enss	Chaplain	Adjutant	Quar Masr	Surgeons	Mates	Midshipmen	Serjeants	Corpls or Bombrs	Gunners	Boatswains Mates	Drummers	Private
44th Regiment of Foot		1	1	4	7	9	1		1	1	1		14	14			15	345
48th Do	1		1	4	7	5	1	1	1	1	1		20	20			17	360
Artillery				2	1					1				4	7		1	20
Detachmt of Seamen												1				1		14
Light Horse				1	1					1			2					22
Ammerican Foot				5	15	3		1	1	3	1		21	20			10	342
Total	1	1	2	16	31	17	2	2	3	7	3	1	57	58	7	1	43	1103

[see next page]

A Return of the Troops Encamp'd at Wills's Creek, distingushing

Sick							Wounded								
Captains	Lieutenants	Midshipmen	Serjeants	Corpls or Bombrs	Drummers	Private	Lieut Cols	Captains	Lieuts	Ensigns	Serjeants	Corpls or Bombrs	Gunners	Drummers	Private
1	1		4	6	2	84		3	6		3	6		1	138
	1			1		43	1		3	4	7	8	8	3	112
		1				4			2			3			7
															7
						2									2
2			3			66		2			7	7			45
3	2	1	7	7	2	199	1	5	13	4	17	24	8	4	311

THE FIT FOR DUTY, SICK AND WOUNDED, JULY 25th 1755 [*Continued*]

Corps	Cols	Lt Cols	Majors	Captains	Lieutenants	Ensigns	Staff					Midshipmen	Serjeants	Corpls or Bombrs	Gunners	Boatsws Mates	Drummers	Private
							Chaplain	Adjutants	Quar Masrs	Surgeons	Mates							
44th Regiment of Foot		1	1	5	15	9	1	1	1	1	1		21	26			18	567
48th Do	1	1	1	7	11	9	1	1	1	1	1		27	29			20	515
Artillery				2	3					1				7	15		1	31
Detachmt of Seamen												2				1		21
Light Horse				1	1					1			2					26
Ammerican Foot				7	17	3		1	1	3	1		21	20			10	453
Total	1	2	2	22	47	21	2	3	3	7	3	2	71	82	15	1	49	1613

THO DUNBAR

CAPTAIN WILLIAM EYRE [1] TO ROBERT NAPIER

(A.L.S.)

Camp near Albany
27th July 1755.

Dr Sir,

Since I did my self the pleasure to inform you that Genl. Bradock order'd me upon this Service from Fort Cumberland I have been here helping to make all the Necessary Preparations for our expedition against Crown Point, and this Morning were all Alarmed with the News of Genl Bradock's being defeated within Nine Miles of Fort duquesne. the Particulars we have not yet learned, but make no doubt but you Will know them before this reaches you: its further said he has lost most Part of the Artillery. if this fatal News prove true, I am afraid it will throw a Damp on the Minds of those raw and undiciplined Troops with us, and what is, as bad, the Indians who now seem very hearty in Our Interest. however be it as it will, we hope soon to make the tryal, and endeavour to get revenge: the first Division march'd a few Days ago, Under Major Genl. Lymon,[2] wch was about 1000 Men with two field Pieces, to make Roads Bridges, &c, between this and a Place Called the carrying Place, about 50 Miles up this River; the Battering Train moves in three or four Days with 1200 Men & the field Pieces with the rest of the Army immediately After. Our Army Will amount to three thousand five hundred, & the Number of Cannon are 6 18 p^{drs}, 2 32 p^{drs}, 8 6 p^{drs}, one 13, & two 8 Inch Mortars, but as all our Artillery are Iron I am afraid we shall not be able to get them along, if the Roads prove bad, particularly the 18 p^{drs}, they weighing from fifty two to fifty three hundred weight, and the 32 pd^{rs} only between 41 & 44 hundred. I have very little help to assist me in the management of the Artillery, no Engineer but my self, and was Obliged to Act as Q^r Master Genl. Since my Arrival, as there was no such Officer Appointed by the Provinces, nor any Body here who was acquainted with that Service, so Major Genl. Shirley has lately Given me A Commission for that Purpose. I make no Doubt but we shall be able to reduce the Fort in a short time if we can get up our Artillery, but they are so extremely heavy, and so

---

[1] William Eyre, ranked as a practitioner engineer in 1744, was with Cumberland at Culloden in 1746, and served as engineer in ordinary in Flanders in 1747. He became a sub-engineer in 1748. For his services with Johnson, Eyre, already a captain in the 44th regiment, was rewarded by being promoted, from England, to the rank of major. He became lieutenant colonel of the 44th regiment in July, 1758. After the war he was made chief engineer in America, and in 1765, as he was returning to England for his long-delayed leave of absence, was drowned off the English coast.
[2] Phineas Lyman of Connecticut.

many other difficulties in our way, as I fear, will make it not easy to surmount, however, I long to make the experiment, and be persuaded there is no thing shall be wanting on My Side to bring things to a happy Issue,

Major Genl. Shirley is lately pass'd here in his Way to Niagara. I wish he could make a little more haste, or I fear he will Miss the opportunity to lay hold of it. His Army is about 2000 & upwards. The Sloop that takes this Letter to New York is just going, so beg you will excuse hurry. My best respects to Mrs. Napier. And Am Dr Sir, Yr Most Obliged, & most Obt Servt

WILL EYRE.

Since I finish'd the Other Side, we have a List Sent up by Capt. Orme of the Unhappy & most Shocking fate of Our Troops, with the loss of the General & Our Artillery. Oh! how I wish for revenge: If the Troops stands firm, and the Indians do not quit us, I make no doubt but we shall be able to return the Compliment. What shall I say? we must return the Blow. I must conclude, adieu once more dear Sir—

[*Endorsed*] 1755 Capn Eyre July 27 Recd Oct 2d.

FRENCH ACCOUNT OF THE ACTION NEAR THE RIVER OHIO ON THE 9TH JULY 1755
(COPY)

RELATION de Laction qui Sest passé Sur La Rre oyo, a 3 Lieues du fort Duquesne le 9e Juillet 1755 entre un Detachement de 250 Canadien et 650 Sauvages, commandé par Mr De Beaujeu, Capitaine, et un corps de 2000 hommes anglais commandé par Le General Braddork

Extrait de La Lettre écrite par Mr De Contrecoeur Commandan au fort Duquesne a Monsieur Le marquis De Vaudreuil Gouverneur Général, daté du dit fort le 14e Juillet 1755 [1]

Je n'ai cessé depuis le commancement de ce mois denvoyer des Detachement de français et Sauvages pour harceler les anglais que Je Savois être au nombre de 3000. a 30: ou 40: Lieues du fort Sepreparent avenir Lassieger, ces Troupes Se Tenoient Si bien Sur Leur gardes, marchant Toujours en bataille que Tous les Efforts que faisoient les Détachement contre elles devenoient inutiles,

Enfin apprenant Tous Jours que ces Troupes approchoient; Jenvoyai Le Sr La Peyrade, officier, avec quelque francais et Sauvages, pour

---

[1] A part of the extract from Contrecœur's letter is printed in Parkman's *Montcalm and Wolfe*, Appendix.

Savoir précisement ou elle etoient, il ma'pprit le Lendemain 8ᵉ que Les anglais etoient a énviront 8 Lieues de ce forts,

Je fis Sur Le champ un autre détachement quy mappris Le même Jours qu'ils netoient plus qu'a 6 Lieues et qu'ils marchoient Sur Trois Colonne,

Le même Jour Je formais un parti de Tous ceque Je pouvois mettre horts du forts pour aller a Leur Rencontres il etoits composé de 250 . . . francais et de 650 Sauvages, cequi faisoit 900 hommes Mʳ De Beaujeu, Capitaine; le Commandoits. Il y avoit deux Capitaine qui etoient Mʳˢ Dumas et Lignerie et plusieurs autre officiers Subaltarnes

Ceparti se mit en marche Le 9 a 8 heurs du matin, et Se Trouva a midi et demy en presence des anglais a environ 3 Lieues du fort, on commancas a faire feu de part et d'autre le feu de L'artillerie ennemie fit Reculer un peu par deux fois notre partie, Mʳ De Beaujeu fut Tué a La Troisieme de charge, Mʳ Dumas prit Le commandement il Sen acquita au mieux nos français plains de courage Soutenu par Les Sauvages, quoiquil n'eussent pas d'artillerie firent a Leur Tour plier les anglais qui Se batoient en ordre de bataille en bonne contenance et ces derniers voyant lardeur des nos gens quy foncoient avec une vigueur infinie, furent en fin obligé de plier Tout a fait après 4 heurs d'un grand feu Mʳˢ Dumas et Lignerie qui navoient plus avec eux qu'une vingtaine de francais, ne Sengagerent Point dans La poursuit; ils Rentrerent dans le fort, parcequ'une grande partie des Canadiens, qui n'etoient malheuresement que des Enfant, Setoient Retiré a La premiere décharge, les meilleurs avoient Resté a LaRʳᵉ aux Boeuf a faire les portage des vivres; d'aillieurs un partie des Sauvages netoient occupés qu'a Lever des chevelures et a piller. Si les ennemis fussent Revenus avec Les 1000 hommes de troupes fraîches qu'ils y avoient en Reserve a quelque distance d'eux, et dont nous ne Savions pas L'eloignement, nous nous serions peut-être Trouver fort embarassé

Mʳ De Courtemanche, Lieutenant, coucha Sur Le Champ de Bataille, ainsi que les officiers qui etoient de Retour dela poursuitte des fuyards, sur les quels il avoient Tiré Jusqu'a La nuit, avec les sauvages qui les avoient Suivis.

Mʳˢ Dumas et Lignerie ont bien Remplacé Monsieur De Beaujeu dans l'actions, Tous les officiers en général Sy Sont distingues, Les Cadets ont fait des merveilles ainsi que nos Soldats,

Tous les Sauvages du Détroit et de michilimakinak Sont partis des le Lendemain de Laction, Sans que J'aye pu les arrêter, ces Sauvages comme les domiciliés et ceux de la Belle Riviere ont Tres bien fait, il est necessaire de les Recompenser

J'envoie aujourd'hui un petit Détachement pour decouvrir ceque sont devenus les anglais; et Savoir S'il ont dessein de Revenir nous attaquer ou de Sen Retourner

Si ont veut conserver cette Riviere, il faut y faire des Etablicement plus considerables

Cy-Joint &c.

ETAT de Lartillerie, munitions de guerre, et autres Effets appartenant aux anglais, qui SeSont Trouvé Sur le Champ de Bataille aprés Laction

SÇAVOIR

4 Canon de fonte aux armes d'angleterre du calibre de 11^{lb}

4 idem de $5^{lb}\frac{1}{2}$

4 Mortiers ou aubussiers de fonte de 7 pouce $\frac{1}{2}$ de diamêtre

3 autres mortiers de grenade . . . de 4 pouce $\frac{1}{4}$ idem

175 Boulet de 11^{lb}

57 aubus de 6.$\frac{3}{4}$

17 Baril de poudre de 100 Chaque

19740 Cartouche Chargé pour mousquets

Les artifices pour Lartillerie

Les autres outils necessaires pour un Siége

grandes Quantité de fusils, de Service et hors de Service

Quantité de Chariots brisées

4 a 500 Cheveaux, dont partie Tué

Environ 100 betes a Cornes

un grand nombre de baril de poudre et de farine enfonces

Environ 600 hommes morts, dont grand nombre d'officiers,
    et des blessé a proportion

20 hommes ou femme fait Prisonnier par les Sauvages

un butin Tres considerable, en meubles, hardes et ustenciles

Quantité de papier qu'on a pas eû le Temps [?] de faire Traduire

on y a Reconnu entrautre le plan du fort Duquesne avec Ses Exates proportion

N^{ta} Les Sauvages ont Pillé beaucoup dor et dargent monnoyé—

LISTE des officiers, Soldats, Miliciens et Sauvages de Canada qui ont été Tués dans Laction sçavoir

Morts

M^{rs}

De Beaujeu, Commandant

De Carqueville, Lieutenant

De La Peyrade, Enseigne

3 officiers . . . . ⎤
3 Canadiens . . . . ⎬ 23 hommes Morts
2 Soldats . . . . ⎪
15 Sauvages de differentes nations ⎦

Blessés

M^{rs}

Le Borgues Lieutenant, un bras Cassé ⎤
Bailleul Enseigne . . . Legerement   ⎪
hertel Ste Thereze ⎱   ⎬ 16 hommes Blessé
Montmidy . . . . . . ⎰ Cadet idem   ⎪
12 Sauvages . . . . idem ⎦
Pour Extrait a Quebec Le 8e aoust 1755

[*Endorsed*] Relation Française de l'action du *9:* juillet à *Monongahela*, près de la Riviere *Ohio. 1755*

SUMMARY OF LETTERS FROM SPENCER PHIPS, THOMAS FITCH, ARTHUR DOBBS, AND RHODE ISLAND [1]

(COPY)

Massachusets Bay Presid^t *Phips*   Is raising *800:* Additional Men. for
Augt 30th *1755.*   Gen¹ *Johnson*

None of President *Phips's* Letters apply for Assistance from England;—But a long Memorial from the Province has been delivered by their Agent Mr *Bollan,* supported by a long Letter, setting forth the great Number of Men they have raised, & their Large Expences, & desiring Assistance in general—They also represent, that many Inconveniences, may arise from recruiting the regular Troops in *America;* as it may lessen the Number of Inhabitants, & discourage the Eagerness of the People, to inlist for particular Services—

Connecticut. Letter from Mr *Fitch.*   Have raised & Maintained *1000:*
& Address Augt 1^t *1755.*[2]   Men for the Expedition to *Crown
                                           Point;* are going to add *500:* more.
—have permitted New York to raise *300:* Men in their Country—represent the want of Arms, & desire such Supply as the King shall judge

---

[1] This document is in memorandum form.
[2] Printed in Conn. Hist. Soc. *Coll.,* I, 265–269.

proper—they have contracted large Debts for this & other publick Services, & desire Relief therein

N° Carolina Govr *Dobbs* Augt 25: *1755*.[3]

12. 12 Pound^rs
8. 18 Pound^rs
14. 18 Pound^rs
16. 9 Pound^rs
30. Suivels
30. Musquetoons
20. Barrels powder.

To fortify Cape Look-out

Has given Directions for a Battery & Barracks at Ocacock Harbour, for which there is wanting. *12. 12* Pound^rs & *8: 18* Pound^rs— And for *Johnston* Fort at Cape *Fear* River. *14: 18* Pound^rs *16. 9* Pound^rs *30* Suivels, & as many Musquetoons, with Bullets, & Stores for all the Guns.—Mr Dobb also desires *20:* Barrels of Powder— He likewise represents It will be necessary to fortify Cape Look out **Harbour.**

Rhode Island—*April 17—1755:* & Agents—Petition in *July 1755* [4]:—

20: Cannon, with Stores—

Have raised *400:* Men, Given *10,000£,* & the Town of *Newport 5,000£* for repairing, and enlarging the Fort at *Newport,* in which there are *24:* Cannon purchas'd by themselves—*20:* more from *18: to 24:* Pounders are wanted, which they desire to be sent, with *50:* Shott for each Gun, & other proper Stores.

These Cannon were applied for, several Years ago; in *1735,* the Board of Trade reported for sending them: In *1744,* the Report was referr'd to the Master of the Ordnance, to make an Estimate, which came to £*1812:14*^s—

SKETCH FOR NEXT YEAR'S CAMPAIGN IN NORTH AMERICA.[1] SEPT^R 6: 1755

(COPY)

1°.

The unfortunate Miscarriage of His Majesty's Forces in the designed Attack upon Fort du *Quesne,* in *North America,* & the Death of Major

[3] Printed in *North Carolina Col. Recs.,* V, 419.
[4] References in *Rhode Island Col. Recs.,* V, 411, and Kimball, *Correspondence of the Col. Governors of R. I.,* II, 156.
[1] In the handwriting of Robert Napier, this document is in memorandum form.

Gen¹ *Braddock*, make it necessary to alter the *Scheme* proposed for the next year's Campaign in that Country; ² which, if the attempts upon *Niagara* and *Crown-Point* Succeed, as those have already done upon Fort *Beau Sejour* & *Sᵗ John's*, will still put us in a condition to attack *Montreal* and *Quebec*, & afterwards to go up the River, & attack Fort du *Quesne*.

2.

In order to which, an additional Force of (at least) *1000:* Regular Troops should be sent from Britain, as soon as conveniently can be, together with an *experienced* & *active* General Officer to command in chief, who should repair imediately to *Albany*, as the most centrical & convenient Place for getting Information, and also the most proper for making his chief Magazines.

3.

The Troops to be sent over, should, likewise be stationed at *New-York* and *Albany*, in which Neighbourhood the rest of those Forces should also have their Winter-Quarters, in order to begin the operations next year, as early as possible, which the advantages of the Rivers in those Parts, will greatly contribute to.

4.

To the *1000:* Men to be sent from *Britain*, (as above mentioned) a *1000:* may be added from the two Regiments of *Halket* & *Dunbar*, leaving the Remainder of those Corps, & Part of the *seven* independant Companies to recruit in *Virginia*, & cover the back settlements there: the General will also be able to draw a considerable number from the *three* Regiments in *Nova Scotia* after leaving about *1500:* for the necessary Garrisons in those Parts. These Forces, with the Regiments of *Shirley* & *Pepperell*, & such additional Provincial Troops and Irregulars as he may find necessary to be granted by the different Provinces, will make up such a Corps as, 'tis to be presumed, will put him in thorough Condition to do his Business effectualy in those Parts, notwithstanding the Reinforcement sent lately to *Canada* from *France*.

5.

If the Attacks upon *Niagara* and *Crown-Point* have met with the Success which 'tis hoped they will, the obvious Business of next Cam-

---

² Probably the plan of August 11, 1755, Add. MSS. 35,909, f. 208.

paign is the Reduction of *Montreal* and *Quebec* with the Forts which lie between those Places: in order to which we must be masters of Lake *Champlain* by having a proper Number of armed Vessels upon it: and, as this Lake empties itself into the River *St Lawrence*, by the River *Sorrell*, between *Quebec* & *Montreal*, it will naturaly occur to the General that he must make himself Master of the last mentioned River; by which Means he will have the Advantage of Water Carriage from *Crown Point* to the *St Lawrence*, & have it in his Power to keep either *Quebec* or *Montreal* in check, whilst he carries on his attack upon either of those Places. And it is not to be doubted with the Force he will have, he will have, the Benefit before mentioned of water Carriage behind him, & the assistance of such a Number of His Majesty's ships of war, as shall be thought sufficient to block up the mouth of the River *St Lawrence* he will soon be able to reduce those Places, & by that means, make himself master of all *Canada*.

6.

The Providing in time (so that the operations may begin as early as possible in the Spring) the necessary stores, ammunition & Provisions, as also Vessels, *Batteaux* & Floats for transporting them, must be diligently attended to; together with a good & sufficient Train of Artillery; and 'tis presumed, that this may be done from what is in *Nova Scotia* & the Provinces. But, 'till such time as a particular account can be got of the Numbers, Natures & Condition of the Artillery *there*, nothing can be said more on that head: nor can it be said what number of small arms will be necessary 'till a like account can be had of those that are already there. It is, however, proper to mention in this place, that 'till such time as the Governm^t gives some orders to the Governours of the Provinces to take care of, & keep up the Arms that are from time to time sent over there, in proper condition & Repair; the sending over such large Numbers as they demand, is putting the Governm^t *here* to very great Expences, to little Purpose.

7.

On the Supposition that we have already succeeded in the Attack on *Niagara*, that we have established ourselves strongly there, & that our naval Force on Lake *Ontario* is sufficient (which will fix & confirm the *six* Indian Nations in that Friendship & Alliance they have so lately promised) it will be equaly necessary & very possible to establish a like naval Force upon Lake *Erie* also.

8.

The making ourselves masters of Fort du *Quesne* has not been mentioned 'till now; as the great Tediousness, Expence and Difficulties which were most unexpectedly found in our attempt, by the way of *Virginia,* makes it seem necessary to alter the manner of proceeding to that Place. To avoid, therefore, the former inconveniencies *it is proposed,* That the Expedition to that Fort should go from the sources, down the River *Ohïo,* rather than the former way: on that supposition, the being previously Masters of *Niagara* is necessary; upon which it is reasonable to imagine that the French will abandon the Ohïo, as they will be cut off from all Comunication with *Canada:* but, should they not; by means of *Niagara,* there will be a short & easy access to the Ohïo, & the Advantage gained of conveying the Troops & Stores down that River, in order to attack the Fort, 'tis to be hoped, more successfully.

9.

But, whether the next Campaign is to begin by reducing Fort du *Quesne Niagara Crown Point* or *Quebec,* the General will find *Albany* the proper Center to collect his Troops, & to make the necessary Dispositions for taking the Field; he should therefore be sent over as soon as can be, to consult with the several Governors & jointly to concert measures with them, that he may not meet with those unforseen & unexpected Retardments, which delayed our Troops so long this last Spring.

10.

The French will probably endeavour to make a Diversion from the *Missisipi* upon our Southern Provinces: but, with the independant Companies, & Part of the two Regiments left there, together with the Provincial Forces of those Parts, & the Assistance of our most Southern Indians (who have hitherto been, in general, steady) it is to be presumed that any Attempts the French may make *that way,* will be of little consequence, considering also the Difficulties They will meet in coming up the *Missisipi* River. The General, however, by being upon the Spot, will be a better judge; &, by consulting with the Governors of the Southern Provinces, be better able to take the most necessary & prudent Measures for preventing any great Danger in those Parts.

PETER WRAXALL [1] TO HENRY FOX

(COPY)

Camp at Lake George,
September 27th 1755.

Honoured Sir,

The Title I take the Liberty to give you, I have before made use of, explained my Motives for it, and, I hope, they appeared to you, as they did to me, a Justification.

The subsequent Matter of this Letter will, I flatter myself, atone for the Interruption it may give you, if I am mistaken, I am certain my Intentions are full of respect and gratitude.

The Troops which compose this Camp, are those Provincial Levies which were agreed to be raised at the Council at Alexandria, in order to form an Expedition against Crown Point, and to be put under the Command of Col: Wm. Johnson, who had, in Consequence thereof, Commissions given him, by sundry of the Governm[ts] concerned, of Major General, and Commander in Chief.

The Numbers agreed upon at Alexandria, were between 4 and 5000, but the 500 raised by New Jersey were drawn off by General Shirley, to aid his Operations from Oswego. The other Governm[ts] did not come up to their Quotas. The New Hampshire Troops, about 450 did not join us, till about 3 Weeks ago, so that, when General Johnson left Albany, the amount of the Troops, fit for Duty, were about 3000.

I was sent, by General Braddock's Orders, from Fort Cumberland, to assist General Johnson, in his Indian Transactions; he wrote, afterwards, to General Braddock, that I might have leave to continue with, and act under him, in his Military Department. This was consented to. I received, from General Johnson, three Commissions: One, as his Aid de Camp; One, as his Military Secretary; the Other to be Judge Advocate, to the Troops under his Command. These Offices I have acted in. The Colonies made no Nomination, or appointed any Pay, for either of Them, and, I believe, never will do it. I neither have taken, or shall take, any Fees or Perquisites. My Emulation to serve the Publick, and my private Friendship for General John-

---

[1] For Peter Wraxall (d. 1759), who was Town Clerk of Albany, secretary for Indian affairs in New York, Johnson's secretary, and captain of a New York independent company, see C. H. McIlwain, ed., *An Abridgment of the Indian Affairs . . . by Peter Wraxall* (1915), pp. c–cxviii.

son, were, and are, my prevailing Motives, for sustaining Employments, which have given me unremitted Fatigue, for upwards of 3
Months.

The first Post we took Possession of, after we left Albany, was, at
the Great Carrying Place, about 50 Miles from Albany. This is a
Pass of great Importance, as all the frequented Roads, from Canada
fall in there. Here the General ordered a Work to be thrown up,
which was done, after a Plan, and under the Direction of Captain
Eyre, whom Gen¹ Braddock sent as an Engineer, tho' not quite compleated, Troops are in Garrison there, & our General has given it
the Name of Fort Edward, in Honour to Our Young Prince.

From Fort Edward We marched, with 1500 Men, to this Lake,
which is about 15 Miles distance. The French call it Lake St. Sacra-
ment, but the General gave it the Name of Lake *George,* thereby further to ascertain His Majesty's undoubted Right to it. We arrived
here the 28th of August, found all the Land about it a thick Wood,
where never the least Settlement had been made; Not a Foot cleared;
Some Days were spent in cutting down the Trees, & clearing Ground
for a regular Engagement. This Lake runs pretty nearly N. & S., in
the broadest Part about 1½ Mile. It abounds with small Islands, the
Water wholesome & pleasant, & very full of Fish, particularly fine
large Trout. It is navigable for Boats for about 36 Miles, when It
grows very Narrow, and has a perpendicular Fall, which stops all
Navigation; there the small Boats & Canoes in use here are carried
over the Land for about a Mile, and launched into the Lake again;
It soon empties Itself in the River, which leads to Crown Point; This
Fall is about 18 Miles from Crown Point. This Fall, & a little beyond
it, is another grand Pass called Tionderogo, which commands all
the Water Passage between Crown Point, and these Parts. This important Pass our General proposed to take Possession of, & fortify,
and before We received the late Visit from the Enemy, intended to
have embarked with about 1000 Men &c. & taken Post there; It is
about 15 or 16 Miles from Crown Point. From all that I can observe
from Maps, or learn from Information, it would be a better Situation,
and a greater Security for this Country to have a good Fort there,
than where Crown Point stands; but as the River, which leads from
thence to Crown Point, is broad & deep, either that must be de-
molished, and the Enemy prevented from Rebuilding, or Tionderogo
be made very strong & well Garrisoned.

The particular Account of the Actions of the 8th Instant, I drew
up, and was transmitted by the General to the Lieutenant Governor

of Boston, in a general Letter to all the Governments concerned.[2] As I make no doubt that Relation has been transmitted by Governor Phipps, & others to the Administration, & will have reached you before This has the honor to be in your Hands, I shall not repeat it; But make some Observations on the Three Actions of the Day, in order to let you into the Character of Our Troops, and their Merit.

The Party in the Morning, with the Indians, & the sustaining Party sent out upon Our hearing the first Fire, were equal, if not superior in Number to the Enemy. Our People were surprised, by neglecting to have advanced, & flank, Guards. Only the Indians, & some of the foremost of Our Men stood the Attack; among both those there was a great slaughter: The rest did not advance, or make any Motions to sustain the Front, upon which They were beat back, a Panick took Place, & the whole fled in a disorderly Manner towards the Camp, The Enemy pursued, and kept firing upon the nearest Fugitives. Our People run into Camp with all the Marks of Horror & Fear in their Countenances, exagerating the Number of the Enemy, this infected the Troops in Camp, The Enemy were advancing, Our General harangued & did all in his Power to animate our People, I rode along the Line from Regiment to Regiment, decreased the Enemy's Numbers, promised them a cheap Victory if they behaved with Spirit, begun a Huzza which took, & they planted themselves at the Breast-Work just as the Enemy appeared in Sight; some of the Officers, but not many, seconded my Endeavours. The Enemy had been obliged to halt upon some Disputes among their Indians, this happy Halt, in all Probability saved Us, or the French General would have continued his Pursuit, & I am afraid entered with the last of our flying Men, before our Troops recovered from their Consternation. Great Numbers of our Men hid themselves during the Engagement, and many pretended Sickness. I did all in my Power to drive several out to the Breast Work, but for the most Part in vain. I beleive about 1700 Men stood to their Duty, We might be in the whole about 1900.

When the Enemy was beat off and flying, a Trial was made to pursue, but Men & several Officers were backward. However I don't know but a Pursuit might have been dangerous to Us. The Day was declining—The Rout of the Enemy not certain,—The Country all a Wood,—our Men greatly fatigued, provided neither with Bayonets or Swords, undisciplined, & not very high spirited. These Reasons (for my Opinion was asked) induced me to think we had better be content with the fortunate Repulse we had given the Enemy, and

[2] *Documentary History of New York*, II, 691–695.

before Night put every Thing in Order and Security, for the Prisoners said they had 1000 Men more who were expected to be on their March to reinforce them.

The Third Engagement of the Evening seems to be the only considerable Honor on our Side.

The Enemy were double our Number, our brave Party drove them from their Ground, took Possession of their Baggage, & made a great Slaughter amongst them. It must be owned the Enemy were vanquished Troops and had fled from the Attack at the Camp.

I believe on the whole of the Day's Actions the Number of our slain and wounded were not greatly inferior to the Enemy's. Their greatest Loss was among their regular Troops, who made and supported the grand Attack on our Center, and behaved with the utmost Bravery.

We had the Honor to take their General Prisoner; His Aid de Camp surrendered himself, & we killed and wounded most of their principal Officers.

Our General treated the French General with the utmost Humanity & generous Delicacy, had him laid on his own Bed, and tho' the Doctor attended to dress his wound, had all the French General's first looked at & dressed. The Baron de Dieskau from first to last behaved with Magnanimity, with the most decent Composure, & with a frank Politeness, in short, the Philosopher, the Soldier, and the Gentleman shone conspicuous through his whole Behaviour. He is wounded in his Bladder and I fear will not recover. General Johnson at his own Request sent him down to Albany in a horse Litter where most of the other Prisoners are also sent. The Intelligence derived from the Papers (which were very few) and Prisoners taken, amounts to this.

That with the Baron Dieskau and under his Command arrived from Europe to Canada about 2000 Regular Troops part of which were detached to Cadaraqui and Niagara and the remainder (about half) kept to act against Our Designs.

That a chosen Body had been picked out of all the Regular Troops in Canada to support the Baron's Opperations. That there assembled at Crown Point Regular and Irregular Troops about 6000 and upwards of 700 Indians. That they were throwing up new Works and strengthening Crown Point—taken Possession of all the important Passes in Our Way, had a strong Encampment at Tionderogo, secured by Cañon & Works, and by late Intelligence We have reason to beleive they have an Encampment of Observation between this and Tionderogo.

Two Days after Our Engagements of the 8th all Our Indians left Us & went home.

In their public Speech they pleaded as their Reason, the constant Custom of their People after a Battle in which they had sustained any considerable Loss, as they had by the Engagement of the Morning. They disavowed any fear of the Enemy or Treachery towards Us, and declared they were now more than ever enraged against the French and their Indians and were determined upon Revenge— hoped We should not sheath the Sword for they would not, but return when the General sent for them and was ready to proceed. They desired most earnestly that the Cagnawaga Indians, who had broke their Faith with them might never again be permitted to trade either at Albany or Oswego.

The Cagnawaga Indians live in Canada and are the bravest of the French Indians. They are Fugitives from the 6 Nations whom the French Policy and Priesthood have debauched from Us, aided by Our former Negligence and ill management in Indian Affairs. They are freely admitted to trade at Oswego and Albany in behalf of the French, who by their means supply themselves with Indian Goods from Us and so fight Us with Our own Weapons. It is a profitable Trade to the People of Albany & though very prejudicial to the general Interest, yet those People have but one Maxim of Conduct— that private Profit is the highest and only Motive of Action.

The Officers of this Army with very few Exceptions are utter Strangers to Military Life and most of them in no Respect superior to the Men they are put over, They are like the heads and indeed are the heads of a Mob. The Men are raw Country Men. They were flattered with an easy & a speedy Conquest; All Arts were used to hide future Difficulties and Dangers from them, and the whole Undertaking in all it's Circumstances smoothed over to their Imaginations, most of them came with nothing more than a Wastecoat, 2 Shirts and one Blanket, Their Tents ill made, not Weather Proof and some none at all. during the warm Weather and Our first Operations, Things in main went on tollerably; but late Fatigues, some rainy & cool Days the length of time, the brave Behaviour of the Enemy, the killed & wounded among Us, the Approach of Winter Weather—all these matters have broke Our Mens Spirits, injured Their Healths and produced a general and visible Dejection amongst them, a fondness (incurable I beleive at present) to return home for this Winter and an avowed Dislike to proceed any farther till next Spring. Large Reinforcements are said to be on the Way from Boston and Connecticut Governments thro' the Country by way of Albany, but as the Provisions and Ammunition for them is to come a long way round by Water, it will probably be the beginning of Winter before they can be brought from Albany hither. These Reinforcements live and are to live till the Arrival of their Own, on the Provision belonging to the old Troops; so that tho' they add to Our Numbers they diminish Our Provisions & Ammunition, of both which We had no superfluity.

Provided the number of Waggons to transport Our Provisions, Stores & Battoes from Albany & Fort Edward hither, should greatly exceed Our Expectations—should the necessary Reinforcements not arrive here—should the warm Cloathing said to be preparing also arrive—should the flat bottomed Boats for Our Artillery be finished—I say should all these matters take place and be compleated within these three Weeks, and sooner there is no probability they will, and provided the Officers and Men were all disposed to go forward on the Expedition.

Were every thing thus far compassed give me leave to observe
1. By the best Intelligence We can obtain and which may in great measure be depended on, the Enemy's Forces ready to oppose Us are more than We should with the expected Reinforcements be able to march against them. A great part of theirs are regular Troops (We none) over and above these the Enemy have 3 Indians to one against Us should Ours return.
2. We have Intelligence that the Enemy have taken possession of Tionderogo, have Artillery & thrown up works there.
3. We have not any practicable Method of bringing Cannon to attack the Enemy and endeavour to dislodge them from Tionderogo in order to open Our Way, but by Water; all Our Battoes will scarcely transport with 15 Days Provisions and requisite Stores 2500 Men, a Number by the best Accounts not equal to the Enemys.
4. Our Battoes are small kind of Wherrys incapable of sustaining much Wind or rough Water. This Lake when the Wind at North or South blows any thing hard is exceeding rough & very dangerous to a loaded Battoe. At the time of Our supposed Embarkation, there is great probability of high Winds and stormy Weather of Snow and in all likelyhood of some Ice; it would not be practicable to encamp on our Passage—it was always proposed to leave Our Tents behind.

We shall at least be three Days & Nights on the Water with such a Body. are Our Battoes, are Our Men equal to the Chances against them, or rather to the Certainties.

5. We have no Body in our Army nor I believe any one to be procured, but from Our Enemies, who is well enough acquainted with the Landing near to Tionderogo (for it begins at the Carrying Place) to know whether we could land any where but under the Enemy's Batteries; Tho' a Number of Men inferior to the Enemy, & raw Troops, without Sword or Bayonet, uncovered by our own Artillery, exposed to the Enemy's great Guns & small Arms, in this Situation, would it not, all Circumstances considered, be a rash, ill-judged Attempt?

In order to indulge the Argument for our Proceeding; I have supposed We should be ready to embark in three Weeks from the Date hereof, whereas I am persuaded, with the utmost Dispatch, We cannot be ready under 4 Weeks from the Date hereof, & probably in not less than 5. I have supposed the Mens present Dispositions to be reversed. I have not laid any great Stress on the Enemy's regular Troops, which, tho' held in Contempt by the ignorant, I think, where they have Ground to act on, are 5 to 1 against such as our's. To conclude, I have granted a Variety of Particulars, which might, with more Reason be denied.

Instead therefore of prosecuting the designed Enterprize at this Season of the Year, & in our Circumstances, I am of Opinion, that we should,

1. With all possible Dispatch erect a respectable Fort at this important Pass. Mount our heavy Cannon in it; Garrison it with 300, or 350 chosen willing Men,—a good Commanding Officer, the others the best that can be got; 3 or 4 good Gunners, full 3 Months Provisions, & other Stores sufficient. The General would have had such a Fort near built before now, but his Council of War prevented.

2. March with the rest of our Troops, Cannon &c. to Fort Edward, compleat That, garrison it &c.

3. That the Remainder of the Troops return Home (& if the Provinces have a Stomach for the Expedition next Year) hold themselves in Readiness, with better Officers, to march to Fort Edward, and hither by the 1st of April next. That they be augmented to 8000 Men, 5000 of which to proceed by Way of this Lake, & 3000 to proceed by Way of Wood Creek, & by Scouts across which is not above 14 Miles, so to correspond in their Motions, as to make, nearly at the same time, a double Attack upon Tionderogo.

If this Winter affords Snow enough, the Provisions & Stores for these Troops may be brought to Albany upon Sledges, or to Fort Edward, & the future Fort here, which being a cheap & easy Method, will save a great deal of Money.

4. That General Johnson, on his Return Home, keep out constant Parties of Indians, to observe the Motions of the Enemy, & white Men with them to view their Fortifications &c and if they should discover any Designs upon these Forts, to give immediate Intelligence there, & then put the County of Albany in Arms, to march to their Relief, which may be done in 24 Hours even to this.

5. That General Johnson, on his Return Home, be also enabled to use His Power & Influence over our Confederate Indians, to prepare & induce greater Numbers to join us next Year, than did this, & to take further Measures to draw off the Cagnawagas from the French Interest.

6. That the Prohibition of the Exportation of Provisions to Cape Breton, or any of the French West India Islands continue throughout the Colonies, & be strictly supported. That the Exportation to the Dutch, Danish, Spaniards & Our own Islands in the West Indies, be so restrained by the Colonies, & Our Governors in the West Indies so to co-operate therewith, that all Resources may, if possible, be cut off from the Enemy that Way.—If due Care is taken herein,—If the English Squadron, so long as the Season will permit,—continue to block up the Mouth of the River St. Lawrence; and the Exportation of Provisions from Ireland, in French Ships, be prevented—It is presumed Canada will not be able to support any additional Troops, or that those already there, and It's Inhabitants, will be greatly distressed to support their present Military Establishment, either this Way, or at Cadaraqui.

7. Which should have been mentioned before; That Our Artillery be increased, and in all respects put on a more formidable & regular Footing.

8. That Our Navigation on Lake Ontario be continued, & strengthened; If the Designs that Way should not succeed, or be put to trial this Season, that, with the Junction of the regular Troops under Colonel Dunbar, those Measures may be vigorously prosecuted next Year.

9. That Virginia, Maryland, and Pensilvania, keep Possession of Fort Cumberland, & exert Themselves next Spring, to make, at least a Diversion towards Fort du Quesne.

Finally, That this Diversion from Fort Cumberland, the Operations from Oswego, & the Expedition this Way, be all put in Motion next Year about the same Time, and that there be a general Exertion throughout the Colonies, during the Suspension of Our Operations, to put Them all forward at the Time mentioned.

In this Light Matters appear to me, and that Things are not at present ripe to strike *the Stroke*. This Plan vigorously Conducted, if a War should be declared, I am of Opinion, the French Dominions in these Parts may be, if not totally, in a great Measure overset.—The British Indian Interest greatly over-ballance the French, and, by that Means, the invaluable Fur Trade, which is the whole Support of Canada, fall chiefly into Our Hands, and be greatly more than a Repayment to the Colonies for all their Expences, besides enabling Them to cultivate their abandoned Lands, & those, which never will be settled, till these Events are in some Measure accomplished.

A more favourable Period for destroying the ambitious Schemes of the French in North America, & extinguishing their growing Power, cannot be hoped for, than the present, & if neglected, or suffered to slip away, may never again be regained.

Our Fleet must do their Part, & if not sufficient (for I dont know their Strength) must be increased, particularly with 20 Gun Ships, for Cruizers, and must enter into the River St. Laurence, not only to intercept Succours, but to alarm Quebec, if the latter can be done in earnest, it will greatly facilitate all the other Operations.

Sir,

I am afraid I have been too tedious, and, perhaps, to little purpose. I design well, and thought I might be permitted to throw my Mite into the Stock, of Intelligence, from these Parts, at this critical and important Juncture. My Obligations to you, and my Experience of your Goodness animated me, and is my Dependance for Pardon, if I have offended.

This Letter has been wrote by peice-meal. The Post I act in, however imperfectly filled, not only leave me very little vacant time, but unfit me for that Composure and Attention, which I would always wish for, when I have the Honour to write you.

I send you herewith a Sketch of Lake George, South Bay, and the Wood Creek, The three only passes from hence and Fort Edward to Tionderogo and Crown Point. I have never seen any correct Map. This is rather to illustrate some Parts of this Letter, than to ascertain Things with Accuracy.

My Heart is truly grateful, and offers to your Accceptance its best Wishes most fervently.

I am &c^a

PETER WRAXALL.

JOHN BREWSE [1] TO THE BOARD OF ORDNANCE
(COPY)

Halifax 18th October 1755

Right Honble and Honble Gentlemen

As a body of Troops (to which I was joined) has been in motion this Summer in Nova Scotia, I humbly beg leave to give Your Honours some Account of their employment.

In February last Colonel Lawrence our Lieutenant Governour communicated to me His design of reducing the Fort of Beausejour to His Majesty's obedience and driving the French from the Isthmus of Chignecto, and the rest of their incroachments in that neighbourhood; in consequence of this resolution, Lieutenant Colonel Monckton [2] was sent to Boston to procure Governour Shirley's Assistance in raiseing the Troops for the expedition, whilst at Halifax we were getting in readiness all the implements and the Stores for the Train of Artillery. On the 2d of May we sailed from hence in three Vessels, with 50 men of Captain Broom's Company and the abovementioned Stores, and arrived the 9th at Annapolis Royal. Colonel Monckton with the Troops and Battering Cannon arrived there the 26th, under Convoy of three 20 Gun Ships, and the 1st of June we sailed for Chignecto, where we landed the 2d and were joined by our Garrison, making in all 2000 Irregulars and 280 Regular Troops, on the 4th the whole marched from Fort Lawrence with 4 Brass Field Pieces 6 Pounders, and flung a Bridge over the Mesaguash at Pont Buot, where a Body of French and Indians were posted in an Intrenchment with some small Cannon to oppose us, but were soon dislodged, and with little loss on our side. The Troops continued their March to a riseing Ground, within a mile and half of the French Fort, when the Enemy set Fire to the Village and Church. The next day we cleared the Woods for an Encampment from the rise-

---

[1] John Brewse was stationed at Halifax in 1749, and was serving as second engineer in Newfoundland when ordered on the Fort Beauséjour expedition. As captain lieutenant, he was one of ten engineers at Louisbourg in 1758. He became captain and engineer in ordinary in 1759, major in 1772, and as lieutenant colonel was chief engineer of Minorca after Mackellar's death in 1781.

[2] Monckton's journal of the siege of Fort Beauséjour, of which the unique copy is among the Cumberland Papers, is printed in J. C. Webster, *The Forts of Chignecto* (1930).

The maps on the following pages are reproductions of the second and third of John Brewse's drawings referred to in the text. They are from the Cumberland Maps in the Royal Library at Windsor Castle. The original plan of Chignecto measures 14 by 20⅜ inches; that of Fort Beauséjour 18⅞ by 29 inches.

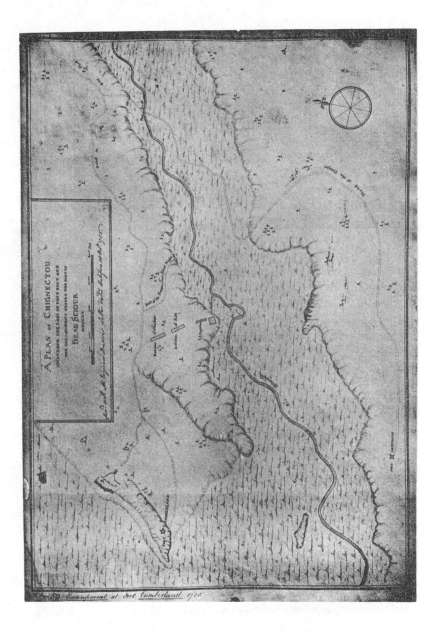

A PLAN of CHIGNECTOU
SHEWING THE BAY OF FUN'S BOUT, AND
THE ISTHMUS OF BEFORE THE FORTS
BEAU SEJOUR
HOPSONS

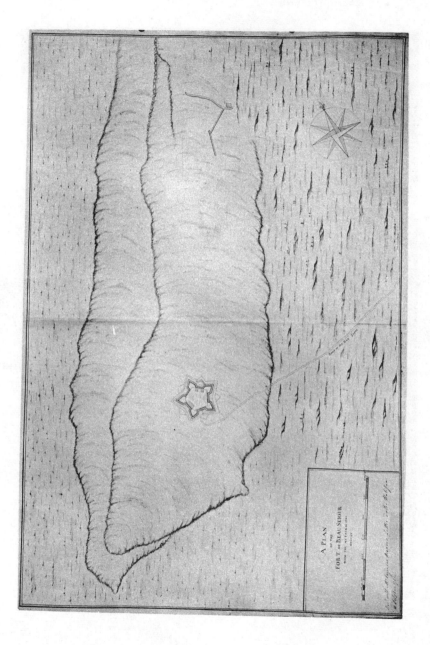

A PLAN
OF THE
FORT OR BEAU SEJOUR
WITH THE ATTACKS 1755
BY THE ENGLISH

ing Ground beforementioned in a Line to the Marsh, thro' which the River Mesagouache runs, and where the Vessels were to lye that contained the Stores and Provisions. From this time to the 12th we continued reconoitering and landing our Cannon, and on the evening of that day we dislodged a Body of French and Indians from the Ground on which the approaches were to be made. In this Affair Ensign Tongue was wounded; He was one of the three Officers appointed to assist me as Enginiers. We remained in possession of the Ground, but the intrenching Tools not coming up 'till midnight it was impossible to undertake the work I had proposed, as we had but three hours till daylight, so that I traced a parallel of two hundred yards and lodged the Men in security, which was all we were able to effect, for the next morning the Garrison kept an incessant Fire from six pieces of Cannon. however on the 14th we run a Boyau or Trench of Approach to the Right, and the next night another to the Left. A thirteen Inch Mortar, and three of eight inches were placed on our left behind the parallel, which had the desired effect, for by ten in the morning on the 16th the Commandant sent out to Capitulate, Articles were exchanged by seven in the Evening, and our Troops in Possession before dark. Colonel Monckton sent a Summons on the 17th to the Commandant of Fort Gaspreau who desired to be included in the Capitulation and a Body of our Troops under Lieut Colonel Winslow took possession on the 18th.

I now transmit to Your Honours four different plans, the first a general Draught of the Road cross the Isthmus from Beausejour to the Fort Gaspreau and the Bay Vert; the Second is a Plan comprehending the space between the Forts and our passage at Pont Buot; the third shews the Fort and our Attack; and the fourth is a particular plan of the Fort itself which Your Honours may observe is a Pentagon and approaches to a regular construction, but so diminutive in all its parts [that] even the little Ditch there is cannot be seen from the Flanks, except thro' the Embrassures, the Rampart is Faced with Sods on a Plinth of dry Stone Work; on the Faces of the Bastions run a Line of Fraises to prevent an Escalade. The Merlons are Caisons of Timber filled with Earth. Above half the Buildings in the Fort were taken down to the Ground and the Roofs taken off the three that remained, the first of which is a Quarter for Officers of 73 by 35 feet, and the other two of 22 feet square each. The French Garrison lay in Casemates in the several Bastions, which are neither dry nor Bomb Proof.

As to the situation of the Fort, it is advantageously placed on every side but that where we attacked, there the Ground rises gradually to the distance of 800 yards, and contains hollows covered with Rocks, which we immediately seized and posted our Regulars in them, who from thence could communicate with the right of the Parrallel.

Since the Surrender of the Fort now Honoured with the Name of Cumberland, Transports have been employed to carry the whole Body of French Inhabitants intirely out of the Country, and the greatest part are already sailed. If my Services in this Business are approved by the Honble. Board, I shall think myself amply rewarded for the past, and highly encouraged to proceed in obedience to their Commands whenever I shall be honoured by them. I am,

Right Honble: and Honble Gentlemen,

Your Honours most Dutiful and most Obedient humble Servant

Jɴᵒ Brewse.

Extract of a Letter from John Watts [1] to William Cotterell.[2] 6 Novʀ 1755

(copy)

Our Governor and Lieuᵗ Govʳ still continue at Albany, but their Stay will probably be but short, as the Season for Operations, as they call it, is pretty well over. Mʳ Shirley is returning to Albany, without having attempted any one thing, with a Force of four or five & forty hundred men, a few Indians included, tho' Niagara was known to be exceeding weak, in a ruinous Condition, and thinly garrison'd. Divisions & Sickness prevail'd in his little Army, instead of military Feats, and now I suppose it will take a whole winter to apologize both here and at home for the inactivity of the Summer, and to make the excessive, fruitless expence go down, it has cost the Nation.—Colᵒ Ellison died among many others, Capᵗ Desury of Pepperell's & Capᵗ King of the Independants. Dunbar's Division (the Remains of Genˡ Braddock's Army) are at Albany, sickly, in their Tents, whither Mʳ Shirley order'd them without making any Preparation for their Reception. Govʳ Hardy is building Barracks for them, but it is much to be fear'd many men will be lost before they are finish'd.

It is imagined Genˡ Johnson's chargeable army are stopt for this Season, the Troops are constantly coming & going ill arm'd, ill cloath'd

1 For John Watts, a member of the New York council, see his letter-book in N. Y. Hist. Soc. *Coll.*, 1928.

2 William Cotterell, a captain in the 45th, was the first provost martial of Nova Scotia, a member of the council there since October 23, 1752, and sometime acting secretary of the province. Loudoun gave him leave to retire in 1757, as his health was broken, and sent him to England to present to the ministry the arguments for Loudoun's decisions.

& worse disciplined, some having served their time out, as they phrase it, and some commencing fresh men. Never to be sure was such a motly Herd, almost every man his own master & a General. My Respects to Governor Lawrence &c.

[*Endorsed*] Extract of Mr Watts's Lre to Capt Cotterell New York 6 Novr 1755

EXTRACT OF A LETTER FROM GOVERNOR SIR CHARLES HARDY [1] TO HALIFAX, DATED AT FORT GEORGE THE 27 OF NOVR. 1755
(COPY)

My last to your Lordship from Albany will have prepared you to receive an Account of the Failure of the Expedition form'd against *Crown Point.* I return'd to this City yesterday, after having used all means in my Power to enable them to move forwards: But on a due Consideration of the whole, I am of opinion, had the Army been in a Condition, as well as Inclination, to have gone forward after the Battle of the 8th of September, they would have found the Pass of *Tionderoga,* at the North end of the Lake *George* so well guarded, and so readily reinforced from the army at *Crown Point,* as would not only have rendred the Attempt very difficult, but greatly hazarded the Loss of the whole army.

Thus, my Lord, have the whole Expeditions of this year ended, much, I fear, to the Disappointment of your Lordship and the Ministry. But I must beg your Lordship's Patience and Permission to lay before you some Truths, and suffer me to assure you what I now assert to you is without Prejudice to any; But I think it my Duty, after the Directions your Lordship honour'd me with before I left Europe, to give you every true and fair Information of the State of things here, for your Lordship's knowledge, and as I do not doubt but you will receive other Accounts of the miscarriage of this Expedition, perhaps principally design'd to blacken the Reputation of the Gentleman who had the Command of it, I think it but a Justice due to him, to acquaint you what has pass'd under my own Observations.

Your Lordship had the earliest Intelligence from me of my going to Albany; on my getting there, as well as during my Residence, I saw the necessity of keeping all the Waggons and Horses of this Country

[1] Sir Charles Hardy (d. 1780) had been in the navy since 1731, became rear admiral of the blue in 1756, and was governor of New York from 1755 to 1757, siding with the DeLancey faction.

employ'd in supplying that Army with Provisions (General *Shirley's* Expedition call'd upon me to assist His Commissaries with Carriages also). But the Reinforcements from the *Massachusets* & *Connecticut* arrived so quick, the first of which repair'd immediately to the Army, without any supply of Provisions being laid in for them, that it became impracticable for this Country to provide a sufficient number of Waggons & Horses to transport the necessary Quantity of Provisions & Stores for so large a Body of Men, for this reason the Connecticut Reinforcements were kept in and about *Albany*. This Difficulty I apprehend to be one principal Cause that the Army was not in a Condition to move, and a Difficulty it was that I could not with all my Efforts surmount, tho' I believe I may with truth say, had I not gone to Albany, Genl. *Johnson* would have been under a necessity of moving the greatest Part of his Forces to the City of *Albany* for Subsistance, and I am not at all clear that General *Shirley* might not have been under some such like Circumstances with his Forces.

Your Lordship will see, had this been the Case, the whole Frontiers must have been open, and in consequence subject to the Incursions of the Enemy, an Advantage I think they would not have overlook'd. Add to this, that the Supply of Provisions and Stores, for these Reinforcements, did not arrive at Albany till many days after their Forces, that had we been furnish'd with Conveyances we had not the Provisions to send up. Thus much for Provisions to which I shall only add, that I was extremely glad to keep them so supplied as to enable them to maintain their Camp.

The Army under such Circumstances most certainly could not think of prosecuting the Expedition to the full, but, that they might not be wholly inactive, I recommended to General *Johnson,* & that repeatedly, to attempt removing the Enemy from their advanced Posts; The General laid these Recommendations before his Council of War, but to little Effect. In short, my Lord, I shall tell your Lordship what I should not care to say publickly, that after the Battle and the Defeat of the Baron *Dieskau,* I firmly believe the army did not care to put themselves in the way of such another *Bout,* and I am as firmly persuaded that General *Johnson* would as readily have lead them to face the Enemy, had he been in a Condition to have done it. There are many other Circumstances, had they been sufficiently supplied, that impeded this army's moving, that are not worth troubling your Lordship with, and that may be comprized under Jealousies that arose after the Battle, and, I am led to think, were spirited up by some Chiefs in Command whose Conduct that day may not turn out so clear. But the principal Articles wanted were a suffict. number of Battoes for transporting the Army thro' the Lake, four hundred of which could not be carried from *Fort Edward*, with[t] taking the Waggons from transporting the Provisions, which was so immediately wanted, also flat bottom Scows for transporting the Artillery thro' the Lake, which were begun but never finish'd.

Thus far, my Lord, I have endeavour'd to give the principal Causes of the miscarriage of this Expedition, & shall add no more upon this Subject, than that as your Lordship may imagine these Evils would not have appear'd had they been provided for in an early time, granted my Lord: But to that I beg leave to answer that the Expedition was concerted in a Hurry, without those necessary previous Considerations. It was expected that the Battoes sent up to *Albany* for this Service would have convey'd a sufficient Quantity of Provisions and Stores; in the first Place, they had not the Provisions and Stores at *Albany*, and secondly, I am inform'd the Waters of *Hudson's* River was then so low, that loaded Battoes could not be carried over the *Rifts* etc. By this your Lordship may see how we came to be under these Difficulties.

I have transmitted to the Secretary of State Copies of Councils of War sent to me while at *Albany*, also a Copy of an Agreement at a meeting with Mr. *Shirley*, and Commissioners from the *Massachusetts* & *Connecticut*, for garrisoning the *Forts Edward* at the great carrying Place, and *Fort William Henry* at the South end of Lake *George*, by which your Lordship may observe how unanimous they are, in not thinking it adviseable to attempt the Reduction of *Crown Point* this Season. I make no doubt but your lordship will hear the Provinces are not so well inclined to raise men for these Services next year. I am not at present sufficiently inform'd of their Disposition as to this matter: I shall endeavour to do all on my part in this Province.

I am extremely sorry to find by our late Advices from *England*, that no General Officer is appointed to be sent here, to take the Command of His Majesty's Forces, and I hope I shall stand excused in saying, I have no Opinion of the Service's being carried on, with any prospect of Success, without some more able & experienc'd General is at the head of them, than this Continent furnishes. I by no means, my Lord, mean to insinuate anything to the Prejudice of General *Shirley*, from any hasty, misguided Opinion. Your Lordship has enjoin'd me to be sincere, and as a Lover of Truth I cannot be otherways, & think it my Duty to tell you, that it is a Task far beyond our present General's Abilities, and if your Lordship should have been told otherwise, I beg you will suspend your Judgment, & I am sure a short time will convince you of this Truth.

I have had many Conversations with Mr. *Shirley,*
Character of Major whom I left at *Albany,* and I must take leave to say I
G¹ Shirley   never met his Equal to transact Business with. Let me
entreat your Lordship not wholly to give Ear to his
Representations, and however hard the Task is to reflect on any Gentleman, the honour & respect I have for your Lordship oblige me to inform you that *I fear he is no better* than an *artfull Deceiver* ready to
advance any thing in his Representations of Things as Facts, when he is
perhaps *more a Stranger to the Facts he asserts than those he lays them
before.* It is impossible your Lordship and His Majesty's Ministers can
be inform'd, if Truths are not the Foundations of such Informations:
my Lord, I much doubt if that has been or is like to be the Case from
that Quarter. The Scene of Confusion I left him in at Albany, is hardly
to be credited.

In some of my last Letters I mention'd to your Lordship his temporiz-
ing with the Indians; I greatly fear that will be an Evil not easily to
be removed, if not speedily remedied. As far as I can judge from the
little Experience I have had in this Country, if the Indians are not
committed to the Care of *Johnson,* and him supported in it, I shall have
great doubt of our being able to have that Dependance on their sincere
Services, so necessary for the Good of these Countries. I think I may
venture to assure you that many of the Persons Mr. *Shirley* employs
to transact Indian Affairs for him are meer ignorant Tools; as an
instance of this, I must observe to your Lordship that his principal
Indian Ambassador is Mr *Broadstreet,* who never saw one of the *Castles*
till his going this year to *Oswego,* and now takes upon him to know
more of the matter than any body in this Country. I will not assert it,
but I have reason to believe these People have been employ'd to withdraw *Johnson's* Influence from them. However of this I may soon be
better able to inform your Lordship, as I have wrote to Johnson to
stop at the Castles in his way from his Camp, and when he comes to
me, I shall inform your Lordship of his opinion as to this matter. In
short, my Lord, I fear the worst if his Majesty does not send out some
able & experienced Officer to conduct his Troops. I have taken the
Liberty to mention as much in my Letter to the Secretary of State from
a thorough Conviction I can with great Truth support this opinion.
And on the other Hand, if able & experienced Generals arrive here,
[in] time enough to make the necessary Preparations for the opening the
Campaign, I shall hope his Majesty's Service may be carried on with a
great Prospect of Success, & I trust the Provinces, under a Confidence of

able Leaders, might be brought to contribute what is in their Power to the promoting these Services.

I must entreat your Lordship's Forgiveness in being thus free, but there appears to me such a necessity of Truths being laid before you, that I could not forbear committing to Paper those Thoughts that my Heart would have dictated, had I the honour to be with you to acquaint you with the deplorable Situation of these Countries, if the Troops of His Majesty are to be no better conducted than they will be under their present Leader. And I must beg leave to assure your Lordship that, after all I have said, I shall to the utmost of my Power, assist General *Shirley* in carrying on His Majesty's Service, though I must say I shall not be out of Hopes that your Lordship will use your Influence to have some proper Officer sent out. Mr Shirley has made a very able Governor of the Massachusetts, and I beg leave to offer it as my opinion, that he is much more able to do His Majesty Service in that Department, than at the Head of his Armies.

SUMMARY OF DISPUTES BETWEEN GOVERNOR WILLIAM SHIRLEY AND GENERAL WILLIAM JOHNSON.
1755 [1]
(COPY)

There is no Letter from Gen[l] *Johnson* to the Secretary of State, but the *Board of Trade* have transmitted One to them, dated the *3ᵈ Septʳ;* full of Complaints against Govʳ *Shirley*, who has, as Gen[l] *Johnson* says, endeavour'd to do him all the Prejudice he can with the Indians; That He has represented him as an *Upstart,* entirely dependant upon him, & that He furnishes him with all the Money & Presents for the Indians, & that He can pull him down, when He pleases. That Mʳ *Shirley* employs one *Lidius* to the Indians, who is a Person odious to them. That Mʳ *Shirley* in order to detach the Indians from Mʳ *Johnson,* has made them such large Offers, that Mʳ *Johnson* has been obliged to yield to very unreasonable Demands from them.

In support of this, Mʳ *Johnson* incloses the Speech of the Great *Mo-hock Indian,*[2] relating what Mʳ Shirley had said to them. Gen[l] *Johnson*

---

1 While the three letters summarized here are printed, in C. H. Lincoln, *Correspondence of William Shirley*, II, pp. 243–248, 309–310, 270–276, the way in which they were edited in the secretary of state's office seems worth reproducing. This document is in memorandum form.

2 *N. Y. Col. Docs.*, VI, 998–999.

thinks, these Proceedings contrary to the Commission given him by General *Braddock,* by which he was appointed sole Superintendant of the Indian Affairs. That He cannot fullfill the King's Expectations, if His proceedings are to be controulled by a Governor, & unless a certain Fund is appointed, & confided to his Disposal, for that Service, & unless he is put on that footing, He desires to decline the Charge. The only Reason he can guess for Mr *Shirley's* Conduct is, his not having provided *100:* Indians to escort him to *Oswego,* which the Indians said was unnecessary as the Road lay thro' their Country.

There is no Letter from Mr *Shirley,* on this Subject, but, in One of the 5ᵗʰ *Octʳ* on the Action at Lake *George,* He refers to Copies of two Letters to Genˡ *Johnson,* for his Sentiments of his Conduct, & says, *He dont yet certainly know, what the Issue of that Expedition will be this Year, but has Reason to think it will be dissatisfactory to all the New England Colonies as well as Himself.*

In Mr *Shirley's* Letter to Genˡ *Johnson,* He does not make any particular Accusation, but seems to hint, that He has taken a wrong Road to *Crown Point,*

That the Fort he is building at Lake *George* is useless, Presses him to go on, & by all means endeavour to make himself Master of *Tironderoge.*

Thinks he must have sufficient Force for that purpose; That his Account of the Strength of the French is aggravated; And differs from him in his Opinion of the Conduct of the French in the late Action.

GOVERNOR CHARLES LAWRENCE TO HALIFAX
(COPY)

My Lord,

Since my Letter to your Lordship of the *18ᵗʰ of October,* by the hands of Admˡ *Boscawen,* I have had the Honour to receive your Lordship's most obliging Favour dated in August, full of the highest Encomiums on my Conduct & management; My Lord, I am happy, excessively so, in what you are good enough to think & say of me, nor is any thing wanting to make me compleatly so, but a Consciousness of having in truth merited half the Praise your Lordship's Partiality in my favour has conferr'd upon me, for I should then be secure of that which is the highest Point of my Ambition, the Continuance of your Lordship's Approbation and Applause, & consequently of your Countenance and Protection. I wish to God I could give myself Credit for having crown'd your Ldsp's Labours, for the happy Establishment of this Province, with Success; That indeed would be to have gain'd such Glory and Advantages as your Goodness would attribute to me: But I fear a considerable part of so great a Work is yet to be accomplish'd. The Prospect may, I think, fairly be said to be now open that leads to Success, and no Circumstance in my Opinion, my Lord, brightens it more than that happy, tho' expensive one of extirpating those *perfidious Wretches, the French Neutrals,* some of which that have escaped Us being even still audacious enough to declare that the French will infallibly make themselves masters of the Province the next Spring. I must confess I am not without my Apprehensions of their attempting it, for altho' the Removal of the Neutrals with the Loss of *Beausejour* and their other Possessions, must have extremely disconcerted their measures to the Northward, and rendred their Views within this Province much less valuable, yet as our Military Operations to the Westward (if Credit can be given to the inclosed Letter & Extracts) have amounted to little more than the levying & disbanding of Troops, the French, who at first perhaps trembled for *Quebec,* will now certainly (when they find *Crown Point* & *Niagara* out of danger) meditate some Revenge upon *Nova Scotia* for any little Efforts of Ours to gall them. And this Consideration, my Lord, leads me to renew my Application regarding the Augmentation to be made to the Troops: The Officers recruiting on the Continent having met with every Obstacle the People could throw in their way (an Event I was apprized of & prepared for) have hitherto made little or no Progress, nor can I at present flatter myself with any sanguine hopes of our succeeding better here amongst the New England Irregulars, as a thousand Stories are daily propagated by their Officers to discourage their becoming Soldiers. The Meth[od] of this will appear pretty clearly from the publick Prints upon the Continent, and more fully still from Lieut. Govr *Phipps's* Lre [letter] and the Vote of their House, which, false as their Suggestions are, I inclose for your Lordship's Perusal. But if We have the Resentm^t of the French to apprehend, and are at the same time without any Prospect of accomplishing what will be so essential to Our Security, the Augmentation to the Troops, more especially when the New-Englanders (who will serve not a moment beyond their Term) are dismiss'd, I beg leave to say, my Lord, if this be the Case, We have nothing to depend upon but the Expedient I proposed and pray'd your Lordship's Consideration of in my last, the compleating the Regiments here by Draughts from those at home. I cannot quit this Subject, my Lord, without assuring you again that I fear the Divisions which We are told subsist between the Colonies, and the Disappointment of their Hopes & Expectations from those Expeditions for which they have rais'd & maintain'd at great Expence such numbers of men, will render the Difficulties insuperable that any future Attempt must meet with, to unite the Provinces in new Enterprizes against the French in the ensuing Spring: And when the French have no longer any thing on their Hands to the Westward, it will require a very considerable additional Strength to our present one, to secure Our safety here to the Northward, where we are a Frontier, and the immediate Object of their Envy & Resentm^t.

I doubt not but your Lordship's Board will approve and carry thro', the Estimate for finishing the Fortifications on *George's* Island, without which this Town would be much more secure, were there no such plan'd, since in the present State & Condition of it, nothing would be easier than for an Enemy even of inconsiderable Force to make themselves Masters of it, turn the Guns upon the Town & beat it about Our Ears, without having any thing to apprehend. As the Removal of the French Inhabitants has proved a Work of much more Trouble & Time than could be imagined, so great a Progress has not been made as I could have wish'd in the necessary works & repairs about the Forts on the Isthmus of Chignecto, wherefore I cannot as yet well ascertain what the Expence there will amount to, but, if I am not extremely mistaken, the ten thousand Pounds, transmitted by order of the Lords Justices, will be abundantly sufficient for answering all the Ends proposed from it. In which Case I intend (upon the Strength of Sir Thomas *Robinson's* Letter, which is clear as to the repairing & securing whatever We have taken or, in his own words, may take) to possess ourselves of St. John's River, and repair the Fortifications in the Spring, if I have Strength to undertake it. Nothing, my Lord, is more necessary; nothing will contribute in so great a degree either to our own Security or to the Annoyance of the French, in case of a Rupture, as a good Fort in the Heart of the *St. John's* Indians, who are a warlike well-spirited Tribe, who are the Terror of the Micmacs, our nearest neighbours, and who, I conceive, with a little Address may, whilst the Imposition of *Canada* live fresh in their memory, be easily brought to abandon the French and attach themselves entirely to Our Interest, whereas if they are now neglected, they are probably lost for ever.

There is nothing I find myself so perplex'd about, as the Business of calling an Assembly. The present Posture & Situation of Our provincial Affairs, the uncertain Event of the Differences between Us and our treacherous neighbours, with a thousand other untoward Circumstances render in my Opinion all Proposals and Projects for an Assembly at this critical Conjuncture chimerical. But as I have laid my Thoughts at large on this matter before your Lordship's Board, in Obedience to their Commands, I shall make no further mention of it here, than to entreat, my Lord, that, if possible, every Consideration of that sort may be dispensed with for the present, and give way to Matters of more immediate Utility and at least of as much real Importance to the Wellfare & Prosperity of the Province. For I know nothing so likely to obstruct and disconcert all Measures for the publick Good, as the foolish Squabbles that are attendant upon Elections & the impertin^t Opinions that will be propagated afterwards amongst the Multitude by Persons qualified, in their own Imaginations only, as able Politicians. I am morally certain, my Lord, that if an Assembly (supposing it practicable) had been call'd a twelve month ago, every thing that has been undertaken within that time would have remain'd unattempted, and the Province, if not in the Possession of the French, at least a much easier Prey than they will ever find it for the future, unless I flatter myself extremely.

If on this or any other Occasion, either to your Lordship or the Board, I have been guilty of any Omission as to Points that should have been wrote upon, or the Explanation of them, I promise myself your Lordship's Goodness, in consideration of the Multiplicity of troublesome things I have had lately on my Hands, will hold me in some measure excused. As to every thing hitherto done, or that will hereafter be undertaken, whilst I have the honour to be entrusted with this important Charge, my Lord, do me the Justice to beleive that I will not only act at all times with the strictest Justice & Integrity myself, as well as with all imaginable Care & Oeconomy, but will keep a constant & vigilant Eye over such as are any way concern'd in the expenditure of the publick money. By such a Conduct and by that alone I persuade myself I shall preserve the Continuance of your Lordships favour & Friendship, and the Liberty of subscribing myself most respectfully

My Lord &c &c

CHA^s LAWRENCE.

Halifax, Decr 9. 1755

CONSIDERATIONS UPON THE SCITE, INTERESTS, AND SERVICE
OF NORTH AMERICA, BY THOMAS POWNALL [1]

(D.S.)

THE following Paper proposes to consider

First—The Scite of the Country

Secondly—The Interests of the Possessions & Settlements as the Basis

Thirdly—of the State of the Service in America

It becomes necessary to a right Understanding of these to recurr back & run up to the First Principles on which they are founded, not only because the Subject is New; but because It has been misconceived, Perverted & Misrepresented.

1st . . . . PRIOR to any Observations on the Settlers & Settlements, it will be necessary to take some Notice of the peculiar State & Scite of the Countries in which they have settled; For it is the Scite & Circumstances (I mean those that are unchangeable) of a Country which give the Characteristic Form, to the State & Nature of the People who inhabit it.

The Consideration of the Continent of America may be properly divided into two Parts from the Two very different & distinct Ideas that the Face of the Country presents, but more especially from the Two different Effects which must necessarily & have actually arisen from the Two very different Sorts of Circumstances in each Tract of Country.

All the Continent of North America as far as known to the Europeans is to the Westward of the endless Mountains a High Level Plain. All to the South East of these Mountaines slopes away South Easterly down to the Atlantick Ocean. By a level Plain I must not be understood as tho' I thought there were no Hills or Vallies or Mountaines in such, but that the Plain of a Section parallel to the Main Face of the Country would be nearly an Horizontal Plain; as the Plain of a like Section of this other Part would be inclined to the Horizon with a large Slope

---

[1] Thomas Pownall (1722–1805), after some years in the Board of Trade office, went to New York in 1753 as Governor Osborn's secretary. After the governor's suicide, he remained to study the colonial situation as a whole, presented several papers to the Albany Conference in 1754, returned to England in 1756 to present Johnson's side of the dispute with Shirley, and came out with Loudoun as the latter's secretary extraordinary. In 1756 Loudoun sent him to England to present his case before the ministry, and in 1757 Pownall returned as governor of Massachusetts, having won Pitt's confidence. This paper is the original draft of the report to Cumberland which Pownall expanded for publication in the *Administration of the Colonies* (1774), II, 174–233.

to the Atlantic Ocean. The Line that divides these Two Tracts, that is the South East Edge of these Plains or the highest Part of this Slope, may in general be said to run from Onondaga along the Westermost Alleganni Ridge of the Endless Mountains away to Apalatche in the Gulf of Mexico.

In considering First the main Continent high Plain; It will appear that altho' it be raised thus high above the level of the Ocean, Yet the Element of Water seems to claim & hold a equall Dominion with the Land in this Extent. For by the Great Lakes which lye upon it's Bosom, on One Hand, & on the other by the Great River the Messesippi & the Multitude of Waters which run into it there seems to be a Communication an Alliance or Dominion of the watery Elements which commands thro'out the Whole. These great Lakes appear to be the Throne & Center of a Dominion whose Influence by an Infinitude of Rivers Creeks & Streams extends itself thro' all & every Part, supported by the Connection & Communication of an Alliance with the Waters of Messesippi.

With very few exceptions in Comparison to the Whole, it may be observed, that this Multitude of Waters is properly speaking but of Two Masses. The One composed of the Waters of the Lakes & their Suit, which disembogue by the River St Lawrence. The other that Wilderness of Waters that all lead into the Messesippi & thence to the Ocean. The Former into the Gulf of St Lawrence, the Latter into the Gulf of Mexico.

There is not in all the Waters of Messesippi at least as far as We Know but Two Falls of Waters, The One at a Place called by the French St Antoine high upon the West or main Branch of Messesippi; The other on the East Branch called Ohio. Except these & the Temporary Rapidity arising from the Freshes of Spring & the Rainy Seasons all the Waters of the Messesippi run to the Ocean with a Still, Easy & Gentle Current.

As to all the Waters of the Five great Lakes, & the many large Rivers that empty into them; The Waters of the Great Outawawa River, The Waters of Lake Champlain, of Trois Riviers, & the many others that empty into the River St Lawrence above Quebec, they may all be considered in One Mass as a Stagnation or Lake of a Wildernesse of Waters spreading over the Country by an infinite Multitude & Variety of Branchings Bays Straits &c^a; For altho' at particular Places of their Communication & mouth of their Streams, they seem to pour out such an immense Ocean of Waters, Yet when all collected & assembled together at a general Rendevouz where they all disembogue themselves into River St Lawrence, the whole *Embocheur* of this Multi-tude of Waters is not larger than the *Seine* at Paris.

About 12 French Leagues above Quebec over against a Place called *La Loubiniere,* The River St *Lawrence* appears to be of a very con-siderable Breadth; But when the Tide (which runs up much higher than that Place) has at it's Ebb entirely retired That Breadth which One would have judged to have been That of St Lawrence River, remains all Dry except a small Channell in the middle which does not appear to be much larger than the Seine at Paris, nor the Waters of it that pass there to have more or a greater Current.

Not only the Lesser Waters of each respective Mass, but the main general Body of each go thro' this Continent in every Course & Direction.

Attention to these general Facts will lead any One to Know that this great Extent of Country is as I have defined it a high level Plain & a more curious & accurate Scrutiny into the particular Facts whence these general Observations are formed, will confirm him in that Knowledge.

If You add still farther to these Observations the Information We have of those immense unwooded & unwatered Plains that to the West-ward of Messesippi extend still farther Westward than any European or Indian has penetrated them the Thing will appear in a stronger & fuller Light.

If We give Attention to the Nature of this Country, & the One united Command & Dominion which the Waters hold thro'out the same, We shall not be surprized to find the French (tho' so few in Number) in Possession of a Power which commands this Country. Nor on the other Hand, when We come to consider the Nature of this eastern Part of America, on which the English are settled, if we give any Degree of Attention to the Facts, shall we be surprised to find them, tho' so numerous, to have so little & so languid a Power of Command, even within the Country where they are actually settled. I say a very strong Reason for this Fact arises out of the different Natures of the Country, Prior to any Consideration of the Difference arising from the Nature of their Government or their Method of taking this Possession.

This Country by a Communication of Waters that is extended thro'out, & by an Alliance of all these into a *One Whole* is capable of being & is naturally, a Foundation of a One System of Command. And accordingly such a System would & has actually taken Root therein, under the French Hands. Their various Possessions thro'out this Coun-try, have an Order & Connection, & Communication an Unity a System. & is forming Fast into One Government as will be seen by & by.

Whereas the English Settlements have naturally neither Order Connection, Communication Unity nor System.

The Waters of this Tract on which the English are settled are a Number of Rivers & Bays unconnected with & independent of each other, either in Interest or Communication

As far as the Communication of the Waters of any River, or Communion there may be between Two such extends, so far extended will arise a Communication Unity or System of Interest & Command. And therefore the Settlements on this Tract of Country would be naturally, as they are actually, divided into Numbers of little weak unconnected independent Governments.

Which State & Circumstances of these our Settlements are also equally Consequences of the Scite & Nature of the Country on which they are found prior to, or apart of all Considerations of the Effect of Government or Administration.

The Consideration of which Country so far as it is connected with, or has any Effect upon the Interests & Politicks of the English Settlements, presents itself to View; divided in Two Ideas. 1st . . . The Country between the Sea & Mountains. 2dly: . . . The Mountains

The First Part is almost thro'out the Whole capable of Culture & is intirely settled. The Second a Wilderness in which is found here & there, in smal Portions, in Comparison of the whole, solitary detached Spots of Ground fit for Settlements, the Rest is Nothing but Cover for Vermin & Rapine, a Nest & Den for wild Beasts & the more wild Savages that lurk in it

This whole Country instead of being united & strengthened by the Alliance of Waters which run in it, is divided by these several various Waters detached from & independent of each other, into many separate detached Tracts, that do naturally & have actually become the Foundation of as many separate & Independent Interests, on which many & Independent Governments have been formed.

Thus far of the Scite of the Country as it becomes the actual Foundation of a *Natural Difference* between the English & French Possessions in America.

Secondly . . . . . of the Manner in which the English & French have taken Possession of, & settled in this, Country.

The French in their First Attempts to settle themselves in these Parts endeavoured to penetrate by the Force of Arms, to fix their Possessions by Military Expeditions, 'till thro' the perpetual & constant Abortion of these Measures, & the certain Disappointment & sure Loss that attended Them, they thro' a Kind of Despair, gave over all thoughts of such

Whether by the dear bought Experience that they learnt from hence, or whether thro' Despair leaving their Colony to make its own Way, or whether, rather the right good Sense of Mon Frontenac & Mr Calliere lead them to it is neither easy nor material to determine

But so it was, They fell afterwards into that only Path in which the real Spirit & Nature of the Service led.

The native Inhabitants, the Indians, of this Country, are all Hunters, all the Laws of Nations they know are the Laws of Sporting, & all the Idea they have of Landed Possession that of a *Hunt,* The French Settlers of Canada universally commenced Hunters, & so insinuated themselves into a Connection with these Natives.

While the French kept themselves thus allied with the Indians as Hunters & communicated with them in, & strictly maintained all the Laws & Rights of Sporting, The Indians did easily & readily admit them to a local Landed Possession. A Grant which rightly acquired & applied they are always ready to make, as none of the Rights or Interests of their Nation is hurt by it; but on the contrary, they experience & receive great Use Benefit & Profit from the Commerce that the Europeans therein establish with them. But this will more clearly & better appear by a more minute & particular Attention to the French Measures in those Matters.

1 . . . . . No Canadien is suffered to hunt or Trade with the Indians but by *Conge* from the Governmt & under such Regulations as that License ordains. The Police [Policy] of which, is this, The Government divides the indian Countries into so many Hunts according as they are divided by the Indians themselves. To those several Hunts there are Licences respectively adapted, with Regulations respecting the Spirit of the Nation whose Hunt such is, respecting the Commerce & Interest of that Nation, & respecting the Nature of that Hunt.

The Canadien having such License ought not to trade & hunt within the Limits of such Hunt, but according to the above Regulations, And he is hereby absolutely excluded under severe Penalties to trade or hunt beyond those Limits on any Account whatsoever. It were needless to point out the many good and beneficial Effects arising from this Police, by giving thus a right Attention to the Interest of the Indian, in observing the true Spirit of the Alliance, in putting the Trade upon a fair Foundation, & by maintaining all the Rights & Laws of the Hunt which the Indians most indispensably exact.

But the Consequence, of the most important Service which arises out of this Police; is, a regular, Certain, Definitive, Precise & assured Knowledge of the Country.

A Man whose Interest & Commerce are circumscribed within a certain Department will pry into & scrutinize every Hole & Corner, of that *Endroit*. Again when such a Hunt is by these Means as full of these *Coureurs de Bois* as the Commerce of it will bear, whoever applies for a *Congè* must betake himself to some New Tract & Hunt, by which again begins an Opening to new Discoveries, & fresh Acquisitions.

When the French have by these Means established a Hunt, a Commerce, Alliance & Influence amongst the Indians of that Tract, & have by these Means acquired a Knowledge of all the Waters, Passes, Portages, & Posts that may hold the Command of that Country, in short a Military Knowledge of the Ground, then & not before, they ask & obtain Leave of the Indians to strengthen their Trading House to make a Fort & to put a Garrison into it

In this Manner by becoming Hunters & creating Alliances with the Indians as Brother Sportsmen by founding that Alliance upon & maintaining it (according to the true Spirit of the Indian Laws of Nations) a right Communication & Exercise of the True Interest of the Hunt, they have insinuated themselves into an Influence with the Indians, have been admitted into a Landed Possession, & by locating & fixing those Possessions in Alliance with & by the friendly Guidance of the Waters whose Influence extends thro'out the whole They are become possessed of a real Interest in, & real Command over the Country. They have thus thro'out the Country 60. or 70. Forts, & almost as many Settlements, which influence the Command of this Country, not One of which without the above true Spirit of Policy could they support with all the Expence & Force of Canada. Not all the Power of France could, 'tis the Indian Interest alone that does maintain these Forts.

Having thus got Ground in any certain Tract, & having One Principal Fort, they get Leave to build other trading Houses, at Length to strengthen such, & in Fine to take Possession of more & more advanced Posts, & to fortifie and Garrison them as little Subordinate Forts under the Command of the Principal One

I have not been able to get an exact List of these but the following is sufficient to sketch out the Manner in which they conduct this Service.

St Frederic	{ St John Carillon	
Frontenac	{ La Presentation Les Condres Quintez	Tho' these Principal Forts have subordinate Forts independent on them; They are
Niagara	{ Torento & One other	Yet independent of each other & only under the Command of
De Quesne	{ Presq'isle Riviere au Boeuf One other	the Govr Genl: There is a Rout of Duty settled for these & the Officers & Comanders are removed to better & better Commands.
Le Detroit	} Two	
Nipigon	{ Two or Three upon the River Michipocotoz One Other on Long River	

St Joseph & One other

Le Petit Paris { Many more which bear the Names of the Rivers

Alibi

Saquenay. In all about 60.

The present Establishment for this Service is Three Thousand Men of which there are generally Two Thousand Three or Four Hundred Men Effective.

Most of these Forts have fine Settlements & large Stores round them, & they do I believe entirely support themselves. It being usual for both Officers & Men to defer receiving their Pay 'till the Garrison is releived which is generaly in Six Years. And scarce any thing is sent to these Garrisons but dry Goods & Ammunition.

There is a fine Settlement at Detroit of near Two Hundred Families: a better still at St Joseph of above Two Hundred; a Fine One at St Antoin & many fine Ones about Petit Paris. But the French Government does not encourage these, & have, by a positive Ordonnance absolutely forbid any One to make a Settlement without especial License which They found necessary to do to restrain the Canadians from totally abandoning Canada.

By these Means, I repeat it, have they created an Alliance, an Interest with all the Indians on the Continent: by these means have they acquired an Influence & Command thro'out the Country. They Know too well the Spirit of the Indian Politicks to affect a Superiority of

Government over the Indians; Yet they have in Reality & Truth, of more solid Effect an Influence an *Ascendency* in all the Councils of all the Indians on the Continent & lead & direct their Measures, Not even Our Own Allies the Six Nations excepted. Unless in that Remains of Our Interest which partly the good Effects of Our Trading House at Oswego & partly Gen¹ Johnson has preserved to the English by the great Esteem & high Opinion the Indians have of His Spirit & Truth.

The English American Provinces are as fine *Settlements* as any in the World, but can scarce be called *Possessions* because they are so settled as to have no Possession of the Country. They are settled as Farmers Millers Fishers &cᵃ upon Bays & Rivers that have no Communication nor Connection of Interests consequently the Settlers belonging to these Rivers Bays &cᵃ have no *Natural Connection*.

But farther the Settlers upon any One River or Sett of Waters (which Waters having a Connection might become the *Natural Seal* of One Interest) are yet so settled that they have no Connection nor Union amongst each other scarce of Communion much less of Defence.

Their Settlements are Vag[u]e without Design, scattered, Independent, They are so settled, that from their Situation 'tis not easy for them to unite in a System of Mutual Defense, nor does their Interest lead them to such a System, & even if both did, Yet thro' the Want of a *Police* to form them into a Community of Alliance Unity & Activity amongst Themselves they are *Helpless* & *Defenseless* & thus have the English of this Sort for many Hundred Miles a long *indefensible Line of Frontiers* prior to the Consideration of the Nature of the Enemy they may be engaged with.

First. The French can collect in a short Warning at any Time, in any of their advanced Posts a Force sufficient to break up the Settlements & return again within their Lines before any Force can be collected to attack them.

But there is something more particularly critical in the Situation of the English Settlements with Respect to the Indians.

The English are settled up to Mountains the very Mouth of the Denns of these Savages; in which Situation the Building a Line of Forts as a Barrier against them would be as little effectual as building a Line of Forts to prevent the Bears Wolves & Foxes from coming within them.

Thirdly. . . The State of the Service as arising from the above Facts

It appears from the First Stroke of the Eye, That the English without some preparative Measures, will not be able to carry into Execution any Military Expeditions, ag^t the French, in the upper Part of America.

The First of these Measures is the Settling the Police of Our Alliance with the (Kenunctioni) Confederacy upon a permanent solid & effectual Basis; so as to restore and reestablish Our Interest with them.

The French Power in the Upper Plain will as things are now circumstanced prove too Strong for the English.

The Second is taking Possession of & Fortifiing such a System of advanced Posts. Viz: Magazines whereat to collect Stores & Provisions, Camps from whence within a reasonable Distance & by a practicable Way to make Our Sorties.

Thirdly the securing the Dominion of *Lake Ontario* for the present & laying a Foundation for the like Dominion on Lakes *Erie Huron* & *Michigan.*

The First of which has not yet even a Thought of a Foundation, and the Two other far from being carried into an Effect that can be *sufficiently depended upon* so as to build upon them a *well grounded Scheme of Action.*

It also appears from the above that the English Settlements as they are at present circumstanced are absolutely at a Stand, they are settled up to the Mountains, & in the Mountains, there is no where together Land sufficient for a Settlement large enough to subsist by itself, to defend itself & preserve a Communication with the Present Settlements.

If the English would advance One Step farther, or cover themselves where they are, it must be at Once by One large Step over the Mountains with a numerous & Military Colony

There are a farther Detail of Matters arising from the above State of Facts but too minute & particular to enter into this general Idea.

T. POWNALL

[*Endorsed*] Mr *Pownall's* **Considerations** upon the *Scite, Interests* and *Service* of *North America. 1755.*

TROOPS IN THE PAY OF THE PROVINCE OF PENNSYLVANIA AND WHERE POSTED.

FEBRUARY 23^D 1756 [1]

(COPY)

Capt. John Potter with 50   Near the Maryland Lines where he is to build a small Fort.

---

[1] This document came into Cumberland's possession in connection with the discussion in London offices, early in 1756, of the advisability of parliamentary action towards Pennsylvania. See W. T. Root, *Relations of Pennsylvania with the British Government*, Ch. X; S. M. Pargellis, *Lord Loudoun in North America*, pp. 56–57.

Capt. Hans Hamilton with ...	75	At Fort Littleton near the Sugar Cabbins.
Capt. George Croghan with ...	75	At Fort Shirley near Aughwick.
Capt James Burd with	75	At Fort Granville near Kishyquohillis a branch of the Juniata.
Capt James Patterson with ..	75	At Pomfret Castle about 15 Miles from Fort Granville & 12 from the River Sasquehanna
Capt Thomas McKee with ...	30	At Hunters Mill.
Capt Frederick Smith with ..	50	20 at Monaday & 30 at Swahatara
Capt Christian Busse with ...	50	At Fort Henry in the important Pass called Tolikaio.

These Men have been regularly inlisted by the Governor in the Kings Service, for a certain time, to serve within the Province of Pennsylvania, & the Provinces bordering upon it.

Capt Jacob Morgan with	50	At Fort Lebanon in the Forks of Schuylkill, he is ordered with 30 of his Men to erect a Blockhouse halfway between Fort Henry & Fort Lebanon.
Capt Foulke with	63	Posted at a new Stuccado between Fort Lebanon and Fort Allen.
Capt Wayne with	50	Posted at Fort Allen which stands where the Moravian Town of Gnadenhutton was.
Capt Orndt with	50	At a new Stuccado about 12 Miles East of Fort Allen.
Capt Craig with	41	At Fort Hamilton about 5 Miles from Delaware.
Capt Van Etten with	30	At the Minisinks.
Lieutenant Wetterhold with ..	26	At a new Stuccado round Broadhead's House near Minisinks.
Ensign Sterling and	11	At a Stuccado round Teets house at the Wind Gap.
A Serjeant and	5	At Uplinger's House.
An Ensign with	15	At Druckers Mill.
A Lieutenant with	15	In Allen Township.
Capt Trexler with	53	Within the Mountains.
Capt Martin with	30	In the Settlements above Easton.

These were inlisted, by the Commissioners named in the Act, as Militia.

List of Applications for Stores &ᶜᴬ Depending before the Committee.[1] May, 1756
(copy)

New Hampshire—   For a Strong Fort to be built at the Head of Connecticut River and a Communication opened from thence to the East Side of Lake Champlain. For a Naval Force to be built on Lake Champlain. For Fort William and Mary and the several Batterys to be put in good Repair and the Cannon unfit for Service to be exchanged. For a Uniform Set of Arms for a certain Number of Horse & Foot to be placed in the said Fort to be used occasionally and for Barracks to be built for at least 1000 Men.

Rhode Island—   For so many Cannon Mortars and Field Pieces as may be sufficient for the Fort there and its Appendages with the usual proportion of Ordnance Stores, and such a Quantity of Small Arms and Powder as to His Majesty shall seem meet.

New York—   For Cannon and Stores for the New Works already built and such others as it will be necessary to build, and also Cannon of a smaller Size for Out Forts and Blockhouses, and for Forts in the Indian Castles.

Virginia—   For Fort George, York Battery and Gloucester Fort to be rebuilt under the Direction of a skilful Engineer and supplied with Cannon and Stores. For a Fort to be built at Cape Henry and supplied with Cannon and Stores, and for Forts to be built along the Ridge of the Allegany Mountains at the Passes and Garrisoned with a competent Number of Soldiers.

Georgia—   For Forts to be erected and supplied with Cannon and Stores and Garrisoned with regular Forces and for Two Troops of Rangers.

Jamaica—   For the Regiment now there to be augmented to 1000 Men and another Regiment to be sent

[1] This is a summary of the Board of Trade representation of May 11 referred to the committee of the Privy Council May 17, 1756. *Acts Privy Council, Colonial, 1745–1766*, p. 335.

thither together with a Supply of Ordnance Small Arms Stores and an Engineer.

Leeward Islands— For a Strong Squadron to be sent thither, the Regiment to be augmented and the Men allowed the Navy Allowance and for a Sum of Money to be granted to the Island of Antigua for compleating the Barracks.

For the Fortifications at English Harbour in Antigua to be repaired and kept up.

Virgin Islands— For a Small Ship of War to be Stationed there and for a Supply of Cannon Ammunition and Small Arms.

North Carolina— Two Reports of the Board of Ordnance with Estimates of the Expence of Stores for Fort Johnson and of Thirty Barrels of Gunpowder and a proportionable Quantity of Balls.

New Jersey— No Fortification or Place of Defence in the Province, nor any Cannon Small Arms or Military Stores belonging thereto.

Pensilvania— The Govr represents that this Province is in no Condition to defend itself, but must fall an easy Prey to almost any Invader, without the British Parliament interposes and by proper Laws establishes Order & Discipline amongst the People.

[*Endorsed*] List of Applications for *Stores* &c^a for the Several Colonies of North *America*. May, *1756*.

Captain William Eyre to Robert Napier

(A.L.S.)

Schenectady, 1st May 1756

Dear Sir

Inclosed I send you a Plan and Sections of Fort William-Henry, which will shew the Construction of that Fort better than that I gave Mr Pownall for your perusal, which no doubt you have seen before this Time.

I have made a Design by General Shirleys order for the further strengthening of Fort Edward, which I sent him to Boston, a Copy of which I gave to the Government of this Province by Sr Charles Hardy's desire, and shall by the Next Opportunity send you An Other.

We have lately been much alarmed for the Danger that Oswego was in, chiefly for want of Provisions, besides it's other Weakness's which we hear are not a little.

A Detachment of Our Reg^t with one from the 48th were sent two Days ago to Fort William-Henry, the Garison there consisting of New England Men, having declared the[y] Would Abandon it; and I think its more than Probable they will quit it immedeately upon the Regulars marching in, As the[y] seem not to be fond of red Coats.

I do not recolect whether I mentioned in my last a Complim^t This Province were pleased to make me; the General Assembly voted me thanks for my Services last Campaign, and as a Testimony of their Esteem, order'd a handsome Piece of Plate to be presented to me with the Arms of the Province, and a Genteel Motto Engraved on it, to shew the Sense (they are pleased to say they have) for my Endeavours last Summer.

I am sorry that things are not in more forwardness, I am afraid the most Part of this Campaign will be lost before we shall be in any Condition to strike a Blow, or even Attempt one.

I shall acquaint you with our first Motions, and every Other incident that may happen, tho' I make no doubt but you will have it from many more Hands clearer than I can send you.

This, I send by Col Dunbar as I hear he goes in the next Packet.

My best Respects to Mrs Napier. I am, Dr Sir, Your much obliged and Most Obe^t humb^l Servt.

WILL: EYRE

P.S. The Strength of our Regim^t is between Eight & Nine hundred Men at present, And I believe the 48th is pretty Nearly the Same.

[*Endorsed*] Engineer Eyre May 1 with a Plan of Fort Wm Henry R Jun 16 1756.

SIR CHARLES HARDY TO HALIFAX

(COPY)

Fort George New York 7th May 1756.

My Lord,

I have the Honor of your Letter of the 17th of January; the Opinion Your Lordship is pleased to mention of my Endeavours for the Public Service gives me the greatest Satisfaction in meeting with your Concurrence; I shall esteem myself happy if I equally succeed in that Part of my Administration that more particularly relates to His Majesty's Instructions; I have made some Efforts, which I could not persevere in, without endangering that necessary Influence over an obstinate Legislature, for the promoting the King's Service, in support of the Common Cause, in

Conjunction with, if I may use the Expression, much more stubborn Colonies; So circumstanced, His Majesty's rights & just Prerogatives remain in much the same State I found them, & if I may take Leave to offer my Opinion, Prudence requires such a Conduct at this critical Juncture; But Your Lordship may depend I shall embrace every Opportunity to enforce my Instructions, in recovering from the Assembly their unjust Encroachments upon the royal Prerogative; I have reason to think they expect as much, whenever Opportunity offers, however well we rubb on together now.

To enter upon an Inquisition, or Enquiry into the Causes of Differences between Men, or Provinces, at this time, would be an endless Task, as well as difficult, & must tend rather to heighten the Jealousies and private Piques, (founded perhaps upon private Interest) & produce still heavier Charges & recriminations, than answer any good Purpose; To consider the general Good ought to be the Attention of every honest Man, & no time ever more strongly called for an Exertion of the united Strength of this extensive Dominion to defend His Majesty's just rights, & remove a perfidious & vigilant Enemy from their Encroachments, an Enemy watching every Neglect, & improving every Advantage, & tho' small in Number, when compared to our numerous Inhabitants, still acting as one Body, under one Order of Controul, & united in that Order, put Us poor disunited Millions in Defiance, committing by the Means of their Indians, the most unheard of Barbarities, & laying waste our Lands without opposition.

This, My Lord, is the State of unhappy divided America. Your Lordship is desirous that a strong Army may appear in the Field; the Provinces that were concerned last Year, are raising a great many Men, intended to be 10,000 & I believe will fall little short of that Number; This may in appearance promise great Things, but I cannot flatter myself in much Success; Our Measures are slow; one Colony will not begin to raise their Men in an early time, doubting whether their Neighbours will not deceive them, in compleating their Levies so largely as they promised; By this Means we get late in the field; Our Magazines are not filled so soon as they ought; The present time too much evinces this Truth, as Your Lordship may readily imagine, when I tell You there was not one Man at Albany of the Provincial Forces the 30th of last Month, & consequently no Provisions & Stores could be sent to Fort William Henry for want of proper Escorts for the Convoys; and without, the French Indians make it impracticable to go; & when the whole Army is assembled for the Expedition against Crown Point, if to be executed by Provincials only, I much doubt if they can possibly succeed in such an

Enterprize; They must expect to encounter many more Difficulties than last Year; the French we shall find much stronger posted on Lake George, & Crown Point greatly strengthened by additional Works.

I am glad Your Lordship is of Opinion that Provincials alone are not capable of attacking fortified Posts; I wish they thought so too; There are other Evils attending those Forces, that want a remedy, namely, the want of sufficient Laws in the several Colonies to subject their Troops to military Discipline; This Province is singular in having such a Law, but, I fear, should the Law be rigorously executed, even if necessity called for it, it would have ill Consequences with the Forces ours may be acting with, even to cause a total Desertion in their Corps, or if not, it must end in such with our's. I am aware Your Lordship will say a late Act of Parliament subjects all Provincial Forces to military Discipline, & the Articles of War, when they are joined with the King's Forces; possibly the very reason why they will not, or do not like to join His Majesty's Forces; one would imagine the New England Governments acted now upon this Principal, & that they foresaw such a Junction; The General Court of the Massachusets, when they voted their Quota for the Crown Point Expedition, expressly say, "And that the Forces of this Government shall not be compelled to march southward of Albany, or Westward of Schenectady"; & I believe the other Governments have the same Resolution; this appears plainly to avoid joining the King's Troops; & I am the more confirmed in this Opinion, from what passed at a Meeting of the Commissioners at Albany to settle the Garrisons for Forts William Henry & Edward; At that Meeting I observed to Genl. Shirley, that I was of Opinion, that all Forces raised in the Provinces should be under the Command of His Majesty's Commander in chief, & that I was not without some Hopes of seeing such a Regulation; The Boston Commissioners took up the Argument, and advanced, that they hoped never to see the day, that their Troops should be under the Command of the King's Officer. The Absurdity of this Doctrine is very evident; & I think the Mischiefs arising from it are great, & tend manifestly to the Prejudice of His Majesty's Service; I shall beg Leave to lay before Your Lordship one Case that may offer, which will serve fully to prove this Argument.

The four New England Governments, & New York, have agreed to raise 10,000 Men for the Expedition to Crown Point; His Majesty has been graciously pleased to order such a Number of His regiments for the American Services, & probably may think it necessary to employ one or two Battalions upon this Service; The other services the Commander in chief may have in view must be disappointed, or not attended to if the one or two Battalions are not replaced by as many of the Provincial Forces; Pray, My Lord, where are they to come from? Under the Vote for raising the Men I have recited, the Men have it in their own Choice, & are supported in it by a Law of the Colony from whence they came, the Consequence is plain, that His Majesty's General cannot spare any Part of the regular Forces for a material Service, that cannot be executed without them, or if he does, he must forego every other for want of sufficient Force.

The Troops of this Province, 1,300 in Number, or, if necessary, 1,700, tho' voted for the Crown Point Expedition, are, I thank God, not under the restriction above, & I think, if the Commander in chief should think proper, to assist the Crown Point Expedition with one or two regiments, I can order them to join the King's Troops, or, if I should be mistaken in my Power of changing their Destination, I trust I shall have no Difficulty in obtaining the full Consent of the Legislature for it. One more Difficulty I beg Leave to mention to Your Lordship, with regard to the King's Forces & Provincials joining, that is in the first Place, (& particularly on the Crown Point Expedition) the Command. I have already mentioned the Sentiments of the New England People on this Point, & shall proceed to consider the Rank of the Officers, as established by His Majesty's Order in Council, in which no rank is allowed to the Field Officers of the Provincial Forces; their Captains and Subalterns are, by that order, to rank as youngest Captains and Subalterns of His Majesty's Forces; So far very proper & well, But what becomes of the Field Officers? They think themselves much injured in this Particular, & tho' they cannot expect to have Command over the Field Officers of the same rank, they still hope to be on an equal foot with them, as the Captains and Subalterns are with those of their Rank; I shall only add to this, that, on the other hand, the Captains of the regulars will think it hard to be commanded by Field Officers of Provincials, & the Field Officers of the regulars will likewise think so in having them on an equal foot; if this knotty & difficult Point could be once settled, I am of Opinion it would make the two Corps act more chearfully together. This brings me to offer to Your Lordship my Opinion of raising Men for His Majesty's Service in the Colonies; the present Method is attended with great Delays, & many Difficulties, most of the principal ones I have already mentioned, & are all to be obviated by what I shall now lay before You. All Men raised in the Provinces for His Majesty's Service, should be raised by the Commander in Chief, who may give Blank Commissions, in such Numbers he thinks proper, to the several Governors, to fill up with the Names of such Persons as may be qualified, & may have an Influence with the People of his Country; which in most Instances has more of Appearance in it than reality, which I shall make appear to Your Lordship presently. The Governors should be required to give the Officers all the Assistance in their Power; And the Assemblies should have nothing to do with raising the Men, but make the Grants to His Majesty, which should be drawn from the Treasury by the Governor, upon the application of the Commander in chief, and invested in him, & applied by him for the Purposes it was granted, and to leave the assemblies no Room to think of any Misapplication of their Money, the Commander in chief should render a true & faithfull Account to the Governors of all Moneys he received, who should lay the same before their respective Legislatures: by this Measure the whole force would immediately be under the Command of His Majesty's General, & consequently their Destination for any Services he may think it for His Majesty's Service to undertake; &, if His Majesty pleases, those Services to be concerted at a Council of War of the General and the Governors, previous to the opening the Campaign: This regulation may be attended with Difficulties, but, I believe, this, or something like it, to be the only Means by which we can avail ourselves of the many Evils arising from the disunited State of the Colonies in North America, in Matters of War.

With respect to the Augmentation of His Majesty's Forces, it is not altogether so bad as has been represented, the old regiments have recruited beyond Expectation, &, I believe, I may say, were once full 900 each, & as a Proof that American Officers cannot recruit or raise Men sooner than European, Shirley's & Pepperell's have never equalled them in Number; It is a Service that requires Knowledge; & the old Corps have shewn by their Vigilance & good management, that they can get Men, when the American Influence cannot. The great Dispute on this recruiting Service has been enlisting Servants, This has been carried to a great Height in Pensylvania and Maryland: I have always declared it was my Opinion, that His Ma^{ty} has an undoubted right to the voluntary Services of His Subjects; Govr. Morris thinks so too; but the Lawyers differ in it; they hold indented & bought Servants to be Property, &, as such, have no Will of their own, & cannot be withheld from their Masters; I much doubt if His Majesty's Attorney General was to try a Cause of this Sort, but he would find both Court of [and?] Jury of this Opinion; We have had very few Disputes of this kind in this Province. The only strong Argument in support of the Property of Servants is, that, if they are taken away, it may oblige the Colonies to furnish themselves with Negroes, which should most certainly be avoided, if possible; & I had rather the Servants were taken away, when the publick Service calls for it, tho' it may fall hard on some individuals, & no Importation of Negroes be allowed. This is a Point I am not [critical?] enough to determine, & it must be settled at home, & it might not be improper to instruct the Governors upon it, especially those Proprietary Governments, who are chiefly concerned.

It has given me great Satisfaction to find Lord Loudoun appointed to the chief Command in America; & tho' I have not the Honor of knowing His Lordship, he is a Soldier, as such, if he is not too violent, but will lower himself a little to the Disposition of the People of these Countries, (which there will be an absolute necessity for his doing, in some small Degree, to gain their Confidence) he will soon put Things in a proper Train; But, I fear, his Arrival here with his regiments will be full late; I could wish he had been here some little time to have looked round him, before he entered upon immediate Service.

Your Lordship's Determination of putting the Affairs of Management of the Six Nations into the Hands of Sir Wm. Johnson, is the only Means of uniting those Castles; It may be proper Sir William should, in some Degree, be under the Controul of this Government, in order to support its Influence with the Indians; Sir William Johnson has been truly represented to Your Lordship as the properest Person to be Agent, or Colonel, over them; He is both honest & brave, & I should do him great Injustice if I did not acquaint Your Lordship with his late Conduct; He is Colonel of the Militia of the County of Albany, consisting of two Battalions, has very lately made three Marches with Part of the Militia, & Indians upon Alarms that Oswego and some Magazines on the Mohawks river (one at the Oneida Carrying Place was destroyed before he could get to it's relief) was likely to be attacked by the French & their Indians; The Fort destroyed I suppose Genl. Shirley has transmitted an Account of, & as he is likely soon to lose his Command, shall say little to those Matters, any more than he left this City for Boston, without leaving the proper Orders for the Troops moving on any Occasion, which laid the Officers commanding them under great difficulties, created a great deal of Trouble to them, and me, & has occasioned our Militia to be harrassed; for I judged it necessary, from such a Neglect, to order Sir Wm. Johnson to march with the Militia to support any of the Posts, that might be in Danger. And a very extraordinary Circumstance happened so lately, that I cannot help informing Your Lordship of it; From the original settling the Garrisons of Forts William Henry & Edward, I have urged Genl. Shirley to let some of His Majesty's Forces take up their Winter Quarters in them, and have repeated this Application to him at Boston, but all to no Purpose; the Garrison of Fort William Henry were all New England Men, who were promised to be relieved early in the Spring, but, finding themselves deceived, declared their Intentions to the Commanding Officer of abandoning the Fort, & fixed their Day; Upon his sending this Intelligence to Albany, Colonels Gage & Burton judged it necessary to send 80 Men from their Corps, with proper Officers, all they could then spare, for the Security of that fort; These are joined by 125 of the Militia; Thus had this important Fort like to have been in Danger of falling into the hands of the Enemy; and even this I think too small a Garrison. I have wrote so to Genl. Shirley, who is now at Albany, and hope he will reinforce that Post, till the Provincial Forces can arrive to releive them.

The French Schemes, at present, seem to be to harrass the Parties going with Provisions to Oswego, and to Lake George, from the Number of Indians, that have lately infested the Waters & Road; What our Indians are about I do not comprehend; I have repeatedly urged Sir Wm. Johnson to press them to keep those Passages clear, & they have as often promised him, without effecting it, as Your Lordship will see by his late Conferences, a Copy of which I send Your Lordship's Board, to which I must beg Leave to refer, where Your Lordship will see what Steps have been, & are further to be, taken, to accommodate the Breach between Us & the Delaware Indians; if this can be happily accommodated, I hope it may give another Turn to our Affairs, & encourage the Cherokees to join the Southern Provinces.

I am &c &c.

Harry Gordon to Robert Napier
(A.L.S.)

Albany June 22nd 1756.

Sir

My Brother has informed me of your good offices in recommending me to His Royal Highness The Duke for a Lieutenancy—I think myself very deeply indebted in Gratitude to His Royal Highness for his Approbation and to you Sir for your Recommendation. I shall continue as much as [is] in my Power to exert myself, with Zeal, for the Service of the best of Princes, and endeavour to recommend myself to His Royal Highness's future Protection and to your Favour.

I send you by this Packet a Plan or rather a Sketch of the Country from Fort Edward on Hudsons River to Crown Point on Lake Champlain. This you may depend upon for conveying a true Idea of the Nature of these Places—I collected it while I was up at Lake George, where I beg'd Leave to goe to, upon hearing of the bad Condition that Fort and Garrison were in. The Plan was taken originally from a Draught Lieu^t Rogers Brother of the famous Capt had made—but if you desire to know particularly, I must refer you to a writing I have sent by this Packet, which I had not Time to copy as the drawing a Copy of the Plan for Lord Loudoun, and Designs for the Improvements of the Forts Edward and William Henry, which General Shirley has ordered, has kept me very hard at Work since I came down.

I intend to forward you by next Packet Copies of these Plans and Designs but have only had Time yet to draw them for General Shirley —that you may know the State of them you may peruse the writing above mentioned and a Copy of my Report which I have inclosed.

Mr. Mackellar is at Oswego and has sent down a much worse Report of that Place and we are only indebted to the Want of Ability or bad Conduct of the Enemy for its being in our Possession; as of itself it could have made no Defence—I wish Mr. Montresor may send you a Copy of his Report which could be of no bad Consequence if taken by our Enemies—but would expose their Folly in allowing us till this Time to put it in a proper Condition.

Our New England Friends are coming up very fast, their Returns are now 6400 and they expect 1500 more. Provisions are likewise ready so that I imagine we shall set forward very soon. I wish an Expedition had been encouraged from Virginia, a small Train of Artillery with Men of that Business and an Engineer would have brought 2 or 3000 Men together from those Provinces. If they had not taken Fort de Quesne they would have caused a Diversion and secured a good Fort to the Westward of the Mountains, which would have better covered these torn Provinces.

I am, with great Gratitude & Respect, Sir   Your most obliged and most obedient Servant

HARRY GORDON.

P.S. Young Williamson has assisted me much in my drawing he has all the Appearance of turning out extremely well.

REMARKS ON FORTS WILLIAM HENRY AND EDWARD, BY HARRY GORDON

(A.D.S.)

Remarks upon the Forts of William Henry and Edward of their Situation and what Works are most necessary to be added for the Strengthening of them—by Order of H. E. General Shirley.

Fort William Henry is situated at the South End of Lake George formerly called Lake St. Sacrement— It is a Work that consists of 4 Bastions with intermediate Curtains—and a Ditch eight foot deep and about thirty wide from the North-West Bastion to the South East one. The Work of the Ramparts and Parapets is faced up with large Logs of Timber bound together with smaller ones. The Rampart is in most Places fifteen Foot broad on the Curtains—the Bastions are filled up— The Parapets are, in the Faces of the Bastions most exposed, from fifteen to eighteen Foot thick, and on the Curtains from twelve to fifteen— The Rampart is between ten and eleven Foot high, and the Parapets from five to five and a half— There are Barracks for between three and four hundred Men— A Casemate under the left Flank of the South East Bastion, and another under the East Curtain. Likewise a Magazine under the N. E. Bastion towards the Lake and another smaller under the N. W. Bastion.

This Fort stands upon a high sandy Bank twenty Foot above the Lake which covers one Front— A Morass another which winds within fifty yds of the third; so that an Attack cannot be well carried against any but the Western Front. There is a rising Ground about 300 Yards distant before the South West Bastion which rises to between sixteen and eighteen Foot higher than the Ground the Fort stands upon— likewise the rising ground across the morass is higher.

In order to strengthen this Fort it is necessary to raise the Faces exposed to the rising Grounds three Foot higher—to cover and defend the South West Bastion and Curtain, from the Batteries an Enemy might raise upon the rising Ground, so as not to be battered in breach from thence— To effect this a Ravelin ought to be raised before the said Curtain, and a Countergarde before the S. W. Bastion. A Communication ought to be made to the Ravelin—which ought to be sunk under the Curtain to come out at the bottom of the Ditch—and to cross it by a Caponiere with steps up to ascend the Ravelin— A covered Way pallisadoed ought to be carried from the left Face of the Counterguard to a detached Redout, made last Year, very properly to scour the Bank above the Morass which was not seen by the Fort— This Redout for Want of the Communication being properly secured, is at present insultable, but may be made very necessary to scour the left Face of the Countergarde.

These proposed Works will entirely cover the exposed Front of the Fort (and without them a Breach may soon be made without shifting the Batteries from the rising Ground—but if these Works are added the Enemy must first destroy them and afterwards make their Batteries in them to make a Breach in the Bastions. A Casemate should be made under the left Face of the Ravelin which cannot be battered but obliquely. The covered Way will serve for a small retrenched Camp, or a Cover for Magazines of Provisions &ca.

Fort Edward is situated on Hudsons River 14 Miles below the other Fort above described. It is a Work of four Bastions as the other—that on the River below is rather a half Bastion, one Side is close to the River another to a small Rivulet which winds towards the third. The Gate is in the Curtain towards the Plain. There is a Gate likewise in the Side thats towards the Rivulet. There is a Ditch on the North and East Sides, and a Row of Pallisades (which has been the Preservation of the Fort) goes quite round between the Ditch & the Parapet—with their Points inclining towards the Country. There is no Rampart to the Fort and the Parapet is not above eight Foot thick in some Places it has washed to six a Top. The Parapet is from eight to ten Foot high reared up of Sand, without any regular Banquet—or any kind of facing. There is a Magazine in the East Bastion, which is only covered with one layer of Logs. The River Hudson divides itself a little above the Fort and forms a large Island opposite to it. The Branch of the River between the Fort and the Island is about sixty Yards across. The Island a hundred, and the other Branch seventy.

In order to strengthen this Fort the Parapets ought to be faced with Logs as at Fort William Henry, and made from 14 to 16 Foot thick— the Rampart on the East & South Sides ought to be raised so as to have Casemates under the Curtains—and proper Cover for 2 Magazines under the 2 Bastions—A Ravelin constructed before the Gate of the North Curtain—and a Redout detached before the East Curtain to discover the Banks of the Morass which are high—this Redout to communicate by a Sally Port under its Curtain and a covered Way well pallisaded— a covered Way may be carried from the Redout to the Ravelin and prolonged to the River. A Hornwork ought to be made in the Island with its Lunette across the Western Branch. This Work will secure the Passage of the River and cover Storehouses to lodge Provisions &ca. Care must be had to raise the Floors of the Storehouses as the River has been known to rise over the Island. Landing Places must be made for Boats in the Island. The Curtain towards the River must be secured against Floods as the Ground the Fort stands upon is rather lower than the Island. A small Redout may be made across the Rivulet the better to Flank the Hornwork.

These Works as the Timber is nigh may be soon Constructed, and without them the Passage of the River (The Design of this Fort) cannot be covered properly for communication nor prevented our Enemies as they may goe along with any Number of Battoes or Canoes down the Western Branch without being discovered by the Fort. If it is supposed ever to be attacked the Out Works will add greatly to the Strength of it —seeing, in such Case it would have all the upper Inhabitants of the Province of New York to defend it—whose principal Frontier this Fort certainly is—and with the addition of these Works, it could with great Numbers & Risque only, be invested.

As to the Works to be added to Fort William Henry—they seem to me so necessary for a Defense—that without them the Enemy can in one Night open Trenches make a Battery within 280 Yards of the Bastion which entirely commands it and which without shifting may soon make a Breach.

HARRY GORDON   Engineer

MEMOIRE NARRATIF DE MR. T:T: [1] TOUCHANT LES SERVICES QU'IL A RENDU À LA NOUVELLE ECOSSE

(A.L.S.)

Monsieur,

La bienveillance que Vous me temoignés m'engage à Vous écrire, et cette généreuse sensibilité pour les peines d'autrui que l'on remarque en Vous, et qui fait l'essence de tout honnête homme, me persuade que touché de ma Situation, Vous vous porterés à m'accorder l'honneur de vos bons offices. Mais comme la prudence veut du discernement dans les graces que l'on fait, et qu'elle défend de s'intéresser pour celui que l'on ne connoît pas, Je vais rappeller icy quelqu'unes des circonstances qui m'ont conduit à l'état où je me trouve.

A la fin de la derniere guerre pendant laquelle j'ai exercé differentes emplois distingués, Je fus invité par le Comte de Raymond de l'accompagner à l'Isle Royale dont il étoit Gouverneur. Je lui servis de Secretaire. Je le fis valoir, Je lui fus de la plus grande utilité. Il n'executa

[1] Thomas Pichon (1700–1781), a native of Vire, Normandy, went to Cape Breton in 1751 as the secretary of the governor, Count de Raymond. In 1753 he became Commissary at Fort Beauséjour, and shortly afterwards began to sell information to the British. He used the name of Thomas Tyrell, and as such settled in England in 1758, where he lived until his death. His papers are preserved in the Public Archives of Nova Scotia and at Ottawa, and are to be printed shortly by Dr. J. C. Webster. There are four Pichon items in the Cumberland Papers: two are copies, with insignificant changes, of papers in the Pichon collection; a third, describing the soundings of Louisbourg harbor, will appear in Dr. Webster's volume; the fourth varies sufficiently in phrasing and subject-matter from a similar *mémoire* in the Pichon collection to justify its inclusion here.

cependant aucune des promesses qu'il m'avoit faites en France. Je re-
fusai de l'y suivre et il me laissa à Louisbourg en affectant d'ignorer ce
qu'une généreuse Equité exigeoit delui. L'Intendant de cette Isle m'envoya aussitôt au fort de Beausejour, aujourd'hui de Cumberland, pour
y faire les fonctions de Commissaire, d'ordonnateur et de subdelegué
de l'Intendance. M. Scott [2] que j'avois vû à Louisbourg et qui comman-
doit au fort Lawrence proche le fort françois, m'invita à l'aller voir.
Dans nos conversations sur les intérêts respectifs des deux Couronnes
dans l'Amerique du Nord, il me fit entendre qu'il pouvoit occasionner
ma fortune qu'il en connoissoit des moyens très sûrs, et que Je n'aurois
jamais lieu de me repentir de m'être dévoué pour ce qu'il me proposoit.
Les assurances réiterées qu'il me donnoit, de me mettre dans le plus
agréable bienêtre, que rien ne manqueroit à ma Satisfaction et que ce
qu'il me promettoit, il le faisoit au nom du Gouvernement en général,
m'engagérent à me livrer entierement à tout ce qu'il desiroit de moi.

Nous établîmes une correspondance qui fut des plus suivies. Il fut
successivement averti de toutes les ménées des prêtres françois pour ex-
citer les Sauvages à faire coup Sur les Anglois, Ce que j'ai toujours
détourné. Il le fut également de tout ce qui se passoit concernant la
Colonie et les Commandans de cette partie de l'Acadie &c. Il eut des
memoires aussi instructifs qu'interessans Sur l'état actuel des forts
françois, sur les habitans refugiés et sur ceux qui restoient dans la partie
de l'Acadie déja sous la domination Angloise. Il Sçait quelle confiance
ces bonnes gens avoient en moi.

Je lui donnai peu avant son départ un mcmoire fort détaillé sur les

[2] George Scott's parentage is unknown. He may have been a native New Englander.
He was commissioned ensign in the British army January 24, 1741. On September 1,
1745, he became captain-lieutenant, perhaps in Shirley's regiment of foot raised after
the capture of Louisbourg, which went on the establishment that month. On April
30, 1746, he became a captain in Shirley's regiment, went on half-pay when the regiment was broken in 1748, and three years later exchanged with Captain John Winslow
of the 40th regiment (June 28, 1751). In 1753 he was listed as a justice of the peace and
commandant of the garrison at Chignecto. Selected in 1755 to command the second
battalion of Shirley's regiment of New Englanders sent to Nova Scotia, he was praised
by Monckton as an officer "on all occassions of the greatest Service to me, as well from
his Knowledge of the Indians & Inhabitants as from his activity & good Conduct."
(Monckton's Journal of the Siege of Fort Beauséjour, printed in J. C. Webster, *The
Forts of Chignecto*). On July 28, 1757, he wrote Loudoun an anonymous letter,
which he afterwards acknowledged, containing cogent arguments against proceeding
with the projected attack on Louisbourg. He was rewarded with the post of Major
of Brigade. Later that winter he drew up a plan for clothing and accoutering troops
serving in America, and reducing the number of firing motions (Henry E. Huntington Library, LO 6927). In 1758 he was put in command of a body of rangers and light
infantry appointed to act as rangers, and in 1759 he commanded the rangers in Wolfe's
army. He became lieutenant-colonel in America July 11, 1761, though still gazetted as
first captain in the 40th regiment. In 1766 he received a grant of 20,000 acres in East
Florida (*Acts Privy Council, Colonial, 1766–1783*, p. 590). The *Army List* of 1767 is
the last in which his name appears.

mesures que je croyois qu'on pouvoit prendre pour reussir à s'emparer des forts françois, Je peux avancer icy qu'on a Suivi dans la plus grande partie le projet que j'en avois fait. Je devrois donc être regardé comme un des instrumens qui a servi à cette importante Conquête.

Le Capitaine Hussey Successeur de M. Scott et chargé dela même correspondance, recut également quantité de Lettres et de memoires, copies de tout ce qu'envoyoit l'abbé le Loutre à la Cour de france et de ce qu'il en recevoit.

M'étant procuré avec autant de peines que de dépenses les noms des Sauvages repandus dans l'Acadie, le recensement noms par noms des habitans françois et de leurs familles, je les fis passer à ce Capitaine.

Je lui remis presque à Son arrivée le plan que j'avois fait faire de l'Isthme et entier des Bayes Verte et Beaubassin de leurs environs, des deux forts françois qui y sont Situés, et les distances les plus exactes de chaques endroits. J'y joignis un memoire et des observations particulieres. Cet ouvrage fut très utile pour la reduction des deux forts.

Je pourrois m'en rapporter sur tout cecy aux temoignages de Mrs Boscawen, Lawrence, Scott et Hussey, Si j'ignorois que vous êtes déjá instruit, Monsieur, de bien d'autres détails que j'omêts. Mais l'on n'a guères sçû qu'en partie tout ce que j'ai risqué pour continuer la plus difficile correspondance que je vous assure m'avoit couté considerablement pour rompre en visiere à plus d'un envieux observateur.

Je fis ralentir les ouvrages qu'on avoit projetté de faire et d'ajouter tant au fort de Beausejour qu'à celui de Gasparaux pour leur défense.

Le premier ayant été en quelque façon investi et l'effet des bombes s'étant fait sentir, les habitans au nombre de cinq cent que l'on y avoit enfermé pour aider à le défendre, forcerent par mes conseils le Commandant Vergord à demander à Capituler ce qui abrégea beaucoup ce Siége. Ce fut aussi par mes conseils que le Commandant du fort Gasparaux se rendit sur la Seule Lettre qui fut portée par un habitant et que j'avois aidé à dicter.

Un grand nombre des Acadiens les plus guerriers et dont les familles sont les plus nombreuses, projettoient de se retirer avec les Sauvages Abenakis Sur la Riviere St Jean; leur secret m'ayant été découvert, on trouva les moyens de les retenir.

Depuis la reduction des deux forts, M. le Colonel Munckton et M. Scott furent toujours informés dans le plus grand détail de tout ce qui pouvoit interesser par rapport aux habitans &c.

Lorsqu'il fut question de l'expedition de la Riviere St Jean où les françois alloient commencer un nouveau fort, j'ai remis à M. de Munkton le plan tout nouvellement fait pour la Cour de france, tant du premier fort françois que des Côtes dela mer, de l'embouchure de cette riviere, de son entrée et de ses profondeurs.

Etant convenu avec Mrs de Munkton et Scott, pour cacher necessairement l'espece d'intelligence où Nous étions, et afin que je fusse toujours à portée de continuer à être également utile, que je Serois fait prisonnier de guerre, je fus transferé au fort Lawrence, ensuite à celui de Pegiguitk. J'ai recû dans ces divers endroits la visite d'un grand nombre d'Acadiens qui me demandoient conseil sur le parti qu'ils avoient à prendre. En qualité de prisonnier je ne pouvois, leur disois-je, leur en donner, ce qui les jettois dans la plus grande inquiétude. Je leur representois cependant qu'ils devoient connoître bien mieux que moi, leurs veritables intérêts, considerer l'avenir; qu'ils avoient des familles dont la transmigration dans d'autres pays, fût-ce en france, ne pourroit que leur préjudicier considerablement; qu'il étoit triste pour eux de n'avoir pas été en état de faire comparaison des deux dominations, Angloise et françoise; que la premiere étoit infiniment plus douce que l'autre à tous égards, &c.

Transporté depuis à Halifax et y ayant trouvé beaucoup de prisonniers françois, Je continuai de passer pour prisonnier, et Je fis entendre aux principaux qu'en consequence dela capitulation de Beausejour Je devois être renvoyé à Louisbourg aussitôt après l'examen de quelques papiers qu'on supposoit m'avoir été remis par l'abbé le Loutre. Dans cette idée plusieurs de ces françois me chargerent de Lettres, memoires &c. pour faire passer à Louisbourg et en france. La fameuse Savonnette qui contenoit le plan d'Halifax et un projet pour surprendre ce poste &c, ouvrage de M. Hocquart et des trois Ingenieurs françois, me fut aussi remise. Je la rendis aussitôt à M. l'Amiral Boscawen ainsi que les Lettres et pacquets cachettés des autres françois. La découverte de ce projet de M. Hocquart, des Ingenieurs, &c de s'emparer ou de détruire Halifax, de bruler les vaisseaux qui devoient hyverner dans ce havre &c, parut d'une telle importance qu'il en fût ordonné un jour d'action de grace à Halifax.

L'on m'a Souvent flatté dela Satisfaction qu'on m'assuroit avoir de toutes mes operations, ne puis-je donc pas paroître desirer l'accomplissement des promesses qui m'ont été faites, de me procurer un état Solide et avantageux? Ne puis-je pas me flatter de le meriter? La Conquête, pour ainsi dire, de toute la nouvelle Ecosse, l'importance dont cette partie del'Amerique doit être pour toutes les autres Colonies Angloises, ainsi que pour la grande Bretagne, par les consequences qui en resultent et par les avantages qu'on en doit tirer dès à present et pour l'avenir; tout ne Semble t'il pas m'autoriser à demander une recompense proportionnée?

J'avois un état en france où J'ai encore du bien. Je devois être chargé dela Subdelegation, del'Intendance dans plusieurs Colonies del'Amerique du Nord, postes qui m'auroient assurement été avantageux. Je les ai abandonné, J'en fais de même de tout ce que j'ai en france où Je ne dois plus penser à retourner. J'ai fait en outre des pertes très considerables lors et par la prise de Beausejour, &c.

Voilà, Monsieur, ce que je n'ai point craint de confier à votre discretion; votre façon de penser Sage et judicieuse m'est connue. Je me persuade que ces détails que j'aurois desiré pouvoir abreger, vous exciteront à continuer de vous interesser pour moi. Je voudrois bien continuer d'être de quelque utilité. Ce fut dans cette vûë que M. Boscawen, qui connoît tout mon zéle à cet égard me fit venir à Londres. Je compterai donc beaucoup Sur vos démarches si vous avés la bonté d'en faire pour moi; vous obligerés un homme reconnoissant et qui s'étudiera toute sa vie à vous donner des preuves de son attachement.

J'ai l'honneur d'être bien respectueusem^t
Monsieur, Votre très humble et très obéissant Serviteur
T.T.........

Le 27 Juin 1756

BENJAMIN FRANKLIN TO SIR EVERARD FAWKENER [1]

(COPY)

New York, July 27, 1756.

Honourable Sir,

I wrote you a very long Letter by the Harriot, Capt. Bonnell, to which I have now little to add. It was in answer to those I had been favour'd with from you.

Being requested, by a Letter from Mr Pownall before he left England, to be here at Lord Loudon's Arrival, I came accordingly about the time he was expected, but waited near 5 Weeks before he arrived, which was not till last Friday. I am pleased, however, that I staid so long, as I have had the Satisfaction of several Conferences with his

---

[1] Sir Everard Fawkener was one of the Postmasters General, and Cumberland's private secretary. He died in 1758, at the age of seventy-four, and his widow, the natural daughter of General Churchill whom he had married as a young girl in 1747, became the wife of Governor Thomas Pownall.

Lordship on American Affairs, and hope I may be able, on my Return, to do him a Piece of Service that he requests of me. He seems to me very well fitted for the Charge he has undertaken, and I promise myself the King's Affairs on this Side will prosper in his Hands. He sail'd yesterday for Albany, and I return home tomorrow.

The publick Papers, which I inclose, contain all the material News. The Provincials under General Winslow, are on their March to Lake George, in order to attack Crown Point. They declin'd the Assistance of the Regulars, who therefore only follow them, and take the Posts they leave, to be ready to support them in case of any Accident. The Provincials, it seems, apprehend, that Regulars join'd with them, would claim all the Honour of any Success, and charge them with the Blame of every Miscarriage. They say, that last Year, at Nova Scotia, 2000 New England Men, and not more than 200 Regulars, were join'd in the Taking BeauSejour; yet it could not be discovered by the Acc^t sent home by Govr Lawrence, and publish'd in the London Gazette, that there was a single New England Man concern'd in the Affair. It is suppos'd by some, that they will now exert themselves to the utmost; and that the Joining to them a Regiment or two of the Regulars, would have discouraged and dispirited them exceedingly, and thereby *weaken'd* more than it would strengthen them. The general Opinion, however, of the Regular Officers, is, that they will be beaten and re-puls'd; for they must expect to meet at Crown Point almost the whole Force of Canada. A few Weeks will now determine this Matter.

The Naval Force of the Enemy on Lake Ontario, is represented as superior to ours; but as we have more Vessels fitting out, and almost ready, 'tis hop'd the Scale will soon turn there in our Favour. The Check the French receiv'd in their Attack on our Battoes, it's thought will have a good Effect; and discourage them a little in their Scheme of cutting off our Communication with Oswego. It is agreed by all, that Bradstreet & his Battoe-men behav'd very well.

The last Act of Parliament,[2] that authorizes the Enlisting of bought Servants in America, tho' it directs that the Officers who inlist them, shall pay the Masters the prime Cost of the Servant, deducting for the time he has serv'd a proportional Part of the Sum (which perhaps is the best general Rule that could be fix'd) or return the Servant, the Master paying back the Enlisting Money; will nevertheless intirely destroy the Trade of bringing over Servants to the Colonies, either from the British Islands or Germany. Because no Master for the future can af-

[2] 29 Geo. II, c. 35.

ford to give such a Price for Servants as is sufficient to encourage the Merchants to import them, while the following Inconveniencies and Hardships still remain on the Master, viz

1. Many of our Servants are purchased young of their Parents, who, coming with large Families, bind some of their Children to Tradesmen and Farmers, in order to raise a Sum to pay the Freights of the whole, and keep themselves free; their Children too being by this Means well provided for, as they are taught some Business with which they may obtain a future Livelihood. Now the last Year or two of such a Servant's Time is of more Value to the Master than three or four of the first Years; and the Allowance of a Part of the first Cost, in proportion only to the Time remaining unserv'd, is therefore by no means an adequate Compensation to the Master.

2. When a Man's Servants are taken from him, he knows not where to find Hands to assist him in cultivating his Land, or carrying on his Business, hired Labourers or Journeymen not being so readily obtain'd here at any time as in England, People chiefly depending on their bought Servants, and in the present Case the Labourers and Journeymen had been before rendered much scarcer by the long continued Recruitings. Thus many Masters are reduced to the greatest Distress in their Affairs, by a total Stop put to their Business. And where the Business is carried on in different Branches, depending on one another, the Taking of one Servant may render useless several that are left. For instance, Taking the Spinners from a Ropewalk, the other Servants who know not how to spin, tho' they do not inlist, cannot go on with the Business, and must stand idle. Taking the Compositors from a Printing House (my own Case) the Servants who are Pressmen, tho' left behind, not knowing how to compose, must remain idle. Therefore the Allowance directed by the Act for the Time the Spinner or Compositor had to serve, is by no means a Composition for the Damage done.

3. If the Officer declines paying the proportional Sum, directed by the Act to be paid, he is to return the Servant, and the Master is to pay back the Inlisting Money. The Servant very probably has spent it in Drink with the Serjeant and his Fellow Recruits, so it must be out of the Master's Pocket: Then there being no Provision to prevent the Servant's Inlisting again, he may repeat the Frolick as often as he pleases. If the same Officer should generously refuse (for he is not forbid) to inlist the same Servant twice, another Officer may inlist him, not knowing that he had been inlisted before, and discharged; and so the Master may be continually harass'd with the Expence and

Trouble of Recovering his Servant, till he chuses rather to lose him intirely.

Upon the whole I see clearly, that the Consequence will be, the Introduction of Slaves, and thereby weakening the Colonies, and preventing their Increase in White Inhabitants.

How much better would it be to recruit in Britain, Ireland or Germany: For by that means the Colonies would be strengthened!

I write this in Obedience to your Commands that I should give my Opinion freely to you, on Publick Measures relating to America.

I hope Mr Hunter is with you by this Time, and that the Voyage will answer the Expectations of his Friends, in restoring his Health. He sail'd about the 20th of June, in the Anna, Capt. Randolph, from Virginia. He will settle our Accounts with the Office, and inform you of everything relating to it on this Side. I am, with the greatest Respect, Honble Sir, Your most obedient and most humble Servant

B Franklin

A Journal of the Transactions at Oswego from the 16th of May to the 14 of August 1756. By Patrick Mackellar [1] Eng'r en Second to the Expedition

(A.D.)

May 16 I arrived at 2 a Clock in the afternoon, with Lieut. Colonel Broadstreet,[2] & a Convoy of Battoes with Provisions Naval Stores &c.

[1] Patrick Mackellar (1717–1778) got his training as an engineer at Minorca, where he was stationed from 1739 to 1754. Of the British engineers who served in America in the Seven Years' War, Mackellar was probably the ablest. Engineer en second with Braddock's expedition and at the siege of Louisbourg in 1758, he acted as chief engineer at Quebec in 1759, in Canada in 1760, at Martinique in 1762, and at Havana in 1763. Four of these sieges demanded the use of European methods; only at Oswego was Mackellar called upon to adapt his knowledge to meet frontier requirements.

[2] Captain John Bradstreet (c. 1711–1774) of the 51st regiment may be identical with that Jean-Baptiste Bradstreet, born December 21, 1714, and baptized March 12, 1716, the son of Lieutenant Edward Bradstreet of the 40th regiment in Nova Scotia (died December, 1718) and Agathe de la Tour (Murdoch, Hist. of Nova Scotia, I, 263, 354). John bought an ensigncy in the 40th regiment in 1735, played an important part in the Louisbourg expedition of 1745, and became a captain in Pepperrell's regiment raised in 1746 and lieutenant governor of St. John's, Newfoundland. In 1755 Shirley put him in charge of transportation to Oswego, recognizing, as did later commanders in chief, his unusual qualities as a leader of irregulars. His title as lieutenant colonel was at this time unofficial; he was one of several officers who suffered from Shirley's unauthorized promotions. Not until December, 1757, when he became a deputy quartermaster general, did he gain the rank he had coveted for eleven years. Ambitious and aggressive, his superiors realized that he

In the Evening I visited Fort Ontario and took Memorandums of its Defects.

17th In the Morning I visited Fort Oswego and Fort George and took Memorandums of their Defects. About ten a Clock, I reported the Defects of the Three Forts to Lieut. Colonel Mercer and shewd him my Instructions; I then demanded eight Men to assist my taking a Survey of the Place, and all the Men that coud be spared, to begin the Repairs of the Works next day; He told me that the Master Builder demanded more Men to carry on the Business of the Shiping, than he coud possibly spare from the Dutys of the Garrison, that he was obliged from the Misfortunes that had happen'd of Scalping and taking the Workmen in the Woods, always to send strong Covering Partys along with them; but that he woud call a Council of War in the Afternoon, and settle what ought to be done.

In the Afternoon He called a Council of War, vizt Lieut. Colonels Littlehales and Broadstreet and Captain Broadley[3] Commanding Officer of the Vessels upon the Lake, I was desired to attend. Before the Council of War, He represented the weak condition of the Garrison, the impossibility of sending sufficient Covering Partys with the Workmen into the Woods, and to give Men for the Repairs of the Fortifications at the same time; He likewise represented the Want of Money. It was resolved, that the Business of the Shiping was the most essential and therefore to be forwarded with most Despatch, that the Repairs of the Works shoud be postponed, that the Party at the Falls (left there by Colonel Broadstreet to build a Fort) shoud be called in, if Colonel Schuyler's Regiment was not arrived there, in its way to Oswego; and that the Want of Money shou'd be represented to General Shirley by the first Opportunity, and that the Commanding Officer shoud endeavour to prevail with Mr. Lewis[4] the Commissary to continue the payment of the Workmen, untill his Excellency's pleasure shoud be known.

This morning Lieut. Blair of the 51st Regiment being posted with a Party of Men above the Rift to cover the Battoes was attackd by a Party of Indians; Lieut. Blair and one of his Men were killed and another Mortaly Wounded; upon the Alarm of the Fire, there was a

---

"had to be rode with a bridel." In 1758 he planned and carried out the successful expedition against Fort Frontenac. Appointed colonel in America in 1762, he died a major general in the British army.

[3] For the conduct at Oswego of Captain Housman Broadley of the Royal Navy, see W. L. Grant, "The Capture of Oswego by Montcalm in 1756: A Study in Naval Power . . . ," Royal Society of Canada, Transactions (1914), ser. III, Vol. viii, p. 193.

[4] Francis Lewis, later a signer of the Declaration of Independence.

Reinforcement sent from the Garrison, (of which one of our Mohawk Indians was killed); upon their Appearance the Enemy went off and left two of theirs killed who were scalped by our people.

18th   I visited the Powder Magazine and took Memorandums of its Defects. Colonel Broadstreet return'd this Morning for Schenectady with his Battoes.

19th   This day very rainy which put a Stop to the Work of the Shiping.

20th   Lieut. Cooling came in with the Party left at the Falls according to the Resolution of the Council of war of the 17th Instant. Mr. Sowers the Engineer came by Water, and had a Battoe of Tools oversett.

21st   I reconoitred the Ground round Fort Oswego and Fort Ontario.

22nd   I reconoitred the Ground along the Lake to the Westward and up the River towards the Rift.

23d   ———

24   About eleven at Night a Party of Indians attacked a small Encampment of Battoemen at about forty yards distance from the Town, they took two Prisoners, killed four, three of whom they scalped, they likewise scalped a Soldier who lay drunk asleep (he afterwards recover'd) and wounded two more. When they found the Garrison alarm'd they went off, but had pursued some of the Men into the Street. The Garrison continued under Arms till two in the Morning.

25th   In the Afternoon Colonel Schuyler [5] & Major Kineer arrived, the former with about 170 Men of his Regiment, the Major with a Party of (   ),[6] they brought a convoy of Battoes with Naval Stores and Provisions.

        There arrived likewise a Drove of Oxen.

        I writ the following Letter to Mr. Montresor Chief Engineer:—

                                        Oswego 25th May 1756
        "Sir
        I arrived here the 16th, but untill now, have not had an opportunity of writing to you, since I examined the Condition of the Fortifications, which I send you an Account of that you may be prepared to speak to the Commander in Chief about them and receive his farther Directions.

[5] Peter Schuyler of the New Jersey regiment.
[6] Space left in manuscript.

"Old Fort Oswego is according to the Plans you have seen, a Blockhouse surrounded with a Wall at a Small distance from it, both of dry rubble but pointed upon the Joints here and there with Mortar; there are three Guns mounted within the outward Wall to fire through Loopholes in the rounding towards the River, but they must not be fired for fear of bringing down the Wall, which is already crack'd in three places from top to Bottom, these are the only Guns within this Work.

"The Hornwork built last Year and the Raveline before it, are badly laid out, the Flanks of the half Bastions do not defend the opposite Faces, the Wings are enfiladed from end to end, the Terreplain seen almost throughout, the North wing towards the Lake quite open, with only a small Cliff of Earth and Rock where any Body may run up and down; the South wing towards the Town was closed somewhat in the form of a Tenaille last Winter, in Fascine and wattled Work fitted with Earth, which I think some Improvement, it has eight or ten Embrazures towards the Town; the Gorge of the Raveline is so close upon the Curtain, and the whole of it rais'd so high that it obstructs the Fire, at least of two thirds of both the Flanks and ye Curtain, and makes no Defence itself, there being only a Rampart raisd to a great Hight without any Parapet, the retaining Wall within which is of dry rubble, and the scarp without which is of Sod, have both given way; The Faces of it terminate upon the Curtain some Toises within the Flanks.

"The Fort upon the Hill on the Town Side called Fort Oswego seems to have been designed a Square with Bastions, but there is so little of it done and that so roughly, that one cannot say what it might be if finished, the Ditch is sunk on two Sides about five feet deep and the Earth thrown in and supported with Wattle Work about three feet high, this gives a rough Form to one Bastion and two half Bastions; the other two sides are not touched upon but for the present inclosed with a bad Pallisade which is continued round the whole leaving out the Figure of the Bastions; there are Huts within for lodging the Men and Officers, tho in my opinion the Work is by no means tenable, and quartering Men there is I think runing a great risk of losing them.

"The Town if it may be called so, is open to the south and

west Sides, and of Course exposed to the Enemy's Scalping
Partys, one of which a few Nights ago came in to the very
street and scalped killed wounded and took eight Men Battoemen and Soldiers.

"The Powder Magazine is so bad that I think the Powder
must be considerably dammaged, it is so crouded at present
that it cannot be narrowly examined, but it being sunk four
feet in the Ground, and the top one side and one Gable End
coverd with Sod, there must certainly be a great deal of Mois-
ture got into it.

"The Fort on the east Side of the River called Fort Ontario
is stockaded with good Timber and the joints squared, but
the Plan is bad, its other Defects are as follows.—The Barracks for the Men and officers are mostly built against the
Stockade which loses so much of the Fire, the Gate is placed
in an Angle and flankd on neither Side, which must be the
Case in a Star as all the Angles are dead; there is no Banquet,
nor Loop holes cut, but for the Canon, however there is a
Gallery carryd round the top where the Buildings do not
interfere, which has a good Command and renders the Work
capable of a tolerable Defence against small Arms.

"I intended according to his Excellency's orders to have set
about repairing the most material & least costly of these Defects immediately after my arrival, and spoke to Colonel Mercer the Command^g Officer upon that head, who immediatly
consulted some of the principal Officers, and it was agreed,
that as they were under apprehensions of a siege, the work of
the Shiping was the most requisite to be forwarded, and that
as the Weakness and Sickliness of the Garrison would not
admitt of their giving a sufficient Number for that service, the
other Works must be postponed untill the Hurry of that Business shoud be got over.

"The principal Defects I intend to go upon when I can
get Workmen, are those of the Horn Work and Fort Ontario;
the former of these notwithstanding its Defects, is the only
work on this Side that we can mount Guns upon; the Repairs I intend [in] it, are Traverses to secure the Enfilade,
securing the North Wing, and making platforms and Embrazures where necessary; I think the Raveline must be de-
molished intirely.

"The Repairs in Fort Ontario are soon done except that

of removing the Buildings, which cannot be done without removing the Troops, it is besides too expensive a Work to go upon without a particular Order.

"Fort Oswego I can consider as a Work begun only, and what is done does rather more harm, than good, I shall therefore defer doing anything to it, untill I receive his Excellency's orders, it is in fact the same as building a new Fort.

"The Powder Magazine and that of inclosing the Town will likewise be Articles of too much Expence to enter upon without orders, and sending Plans which I cannot do at present.

"I shall as soon as the hurry of the shiping will allow me a few hands, take an exact Survey of both sides, where I shall lay down whatever I may see necessary both in the building and fortifying way, for his Excellency's and your Perusal; in the former of these I do not expect to succeed to my own satisfaction, the Situation is very unfavourable, for the Ground where a Fort woud be of most general use, is overlooked on two Sides and mostly within Musquet Shot—, and building little Forts here and there at a distance from each other, ought I think to be avoided for many reasons if possible. I shou'd be very glad you had seen the Ground.

"I writ to you from the Carrying place, to acquaint you with the Orders I had received from the General of laying out three Forts. That at the head of Wood Creek where Bulls Fort stood, I hear is finished but the Ditch not according to my plan; that at the mouth of Wood Creek, there was no time nor hands to enter upon, and that at Oswego Falls we were obliged to leave off, after digging the Trench and cuting some of the Stockades, the Party for that service being wanted to reinforce this Garrison.

"I was very unfortunate in the Tools I brought along with me, all the Spades and a good many Pickaxes and felling Axes were destroyed or lost at Herchkermers, Williams's Fort and Bull's Fort; and at the Falls there was among many others no less than three of the Tool Battoes oversett or sunk, some of the things were recoverd, but lost the Hambro' Line, the Nails and the best part of our remaining Pickaxes and Felling Axes; these Articles with some Spades, we shoud be glad to have a supply of as soon as an opportunity offers, and I shou'd be glad the felling Axes were of a different kind from the last, which are the worst I ever saw.

"When you get a Supply of Stationary Ware we shall be glad of some, We have scarce any left, and pray dont let the Paymaster forget to send us some Money, which we find a more Necessary Article than we imagined.

"I have been ill for these three Weeks past, first of an Ague and now of a Flux, I am weaken'd a good deal, but I think recovering.

"I shall write to the General by this opportunity, but as I cannot trouble him with all the particulars in your Letter, you'l be so good as wait upon him, and if he desires to know them you'l please to inform him. I am" etc.

26th The Garrison upon the Business of the Shiping
          I this day writ the following Letter to his
          Excellency General Shirley.

                                        Oswego 26th May 1756
Sir

I arrived here the 16th Instant & Communicated your Excellency's Orders Concerning the Works to the Commanding Officer, who after consulting some of the principal Officers then upon the Spot, finds that dispatching the Shiping, is at present of more immediate Consequence than repairing the Works, and as the former Requires all the hands off Duty, the latter has been postponed.

"I have since that time examined the several works and find them very defective, especially those on the west Side; it woud give your Excellency too much trouble to read the particulars, but I have transmitted them to the Chief Engineer, who will lay them before your Excellency if required. I can consider Fort Oswego only as a Work begun, and as it requires a good deal of Expence to finish it, I shall forbear doing anything to it, without your Excellency's farther Orders. When the hurry of Business for the Shiping is over, I shall go on with some of the Repairs in the other Works that are most necessary and least Expensive. The Commanding Officer will use his Endeavours to reduce the price of Labour, it chiefly depends upon him; the want of ready Money may be some obstacle to it, but this difficulty I presume your Excellency will soon remedy.

"As soon as I can get a few hands, I shall take a plan of the whole and lay down such particulars as I shall think Necessary, with Estimates for your Excellency's Consideration.

"Colonel Broadstreet woud inform your Excellency that Wood Creek Fort was left in hand, I hear it is finished since; he had not Men to begin the Fort at the Mouth of Wood Creek; and after the Fort at the Falls was begun upon, there was a Necessity of taking off the Party to reinforce this Garrison. I am Your Excellencie's." &c.

There was an alarm on Ontario Side this afternoon of some Indians being seen skulking about the Swamp, but they went off without making any attempt.

27th   The Garrison employed upon the Business of the Shiping.
A Convoy of Battoes arrived this afternoon with Provisions and Naval Stores.

28th   The Garrison employed upon the Shiping.
Captain Richmond of the New York Independents marchd off this Morning with his Company for the German Flatts.

29th   The Garrison employed upon the Shiping. There was an attack in the Woods on Ontario side in the Afternoon, & two of our Men kill'd.

30th
31st   } The Garrison upon the Shiping.

June 1st   The Garrison employed upon the Shiping.
a Corporal and eight Men orderd by the Commanding Officer to begin the Survey but the Weather too bad.
There were some Indians fired at from Fort Ontario and went off.

2d   The Garrison employed upon the Shiping
The Survey begun by Mr. Sowers I being ill of the Flux.

4th   The Garrison employed upon the Shiping
Mr. Sowers upon the Survey.
The garrison and Vessels fired at one for the Prince of Wales's birthday.
Some Indians who had been in the Woods reported, they had seen a french Vessel passing 12 mile point; there was a Schooner sent in the Evening to discover her, but did not.

5th   The Garrison employed upon the Shiping.
The Survey continued.
The two Vessels Commanded by Captains Bradley and la Forey, and the small Schooner went out this Morning.

6th   The Garrison employed upon the Shiping.
The Survey continued.

7th   The Garrison employed upon the Shiping.

I went out to examine the Survey & finding it disagree I began a fresh Survey.

8th The Garrison upon the Shiping.
I continued upon the Survey.

9th The Garrison upon the Shiping.
I finished the Survey of the West side.

10th The Garrison upon the Shiping.
I began the Survey of Ontario Side.

11th The Garrison upon the Shiping.
The Survey continued.

12th The Garrison upon the Shiping.
I finished the Survey.

13th
14th } The Garrison upon the Shiping.
15th

16th The Garrison employed upon the Shiping.

The Battoe Guard consisting of a Serjeant a Corporal and 12 Men, were at four this morning cut off by a Scalping Party of Indians, believed to be about 150. Two private Men made their Escape, the rest were killed or taken. They kept about the Skirts of the Wood for about an hour and half, during which time we fired some Shot and Shells at them.

The Vessels returnd this Evening.

17th The Garrison employed upon the Shiping, and clearing away the Wood round the Forts. The platforms having given way with yesterday's firing, there were 20 Men employ'd this day to make new ones as p acco^t.

A Scoute of five Whale boats sent to the Eastward returnd this Evening with an account of their being fired upon from the shore (about 20 miles to the Eastward) by a party of Indians thought to consist of 1000.

18th The Garrison employed as Yesterday.

A Convoy of Battoes and Whale boats arrived by whom I received the two following Letters from the General and Chief Engineer.

Albany June the 10th 1756
"Sir

"I received your favour of the 25th of May with a very clear Description of Oswego with its Forts &c. and accordingly waited on the General, who desired to know the particulars relating to the present Condition of the Fortifications, with your Opinion on them referr'd in my Letter, and after an exact Examination of the State of the Several Works, with their Situation, and the Services that can be expected from them, considering the advanced Season of the Year, I have with the Approbation of his Excellency General Shirley proposed the following Articles to be executed in your department at Oswego immediatly. Notwithstanding your doing this the General desires that you will as soon as possible make proper Designs of larger and more respectable Fortifications and transmitt them here.

1st Fort Ontario's Situation both Commands the Lake River and its Environs, and is by your Letter Capable of making a tolerable Defence against small arms, shou'd be the immediate point in View by the Securing it and strengthening it nearly to the plan and profil herein inclosed (order'd to be sent to you) making such improvements and ammendments as you may see farther Necessary for its Defence.

"The Gate to be removed where you think proper for its Security and if some little Couvre-port was thrown up in front of it, that would not be amiss.

2nd "The Magazine for Powder I imagine you will think necessary to be considered upon at the same time, and to be constructed on such a Situation as will keep it dry and free from any Inclemencies of Weather, with room to Shift and Skreen the Powder (if thought necessary) also placed in Security from Shot and Shells, and to lye Convenient for the Supplying your principal Works, which are supposed to have a small Magazine in Each.

3— As to the Horn Work, the Repairs you have proposed seem to me just and right, and think as you do, that there is no Occasion for such a Ravelin on so short an exterior Side.

4— Oswego Fort as it is only sketch'd. It is a Field open for your Constructing and Securing it properly.

5— Since the Scalping that has happened in the Street at Oswego, the General is of opinion that some few Stockades placed properly woud prevent Such Accidents for the future.

"His Excellency has often mentioned, that he had some thoughts Concerning the Removal of the Town of Oswego from where it is at present to the east Side, also of a Morass underneath, that whether a small Harbour for Boats coud not be made on that Spot, and desires your Opinion about it.

"As to Tools, there are a great Quantity sent to Oswego of all kinds wanted except Nails which will be sent you. I spoke to the Paymaster about Money, and as he cannot send any up, desires that you'l draw on him here at Albany.—

"There are no Ships from the Ordnance, & of Course no Stationary, I shall get some from New York and supply you with a little Writing paper.

"His Excellency will send you Orders for the executing these several Articles above mentioned which you will receive at the same time.

I am &c. (Signed) Ja^s Montresor Ch Engin^r."

underwritten

Sir

You are hereby directed to compleat the Works at Oswego in the manner pointed out to you by Mr. Montresor in this Letter I am Sir &c.

(Signed) W. Shirley"—

Albany 10th June 1756

Sir I have only to add to the inclosed that with regard to the Money you shall want to pay off the Workmen, You will take it up of the Traders at Oswego, or such other persons there as can furnish you with it, and draw upon the Paymaster at Albany for it, and your Bills shall be punctualy answerd; I doubt not of your transmitting Accounts of the Money paid to the Workmen in a Regular Way, so as to be good Vouchers to annex to the Warrants that shall be drawn for discharging those accounts I am Sir (signed) W. Shirley."

"To Mr. Mackellar".

19th   The Garrison employed upon the Shiping, clearing away the Woods, and making Platforms, the latter as p^r Account.

I writ of this date to the Chief Engineer to acquaint him of my having finish'd the Survey, and to desire he woud let his Excellency know in answer to his Letter of the 10th received yesterday, "that there was not money to be had at Oswego for Bills, from Traders or any Body else sufficient for carrying on the Works, and that an Engineer is not a proper person to receive or pay Money, as his certificates are the proper Vouchers for laying it out."

This Letter sent by a Convoy of Battoes which returned to Schenectady.

20th   The Garrison employed upon the Shiping & clearing the
Woods, and upon the Work by the advanced Guard, the latter
as p Account.

This morning I laid out the Work round the advanced
Guard, to cover the Town, in place of the pickets orderd by
the General in the Chief Engineer's Letter received the 18th
Inst, the former being the most Expeditious.

21st   The Garrison employed upon the Shiping, clearing the
wood and upon the Work by the advanced Guard, the latter
as pr Accot.

22nd   The Garrison employed as yesterday, the Morng being very
wet they wrought only for the afternoon.

23rd   The Garrison employed as Yesterday upon the Work round
the Advanced Guard as pr Accot.

The two large Vessels the two Schooners and eight Whale
Boats with a Party of Men and Officers went out this Evening
to Cruize and Scout.

24th   The Garrison employed as Yesterday round the advanced
Guard as pr accot.

25th   The Garrison employed as Yesterday round the advanced
Guard as pr accot.

Mr. Ogden of Colonel Schuyler's Regiment who had gone
out in one of the Whale Boats the 23d Inst. return'd early this
Morning, and brought an account, that having gone to the
eastward with the little Schooner and the other seven Whale
Boats they were fired upon Yesterday Afternoon, by a considerable Body of Indians from one of the Islands off Portland point. Captain McPhun in the little Schooner with a
Whale Boat came in soon afterwards, and Lieut. Moncrieff
one of the Officers who came with him, says that Captain
Bickers of Schuyler's Regiment, going in near the Shore, was
fired upon as related by Mr. Ogden, and a good many of his
men being killed, His Boat coud not get off, that some Indians
immediately put off from the Shore, seized the Boat and
carried her in, they saw only two of her hands, which were
eleven in all taken out alive, they think Capt. Bickers and
Mr Loe a Voluntier are killed; that He and three other Whale
Boats immediately got aboard of the Schooner, she having
stood farther out, and scuttled three of the Whaleboats, least
they might fall into the Enemy's hands, and brought the
fourth along with them, they judged the Number of the Indians to be about 150. Ensign Grant came in the afternoon

with two other Whale Boats, and says they were pursued by some of their Canoes.

26th The Garrison employed upon the Shiping and upon the Work round the Advanced Guard; the Number upon the latter as pr account.

Captain McPhun went out this Evening in the little Schooner.

27th No Men employed upon the Works.

Captains Broadley and La Forey came in, having been met upon the Lake by four French Vessels one of whom carryed 14 Guns, they judged the Enemy considerably superior to them in force;

They think Captain Farmer [7] in the great schooner is taken. This proved true.

28th The Garrison employed upon the Shiping and work round the Advanced Guard, the latter as p^r Account.

Captain McPhun was chased into the harbour by one of the French Vessels which we took to be the Commodore La Force

Colonel Broadstreet sent an account of his arrival at the Three Rivers with a large Convoy of Battoes and demanded a Party of 100 men to be sent immediatly to the great Falls to cover the building of a Fort there.

There was a Council of War called to resolve whether they cou'd be spared, I was askd my opinion as to the number requisite to put the Works in a State of Defence, I answer'd it woud require at the rate of 400 men for three Months. It was unanimously agreed that the Party demanded by Colonel Broadstreet coud not be spared, as carrying on the Works woud require a greater number than coud possibly be spared even with the reinforcement then acoming which consisted of about 230 Men including Captain Patoun's Party at Onondago.

29th The Garrison employed upon the Shiping, and Work round the advanced Guard the latter as pr account.

30th The Garrison employed as Yesterday.

The Work round the Advanced Guard finished about 9 a clock, and the Men employed for the Remainder of the day in making Fascines.

July 1st A Part of the Garrison employed upon the Shiping and the

[7] Jasper Farmer, son of a New York merchant of that name.

Men allowed for the Works in bringing Fascines as p^r Account.

I took the Soundings of the Harbour and Entrance.

Colonel Broadstreet arrived this day with a Convoy of about 600 Battoes with Provisions for the Garrison and Guns and Rigging for the Vessels.—Captains Moore and Paget with a Party of 150 Men, and Mr. Pitcher Commissary of the Musters came with him.

2nd   The men allowed for the Works employed in making and bringing Fascines; This Morning I began a Fascine Battery upon the North Wing of the Horn Work towards the Lake for securing that wing and defending the Entrance of the Harbour.

A Council of War called about Noon to represent the want of Money for carrying on the Works and in regard to detaining a company of Pioneers, to work here, which came with Colonel Broadstreet, to Work upon the Fort at the Falls. It was resolved as to the former to send an Express to the General, and Mr. Lewis the Commissary, at the Request of the Commanding Officer, agreed to pay the Workmen for some time longer, tho' he had already advanced a good deal of Money upon that account, and had no publick money in his hands for a considerable time past. It was thought adviseable to send the Pioneers away, least their high pay might create a murmuring amongst the Soldiers.—

I writ a Letter this day to Mr. Montresor representing some Difficulties about the Ditch and Loghouse proposed by his Letter of the 10th of June at Fort Ontario, and the want of men and Money.

3rd   No men allowed for the Works upon account of the Musters.—

Colonel Broadstreet set out this Morning with his Convoy of Battoes for Schenectady.

A Brig of 16 Guns and a Sloop of 12 guns launched this Morning about 10 a Clock.

Between three & four in the afternoon there came an Express with an Account of Colonel Broadstreet's Convoy being attack'd about seven miles off, Captain Paget with a Party of 150 Men was sent to reinforce him. About ten at Night there came another Express from Colonel Broadstreet with an Account of the Enemies quiting the Field and of his having taken two Prisoners, and by the Account of one of them, the strength of the Enemy consisted of 180 Regulars 400 Canadians and 100 Indians, by the Account of the other, they consisted of a great many more.

4th   The Morning very wet. No Men allowed for the Works on account of the Musters.

Captain Moore with a Party of 200 Men was sent out about 2 a Clock, there being an Account that the Enemy were encamped on the East Side of the River seven or eight Miles up.

This Evening arrived a small Convoy of Battoes for Mr. Lewis with Merchandize, one of whom brought in a french Prisoner who surrender'd himself two miles above the Town. This Prisoner says, "that about three Weeks ago they left Montreal with 800 Men and came in 13 days to la Baye de Niaouré, that they were encampd there the 24th past, when the little Schooner appeared off the Islands to the northward of them, that 200 Indians put off immediatly to the Island where the Whale Boat was afterwards taken, that in the afternoon when they saw the Indians fire upon our Whaleboats, there were 200 Regulars sent off to their assistance. That Captain Bickers and five of his Men are alive, that Mr. Loe and all the rest are kill'd. That six days ago, they came from la Baye de Niaouré with 60 Canoes and Battoes to Riviere au Sable, that 200 men remain there to guard the Craft, and 600 came forward to Scalp and take Prisoners about this place and attack our Battoes upon the River; that yesterday the Indians went off immediately after the first fire, and that the rest of the Engagement was continued by the Canadians and Regulars, that they all went off in about two hours after the Engagement began, that they brought only eight days Provisions w^t them, that he himself had eat nothing for two Days which with his having lost his Way, was the reason of his surrendring Prisoner, that there are seventeen ships arrived this year from France in Canada with Merchandize Troops and Provisions, but does not know whether any of them are Men of War, that they have plenty of Bread and Pork, Chiefly from France and a little from our Colonies, that there are four Battalions in Canada King's Troops & 1500 Colony Troops, two Battalions at Cataraqui, and one Battalion with 500 Canadians at Niagara, that the Battalions consist of 500 Men each. He says the Indians are Lords and Masters of the Country, and that they must all do as the Indians woud have them. He says the Party will get in four days to Riviere au Sable, and that they are to remain at La Baye Niaouré untill they receive the General's Orders, which they can have in six days from Montreal."

5th   No Men for the Works.

A Council of War called about 12 a Clock. The Commanding Officer represented "that Mr. Lewis the Commissary had acquainted him with his having received a Letter from Mr. Alexander General Shirley's Secretary of the 20th of June in which Mr. Alexander told him that he woud not be concerned with any Payments made on account of the Fortifications or any other Works about the Place, the Shiping excepted, and directed that the People concernd in carrying on these Works shoud apply by Memorial to the General for Money for their respective Branches; that Mr. Lewis thought this Letter countermanded the order he had received from Mr. Alexander in October last for making those payments, and woud therefore pay no more, not even the Bills that were due at the time of his receiving the Letter." Mr. Lewis being called upon, produced the said Letter and the Paragraphs relating to the above particulars were read and found answerable to what the Commanding Officer had set forth, and Mr. Lewis being publickly ask'd whether he would advance any more Money for the Works as usual, answer'd that he did not now think himself safe in doing it and therefore would not. The Commanding Officer then took Notice of some Desertions that had lately happen'd, and produced an Anonymous Letter that was found in Fort Ontario some days before, tyed to a Stone, as if it had been thrown in, it was directed to the Officers in General; the Substance of it was as follows. "Gentlemen, You seem surprized at our Desertion, but youl "not be surprized if you'l Consider that we have been starved "with Hunger & Cold in the Winter, and that we have received "no pay for seven or eight Months; Now we have no Cloaths "and you cheat us out of our allowance of Rum and half "our Working Money". The Commanding Officer then put the Question, whether it would be adviseable to make the Men Work and trust for the payment? It was resolved that it would not, and that the Works coud not be carryed on without ready Money, and that Memorials should be drawn by those directed in Mr. Alexander's Letter to apply to the General for Money.

Captain Patoun with 112 Men from Onondago being joined by Captain Moore's Party that went out yesterday came in this Afternoon.

6th   I drew up a Memorial to the General for Money to carry on the Works, agreeable to the Resolution of the Council of War held Yesterday.

7th   I sent the Memorial to the General inclosed in a Letter of this date; the Copies of which follow.

"To His Excellency William Shirley &c.

"The Memorial of Patrick Mackellar Esqr &c.

"Sheweth

"That on the 5 Instant, it has been resolved by a Council of War at this place to employ no more Work men upon the Fortifications for want of Money.

"That to repair the old Works and put them in a proper posture of Defence with some additional New Works to secure the Town &c. it will require 400 Men for three Months which will amount to £900 Sterling.

"That delaying these Works may be of dangerous consequence, in case of being attackd, which is not unlikely to happen, as the Enemy are Masters of the Lake, are making preparations at Cataraqui, and by Report have superior Numbers.

"The Memorialist therefore prays his Excell^y may remitt the above Sum as soon as possible, and appoint a Paymaster for receiving and paying the Same".

"Oswego 7th July 1756—

"Sir,

"Mr. Lewis the Commissary having by a Letter of the 20th June from Mr. Alexander your Excellencie's Secretary, refused to advance any more Money for carrying on the Works, and a Council of War of the 5th Instant having in consequence of that put a Stop to them, I have according to the Directions of that Letter, tho contrary to Method, sent your Excellency the inclosed Memorial. I am &c.

To His Excellency General Shirley"

8th   The two Regiments were musterd by the Commissary.

An Express sent to the General returned in the Evening

with an alarm of his having discover'd some Enemy Indians four miles up the River. He was sent off again in the Night.

9th Some of our Indian Squaws having brought an account of having discoverd Enemy Indians, there were two Captains sent out with Scouting Partys but they made no Discovery.

10th
11th
12th
13th Nothing Extraordinary.
14
15th

16th An Express to the General, and some of our Onondago Indians, set out this Morning; One of the Indians returnd in the Evening with the Death Cry and an Account of having discover'd a great Number of French and Indians up the River. Our Guards and Centries were doubled.

17th A scouting Party sent out this Morning to look for the Enemy, which the Indian reported last Night, but returned without making any Discovery.

In the Evening an Indian from Cataraqui who had been with our Indians that went out yesterday and got drunk with them, came in without Arms and profess'd Friendship, and said that the Missisaguas his Countrymen were not concern'd in any of the Mischiefs done about this place, but wanted to be in Friendship with us, and come and traffick with us, that they were in great Want of every thing, but that the French told them it would not be safe to come near us, however, he ventured to come and try and was now at our disposal. The Commanding Officer having made him a favourable Answer, he said that he left four more Indians in the Woods, two of whom were our Friends, and he would bring them in to witness his good reception, but the other two he believed were French in their Hearts, and they shoud not come in, nor woud he suffer them to do any harm.

18th The Indian mentioned yesterday went out this Morning, as he said to bring in his Friends, but soon afterwards was discover'd reconoitring Fort Ontario from behind some Loggs, he was fired at by one of the Centries and some Men who happen'd to be accidentaly paraded; as soon as they fired they ran and surrounded him and took him Prisoner.

Ensign Grant with a Scout of Whale-boats was sent to the Eastward.

19th
20th } Nothing extraordinary.

21   The Indian Prisoner says that the French certainly intend to attack us next moon, that they lately sent 500 Men from Cataraqui accross the Lake but does not know their destination, that 1200 more had moved towards the eastward to Cross at the Head of St. Laurence, who he believes are intended against this place, that they have a great french Warrior and a Number of Canon at Cataraqui; they have four Vessels one of 14 Guns, one of ten Guns and two of four Guns each.

22   Ensign Grant returned this Morning from a Scout from the Eastward, and reports his having discover'd a pretty large Encampment upon the Lake fifteen Miles on this side of Portland point.

The Commanding Officer call'd a Council of War; and acquainted them with Mr. Grant's Report and the Indian's Information, and as there was no Answer from the General upon the Resolutions of the Council of War of the 5th Instant, proposed whether it would not be adviseable to employ the Troops in repairing the Works, & that the Captains and Commanding Officers of Companys shou'd speak to their Men to induce them to Work and trust for the Payment untill there shoud be a remittance sent up, which was unanimously resolved upon. The Captains were called soon afterwards and acquainted with the above Resolution.

A Snow of 18 Guns lanched this Afternoon.

I marked out a Ditch round Fort Ontario according to the General's order received the 18th past.

23rd The men allowd for the Works (as p^r Account) are employed in sinking the Ditch round Fort Ontario making Foot Banks and platforms, cutting Loop holes and securing the Gateway; at Fort George in making Platforms, Footbanks, repairing the Parapet and sinking the Ditch.

The little Schooner and some Whaleboats were sent to the Eastward but returnd without making any Discovery.

24th The Men allowed for the Works employed as yesterday on both Sides, No. as p^r Account.

25th   The Men allowed for the Works employed as before p^r Account.

The small Schooner was sent to the Eastward, but returned without making any Discovery.

26th   The Men allowd for the Works employd as p^r Acco^t.

The small Schooner with a Party and some Whale Boats were sent out first to the Eastward, and afterwards to the Westward where some of the Party landed and discover'd a Road which they suspected had lately been made by the Enemy; the Party return'd in the Evening by Land and reported it.

27th   The Men allowed for the Works employ'd as before as p^r Account.

There was a Captains party sent out to reconoitre the road discoverd yesterday, but it proved to be a path made by some of our Indians who had lately been out that way to get Bark.

28th ⎫   The Men allowed for the Works employed as before vizt
29th ⎬ at Fort Ontario, making the Ditch &c. and at Fort George
     ⎭ repairing the parapet &c.

30th   The Men allow'd for the Works employed as yesterday.

This morning the New Brig of 16 Guns, the New Sloop of 12 Guns and one of the old vessels of six Guns went out with a Command of Men on board.

31   The men allowed for the Works employed as before.

This morning the Vessels came in, the Brig having Sprung one of her Masts and the old Vessel her Boom.

August

1st   The Men for the Works employed as before.

2nd   The Men for the Works employed as before.

An Indian Spy arrived from Niagara sent there by Colonel Broadstreet, says they have built a New strong Fort there with a Ditch round it & have a good Number of Guns mounted, but says their Garrison is not very strong. The French Vessels from Cataraqui arrived there with a great deal of Merchandize some days before he came away and were then ready to return.

3rd ⎧   The Men for the Works employed in sinking the Ditch &c
    ⎨ at Fort Ontario, repairing the Parapet and making Platforms
4th ⎩ &c at Fort George.

5th   The Men for the Works employed as yesterday.

The New Brig Sloop and one of the Six Gun Vessels went out upon a Cruize.

The Indian who came from Niagara the 2nd Instant, being sent to scout to the Eastward brought Intelligence that he had seen 28 Battoes the day before coming along the Lake.

6th   The Men employed as before on both Sides.

The Vessels being seen off near the Harbours Mouth, the Commanding Officer sent out Lieut. Schuyler in the small Schooner to Acquaint the Commanding Officer of the Discovery the Indian had made yesterday.

7th   The Men employed as before on both sides.

The Vessels seeing a Storm rising, came into the Harbour about Noon. The Brig run aground being taken aback with a sudden squall.

The Small Schooner went out this Morning but returned without making any Discovery.

8th   The men employed as before on both sides.

The Brig was got off this Morning and had Suffer'd but little dammage.

7th[9th]   The Men employed upon the Works for the Afternoon only. The Execution of two Deserters took up their time in the Morning.

10th   The Men employed as before.

A Man scalp'd this Afternoon near the Lake on Fort Ontario Side.

11th   The Men employ'd on Fort Ontario Side upon the Ditch, Securing the Gateway and making a Bridge before it. Upon Fort George repairing the Parapet towards the Town and making Platforms.

The small Schooner being sent out early this Morning discoverd an Encampment to the Eastw^d within four mile point, about a Mile and a quarter from Fort Ontario; She immediately put back and made the Signal concerted for her Discovery.

Soon after two Vessels, one of 12 Guns and the other of six Guns, the only Vessels then ready, were sent out to make the Enemy decamp; when they got opposite to them, they were fired upon with Canon, the Vessels returned the Fire and a Canonading ensued on both Sides for about an hour and half, the Vessels finding their attempt fruitless then bore away. The people belonging to Fort Ontario, who had been at Work upon the Ditch retired within; the Commanding Officer sent them a Supply of Ammunition and Provision and some additional Gunners; I offerd my Service to go there, the Commanding Officer told me, that he thought I could be of no use there and that my service would be wanted more where I was.

Between two and three in the afternoon, we found the Enemy had got along all the Skirts of the Wood and some of them behind the Ridge to the Eastward of the Fort and behind some Loggs that lay about Upon the Ground; from this time a firing of small Arms began upon both Sides, which continued till dark, the Fort now and then firing a Gun or throwing a Shell when they discovered any Number of the Enemy together. They heard them felling Trees to make a Road for their Canon from their Encampment to the Fort, and saw they had begun a parallel (under the Cover of the Ridge to the Eastward) which run towards the Lake slanting to the Northwest.

This Evening there arrived an Express by two Indians from General Abercromby to the Commanding Officer desiring him to go forward with the Repairs of the Works, and that he would send him a Reinforcement and a Supply of Money as soon as possible.

12th   The Night pass'd with a few Shots on both sides without any Attack, at Daybreak there was a Smart Fire of small Arms for near an hour, then slacken'd a little, and continued encreasing and diminishing by turns till Evening.

This Morning the People at Fort George were employed in repairing the Parapet towards the Town, sinking the Ditch before it and laying Timber and Plank upon the Powder Magazine to make it Bomb Proof.

The two Indians with the Answer to General Abercromby's Express set out this morning between 8 and 9, we afterwards learned, they cross'd the River to the French Camp and deliver'd our Letters which contained the Strength and State of the Garrison.

This Evening a Body of the Enemy fired accross the Water, from behind the rising above the Swamp, at our Workmen, and another Party at our advanced Guard, but after our firing a few Shot and Shells at them, they retired into the Woods.

Late this Evening Colonel Schuyler with a Detachment of 200 Men of the 50th Regiment and his own, was sent to Fort Oswego to guard that Post.

13th   There were a few small Arms fired during the Night without any thing farther remarkable, at Day light there was a Smart fire of small Arms for some little time as the Day before and continued in the same Manner.

The Men at Fort George employed in repairing the Parapet towards the Town and sinking the Ditch.

Between four and five I went to Fort Oswego and mark'd out a Trench within the Pallisades to be sunk two feet and the Earth to be thrown up against the Pallisades (to make a Breast Work for the Men to fire over) and set the people to work upon it. About eight I was called to attend a Council of War, where it was proposed, whether it would not be adviseable to withdraw the Garrison of Fort Ontario (as the place was defenceless against Canon) and reinforce Oswego Side. I was asked whether it was Canon proof, I answerd "that they "might fire at it for some time before they coud make a Breach, "but that I had seen Canon Shot go through much larger "Trees than any that were there and fly a considerable way "afterwards, but that it would have an unmilitary Look to "withdraw the Garrison before there was any Canon fired"; while they were deliberating, there came an Express from Fort Ontario with the Opinions of a Council of War held there, setting forth that they heard the Enemy drawing up their Canon and then near at hand, and as they presumed their Batteries were prepared to receive them and as their Fort was not Canon proof, proposed whether it woud not be adviseable for them to retreat and join Oswego Side. The Council of War then sitting Resolved that the Garrison ought to be withdrawn, and left the Manner of doing it to the Commanding Officer.

It was then proposed whether the Vessels ought not to go out and endeavour to distress the Enemy, and keep the Lake untill the fate of the Garrison shou'd be decided, and in case of its being taken, go to the Westward and sink the Vessels, and the Men to make the best of their Way to the back of our Colonies? or whether they shou'd remain in the Harbour, assist in the Defence of the place and share the fate of the Garrison? I was asked whether the Vessels cou'd be of any use

for the Defence of the place? I answerd that "their Fire
"towards Oswego side was obstructed by the Town and there-
"fore cou'd be of little or no use, nor did I know any use they
"cou'd be of in the Harbour but in covering the Retreat from
"Fort Ontario if attacked, but if they kept them in the Har-
"bour proposed pointing Guns into their Hold to be ready to
"sink them and prevent their falling in to the Enemy's
"Hands". It was agreed, that if they went out, it was too late
to annoy the Enemy, and if the Place was taken, they must
deliver themselves to the Mercy of the French or perhaps their
Indians without any Terms, and if they were to sink the Vessels to the Westward, they were liable to fall into the hands of
the Indians in their Way through the Woods or perhaps perish in the Woods if they lost their Way; It was therefore resolved that they shoud share the fate of the Garrison.

The Trench laid out this Morning in Fort Oswego was
finished about eleven, the Men were then sent to get Fascines
and Pickets for an Intrenchment which the Commanding Of-

---

*The map opposite is a reproduction of the essential portions of Mackellar's
original drawing in the Cumberland Maps in the Royal Library at Windsor
Castle. The original measures 25 by 25½ inches, on a scale of 200 feet to an
inch. The reproduction has been reduced to a scale of 360 feet to an inch.*

PLAN of OSWEGO with its FORTS as BESEIGED by the MARQUIS of MONTCALM
August 1756.

References.

A Block House
B Traders Houses
C Hospital and Bolting House
D Bake House
E Ditch within Fort Oswego made the 13th of August
F Retrenchment at Dº. Fort laid out the 14th in the Morning
G Batterys of Pork Casks made the 13th in the Evening
H Carpenters Houses
I Smith's Shop
K Parallel begun by the French in the Evening
L Batterys against Fort Ontario
M Approaches made the 13th in the Night
N Battery en Barbette made the 13th at Night against Fort George
P Dock

N.B. $\left\{\begin{array}{l}\text{Fort George ......20} \\ \text{Fort Oswego .....70} \\ \text{Fort Ontario .....50}\end{array}\right\}$ above the Level of the Lake.

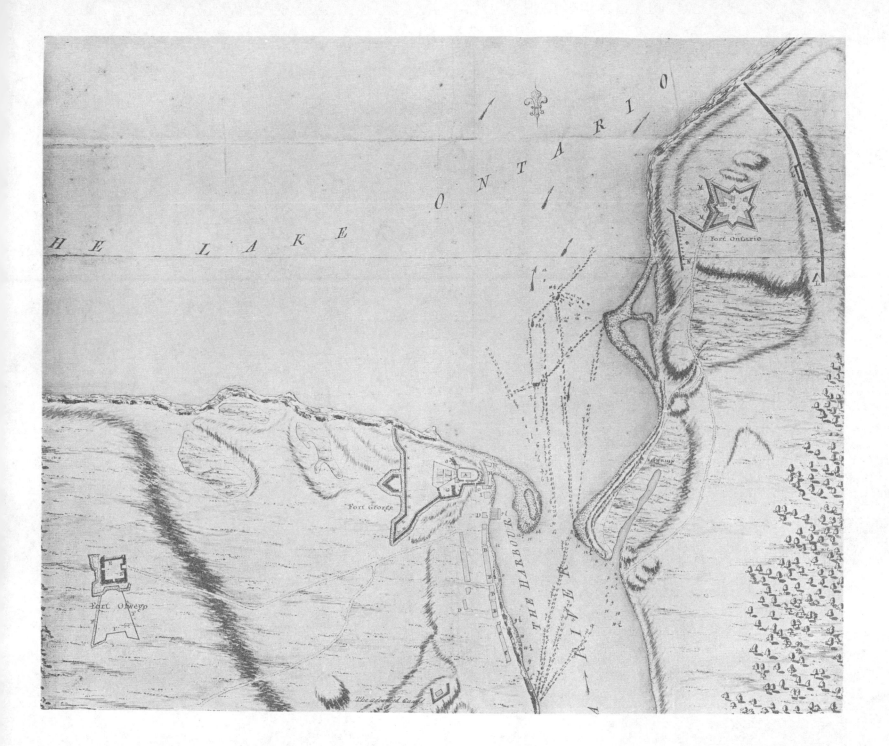

ficer proposed for the Garrison of Fort Ontario, and for the Whole to retire to in case of being drove out of Fort George.

Between two and three in the Afternoon the Garrison of Fort Ontario was withdrawn & landed on Oswego Side without any Annoyance from the Enemy and I believe without being discover'd, which I judged by the Manner of their going or rather stealing up to the Fort after its fire ceased.

Before they left the Fort, they spiked the Guns and threw the Remainder of their Ammunition into the Well. When they landed, they were sent up to Fort Oswego to join the Detachment there and assist them in Carrying on the intended Work, but when they joined they mis'ed and fell into a Confusion, which the Officers with all the fair Means they cou'd use, coud not get the better of, and they perhaps thought it an improper time to make use of severe Measures, so that there was no more Work done there that Night.

In the Evening we made a Battery or Blind of Pork Casks on each side of the Blockhouse to Cover the Gunners from Grape Shot and Swivels; behind that on the north Side there were two Guns and a Mortar, and one Gun and two Mortars behind the other on the south Side. We kept firing at the Enemy after they took possession of the Fort till eleven at Night.

Late in the Evening, I discover'd from the Advanced Guard, the Enemy drawing up their Canon behind Fort Ontario.

14th   At Day Break in the Morning, we discover'd a Battery en Barbette erected along the Edge of the Cliff in the front of Fort Ontario, which we then began to fire upon, they immediately returnd our Fire, at first only with three Guns tho' they had six mounted, this Battery commanded all the Inside of Fort George, excepting a little Space that was cover'd with the Blockhouse towards the Town; We fired with four Mortars and six Guns, three of which (standing upon the North Flank and Curtain of the Horn Work) were reversed upon the Platforms, One from the Indian Council House, and two from the Battery of Pork Casks on the North Side of the Blockhouse, which last two, were the only Guns that had any Cover.

A little before five I went up to Fort Oswego and laid out the designed Intrenchment, and took about 200 Men to digg

the Ditch, the rest being employed in getting Fascines and
Pickets; when the Enemy discoverd us at Work, they directed
a good part of their Fire upon us, but being obliged to fire
at an Elevation upon Account of the distance, did us no harm.
The Commanding Officer came up between seven and eight
and approved of the Work laid out.

Between eight and Nine Lieut. Bailey of the 50th Regiment, came up to tell me that Colonel Littlehales wanted me
at Fort George to attend a Council of War, that Colonel Mercer the Commanding Officer was killd, and that a great Body
of French and Indians had crossed at the Rift in order to
surround us; all the Workmen were at the same time orderd
to lodge their Tools, take their Arms and march down to
Fort George, except the Guard which consisted of 100 Men
and was to remain in Fort Oswego.

When I went to Fort George I found Colonel Littlehales
(then Commanding Officer) the Field Officers and some of the
Captains without the South Bastion, the Detachment from
Fort Oswego were posted in the Ditch round the Work, and
some sent in within the Work, there was likewise a Captain
and 100 Men sent to reinforce the Advanced Guard, the Enemy coming then in a large Body towards that place, who
soon afterwards march'd off from the left along the Skirts of
the Wood, towards Fort Oswego, the Guard left there was
then sent for to Fort George and a Party sent to bring the
Tools; soon after the Guard left it the Enemy took possession
of it, and took up the Brow of the Hill from the River to the
Lake; the Enemy's Canon were by this time increased to nine
or ten in Battery. The Commanding Officer then askd my
opinion in the presence of the Council of War in regard to
the place, whether it was tenable? and whether it coud stand
a Storm? I answerd as to the former "that I did not think it
tenable long, but desired they would consult their own
Judgement and not take my opinion for a Rule"; and as to
standing a Storm, "I thought that must depend upon the Behaviour of both Sides, and as they knew their own Men best,
they ought to be the best Judges". Captain Hind was called
upon and asked the State of the Artillery. He answered that
"there was one of the Iron Mortars burst, that the Carriage of
one Gun was disabled, and the Carriages of four more he
judged must be disabled in a few Rounds." Circumstances

then being stated viz. our being exposed to the Enemy's Fire of a Superior Number of Canon in our Flank and Rear, and our being inclosed upon the other Side by a Superior Number from the River to the Lake; It was proposed whether we should Capitulate or Stand a Storm; it was agreed that our Standing a Storm was most becoming, but that it woud be to little purpose as the Enemy were certain of Carrying the Place in a Short time, whether the Storm Succeeded or Not, and that if there was a Chance for any Terms, it must be before an assault was made; it was therefore resolved to beat a Parley, and send to the French General to know what Terms he woud give. The Parley was accordingly beat and immediately answerd by the Enemy from Fort Ontario. There were then two Officers sent with a Flag of Truce accross the Water. Upon their Arrival at Fort Ontario they were forwarded to the Camp, and a French Officer sent from the Fort to know what Terms we desired; whilst we were assembled to write them out (it being a little after ten) there arrived an Aid de Camp (Monsr de Bougainville) from the Marquis of Montcalm with the Terms which he Agreed to give us, which were to deliver up all the Forts and surrender Prisoners of War, with Promises of good Treatment, and desired an Answer by Noon.

It was then proposed to ask to be sent to the Carrying place, but the Aid de Camp said it woud not be done, nor any other Terms given but those that were offer'd, so that the Capitulation was made out & signed and sent to the Marquis of Montcalm.

Soon afterwards Monsr De la Pauze his Major General brought it back in French with the Marquis's acceptance under some Conditional Articles of delivering up the Artillery Stores Vessels and their Appurtenances, and impowering Monsr De la Pauze to settle the Manner of performing the Capitulation, and to protect the Garrison from Insult. When every thing was settled, some of their Regulars marched in & posted Centries round the Work, and took Possession of all the Magazines both in the Town and Fort, and our People deliver'd their Arms; we were then carryd in Detachments to Fort Ontario escorted by Centries, and had a Strong Guard of Regulars to prevent the Indians from rushing in upon us, which they several times attempted. That Night they took Re-

turns of all the different Corpses, and next day put the Officers with their Servants on board of twenty Battoes with as
many Women and Soldiers as made eleven to each Battoe
besides the four Battoemen; There was an Officer and a Surgeon for each Regiment kept with the Men. All the Officers
were then required to sign a Parole of Honour not to serve
against his most Christian Majesty untill they were exchanged
by Cartel or otherwise; when the Parole was signed we set out
for Montreal, without any Guard, where we arrived the fifth
day.

Workmen on the Fortifications at Oswego
The Three Corpses.

Time	Overs^s	Serg^s	Corp^s	Dru^s	P. men	How employed
June 17	"	"	"	"	20	Platforms in Ft. George
18	"	"	"	"	20	Do
19	"	"	"	"	20	Do
20	"	1	"	"	20	Work at ye Advanced G^d
21	2	3	3	"	60	Do
22	2	3	3	"	40	Do 2 ye No $\frac{1}{2}$ ye day
23	2	3	3	"	60	Do
24	2	3	3	"	80	Do
25	2	3	3	"	80	Do
26	2	3	3	"	90	Do
27	"	"	"	"	"	
28	2	3	3	"	71	Do
29	1	2	2	"	72	Do
30	1	2	2	"	70	Do this Work finishd
Tot^l June	16	26	25	"	703	
July 1st	1	2	2	"	50	bringing Fascines to Ft George
2nd	1	1	1	"	45	Do & Battery to the Lake
Tot^l	2	3	3	"	95	

Workmen at Oswego 1756
50th Regiment

Time	Overs^s	Serg^s	Corp^s	Dr^s	P. men	How employed
July 23rd	1	7	"	2	150	Fas^s &c. [?] Fort George
24	1	7	"	2	143	Do & repair Do
25	2	3	"	2	60	Do
26	4	7	"	2	144	Do
27	3	3	"	2	98	Do
28	3	5	1	2	129	Do
29	3	4	"	2	89	Do
30	3	4	"	2	$41\frac{1}{2}$	Do 2 ye No $\frac{1}{2}$ ye day
31	3	4	"	2	84	Do
Tot^l July	23	44	1	18	$938\frac{1}{2}$	

Time		Overs^s	Serg^s	Corp^s	Dr^s	P. men	How employed
Aug^t	1st	3	4	"	2	84	Fas^s &c. [?] Fort George
	2	3	3	"	2	68	Do
	3	3	3	"	2	58	Do
	4	3	3	"	2	49	Do
	5	3	2	"	1	43	Do
	6	3	3	"	1	43	Do
	7	3	3	"	1	56	Do
	8	3	7	"	2	134	Do
	9	3	$2\frac{1}{2}$	"	1	$60\frac{1}{2}$	Do 2 y^e No $\frac{1}{2}$ y^e day
	10	3	5	"	2	114	Do
	11	3	4	"	2	113	Do
	12	3	4	"	2	126	Do
	13	3	4	"	2	140	Do
Tot^l Aug^t		39	$47\frac{1}{2}$	"	22	$1088\frac{1}{2}$	

Workmen at Oswego 1756.
Schuyler's Regiment.

Time		Overs^s	Serg^s	Corp^s	Dr^s	P. men	How employed
July	23rd	1	2	"	"	$40\frac{1}{2}$	Fascines & Rep^s Ft George
	24	1	2	"	"	47	Do
	25	1	1	"	"	20	Do
	26	1	1	"	"	34	Do
	27	1	1	"	"	12	Do
	28	1	2	"	"	30	Do
	29	1	2	"	"	$15\frac{1}{2}$	Do
	30	1	1	"	"	$10\frac{1}{2}$	Do 2 y^e No $\frac{1}{2}$ y^e day
	31	1	1	"	"	16	Do
Tot^l July		9	13	"	"	$225\frac{1}{2}$	
Aug^t	1st	1	1	"	"	14	Fort George
	2	1	1	"	"	18	Do
	3	1	1	"	"	23	Do
	4	1	1	"	"	18	Do
	5	1	1	"	"	15	Do
	6	1	1	"	"	20	Do
	7	1	1	"	"	15	Do
	8	1	2	"	"	29	Do
	9	1	2	"	"	15	Do 2 y^e No $\frac{1}{2}$ y^e day
	10	1	2	"	"	27	Do
	11	1	2	"	"	31	Do
	12	1	2	"	"	29	Do
	13	1	2	"	"	34	Do
Tot^l Aug^t		13	19	"	"	288	

Workmen at Oswego 1756.
51st Regiment.

Time	Overs^s	Serg^s	Corp^s	Dru^s	P.Men	How employed
July 23rd	2	2	"	"	62	Ditch of Ft. Ontario &c
24	2	2	"	"	118	Do
25	4	3	"	"	180	Do
26	4	3	"	4	200	Do
27	4	3	"	1	120	Do
28	4	3	"	1	148	Do
29	4	3	"	"	123	Do
30	4	$1\frac{1}{2}$	"	$\frac{1}{2}$	$53\frac{1}{2}$	Do 2 y^e No $\frac{1}{2}$ y^e day
31	4	3	"	1	109	Do
Tot^l July	32	$23\frac{1}{2}$	"	$7\frac{1}{2}$	$1113\frac{1}{2}$	
Augt. 1st	4	3	"	"	126	Do
2	4	3	"	"	124	Do
3	4	3	"	"	125	Do
4	4	3	"	1	108	Do
5	4	3	"	1	119	Do
6	4	3	"	1	116	Do
7	4	3	"	"	114	Do
8	4	3	"	"	116	Do
9	4	$1\frac{1}{2}$	"	"	$71\frac{1}{2}$	Do 2 y^e No $\frac{1}{2}$ y^e day
10	4	3	"	"	147	Do
Tot^l Augt.	40	$28\frac{1}{2}$	"	3	$1166\frac{1}{2}$	

Abstract of the Number of Private Men employd on the Fortifications at Oswego in June July & August 1756

June from the 17th to the 30th {	for the three Corpses		703
July 1st & 2nd—	for Do " " "		95
July 23rd to 31st {	50th Regiment "	$938\frac{1}{2}$	
	51st " " "	$1113\frac{1}{2}$	
	Schuyler's " "	$225\frac{1}{2}$	
			$2277\frac{1}{2}$
Augt. 1st to 13th {	50th Regiment "	$1088\frac{1}{2}$	
	51st " " "	$1166\frac{1}{2}$	
	Schuyler's " "	288	
			2543
	TOTAL " "		$5618\frac{1}{2}$

From the foregoing Journal, the following Particulars, relating to the Engineer's Conduct, appear vizt.

May 17th   The day after his Arrival at Oswego, He represented the

Defects of the Works to the Commanding Officer and Applyed for all the Men that coud be spared, to begin repairing them; there was a Council of War called in consequence
of that Application, which postponed the Fortifications &
carryed on the Shiping.

25th   He sent an Account of them by Letter to the chief Engineer setting forth their Defects.

26th   He writ to General Shirley referring him to the Chief
Engineer for a full Account of the Works, and mentioning
the want of Money.

June 18th   He received the Instructions relating to the Works, agreeable to which Instructions, all the Works that he carryed
on, were done.

Do   He received a Letter from the General desiring him to
draw upon the Paymaster for Money for the Works.

19th   He writ to the Chief Engineer desiring him to acquaint
the General, that there was no Money at Oswego.

28th   In a Council of War he estimated the Number of Men
Necessary for repairing the Works at 400 Men p^r day for
three Months or 90 days which is equal to 36000 Working
days of one Man, and by the preceeding Account kept of
the Whole that were employ'd, there is only 5618½, which
is not one sixth part of the Demand, and their Working
time was often broke with Alarms, consequently the Execution of the Works in the Instructions must fall so much
Short.

July 7th   When the Works were stop'd by a Council of War of the
5th Instant for want of Money, He applyed by Memorial
to the General for Money & represented the danger of
Stoping the Works.

If the Council of War of the 17th May postponed the
Fortifications to carry on the Shiping, and that of the 5th
of July put a Stop to them for want of Money, The Engineer hopes it will not be laid to his Account, as he had
neither Voice nor Sway in their Councils, but only attended to answer Questions for their Information. At
both these Councils He spoke against stoping the Works
and the danger attending it in case of being attackd.
When the Works were carrying on, he frequently complained of the smallness of the Numbers allowd him, and

was always answerd, that there cou'd be no more spared, and that the Men were greatly harrassed.

From the Resolutions of both these Councils it Appears, that there was upwards of fifty days Work intirely lost, and for many other days, the Numbers allowed very Small, which in three Months time that the Engineer had been there, makes a considerable difference in Works, to lengthen the Siege of so Defenceless a place. The former of these Councils, the Commander in chief had early Intelligence of, and the Want of Money he was acquainted with at the same time and was not a Stranger to it for some time before.

Upon the whole then it Appears that the Engineer gave early Accounts of the Defects of the Works both to the Commanding Officer upon the Spot and to the Commander in chief, and had not one sixth part of the Demand he made to put them in repair, which he is very certain was within Compass; when there were Men allowed for the Works, He himself as well as all the persons Concern'd gave due attendance and did all they cou'd to forward the Work in hand. His personal Behaviour and diligence then and throughout every part of the Expedition, he leaves to the Accounts of all the Officers and Engineers who from time to time were Eye Witnesses to it.

An Account of the Strength of the Garrison, & State of the Works at Oswego, at the Time of Its Being Invested, Together with an Account of the Naval Force at That Time, & the Seige of the Place, in August, 1756

(D.S.)

The Garrison Consisted of twenty seven Officers, twenty nine Serjeants & four hun^d & eighty one Rank and File of His Majesties 50th Reg^t of Foot; Twenty Two Officers, Twenty eight Serjeants, and Three hundered and ninety Rank & File of the 51th Regiment; Seven Officers, Ten Serjeants, and One hundred Twenty three Rank & File, of the New Jersey Reg^t Comman^d by Col^o Schuyler (Including the Sick of these Corps) Together with 1 Capt 1 Lieu^t & 16 private men of the Royal Reg^t of Artillery; The Remainder of these Regiments being Posted at the Oneida Carrying Place, and other Passes between Schenectady and Oswego, for guarding the Magazines there, and keeping open the Communication between those two places.

The Works consisted of three Forts Viz^t. The old Fort, or Tradinghouse; w^c was in a ruinous Condition, nor designed at first or ever capable of resisting Artillery, built severall years ago, at the Entrance into the Harbour from Lake Ontario, and Commanded to the Eastward by a high Point of Land, about the distance of Five hundred Yards, on the Opposite side of the River, and to the Westward by another Eminence at the same Distance on the Land side, and two New Forts, erected on the aforementioned Eminences; The Fort Ontario to the Eastw^d unfinished and the other to the Westw^d scarcely begun, & which was evacuated the 13th of June 1756 (The Day the Batteau Guard was cutt off, on the East side of the River, a Surprize being apprehended from the Enemy, who were frequently in great Numbers about us) and not one of these Forts being tenable against Artillery. So that the Garrison depended wholly for its Defence, upon a Naval Force on the Lake, Sufficient to prevent the French, from bringing Artillery againest the Forts, which could only be done by Water Carriage.

The *Naval Force* consisted of one new Brigantine, mounted with Fourteen Carriage Guns, Six & four Pounders, and fourteen Swivells; a new Sloop mounted with Six Carriage Guns, Four & three Pounders, and twelve Swivells; a Sloop and a Small Row Schooner (Both built last Year). The former mounted Six Carriage Guns Four Pounders, and twelve Swivells, and Two Haubitz, and the Latter with twelve swivels; as Likewise one large Snow, intended to carry Eighteen Six Pounders, & a Number of Swivels, and a schooner Capable of carrying Eight four Pounders, with swivels, both useless, as they had neither men nor Guns for them.

On the *10th of August* a few of the Enemy's Indians appeared under Fort Ontario, and scalp't a man of Pepperrells Reg^t who were Garrisoned in that Fort. *On the 11th* in the morning a small Schooner was ordered out to view the Coast to the Eastward of the Garrison, which very soon Returned, and fir'd a Gun (the Signal agreed upon for discovering the Enemy). upon this an Officer of the 50th Reg^t was sent out in a Whale Boat to reconnoitre', who on his Return reported, that he discover'd an Encampment Sufficient for fifteen hundred men, but he believed their whole force, to be between four and five thousand, as they were Regulars who were Encamp'd on the Beach, and he supposed the Irregulars to be concealed in the Woods. this acco^{tt} we found afterwards to be prettie exact, as the Enemy had One Thousand Seven hundered and Fifty Regulars, and Three Thousand Five Hundered Cannadians & Indians. Two Sloops of Six and four Pounders were upon this Report, Order'd out to annoy the Encampment of the Enemy; But were soon oblidged to bear away, as they were smartly fired upon, from a Battery of twelve Pounders, and most of their Shott took place. The afternoon of the same Day, the Cannadians and Indians began to fire on Ontario Fort, with their small Arms which they continued 'till dark, and which was briskly returned from the Fort. This night the Enemy opened their Trenches, and began their Parallel to the Northw^d of the Fort, at the distance of about two hundered and fifty Yards, under cover of a rising ground. On the 12th at Daybreak, we discovered about two hundered of the Enemy's Battoes coming round a point, about four miles to the Eastw^d of Ontario, their Fire from their Musquetry recommenced, and the Enemy were plainly discovered at Work, their Cannon bringing up, and a Battery ready to be opened upon the Fort, without a possibility of disturbing them, which was attempted by a few Recochett Shott, and throwing all our Shells, but without Effect, as their works were greatly elevated above ours; The Garrison was pent up in a Pickitted Fort, with a Ditch begun but not Compleated, & too weak to admitt of a Sortie, & but one Entrance to the Fort, the Picketts of this Fort which were fourteen feet high, were below the Level of a little hill to the Eastw^d about eighty Yards, on which their Battery was raised, so that we could not bring one Gun to bear upon the Enemy. This was immediately reported to Colonel Mercer, with the Opinion of the Officers thereupon, which was, That they could not hold out above an hour or two, after opening the Enemy's Battery, Col^o Mercer agreeable to this Opinion made a Disposition, and sent Orders for the Evacuation of that Fort, which was performed in Good Order, about four o'Clock in the Afternoon, without the loss of a man. The same Night the Enemy took Possession of that Post, and began a Battery to the Westward of it, which they had to forwardness, and opened with eleven pieces of Cannon, at Day break *the 14th,* at which time the Cannonading began, and continued very hott for some Hours: About eight o'Clock we discovered the Enemy Fording the River about a mile above us, in three Columns, and we have reason to believe they had passed over five or six hundered the night before; Our men were oblidged to quitt our Works (except the Officers and men on the Plattforms) and go into the Ditch as we were Enfiladed by the Enemy's Battery, without any cover, The Guns reversed on their Plattforms, and the Parapetts intended for our Defence were in our Rear, and the whole of our Works so overlook't, that the Feet of our men were plainly to be seen from the Enemy's Battery, and some of our Sick lying in their Tents, were killed by their Shott; Besides the Guns that were reversed on their Plattforms, we had a Battery of Three Guns, which played upon the Enemy, made of Pork Barrells, three Barrells in heighth, and three in Breadth, these three Guns were all dismounted through the badness of the Carriages Remounted on Fresh Carriages in the midst of the Enemy's Fire, and dismounted a second time which rendered them usless having no more Carriages. During the Fire our seven Inch Mortar burst, & it is to be observed our Magazine which was only cover'd with Plank & Turff, so far from being Bomb Prooff, was not Proff againest a Six pound Shott.

About 10 o'Clock we discovered the Enemy, to the amo[t] (as we afterwards learned) of Three Thousand Five Hundered, Filing off and Surrounding us, & the Marquiss De Montcalm with the Regulars on the East side of the River, ready to pass over to make a General Assault, Colonel Littlehales on whom the Command devolved then called a Council of War, and demanded the Opinion of the Engeneers as to the State of the Garrison, Which they declared was not Tenable. upon which the Chamade was Beat, and an Officer sent over with a Flag of Truce.

> JNO BARFORD, Capt
> GUSTS KEMPENFELT, Capt.
> WILLIAM JOYCE, Lieut
>
> J: How
> JAMES McMANUS. Lieut
> DAV: HALDANE, Lt & Adjut.
> TREVOR NEWLAND, Lieut
> JNO STEWART: Lieut
> ARCH. HAMILTON, Lt
> WM COOK, Lieut
> RICHARD MARSHALL, Ensign
> THOMAS GRANT, Ensign [1]

[1] All of these officers were in Pepperrell's 51st regiment.

HENRY FOX TO GOVERNOR CHARLES LAWRENCE
(COPY)

WHITEHALL 14th Augst 1756.

Sir,

I have received your Letter of the 28th of April, and the King having observed, that by the Departure of the two New England Battalions, upon the Term of their Enlistment being expired, and by the Sickness among the Regulars, there might not be a sufficient Force for the Security of your Province against the Enemy; His Majesty has given Directions, that a Number of Men should be forthwith draughted from the several Battalions of Foot in Ireland, & be sent, under the Care of proper Officers, to Nova Scotia, to compleat the three Regiments there to their proper Complement, & it is The King's Pleasure, that you should, as soon as possible, augment your Garrisons on the Isthmus, and proceed in finishing those Works, which you were directed, so long ago as the 13th of Augst last year to make at Fort Cumberland, and for which purpose, the Sum of £10,000. was entrusted to you, by the Order of the Lords Justices.

You do not seem to have sufficiently attended hitherto, to the keeping a Strong Garrison upon the Isthmus which appears to The King to be an Object, of the utmost Importance, & superior, at this time, to any other within your Government, even to that of Halifax itself, which is not in equal Want of a numerous Garrison especially whilst it continues to be so well guarded by the Naval Force now in those Seas. It is also very necessary not to suffer the French Inhabitants, (particularly if mixed with the Indians, and commanded by French Officers) to remain near the Bay of Fundy, as there is no doubt of their surprizing the Forts on the Isthmus, in Case the insufficient Force in those Garrisons should give them the least Prospect of Success.

But it is hoped, that as soon as the Reinforcement from Ireland shall arrive, you will not only be able to execute the Services abovementioned, but also to send a sufficient Number of Troops to the River St John's for the Security of those Parts.

I am &c.

H. Fox.

LOUDOUN TO CUMBERLAND
(L.S.)

Albany 20th August 1756.

Sir,

1. I shall not trouble Your Royal Highness, with a repetition of any thing that is in my Letter to Mr. *Fox,* and must beg your Protection, if I am found fault with, for delaying to write from *New York;* I could have told You nothing but that I was arriv'd; and here my Letters have been detained from day to day, by the *Quibbles* of the *Provincials:* for without them, I had nothing to Stop the progress of the Enemy, if they had invaded Us, which they certainly would have done; and now that I have settled matters with them, as far as I can, my next care must be, to prevent their throwing themselves away, as the Consequence of that will be, letting in a Torrent I am in no Condition to Stop; If I can manage this point with the *Provincials,* and be able to stop up the Entry into this Country, by *Wood-Creek* and *South Bay,* which, by any Accounts I have yet got, will be very difficult; and can preserve *Oswego,* and the communication with it; and get our Naval Force there, on a more respectable Footing; I hope Your Royal Highness will not think We have been Idle: But how far we shall be able to Effect that point, I dare not yet promise; for we are at present groping very much in the dark.—no Intelligence; no part of the Country reconnoitred; few Men to Act; with no one thing provided for moving them, but Provisions; which I have the greatest difficulties to transport to the Places where wanted. The real State of the Troops here, in Major General *Abercromby's* and Mr *Webbs* Regiments, are as returned, but in want of maney things, and must soon be naked, as you will see by the *returns* transmitted; those two I hope soon to compleat: Major General *Abercromby's* from the *Carolina* Companies, which Mr *Dobbs,* in a Letter I have just received from him, offers in the handsomest manner to turn over to Us; and Mr *Webb's* I hope to compleat from the *Provincial* Troops, when they are dismissed; besides getting a good many of them for the Royal Americans. As to the *50th* & *51st* Regiments, I shall soon be able, from Mr *Webb's* return, to give you an Account of them: but by all the Accounts I have yet got, I shall have them to raise and discipline; the Independent Companies just as bad; So that Your Royal Highness sees, I have little to depend on at present, but Major General *Abercromby* and Mr *Webb's* Regiments, with the *Nine hundred* Men of Lieu^t Genl *Otway's,* and the *Highlanders;* and you see, Sir, how I am forced to divide them.

2. From the *Indians,* you see we have no support; Some *Rangers* I shall be obliged to keep all the Winter, till I can make some of our own people fit for that Service. When I arrived, I found there was a disposition in the Soldiers, to go out with Indians and *Rangers,* and that some of them were then out; I shall encourage it all I can, and if the parties that are now out, have success and escape, we shall soon get a knowledge of this Country, and be able to March with much more safety than at present; for I am convinced, that till we have every thing necessary, for carrying on the War here, within ourselves, Independent of Aid from this Country, we shall go on very slowly.

3. We are employed at present, in finding out and Collecting the things that have been provided, as we hear, for the Army, and pre- paring every thing wanted; which in reality is *every thing.* You will see the Reports we have of the Fortifications at *Oswego,* Fort *William- Henry,* and *Edward,* much to be done at each of them; The Fort here ruinous; the Town is Palisaded round, these all Rotten; *Barracks, Hos- pital, Store-Houses* still to be built; not one shilling to do this with, but *one thousand* Pound Currency, rais'd by this Province for Bar- racks; Not a bit of wood for all these Operations to be had, but at double price; for tho' the Country is all Wood, 'tis all granted away, and so become private property, and nothing reserved for the King; with all those difficulties we are struggling, but must get through before winter, and shall acquaint you from time to time, with the manner in which we get the better of them.

4. The next difficulty will be, settling the *Money* matters of the Army, which is I doubt, as much in a state of Confusion, as the other Affairs; and if I can make the necessary provision, and set things on a clear footing, before next Campaign, I shall think myself very happy: for those purposes, I imagine, I shall remain here, most, if not all the Winter.

5. The Case of the *Commissions* granted by Major General Shir- ley, I have mentioned in my other Letters; I hope Your Royal Highness will approve of my general resolution on that Subject, and send me your Orders, in relation to the *Company Sold.*

6. As to the 3^d *Article* in my *Instructions,* I understood, that Your Royal Highness had agreed, that the Non-Effective fund, should stand here on the same footing, as it does in Europe; and without it does, it is impossible to recruit the Regiments, except by Warrants from me, which I never can pass, whilst that Article stands in my Instructions;

So that the Recruiting must either totaly Stop, or I be undone in carrying it on. And the *Royal American* Regiment's Affairs, will come under the same misfortune, both as to the Original Accounts charged on it, and the Expence of Transporting the Recruits and Officers from Germany; which Accounts I never can pass, as long as this Article remains in my Instructions; therefore, I most humbly beg Your Royal Highness's Protection.

7. The Expences here, are immense; the Prices of every thing in this Country are dear, by the managem^t of our Predecessors; all those Prices to the Publick are exorbitant; that of Indian Affairs in particular: for last year, during the Struggle, to take the Managem^t of them out of Sir William *Johnson's* hands; those people who formerly, as *Sir William* informs me, did not cost above Six pence a day, were paid four, Six, Eight and *ten* Shillings a day, and some up to *Nineteen* Shillings; those People are naturally Avaricious, and this has made them insatiable.

8. There has an unlucky affair happened, in relation to one *Jerry*, which I have not mentioned in my Publick Letter, but reserved it for this to Your Royal Highness. This *Jerry* was one of the Indians, who attended Major General *Braddock* last Year; he deserted from them, and Scalpt several of their People; he was afterwards taken, by the few Indians who remain'd with that Army, who would have killed him, as I am informed, but that Colonel *Dunbar* prevented it, for fear of Offending the *Indians* in their Neighbourhood; he had lately Join'd himself to the *Tuscorora* Indians, and came along with them and some *Mohawks*, who came here with Sir William *Johnson*, to make me a visit. this Man has since been Murdered, and his Head found next morning on a Post, at the Head of the 44th Regiment, at *Schenectady*. The enclosed Copies of Letters, will shew you my opinion of this Affair, and the Steps I have taken upon it. The first Order I writ, I kept no Copy of; but I hope what are here sent, will suffise to shew, that I have so far done my duty in it.

9. Whilst I was writing this, I received two Letters from Major General *Shirley*, with a heap of Papers, all which I have order'd to be Copy'd, and shall send them to the Secretary of State; if Mr *Shirley* had not been ready to Sail, I should have kept them till next packet, and have explained the *falsehood* contained in them, at large; but as time will not allow me to do that now, and he may gain Credit by such Assertions, before the truth is known, I only writ *Marginal Notes* on them. I think the Second Letter, when Your Royal Highness compares the first part of it with the last, and many particular paragraphs,

will Justify me, when I say, what I have been told by many People since I Landed, (which I intended not to have mentioned, till I had vouchers to have sent along with them;) that he has been the *first contriver and fomenter* of all the Opposition, the *New England* Men make, to being Join'd to the Kings Troops; in order to raise a party for himself, and to shew the King's Ministers, that nobody can serve the Crown in this Country, but himself; and since he has failed in part, of keeping up the difference so wide as he hoped, between the Kings regular Troops, and those raised in the Provinces, he is now endeavouring to raise a Flame, all over the Provinces; and in order to make me personally ill with the *New England* People, which he shall not be able to do; he has told them, that I used the harsh words, you see in the Extract of his Letter to Mr *Winslow:* As I knew at that time, that the dispute with the *Provincials,* was totaly owing to him, all I said on the Subject, was, *that I was sorry to find, that the New England Troops had declined a Junction with the regular Troops:* And his answer was, *that they were Jealous of their Rank; but that when they were got up to Tiendorogo, and found things difficult, then they would agree to a Junction.* I said no more of the Troops; but added, *that if there were any particular persons, who had either contrived that measure, or that now fomented the difference, I believed they would be looked on at home, as little less than fomenters of Rebellion;* which struck him all of a heap: and there the Conversation ended.

10. I have said above the *New England* Troops, because they are the *only* People, with whom there is any dispute about a *Junction;* for, the *New York* Troops, have orders to be under the Commander in Chief; the New *Jersey* Regiment has been last year, and are now this year, at *Oswego,* and are entirely under my Command; as are the Companies raised by North *Carolina.*

11. I have sent a Copy of the Letter he writ to Sir *Charles Hardy,* to shew the *double part* he has acted; the Provincials, when they were with me, did assure me, they have a Letter under his Hand, assuring them that they should not be Join'd with the regular Troops, but that they had left it in Camp; if there is such a Letter, I shall one day get hold of it, and send it.

12. I ask Pardon, for troubling you with so much about Mr *Shirley;* but it is pretty strange, that he says he has provided every thing, for we, either he or I, must be most infamous tellers of untruth; but when I can collect those great Provisions made, you shall have a return of them. I hope the *Treasury* will not be in a hurry, of passing his Accounts; from what I have already seen, I shall have something to inform them of, worth their knowing before they pass: I have in my hands, what never was intended for me, an Account with *five per* Cent Commission; and I am informed, that Commission raises in many cases to *ten* per Cent, and in some, to *thirteen* per Cent; but this is pretty well guarded against discovery, yet I think I shall gett at it.

13. I believe I shall have a good deal to say, on the Article of *Arms,* but I am not ripe on that Subject, as I have had no time to attend to those things yet; but the Winter will bring many things to light.

14. As there will be another Packet to Sail soon, I will trouble Your Royal Highness no farther at present.

15. Since writing the above part of my Letter, the Intelligence of the loss of *Oswego* has arrived; this last Account, Your Royal Highness will perceive, comes only by a Man who has made his Escape from thence; but when I add to that, the Intelligence of an Indian, who came to Sir William *Johnson,* the day before, and gave an Account that he saw the Enemy, throwing up works before it, and from the knowledge of the badness of the Garrison, and the defenceless Situation of the Fortifications, which the Enemy must have known, from the great numbers of deserters they had from thence; and having no Express this day, to contradict that of yesterday; and knowing, that there has been but one Letter from thence, since Major General *Abercromby* arrived, which was directed to Major General *Shirley;* and that all the Messengers we have sent, have been prevented from getting there by the Enemy: We have concluded it to be true, and have taken our measures accordingly; the general purport of which, Your Royal Highness will see, from my Letter to Mr *Webb,* and the Copies of my Letters to the different Governors, and to Mr *Winslow.*

16. There are now about *five hundred* Recruits raised for the *Royal American* Regiment, and I have given Orders, to send up the Men they can raise, by *five hundred* at a time, in order to croud up men here as fast as possible, to enable us to Act, in whatever shape we may be able.

17. I must endeavour to remedy that total want of *Intelligence* in this Country; the distances are so great, and no way has ever been tried, but by Indians, who are in no Shape to be relied on, that we really know nothing at present: And I am at a loss to Judge what Step the Enemy will take on this Success; I think they will not Fortify *Oswego,* as they have a better *Port* on the *Lake,* and should rather imagine, they will erect a Fort at the *Falls, twelve* Miles on this side of it, in order to Stop our getting there again: but the Question is, if they are to build a *Fort,* whether they will remain to do that now, or will push on, and secure as many of the Forts on the way thither, as they can; as they are plentifully provided in Boats to Transport them. there is another Plan they may have, which is to send off a Detachment cross the Lake, down the River *St Laurence,* across from *Le Préau fifteen* miles good Road to Lake *Champlain;* those will be very troublesome there, but I should hope, if we have Success with the Colonies, we might still make a push for *Oswego,* if they leave that Post weak.

18. Your Royal Highness sees, what situation we found things in, at our outset; and all I can promise, is, we will do our utmost to make them better.

19. Arms will be greatly wanting, for I expect a very bad account of what was sent here before.

20. As there are so few Officers of those two Regiments, *50.* & *51st remaining,* I shall not take any Step towards Recruiting of them, till I receive Orders upon it; but shall compleat the other Regiments out of the Few Men left. And as you are not likely to get back the Officers, as the French *give up no Prisoners* in this Country, Your Royal Highness will be so good as to consider, in what manner you will replace the loss of those two Regiments, which we should have made two thousand Men on this Establishment.

21. Your Royal Highness sees the yet uncertainty of our Accounts of this Affair, and the reasons for which we give it Credit, and the Measures we have taken; which I hope will meet Your Approbation whatever is the case. In the first place Sir John *St Clair* is afraid, the Carrying Place, which is *80:* Miles on this side of *Oswego,* is to[o] far advanced for us to support; we differ, but have given *discretionary* Orders to Mr *Webb;* and in them you see our Reasons. the Steps taken with the Southern Colonies, to make them secure their Frontiers, and compleat the *Royal American* Regiment, can have no bad Effect; and the engaging for the Money, is what we must have paid in all events, for we should never have had a Shilling from them.

22. If we succeed with the New England Colonies, and get a number of Men, in one event, we may be enabled to make a push; in the other to prevent any great Evil happening.

23. This Post of *Albany* is a *material one;* here are our Magazines, here is the only Communication with the low Countries; here Centers the Communication with *Crown Point;* and here Centers the Communication with *Oswego,* and all the Country above this, on that Road; from whence we draw a great part of our Provisions; and from this, the People advanced, must be totaly supplied.

24. It is defenceless by it's situation, and at present has only a rotten Stockade, which we are repairing, for at present we are not able to do more; it is liable to Attack, not only by the way of *Lake George,* where we have a Fort, but by *Wood-Creek* and *South-Bay;* from whence they can come, either by *Fort Edward* or *Saratoga.*

25. Mr *Webb* is sufficient for the Command on that side, and the *Provincials* and we are not so well settled, as to be able to *Join,* without creating Confusion; nor are they strong enough to Act; here is the place where we have every thing to collect, and indeed almost every thing to get; the People of the Country to be brought to be Serviceable, which is not the case at present; and every thing to forward from hence. At present I think I can be of ten times the use I could be in any other place; and therefore propose remaining till some Incident sends me off at once to any Quarter where I may be wanted.—I know the *Citty* will think this wrong, but if I can be so happy, as to have my Masters, and Your Royal Highness Approbation, the other will give me no trouble.

26. I have sent home, an Extract of Col° *Mercer's* Letters of last Winter, shewing the Situation of that Garrison; the Originals of which, shall not get out of my hands, till I find a safe opportunity of sending them home; I am told there are many more of the same sort, which I will endeavour to come at; I am likewise informed, that there was a Subsequent Letter procured from the Colonel, shewing his surprise such a Report should ever have been raised; that Letter I will endeavour to get, if Mr *Shirley* has not carry'd it home; but I hope it will deceive nobody, as I dare say you will believe me, when I assure you the Originals are in my hands, and this moment another Letter, of which I have sent a Copy.

27.[1] I shall likewais beg leave to Say that I hope the Dates of letter[s], Commissions, &c will Desave [deceive] nobody, for I shall be able to show very soon that those have been made Free with on all occasions to serve Purposes. Many Instances I have Seen, but I have one must come out at one [once], for the Officer must at least be Brook if this does not appear tis the Pay of the Regt by his [i.e., Shirley's] Secretary's Memorandoms the Warrants for the Pay were Regularly Granted, tho I know—that is I have the greatest reason to believe— they were not and I imagine no Man in his Senses will give his Aid to Prove he had Eight Months Pay in his Hands of the Regt without paying them espatialy when it will appear he had an opportunity of Transmitting it to the Regt.

1 The remainder of the letter is in Loudoun's handwriting.

28. Since I writ the Above there are four Men of M G *Shirlyes* Regt and two of M G *Pepperells* Regt come in from *Oswago* they had all formerly Deserted from the French. I have sent there Examination Inclosed I have yet no furder Information of this Affair or of the Motions of the Enemy so that all I can do at Presant is to Collect and Prove every Necessary thing I am able, to be in readiness to give the Propper Aid where it shall be wanted.

29. I have Just received a letter from Governor *Morris* with an account that Fort *Granvil* has been taken by a Body of French and Indians Commanded by a French Officer and that the *Fort at M^c-Dowals Mill* has been abandoned by the Provincials. Those things will I am afraid stope the Recruting and oblige me to leave a Battalion in Pensilvania where I hear they are endeavoring to find out every Evesion to Disapoint the Recruting Act and I shall only ad that I have sent a Message to Mr *Shirly* by his Secretary that if he does not go home I will send him in a Shape he will not like. He does me infinit Mischiff but I am not yet Ripe to Send all the Evidence against him.

I am Sir Your Royal Highness Most Duttefull And Obedient Servant.

LOUDOUN

[*Endorsed*] Albany, August 20th, 1756. Lord Loudoun to H:R:H: inclosing 17: papers.

LOUDOUN TO CUMBERLAND

(L.S.)

Albany, 29th August 1756.

Sir,

Enclosed I send Your Royal Highness, a Copy of a Letter I received from Major General Webb, with my Answer to it; I should not have done this, but that I thought it necessary, now on my outset, to make Your Royal Highness entirely Acquainted, with not only the things I do, but the manner of doing them.

The delays we meet with, in carrying on the Service, from every parts of this Country, are immense; they have assumed to themselves, what they call Rights and Priviledges, totaly unknown in the Mother Country, and are made use of, for no purpose, but to screen them, from giving any Aid, of any sort, for carrying on, the Service, and refusing us Quarters.

By the Mismanagement of the Commissary of the Transports, in Enlisting part of the Sailors in the Transports, and not employing them afterwards, and allowing the others to run away, I am now beginning to receive some of the Recruits for those two Regiments, and cannot for my heart, get up either Artillery or Ammunition, or hardly any thing, from thence.

As to Quarters, this is the only Town has ever given any; Sir Charles Hardy, got them to Quarter the two Regiments, that came from Plymouth; but they very soon repented of what they had done, and when a detachment went out, would give no Quarters to those returned from any Command: I endeavoured all I could, by gentle means, to get the better of this obstinacy, for near a fortnight, till at last, the Mayor sent me a Message, to inform me, that he understood the Law; that I had no right to Quarters, or Store Houses, or any thing else from them, and that he would give me none. The Mayor is a Fool, and has made a great fortune by Supplying the French in Canada, which is now stopt since we come here, which provokes him; therefore I did not stop there, but sent for the Recorder, who is a Man of more sence, and told him the custom, in time of War, in all Countries, even in England itself, and the necessity there was, of Troops been lodged, and having all necessary things found for them here, in a Frontier Place; that I would in every thing, take the Civil Magistrate along with me, if they would Assist me; if they would not, I must follow the Custom of Armies, and help myself, for that I could not sit still, and see the Country undone, for the Obstinacy of a few Men: the Recorder did all he could, to change the Mayors Resolution, but to no Effect: So I have since that, Quartered the Men, by my own Quarter-Masters, and hitherto have billetted none, but where we had Billets from the Magistrates: On this occasion they have shut out several Officers, but have always made it up, till last Night, that another Cannadian Trader, threw an Officer's Baggage into the Street, and Barricaded the Door; and I sent a file of Men, and got the officer into Possession: my resolution is, if I find any more of this work, whenever I find a leading Man, shut out one of the People, to take the whole House for an Hospital, or a Store House, and let him Shift for himself.

There are two Officers here, wore out and incapable for the Service, in this part of the World, whom I have given leave to go home; the one is Captain *Muloy;* of Major General Abercromby's Regiment, who was the Serjeant that defended *Revon,* in 1745; the other, is Lieutenant Wender of Major General Shirleys, who is likewise very Old, and has lost a great part of his Scull; they both hope to be put into the Invalides; and are only absent with leave, which I should not have granted, if they could have been of any use to us here; So Your Royal

Highness will determine about them, as you shall see propper: they have both been very Gallant Men in their time.

Since closing my Letter to Mr Fox, I have received a Letter from Mr Webb, Acquainting me, that his Party, sent out to bring Intelligence from Oswego, are returned; that they got as far as the Onondaga Indians, who assured them, that Oswego was burnt; that the french were gone off; that they had cut down a great many Trees on the River, above Oswego, before they went; that the ground at Oswego, lay cover'd with dead bodies, which raised such a Stench, they could smell it at a great distance; that they saved very few but Sailors, and a few Officers; that they said, that they were very much obliged to the English, for furnishing them with so many Cannon, to take their own Forts; that they hoped soon, to take Fort William Henry, and to be at Albany after that: but as those Onondago Indians, would not allow them to go on further, for fear as they said, of meeting with some parties of French Indians, who may be left behind; I by no means like this Intelligence.

Sir William Johnson Acquaints me, that the Party he has sent out, has orders, not to go by any of the Indian Castles; I shall be very impatient, till they return, and that I know something with certainty, of their Motions: Sir William Johnson is very Ill, of a Bloody flux; he will be a great loss to us, if we lose him.

Affairs here, are in a very bad situation; Your Royal Highness knows what Troops I have; the New England Men, by all Accounts, frighten'd out of their Senses, at the name of a French Man, for those are not the Men they use to send out, but fellows hired by other Men who should have gone themselves; and the Forts much worse than we imagined; but those two things I shall be able to Inform you of, with Certainty, when Colonel Burton and Mr Montresor return, whom I hourly expect.

The Enemy I am afraid, are much stronger than You think, and all Accounts agree, that there is a Battalion of the Irish Brigade here; they Scattered Letters all round Oswego, this last Spring, promising great Rewards, to any Soldiers that would come over to them; which drew great numbers of the Irish Recruits, from the two Regiments there, which were mostly Roman Catholicks; And I will be far from venturing to assure You, that there are no Roman Catholicks in the other Regiments, tho' all possible care has been taken to prevent it, by Lieutenant Colonels Gage & Burton, and I find, most of the deserters from them, are Irish.

I have yet no returns, to the Circular Letters I writ, on the taking of

Oswego: I hope they will fill up their New England Men, with better than they were first; but I must leave the Second Battalion of the *Royal Americans,* at least for some time, in Pensilvania; the first I think, I shall compleat immediately, and soon get here, if I can move any thing in this Country, which I think, if I had a little more leisure on my hands, I could do.

They will give you, not one Shilling, to carry on the War; they will give you no one thing, but for double the Money it ought to cost; that I cannot help Just now, but I hope a time will come, that with a little Sweet and a little Sower, they may be brought about.

I am, Sir, your Royal Highness most dutefull and obedient Servant

LOUDOUN

Albany, August 30th, 1756. I have just now received an Express from Sir William Johnson acquainting me that an old Indian is just arrived with him on whose Fidelity he can depend; who says the French are preparing at Oswego to attack the Great Carrying Place. That was what I suspected they would do, the Moment I saw the Onondago Indians would not let our Party proceed.

I have given Orders to send Mr. Webb 250 of the Highland Regiment, with Rogers Company of Rangers of 50. I send Buchanan of the Train with 12 of the Gunners and Orders repeated to send away all the useless things they have with them, such as Cannon dismounted, Shot for Guns at Oswego, and all the Atterail of Stores gone there. This is all the Supply I am able to give them.

I beg your Royal Highness will turn in your Mind what is to be done. I imagine it must end in an Expedition up the River St. Lawrence. Can you give us a Fleet to Support us? I will let you know, as soon as I can see how things will turn out, what Prospect of Success there may be.[1]

[*Endorsed*] Albany, August 29: 1756. Lord Loudoun to H:R:H: inclosing *Two* papers.

LOUDOUN TO CUMBERLAND [1]

(A.L.S.)

Albany Octr 2d 1756

Sir

I have made my Secretary coppy most of the Letters I have the Honour to write to you in order to save you the Trouble of reading a very

[1] The postscript is in Loudoun's handwriting. See the note to the following letter.
[1] Loudoun's autograph letters present a problem to the editor, for he wrote so execrable a hand that it is often impossible to tell how he spelled, and he never

bad Hand, but what follows I thought your Royal Highness would rather choose to have from me directly.

1st ꞏ I shall begin with the Deputy Quarter Master General, who has lived very ill with both my Prediccesors, but I hope that is all over now, for so far as I can judge we are on a very good footing and I have talked to him on all sort[s] of Business either such as belonged properly to the Bussiness of his Department, or where I could get light from the Experience he has had in the Service. Some times our Oppinions vary but realy very seldom; when they do, I take my own Way if his Arguments do not convince me. I think the only one was about defending the Great Carrying Place, which he thought at too great a Distance; that you see Mr Webb settled for us both without my Knowledge till it was done, and I wish it had been still to do for the appearance it had among the Indians.

2dly In this Country the Qr Mr General has a great deal of Bussiness, more than in any Service I ever was in, which arises from the Variety of Services going on at the same time in so many different Places; the Supplying the Garrisons and Troops at the two Forts, supplying the Parties on the Mohawk River and carrying on the Works here, of Hospitals, Store Houses, and Barracks, besides the stockading the Town and making some little Works, which is all it can admit of, not one Carriage provided, nor in my Power hitherto to make a Contract to carry on those Services, makes an infinite deal of Work, and Sir John is not at all well, and I think cannot hold it a great while, for he has still great Pain from his Wound, and every little burdern [Accident] lays him up, and if he were gone, from any thing I have yet seen of the People here I do not know where to find one to put in his Place. The likliest Man I see is Major Robertson.[2] He had one Depute when I arrived whom he did not choose to post[part with], Mr Leslie, but as I found they were not able to carry on the Bussiness, I was obliged to give him Captain Christie as an Assistant.

---

punctuated. The copies of the Windsor Castle originals which were made by the staff under Miss Mackenzie's direction have been collated with the copies in Loudoun's Cumberland letter book in the Huntington Library, which were made at the time by Loudoun's secretary, John Appy. In many cases Appy was not as careful nor as accurate as the staff at Windsor Castle. Moreover Appy's love for excessive punctuation, which can be seen in the L.S. Loudoun to Cumberland letters in this volume, often completely altered the meaning which his chief intended. The editor has thought the wisest solution to this problem to present a mean between the modern and the contemporary copy, giving Loudoun every benefit in spelling and holding Appy to a judicious use of commas. By this device the sense is better presented. The words in brackets are Appy's reading in cases which seemed doubtful. This plan has been followed for all of Loudoun's A.L.S. letters in this volume.

[2] James Robertson of the 60th regiment, later deputy quartermaster general and governor of New York.

3ᵈ   I have here told you the footing I imagine I stand in with Sir John; but you will know better how that realy is from his own Letters.

4ᵗʰ   M. G. Abercromby is a good Officer, and a very good Second Man any where, whatever he is employed in.

5ᵗʰ   Mr. Webb, by being detatched, has been little with me, and I was afraid the things that happened on that Command might have soured him; but now that he is returned I do not find it has. I proposed at first to have carry'd him up with me, but[and] that he should have commanded at Saratoga, for[but] there is so much to do here and the People of the Place so extreamly unruly, that I have determined to leave him here.

6ᵗʰ   As to the Corps Col. Monro does what he can to keep that Regiment ³ right, but they must have many Examples made before it will do. None of them have ever been in Service. These Men are large Bodied but the most unruly[urnuly] I ever met, and I think by next Campaign I shall make the pressed Men better than the old ones; and the Officers want full as much to be reclaimed as the Men, and I have not hitherto been able to bring them to act like other Troops. They have overdrawn their Provisions; they have lost the Live Stock I delivered to them, and they have taken others in their Place; all which I have ordered to be paid to the last Shilling, which I hope will do them good as it will amount to above one hundered Pound.

7ᵗʰ   Lt Col Gage is a good Officer and keeps up Discipline Strictly; the Regt is in Rags but look like Soldiers.

8ᵗʰ   Lieut. Colᵒ Burton I did not know before, but he is a diligent Sensible Man, and I think will be of great use here.

9ᵗʰ   Both those Regiments have some Men in them that with all the Severity they are able to use, they are not able to lave of [cure of] Theft and Drunkenness, but I must do them the Justice to say, they have no Bowels on them.

10ᵗʰ   The Highland Regiment will be a good one next Year, but they have not near two hunderd Men left of their old Ones.

11ᵗʰ   Lieut. Colᵒ Bouquet is a diligent Officer and seems to understand his Bussiness, and if we can keep the Men now we have got them, will make a good Battalion next year, but I doubt we shall be very much disapointed in the Engineers. When I know from my own Knowledge I shall acquaint your Royal Highness just as it appears to me.

12.   I have in my Letter to the Secretary of State mentioned my Opinion of the Operations for next Campaign; that Quebeck is the

³ The 35th regiment.

Point we should push for, by the River St. Lawrence. I need not explain to you the Consequences would arise from our Success there. But I realy see no other Point we are so likely to succeed in as in that, which is the main Point; for where ever we make our Point, we must fight the whole Force of Canada before we arive at it; as their Power over these[their] People can bring the whole to what ever Place they are wanted. There, if we have a proper Fleet, and that comes in time, we can arrive with our whole Force at once; if we can land and establish our selves, we have nothing then but the Siege to make; if we succeed in that I imagine the Bussiness is done, for there we shall I do suppose [meet] all there Regular Forces, which so far as I have yet learnt is Six Battalions from Europe, besides their Marine and their People of the Country, with their Indians which are very numerous. Their Town is mostly built of Wood, and probably must be burnt about their Ears.

*13*th   The Troops we have for the Execution of this Plan your Royal Highnes knows, and what they are. In my opinion I must leave at least two Battalions here, to defend the Forts and prevent their coming in whilst we are going round to attack them, otherwise they could make a very distressfull Attack here and be back time enough to meet us there.

*14*th   I know in England they will say we may have all the Men in New England to go on that Expedition, to what their Hearts are set on.

*15*th   But then Mr Shirley has instilled into his Party whom he has bound to him by all the Ties Knaves can be tied by, that is, Proffits Received, a Belief of Power in him to protect them and continue Proffits to them, to oppose and dissappoint every Scheme that can be proposed for the Publick Service except Mr. Shirley is to execute it. The Crushing of him, if that is thought proper, will end them, but from his staying here so long, that must probably come too late to have its Effects this Year.

*16*th   There is another Objection, I believe, to having great Aid from them, which arises from this, That so far as I can see, all the Expeditions they fit out have their first Foundation in an Intention to enrich particular People, then a Popular Point is taken up, and the People Run madly into it.

*17*th   That motive now ceases, if they go with the Regular Troops, for these the Kings General must command, and these Profits cannot arise unless he is a Knave likewise.

*18*th   These Men receive a Bounty when they enlist, but no Pay till the Campaign is over. They allow of no Suttlers or Traders of any Sort, but the Officers supply them with every thing they want, by which Means they receive most of their Pay when they come back; this you see does not promise much from them in the present Situation, and yet as Canada has been so much Preached up to them, numbers of these Enthusiastical People might engage, and if they did, they will be a very great Expence to transport them by Sea, and furnish them with Provisions considering the use they would be of, which, so far as I can see, is, when first brought out, will undertake any rash thing, but if they do not get forward they immediately languish to go home, and when ever they grow Sick their Hearts break and they Die. They say their time is come, and there is no help for it, and from that Principle never struggle to live.

*19*th   If they could be brought to cross the Country in small Bodys, for great ones can not be maintained that way, and break up all these Settlements, they would strike a Terror into the Enemy, and in case we miscarried, would storme [show] them next Year, if the Fleet will prevent their having Supplies from Europe, and the People here can be brought not to supply them, which will be difficult, as the Councils can take off the Embargo and are the People that supply them, as happen'd in Philadelphia this year before Mr Denny arrived.

20th   I have throw'n out those things for your Royal Highness's Consideration, and would beg leave further to add, that if you should approve of going to Quebeck, I should hope it would not be talked of, but when ever you are to send, it should be said it goes to New York, and that you will consider what Troops are necessary for it. And altho I can have 24 lb Cannon from the Colonys here, they are all Iron and so heavy that without Horses, which I suppose we shall not get there, or the Enemy will drive them off, so I should hope you would send what you think necessary of Brass. Ball for 24 lb are much wanted in this Country.

21.   In case the Project is approved of, I believe it would be necessary to acquaint Mr. Baker the Contractor, that he may provide accordingly.

22.   I can give you no certain Accounts of the Road to Tienderoga, as it has never been reconoitred properly, but by all the Accounts I have been able to get, it is not to be done with Troops whilst the Enemy are so supperior in Irregulars, for in reality we have none but our Rangers. Before winter is over, if they do not drive us from the Forts, I shall be able to give you an Account with more Certainty.

23.   The retaking Oswego by land labours under many Difficultys. Tis 217 miles from hence, and as the Enemy have now learn'd so many Avenues from the Indians by which they can at several places attack our Convoys, it requires an Army to secure the Communication for

carrying up our Cannon and Provisions. And when there, as they are Masters of the whole Vessells, and such a Number of Boats on the Lake and we were to oppose to them, if they chose it they can before we are cover'd land what Forces they please, within what Distance of the Place they please, and give us Battle, tho I think they would rather choose to starve us, as we could not leave People enough to keep up the Communication at every Place where they could attack us.

24th   Things appearing to me in this Light is the Reason I have proposed going to Quebeck, and I have been the more particular in them, that your Royal Highness might be the better able to judge whether they have not weighed more with me than they ought, and that the King's Service might not suffer from my misjudging.

25th   I ought to have mentioned above that if a Siege is to be undertaken Powder will be wanting, for the Provincial Troops make an intolerable Consumption of it.

26th   I hope your Royal Highness will pardon the Incoherence of this Letter, as I really believe tis the fortieth time I have been interrupted in the Writing of it, and as I am just setting out for Fort Edward I cannot write it over again.

27th   I must acquaint your Royal Highness that I have hitherto had no formal Council of War but have on all Occasions consulted with the General Officers, the Qr Mr General, and such of the Field Officers as I could get any Benefit from talking to. But I found when I had several of the Field Officers together and came to talk to them of what was fit to do in one Case, and what in another, but I got no Aid, so I have gone on in the Method I have told your Royal Highness.

28th   I have this Moment a Warrant of Mr Shirley's put into my Hands, drawn on the Paymaster for an Account of building Barracks on Schenectady last Year. The Warrant is dated June 20th 1756. Mr. Webb arrived here June 7, and in three Days after, Mr. Shirley received his Letters acquainting him he was superseded in the Command, and the Man who got this Warrant left me at Albany to go to New York to settle this Account for which the Warrant is granted. Mr. Shirley will find himself mistaken if he expects to draw any Money out of the Deputy-Paymaster's Hands till the King gives him a new Commission to Command. I am, Sir, Your Royal Highness's Most Dutyfull And Obedient Servant

LOUDOUN

[Endorsed] Albany, October the 2d 1756 Lord Loudoun to H:R:H: private. Rd Novr 21t V:15:8.

Loudoun to Cumberland

(L.S.)

Albany 3ᵈ October 1756

Sir,

The Situation of things here at present, is bad; the *Provincials* extremely disheartened, Sickly and deserting; which last some of their Officers are in Confinement for; no less than *forty* went off at once; most of those we retook; but the numbers that go off in one's and two's, are very great: Your Royal Highness will see, I have reinforced Fort *William Henry,* with all the *Provincials,* except the *New York* Regiment, and the *New Hampshire* Men; if I find I can spare the last, I will send them up likewise.

I have now at *Fort Edward,* Majʳ Genˡ *Abērcrombie's* with the *42ᵈ, 44ᵗʰ,* & *48ᵗʰ* Regiments; and *500:* of the *Royal Americans,* under Lieutenant Colonel *Bouquet,* at *Saratoga;* the other *500:* of them, March to October *1ˢᵗ*; I had it not in my Power, to get Waggons for their Tents till then.

Your Royal Highness will be surprised, I have chose to take the *Royal Americans,* rather than Lieutenant General *Otways;* this last are entirely Raw Officers and Soldiers, and every thing new to them; the prest Men, I dare not yet trust so near the Enemy; I had Six of them deserted together, to go to the French; two of them, after losing themselves in the Woods, and being Starving with Hunger, Surrendered to some of the Parties above; those I tried and hanged directly; the other four, were taken at *Wood-Creek,* by our Ranging Companies; they are not yet come my length.

As to the *Americans,* I have without distinction, of what Battalion Officers belong to, put into this, all the good Battalion Officers for the present, that were within my reach, and have left out the Engineers and Artillery Officers, who Lieutenant Colonel *Bouquet,* on trial, assures me do not answer in the Battalion; I have done this, without any affront to them, for I shall employ them otherwise, where they will be of use: In this Situation I expect more Service from them, than I could have had from the other; and they do bring them on surprisingly.

Our Situation at Fort *William Henry,* is, the *Provincials* in an Intrenched Camp, under the works of the Forts, which are by this time finished, and the Barracks and Store Houses near compleated. they have of Artillery, *two 32:* pounders, *Eight 18:* Pounders, *two 12:*

Pounders, *Four 6:* Pounders, *four 4:* Pounders, Iron: — Brass, Four *6:* Pounders, *two 8:* Inch Mortars, fourteen Swivels, *One 13:* Inch Mortar, *two 10:* Inch Mortars, *two 8:* Inch Hautsbitzers, and *one 7.* Inch Hautsbitzer, *three 7.* Inch Mortars, with a great Quantity of Ammunition.

This is what they had amassed, for the Attack they proposed on *Tienderoge,* a great part of which I proposed to have brought back, but could not get Horses to Transport it, and if I had them now, the *Provincials* would desert if I took it.

At Fort *Edward,* there are *two 18:* Pounders, *four 9:* Pounders, five *6:* Pounders, *One 4:* Pounder; and *Six field Pieces* with the Regiments, *6:* Pounders each; in an Intrenched Camp under the Forts. With the *Americans,* there are *two Six* pounders, and *a 3:* Pounder field Piece; as I have divided them into two Battalions, Colonel *Bouquet* and Major *Young* with the *one,* Lieutenant Colonel *Haldiman* and Major *Robertson* with the other; I expect Col: *Haldiman* every hour, the other three are here.

The Camp at Fort *Edward,* is under the Cannon of the Fort; the Cannon Mounted, but the Fort far from being compleated.

At *Saratoga* they are intrenched, with a small Stockaded Fort within it; this is to prevent the Enemy cutting in, behind us, and are within reach of Joining us in few hours, if wanted at Fort *Edward.*

It looks odd on the Map, to see the *Provincials* advanced before the Troops; but I look on Fort *Edward,* as the likeliest Post to be Attacked; and if that is taken, Fort *William Henry,* with all the People there, falls of Course; therefore I have chose to be there with the Troops.

From Fort *William Henry,* I am just informed, the Enemy seems to be pressing up upon them, and they have seen Boats, *two* and *three* at a time, Skulking along the Shore, which are probably Supplying them with Provisions; I have given them all the directions I can, and have again sent up Captain *Loring,*[1] to Command that Fleet they have built, but make no use of.

This is our Situation, and I would gladly hope, when they see our Posts in this Condition, they will not Attack them; but if they should advance the *Six* Battalions of *Regulars* they have at *Tienderoge,* to keep us in Auwe, and take the Measure of sending their *Indians* and *Canadians,* down the other Side the River, they may destroy the whole back Settlements, and God knows where they may Stop; And it is not in my Power to prevent it.

Your Royal Highness sees, the Aid Mr *Shirley* has been pleased to

---

[1] Joshua Loring, a native of Boston, whom the Admiralty had named in March as Master and Commander of the brigantine *Loudoun* on Lake Ontario.

Contribute; the *Massachusetts* Men, I cannot have at Fort *William Henry*, in less than a Month; the *Connecticuts*, will be between a fortnight and three weeks; however, in case of their taking this Measure, I shall write for them, that they may be in some sort of readiness to Act: If this should happen, nothing further appears to me, to be in my Power to do at present; when any thing does occurr, I will do it.

Desertion and *drunkenness*, are the diseases of this Country; I will stop at nothing to cure them both, if I should Stave every drop of Liquor in it: I have lost above thirty of the *Americans* since they came here.

The backwardness of the People in this Country, to give any Assistance to the Service, is incredible; And if you cannot destroy, that Influence Mr *Shirley* has in it at present, no Servant the King can send, can be of half the use he otherwise would be; I hope you will do this effectually when he arrives, in the meantime, my best endeavors shall not be wanting here; and when time permits, You shall have all the Information I can give You.

On the *Mohawk* river, I have left some small Posts; and am Fortifying *Herkermer's* House, in place of building a Fort; You have Major *Eyre's* Sketch of it enclosed.

As to Engineers, I doubt I shall suffer greatly, by the loss of Mr *Mackeller;* for, I do not find, the Foreigners will turn out to be the People in that branch we expected; I send you enclosed, the *List* Colonel *Bouquet* gave me, of himself, without my asking for it, on suspecting that to be the case; this he did, when he came to apply, to have other Officers Appointed for the present, to the Battalion going on Service.

I am afraid, from Lieutenant Colonel *Bouquet's* report, Colonel *Prevost* has not kept up to his bargain, in recruiting, from the hundred and Seventy arrived; I have not had time to look fully into it, but shall as soon as he arrives, and Acquaint Your Royal Highness with it: I shall go very gently with it, but I must not let him go too far.

Mr *Shirley* has taken on himself, to Stop the Man of War with my Letters to the Government of the 29th *August;* the Captains receipt to me for them, is enclosed to Mr *Fox;* he has sent many Letters, whilst at this distance, I have no opportunity of knowing, of the Ships going: If it is no Crime stopping the Publick Letters, I shall say his time was very Ill employed here, as it was only in raising parties, and stopping all Aid to the Service; and by the Councils Letter to me, which is every word dictated by him, you will see, he is still endeavoring to keep up the difference, between the *regular* and *Provincial* Troops.

Your Royal Highness will see in my Publick Letter, the *Plan* I throw out for Consideration, of attacking *Quebec;* I have in that, mentioned neither the *number* of *Ships* nor *Men,* necessary for that, as I know Your Royal Highness to be, a much better Judge of it than I am, and shall be ready, to execute whatever orders I receive from You: I must only beg, that if you go into it, there be a *good Man* at the head of the Fleet, that will not create Confusion; and that the Fleet come very much earlier than any have done of late, for the French have always been here before us.

Lieutenant *Kennedy's two Prisoners,* are arrived, whilst I am writing, and I have enclosed their declaration to the Secretary of State; It was a *hardi* thing taking them; they had a French Camp within a mile of them; the Waggons continually passing the door; and they took them in open day: Mo^r *Levy* was not gone from the House, an hour before. the *Indians* killed a Servant that made resistance, and had Seized the *Landlady* of the House, in order to *Scalp* her, when Lieutenant *Kennedy* came in and saved her, and an *Old Swiss,* whom they brought along with them; and after a March, thro the deserts, arrived here in *28:days.* They say, the Lady was handsome when she set out, but she is much altered, thro' Hunger, Wett and all sorts of Weather, added to Fear, which was not without good Grounds; for as they had been pursued for five days, by about three hundred Indians, as they imagine, they had been obliged to throw away all their Provisions, and were reduced to such Streights, from hunger, that they several times proposed *to eat* the Lady; but Lieut^t *Kennedy* got her Saved.

She computes the French at *Tienderoge,* to be about *Six thousand five hundred,* but the *Canadians* are very Sickly, and great numbers of them die; the Troops tollerably healthy: she is the first that has mentioned their being scarce of Provisions. I never saw People so thoroughly wore out, as those People are; the Indians are but just alive; Lieutenant *Kennedy* is better than they are, but extremely weak; the Woman has stood it the best, but they had a long March before they met her; they reckon, the way they came, that She walkt about *Six hundred Miles.*

Your Royal Highness will see, that the distress at *Oswego* last Year, was wholy owing, to Mr *Shirley's* going on a Trading Voyage, in place of a Military Expedition; and that you will see from Colonel *Mercer's* Letters, most of them sent down open, to endeavor to get any Supplies, from the People on the different Posts, before the Letters could arrive at the Persons they were directed to. You will see, that the *distress,* the *desertion, diseases* and *deaths* of the Garrison, was on the one hand, owing to their want of Provisions; and on the other hand, from their want of Barracks and Bedding, most of them having lain in bark Hutts, without the Garrison, all Winter; all which will appear plainly, from the Scraps of Information I have got, in following other business. there was a third cause, which I have not yet fully got into, which was their want of Pay from the *24*[th] *October;* in these, I doubt there are more People concerned than him, which hitherto has prevented my seeing into it; there must have been a great neglect in not sending Money to *Oswego,* in the beginning of Winter, but this goes further, for they had opportunities of sending it long before it went; *first,* Colonel *Schuyler* went up with *250:* Men, then Captain *Bradstreet* went up with a *great number of Batteaus* and Batteau Men, and the Recruits; and it was his *Second* Journey, before M[r] *Shirley's* Regiment's Money went; and *that* for Sir William *Pepperel's* Regiment, waited 'till his *third* Journey: I do not see, what can be said to Justify this, and still less what I am told, that their Recruits, who were many Months at *Schenectady,* in the Spring, had no Money; but were Supplied with Shirts and Shoes & ca, 'till that they were so disgracefull, that Colonel *Chapman* would not let them do duty in the Condition they were, and the Officers borrowed of Captain *Kennedy,* of the *44*[th] Regiment *Twenty five* Pounds.

Those things, seem to me Military Crimes, that ought to be enquired into, in order to lay before His Majesty, and as soon as the Campaign is over, I propose to Appoint a General Court Martial, to enquire into the Causes of the loss of *Oswego,* the result of which I shall transmit home.

Part of Lieutenant Colonel *Mercer's* Original *Letters,* I have sent with M[r] *Pownall,* and some of M[r] *Lewis's* Accounts; one Packet fell into my hands by the directions of it, the other found in *Oswego,* by the Men, I mention to have brought us the Account, of the Situation the Enemy left things in, and is the Account of M[r] *Shirley's* Son in Law, his Secretary M[r] *Alexander,* and M[r] *Livingston,* whom he employs on all occasions, where he means to have his own nearer friends **not appear;** You will see in the large Packet, *the Commissary* in the King's Pay, as appears in his Wife's Letters to him, *charging five per Cent* on the *Publick* Money. the large Articles of Commission, I have not yet had time to follow out, as they arise in *Virginia* and *New-York.* I am, Sir, Your Royal Highness's Most Dutifull and Obedent Servant

LOUDOUN

[*Endorsed*] Albany, October 3[d] *1756.* Lord Loudoun to *H:R:H:* inclosing *18:* Papers.

MEMORIAL OF WILLIAM JOHNSTON
(COPY)

TO HIS EXCELLENCY JOHN EARL OF LOUDOUN, General and Commander in Chief of all His Majesty's Forces in North America. &ca. &ca. &ca.

The Memorial of William Johnston Deputy Pay
Master General to the said Forces.

MAY IT PLEASE YOUR LORDSHIP,

The Lords Commissioners of His Majesty's Treasury by a Minute of their Board, dated the 12th August last having taken into Consideration General Abercrombie's Warrant Authorizing your Memorialist to Issue the dollar at 4s8d Sterling, and all other Coins and Species of money in Proportion, are of Opinion, there is no Reason or Foundation for varying from their Resolutions of the 19th February 1755. and of the 11th March last Ascertaining the Rates at which the Several Species of Gold and Silver were to be received and Issued by the Deputy Pay Masters in North America, and have therefore given directions, that the said Deputy Paymasters do follow the Rules, as to the Receiving and Issuing the Same, in the manner thereby Prescribed; And Mr. Sawyer by Direction of Lord Dupplin, having transmitted a Copy of the said Treasury Minute to your Memorialist and Signified to him, that it is the Paymaster Generals Orders, that he do Act agreeably therewith, and give Copies thereof to Your Lordship, and General Abercrombie, or the Commander in Chief for the time being: In obedience to these Orders; I beg leave to lay before your Lordship a Copy of the said Treasury Minute; and as this Regulation will differ from that made in Virtue of your Lordships Warrant, I humbly Pray your Lordship will be Pleased to give me Directions how I am to Conduct myself in receiving and Issuing the Several Species of Gold and Silver for the Future. All which is humbly submitted to your Lordship

Wᴹ JOHNSTON

Albany 25th October 1756.

Copy of a Minute annexed.

MY LORDS,

The Lords Commissioners of His Majesty's Treasury having taken into Consideration Your Memorial together with Major General Abercrombie's Warrant, with an Account of the different Species of Money Remaining in the hands of your Deputy Paymasters in America; on the 19th June last, are Pleased to order me to Signify to your Lordships, that they see no Reason for varying from their Resolutions of the 19th February 1755. and of the 11th March last, and do therefore desire you would take care that your Deputy Paymasters in North America do follow the Rules, as to the receiving and Issuing, the Several Coins of Gold and Silver at the Rates, and in the manner thereby Prescribed. I am, My Lords, Your Lordships Most Faithfull Hum. Servant.

J: WEST

Treasury Chambers, 12th August 1756.
[To the] Pay Master Forces.

[Enclosure No. 4 in Loudoun to Cumberland, Nov. 22–Dec. 26, 1756.]

OBSERVATIONS ON THE VALUE AND RATES OF THE GOLD AND SILVER TO BE PROVIDED FOR THE USE OF HIS MAJESTY'S FORCES SERVING IN NORTH AMERICA, UNDER THE COMMAND OF THE RIGHT HONBLE THE EARL OF LOUDOUN

(COPY)

The Lords Commissioners of His Majesty's Treasury, by their several resolutions of the 19th February 1755 and the 11th March 1756. directs the Gold and Silver to be issued to the Troops in North America in the Following manner, Vizt.

In the Province of Pensilvania they are to receive the Gold at the Rate of £4.–.7¼ per Ounce, and Silver at the rate of 5s4½ per Ounce, mill'd dollars at 5s4½ per Ounce is very near equal in proportion to 4s8d pr dollar, For example. 1151 Mill'd dollars will weigh upon an Average 1000 Ounces, which at 5s4½ per Ounce will amount to the sum_____268.15.
The same Number of dollars at 4s8d each will amount to_____268.11.4
The difference is only_____3.8.

The disproportion between Spanish Gold at £4.–.7¼ per Ounce, and Spanish Dollars at 5s4½ per Ounce or 4s8d each is very considerable for instance—A. has a demand on the Deputy Paymaster for £100 Sterling, which he receives in Spanish Dollars, either by weight at 5s4½d per Ounce or by Sale at 4s8d each, if by Sale he receives 428 Dollars and 4/7 of a Dollar for his £100 Sterling. As the Dollar is Current at 7^s6^d each in Pensilvania, these Dollars will Amount in that Currency to the sum of_____$160.14.3\frac{3}{7}$.

B. has a Demand for the Like sum in Sterling, and receives it from the Deputy Paymaster in Spanish Gold by weight. 24^{ozs} 16^{dts} 6^{grs} at $£4.-.7\frac{1}{4}$ per Ounce is equal to $£100$. This will Produce 116 Pistoles and $^{36}\!\!/_{51}$ parts of a Pistole of 4^{dts} 6^{grs} each which is the Standard weight, but they often weigh more, and as it's value is 27^s Currency, the amount of the whole will be only____$157.11.-^{36}\!\!/_{51}$

In this case A. having received his $£100$ in silver, and B. the like sum in Gold, the latter looses the difference of Value being_____ $\Big\}$ $3 \cdot \cdot 3 \cdot \cdot 3$

If the Pistoles are 4^{dts} 8^{grs} they pass for no more than 27^s, and if we take them at a Medium at 4^{dts} 7^{grs} each, the difference or disproportion in Value between them and Spanish Dollars is still more for example 428 dollars & $\frac{4}{7}$ parts of a Dollar at 4^s8^d each, is equal to $£100$ Sterling. This converted into Curr^y at 7^s6^d per Dollar will produce $£160.14.3\frac{3}{7}$ as above 24^{oz} 16^{dts} 6^{grs} of Gold $£4.-.7\frac{1}{4}$ per Ounce will amount to $£100$; this reduced in to Pistoles of $4^{dts}7^{grs}$ each will produce 115 Pistoles and $^{59}\!\!/_{103}$ parts of a Pistole which at 27^s each amount to only $£156.-.5^{61}\!\!/_{103}$. Consequently the person who receives $£100$ Sterling in Gold at the Rate of $£4.-.7\frac{1}{4}$ p^r Ounce will loose or receive less by $£4.13.10$ than another who might happen to be paid the like sum Sterling in silver.

The disproportion of Value between Gold and Silver if received by weight in the Province of New York is still more unequal than in Pensilvania; but as it is now fix'd to be received and Issued by Sale, we will confine our Observations to the last Regulation made by the Lords Commissioners of His Majesty's Treasury, ascertaining the rates at which the several Coins of Gold and Silver are to be received and Issued by the Deputy Paymaster in North America Viz^t the half Johannis of $£1.16.-$ to be received & paid at $£1.17.4$, the Moydore of $£1.7.-$ at $£1.8-$ The Pistole of 16^s6^d at $17^s1\frac{1}{2}^d$ and the Spanish Dollar at 4^s8^d.

Agreeable to this Regulation we will suppose that A. demands of the Deputy Paymaster $£1.17.4$ Sterling for which he receives an half Johannis B. has the Like Demand and receives it in Spanish Dollars; Eight Dollars at 4^s8^d each is $£1.17.4$, consequently B receives Eight Dollars. A is under a Necessity to Change his Gold into small Silver or Dollars before he can make a distribution of it to the Troops, and as an half Johannis in this Province is Valued and pass'd at $£3.3.-$ and a Dollar at 8^s, A receives for his half Johannis so Changed one

Shilling Currency or ⅛ Part of a Dollar less then B. received for the same sum in Sterling, the Value of the half Johannis being so much less in proportion then that of the Dollar.

In like manner let it be suppos'd that A. demands of the Deputy Paymaster £1.8.— Sterling for which he receives a Moydore. B having a demand for the same sum receives it in Dollars; Six Dollars at 4^{s}8^d will produce £1.8.— A. being oblig'd to Exchange his Moydore into Small Silver or Dollars for conveniency of payment, receives for His Moydore so Exchang'd only £2.6.— Currency which is Equal to Five Dollars and three Quarters consequently he looses or receives less then B. two shillings Currency or one fourth part of a Dollar; the Difference of Value between Moydores at £1.8.— and Dollars at 4^{s}8^d each being so much in Proportion, in the Province of New York.

If spanish Gold or pistoles are to be issued at 17^{s}1½^d Sterling each the disproportion of Value between that and Dollars, is more Considerable then the Portugal Gold, for Example.

The Deputy Paymaster pays A a Spanish Pistole, of 4^{dts} 6^{grs} and Charges him 17^{s}1½^d sterling for which he can purchase only £1.8.— Currency B. receives three Dollars and half and is Charg'd only 16^{s}4^d Sterling with which he can Purchase as much as A. Three Dollars and half being equal to £1.8.— Currency. Consequently A will loose 9½ Sterling upon every Spanish Pistole he receives: Vide a Table or State of the monies annexd.

The Deputy Paymaster has now in his Charge £16,000 Sterling in Spanish Dollars for which he has Pass'd his receipt to Mr. Mortier at the Rate of 4^{s}8^d Sterling each: By changing these Dollars into Spanish Pistoles, and issuing them to the Troops at the rate of 17^{s}1½ Sterling each, he has an Opportunity to defraud the Troops of 9½^d Sterling upon every Spanish Pistole so Changed, which in the above sum will amount to £775.10.— Sterling. This is a Latitude, from which the Deputy Paymaster and the Contractors Agents ought to be restrain'd, and shews the Absolute necessity of having all kinds of Specie, whether Gold or Silver, received or Issued to the Troops in an exact and equal proportion of Value, one with another.

If the Regiments in great Britain were paid at the rate of £1.2.9 for an English Guinea and all other Gold Coins in Proportion, and the value of the Silver Coins to remain, as it now stand; the Regiment that received their Subsistance in Gold, would receive less by 1^{s}9^d in each Guinea than another Regiment that happend to be paid in silver. The same Argument will hold good in America, if the Troops are to be paid in the manner prescribed. from this state of the Case, it is obvious that a new regulation for receiving and issuing the Gold and Silver to the Troops, became necessary, either by raising the Value of the Dollar or lowering that of the Gold, in order to make it bear an exact and equal Proportion in Value; and as the Dollar was fix'd and ascertain'd to be received and issued at 4s8d sterling, and the least liable to vary in it's value, It was propos'd to be made the Standard by which all other Coins or Species of Gold & silver were to be issued and paid, provided the said Dollar was not Clipped or otherwise diminished in the Value it now bears.

In the Province of New York the par of Excha upon Dollars at 4s8d each is 171¾, and the Current price of Exchange being 185, the profit arising by the Contract is £14.4/7 upon every £100 Sterling but whether the Exchange be higher or lower the Profit or advantage in providing Dollars at 4s8d or any other monies in that Proportion, can be ascertain'd with great Exactness; in Pensilvania the Par of Exchange upon Dollars at 4s8d is 160⅝/7 and the Current rate of Exchange at present is 175, so that the Profit arising by the Contract in this Province is £14⅔/7 upon £100 Sterling.

If the Gold and silver to be provided for the use of His Majestys Forces in Virtue of the Contract are to be Issued in different Proportions of Value, in all Probability great inconveniences may arise, and it will be impossible to ascertain, with any Tolerable degree of Exactness, the profit arising by the Contract that now Subsists.

A Table shewing the difference of Value in Sterling between Spanish & Portugal coind Gold & Spanish Mill'd Dollars

Species	Value in New York Currency			Value in Sterling			Difference of value in Sterling		
	£.	s.	d	£.	s.	d	£.	s.	d
Half Johannes	3.	3.		1.	17.	4			
7 Dollars & ⅞	3.	3.		1.	16.	9		.	7
Moydore	2.	6.		1.	8.				
5 Dollars & ¾	2.	6.		1.	6.	10		1.	2
Spanish Pistole of 4dts 8grs ..	1.	9.			17.	1½			
3 Dollars & ⅝	1.	9.			16.	11		.	2½
Spanish Pistole of 4dts 6grs ..	1.	8.			17.	1½			
3 Dollars and ½	1.	8.			16.	4		.	9½

Albany 25th October 1756.

[Enclosure No. 5 in Loudoun to Cumberland, Nov. 22–Dec. 26, 1756.]

OBSERVATIONS FROM QUEBEC DOWN Sr LAWRENCE'S RIVER OCTOBER 1756, BY JAMES PITCHER [1]

(A.D.)

On Sunday the 3^d of October left Quebec with the Wind at South west, but soon chang'd to the north west, We at first steer'd over for the Northern Shore to an inlet or Bay, seemingly so to be from the Harbour but found it to be a Beautifull Fall of Water, which had by time wore the soil away, When we had sail'd to bring this quite open, steer'd away between the Island of Orleans, and the Southern Main, keeping near midway between, but rather nearest to the Island, at the East end of which, (being Seven or Eight Leagues long) We came to an Anchor in about Seven fathom water, the Island is covered with Wood, but seemingly a poor barren soil, like the rest of the Country.

In the morning of the 4th about nine aClock when the Ebb had almost done, we made sail, and about noon came to what is call'd the Traverse; Our first Course steer'd was about East, till we brought the highest hill in the Country to the Westward, in one with the Westermost Point of Madame Island, which is the nearest to the Island of Orleans.

Then we keep'd away more Southerly for the highest of a parcel of Rocks, which appears a little above Water, and lies much about the middle of the River, till we came about the middle of the second Island, when we had the low end of the highest Land to the Westward of the Humocks, and the west End of Madame Island in one, Then steer'd away for a barren hill on the North Shore, about NE, till we brought the North east end of Orleans, & the Main high land in One, then steerd down the North Shore, keeping about one Mile distance till about four aClock in the afternoon, when we came to an Anchor in about twelve fathom Water, about 10 Leagues from Orleans.

On Tuesday the 5th, being the third day about seven in the morning, when it was near low Water, we made Sail and steer'd about E B S, till we came near the Island of Aucudia, then steer'd in for the highest hill on the North Shore, and stood in so close that when we steer'd away for the NE Point of the Island, it brought Us midway between

---

[1] James Pitcher, muster master general, had been in charge of the musters on the Cartagena expedition of 1740. He was taken prisoner at Oswego, exchanged, and returned to North America for the duration of the war. His comments describe the usual channel followed in navigating the St. Lawrence, south of the Isle d'Orleans, through the Traverse, north of Isle aux Coudres, south of Isle du Bic. The map of the river in Thomas Mante, *History of the Late War in North America* (1772), shows the course.

the Westermost point of the Island, and the Eastermost point that Forms the Bay; which is the Channel through a very rapid Whirlpool, but no danger, if the proper cautions are taken; after we were through came to an Anchor near midway between the Island and the main, the West end of the Island bearing SW B S and off of which is Rockey and foul Ground here we discharg'd the Kings Pilot.

NB

"To Pass this Whirlpool, remember to take the midway and the "advantage of a Fresh Breeze of Wind, and near high Water, but "never to attempt it either going up, or coming down, on the "Ebb,

"The Capt of the Ship inform'd Us that three Years ago the "French lost at this place Four men of War, having little wind at- "tempted to pass; but the Eddy over powering the Command the "wind had of the Sails, lost their Steerage and drove them on the "North Shore, but this I could not give Credit to, as they must "pass, one after another, when the first was foil'd, I should im- "agine the rest would have desisted till another oppertunity.

Our Course from here was East about seven Leagues, when we came to Several Islands lying near the South Shore, against which on the main are several houses & a Church, We had another long Island on Our left distance from the others about three leagues, at the East end of which, in the Evening We came to an Anchor in about six fathom Water. Clay Ground this Island is high,—In the morning of the 6th we made Sail and steer'd NE & NE B E, to several small Rockey Islands, from where we weigh'd Anchor, ab^t 6 Leagues, from thence E N E & E B N, keep^g pretty near the Sth Shore about Eight Leagues, when we came to a Point, on which are some lofty Barren, Rockey Hills, & Off of this Point are two Islands, the nearest about 1½ League from the Shore and is called Beak Island, from the East end of which is a ledge of Rocks, and some of them above high water for near two Miles, we sail'd between this Island and the Main having deep water, and Continued our Course about ENE Thirty Leagues, here the River is about Seven Leagues over, and high Land on the Southern Shore, Continued the same Course, and the River extending itself wider that in sailing about Thirty five leagues we lost sight of the Northern Shore, and came to the point that Forms the Entrance of St Laurence's River, and of Gaspia, this Point is low but high Land back in the Country, from this Point we steer'd S E & SE B S about Forty five Leagues, when We saw the Magdeline Islands bearing from Us West, distance about Four Leagues, these Islands the French reckon Fourty two Leagues from the

Point of Gaspia,—The 11th of October being the ninth day since We left Quebec, We continued Our Course S E^t, about Fifteen Leagues, when We saw the Island of St Paul, bearing from Us about S S W distance about Four Leagues; This Island is smal and lies in Lattitude 47°04', and is reckoned by the French Eighteen Leagues from the Magdelines, from this Island we took Our Departure and steer'd away S E B E^t, which carried Us out of the Gulf,

The Tides flow at
Quebec about 16 feet.

[*Endorsed*] J. Pitcher October 1756. Some Observations made on Sailing down the River St LAURENCE from QUEBEC. R Dec. 22^d.

CUMBERLAND TO LOUDOUN

(COPY)

Kensington, October 22^d 1756

My Lord Loudoun, Great as our Impatience has been to hear of your safe Arrival in *North America*, your Excuse for not writing 'till you had began to inform yourself, *partly*, of the Situation of Affairs, imbroiled & concealed, by the ill Conduct & bad Behaviour of your Predecessors, is so reasonable; and the Difficulties of Information are so great, that, I am rather surprised at the Quantity of your Informations. I long feared that our Affairs in that Part of the World, were bad in themselves, & worse by the Management of them. But, I little imagined that Ignorance, Avarice, & Confusion were so prevalent as your Letters, not only mention, but prove them to be. I can not enough commend your Coolness of Temper & Moderation, in what you have already had to do with the *Provincials*. For, execrable Troops as they are, I fear, our present Distresses, will make them, for some time at least, necessary to you.

By all I can judge at this Distance, you seem to have taken the only Steps left you to take, to prevent the utter Devastation of the King's Provinces in *North America*. But, I can not help flatering myself, that, when once you have recruited your regular Force in that Part of the world, you will be an over-match for our Enemys.

I am sorry to observe the little assistance you are like to have from the *Indians*. But, if you encourage the Inclination you have found in the Soldiers to go out with them & the Rangers, you will soon be able to do without *Indians;* & will have Reports & Informations that you can depend upon, & by which you may regulate your Measures.

By all your Reports of the State of *Fortifications* in that Part of the world, I easily conceive how much is necessary to be done. I shall apply to the proper Offices to see what can be done with regard to the *wood* which is all *granted away*, & which they sell you at double Price.

In the Case of Commissions, granted by Major Gen¹ *Shirley*, I entirely approve of your Resolution. But, I think it is hard that the Officer who bought the Company, should not have his Comission confirmed, tho' it is certainly not a valid one. I shall also apply, that the *third* article of your *Instructions,* may enable you to put the non-effective Funds of the Regiments upon the same Footing as they stand at home.

I highly approve of your Conduct, with regard to that *Jerry,* the Indian, who was murdered by some of the 44: Regiment; tho' I can not say that the Answers from the com'anding officers were, either as decent, or as proper, as they ought to have been.

The Account you give of the growing Expences of the *Indians,* is but a trifling Part of Mʳ *Shirley's* bad Conduct. The whole account you have sent upon his head, makes a just Impression here; & I can assure you that he will meet with a very different Reception in England, from what he expects.

I am extremely concerned at the latter part of your Letter, which mentions the Intelligence of the Loss of *Oswego,* which I fear is too true, from the distressed Condition Mʳ Shirley had left it in. I must entirely submit my Judgement with regard to what the Enemy may do, in case they have taken *Oswego,* to yours, which is better informed; & I am glad that you still hope, that if you meet with Success this year, with the *new England* Colonies, to make a Push for the retaking of *Oswego.*

What Arms can be sent you, shall, as soon as we can spare them: but, Arms grow scarce, even here.

If the News are confirmed relating to the taking of *Oswego,* I shall humbly propose to His Majesty the *Breaking* of the *50:* & *51:* Regiments, & *incorporating* the officers into the other Corps, at present in *North-America.* In the mean while, you have certainly judged it right to turn over the Men not taken Prisoners with those Regiments, into the other Corps.

I am glad to see that, by your stile of writing the *Royal American* Regiment will soon be complete: and, I hope, before now, *Offarrell's* Regiment complete *700:* Rank & File; with *1200:* Soldiers, draughted from *Ireland,* will be Sailed from *Cork,* for the Northermost Ports the Season of the Year will allow them to reach. Their original Destination was for *Nova Scotia*. But, your Accounts arriving before they were sailed, they are now put under your orders, for you to employ them, either in your own Defense; or, if you can spare them, to send them, early in the Spring, to *Nova Scotia*.

Your Intention of fixing your Residence at *Albany*, seems certainly right, as it is the most centrical Part; & from whence you can be more *à portée* to send Succours, or give necessary orders.

Private.   St James's, December 2d 1756

My Lord Loudoun, I Shall be Kinder to you than you have been to me; for, I shall make use of my Secretary to save you the Trouble of reading my bad Hand. But, joke apart, I think you very much in the right to have trusted no one with what is in this Letter; & I shall answer it as the Articles in it stand.

I am glad that Sir John *St Clair* does his Duty in such a manner, that you approve of him in the Capacity in which he acts, & that he has so seldom disagreed in opinion with you. It is every Man's Duty that commands in Chief to ask the opinions & advice of those who can give him new Lights from their Experience & Knowledge of the Country and Service. But, where the[y] difer, & do not convince, the Person commanding ought certainly to follow his own opinion, as it still appears to him the best, after having heared other opinions: and I would as little be talked out of my own opinion, as I would be deaf to Conviction. So that, you see your manner of acting has exactly coincided with what I think a Man in your Situation ought to do. It is very plain that the Duty of a Quarter Master General in *North America* is rather too much for any *one* Man to execute: And, as there are so many diferent Services, I am rather surprised that you have not employed such Persons as you find most proper to assist him in the diferent Branches of the Service you are engaged in, as you are so much divided, & in all Probability will be obliged to act by diferent Corps, each of which require a Man to do that Duty. I can assure you, in return, that His Letters are as full of Satisfaction & Regard to you, as I could wish: and tho' he has mentioned his having been of a diferent opinion with you, concerning what was necessary to be done at the *Great Carrying-Place;* yet, he mentioned it with that Deference which an Officer owes to the opinion of his commanding Officer.[1]

The Character you give *Abercrombie* is that which I always had of him. *Webb,* by having been so much detached, has not, yet, had time

---

[1] St. Clair's letters are not among the Cumberland Papers.

to be known to you; &, had you known him as well as I do, you would not have feared that he would have returned soured from his Command. He is a sensible discreet Man, as well as a good Officer; & I can venture to assure you, you will find him as usefull a Help as any I could have sent with you.

As to *Otway's* Regiment, I am not surprised at the scandalous Account you give me of them. They have never seen any manner of Service; &, I am afraid, your Letter convinces me of what I feared before, that it was composed of a Set of ignorant, undisciplined Officers; & 'till you make Examples of the officers, you will never make a Regiment of it.

The two Lieu[t] Colonels you mention are, I believe both of them good Officers [2]; & by your Care, I don't doubt but those two Regiments will, by next year, be as good as any in the King's army.

As to the *Highland* Regiment, they have an excellent officer at their head: and, if they have but a Couple of Hundred of old *Flanderkins* in the Battalion, I shall look upon it as a pretty good one.

Bouquet had a very good Character in the Service out of which he came. I am glad you find him a diligent officer.

I am sorry you seem to fear your being disappointed in the *Swiss* Engineers. But, consider the Ranks they come into our Service in, and whether a *Vauban,* or a *Coehorne* would have come a Captain or a Subaltern into an *American* Service?

Your Opinion for the *Operations* of the next Campaign, which you have mentioned in your Letters of this Date, have very much coincided with the Opinion on this side of the water, and already, for some time past, a *Naval Expedition* has been intended for *Louisbourg.* The Success of that Operation, a Plan of which I will transmit to you herewith, would very properly lead on to the main Point of the River S[t] *Lawrence.* I am sensible by the Events of these two last Summers, that your **Observation is very** just; that, in whatever Part we attack *Canada,* the Constitution of their Government gives them the Advantage, that they can transport thither, not only their whole *regular Force,* but *all* their *Provincials,* who are, God knows, many Degrees above ours: and, their Force is certainly what you reckon it; *six European* Battalions that went from old *France,* at about 560: Strong; out of which Strength they lost what *Boscawen* took, & what fell with *Dieskau* in his Expedition; some marine Companies, the *Canadian* Militia, & some *Indians.*

The crude Thoughts that occur to me, at this Distance, on considering that *Plan,* must be very imperfect. But, yet, I propose the sending

[2] Thomas Gage and Ralph Burton.

you over a Plan for your Opinion thereupon; which, if you should approve of, you will immediately prepare matters for, & send us back your aprobation, that we may go on, here, without losing time.

I see the Necessity of leaving a Couple of Battalions of *Regulars* to defend the Forts; and, if a Number of *Provincials* were joined to them, & so posted as not to fear an attack where they are posted, They must either keep a great Number of the Enemy at *Tienderoga*, who would, else, be employed in the Defense of Quebec; or, if the Enemy should withdraw their whole Force from that Part, that Body might march on & take Possession of *Montréal*, a Place I have very good Grounds to believe not tenable against a *Six* Pounder. It also appears to me that some Force ought to be left for the Defense of *Pensilvania* & *Virginia*, as *Oswego* is now gone; and a Battalion is as little as you can leave for that Service. We begin, here, to know the *New-England* Men; and we have had so many Disappointments from them, that the *Cry* here, at least among knowing, sensible People, is no longer in their Favour: and the additional Disappointments that you seem to fear, from the various Lies & Stories which that Fellow *Shirley* has instill'd into the Minds of the People of that Country, will certainly have some Effect, 'till it be known amongst you, how he has been received, & how he will be treated here. But, still, if a Number of them could be got for the Purpose above-mentioned at the Forts, & small Bodies of them could be brought to cross the Country, & break up, as much as they could, the *then* unguarded Settlements of the French, they would certainly strike an additional Terror, & would, as you observe, starve them the next year, if we had the Misfortune to miscarry.

You are extremely in the right, in recomending the not mentioning the Design to be upon *Quebec*. Much Assistance you can not flater yourself with from this Country, when you are informed that, through the lowest Clamour, it is become adviseable for His Majesty to send away the foreign Troops that were sent for over last Spring, for to assist to defend the Mother Country. Artillery can be easily convey'd to you on board the Squadron intended for that Service; & therefore, you undoubtedly will need no Artillery with you. I shall certainly remember your Hint, concerning the 24^{lb} *Ball*. If it is necessary, Mr *Baker* the Contractor shall be acquainted with the Expedition. But, as yet, I see no Necessity for it.

I am sorry that you have not yet been able to find any certain March to *Tienderoga*. But, I hope that you will, in time, teach your Troops to go out upon Scouting Parties: for, 'till *Regular* Officers with men that they can trust, learn to beat the woods, & to act as *Irregulars*, you never will gain any certain Intelligence of the Enemy, as I fear, by this time you are convinced that *Indian* Intelligence & that of *Rangers* is not at all to be depended upon. The many Dificulties of the re-occupying *Oswego* were plain enough by the almost Impossibility we have been in of maintaining of it; and the Lights which you have given me in this your *Private Letter* have greatly strengthened my Opinion that *Quebec* is the proper Thing to undertake.

You are much the best Judge of when it is proper to hold Councils of war, or not: for, I have seldom seen any good come from them: and especialy, as you have consulted those whom you thought best able to give you Lights, it has been the less necessary. In general Councils of war have not been held for to annoy the Enemy, but to excuse the General, when, either Misconduct or unavoidable Misfortunes have prevented the Execution of the Service that has been expected from him.

The late Treasury had already taken Notice of Mr *Shirley's* having drawn upon the Pay-Master, after his Command was finished, & the new Board shall not fail to be warned upon that Subject.

St James's, December 23^d 1756.

I must conclude this long Letter, with acquainting you that Mr *Shirley* is, either already, or immediately to be brought before His Majesty's Council, whose Report will give a better Guidance for what further Prosecutions, either Civil or Military he may be liable to. I don't doubt Mr *Pitt* will acquaint you by this opportunity, of the Sentiments of His Majesty's Servants, relating to the Reinforcements intended to be sent to you. I shall do all that is in my Power to press the sending them out early, & with such Artillery, Amunition &c, as may make them answer the Purposes they May be intended for.

I must not omit to mention that your sending of Mr *Pownal* here, has been of great Service, & will be more so, when we come to fix upon a *Plan*. By the little Conversation I have as yet had with him, he has fully answered the Expectations I had of him, from the Character Lord *Halifax* gave him. I hope we shall soon be able to send him back to you, as I am sensible he must be a great Loss to you from his Capacity & the Knowledge he has of that Country.

I can, with great Satisfaction assure you that His Majesty in particular, as well as every well-informed Person, is highly Satisfied with your prudent Conduct during this dificult Campaign: and you do me the Justice to believe that I sincerely rejoyce at the Aprobation given to One, whose Measures, Temper & judgement have been so entirely agreeable to my own Sentiments. You shall find all the Readiness possible in me, to support & assist you and your Cause here at home, with all the Strength & Warmth I am capable of. I remain your affectionnate Friend,

[*Endorsed*] Letter from *H:R:H:* to Ld *Loudoun:* October 22: *1756:* continued Decr the 2^d and concluded December the 23^d *1756. N:B:* This Copy was intended for a *Duplicate;* but was not sent to his Lordship.

JOHN THOMLINSON [1] TO GRANVILLE [2]

(A.L.S.)

My Lord (Granville)

As our Foreign Trade is certainly the Source of all our Wealth, and consequently our Strength, Then our American Collonies and plantations, must absolutely be of the utmost conciquence to the defence, wellfare & hapiness of These Kindoms, As the Trade with Those collonies & plantations are of greater advantage to us than all other Foreign Trades we are in possession of, as this very Trade brings in afar greater Ballance to the increace of our National Stock, Than all our other Foreign Trades put together; And also Employs More Shipping, breedes & Employs more Seamen, More Artificers Manufacturers, &c &c, than all the Rest; and with this particular advantage, That however our Other Foreign Trades may be obstructed, this Trade must still continue soley our Own; And this our most daingerous Rivalls in Trade, and most implacable Enemies the French, well know, And are makeing every effort in their power to wrest this inestimable Fountain of wealth & strength out of our hands, and should they ever succeed, how must we then be distress'd to keep up our Fleets & Armys in so respetable a manner as we have hitherto done; and on the other hand thus loseing so large a Fund of wealth and strength, navigation & Trade, to our most bitter Enemies, will enable them to increase their Navigation & Trade, in proportion to our loss, and thereby be enabled to increase their naval strength to such a degree, as to ingross and Commond all the Foreign Tãde in the World, And altho The Kingdoms & States in Europe, may not at present Attend to These Ambitious Schemes of France; but supinely set under them, or unnaturally

---

[1] John Thomlinson of East Barnet, merchant of London, was one of the army money contractors and since 1734 colonial agent for New Hampshire.

[2] John Carteret, Earl Granville, was the proponent of a vigorous continental policy when secretary of state, 1742–1744, and was lord president of the Privy Council from 1751 to 1765.

enter into them for some present End, yet if Their good friends the French shall ever Carry their point so far, as to reduce these Kingdoms to their Wish, Their insatiable Thirst of Universal Empire cannot End here, but thus haveing gott the Means into Their hands; without the spirit of prophetsie I think I may venture to say, Their turn will be Next; and that the first Victims, may probebly be, Spain, Holland & Germany, however your Lordship can see much better & farther into these Matters than I can.

And this My Lord I only disign'd as An introduction to what I set down to offer to your Lordships consideration, at this most Critical juncture, which is a method or plan, which if carried into Execution with resolution Vigor & Despatch, as his most Gracious Majesty has recomended From the Throne, (from my knowledge of the North America Collonies and the long Experience I have had in their Affairs) will in my Opinion not only put an End to all our present daingers, and Difficultys There, but Entirely prevent the like ever happeñing.

The News papers My Lord, Bruite it about this Kingdom, and concquently All over Europe, so that it is in the mouth of Every man you meet, That we are about to send to North America, a great number of Land Forces, and a strong squadron of ships, and it is likewise said & believed, the French are doeing the same, however, if They are not, they undoubtedly will; upon finding what we are doing send a greater Number of Land Forces, and ships of War, out of Brest, or some other Ports, and if possible to be in North America Before us, and may slip out, without our Cruizeing squadrons seeing them, as was the Case the last year when Their ships of war frequently went out, and in, Notwithstand the Vigelence of our cruizeing squadrons, or it may be, this armement may be Esscorted to sea beyond the Cruize of our squadron; by a Fleet superior to any we may then have off Their Ports, as was the Case before, and whither or no it may proceed from the deffrence of our, and the French Constitutions I cannot say, but this is generaly said & believed that all their Expeditions and undertakeings, are resolved on, and all the necessary prepropareations made, and carried into Execution with such impenetrable secrecy as not to be discover'd untill the Blow is struck,—While on the other hand, every resolution of this sort Taken here, of sending Land Forces or Even single ships of War, upon Any Expedition, or Ocasion whatever, or whenever Any Fleets of merchant ships, or single Rich ships are Expected home, or goeing Out, imeadially Every news gatherer, every Busie inquisitive Fellow, or spye, do's know the WHAT, the HOW, the WHEN, and the WHERE, and then by the Villanous And meschivous News papers, every thing we do, or design to do, not only our Friends, But also our Enemies all over the World knows of it, and are thus advertized and caution'd to prepare to defeat Every thing we undertake.

But My Lord besides this Fatal Licenciousness, (which surely might be cure'd) there is another Evel which generally Attends all our Undertakeings, whether it proceeds from the Forms [?] of Offices, or what I cannot say, But generally all our Expeditions are so Teadious in their preparations, that the proper season for putting them in Execution has offten been lost, And at other times the Enemie thus advertize as above, have had sufficent time and oppertunity to make such preparations, as to defeat all our purpose's, And in this now particular Case, more than in most other, Time and season must be Attended to, And give me leave My Lord to say, that Now, TIME is, and a Most Critical & precious Time indeed, For if now that Vigour & dispatch which his Majesty has so graciously recommended, is made Use of, so that a sufficent number of Troops may be Embarked, togeather with a strong squadron, and ready to put to sea with the first fair wind after the first of February, so as to be able to get to North America by the first of April, that they may have the whole summer before them, and which may probably be before the French Armament may arrive there, and I will hope That at this Crittical time when so much is depending, a very sufficent Body of Troops, as well as ships of War, will be sent, and at the aforesaid time, and Then I am satisfied in my own mind, that (under the Favour of Divine providence) they will soon remove the dainger which at present threaten us, and prevent the like ever hapening, and it has ever been my way of Thinking, That Missfortunes and ills, are Easier and better prevented, Than Cure'd when sufferd to come upon us; And Theffore at this important Cricis, will it not be more prudent, at once to remove the daingers and difficultys we now labour under, for ever, Tho at A Milion Expence, than let this most favourable Opertunity slip, so that our Enimies may get such footing in our Collonies, as may in time cost these Kingdoms Twenty Milions, and at last not be able to dispossess them, or recover our loss.

And now My Lord, Tho I have mentiond my hope that a sufficent Body of Troops, and a strong squadron will be ready to sail for North America, by the first of February, I will not pretend to say what number of Troops, or ships of war, But only submit to Your Lordship my private opinion, what may be necessary to be done, in the fitting out, & Destination of this very important Expedition, and the reasons for this opinion Your Lordship will see, arrives from some things I have Mentiond above.

Then in the first place my Lord, Tho as I have said the report has already been spread universally, that this Expidition is for North America, Yet might it not be proper and Necessary at this time, to do what has been done in other Case's of far less concequence; That is, That some hints may be Thrown out; that this first Expedition, is not for America But for some other purpose; supose, for the retakeing Minorca, or the takeing the Island of Corsica, This report would soon obtain, and be spread all over Europe, and might it not have the good Effect of diverting the Attention of the French from America, in a good measure, or At least retarding & Delaying their Expedition Thether, if so, we gain a great point, and it will be very Easie to put This report out of All doubt, with the News Mongers, spyes &c, By giveing orders to the Navy, & Ordnance Boards, to take up & hire The Transports for carrieing the soldiers, artilery &c &c, for Minorca Corsica, or *to all or Any Other ports or place's, where they shall be orderd by the Commander in Chief for the time being.*

And My Lord The Thus Chartring These Transports For One Voyage, And after they are gott to sea ordering them to proceed upon Another, Cannot in my humble opinion be of the least hurt or damage, to them, as the very same Fitting out, as to stores provision Men &c, must be nessasary in one Voyage, as in the other, And so will be in all the ships of war, which are to Accompany them, and the same orders and Instructions will very properly Op̃erate, untill they are a proper distance at sea, where it may be thought proper to direct their Final Orders & Instructions to be opened; And which in my humble opinion may be when the Fleet has proceeded as near as they could, upon a West South West Course one hundred Leagues West from the Lands End of England; And the Final orders to be There and then opened & in my opinion should Then be, That they all proceed a direct Course for New York, untill they Attain the Meridian of Halifax in Nova Scotia, where in all probibility they will be out of the way of any French squadron, Then and there, it may be proper for the Commander to put the Fleet of Transports store ships &c, under a proper Convoy to see them safe to New York, And then to proceed with His Squadron directly to Louisbourg, (takeing care to avoid the daingerous Isle of Sables, which lyes directly in his way) and for some time to Cruize of that Harbour, spreading all the ships under his Command, from Louisbourg aCross the straits between that place and Newfoundland, and so, as to be within call; and thus they can hardly miss any of the French ships of war, or Transports, if we have the good fortune to be there before them, For it cannot be supposed that they will attempt the straits of Betile [Belle Isle], before the summer is pritty well advanced, and Therefore, I am of opinion They must come this way, and that all or some of Them, will Certainly Call at Louisbourg, for information, & other purpose's, & espicially to learn if the Gulf & River of St Laurence is so free from Ice, that the navigation is safe for such large ships, and here our Fleet will soon meet with and take some of The French ships, or Vessills, whereby they will get intilegence if the French Fleet is arrived, and where they are, or if not arrived when Expected, and take their measures accordingly, and they also will be here ready as the season advances, to proceed up the river of St Laurence, or where Ever it may be found necessary.

And now My Lord, by the time this Fleet shall be arrived off Louisbourg, and thus properly station'd; I will hope, that the Fleet of Transports may be safe at New York, and there find every thing prepared to Carry the Troops &c, up Hudsons River to Albany, or whereever Lord Louden may order them to join the army, and which I hope They will meet all Assembled, and in good order, and spirits, and fit for Action, And of sufficient Force to drive the French before them, And Then, after we shall have The good fortine to become Masters of the Fortress & Garison of Crown Point, I think our Troops will not have much difficulty in getting by the way of Lake Champlain, and otherways to the Banks of the River St Laurence, and then, by the blessing of God, Monreal & Quebeck will soon be in our hands, and then all the French Forts & settlements in those parts must fall of Course, and the great work in this part of the World will be over.

And I must hope, That as soon as our Arms are blessed with success so far as to have got possession of Crown Point, And Lord Louden can form a judgement, at what time his army may arrive before Quebeck, and that if he shall find it necessary, he will send directly Expresse from Crown point, to the Commander of our Fleet off Louisbourg, acquainting him with his Lordships Plan of Operation, and the time it may be necessary for the Fleet to be before Quebeck; and may in my opinion be the soonest and best done, by sending his despatches to Governor Wentworth, who lives at Portsmouth in the province of Newhamshire, & near The mouth of the River Piscataqua, and where there are constantly ships and Vessills, so to be ready to carry these dispatches to the Fleet, and this being the nearest port to Nova Scotia.

And with great submition to your Lordship, may it not be necessary to do, if not already done, and that is, for the government to send away a nimble ship, and also duplicate by the first New York packet, or otherwise, Orders to all the Governors in North America, to raise as many men as possible, to Join Lord Loudon by the first of April, And I am of opinion that they will raise a great number, provided they shall at the same time be promised, to be reimbursed the Expence of these Extraordnary Forces, and as I have said before, That let it cost what it may, it will in My Opinion be far better to finish this most intresting Affair in One Year, Than to prolong it to a great length of Time, And a Monstrous Expence.

My Lord, nothing but my Zeal for my King and Country, and deffence security peace and happiness of his Majestys Domions, and of Every individual Therein, could have induced me to have taken this liberty, of troubleing Your Lordship, with so long & incorect a Letter, and on such a subject, as I could not let any body see or make a fair Copy of, And if there should be any thing in it, that can be of any service to the publick, Then my End is answer'd; But if not, I am Well satisfied from the Experience I have had of Your Lordships candor that you will beleive it is well mean't, & Therefore will take the Will for the Deed.—I am with the greatest deffrance and regard, May it please Your Lordship, your Lordships Most Obed[t] hum[ble] servant

JOHN THOMLINSON

East Barnet the 13th of December 1756

To the Right Honourable John Earl of Granville President of His Majestys most Honourable Privy Council.

[*Endorsed*] East-Barnet; Decem[r] *13: 1756* M[r] *Thomlinson,* to Lord *Granville;* with considerat[s] upon the intended Expedition to North *America.*

CUMBERLAND TO LOUDOUN

(A.L.)

most private,

S[t] james's Dec[r] 23[d] 1756.

my Lord Loudoun, I write this *private Le*tter to you to assure you of the thorough Satisfaction your Conduct has give me & will not fail to Support you to the utmost of my Power through the many dificulties you find in the executing of your orders & in opposition to the public Service.

Nothing can be worse than our Situation here at home, without any Plan, or even a Desire to have one. great Numbers talked of to be

Sent you, but without any Consideration of how, & from whence, without considering what they Shoud carry with them. But, that you may know what can be done for you, I write in my own Hand, trusting to your Honour that you will burn this as Soon as read.[1]

The King will Spare you *five* old Battalions from *Europe* & *two thousand* new raised *Highlanders,* which will make *6000:* men, officers included: & I will Send a proper Train of Artillery with them. Prepare your own Plan for one army up the *St Lawrence* River, & for the other to keep the Enemy in check, from where your army now is. I will Send you my Thoughts more fully with a Plan of mine for your operations, which you Shall be left at Liberty, either to adopt, in part, or not at all, as you Shall find it proper, from your better Information. I don't doubt a moment of your burning this Letter. So don't answer it; but Send your Plan & Thoughts without taking any Notice of this *most private Letter.* I remain very Sincerely your most affectionate *Friend.*

LOUDOUN TO CUMBERLAND

(L.S.)

Albany 22^d November 1756.
concluded at *New York;* 26: Decem^r 1756.

Sir,

I have in my Letter to Mr *Fox,* given an account of the Quarters I have put the Troops into; but it is necessary, I should likewise Acquaint Your Royal Highness with my reasons, for making that distribution of them.

In order to save Your Royal Highness trouble, in looking back to my Letter, I have sent you a return of the Situation of the Troops.

I determined to Garrison Fort *William-Henry* and Fort *Edward,* with the *44th* & *48th* Regiments, because I found those two Regiments, much more Soldiers, than any Troops I had to place there, and I thought them the only People, on whom I could depend, for making a propper defense, in case of an Attack. If I take another Rout, I shall relieve them in the Spring; if I do not, they are ready to take the Field: If I had taken but one for that purpose, it would have prevented their recruiting; and the other of them, had not so many men as were necessary for the Garrisons.

---

[1] The signed letter of which this is the autograph draft is in the Loudoun Papers in the Huntington Library.

The remains of them I bring to Albany, and I shall keep them both there, along with the 35th Regiment, who I likewise keep at Albany, to be immediately under the Eye of Major General *Abercromby*, who will look very well to them; and I hope, by their doing duty along with the officers and Men of the 44th and 48th Regiments, we may by the next Campaign, Improve both their Officers and Men; and I do assure You, there has been no pains Spared: They are a fine body of Men, and will be a good Regiment; and in order to forward that, I am now picking out some good Officers, to fill up the Lieutenantcies that are left vacant in it.

There was a great push made, to persuade me to throw in the 42^{d} Regiment into the Forts, but as they have very few of the Men remaining, that were with You in *Flanders;* great part of those that came from *Ireland,* new; and *five hundred* recruits thrown in just now; I dared not trust the defense of those places to them this Winter. I sent them to *Schenectady,* where they will have most of their Men together, having only two hundred and Fifty Men detached, where they are among the *Indians,* and are likelyer to agree with them, than any other of the Troops, as the Indians have an Opinion, that they are a kind of *Indians.*

The *Royal Americans,* I have been obliged to turn into several Shapes: I have now divided them into the *four* Battalions, and from the duty they have had this Summer, those we had, are better able to assist in disciplining the Recruits, than they would otherwise have been. The Quarters I have chose for them, are in the Heart of our only recruiting Country, and are the most convenient for taking the Field next Campaign, where-ever it is to be. If You approve of the Plan, of going up the River St *Laurence;* I can at once, from *New-York* and the *Jerseys,* put those *two* Battalions in Sloops, and carry them Land locked, to *Bristol,* and from there, March them *Fifty* Miles of good road, to *Boston;* the other *two* Battalions being more South, I can March so, as to take up the Quarters in the *Jerseys,* the day the others embark, and so put them on board likewise. I have mentioned landing them at *Bristol,* or in that Bay, for I should not chuse, early in the Spring, to venture to turn that long Point of Land, to carry them round to *Boston* in Sloops; for should they meet with a *North* West wind, they must stand Streight for the West Indies.

The Objection is still stronger, to putting the Troops to the Southward, at once into Transports, because they must stand without all the *Nantucket* Shoals, which is a bad Navigation; and without a Convoy, would run the risk of being pickt up by the Enemy; this is the

Situation, if the Campaign is to be on that side: If it is to be pushed on this way, the convenience of Water Carriage, answers the same from *New York* and the *Jerseys* here, that whenever the Sloops are Collected, the whole or any part Sails up the River to *Albany*.

My reasons for distributing the Independent Companies, are, as they are in so bad a Condition, I dare not trust them quite to themselves, to set them right; therefore, have in some degree, Join'd each to a Battalion, that they may be under the Eye and Inspection of the Commanding Officer of a Battalion; from where I hope to have them compleated with good Men.

As the Provinces *South* to this, where the *Royal Americans* and *three* of the Independent Companies are Quartered, are the only one's from where we have hitherto got Recruits, I was under a necessity, of allowing the 35th 44th & 48th Regiments to Recruit there likewise, or I could not in any other Shape have compleated them; which I am in hopes to do, altho' the Recruits have come in very Slow of late.

By being obliged to have so many Corps recruiting there, the whole Country is as full of recruiting Officers as it can hold; which Joined, with what I understand, was one of the motives for raising Majors General *Shirley* and *Pepperell's* Regiments, that out of the numbers of Men in New *England* they could be immediately compleated, tho' that did not happen, and the most of them were raised in the South ; Yet as Mr *Pepperell* is on the Spot, and Mr *Shirley* has still a party Subsisting, both which, I will endeavor to pique on compleating those two Corps; I thought it right, not to over load the *South* with more recruiting Officers, at least till I had got sure of the Corps already recruiting there, compleated, and made the Experiment in New England; besides, till another Packet arrives, I do not know certainly, what Orders I shall receive about those *two* Battalions.

Captain *Richmond's* Independent Company, I am assured by every body, will be compleated there; and for that reason I send them there.

I have on purpose avoided, sending any of the Independent Companies to *New York*, as the Governor used to have the Command of them; and from many Incidents, I see is still very unwilling to believe, he has it not yet.

I have been forced to keep the Troops too late in the Field; *first*, from the Enemy keeping so long in a body in our Neighbourhood; then, to finish the Forts so far as to make them defensible; and thirdly here for want of barracks, in which I have been very ill served; for Mr *Montresor*, whom I employed as being Chief Engineer, has shifted so often from one thing to another, without Acquainting me, tho' on the Spot, and making Alterations, & carrying on works without Acquainting me, which has thrown the Barracks so far back, that I am forced to put the Troops into Quarters, which are not able well to contain them; this I believe he will not try again, but business will not go on under his direction; it is all very well when he is with you, but as his Practise has plainly been all, in drawing & directing in his room, it neither goes on nor is well directed, when he is from you.

Your Royal Highness will see in my Publick Letter, the Situation of the *Forts;* to which I shall add, that those *Wooden Forts* are so far good, that they consume a great deal of Timber, and by that, clear round themselves; but on the other hand, they occasion a great deal of labour, in driving home those logs, squaring them, and dovetailing them together at all the Angles; And from what I can yet Judge, will not last long, before they are rotten and decayed: my opinion is, not above *five* or *Six* years, and I see none, that imagine they will last above Seven Years.

I form my Judgement in this case, from what I see; *first,* all the Timber one sees lying in the Woods, with which they are quite full, is all rotten; even that, which was cut in Spring *1755,* to make the Road, is very much Spoilt; but there they are very much Shaded, and under the drop of other Trees, which consumes timber very fast: But I see likewise, at Fort *William-Henry,* in the works that were carried on there last year, that the timber has already suffered; and in the Casemattes there, where the Water has Soaked through; but the great Logs, from not being sufficiently secured with *Oakum,* are very much Rotted; and even the People here, agree that the Timber of this Country, rotts much sooner than the Timber in Europe does; but indeed there is no Justice done to it here, for it is cut when wanted, and directly put to use, whatever the Season of the Year is; For which reason, whenever there is occasion to build a Fort, that probably will remain, if there is Stone & Lime near, I should advise it's being built of them. The Alegation that I have heard, that Lime does not bind in this Country, I do not find holds in private buildings, tho' I am afraid it does in many Publick, both with us and the French; but that seems to be entirely owing, to the buildings being made in the end of the Year, after the Frosts are begun.

When I mentioned the Garrisons, I neglected to inform you, that I had stowed them with *Eight* Months Provisions; the Storm preventing the Troops at Fort *Edward,* longer from Marching than intended, may encroach on that, but I have Provisions in the Magazines on the Road, to supply that, as soon as *Slaying* comes to be good, which is the Cheapest way of doing it; and if the Winter proves good for Slays, I propose keeping those Magazines full, by filling up as they consume them. I have likewise left the Pay for the Garrisons of the two Forts, to the 23^d of February.

As to other particulars, relating to the Troops; there are two, that it is necessary for me to mention to You. I Acquainted you with the manner, in which I proposed to recruit and Cloath the Men of the 44th & 48th Regiments; that I proposed to have compleated the 50th & 51st Regiments, so far as would, in a great measure, have answered the filling up the others, and to have Cloathed them before I drafted them. I had great hopes, of the *North Carolina* Troops submitting to Mr *Dobson's* determination, and having them all turned over; and of recruits from the *New York* and *Jersey* Regiments; but those two last keep up their Regiments, to avoid the intollerable expence they are at in *Levy* Money every year; and the *Carolina* Troops would not Submit to be turned over, without force; which I thought better avoided, as I shall have them turned over as soon as they return, by their own People; and since they were ordered home, I have got a good many of them enlisted in the *Americans*. And as to my Plan of drafting the 50th & 51st Regiments, to compleat the 44th & 48th, with Cloathing, it will not answer; for those Regiments really want more Cloaths than Men; Besides which, another misfortune attends them, that very few of their Coats will make waistcoats; they are so thorough worn, that they are really like *Cobwebs,* tho' they have kept them as decent as they can, with mending them: So that on considering those things, and both the badness of any Stuff can be bought here, to cover those Men, and the excessive price it Costs in this Country, it seems to all of us here, that the best way we could supply that Cloathing, was, by taking as much of the 50th & 51st Regiments, as would do it; that whoever was to Pay that Cloathing, it was both better and cheaper, than what could be got here; and this is a Climate, where Men cannot live in Winter, without Cloaths.

If those Regiments are to be recruited, up to the full establishment, there will be still time enough, to replace that Cloathing from England; if vacancies are to be kept, for the Men that are Prisoners, there will be more than enough of Spare Cloathing.

The other, is the Supernumeraries of the *Highlanders,* which Your Royal Highness agreed should be put in the *Royal Americans,* and drafted from there, to compleat the 42^d Regiment, as wanted: As they have all along looked on themselves, as belonging to the *Highland* Regiment, and I believe the *American* Officers, when they had so many

Men to discipline, not chosing to be troubled with teaching them, have all beg'd of me, to Join them to the 42^d Regiment, and to continue to charge their Pay to the Royal *Americans,* till they fall into the 42^d by vacancies, which I have agreed to; and they are now with the *Highlanders.* I should likewise have told Your Royal Highness, that one Ship, with Recruits from *Germany,* must either be taken, but more probably lost; for she came out with the Ships that arrived a considerable time ago from *Stade;* She was with them in the *Orkneys,* there complained her Provisions would not hold out the Voyage, and then made so much Water, that her Pumps were constantly going; Some of the Officers, M^r *McLane* I think, went a Shore, and bought some Provisions for her, but She would not stay to take them on board, but left them there, and went to Sea: they say the Captain had Letters of Mark on board, and it was imagined, he chose to part with the other Ships, in hopes of taking a Prize, with the assistance of so many Men on board. If there is no account of her come to London, She must be lost.

I come now to the *Prisoners* taken, and sent home; from them, I imagine Your Royal Highness may have all the Information that can be had of that Place; Several of them were there, when Mr *Shirley* was there last year; others of them, have been there all Winter; who can give full information, of what situation things were in, at both those periods; for which, the information I have had, of which I transmitted Copies, will furnish so many of the *Queries:* M^r *McKellar* can give you information, of the situation of the Fortifications; and by all I hear, Mr *Pitcher,* the Commissary of Musters, will be as likely a Man to tell truth as any, of all that could come to his knowledge: And from Letters, from Mr *Lewis'* wife, to him, I imagine, if Mr *Alexander* does not get hold of him, he will reveal all the Clandestine Trade; as her advice is, to Join with the People that are come, and reveal all; for She says, She does not see, why he should ruin himself, for People who have used him so Ill. he was Commissary of the Stores; and had the disposal of the Goods, sent up by Messrs *Alexander Irwin* &ca, and can inform what Quantities of them were sent up in the Kings Batteaus, and at his Expence; by which, the Garrison come to be in such distress last Winter, for Provisions.

It is plain, those *two* Regiments were never regularly Paid; I have suspected many reasons, but I am not yet able, to find out the true State of the Case: I long suspected, that as Mr *Shirley* used to put many of his Warrants into the hands of his People, and allow them to Negotiate them, with the Contractors Agents here, that they had a Share in the drawing for the Money; but this, Major *Craven* assures me was not the Case: He is now drawing up a State of that case, a Copy of which I shall enclose; and as Captain *More*, of the 50th, is sent home, it may be got out of him; for it is very extraordinary, that That Regiment, that never was compleat, should have but so small a Sum in the Pay Masters hands, when I Landed.

I have discharged several of those *two* Regiments, and the Independent Companies, which will not appear in those returns; those for November not being all come in yet.

I am still afraid, I shall have a good deal of trouble in Settling the Quarters; but as this year will be the Precedent for future times, I shall spare no Pains to sett it right. In this place, they realy have hardly any more beds, than they lye on themselves; I am forced to give the Men *Palliasses;* and tho' they have a better Excuse than the other Quarters, from the number of Troops here, I am afraid I shall be forced to do it every where; but I shall take care to keep up my Claim, to every thing included in the *Mutiny Act.*

I am afraid, I shall be blamed for the *Ranging* Companies; but as realy in Effect we have no *Indians,* it is impossible for an Army to Act in this Country, without *Rangers;* and there ought to be a considerable body of them, and the breeding them up to that, will be a great advantage to the Country, for they will be able to deal with Indians in their own way; and from all I can see, are much stronger and hardier fellows than the Indians, who are many of them *tall,* as most of the People here are, but have a *small feeble* Arm, and are a *loose-made indolent* sett of People; and hardly any of them, have the least degree of *Faith* or *honesty;* and I doubt a good deal of their *Courage:* better times, may shew them in a different light.

I believe in a former Letter, I misinformed Your Royal Highness, about the number of deserters, from the *44th* and *48th* Regiments, and made them about *three hundred* from each; I have since perceived, I had Jumbled that wrong in my own head, for it is about *three hundred* from the two; but as the returns come along with that Letter, it would shew that affair as it is.

In the return from *Quebeck,* I imagine those Prisoners that are not accounted for, have enlisted with the Enemy.

Enclosed, I send Your Royal Highness a State of the *Independent Companies;* I think, if you approve of it, they had better be put on the same footing with the other Troops, as to their manner of being Paid, and take off that *ten per Cent,* which is stopped, by reducing the *Surgeons* and *Chaplain;* as they have but *two* of the *first,* for the four Companies, I should think, they had better have a Mate to each; And as for the *Chaplain,* I do not find they ever saw him: If you do not chuse to make that Establishment any more expensive, that may be kept on the same footing, by reducing a few of the Men of each Company: If you chuse to Regiment them, there is likewise a Plan sent for that.

There is one thing, I would beg leave to mention, for Your Royal Highness Consideration, which is, whether you would allow the Captains of those Companies, to continue to draw their own Money, as they have always done, which is a difference to them, of *fourteen* or *fifteen* per Cent; which will make those Companies a better thing to give to an Old Officer, when you chuse to put them there. I shall have great difficulty, to make any thing of those Companies, there are so very few Officers in them, who know any thing of the Trade; but that I shall endeavor to remedy, as fast as Vacancies happen, and I can get People to supply their Places, who can discipline them: Many of the Officers have been Indian Traders, and bought of the Governor, for the convenience of carrying on their Trade: Among those, is Lieu^t *Roseboom,* who is in that sort of Condition, as the Surgeons of our own Hospitals, whom I have sent to Visit him, assure me, I cannot force him to do duty, as he is, what they call, *Hypocondriack,* but in no likelyhood of dying. I hope Your Royal Highness will not disapprove, if I can get him to Sell for *one hundred* or *one hundred and fifty* Pounds, to some of the Serjeant Majors, or a Voluntier, that has the appearance of making an Officer; that I may have some tools to work with.

This brings me to the Payment of the Troops, which was very well settled before; but after I had the honor to be Appointed to the Command here, and the *Royal American* Regiment was to be raised, a new plan was set on foot, for Paying the Troops in *Pensilvania,* in Gold, *by weight;* whereas the former method was, by the dollar, at four Shillings and Eight pence; against which there has been no complaint, and there is a Saving to the Crown, of about *Eight* per Cent, at the Expence of the Troops and Contingencies. Mr *Hanbury* was sent to me, to explain this, and to shew me, that this Alteration was meant entirely for the benefit of the Service, and the Soldier in particular. This was a Plan of Mr *Hunter,* in *Virginia,* who is Mr *Hanbury's* Agent in this Country; Mr *Hanbury* did not understand it himself, so failed in convincing me; and I objected on the general Principal, that if Soldiers were to be paid on one side the River, in one Shape, and on the other, in another manner, it would be impossible to convince them, that they were not cheated; but on the Duke of *Newcastle* & Lord *Duplin's* insisting, that it was certainly a right thing, I agreed to try it; on Condition I was to Change it, whenever I found it liable to Inconvenience: I accordingly did try it. It will be objected, that Major General *Abercromby,* did before my arrival Change it, on the representations made to him before my arrival; but as soon as I come, I superceeded that Order: As I had promised to try it, which transaction Major General *Abercromby* knew nothing of, being gone before it was Settled; and after the trial, I have since been obliged to renew Major General *Abercromby's* Order.

Enclosed, Your Royal Highness has the State of the Affair at large, annexed to the Deputy Paymasters Memorial, which he brought, in consequence of his Order from the Office; and as the State of the Affair is long, I shall beg leave to mention one or two plain Facts.

I shall take Pistoles for the Example; they are of two different weights; All those that do not weigh fully the highest weight, when Paid away, are only markatable at the lowest value, whatever addition of Gold they have, which does not come fully up to the heavy Pistole, and that sometimes, amounts to near two Grains, all which is accounted to the Pay Master when he receives it by weight, and for which he receives not one farthing when he pays them again in Tale: this Your Royal Highness sees, is a very great proffit to the Contractors, or their Agents, which never can appear, or be brought to Account, to the Crown. There is another Fraud attends this new Scheme, which is, that by it we shall never receive any Silver, as after the Contractors Agents have collected the Money in Silver for their bills, they can then make *fourteen* pence on every *Twenty eight* Shillings, by changing it into Gold; there have been several Instances of this, but I shall name only one, which I have no other Proof of, but Mr *Hunter's* Clerk owning it himself, to several People: It is this, he brought *Thirty thousand* Pounds in Silver, from *Virginia,* to Pay to the Deputy Pay Master at *New York;* he, at *Philadelphia,* changed this Sum into Gold, by which, either he, or his Master, made *fourteen Hundred* Pounds clear: This Your Royal Highness will see, is a very great Trade, and is still attended with several further Inconveniences; such, as when we are in Towns, we cannot Change any Piece of Gold, in order to Pay the Men, without Paying the Person that gives Silver for it; and when we are up in the Deserts, there is no Possibility of Changing the Gold, to pay the Men: besides this, when we receive the Money in different Species of *Gold,* there is no possibility of Paying the Men equaly; for tho' they all come to us, at so much the Ounce, the Species have different values, in the different Provinces. This Evil is likewise severely felt, in all sums paid out of the Contingencies of the Army; whereas, those that receive the Gold, know the loss, and Charge in their demands, accordingly. I hope for Your Royal Highness Protection in this Point, for I may Negotiate with those Boards, but I cannot Change, without throwing things into great Confusion.

I have in my Publick Letter, given an Account, of the Quarters being at last Settled here; to Your Royal Highness, I will say more of the matter. I told them from the beginning, that if they did not give Quarters, I would take them; I chose to get them, to settle the Precedent of their giving them; in this Situation, they beg'd for a delay from day to day, to bring in their People; at last they came with their Answer, and I sent for the *Mayor* into my room, to know what it was to be when I met the Corporation; and he told me, he could not bring his People to Consent: I told him since that was the case, as he had several of the Magistrates with him, I would send for some of the Principal Officers, that we might have People of both sides present, to hear what past; in the mean time, till those People came, for it was before Nine in the Morning, I explained to the Mayor, in strong terms, how their Conduct appeared to me; and afterwards asked him his opinion, that as the Troops in Town, were not much above three hundred, whether the People would Submit Peaceably to my Quartering them, or if it would be necessary for me, to March in *more* Battalions for that purpose; for that as soon as I had received their answer, I would send for *three, four, five* or *Six* Battalions, if necessary, to settle that Point; and that I did assure him, if the Order for the March of those Troops was once given, nothing they could do, after taking up so much of my time, should Stop them from coming here, and being Quartered in the Town; and that I would likewise take Quarters for myself, and every Officer, when business obliged him to be here, till the *Motions* of the Enemy, or the Season of the Year, obliged me to move them out: On this, he beg'd a delay till next morning, and that afternoon, he, with the Recorder and Lieutenant Governor, came to me, and agreed to give what Quarters I demanded. Their Plan for Quartering the Officers, was to Pay their Lodgings out of a Fund to be raised; I told them, it was no difference to me, whether they made the Quartering, a burthen on the particular Houses where the Officers lodged, or from a general Fund, but that which ever it was, I must have a Billet on the House.

Here, this opposition seems not to come from the *lower* People, but from the *leading* People, who raise the dispute, in order to have a merit with the others, by defending their Liberties, as they call them.

At *Philadelphia,* things are very bad; I shall not pretend, till I am better informed, to say who occasions it, but the Point being settled here, I hope will enable Mr *Webb,* to set it right there.

But the truth is, *Governors* here are *Cyphers;* their Predecessors sold the whole of the Kings *Prerogative,* to get their Sallaries; and till you find a Fund, independent of the Province, to Pay the Governors, and new model the Government, you can do nothing with the Provinces. I know it has been said in *London,* this is not the time; if You delay it till a Peace, You will not have a force to Exert any Brittish Acts of Parliament here, for tho' they will not venture to go so far with me, I am assured by the Officers, that it is *not uncommon,* for the People of this Country to say, *they would be glad to see any Man, that dare exert a Brittish Act of Parliament here.*

Whilst I am writing, Letters are come in from Colonel *Bouquet,* at Philadelphia, who Acquaints us, that the Magistrates have *refused* Quarters; that Mr *Denny* has Issued a Warrant for them, and sent it to the Sheriff, who has refused to execute it, on which I have sent an Express to the Governor, to thank him for the assistance he has given us, and to beg him, to inform the People, that I send directly Major General *Webb* to Command there, and with orders to take Quarters, in the same manner as they were taken in Brittain, in the Years *1745:* & *1746;* which the Governor Knows, as he served those Campains; that if the Battalion now there, is not Sufficient, I have ordered Mr *Webb,* to March in as many more as are necessary, and Quarter the *whole* on them.

The method I have followed in Quartering, is this; at *Albany,* where I am obliged to Quarter more Troops than the People can support, or reasonably ought, I have taken nothing from the Inhabitants but House room; and as they realy have not Beds, I have given the Men *Paillasse's* to lye on, and furnish them *firing* from the Magazine, at the rate of one fire to Twenty Men, as they have in the Barracks: the Officers, I have given Money for their firing, and I find it Cheaper than giving them Wood, the Accounts of which shall be sent, but I am afraid, it will not be ready till next Packet.

Here, as they have resisted me, and are better able; I make them furnish me *Beds* and *Firing:* As to the small beer, I have established my right to it, but said, I should not insist much on it at present.

At *Philadelphia,* I propose, as they have all along been so troublesome, and are now so obstinate, to take the whole I have a right to;

Imagining, that making a difference between those that comply will-ingly, in carrying on the Service, and those that are refractory, will have a good Effect; and I would gladly hope, that after this dispute at *Philadelphia* is Settled, I shall have no dispute about Quarters; except it be at *Boston,* where I have reason to apprehend, they are not dis-posed to give them.

I have enclosed a List of the *Commissions* I have given, with an ac-count after each of them, in my own hand, of the reasons and recom-mendations. I have in this Provided every English Voluntier here, but I have still with me, some from *Ireland,* some from this *Country,* and a good many from *Scotland.*

I imagine, I have left four Lieutenantcies in the *Royal Americans* vacant, as I do not know with any certainty, how that affair stands, as I have no accounts, of what has been done since I left *London,* but one of Lord *Barrington,* of two Lieutenants that did not accept, and whose Places were Supplied by the King; and a List of foreign Officers, from Colonel *Prevost,* in which he does not inform me, in whose stead they come, or if they are added; but I imagine, with the two I have added here, their number is compleat of foreigners: As soon as I am informed, which I hope will be by the next Packet, whatever Vacan-cies there are, shall be filled up. Captain *Stanwix,* Son to the Colonel, is dead; as soon as I can with decency, I shall fill it up.

I have had an infinite deal of trouble, with the Accounts of the 50th Regiment; it took it's rise in this Shape. In August, Captain *Jocelyn* applied to me, for Subsistence of the detachment of the 50th Regiment, under his Command at *Herkermers.*

Your Royal Highness will see, by my Letters to Major General *Webb,* of August 20th & September 16th, that I, on finding that the Pay of Major General *Pepperels* Regiment, had not got up to *Oswego,* gave an Order to have it returned to the deputy Pay Master; but Major *Craven* Acquainted him, he had little more Money than was necessary for the detachment there; which surprised me a good deal, as both those Regiments had been paid up, by warrants from Major Gen-eral *Shirley,* to the 24th of *August 1756:* On which, till this detachment should Join me, I ordered Major *Craven,* Pay Master of the 51st Regi-ment, to supply the 50th till further Orders: When I come here, I found Captain *Jocelyn* had drawn from Major Craven £1218.15.11; and gives me in a demand of Pay, for the whole detachment, from the 25th of *October 1755,* to the 24th of December *1756;* Except the Sum of £142.2.4., for which he gives Credit, as the only Money received from the Pay Master during that time; but on examining into this last

Sum, it appears that the Pay Master, realy left with the detachment, near £400; but that the different Officers, say they, Settled their Accounts with him, and that the other part of the Money, was their own Pay: And it appear'd that, when I had granted the Warrants for the two Musters, from August 25th to December 24th 1756, for their Effectives, there would be wanting, to clear off Major *Craven*, the Sum of £921.8.4—As I find Captain *More*, the Pay Master, was appointed by the Captains of the Regiment, I have ordered them to Pay Major *Craven*, the Money advanced to them on my order, as they are now Paid, the whole of their Pay to the 24th of August, by Warrants from Mr *Shirley*, and to the 24th of *December*, by me; and I see no other Course I could take, as the Captains having appointed the Paymaster, are answerable for him; and as he is out of my Power, being a Prisoner and gone to England; and as it does not appear to me clearly, what Money the Paymaster, did realy advance to that detachment.

There are other difficulties still; Mr *Shirley*, before he went away, lodged Money in Mr *Apthorp's* hands, who writ to a Banker in *New York*, to Acquaint him Mr *Shirley* had done so; and desired him, to Negociate the Bills Captain *Jocelyn* might draw on him, for the Subsistence of the 50th Regiment, on a Letter of Credit he enclosed, to be forwarded to the Captain. This Mr *Bayard* Acquainted me of, when I was at Fort *Edward*; I immediately writ to him, that the Subsistence of that Regiment, must be drawn by Warrant from me, on the deputy Pay Master, as I was directed by my *Instructions*: And since I come down, I find that Credit amounts to Three thousand One hundred and Fifty Pounds, which Sum it seems, Mr *Shirley* did propose to have paid, into the hands of Mr *Mortier*, the deputy Pay Master, and to have withdrawn Warrants of his, to that amount; which Mr *Mortier* acquainted him he could not give up, as part of them were gone home, and the Pay Office had notice from him, of his having Paid all the others. I see, they hope to get Mr *Apthorp*, at *Boston*, to advance this Money to them, from that fund; but I shall give no order upon it, till I am better informed about it.

I send Your Royal Highness, enclosed, a very extraordinary Account, with as extraordinary a docket; the Original of which, is now in the Pay Office in London, sent over annexed to a Warrant of his.

This seems to me, to be intended, to cover the disposal of the Levy Money of the Regiment; as it appears by the Article of *Twenty thousand* dollars, paid to Lieutenant *Bartman*, who declares, that neither he, nor any of the Officers, were sent out a recruiting that Year, but Lieutenant Irwin, who did not get a Man; And further, that he re-

ceived that Money on the Warrant, and instantly paid it over to
Mr *Shirley,* and shew'd me Mr *Shirley's* receipt for it, in his own hand
writing, of which you have a Copy enclosed; those Sundries, for the
Niagara Expedition, and the others, I suppose are of the same nature;
And I imagine, Your Royal Highness will think the Articles charged
to the Regiment, are as odd, for *Barracks, Bedding, Barrack Utensils,
Ground to* encamp on, Provisions, &ce, which I think do not come
out of the Regiments Subsistence.

I cannot, with absolute certainty, tell Your Royal Highness the
method, in which this Regiment was raised; but so far as I can collect
from the Officers, it was raised in this manner: Mr *Shirley* had blank
Commissions sent him, which he gave to People of this Country, on
Condition of raising so many Men each; but the main of them were
got by Letters, writ to all the Colonels of the Militia, to Enlist out of
their Regiments, as many Men as they could, the Allowance for which,
was, for a Man for *two Years, One* Pound; for a Man that Enlisted for
three years, *Thirty Shillings;* for a Man that enlisted for *five* years, or
for Life, Five Pounds; And the whole of the managing this, and of
making up of the Accounts, was committed to the Generals son Captain *Shirley,* and his Son in Law, Mr *Hutchinson,* the Judge; And I see
no reason to believe, that any Officer of the Regiment, ever saw the
recruiting Account, or in what manner the Levy Money, or non
Effective Money, were disposed of; And the Pay Masters here, have
never given any Officer of either of those Regiments, an Abstract of
their Companies, they having always paid them to Account.

So far as I can see, the non Effective Fund of the *50th* Regiment, to
Christmas, is £*1878.4.6;* And the *51st* Regiment, at the *24th* of *August*
last, had £*7978.3.* As I have had no demand from them for Pay, Major
Craven having still sufficient for that purpose, I have not calculated
their's any further than *August.*

But when those Articles are taken from the Account of the Subsistence of the *50th* Regiment, which have no connection with it, the
non effective fund will be greatly encreased.

And that, when the fictitious Articles are taken from the Account of
raising the Regiment, and the real Articles charged in their Place,
Mr *Shirley* will have much less Money in his Pocket.

There is one word in the *Docket,* which I must explain to Your
Royal Highness, which is where he mentions *four pence* half penny
a Mess; here it does not mean *five* or *Six* Men, but to each Man, *four*
pence *half penny* for his *breakfast;* as much for his *dinner,* and as
much for his *Supper;* making *thirteen* pence half penny, for the

Maintenance of each Man *per day:* And I am led to understand it thus, from an Act of the *Boston* Assembly this Year, by which they Order their Troops to be maintained at the Houses, as they return home, at this rate; And in their Account they have given us, of their Expences for this Campaign, they charge *one shilling* & *Six pence,* their Currency, a day, for the Maintenance of each Man, on their March, till they arrive at *Albany,* where they had Provisions; which is just *thirteen pence half* penny Sterling; And their Men will eat *three good Meals* a day.

I shall inform myself, at Boston, of what barrack bedding and Utencils were provided, as none have been delivered to me; And I am told, that there were few Provided, and those at the Expence of the Province: The reason of few being wanted, was, that all the Men they dared *trust,* had *furloughs* to go into the Country, till they were to March to *Oswego,* except a few, they were afraid would desert. You will be surprised when I tell You, that neither of those Regiments ever had a field day, till Mr *Webb* Joined the detachment on the *Mohawk* river; I own I am impatient till I know your resolution about them.

Since I writ my Publick Letter, I have accounts, that we begin to get some Men in New England; by the last Accounts we had got Seventeen; and now that their Troops are come home, I hope we shall go on.

I must beg leave to Acquaint Your Royal Highness, that Officers, that are worn out in any degree, are totaly incapable of Service in this Country, where the Operations are in Places, where they cannot have any relief, and where the Climats wear that sort of People out immediately: And where they are in high ranks, they are a *Clog* in carrying on the Service in Winter, and are totaly incapable of the Service in Summer: Some of the Foreign Officers do not improve the Corps, and from what I hear, I shall find more of that sort among them, when we meet next Campaign.

But the Point I am weakest in, is *Engineers;* Mr *Montresor,* I dare not trust a Siege to; Major *Eyres* is a very good Man, but will not do for a *first;* Among the Foreigners, there are many nominal ones, but know no more than what they have learnt in a drawing School; the only one they look on as an Engineer, is Lieutenant *Meyer;* they say he is fit for great designs, meaning, making a Plan for such, for he has never served any where. I have at last got hold of him, and from all I can see, he is *Slow.* I desired a return of what Artillery he thought would be necessary to carry to the Field, Supposing we should Attack *Ticonderoga* and *Crown Point,* and should be able from there, to push down into *Canada,* either to *Montréal* or *Quebeck;* but he could not do it, without he knew what the Fortifications of the Place were, and what number of Cannon were in it.

I then put the Question, what *Artillery* was necessary to carry to the *Field,* with an Army of *ten thousand* Men, who might have occasion to make a Siege, and had the enclosed return: I likewise send Sir John St *Clair's* return, on this Subject: I imagine Your Royal Highness will think the one too high, and the other too low.

But I hope Your Royal Highness will be of Opinion, that some brass *24:* Pounders are necessary; And that in this Country, where there are so many *Wooden* Houses, and that the name of a *bomb* frightens every body, that some *brass Mortars,* for *thirteen* Inch Shells, will be absolutely necessary; with more Powder and Ball, which the People of this Country, make a most intollerable and inconceivable Consumption of.

The Artillery that comes, must have all their *Attirail* with them; And Sir John St *Clair* insists, that the Mortars in the *Bombketches,* should have land Carriages with them, in case they should be more usefull a Shore than on board; And we are extremely at a loss for *Gunners* and *Bombardiers,* and a Man at the Head of the *Artillery;* Captain *Broom,* at *Halifax,* I am informed is worn out; Captain *Ord,* the Commanding Officer with me, is very Industrious, but has no execution; I have kept Lieu^t *Buchanan,* because he and *McLeod,* are all I have to trust to: there are several Younger one's that will do in time, and there is one *McCullogh,* who was a good Man, but ever since he was Wounded at the *Monongahela,* has been at times disordered in his Judgment; I am to allow him to go home, for the recovery of his health. I imagine I have some good Gunners among the Foreign Officers, and I am training as many Men in the Battalion as I can.

If it were possible, to get M^r *McKellar* Exchanged, I imagine he is better than any of them; and his having been through all those Places, would be a great advantage to the Service.

As Our Recruits come in very Slow now, I cannot Answer for compleating the Troops here, tho' I would still gladly hope to do it; I may meet with blame, for not giving more Levy Money, but I do not find, that those that are enclined to List, part with us on that Account, which is the reason I do not augment it, as I would not raise the Price of Recruits, that must be wanted hereafter; whenever it appears necessary, I will Augment it directly, and in the *Americans* we are very able to do it.

But this scarcity of Men, with the want of the *50th* & *51st* Regiments, with the prospect, of a great many of the recruits we get, coming late, obliges me to suggest to Your Royal Highness, that if any Battalions can be spared, they will be very necessary, to ascertain You Success here; And if that is done, I should hope your great work in *North America* is over; not only with the *French,* but with the *Indians* likewise.

As I do not imagine, You will draw any Forces from *Nova Scotia,* whilst the French are strong at Cape *Bretton,* and constant supplies going there from Europe; and the Plan remains, of driving the Indians & French Neutrals from *St Johns;* I should hope you would Pardon me, if I should throw out, that *four* Battalions would be necessary, as they would be only *two* more, than were destined for this Service; for I do not reckon either the *50th* or *51st,* any part of our Strength for this Year. In the *50th* we have but Six Officers, and part of them not able to serve.

Next, I must beg leave to mention, that if the *Fleet is not sufficient,* or *comes too late,* both which things will happen, except Your Royal Highness interposes, the whole Plan will be in danger of miscarrying; besides this Country being ravaged whilst we are gone.

My Plan for the Provincial Troops, is not to take many of them, and if I can manage that Point, so as to have all those from *New England* as *Rangers,* and to send them into the Enemy's Country, by Number *4,* where I will erect a Magazine for them, and send them into the Enemy's Country, by *Otter Creek,* and the lower end of Lake *Champlain,* to make all the disturbance in their Power; and if they can break up the Settlements on this side the River, and drive in the Inhabitants, they will distress them greatly in their Provisions; when we arrive before *Quebeck,* we can Transport them over, and when their business is done on this side, turn them loose on the other; by which means, no Enemy can move towards us; but we must have early notice of it, and be able to harrass them on their March.

The number I propose to ask from the *four New England* Governments, is *four thousand,* all *Rangers,* without any of their Generals; but I would compound for *two thousand,* if it would not prevent my having difficulties here, and in the *Jerseys,* to get Men to defend the Forts whilst we are gone; but this will be a difficult point to carry, for from all I have yet seen, most of the Expeditions they have engaged in, has been principaly, on Account of the *Generals* who were to Command them: how I shall be able to manage this, with Mr *Shirleys* party to oppose me, you shall know from *Boston.*

You see that, from what I have said of my Plan, I take it for granted, at a Peace, you will give up the river *St Laurence,* if we are so happy, as to be able to take it; but if you should not, you can have very little dependence on the present Inhabitants.

The Men from *this Province,* and the *Jerseys,* I propose to employ on this side, by the Forts, to keep the Garrisons at *Ticonderoga* and *Crown Point* in Awe, and prevent the Enemy from drawing any force from them.

I have not yet fixed in my own mind, what Troops I will leave in the Forts; whether Battalions or Companies from these go with Us; that I shall determine, when I see how the Regiments turn out.

Whilst I am on the Subject of *Forts,* it is absolutely necessary that there should be a *large scope* of Ground reserved to the King, round every Fort he has, to supply timber for repairing them, and Wood for firing; at present, he has not one bit of ground any where, for they pretend even at Forts *Edward* and *William Henry,* that the Ground is Pattented; but I believe the Claimants have no manner of right: When any Act of Parliament is passed, in relation to this Country, I hope this will be remembered.

I have hitherto, forgot to Acquaint Your Royal Highness, that the *Small Pox* is Spread over, I think, the whole of this Country, except *New England,* from where I have not heard of it yet: It is at *Albany,* It is *here,* and it is at *Philadelphia,* and among the *Six* Nations; they got it from the *French,* at *Niagara;* and the French in *Canada,* had it all last Year; when it first broke out, it made a very great Alarm in the Country, but now that is over, except among the New England Men. Some of the Troops have had it, but as the kind is good, we have lost very few; I am preparing, to *Innoculate* such as have not had it, & are willing to undergo the Opperation; in order to prevent their falling down during the Campaign.

I am, Sir, Your Royal Highness most Duttifull and most Obedeent Servant.

New York 26th December.

LOUDOUN.

[*Endorsed*] Letter begun at *Albany, N:A:* November 22: concluded at *New-York* December 26: 1756. Lord *Loudoun* to *H:R:H:* inclosing 22: Papers.

List of Commissions Given by His Excellency the Earl of Loudoun, in the Following Regiments Viz^TT [1]

Rank	Officers Names	Dates of their Commissions	

35th Regiment.

Rank	Officers Names	Dates	Notes
	John Cockburn	26th Novemr 1756.	was 2d Elest Ensign in the 44th Regt a very good Offier Putt in to Improve the Regt fitt for an Adjutant
	Matthew Fleeming	27th ditto	An Offier formerly in the Service Strongly Recomended
Lieutenants	James Sinclair	28th ditto	Had a Commission given him hear by Sir John St Clares Recomendation and altho he sett out from Briton as Soon as he receved the account of it found on his Arival that Sir John had growen Impatient and got him Supperseeded Since Provided for and now Promotted is very Dilegent
	James Field	29th ditto	Recomended by Mr Fox
	Thomas Cumberford	15th December	Eldest Ensign formerly a Quartermaster of Dragoons
Ensign	Charles Portis	1st ditto	Quartermaster to the Regt

————

42d Regiment

Rank	Officers Names	Dates	Notes
Lieut	James Campbell	14th Decemr 1756	Eldest Ensigne in the Regt
Ensign	James Mackintosh	15th ditto	Volunteer in the Regt very uesfull in Recruting last Spring

————

1 Neither the 1757 or the 1758 edition of the printed *Army Lists* incorporate Loudoun's promotions. The 1759 list for the first time brings the regimental lists of officers serving in North America up to date. John Cockburn, for instance, the first name below, continues to be ranked as the eldest ensign in the 44th regiment until the 1759 list, when he is gazetted as a lieutenant in the 35th regiment as of November 26, 1756. But the 1759 list records names as of December, 1758, with a few exceptions running into the early months of 1759, so that it is useless as an authoritative record of prior promotions. The notes are in Loudoun's handwriting.

LIST OF COMMISSIONS

Rank	Officers Names	Dates of their Commissions	

44th Regiment

Ensigns
- Primrose Kennedy ..... 25th Octob^r 1756. — Son to the Elest Capt over whom Major Eyre was Prommotted he was bread to the Sea and now has the care of the Vessals on lake George
- Andrew Watson .... 26th November — nephew to Major Gen: Abercromby Removed on his Desier from the 62^d Regt

———————

45th Regiment.

Ensigns
- James Ormsby .... 30th Novem^r 1756. — Removed from the 47th to the 45th Regt His Commission from Mr Shirly in the 47th is Dated June 24th after he was Supperseeded on the Spot
- John M^ckane .... 2^d December. — Formerly in the Horse brought over and Recomended by Mr Webb

———————

47th Regiment

Ensigns
- Milborne West .... 28th Novem^r 1756 — Caryed Armes with M G Braddock and wonded on the Monengalea had a Commission from Mr Shirly after he was on the Spot Supperseeded which I could not allow but have Provided for him now
- Garnett Ewer .... 5th December — Recomended by Ld Geo: Sackvile

———————

48th Regiment.

Ensigns
- John Crofton .... 24th October 1756 — Removed from the 62^d in which Regt he was Proveded on the Recomendation of Mr Webb to whoes care he is Committed
- Charles Davers .... 26th ditto — Recomended by the Duke of Grafton
- John Hedges .... 29th November — Recomended by the Duke of Marlborough

———————

Rank	Officers Names	Dates of their Commissions	

62ᵈ Regiment.

Rank	Officers Names	Dates of their Commissions	
Chaplain	John Ogilvie	1st September 1756	Has a very Small Living hear is one of the missionarys to the Indeans Preaches to them in there owen Languegh and very uesfull among the Mowhaks Recomended by Sir William Johnson
Lieutenant	Brereton Poynton	30th ditto	This Ensigne and the thirteen that follow were the Eldest in the Regt there are no Ensignes in this Servce above a Month older than them tho there Commissions are Dated in June as they are all granted by Mr Shirly who did not Receve the Power of giving Commissions till the end of Novr in which case I thought it would have been hard to have brought Strangers over them by which the Servie would not have been benifitted
Lieutenants {	James Allen	1st Decemr 1756	
	Thomas Barnsley	2d ditto.	
	[George] Mackintosh ...	3d ditto.	
	Thomas Campbell.	4th ditto	
	Ralph Phillips	5th ditto.	
	Samuel Mackay	6th ditto.	
	Francis Mackay	7th ditto.	
	George Archbold	8th ditto.	Those above this have all Served but the Eldest who was a Cornet before
	James Monro	9th ditto.	
	William Ridge	10th ditto.	
	William Hay	11th ditto.	
	Alexander Shaw	12th ditto.	
	Thomas Meredith	13th ditto.	
	[John] Parker	16th ditto.	A Capt in the New Jersey Regt and now commands them was in the Kings Servie and with Admiral Boscawen in the East Indies
	[Henry] Babcock	17th Decembr 1756	Major to the Road Island Regt uesfull to me in breaking the Consent of the General and Field offcers in the Provenceals when they would not Submitt to be under my Comand

Rank	Officers Names	Dates of their Commissions	
		62ᵈ Regiment	
Lieutenant	Claas	18th ditto.	a German has been employed in the Provenceal Troops and among the Indeans with Sir William Johnson who I think will be uesfull to me on many occasions
Ensigns	Alexander Stephens	27th Novemʳ 1756	Vollunteer with General Bradock wounded on the Monongahela Mr Shirly gave him a Commission in Nova Scotia to be Ensigne when the Company was Sold in England and after attending his Duty about Six Monthes the Ensigne Mr Pritchard arived with the Kings Commission
	Thomas Vinter	3ᵈ December	Recomended by Sir Charles Hardy
	Archibald Blane	4th ditto.	A Relation of Mine from the Shire of Air
	Donald Campbell	6th ditto.	Recomended by great Numbers of People in this Provene His Father came hear and Made a Bargine for Land on the Fronteer with the Governor Returned and brought over a great number of People to Settle them and £4000 in money the Governor brooke the bargen and he and those People were Ruined [2]
	William Ramsay	7th ditto.	Vollunteer from the Shire of Air
	John Wilson	8th ditto	Son of the Chief Justice of St Chrestophers his Recomendation to me not yet arived from England but as he has been the first man to Sett an Example to the men in Daily Duty I thought him a Propper man to Prefer

[2] A memorial of Campbell on this subject is in *N. Y. Col. Docs.*, VII, 629–631.

Rank	Officers Names	Dates of their Commissions	

62^d Regiment

Rank	Officers Names	Dates of their Commissions	
Ensigns	Alexander Baillie	9th December 1756	Recomended to me by Lady Stair
	Simon Fraser	10th ditto.	A Relation of M G Abercromby recomeded by him
	Lauchlan Forbes	11th ditto.	Recomended by Lt: G: Bland
	Thomas Pinckney	12th ditto.	Son to the Tresorer of South Carolena Recomeded to me in London by the People of that Province
	William Brown	13th ditto.	Has lived several years in this Country Recomended by Sir Richard Grosvener
	John Mackie	14th ditto	Nephew to Mr Mackie and Major Young
	Charles Williamos	16th ditto	Recomended by Mr Points is from Sviserland a very Pretty young Man
	Alexander Shaw	17th ditto	Recomended by Ld Cathcart and Mr Osvald
	Henry Stratford	18th ditto	Recomended by Sir Charles Hood
	Isaac Motte	19th ditto	Of this Country Recomended by the Marquis of Winchester Thos that had not Served till this Campaen Draw for there Rank

New York Independ^t Company Commanded by Captain Marshall.

Rank	Officers Names	Dates of their Commissions	
Lieutenant	William Gullen	25th Novemr 1756	He was Sargent Major to the Royal brought over by M G Abercromby and put in hear that there may be one Offier in the Company that can Disiplin the Men

----

Dep^y Commissary of Musters.

Rank	Officers Names	Dates of their Commissions	
	John Billings	10th Septemr 1756	He had a Deputation and Instructions from Mr Pritchard Muster Master on Mr Pritchards Levy taken in Oswago I gave him a Commission on the bake of that Deputa-

Rank	Officers Names	Dates of their Commissions	
			tion to Act in the Mean time Since that I have a letter from Mr Pritchard desiring me to appoint a Deputy to him with instruction

――――――

Staff Officers

Rank	Officers Names	Dates	
Quarter Masters	Lieut Francis Pringle ... Lieut Donald Campbell . Lieut Joseph Ray	18th August 1756	The Commissions to the Lt and Ensignes I have begone to Date from the 25t of Nov that they may not enterfear with thos given by the King
Adjutants	Lieut James Dalyell .... Ensign James Allen ..... Ensign Thoms Barnsley .	18th August 1756	The Adjutants and Quarter Masters I have Dated from the time I appointed them to Act in Order to trie if they were Propper for those Commissions as those are Commissions give no Rank so will not Enterfear with the Kings Commessions

Royal Regiment of Artillery

Rank	Officers Names	Dates	
Lieut Fireworker.	John Mean	1st October 1756	Recomended by Capt Ord

[Enclosure No. 5 in Loudoun to Cumberland, Nov. 22–Dec. 26, 1756.]

INFORMATION OF CAPTAIN JOHN VICARS OF THE 50TH REGIMENT COMMANDED BY MAJOR GENERAL WILLIAM SHIRLEY [1]

(D.S.)

Having Obtain'd a Commission in the 50th Regiment, I came in the Transports that were sent out with the Troops, on Major General Braddocks Expedition, and went with them to Virginia, and from thence went round to Boston where I. landed April 7th 1755.

When I arrived, their were about 300 men of the Regiment in Castle William, who I imagine were men, they were affraid would desert, they were in Barracks in the Fort,

[1] This document was dictated by Vickers to Loudoun, in answer to the latter's questions.

some time after my arrival we Encamp'd and the other men of the Regiment were Call'd in.

When we march'd from thence for Oswego we were about 800, the Regiment never was Compleat,

I know nothing of the Expence of the Recruits, as I never was employed in Recruiting, nor ever saw any Account of it, Before the Regiment left the Island where they were Encamp'd, Judge Hutchenson Major General Shirleys Son in Law, came to Camp and pay'd of what demands the men had to a Certain day, but I have forgot to what day it was, from that day, the Officers had the paying of the men, I was by when the Judge payed my Company, and saw him paying the other Companys,

In the End of July or begiñing of August 1755, I commanded the Escort that Major General Shirley took with him from Albany to Oswego where I remain'd till the 3^{d} of July 1756.

The Escort Consisted of 80 men of the 50th and 70 men of the 51st Captain Delancey Commanded them

I know nothing of the Number of Battoes that were up with us but that I had 8 for my detachment,

I recolect no want of Provisions on the march up, but think we were short in provisions the Latter end of the time Mr Shirley was at Oswego.

I know nothing of what Provisions they were we had at Oswego, whither they were those Provided by Major General Shirley, or those Provided by the Province of New York for the Independent Companys

I know we were short of Provisions soon after the General Left Oswego, and had the poor fellows Lived they must have Eat one another

That General Shirley gave furloughs to a Great many men before he left Oswego, and that Lieutenant Colonel Mercer was forced to give a great many afterwards to save the Provisions, that I believe their were about 300 men on Furlough from the two Regiments

I was a Member of Several Councils of War in which we met to deliberate whither we should Abandon the Place on Account of the Want of Provisions, in one of Which it was agreed if no supply arrived in ten days we should Abandon the Garrison, and retire to the German Flatts, but in Five days after there arrived Four Battoes with Provisions.

I know Lieutenant Colonel Mercer writ after to show the State of the Garrison & to desire to have Provisions and a Reinforcement of Men as he Expected to be Attack'd

I am sure Colonel Mercer never writ a Letter in which he said the

Garrison never was in Want of Provisions, for he was too honest a Man to write what every man in the Garrison could Contradict

When General Shirley left Oswego, my Company Consisted of 50 men, that before may their were 39 of them dead, and one taken Prisoner, I think each of the 8 Comp^{ys} at Oswego lost above 30 men.

I am of Opinion this mortality was owing to bad Barracks and want of Beds, which threw the men in to Scurveys, and the Water which gave them Fluxes

There were no Barracks in the Fort of Oswego, only a Guard Room, and one Room for the Commanding Officer, all the Garrison Lay without the Forts, where there were two Shingled Houses in the one of which Lieutenant Colonel Littlehales lived, in the other Captain More the Paymaster Lived whilst he stayed, when he went away, two Lieutenants of the Ships got it, there was a Barrack of three Rooms in which there was two Tire of Bed steeds but no Beding, as the Barrack was made of Green Boards, they all Split, and the Snow drove in Constantly on the men, the rest lived in Bark Hutts, and Lay on the Ground all Winter, The two Shingl'd Houses of two small Rooms each & all the Hutts belonged to the Indean Traders and Suttlers

The Recruits that came up this Year were very bad, a great many of them spoke French and were the people that Inveig'led the men to desert, one dutch man in the Train Carried off 3 men.

When I left Oswego the Garrison were pretty healthy as it Consisted mostly of Recruits Just come up, the men that Compos'd the Garrison in the Winter being mostly dead.

In January we were inform'd by the Indeans, that we were to be Attack'd the Garrison was then so Weak, that the strongest Guard we proposed to mount, was a Subaltern and 20 men, but we were Seldom able to mount more than 16 or 18 men, and half of those were forced to have Sticks in their hands to support them, the men were so weak that the Senterys often fell down on their Posts, and Lay there till the Relief came and lifted them up—

That two or three times when we expected to be Attack'd in the Night the Carpenters mounted Guard

Before the Recruits arrived my Comp^y was only ten men, the other Companys were Little Stronger

The Lieutenant Colonels Company was with Lieutenant Bull at the great carrying place, where they were all either killd or taken, when that Fort was Burnt, the Granadiers went down the Country with Major General Shirley and I met them going up when I came down

The Regiment was paid at Schenectada in their way up in the end of July or beginning of August 1755, to the 24th of October, that the Paymaster left at Oswego some money in the hands of Lieutenant Carden—who gave some money to Officers that Wanted but I do not know to what Extent, I received 200 dollars of my own Personal pay, but none for the men, as none of the Regiment were payed up farther then the 24th of Octr 1755, till Captain Moore the Paymaster arrived at Oswego Four days before I left it, when I received Bills from him for 8 months personal pay up to the 24th of August 1756. But there was little due to them when I came away, as we had Supplied them with Chocolate, Tea, Sugar, Coffee, shirts, shoes, and Stockings, we carried up of those some things to supply them with, but the main of them were supplied by Mr Alexander the Generals Secretary, who carryed up a great Quantity of Goods from Boston, & deliver'd them over to each Corps, I think those Goods of Mr Alexanders, went up with the Regimts.

I suppose the Paymaster payed him for them, but I do not know the price as I never Received an Abstract

When those were Expended, we bought the Goods from Mr Lewis the Commissary for ready money, who I heard was Mr Alexanders Partner, I do not Recollect the prices, but I know we bought Breeches for Fourteen Shillings Currency, or eight shillings & two pence Sterling, we took so much Care to Supply the men, that Several of my Compy died in my debt—

The Recruits that came up Grumbled for want of their pay, and I have been told that Several of the deserters that were taken at their Tryal plead that as they neither Received their pay nor Sufficient Provisions they went away to prevent their Starving

Fort Ontario was a Good place against Indeans, the Barracks were better than those at Oswego, by which Sir Wm Pepperrells Regiment lost fewer men than the 50th at Oswego, but the Barracks were Built so near the Stockead's they could make no defence. behin'd them, there was a Stage made Round near the tops of the Stockad's where the Cannon were Placed, as I was in a Bad State of health, I never was in it after the Barracks were Finished.

There were no Works in Oswego Toward the Attack where Cannon could be used but from the Old Stone Trading House where they formerly had two Cannon, But the Firing them on the Rejoicing days, shook the Wall so much that Several Stones fell out of the Wall for which they were oblig'd to remove them

The Fort call'd new Oswego or Fort Rascal never was finished and there were no Loop holes in the Stockad's so that they could not Fire

out of the Fort but by opening the Gate and Firing out of that
    There was a kind of a ditch about half way Round it which was
made by taking out some Earth to fix the Stockad's.

                                                    JOHN VICKERS

New York, January 4th 1757—

[Enclosure No. 1 in Loudoun to Cumberland, Jan. 6, 1757.]

LOUDOUN TO CUMBERLAND
(L.S.)

                                    New York 5th January 1757

Sir,
    I have received Mr *Fox's* Letter, Acquainting me, with Major Gen-
eral *O'Farrell's* Regiment, and the *twenty-four* additional Companies
from *Ireland,* being ordered here. I shall immediately compleat Major
General *O'Farrells* Regiment, out of the additional Companies.
    As to the Troops in *Nova Scotia,* I have reason to believe; by their
returns, dated October *1st,* they wanted to the Establishment, *four hundred* and *two,* which according to Your Royal Highness liberty to us
in *Flanders,* is in reality, no more than *two hundred Eighty two.* from
Col¹ *Monckton,* I am informed, of *Sixty* Men Joined that Regiment,
and *forty* Recruits on their March to it, after that return was made up:
And I know there are a great many Recruits gone from this Country,
to the other two Regiments, but have received no returns of their
Numbers; tho' I think they must be fully compleated.
    But by Enquiring of Captain *Cotterel,* who is here, for the recovery
of his Health, having lost the use of his hands, by the *dry belly-Ache,*
which is a *West India Disease,* I find they are Subject to in *Nova Scotia;* he acquaints me, that when the Regiments were low in Numbers, they had Enlisted a good many French, that were Prisoners,
about *two hundred,* who not answering as Soldiers with us, they were
determined to deliver back as Prisoners; on which, I propose to reserve *three* hundred Men of the Additional Companies, for those
Nova Scotia Battalions, and to send them there, as soon as the Season
will permit; and in the mean time shall put them in Quarters, the most
convenient for that purpose. As to the remainder of the Additional
Companies, I have not quite fixed what I shall do with them, till I see
them; What Serjeants, Corporals, Drums and Old Men, they have, I
shall put into the *Americans,* as they are more wanted there, than in
the other Corps: As to the new raised Men in those Companies, of

which I suppose, the greatest Number must consist; I at first proposed, out of them, to have compleated, the 35th the 44th and the 48th Regiments, as they could presently have disciplined them, and as it would have taken their recruiting Officers, out of the way, of crowding our Recruiting Quarters.

But on the other hand, when I consider, that there is a great doubt, of our being able to compleat the four Battalions of the *Royal Americans,* in time for the Field; and the little time there will be, for disciplining the Recruits that we get, just before we take the Field; and the Inconvenience of having Battalions in the Field, of very unequal Numbers; I believe I shall put the whole of them, into the *Royal Americans:* but I will see them, before I determine any thing certainly.

There is another reason, that I believe must determine me, to put them into the *Americans;* and I think it necessary to mention it to Your Royal Highness, as I may meet with blame from some People, if they think I have taken from *Nova Scotia* one Man, that they imagine might have been there.

I know nothing of the Numbers, Major General *O'Farrells* Regiment, or the additional Companies, consist of, or when they come on this Establishment, but from the words of Mr *Fox's* Letter, of *October 2d;* in which he says, speaking of those Troops, now Embarked at *Cork,* I presume they come on this Establishment in *September,* for *Ireland* will Pay them no longer, than they are with them.

As the Regiments in *Nova Scotia,* have not yet sent me an Account of their non-effective Fund, I do not know what that is, or whether they could out of that, Pay the Money ordered to be Paid to the Regiments they come from; but Your Royal Highness will plainly see, by the returns of the 1st *of October,* when they wanted realy, but *two hundred Eighty two Men* on the Spot, and had at that time a great number of Recruits in this Country, so that whatever Vacancies they may have, by Men discharged since, they have not Money to Pay those Men, from any time in *September,* nor can the 44th nor 48th afford it, out of their non-effective Funds; And the *Royal Americans,* have Money enough for the purpose.

Your Royal Highness will be surprised, to find no returns for *December;* the reason is, we are so dispersed, (that I have not been able to collect them,) as You will see, from the Account I have given you of their Quarters. There is no returns from the *Royal Americans;* this is occasioned, from their having blundered in making them, so that I cannot set it right, till I have their Answers: They left out of their returns, the *Highlanders* that we Pay; the People belonging to Colonel

Prevost, that were taken in their Passage, who whilst they are Prisoners, I imagine must remain on our Returns; And they have even left out, some of the Recruiting Parties, that were delivered over to the different Battalions, when they were divided: but as near as I can inform Your Royal Highness, they are about *Eighteen hundred* Men, at present, without including the *Virginia* and *North Carolina* Recruits, of which I have no Account.

January 6th.   Colonel *Rollo* arrived in one of the Transports, which Sailed from Cork *November 6th,* and parted from the Fleet on the *18th,* in a Gale of Wind; they have on board, One *hundred and Seventy Eight* Men, composed, of one Company of the Regiment, and part of the Drafts; by him I understand, Your Royal Highness has eased me of the trouble, of disposing of the Serjeants and Corporals of the Additionals, who would have been extremely usefull here, if they could have been spared; for there is the *50*th and *51*st Regiments, have not one that deserves the name; and I can say very little more, for the *four* Battalions of the *Royal Americans;* for very few of the foreigners, we have got in that Station, are good for any thing.

By the Account I hear, of the manner of Drafting those Men, which was, that most Regiments threw the *twelve* Companies into one body, and compleated the ten Companies out of that, and then sent us what were left; I do not doubt, we have got the whole Vices of the Irish Army; those I shall endeavour to reform; but I am afraid, we have likewise got the whole Diseases. I shall have every Man examined, and if I find, there are any considerable number unfitt for Service, I hope You will not think me in the wrong, if I return them to their own Corps, as Invalids are totaly useless here; as with all the care we can take, we shall find Men enough in the Corps here, for the Garisons during the Campaign, that are not able, to undergo the fatigue of a Campaign in the Field, in this Country.

I am likewise informed, that there was a very great Desertion, during the time of the Muster, the day they embarked; So that when I have compleated Major General *O'Farrells* Regiment, and set aside *three hundred Men,* for the Regiments in *Nova Scotia,* I shall have about *four hundred* Men remaining, who I shall put in the *Royal Americans.*

Colonel *Prevost,* hath the returns of those Companies, who is not yet arrived; when he comes, and I receive my Letters, I shall send Your Royal Highness a return of them, and an Account of what they are.

I shall leave, in Writing, my Orders, for the division of those Companies, to make it as equal as I can; but I have many People, I cannot depend on their executing in a *fortnight*, what another Man might do in *two* Hours; if Mr *Webb* is recovered, it will be well done; but if he is not, my friend Colonel *Dusseaux* will Plague their hearts out; for he does so much, that he never executes any thing: the Officers of his Battalion, are far from happy; And the Adjutant, who came from Colonel *Leighton's* Regiment, one *Allen,* who is a very good and diligent one, I believe will throw up his Adjutantcy; for, before he can execute, one half of one Order, he has another Order, and so on, with infinite abuse. It is my Duty, to let Your Royal Highness know the truth in every case, but I do beg, you will not mention this from me, as you know, where it would hurt me greatly.

I mentioned Mr *Webb* being Ill; he was about a fortnight ago, attacked with a very Slight fit of the Palsy, which did not last a Minute, and to another Man, would have been of very little Consequence; but all his People have died of that Disease, and he is still low and down, and I cannot get his Spirits up; I am very much afraid, he will not soon be able to do much business; if that is the case, he will be an infinite loss to the Service, for the Country is so immensely wide, we must have People we can depend on, in different Places, and hands I find great want of; And yet I do not Ask further of your Royal Highness, than to shew you that is the case, and that I am still of the same opinion, that any Man that were to come, that did not do us good, would do us a great deale of mischief.

I was this day with Sir Charles *Hardy*, about *Cannon*, and I find they have no *24*. Pounders, but two long *Iron* ones; They have forty Six *32*. Pounders; bad long Guns, ill fortified; Of *18*. Pounders they have *Sixteen;* but not a Gun in this Country, has a Carriage can be trusted to, indeed they are in general, totaly Rotten; nor is there a bit of Wood to make them of, but what is Green. There is very few Cannon Ball, for any of the different sorts; they make ball in this Country, but what has hitherto been made, is not good; I am endeavouring to get some made, and to amend that fault.

On a full Enquiry, I find almost all the 24^lb in this Country, are either at Newfoundland, laying without Carriages or Men to fight them; or at *Annapolis Royal,* where I suppose they are not much better; or at *Halifax:* there I dare not meddle with them. but the truth is, almost the whole Iron Guns in this Country are Honey Combed and rotten; having lain in the Dirt many Years, without the least Care. As this is the Case, I shall make all the Preparation in my Power, but do most humbly beg, Your Royal Highness will consider our Situation; for I am sure, if you do not Protect & Support us, none else will;

And if my Plan is approved of, Cannon will be absolutely necessary.

I set out on the *8th* for Boston; the Moment that Meeting is over, I shall have the honor, of Acquainting the Kings Ministers, of what is Settled at it.

I have Sent the Original Papper Signed by Capt Vickars to your Royal Highness incase there should be occasion to Produce it

Since writting the Above I have Disembarked the men who came in the Transport and if the others are as good as what are come in this they will do very well so I hope the Information does not hold

Mr Webb has begone to get Spirits again and I now think we Shall have the Use of him again I have the Honour to be

Sir your Royal Highnesses most Dutifull And most Obedeent humble Servant

LOUDOUN

[*Endorsed*] New-York; January 5/6 *1757.* Lord Loudoun, to *H:R:H:* inclosing *3.* Paper.

CONSIDERATIONS OFFERED BY [?] UPON A SCHEME FOR ATTACKING LOUISBOURG & QUEBEC. 1757 [1]

(COPY)

1.

The French, being already possess'd of the Lakes & Rivers at the Back of the English Settlements from Quebeck to the Missisippi, can easily bring their whole Force to act either offensively or defensively at any one Point; and are therefore in no great Danger from any Attack from the British Provinces, which cannot be executed but by a March by Land thro' desert Countries & dangerous Passes: And if here & there some Water Carriage may be had, that is so difficult and dangerous that the English Troops may be easily attacked by the French from the numberless Posts they are already possess'd of.

---

[1] This document is in memorandum form. Since it presents a strong argument for Loudoun's plan of attacking Quebec directly, it would seem to have emanated from some one fully as close to Cumberland as to Pitt, perhaps Fox and perhaps Bedford. It is not Pitt's plan, for he on February 4 had sent positive orders to Loudoun to attack Louisbourg first, and then Quebec, and had yielded only after a cabinet of March 13, in which Cumberland sat, allowed Loudoun to use his discretion as to which of the two places should be attacked (Minutes, Mar. 13, 1757, Chatham Papers, Vol. 95).

2.

The Military Situation of France in Europe is such, that, if the Sea be left open to her, she may fill that Country with regular Troops, and the political Constitution of her Colonies affords them a Militia equally good for offence and defence & greatly Superior to that of the English, the different Degree of Populousness in the two Countries consider'd.—from these two Circumstances there is the utmost Danger to the British Colonies, if France shoud think proper to undertake the Risque & Expence of a Conquest; for the Risque and Expence of transporting Troops & Provisions seem to be at present the only Bar to this imminent Peril.

3.

Should France Even chuse not to risque any farther Expence, she is probably in the present Circumstances stronger than the English can be without a very extraordinary Exertion of their Strength: for Should she chuse to remain upon the defensive merely, possess'd of the Posts she now enjoys, she may possibly be able to Suffer the English to act offensively by Land, & yet maintain her Posts, & consequently her Authority with the Indians, till the English shoud be tired with the fruitless Expence, & forced by a Peace to Secure her in the Possession of these Encroachments.

4.

The only Method, by which it seems possible for England to avoid so fatal an Event, seems to be that of preventing the French Colonies from receiving Supplies of Men, Stores, & Provisions by Sea, which are absolutely necessary for supporting & maintaining that Body of Troops which they employ, Canadian or European, & that Number of Posts which they possess in America.

5.

The doing this by *cruising* merely has already been tried in a certain Degree ineffectually, & is perhaps to an absolute Degree in the Nature of Things, impossible; for so numerous are her Armies in Europe, that she may afford to send over Troops at five to one Risque of the Embarkation's Success. And with Respect to Provisions, as the Missisippi & St Lawrence Rivers must still in a certain Degree be open against the most vigilant Cruise, & the Provisions & Shipping of England, as well as neutral Powers, can always be had with a certain Degree of Temptation, it is not perhaps a Paradox to assert that the whole Navy of England could not prevent the necessary Supplies, if France should determine to have them at Such a Risque.

6.

It seems therefore. . . .

7.

Two Ideas naturally occurs on this Subject,—Missisippi & St Lawrence Rivers. With Respect to the first, as it's Entry is narrow & difficult, cruising might possibly be employ'd with Effect. As to the last, cruising having hitherto proved ineffectual, there seem to be but two Supplemental Objects—Viz—the Attacking of Louisburgh or Quebeck, but as the first of these is probably as strong to the full & well fortified as the last, & consequently woud require as great Force, Expence, & Risque, tho' the Consequences woud not be in any Degree so advantageous; whereas if the attempt on the last can be supposed to prove effectual, it woud necessarily put an End to the War in America, give a Secure & lasting Barrier to the British Colonies, by breaking up every Post on the Lakes & Rivers, which the French now by usurpation Enjoy, & enable the English to take Posts of a like Kind in a Territory, whereof the Title woud not be disputed with them; and at the Same Time probably put an End to the War in Europe, by affording England an opportunity of restoring a proper Equivalent to France for the Conquests she has made there, without any Loss either of Interest or Reputation: Nothing seems more obvious than that the Preference ought to be given to the Attempt upon *Quebeck* to one on *Louisburgh;* unless it be supposed to be attended with Difficulties unsurmountable.

8.

The Necessary Requisites for Such an Attempt seem to be; first, a considerable Fleet to Secure the Superiority at Sea in those Parts, while the Same Superiority is maintain'd in Europe to preserve great Britain & It's Trade from Insult from the Brest & Toulon Squadrons— In this there seems to be no unsurmountable Difficulty.

9.

Secondly a Sufficient Body of regular Troops with a proper Train of Artillery for taking & bombarding the Place. The Body of Troops raised & sent for this Purpose in *1711:* consisted of Seven Battallions amounting, with Recruits, to *5300:* men, together with Independant Companies from New England amounting to *1500:* Men. Such a Number now woud probably not be Sufficient. possibly *twelve thousand* woud. The Number of regular Troops in Canada is Supposed to be considerable—Six Battallions have been mention'd as having been lately Sent over, but the Troops they have there must be distributed in a Variety of Posts over a wide Extended Country— The Men by the Advantage of Water Carriage might possibly be drawn together upon an Alarm, but Stores, Provisions & Artillery not so easily—if withdrawn from their present Posts, these must be abandon'd. and therefore it may be prudent to have a Number of Troops collected together in one Body, or seperated into Several, as occasion may require, to take Advantage of Such Absence, if Such Posts were broken up or abandon'd the Possession of them woud probably be soon Secured by Provincials, who woud flock theither on Such Success—

10.

The River, as is said, is navigable for large Vessells greatly beyond *Quebeck,* & therefore if the Troops from the Out Posts were not assembled in the Town before the Attempt was made, there woud probably be great Difficulty in doing it afterwards; & still greater in getting together Provisions Stores &c which cannot be convey'd but by Water.

11.

The Town, it is said, consists chiefly of Wooden Houses, therefore if the Ships can approach it, they might by a Bombardment easily fire it, & by that Means be greatly assistant to the Military Force.

12.

Thirdly, a Sufficient Number of Transports. In this there can be no unsurmountable Difficulty. 27 Transports were employ'd in Sir Hovenden Walker's Expedition, containing 7429 Tons, & carrying the Seven Battallions of 5003 Men—three more Ships of 448 Tons carried 300 Recruits. there was one Hospital Ship, one for Cloathing, & Eight for the Artillery & Provisions. They went first to new England, & afterwards proceeded to the Gulph of St Lawrence. The Expedition failed for want of proper Pilots, but there was no Complaint made as to the

Health of the Men from being over crowded, or from any other Circumstance relative to the Transportation.—But as it is the opinion of many who have been Supposed Judges of such affairs, that for so long a Voyage a greater allowance of Tonage ought to be made in Proportion to the Number of Troops sent than in Sir Hovenden Walker's Expedition; that alteration, if thought proper, may be easily made— And here it may not be improper to observe that for the Sake of Secrecy it might be right to hire the Transports per Month for a certain Time without Specefying the Place of their Destination, as has, it is believed been generally done. possibly the Same Transports now taken up for & employ'd in carrying over his Majesty's Electoral Troops might be continued in the Service without giving any Alarm to the Publick—

13.

Fourthly—a proper Pilotage for carrying the Ships of War & Transports up that dangerous River to Quebeck is of absolute Necessity. Upon this Rock the Expedition of *1711:* split, & probably failed from this Circumstance alone. but it is to be hoped that the Want of this will prove no unsurmountable Difficulty. We were in Possession of Louisburgh for two years of the last War; & we have been Establishing the Colony of Nova Scotia ever Since the quitting Possession of it. We have had a Naval Force almost constantly employ'd in those Parts, as well for maintaining the Exclusive Possession of the Bay of Fundy as for Exploring the Gulph & River of St Lawrence. A Squadron has been kept there for an year & an half past; & possibly we have Pilots for at least Part of that Navigation in our own Fleet. but shoud that not be the Case, we are Supposed to be possessed of Eight or ten Thousand french Seamen, now Prisoners, Many of them taken on Board Ships going to, or coming from Quebeck. it will not therefore be difficult to pick out from among them with prudent Management a proper Number of good Pilots.

14.

But whether this or any other Plan for the carrying on the War in America Shall be adopted, it is highly necessary that it be immediately fixed upon, & Such orders given & Such Attention had in Every Branch of the publick Service concerned in the Execution of them as that no Delays shall happen on any Pretixt whatsoever.

FIRST NOTE BY ADMIRAL KNOWLES,[1] RELATING TO THE
EXPEDITION TO NORTH AMERICA, 1757

(COPY)

Mem[dm] of things to be wrote to Col: Lawrence about

That it be recommend to Col: Lawrence to find occasion to send a
flagg of Truce to L[ouisbourg] in the Spring as early as a Vessell can
pass, with Cap[tn] Scott of Col: Hopsons Regm[t] or some other discreet
Officer, as he shall judge most proper who was well acquainted with
the Garrison, when it was restored to the French, in Order to make
his Observations what New Works have been errected either at the
Town, or any other part of the Harbour, particularly at the Lighthouse, or near it, & if any Battery is errected there whither it be inclosed & fortify'd on the back or not, & what additional Number of
Cannon there may be Mounted at the Town on the side next the Harbour between the Colliers Battery & the West Gate Bastion, & whither
the Wall from Billings Gate to the Spurr has been heightened or not,
with the best Account he can gett of the Strength of the Garrison, &
Number of Inhabitants, and to gain what further intelligence he possibly can for the benefit of the Service

To prepare Gabions Fascines & Picketts, 3 Inch Plank & Joist for
Plattforms

On Baptist de Yeon, alias Babtist John, an Inhabitant of L—— when
it was taken, is supposed now to be a Pilot on board one of the Men
of Warr at Nova Scotia, to have him detain'd, & other good Pylots
secured, with as much privacy as possible,

Col: Lawrence may have a hint to give out these things are providing for his own deffence, & that he may expect a Visit from Cape
Breton in the Spring, or from Quebec, Or to assign such other reasons as may be judge proper, to disguise these preparations

SECOND NOTE FROM ADMIRAL KNOWLES, RELATING TO
THE EXPEDITION TO NORTH AMERICA, 1757

(COPY)

M[r] Bastide and two Active Engineers under him.

Of these as many to be got as were at L[ouisbourg] before

[1] Charles Knowles, vice admiral since 1755, had been governor of Louisbourg in
1746 and governor of Jamaica from 1752 to 1756. In 1757 he participated in the
expedition to Rochefort.

A Company of the train of Artillery with an able Conductor & a proportion of Officers & Artificers of the Civil Branch of the Ordnance.

20. 24 Pounders with their Carriages Compleat & some spare & a large Proportion of Cartridges, Ball, Grape &cᵃ Wadds or Junk to make Wadd, Powder Match, priming Horns Budge Barrells &cᵃ Sliding Sledges for transporting the Guns, according to the Model given (will require time to make them) 2000 Mens Harness for Dᵒ fitted

Triangles or Gins for Mounting the Guns with Iron pulleys & Brass Shives fitted & Spare Cordage for Tackle falls & Harness, ropes for transporting the Guns over Rocks & bad Ground and large Crows & Handscrews or Jacks for that purpose with store of both Long and Short Hand spikes both claw'd & not claw'd
4. 10 Inˢ Mortars or Howitzs & 6. 8 Inˢ with Shells Carcasses & Laboratory Stores Compleat
4 Cohorns or Royals with shells &cᵃ for each Ship
100 Musquett Mortars & Shells proportionable
100 Wall pieces & Swivel Guns for the Tops with Grape fitted & some Boxes of Hand granades, Pick axes, Mattocks Shovels Spades Whipsaws, Cross cut Dᵒ Hand Dᵒ, Broad Axes, felling Axes Hatches hammers Mauls Sledges Large & small Iron Wedges of different Sizes. Grindstones fitted. Spikes & Nails of all sorts.

Miners & Miners Tools.
Forges for Red Hot Shot with Tongs, Ladles & every other implement Compleat.
Smiths with Forges & Tools for their Work and a Quantity of Barr & Bolt Iron and Coals.

100 Ladders, scaling & fix'd 24 feet long
Wheel Barrows & hand Barrows fitted a sufficient Number Ballast Basketts &cᵃ
Wool sacks Blinds & Sand baggs a proper proportion

Ammunition for the Troops
Fine Powder in   ½ Barrells

A Proportional Number of Musquet Cartridges made up & filled & spare Reams of Paper for Dᵒ the Cartridges to be pack'd up in small baggs and all the Spare Ball likewise
Plank & Joist for Platforms for the Batterys

Tents for the late Additional Lieut^{nts} to the three Regiments in Nova Scotia & for the Train

5 or 600 of 10 Gallon baggs or Baroccos [Barricoes] for Water

Square Musquetts & Flints in small baggs

The Troops to be compleated with Camp necessarys Copper kettles with Frying pan Covers.

Fishing Netts, Hooks ledds & Lines, to be provided a large Number being Absolutely necessary for the Sick as well as a great Refreshment to those in health.

A Commissary of Stores & Provisions, Assistants Clerks &ca.

A Paymaster of the Troops, Specie for them & as much as possible in Small Coin

As a Number of Petty Officers & Sailors (good chosen men) will be wanted for transporting the Artillery, Provisions, Stores &c^a and serving in the Batterys to Assist the train in carrying on the Seige for which its presumed for w^l be regularly paid, as likewise any of the Troops employ'd on such like extraordinary Services, Provision must be made for paying them Accordingly.

Sea Bedding to be Provided for the Troops & Train & Barrack bedding to be sent so soon after as the Success is known, Matts shou'd likewise be provided made of Rushes, agreeable to the Pattern, for the Men to lay on, in their Tents, there being no Hay, Straw or any other thing to preserve them from the Wet Ground, which will prevent Sickness & save the Lives of many.

An Hospital with proper Store of Medicines Attendants &c^a must be provided, And as some large Tents will be much more convenient as well as Commodious for Lodging of the Sick & wounded Some half worn Sails are recommended to be taken to make them off & Tarpawlins to cover them with all to keep out the Rains & Deals to be supply'd for making Cradles, Grotts, Rice, Barley, Vinegar & portable Soup, good Store to be provided for the Sick and Hospital bedding

Blankets or Watch Coats for the Troops and to be order'd to take with them good Store of Shirts Shoes & Stockings.

Large Brewing Coppers & Wooden Vessell for Brewing Spruce Beer for the Troops when Landed, and a Quantity of Ginger is esteem'd very wholesome to put in it as a preservative against the Scurvy. And during a Siege a small allowance of Rum at the discretion of the Commander in Cheif will be very necessary, for there will be no kind of refreshment whatsoever to be got till the place is reduced.

Spare Ammunition to replace what may be expended by the Men of War

That where the Quantitys of any Materials are not express'd, it is submitted to be proportion'd according to the Nature of the Service intended and the Number of Troops employ'd

A Proportion of Provisions for the Number of Troops employ'd must be sent out with them to last till the End of October before which a farther Supply must be laid in, to serve till the end of June 1757 or the Garrison may be starv'd the 1st Supply must follow so soon as ever the news of Success arrives & the 2d to be sent in the Month of April following to last till June 1758. And 3000 Chaldron of Coals sent out after us & so continued Yearly till the Colling there is establish'd, & a Number of Miners engaged & sent out for the Working of it

MEMORANDUM BY COLONEL HOPSON [1]
(COPY)

Minits in regard to a Descent proposed to be made upon the Island of *Cape Breton* & for Attacking The Garrison of *Louisbourg*.

1757.

The Number of Troops intended for this Expedition to consist of
to be assembled at   and to be Embark'd at   about
ye day of   next, with Camp Necessaries compleat Tents, Provisions &cᵃ, A Train of Artillery & Ordnance Artificers requisite for this Service. Enginiers, with Sufficient Store of Materials of all kinds necessary for making the Descent & likewise for carrying on a Seige, Such as by the List annex'd, & what others may further be demanded by the Chief Enginier.

The Country, round Louisbourg in general consists of Rock & Morass, or Bog, & where there is no Morass or Bog, in some few places there are small spots of Good Earth, though these are very few indeed, The generality of these Spaces being only a mixture of a Rubble Stoney kind of Earth, not to be thrown up or moved without great Labour & the help of a Pick axe

It being apprehended that Cabarouce Bay (by sea about 2 or 3 Leagues to the Westward of Louisbourg, where the New England

---

[1] Peregrine Thomas Hopson was governor of Louisbourg after Knowles's departure in 1747, and governor of Nova Scotia in 1752. In England from 1753 to 1757, he accompanied the expedition of 1757 as major general, remained in Halifax during the winter, and died during the siege of Guadaloupe in 1759, in which he commanded the land forces.

Troops Landed when They made their Descent upon the Island in 1745) is the place where it is now thought the Troops for this Expedition must land, It may be proper here to mention Something by way of Description of ye Ground between that & the Garrison of Louisbourg.

It is thought that Cabarouce Bay is about 3 or 4 miles from Louisbourg by Land, the Way some part Rocky, the rest cheifly consisting of Deep, Boggy Swampy ground upon an Ascent almost the whole way, with several Hauteurs which for ye most part command every thing in ye way by which You must advance towards ye Town.—Here, that is, upon these swamps, it was, that ye New England Troops met with Extreem Difficulties in getting their Heavy Cannon &c^a over in order to come before the Place to attack it, & it was said that it proved but just practicable.

It is conceived that, before the Troops (after landing in Cabarouce Bay) can be in readiness to advance before ye Place, a part of ye Garrison will be sent out in order to possess the Hauteurs and that they will raise several Batteries or Redoutes, which they probably may have Sufficient time to put in Execution. In this case The Troops will find it exceeding difficult to advance, as they must be obliged to make use of their Cannon in approaching, & that under very disadvantageous circumstances from the Reverse Situation of ye Enemy, who having no reason to be apprehensive of their being cut off from their Retreat, may safely dispute the Ground for ye greatest part of ye way from ye place of Landing quite to the Garrison, for should they find themselves Push'd, & obliged to abandon their most advanced Posts, They may easily retire to ye next & so on, whereby the Troops will find themselves under the Necessity of Forceing their way, by means of their Artillery, even to ye Spot where They must first begin their Attack against the Garrison. This it is imagined They will do, even supposing They should not get Intelligence of ye intended Descent, for it is conceived They would have time enough to Execute the above scheme between the time of ye Troops appearing off the Place & that of their being ready to Advance towards it after They are Landed, But if They should get any Intelligence Previous to ye Arrival of ye Troops They then most undoubtedly will execute the Thing, & it is here to be observed, That the motions of ye Troops, almost from the Place of Landing, may be observed by ye Garrison.

There is another thing which certainly They may do, & 'tis Judged they will, That is, send round by Sea to ye place proposed for Landing, Artillery, & thereby Obstruct the Landing of ye Troops; This They may do with the greatest Ease; provided they have only 24 hours notice of the design against them.

Supposing all Difficulties got over, &, that ye Troops are advanced before the Garrison, & one attack is to be made near ye West Gate or Else where, as may be judged promising of success, & it should be found proper to make another at ye same time from The Rock against the Collier's Battery at ye South East part of ye Garrison, in These cases, the Difficulties which, it is conceived, may attend each, are.

Though, before ye West Gate, possibly there may be found Earth sufficient for making a Regular Approach for some Small distance, & for Raising Batteries against the Place, (meaning Of the Stoney kind of Earth among the Rocks, which 'tis doubted whether there is or not on the spot) still it is far from being Earth that will be easily thrown up to answer that service, but will require great Labour in doing, however, allowing there should be, yet the other Attack will be attended with far greater Difficulty, as There is not any Earth at all where it is to be made from, It being an Entire solid Rock only.

It is presumed it would not be improper that some Officers of His Majesty's Navy, such as Admiral Knowles, & Captain James Douglas,[2] who have been upon the Spot, should be ask'd some questions in regard to Cabarouce Bay, & the Depth of Water in every part of it, whereby it may be known of what Draft of Water the Transports should be for ye intended Service, How many, or if any of His Majesty's Ships can go high enough into ye Bay so as to be near enough to cover the Descent of ye Troops, & for other Information in many particulars which most probably may prove of the greatest utility to the Expedition.—There is likewise a Gentleman, Brigad^r Waldo, that was upon ye Expedition with ye New England Troops, who, when it shall be judged proper that He may be asked some Questions about ye Affair, It is thought, will be able to give such Information as will also prove very Satisfactory & tend extreemly for the Service.

Further Admiral Knowles, & Captain Douglas, may be asked whether The Ships, in ye Winds before mentioned, when They Sett in hard, & come suddenly on, can always put to sea from ye Head of ye Bay, or, if they cannot do that, whether the whole Fleet of Transports from ye place where They must lay, or any great number of Them, can probably Ride it out without danger of being ashoar, For should such Winds happen after they arrive in ye Bay, before the Troops &c^a are

---

[2] James Douglas was captain of the *Mermaid* in the 1745 Louisbourg expedition. He was at the sieges of Louisbourg and Quebec in 1758 and 1759, and commanded at the capture of Dominica in 1762.

all Landed, & the ships be obliged to put to sea again, or be in danger
of Driving a shoar by continuing at an Anchor, probably the Expedition might fail of success.—

'Tis certain Sr Peter Warren with the Men of War & Transports in
1745, did lay either in or off ye Bay for a long time, but then it was
thought a very extraordinary thing that He happen'd to have such
Favourable Winds as permitted Him to do it.

It is judged Necessary, both during the Seige, as well as before,
that a Strong Squadron of His Majesty's Ships of War (& Those Large
Ships, in case their might be occasion, during the Seige, to Endeavour
to Force ye Harbour of Louisbourg) should Cruise as closs in before
the Place as possible, so as may be Judged proper with Safety, to prevent any of the Enemy's Ships of War, or others from getting in, for
was it to happen that any of the former should do it The Troops employed in the Attack against the West Gate would be Exposed &
Flank'd by the Fire from those Ships from the West End of the Harbour, where some of Them might be lay'd for that purpose, & their
Rear would likewise be exposed to any number of Men that might be
landed from the Enemys Ships in order to annoy them in that quarter,
which might be very easily be done. Besides, if a Squadron of His
Majesty's Ships should be so disposed of, & thereby intercept any of
ye Enemy's from endeavouring to get in, There then possibly may happen an Opportunity for His Majesty's Troops to attack, either ye Grand
Battery, or Lighthouse Battery, or Both, (if it should, upon View, appear that both these Attacks are promising of success) by which means
the carrying of them will be greatly Facilitated, & if carryed would
afterwards render The Forceing of ye Harbour, by our Squadron much
more practicable.—Here it is to be observed, that if there should be
any Men of War of the Enemy's in the Harbour they can dispose of
them in such a manner as greatly to annoy Our Troops, both in their
Camp, as well as in their Trenches, & also when they come to make
an attack against ye Grand Battery.

It is further judged it will be absolutely necessary that some Cruisers
should be closly employed, & that as early as possible, when ye Season
will admit, upon the Back of ye Island, in ye Golph of St Lawrence,
between the Gut of Canso & the East End of the Island, to prevent y^e
Enemy from Stealing in any Reinforcements or Succours, not only from
ye Island of St Johns, but likewise from Canada.—And—If the Liberty
may be allowed to mention one thing, which is, That—As it is con-
cieved, The Neutral Inhabitants of Nova Scotia who were sent away
last Fall from thence to our other Colonies, (a great part of whom, it

is reported, have lately been sent from thence here to England) would gladly get to Cape Breton, to be near to their Old Possessions in Nova Scotia, in order to assist in yᵉ Recovering them again whenever a good Opportunity shall offer, It is presumed that it would be much for His Majesty's Service in regard to yᵉ intended Expedition, if these People could, by any means, be detained here, untill that may be carryed into execution; otherwise should they once get into Old France undoubtedly they will immediately get themselves Transported to Cape Breton, which will be an easy way of Reinforceing the Garrison of Louisbourg & that at an Easy expence to their Government at home.

The Ships of War that are to Cruise off the Harbour of Louisbourg, & on the Back of yᵉ Island, from yᵉ Gut of Canso to yᵉ East End of yᵉ Island, or rather yᵉ N East end of it, to be at their Stations by a time to be fix'd, or to be so near as to take the opportunity of being there as soon as it is even possible for any Ships to get in, either from Old France or from Canada in yᵉ Spring.

The Men of War & Transports with yᵉ Troops &cᵃ for yᵉ Expedition to be ready by the of   next as may hereafter be judged proper, And to have a Rendezvous, (well considered before given for fear of Intelligence being had by the Enemy) given them & not to be open'd till well out at sea, for as it is conceived scarce probable that all of them can arrive together after so long a Voyage, It possibly might prove of yᵉ Utmost Ill consequence to the Expedition, should they Drop in one after another.—

If the Lighthouse Battery, which 'tis said has been lately Raised, should upon View appear to be open to yᵉ Rear of it so as not to require Cannon being brought for the Attack, which if it should not be so, 'Tis imagined it cannot be attack'd at all, The Way to it being extreemly Hilly & also Rocky, & consequently impossible to take Cannon there, It is thought that, in yᵉ first case, by the help of 2 or 3 of yᵉ smallest Transports, or Sloops or Schooners, if such should be sent from Halifax or Boston upon yᵉ Service, there might a proper number of The Troops be Reimbark'd aboard them in order to be Landed at Little Lorenbeg, a small Boat Harbour about a League to the Eastward of the Light House, from whence They may March, by the help of a Guide yᵗ must be procured for that purpose, (but must have no Cannon nor any Incumberence whatsoever) & probably possess themselves of the Lighthouse Battery, which done would be of yᵉ utmost consequence, should it afterwards be judged necessary for His Majesty's Ships to endeavour to force yᵉ Harbour. This is upon a Supposition that the Troops may sooner or later be able to possess themselves of ye Grand Battery likewise, to do which a great Number of Men, & Heavy Cannon must be employed, otherwise they may be cutt off from their Retreat by A Force sent from the Enemy's Ships if there should be any in ye Harbour & in that case they can transport them across it in a very short time for y^t purpose.

The Landing of the Troops at little Lorenbeg is only practicable when the wind does not set in shoar, & that in Boats from ye Transports, and they cannot be Reimbark'd again to return to their Camp except a proper Wind favours their getting aboard, as no Vessels can lay off that Harbour of Lorenbeg when the Wind comes in from the Sea.

It is thought that a proper View of ye Lighthouse Battery, if it is where it is imagined to be, may be taken by a proper Person who may be sent off the Harbour for that purpose. on board of His Majesty's Ships—

To consider what quantity of Provisions may be proper to send with ye Troops in case of Carrying the Place, so as they may not want for the whole Winter, & even as far as the middle of June ensuing, for none can can be sent, with any kind of certainty, in the Fall of ye Year.

A quantity upwards of 3000 Chaldrons of Coals must likewise be sent, for should the Place be carryed, Wood sufficient cannot be got, as is known by Experience, because when the Place was in our hands not one third of what was necessary for the Garrison could be procured in a whole Summer, tho' We then had ye Assistance of Several French Inhabitants that were left in ye Island, & as to laying in a Store in the Winter That is absolutely impracticable or even any at all. For the first Year or two, if not much longer, all our Dependence must be upon Coal from England, for none can be Raised upon the Island untill the Colliery is well Establish'd, several Miners sent out from thence likewise, with all Impliments proper for Working the Coals, & the Place where the Coal Pits are is well Fortifyed, so as to be above any Insult from the Enemy.

It is also to be considered how the Troops are to be disposed of in case They should succeed in ye Expedition, what Garrison is to Remain there, & where the rest are to be sent, as the Place will not contain the whole, except they should meet with very great Losses indeed.

It is further to be considered in the Attack against the Light House Battery (so named, as it is supposed to be near, but not directly at the Lighthouse) that if the way whereby the Troops must pass to make their attack, is open & Exposed to the Direction of the Fire from The Island Battery, That Service will be attended with a considerable Loss of Men, If the Enemy there cannot by some means or other be Diverted, & thereby be obliged to throw Their Fire another way, wherefore if an Opportunity was to offer when the sea is pretty well down, & at yᵉ same time a favourable Breeze of Wind for making an Attack upon that Battery, By His Majesty's Ships, & to Land a proper Detachmᵗ of the Troops on yᵉ Back if yᵉ Surf will permit & likewise upon ye North West End of it, While The Lighthouse Battery is Attackt, It is supposed that one or yᵉ other, if not both, might Fall into Our Hands, which might also be attended with yᵉ consequence of Our Ships getting into yᵉ Harbour, provided the Grand Battery should have been Carryed by the Troops before, & would entirely prevent any of the Enemys Ships of War or others from getting in, Supposing They should pass unobserved by Our Cruisers, by means of Fogs or any other accident that might happen in their Favour, & must disconcert the Garrison in such a manner as probably might prove the means of our carrying the Place, if Briskly Attackt at yᵉ same time. Here it is to be observed that it is doubtfull whether the Attack of the Island Battery (To be made by the Troops that are to be Landed from some of yᵉ Men of War, in Boats, or from some of the Transports appointed for that service, if that is judged most proper, as reasonably it may be on account of Encumbering the Former as little as possible at that time) may succeed without the help of Scaling Ladders & at yᵉ same time some Sailors, who would not only be of great Service in Expediting the Landing of yᵉ Detachment for yᵉ Attack, but afterwards would be no less so by being intermixt with the Troops in making the Assault. Here The Enemy may be extreemly annoyed in the Battery by The Small Arms from the Ships Tops.

From as much as can be recollected, In the Attacking of the Island Battery The Wind must be at West or, as it thought, rather to yᵉ Northward of it, otherwise it will raise a Sea and cause a great surf upon the Rocks, & prevent our Landing the Men for making an Attack upon it, & if the Wind is so far to yᵉ Northward as North West or away to North East or more Easterly, then The Ships cannot come in to attack the Battery, as that Wind will throw in so great a Sea into yᵉ Mouth of yᵉ Harbour that They could not well lay at an Anchor before the Battery. There would be the same inconveniencess if the Wind was to be any where between yᵉ North East & away to yᵉ South. But these matters are submitted to such as are more versed in sea affairs.—

It is judged that in order to be at any kind of Certainty of Carrying the Place, The Harbour, either sooner or later, must be Forced by

Our Men of War employed to cover the Seige, in order to Distress & Disconcert the Garrison, which most certainly that would do to the utmost degree, & might probably give an Opportunity for the Troops making a General assault at yᵉ same time, as before mentioned.

Caution must be taken in regard to the making any stoppage from the Troops for their Provisions, as they will be so near to those in Nova Scotia who have none made from them on that Acc^t.—

If there is no Stoppage to be made for Provisions, and any of the Troops in Nova Scotia are to be ordered on this Service, It is conceived that, Major General Warburton's Regiment, or a Detachment of it, should be a part of those, as that Regiment is the only one of the Three in that Province that was heretofore at Louisbourg, & are acquainted with yᵉ Country round it, & therefore may be of great service upon yᵉ Occasion.

It is to be observed that there is no Ground for an Encampment with any kind of Regularity, but yᵉ Camp must be very Irregular, & consequently will require a Good Disposition to be made for Its Security, upon this Occasion a Feild Train may be necessary.

The Garrison, after calling in as many of the Inhabitants of yᵉ Island as may be judged proper, may order the rest upon a Service which might Harrass the Troops in their Camp, by annoying them that way, & by Intercepting Their Wood Cutters in going to yᵉ Woods for Fuel, as They have yᵉ whole Country behind open to them, and They, may likewise be employed in annoying the Troops from The Woods at the First Landing.

Upon The whole Considering that The Troops Intended for This Expedition, may have a very long Passage, occasioned by contrary winds, Fogs or otherwise, whereby they may contract a Sickness aboard the Transports That The Fatigue will be great in Transporting The Artillery, Provisions & all stores &c^a, from yᵉ Place of Landing, in which Service The Men & not Horses must be Employed, & The number of Men that must at yᵉ same time be employed for yᵉ security of the Whole, while y^t is put in Execution, The Several Attacks which are proposed to be made besides others that may hereafter appear to be necessary.—The Number of Men that must every day be Detacht to the Woods for Fuel, & yᵉ Parties to cover them.—The Sickness that may happen from Fatigues, as likewise from yᵉ Ground being so very Swampy, & the Surface everywhere in that season of yᵉ year being so exceeding Damp from the snow being but just gone off, These Things Considered, It is submitted what number of Troops may be necessary for the Intended Expedition. There is one thing more that may be mentioned which may possibly prove of bad consequence to the Expedition, which is.—

If The Fleet of Transports, after being Observed by the Garrison, for want of a Favourable Opportunity, of Landing should be obliged to Plye off & on for any time near the Place where the Descent is to be made, which may very probably happen, It is to be observed that ye Enemy will have time sufficient to Raise Batteries upon ye shore, whereby They may make it extreemly difficult for Landing ye Troops—

[*Endorsed*] Colonel *Hopson's Private Thoughts,* relating to the Attack of Louisbourg 1757

PROPOSAL BY ADMIRAL KNOWLES AND COLONEL HOPSON

(COPY)

Some Thoughts concerning an Attack on . . . .

This place may be Assail'd either by Land or Sea, or both.

On Land by a regular Siege, By Sea from a sudden Attack of a powerfull Squadron.

The first has been already consider'd by an Able Officer, whose plan I think in general cannot be mended, the last then, is what requires present Consideration: towards which it will be necessary as speedily as possible to gett intelligence what Number of Troops that Garrison at present consists of, what additional Works have been done since it was in possession of the English, as well to the Town, as at other parts of the Harbour, and of what Force & strength those new Works are both in their Fabrick and number of Cannon.

These Points in strickt propriety, shoud have been known before any judgment had been formed, but as we cannot be furnish'd timely with those Lights, I shall found my Opinion upon the State and Condition of the Place at the Time it was deliver'd up to the French, When I think it wou'd have required a Squadron of twelve Ships of the Line from 90 to 60 Guns to have taken it, together with two Bomb Ketches and 6 or 8 Fregates & small Cruizers. such a Squadron well appointed, with 4 or 6000 Troops to have attended it, and landed immediately upon a general Attack, in such places as shou'd first have been render'd practicable for them by the Men of Warr: might I do apprehend have counted upon certain Success. and I am the more confirm'd in this Opinion, when I consider the strength of the Expedition form'd against it by the French under the Command of the Duke D'anville.

It is laid down as a universal Maxim in Warr, by the greatest Generals, to be particularly attentive; especialy at the opening of the first Campaign, not to let the adversary reap the smalest advantage, least in the begining of the Warr, he suffer it to change from the Offensive to a Warr upon equal Terms; much less dwindle to a deffensive One. a strickt Obeservance of the same Rule becomes a Sea General as well as Land. (for what is lost in one Campaign, may not perhaps be regaind in three or four.) Since (unfortunately) then this true Principle has not been observed, I hope it will be consider'd as a Wise and Prudent Measure to send a sufficient Force for this undertaking to make sure (under God,) of a Conquest; and I hope my requesting such a Force will not be imputed to any other Motive.

What I mean by a sufficient Force is such an Augmentation to what I have already mention'd (both of Ships and Troops) as shall be adjudged upon mature deliberation, (no certain intelligence arriving in the meantime) to be equal at least to the additional strength any Wise Nation wou'd have made to such a Frontier, before the breaking out of a War, indeed it may be said before such Nation did begin a War.

In the Island Battery are 33 Ambrazures consequently it is capable of mounting the same number of Guns, the calibre of wch were 27. and 36 pounders; agains[t] this Battery I apprehend it will be necessary to lay one Ship of 74 Guns, and One of 60, and a three deck Ship at the End to enfilade it, (a two deck Ship being scarce Loffty enough.)

The Grand Battery has 32 Ambrazures, the Guns all 42 pounders, Two 74 Gun Ships are as few as can be appointed to silence this Battery.

On the Flagstaff, or Dukes Battery was mounted 21, 42 pounders and 7 12 pounders in the Flanks.

Bastion de Maurepas, or Prince Edwards Bastion was mounted with 9 Guns in the northermost face, 24 pounders and 3 12 pounders in the Flank; in the south face there were no guns but space for 9, in the flank were 5-12 pounders mounted, nor were any guns mounted in the curtains, tho all capable of recieving them.

In Prince Henrys Bastion on the otherside Maurepas Gate were 5 Guns 12 pounders in the flank, in both faces there were only two Guns at the Angular Point mounted en Cavaliere and fired en barbette; against these Bastions, the Dukes Battery and along the Town Wall next the Harbour to the West Gate (where were 6 or 8 small Guns more,) I think it will require 5 or 6 Stout Line of Battle Ships at the least, and Employment enough for them.

The Pallisadoed Line between the Colliers Bastion and Princes

Henrys Bastion will take two stout Ships more, there being 4 Guns in the Cavalier on the Colliers Bastion 3 in the renterent Angle, 18 pounders, and 9 Guns of 32 pounders in the Face; all which must be silenced before any debarkment of Troops can be made to Storm the Curtain of the Wooden Line, after a Breach is made in it.

Some Ships of Force must at the same time be employ'd to take care of the Transports, and cover the Bomb Ketches, two or three 50 Gun Ships may do for this service.

There is an Island, call'd green Island, which lays aback of the Island Battery, within less than ¼ of a Mile, which must be taken possession of a few days before the general attack, as it is a most advantageous situation for a Bomb Battery, overlooking both the Bastions at Maurepas Gate, and looking down into the Island Battery where no Man can stirr but he's seen, some Wall pieces here & Musquet Cohorns will be usefull.

If there is no French Squadron in Port, and the Weather presents favourable I do not apprehend the Conflict will last long after the Ships are placed but in the intrim the fire may be verry brisk.

If the Attack can be made intirely by Shiping, it will most certainly save a verry great Expence, an infinite deal of Labour and fateague, as well as Time, and fewer lives be lost, I humbly apprehend then must happen thro' Sickness alone during the Course of a tedious Siege.

Shou'd a Battery be errected at the Light house, I immagine it will be made verry Strong, (or they must be verry bad Engineers indeed.) else they are securer without One, for if we can possess ourselves easily of any Work there, neither the Island or Grand Battery can hold it out long, the height of the ground thereabouts commanding both those Batterys: if it is closed and fortify'd on the back, we must land and take it for there is no entering the Harbour before we are Master of that.

The several Curtains and faces of the Bastions it may reasonably be concluded will be compleated with Guns if no additional Works shou'd have been made,

Before any Expedition setts forth it shou'd be know for certain whither any Squadron of the French is gone, or destin'd to go for that place, for shou'd but 5 or 6 Ships of the Line gett there, all attempts by Sea wou'd be vain, for they may keep out a hundred; nor do I think a Siege by Land cou'd be carried on whilest a Squadron is in the Harbour, because after a breach is made the Men who are to assault that breach, must March under the fire of all the Ships: unless there were

Forces enough to build batterys to Sink those Ships or drive them away, and carry on the Siege too.

All which is most Humbly Submit'ed,

[*Endorsed*] Joint *Proposal* by Admiral *Knowles* & Colo¹ *Hopson,* concerning an Attack upon *Louisbourg. 1757.*

ANIMADVERSIONS UPON Mᴿ SHIRLEY'S CONDUCT. 1757 ¹

(COPY)

In the Year 1755 M Sh— by Concertion with & under the Commands of Gen¹ Braddock undertook an Expedition against the French Posts at Niagara which was to have been contemporary with that of Mʳ Braddock's against Fort Duquesne. Upon a Supposition that such Measures must divide the Force which the French had in those Parts.

From the Time that Mʳ Sh— left Gen¹ Braddock after concerting this Plan which was in April; & from the Known State of the lower Port [Fort] at Niagara It does appear that Mʳ Sh—'s Part of the Execution might have been effected. Great Preparations were made & great Expence incurred in Order thereto. Yet the Execution was delayed & protracted before Mʳ Sh. set out, 'till the Time was elapsed in which it was to be executed; & even When Mʳ Sh: did set out upon this Expedition, The Execution was again delayed 'till the very Day before that on which Mʳ Sh: with the Advice of a Council of War determined—That it was too late in the Season to carry it into Execution.

However Mʳ Sh: excused himself upon the Obstructions in the Carriage & the consequent Defect of Provisions. & projecting some Works of Defence to strengthen that Post, came away. These Works were left incompleat & never after compleated. Mʳ Sh: acquaints' His Majᵗʸ'ˢ Ministers that He had secured the Country & sufficiently fortified & garrisoned the Post of Oswego; & in Consequence of this as a Fact, projected an Offensive Campaign from Oswego; the Time which He proposes for the Execution of this was the latter End of March 1756, or the Beginning of April & this Plan is accordingly sent to England to His Majᵗʸ'ˢ Ministers & proposed to—the several Governmᵗˢ of the Colonies & concerted, and the Preparation for it engaged, & the necessary Measures taken & the Expence incurred.

After all this Mʳ Sh: delays and suspends again the Execution 'till May 25ᵗʰ & at that Time when possibly He might begin to see—the Im-

¹ This paper, in memorandum form, would seem to be an outline of one of the possible charges upon which the projected court martial of Shirley could be based.

practicability of His original offensive Scheme. Yet at that Time He must have known from the State of the Forts & Garrison of Oswego & from the French Preparations to attack it, that a *Defensive* Plan was become *absolutely* necessary *there;* Yet at this very Time He calls a Council of War & upon the Supposition that the Posts at Oswego were sufficiently garrisoned fortified & provided, with Advice thereof alters the Destination of the 44th & 48th Regimts & entirely quits all Operations in that Quarter, & puts things into such a Situation that when Genl Abercrombie on the 10th July found it necessary to send what Succours He could to Oswego, the 44th Regt only was not able to march 'till the Second Week in August. Farther Mr Sh:'s second Project by this new Destination was never put into Execution, but had it been so big sending every thing & the Two Regiments up the Hudson's River towards—Crown Point to wait upon the Motions of the Provincials; It would then have been impracticable even to have thought of endeavouring to send any Succours to Oswego.

Some Hints for the Operations in North America for 1757 [1]

(COPY)

Number of Forces to be rais'd by the Several Provinces.

New Hampshire & Massachusetts Bay	12,000
Connecticut	5,000
New York	3,000
Jerseys	1,000
Pensilvania	3,000
Maryland	1,000
Virginia	2,000
North Carolina	1,000
South Carolina	2,000
	30,000
Regulars	10,000
	40,000

[1] To judge from his emphasis on provincial troops, his unnecessary reference to the Kennebec river route, his suggestion for an attack on Fort Frontenac, his personal knowledge of Oswego, and the general hopeful tone of his arguments, the writer of these hints was a man with the colonial point of view, perhaps William Shirley. Shirley was in London at this time. These suggestions resemble John Bradstreet's proposals to Pitt in the autumn of 1757 (Public Record Office, Chatham Papers, Vol. 95).

	Regulr. Train Incld.	
For St Lawrence, or Kennebec River	5,000	20,000
Crown Point &C^a	4,000	10,000
Cadaraque	1,000	2,000
	10,000	
To Harrass the Country, seize, on all } Crafts Battoes &C^a in 3 Partys, Each 800 }	....	2,400
Woodcutters Pioneers &C^a		3,200
Sailors to Man 400 Sloops &C^a		2,400
		40,000

As I cannot but be of Oppinion the whole Provinces in America, will with the greatest chearfulness, enter upon any Measures for the imediate attack of Canada which appears to be the least expensive, surest, and only way of redressing Great Britain for the insults and Encroachments, made on his Majesty Subjects & Dominion in America.

To spare no pains, in finding out proper Persons for Intelligence.

That an Embargo be laid on all Provisions through the Provinces in North America until the Month of May, and then to be carried only to his Majestys Islands and Plantations, and not to any Neutral Ports and the Officers in the said Islands and Plantations, to have a particular Regard and security given for all Provisions, put on board any Vessell, more than is imediately necessary for the Crews of the said Vessells intended Voyage, to be landed in some of his Majestys Islands or Plantations, & Certificates to be produced in a limited time, otherways the Bonds to be prosecuted.

To have a proper Fleet Cruising before and in the Gulf of St Laurence's River, as well as before the streights of Belle Isle, that nothing may pass, others station'd along the Coast to prevent the Enemy from making any desent, or surprizing any of his Maj^ty Settlements (which ly very much exposed.) in order to make a Diversion for dividing our Forces.

During the Winter to have a constant succession of Strong Partys of Irregulars out. (if an open Winter, if not so soon as the Weather will permit) to harrass and destroy all the Provisions about Montreal, Quebec &C^a,—which will terrify the Inhabitants and cause them to move into the Fortify'd Towns, which must of course Consume the Provisions, laid up for the Inhabitants & their Troops. so soon as the season will admit, to make a Diversion towards Crown Point, which will draw them out of Montreal & Quebec.

Then for a Sufficient number of Ships to pass the Gulf of St Laurence to the entrance of the River forming themselves in such a manner that nothing can pass them, the rest of the Fleet to keep their Stations, so that if any thing should get in, they must pass two Fires, which I think will be almost impossible

At the same time to have the smal Vessells of War, with a sufficient number of Sloops, Schooners & Brigantines well Arm'd, with the Troops, Artillery, Provisions &C^a on board proper for the Seige which will work up the River much sooner than large Ships or heavy Transports.

This will alarm the Capital; and by the time the Forces design'd for the attack of Crown Point can receive intelligence of Their landing which may be sent Express to the Fort on Kennebeck River & so through Boston, which I imagine may be done in eight or ten days, if Expresses are properly laid, in which time all that can be spar'd, will be sent to the Relief of Their Capital, then to move to the attack of Crown Point, if success there, A sufficient number of The Forces to imediately advance to the attack of Montreal in which I apprehend there will be no great dificulty as the Ranging Partys may secure all the Enemys Boats, for transporting Our Troops. &C^a.

At the same time Crown Point is attack'd the Forces design'd for Cadaraque, should move from the great carrying Place in Whale boats, and may be there in about sixteen days, which should be under the direction of a Person that has some knowledge of the Sea as well as Land service, for if there is two seperate commands, they never will agree and cause the attempt to fail, this will put us again into imediate Possession of the Lakes, and in all Probability, will cause the six Nations of Indians to join Us. But least the Begotted [bigoted] Indians in the French Interest, which are Numerous on that side should over power Us, if We made any long tarry there, I would advise that the Fort at Cadaraque should be demolish'd and the Vessells brought over to Oswego.

As 1000 would be sufficient for this the other in the meantime may be covering themselves at Oswego against Musketry, at Ontario Fort, & where the Old Block house stood, which will also cover the Vessells from any attempt the Indians may make to Fire them.

An Instruction to all Governors in America to inspect the Arms of the Militia in their several Provinces, that they are in good Order, and properly Provided with Amunition, and to be always Ready, in case of any Desent being made in any of the Provinces, & to assist each other, otherways they will incur his Maj^{ys} highest displeasure.

LOUDOUN TO CUMBERLAND

(COPY)

New York, March 8, 1757

Sir,

I have had the Honour to receive your Royal Highness's very long Letter. begun the 22^d of October, & ending the 23^d of December (*1756*.)

Your *R:H:* has made many Men happy; but you never made anyone more so, than you have done me, by the great Goodness you have shewn me, thorough the whole of this long Letter. 'Tis not in my Power to make you any other Return, than by a constant attention to the Instructions you have given me, & by a zealous & faithfull Execution of my Duty, to endeavour to deserve that Favour *Y:R:H:* is so good as to express for me.

As I am pressed in time to go to *Philadelphia,* I hope *Y:R:H:* will pardon my not being so minute in the Plan I have given the great Lines of, in my Letter to the Secretary of State, as I should otherways have been: but, must postpone it 'till my Return.

In that Letter, I have begun with what I propose (if I do not receive orders to the contrary) to leave, for the Security of this Country, whilst I am absent. And, as the *Distribution* I have made of the general officers, is liable to objection, I beg Leave to lay my Reasons for it, before *Y:R:H:*

In the first Place, I can have no Doubt that it is right for me to embark with the Troops, as they are the main Body of the Force in this Country, & go, on the most material Enterprise; and, that it is right for me to carry *one* general officer with me, in case of any accident or Sickness rendering me incapable of doing my Duty.

But here, it may be objected, that I ought to have left Major G^l *Abercrombie,* as the Second, with so great a Command as the *2: Batt^s* and the *6000:* Provincials, & to have carried Mr *Webb* with me.

But, in this, I was determined by the Situation I found Mr *Webb* in, at the Return from *Boston.* For, tho' I had been informed there, by my Letters from hence, that he was perfectly recovered, I found him so weak that he could not bear any Noise; the Impetuosity of Colonel *Prevost* quite overcome him. And altho' he is now much better, he is not so well as I could wish: and, as he is, at all times, extremely sick the whole time he is at sea, I thought he would probably be so weak, that he would not be able to act when he arrived; in which case, if any accident should happen to me, which every man is liable to, it might have proved very fatal to the whole, as the Com̄and must have fallen to Colonel Dussau, who is unequal to it; & then to Co¹ *Prevost,* whom I should have been sorry to have put at the Head of a Brittish Army; for, he wants one above him to bridle his warmth in command.

Before I leave the Subject of Command, pardon me to ask what I am to do, in case there should come over an elder Colonel with the Troops Mʳ *Pitt* mentions?

Before I fixed upon the command either of the general officers were to be employed on, I fixed the Troops for each Command, to prevent Partiality, where People were to be themselves, & to mention the Troops as they are posted at present I determined to take the *42: 44:* & *48:* Regiments along with me: and, from hence, I take the *22:* Regiment & *two* Battalions of the Royal *Americans.*

With Mʳ *Webb,* I leave the *35:* & the *3ᵈ* Battⁿ of the Royal *Americans* with the *4:* independent Companies & the *Provincials.*

He has since proposed to have the *2ᵈ* Battalion, in place of the *3ᵈ* which is not yet Settled. My Reason for pitching on the *2ᵈ* & *4:* to go with me, was, on account of their Colonels, who, I think, I can best deal with; the one will do under a Superior: but, Colonel *Prevost* requires a Firmness pretty near equal to Obstinacy to deal with him: or, he will govern the world.

I would indulge Mʳ *Webb* in every thing in my Power: but, I believe, I must carry the *2ᵈ* Battⁿ with me, for those Reasons.

Sir John Sᵗ *Clair,* has been extremely ill for some time, with many complaints, & whilst I was at *Boston* was *two* Days speechless, with a Complaint on his Nerves. When I returned, he came to me quite emaciated and supported. He then told me, that *it was all over, & he found he must die; for, he could hold it no longer.* But, he afterwards talked of Business, which revived him greatly; & before he left me, he was determined to make the Campaign. He has, since, had several violent Fits of the Gravel, the Pain of which brings on those nervous Complaints, for what I know no Name. In short, his constitution is totally broke, & there is not the least appearance of his being able to serve this Campaign, if he does live, which I do not expect.

My Plan; for, I am not yet fixed, is to appoint Major *Robertson* to act for the present. He occurs to me from his activity, & having formerly acted under *Y:R:H:* in Scotland, as a Deputy, by which he has had some Practice in the office; and he belongs to the 2^d Battalion. *Y:R:H:* sees I am forced to take some Steps in this; & the next Packet, which I hope will sail in three Weeks, will bring you an account of what I do.

The Returns of *January* go by this Packet. I have not yet got all the Returns of *February;* nor can I divide the Draughts yet, except So far as compleats the 22^d Regiment. So that, neither the Remains of them, nor the last Recruits from *Virginia,* are included in those Returns. But, I expect the *real Strength,* at the time we take the Field, will be the 22: & 42: Regiments *1000:* each: the *35:44:* & *48:*Reg^{ts} *800* each: and the *Four* Batt^s of the Royal *Americans* 700: each. But, from that, must be taken Co^l *Prevost's* Recruits that were taken at Sea; & must remain on our Returns 'till we know what is become of them: and the *Highlanders* that are with the *42:* on our Pay: But, they will very Soon be all incorporated into that Regiment; & the 59: taken by *Zephir,* of the Draughts on additional Companies: and, I might include the 124: Men left in that Ship who have capitulated not to Serve for a year. So that, with those I must leave, (as being bad, which the *Virginia* Recruits realy are, most of them being *Convicts,* & many of them bought out of the Ships before they landed) I can not reckon those Battalions above *600:* each, for present Service.

On this Calculation of the Troops here & Mr *Pitt's* Information of *8000:* to be sent out, I have formed my Plan, which leaves *12,800:* for the *Expedition,* independent of what may be got from *Nova Scotia.* But, as I have seen Ministers Promises come short, I have made, in my own Mind, allowances for accidents, though I stick up to the *8000:* in my public Letter; and think if you realy send out *6000:* good men, we will be able to accomplish what is expected by the *Expedition,* if no new Succours are thrown in, to the Enemy; and, if you send a *Man* to command the Fleet that is practicable in Business.

The general opinion, here, is, that Admiral *Knowles* is to command the Fleet. I am very little acquainted with him. But, pardon me to say, the Character he has, is, that he never agreed with any man, in command, & that, there is no dealing with him but before Witnesses & in writing, which may remain, to shew what realy passes. If those Things are true and He command, there is an End of all Prospect of Success. But, whoever the King is pleased to send, I do assure your Royal Highness, nothing shall be wanting on my part, to Keep up a Harmony & carry on the Service. And, I flater myself you will pardon me for having stated my aprehensions of such an Evil happening, as must arise from a Difference between the Commanders at this Distance from you.

These Digressions have lead me off from explaining why the Draughts have not been in the Returns. Their present Situation seems to arise from a Doubt between Colonel *Prevost* & Lt Colo^l *Rollo,* at the Embarkation, who had the Command, & both seem to have commanded in some Things; and, at the same time to think the other had the right to command, by Colonel *Prevost's* being only to command in America, which, with me, would have been no Doubt, as those Troops were under orders to go to *America.* But, from this I have no Return of what was mustered in Town, nor what Number actualy embarked. So that, I am forced to make up the Returns as they arrive, to find out what come from each Regiment, & what Number the whole amounts to.

It likewise seems they were mustered in the Town of *Cork,* the Morning they embarked, and were kept for that Purpose *four* or *five* hours in the Streets, by which I am afraid we lost a great many of them. I find the *22:* Regiment lost above *60:* Men. As to what additional Companies lost, I do not know, as I have no Return of the Number they ought to be, and, if we are to pay for them, I hope *Y:R:H:* will approve of our paying for no more than were embark'd.

The *22^d* Regiment have brought out *Accoutrements* for *700:* but, as they were not informed that they were to be augmented to *1000:* they were ordered to return from *Cork 200:* Sets of new Accoutrements they had, for their additional companies; and they are now in Cap^n *Desbrisay's* Hands in *Dublin.*

As Troops can not serve without Accoutrements; to remedy this Evil for the present, I have given orders to retain the Accoutrements of the *50:* & *51:* Regiments, in order to supply them. I know that when Regiments are broke, they belong to the Colonel; but, if they are to be pay'd for, the value can not be great. But, if the Demand is unreasonable, I can bring a Proof that the former Regiments, belonging to these *two* Gentlemen, never had any accoutrements, or *Grenadier Caps,* which Colo^l *Hobson* can inform *Y:R:H:* of; with the arts that were used at the Breaking of them at *Louisbourg.* These Things I Shall explain to Major General *Napier* in a Letter from the Road, with the manner in which the *50th* was raised, which I have not time to do just now.

I am distressed by not knowing what Comīssions His Majesty has been pleased to give in the *22^d* Regt. or what the King intends should be done here. I see by a Letter the Regiment received from the Agent two Days before they sailed, that the Lieut^t Colonel is out; & Major *Rollo* promoted; & the eldest Captn Blacket, made Major; and some Ensigns filled up, but no account of what either is done, or intended to be done about the *additional* Lieutenant.

I Send inclosed a Copy of a Letter from Major *Blacket,* who never can be capable of doing Duty; for which Reason, I have allowed him to go home, as he can not be of the smallest use here.

I am pretty much in the same Situation as to the foreign officers that should have come with Colonel *Prevost,* as I have no accounts of them, but from him, who has *varied* in his accounts of them; & by the best account I can gather from him, Several of them have something particular in their Circumstances. The first he mentions is Capⁿ *Boneville,* who is in the Transport reported to be at *Antigua.* The next is Captain *Burnan,* who was in the Transport taken by the *Zephir,* & with Lieutenᵗ *Le Noble,* & volunteer *D'Aulnis,* who went back to France. The account of this affair is very odd; but, I have not yet got to the Bottom of it; so shall suspend my judgement 'till I do. The other two Captⁿˢ *Williomans* & *DuFez,* are both in the Swiss, in the French Service; and, as I learn from the other Foreigners, are not likely to come. These *four,* with Captain Lieuᵗ *Littler,* of the *44:* he tells me *Y:R:H:* has ordered me to give Captain's Comission to, in the Royal *American* Regiment: the last, in Place of Captain de *Shool,* who does not accept.

This Situation puzzles me how to proceed. *Burnan* is gone back to *France,* & by Reports of the Soldiers (for I have not seen Capⁿ (?) *Gruelin,* who was in that Ship, & come on) not much against his Inclination. And, they further Say that *Le Noble* & *D'Aulnis* were sent back from the French man of war, in order to draught the best of the unmarried Men of the Draughts, which they endeavoured to do, & promised to provide for them in France. But, this is only from common Soldiers, one of which having been formerly in *Fitz-james's* Horse, understands French; but, he served in Lieuᵗ General *Blakeney's* Regiment, under *Y:R:H:* in 1746 in *Scotland.* The Lieutenants he tells me *Y:R:H:* approved of are *Raan,* Le *Noble, Perier* & de *Noyelles.* None of those are arrived but *Perier,* who is a Sergent in the Regiment; & I do not find he has any particular Merit.

Mʳ *Calcraft* writes he has sent me a List of the officers you have approved of. If he means what you have approved of since Colonel *Prevost* returned from *Germany,* it has never come to hand: But, indeed, most of the Letters that have been sent by Merchant Ships have miscarried.

In this Situation of Things, I stand still, expecting a Packet every Day, to clear up matters. But, I hope you will not think me in the wrong, if, before we take the Field, I fill up all Commissions, where I have no accounts of the officers having Leave of absence from you; or, an account of their being on the way to join their Regiments, as *Y:R:H:* knows 'tis not possible to carry on the Service without officers.

And, if no account be sent to me of His Majesty's having filled up the vacancies of the 22: Regim^t & yet those officers should arrive here, after the Necessity of the Service has obliged me to promote officers from other Commissions to supply those vacancies; and the vacancies are filled up from whence they were removed; I shall be under a Necessity of sending back any officers that may be sent out, to the War-Office, from whose Neglects the confusion must arise, if there is any.

I shall provide for such officers of the *50:* & *51:* Regiments as appear to me fit for Service; & shall send *Y:R:H:* a List of those here, distinguishing those I think fit for Service, & those that are not. As to Major *Craven,* as he has been Pay Master & has all the Accompts of that Regiment to clear, of which I, at present, see no Prospect of an End, I shall not employ him 'till that is done, except you order otherways.

But, I do most humbly beg that, *Y:R:H:* will not send back those that are gone back to *England,* as the officers here, have a very fatiguing Service attended with many Inconveniencies & no Profits; and that many younger officers have been promoted at home: and, if those People come, it will prevent their having Promotion here. I have no View in what I have said, but the Good of the Service, & that *Y:R:H:* is a much better Judge of that, than I am.

I have no account of any colonel being appointed to the *3^d Battalion.* I have never mentioned this article before, as I imagined it would have been filled up directly: and, I presume to hope that the People, here, have been thought of, where there are some very deserving ones.

Colonel Prevost has been with me from Lt Colonel *Bouquet* & *Haldiman* with an apprehension that other Field officers will come in upon them by Seniority, into the Royal *Americans;* and that, from thence, they will be deprived of ever rising. I shewed them that I looked upon the Succession of Colonel *Jefferies* as the first Nomination. But, as the Colonel was a little *outragious* I dismiss'd him, & sent for Colonel *Bouquet,* & shewed him the general Rule of promoting officers: but, that the King did not tie himself from departing from that, either by passing over the eldest, where he was not fit for the Commission, or in promoting younger officers, for particular Merit. And, I told him that as they had had a considerable Step, on their coming into the Service, I thought they had no Reason to take offence, if it should be some time before the King thought of them. I then repeated what I had told them before, that, as they were Strangers, I looked on them as particularly intitled to my Protection: and, I think he went away satisfied; but desired I might mention their Case to *Y:R:H:* as they can be promoted no where but in the Royal *American* Regiment. These two Lieu^t Colonels will do extremely well, and are very good officers. But, I am afraid Colonel *Prevost* will make himself disliked by every officer in the Army, in spite of all I am able to do: for, the manner he behaves to them is very *new:* and if I can not get him to change it, I think he will very soon get a Reproof from others; or, bring himself to a Court-Martial before the Campaign is over.

He has brought me a Plan of Recruiting the Regiment, which he *does* understand. But, as he required to the midle of May to execute it; which I can not come into at present It was a very profitable one too; for, he was by it to receive £6: for every *Free man;* & £4: for every *Servant;* and the Regiment to pay the Master if it was necessary. And, as this Price is greatly above what we give, or the other Regiments can afford, he was to give no more to the Recruits than we now give; & the Remainder of the Money he was to have, to enable him to *reward* the officers & Men employed under him.

The *Colonel* who approves of no one Thing he does not do himself, attributes our want of Success to the Accounts not being cleared for Recruiting, which is entirely owing to the Management of them by Major *Rutherford,* Major *Prevost* & the *Foreign* officers that arrived before me, where there are strange accompts & much Confusion. But, I will clear them, tho' *he* thinks it is better to pass them as given in. One of the foreign Captains charges in his Recruiting accompts £13: for a *Party of Pleasure on the water:* and *This* will not pass in my accompts. I am at a Loss to know where the Fleet & the Transports from *England,* will be sent to? The first Plan was to have embarked all the Troops, that go from hence, at *Boston,* from the accounts I had had of the goodness of the Harbour. But, now that I have been *there,* I find it a very dangerous one. And, by having so many of the Transports here, I shall make a great Saving, by embarking them in this Port; which has determined that Point.

I have now got all the Forrage. I want but *1595:* Tons; to Supply which, there remains the Ports of *Boston, Rhode-Island* & *MaryLand,* from whence the Returns of Shiping are not yet arrived. *Virginia* is so far off, I shall not be able to benefit of Ships from thence; but, Shall endeavour by the King's Ships to press Sailors.

I must defer giving your Royal Highness an account of the Commissions I have filled up in *Nova Scotia,* as they want Explanation which I have not time just now to give; for, some of them have been vacant *above a year,* as I could not understand the Case, 'till I met Colonel *Lawrence* at *Boston,* who seems a *sensible discreet* man.

I have filled up no Commissions in the Royal *American,* but one Company, which I have given to Cap^n Lt *Littler,* on Colo^l *Prevost's* Information of *Y:R:H:* Intentions: and to make Room for Lt *Bartman,* to whom I have given the Company in the *44:* I have dated his Commission as if it had been given before I received the order for providing the reduced officers of the *50:* & *51:* Regiments. I hope you will not disapprove of this, as he is most earnestly recommended by a very good Friend of mine, Mr *Fox.*

I have been with Sir John St *Clair,* since I have wrote the above. I have told him that he is not able to serve this Campaign: but that he shall continue in his office, & I will appoint an other to do the Duty in the mean time; which has made him very happy: and I have appointed Major *Robertson* to do the Duty. Sir John has £$1:$ p Day. I shall give Major *Robertson Ten* Shillings a Day, whilst he acts.

I must beg of *Y:R:H:* to allow of an *adjutant general* on this Establishment. I can find none in the lower Ranks equal to it; and the Day is not long enough for the Business I have to do. Lieu^t Colonel *Burton* is by much the most proper man for that Purpose.

I have judged it necessary to lay in more Provisions for Mr *Webb,* than he has Troops, in case there should be occasion to march any Part of the *Militia* to support him, whilst we are going round. Therefore I have provided for *12,000:* Men, for *6:* months which requires of

	Bread & Flour Barrels at 200^{lb}	Peas Bushels	Rice Barrels 240^{lb}	Butter Firkins 60^{lb}	Pork Barrels
	10,920:......14,625:...650:.......1950:.......6240				
now in *Albany* & the Ports above	7,860:.......12,650:...463:.......1311:.......7147				
wanting to compleat which is now in *new York*	3060:...... 1971:...187:....... 638:				

The Pork is *907:* Barrels over compleat, which I shall bring down, as soon as the Sloops can sail, the Ice being now broke. I think there will be no Danger of Mr *Webbs* being in any want: and I shall carry *Six* months Provisions with me.

The Province of *Mary Land* voted £*3000:* of their Currentcy for buying Provisions for the Army, which they laid out in *Wheat,* & sent to me for that Purpose; which, as there is a Contractor, I could not use; therefore, I have sold it to Mr *Kilby,* for *four* Shillings & Six Pence, which is a good Price for the Bushel. But, as by the within account it amounts in Sterling money to no more than £*1017:19:9*½ this Money I propose to take into my own Hands, as *contingent Money,* to be accounted for, at the marking up of my accompts, as the £*2000:* advanced in England will not answer the Expences of passing so long an account. If *Y:R:H:* thinks this is wrong, be so good to let me know it, & I will directly pay it into the Paymaster General's Hands. As I have acquainted *Y:R:H:* with it, & shall send a Copy of this accompt to the Province, with Thanks for it, in the King's name, it is not in my Power to defraud the Public of it. I am, Sir, Your Royal Highness's most dutifull & much obliged, obedient Servant,

(LOUDOUN.)

[*Endorsed*] Copy of Lord *Loudoun's* Letter to *H:R:H:* the Duke New-York; March *8. 1757.*

CUMBERLAND TO LOUDOUN

(A.L.)

S^t james's, March *21: 1757*

My Lord Loudoun, Many Reasons too tedious to be discussed at this Distance, have prevented my giving you sooner an Answer to your Letters of Novr 22: & Jany 5–6. which arrived together. But, now I can acquaint you with great Satisfaction that *His Majesty* & People in g^l [general] at home, are extremely pleased with the great Beginnings you have made this year for restoring order and Discipline, not only in the Army but in that part of the Goverment which regards the Quartering &c of the Troops, & which it is not doubted your assiduity & Steadiness will carry you through greatly to the Benefit of the public Service & your own Honour. You will perceive by the orders of the last Date that you are left at full Liberty to make such use of the great regular Force you will have under your *Com^d* as may appear to you most beneficial for *H. M:* Service in general & the most conducive to put a glorious End to the war in *N: America*

The opinions at this Distance are extremely various. But whatsoever Predilection any one may have here, you only, on the Spot, can be the proper judge. The opinion you have all along seemed to have, of the Probability of Success in an attack up the R^r St *Lawrence* upon *Quebec* has greatly help'd to incline me to that Plan of Operations preferable to any other, as I should look upon *England* to be entire masters of *N:A:* as soon as we were possessed & kept Possession of *Quebec:* for, then, all the Smaller Possessions of the French in *Canada* must fall into our Hands immediately. And our back Settlers along that immense Tract would be at Rest from the moment such an Expedition was even to be attempted. on the other Hand, if *Lewisburg* becomes the chief object of your operations this Spring, tho' I don't fear Success there; yet, I fear that the Difficulties & Tediousness of the Preparations for the Siege, would take you so much of the Sumer, that there would be hardly time left for the grand operation. And in that case, tho' we should gain *Lewisburg,* yet we might perhaps suffer so much on the Continent of *N:A:* during the Siege as might make the Ballance of the Campaign but little in our favour, From this Reasoning you will plainly perceive which way my Inclination leads; as I own, I can not help flatering my *Self* that such an immense force as England now pays in *N:A:* under the command of one whose abillities I have so good an Opinion of, ought to strike a decisive Blow this year. But, I must again repeat to you that what appears to me at this Distance, will not in the least prejudice me against whatsoever Plan you may undertake, as I shall be convinced that it is undertaken upon better Information & grounds than we can, here, have.

Mr *Shirley's* affair is now a going to be put into the Hands of a chosen Board of G^l officers; by way of preparing matters for his Court martial; & the many Papers & Proofs you have furnished me with shall be properly employd towards bringing that notorious Criminal to justice

I am glad that you have got through, (though with so much Trouble) the great Point of Quartering the Troops where you are; & I hope it will be a Preecedent for the future. § You will receive this Letter, by the Hands of Lord Howe, whom the King has been pleased to appoint to one of the American Batt^s in the Room of Colonel *Jefferays.* I need not recomend him to you as you know him already. You will find him an intelligent, capable & willing officer, & can not help hoping that it will come to his Lot, to command one of the *Batt^s,* that will be employ'd upon Servies. § By the little Conversation & acquaintance I have made this year with Ad^{rl} *Holbourne* I flater MySelf you will find him of a very complying & easy nature, having promised me that he would jointly with you, consider H.M: Service, equaly at Sea & Land, & give no Obstructions but rather all the Assistance in his Power to *the King's* Service in general.

The g[l] plan of *Winter* Qu[rs] that you have established for this last winter, appeared to me extremely judicious & proper for whatever Service you may undertake, this ensuing Campaign; & I do not doubt but that the whole is by this time quite complete. Your Reasons for keeping the Troops so late in the Field are Self evident, as it would have been extremely dangerous to have retired into W[r] Qu[rs] whilst the Enemy still remained assembled in a Body, and your intended Scheme for keeping the Garrisons constantly suplied with *8:* months Provisions & sufficient pay, is also extremely prudent & proper.

I have ordered the order'd the agents of the Reg[ts] to send you the best accompts they can of what Prisoners have been taken of the diferent Embarkations going over from *Europe.* Lord Barrington has Already answerd' your Qu[ns] relating to the independ[t] companies so that I shall say no more on that Head; as L[d] Duplin has also removed the objections that you made, to the Payment of the Troops in Gold:

As to Artillery, you will find by the List sent over that you are sufficiently equiped for any Service that you may want: & L[t] Co[l] Williamson is sent over to command, who is reekoned a very good & carefull officer.

I can not conclude this Letter without my hearty wishes for your Success this important campaign, *on the* Event of which the whole Ballance of this war may turn, & resting full confident that you on your part will do all that a man can do for the Service of your King & country I remain your very affect.

LIEU[T] COLONEL HENRY BOUQUET [1] TO SIR JOHN S[T] CLAIR. PHILADELPHIA, THE 18TH APRIL 1757

(COPY)

J'ai receu, Mon Cher Chevalier, votre Lettre du 11e Cour[t]. Le mauvais Etat de votre Santé m'afflige plus que je ne puis vous le dire: Il faut donc nous Separer puisque vos Medecins vous envoyent en Angleterre:

[1] Henry Bouquet (1719–1765) was a Swiss whom Prevost had brought into the British service, as lieutenant colonel of the first battalion of the Royal American Regiment. Bouquet commanded in South Carolina in 1757, was with Forbes on the Fort Duquesne expedition in 1758, and served the latter part of the war among the western frontier forts. His victory at Bushy Run, in 1763, shows his success in adapting "la petite guerre" as known in Europe to the requirements of American war. Commissioned colonel in America in 1762, he was made brigadier general in America in 1765, in spite of his foreign birth.

mais pourrés vous Soutenir les incommodités de ce Voyage? Ne vaudroit il pas mieux Suivre l'avis de ceux qui vous conseillent l'Air de la Campagne: En choisissant une Situation Saine et agreable, et surtout ne vous occupant plus l'Esprit de travail et d'affaires, vous pourriés vous y retablir, ou du moins reparer assés vos forces pour entreprendre Sans danger une Si longue Navigation.

Quelque party que vous preniés, mes voeux pour votre guerison vous suivront partout. Aprés votre Santé rien ne me touche autant que l'amitié que vous voulés bien me temoigner, et dont j'ai constamment ressenti les Effets des mon arrivée en Amerique: Je Sens tout le prix d'un Amy et d'un Patron cõe vous, au dessus des prejugés trop communs dans votre Nation. Vous voyés notre Situation, elle est desagreable: Vos Conseils et Votre Exemple me Soutenoient, et m'auroit rendu tout suportable. Il ne me restera après votre depart qu'un Zele invariable, mais qui sera aussi inutile au Service qu'a moi même. Notre Chef Seul ne nous a point traités en Etrangers: Il nous a toujours Soutenus, et honorés de Ses Bontés; mais sa Protection ne peut eteindre une Antipathie si ouvertement declarée; Je vois qu'elle eclate en toute occasion, et je suis inquiet pour l'avenir: Tous les hommes peuvent faire des fautes, et qui peut se flatter de se Soutenir à la longue, si l'on a tout contre Soy, et que l'on ne pardonne rien? L'affaire du Cap^ne Steiner m'a fait beaucoup de peine; il a eu tort certainement, Je ne suis point prevenu en Sa faveur, mais n'a t'on pas grossi ses torts? Un Etranger ne merite t'il pas quelque Indulgence, Si dans aussi peu de tems, il n'a pû Se mettre au fait de toutes vos Coutumes et regles *non ecrites?* Et des qu'il offre de reparer Sa faute par toutes les demarches que Son honneur et son grade peuvent admettre, doit il étre humilié jusqu'a devoir Se rendre meprisable aux yeux de tout un Bataillon? Enfin un Officier qui a bien servi et qui a l'honneur de porter la Commission du Roy cõe Cap^ne doit il etre mis tout à fait de niveau avec un *Mate* sans rang ni Comission?

Je compte sur vous, Mon Cher Chevalier, pour faire envisager à Mylord cette affaire d'un Oeil plus favorable. Nous ne tenons qu'a lui, et s'il nous abandonne un moment il faut que nous tombions: Des qu'il sera mecontent de nous il ouvre la Porte à tous ceux qui cherchent à nous nuire, et nous perdrons la Consideration que Sa faveur Seule nous donne et sans laquelle nous ne pouvons bien Servir.

Vos reflexions sur le 4e Batt. sont bien justes: Le mecontentement général que j'y marque me donne tous les jours de nouveaux Chagrins; Si M^r P[revost] avoit voulu suivre les Conseils que Hald[imand] et moy lui avons donné à son arrivée, il se seroit bien epargné des Peines, et à nous aussi. Ils etoient tels que nous devrions Souhaiter qu'ils fussent connus de tout le monde: Nous sommes fort eloignés d'aprouver les hauteurs qu'on lui reproche, et nous avons agi nous mêmes asses differemment pour ne devoir pas etre Soupçonnés d'avoir aucune part à ce qui s'est passé: Cependant nous en ressentirons le Contrecoup, et les Etrangers seront sans distinction envelopés dans la prévention que l'on a contre lui. Hald. . . . et moy nous sommes faits un Plan fixe de n'entrer jamais dans aucun Party quelconque, et nous nous bornons à Servir pendant la Guerre avec l'aplication et l'activité qu'on peut attendre d'honetes Gens qui veulent le bien.

Nous Sommes entrés dans ce Service avec l'Esperance d'y faire notre Chemin Sans traverses, dans le Seul Regiment ou nous pouvons Servir: Je crois que nous nous sommes trompés làdessus, et que nous trouvant à la queüe des Lt Col: nous ne pouvons plus esperer de parvenir au Commandem^t d'un Batt. mais de quelque façon qu'on nous traitte à cet égard; Je conserverai toute ma vie la plus profonde reconnoissance des Graces dont le Duc nous a comblés par toutes ses Bontés dans le Cours de cette affaire, et si nous ne rendons pas tous les Services, dont il nous a crus capables; J'Espere que S.A.R. aura quelque Egard aux Circonstances oú nous nous serons trouvés: Lorsque nous deviendrons inutiles à la Paix Si l'Antipathie Nationale continüe encore, nous pourrons alors nous retirer honorablement et sans ingratitude.

Pardon, Mon Cher Chevalier, de vous fatiguer de details aussi desagreables: mais j'en ai la tete remplie et ne puis en parler qu'a Vous.

Je vous suis bien obligé des bons avis, et des Lumieres que vous me donnés sur mon Expedition de la Caroline: J'ai été très flatté de l'honeur que Mylord m'a fait en me confiant un Commandement de cette Importance.

Je connois le Gouverneur Littleton, et j'espere d'agir aisement de concert avec lui. J'ai reconnu en toute occasion la verité du Caractere que vous donnés aux Americains, Et J'ai trouvé par mon Experience à Philadelphie, qu'avec beaucoup de patience, de Douceur et de fermeté, il n'est pas impossible de reussir avec Eux: J'y arrivay dans des Circonstances assés Critiques, Sans Ordres, ni instructions, et tous les Esprits prevenus contre Nous: Cependant j'ai eu le bonheur d'en faire le meilleur Quartier de l'Amerique, en contentant tout le Monde. Je sçais que ce n'est pas à moy que l'on en donne le Succés, mais je m'embarasse peu du relief, pourvu que le Bien Se fasse: En cas de besoin Fr[anklin] et toute la Ville pourroient repondre la dessus.

Le Retard que Souffre mon Embarquement me fait craindre que ma disposition ne Change: Le Gouverneur D[enny] s'est engagé à fournir à

Mylord 200. hoꝰes pour cette Expedition mais aiant negligé d'en informer à tems l'Assemblée, je doute qu'ils puissent étre prets: Conr: Weiser s'est si bien employé pour m'obliger qu'il a trouvé son Contingent dans le Batt qu'il Commande, mais le reste ne sera pas si facile à avoir.

Dans quelque Endroit que J'aille, je serois bien Charmé d'y avoir de vos nouvelles: Je vous prie de me faire sçavoir si vous partés ou non, afin que je puisse vous ecrire consequemment: Des Details qui pourroient vous interesser dans ce Païs, vous seroient tres indifferens en Angleterre.

Adieu, Mon Cher Chevalier, Ne m'oubliés point, vous trouverés toujours en moi un Ami aussi Sincere qu'inutile. Je vous remercie de ce que vous dites du Lt Howarth un honete homme est toujours d'un grand Secours. Adieu, Personne n'est plus à vous que Votre très hble Ser

HENRY BOUQUET

This is the Original Letter from Lt Colonel Bouquet dated April 18th 1757. given in to Lord Loudoun the 21st of May which was the morning after I was called in by Col^o Prevost to be present at the Colonels reading the Copy of a Letter (to Lord Loudoun) the Original of which he said he had sent to His Royal Highness.

JOHN S^T CLAIR Lt Col:

to the Royal American Regiment & D.Q.Mr Gen[1].

[*Endorsed*] COPY of a Letter from Lieu^t Colonel *Bouquet* to Sir John St *Clair*. Philadelphia *18th April 1757*.

LIST OF COMMISSIONS GRANTED BY HIS EXCELLENCY THE R^T HON^{BLE} THE EARL OF LOUDOUN [1]

Rank	Officers Names	Dates of their Comms.	
		35th Regiment	
Quarter-Master	William Hamilton	24th Feb. 1757.	
Adjutant	Lt James Cockburn	25 March	
		40th Regiment	
Ensign	Robert Catherwood	2. April 1757	Recomended by Col Hobson and comes in Place of Ensigne Lylle a Shipe Master in the Jerseyes Put in by Mr Shirly who Desired to

<hr>

[1] The notes are in Loudoun's handwriting.

Rank	Officers Names	Dates of their Comms.	
Adjutant	Lt John Adlam	7. Febry	Resigne on Receiving £50 which he sayes he lost in Recruting for Mr Shirleys Regt which Mr Catherood Payed Capt Lt Ross on his Being Promotted Sold the Adjutan for £300 the Money he Payed for it Recomended by Lt Col Lorrance
Surgeon	William Catherwood ...	7. ditto	Was Surgeons Mait to MG Warburtons Regt Recomended by Col Hobson to Succed Sheen Dead

------

44th Regiment

Captains	George Bartman [2]	25th Decemr 1756	Was a Lt in the 50t Reomended by Mr Fox in the most ernest Manner I have explaind this furder in my letter of March
	Honble William Hervey	27th ditto	Purtchesed from Capt David Kennedy as furder Explaind in my letter
Capt Lieut	Richard Bailley	25th Decemr 1756 [3]	Eldest Lt Promotted on Capt Lt Litler being appointed a Capt in the Royal American Regt
Lieutenants	John Elwes	25. ditto	Eldest Ensign Promoted in the Succesion ocesiond by Capt Lt Litlers Being Promotted in an other Regt
	Roger Kellet	27. ditto	Purtchesed in the Succession of Capt Kennedy
	John Duncan	25th April 1757	Purtchesed from Lt

---

[2] A natural son of Thomas Hervey, brother of the Second Earl of Bristol.

[3] Millan's *Army List* for 1757 ranks Richard Bailey as captain lieutenant as of January 8, 1756. His commission, as well as those of William Littler to be captain in the 44th, John Elwes, and Stephen Kemble, was made out by Shirley in June, 1756, after he had been notified of Captain William Eyre's promotion on January 7 to a majority in England. Since the same post brought word of Shirley's recall, Loudoun refused to allow Shirley's commissions, and restored these officers to their former rank.

Rank	Officers Names	Dates of their Comm^s.	

			James Puttenger who Purtchesed his Lieutenance and is Renderd intierly unfitt for Servie by Drink
Ensigns	James Abercromby ..... 25th Decem^r 1756		Appointed in the Place of Ensigne Rodes of this Country who grew weare of the Service and Resigned He is a Son of M. G. Abercromby
	David Jenkins .... 27th ditto		Purtchesed for £200 on Capt Kennedys Seal
	Turbot Francis .... 25. April 1757		Purtchesed on Lt Pottengers Lead £200

45th Regiment

Ensign	Hans Wallace .... 18. April 1757	Payed Lt Rossaboon on his Retiring £116–13–4 Ensigne McKane got Lt Rosabomes Commission and Mr Vallae got McKanes Ensince

47th Regiment

Captain	John Mercer .... 10th Decem^r 1756.	Major Hall bought in England of Major Markum in the End of the year 1754 or 1755 The Succession was left to Mr. Shirly to fill up by the Elest he never took any Stepes in it and Ld Loudoun never understood the Case till he meet Mr Lorronce at Boston in the last winter
Captain Lieu^t	Thomas Smelt .... 10. ditto.	
Lieutenants	George Mountain ...... 9. ditto.	They Desired to have the Commissions antedated in order to lighten the Price to the Major who payes the greatest part of the Price But Ld L: refused to do that but Promised to state the case that H R H may give his orders on what time the Pay Should Commence
	John Morris .... 10. ditto	

Rank	Officers Names	Dates of their Comm^s.	

| Ensigns | { Nicholson .... 10. ditto. | | |
| | { David Roche .... 7. Feb^{ry} 1757 | | |

Royal American Regim^t

Rank	Officers Names	Dates	Notes
Lieut Colonel	John Young .... 26. April 1757.		Succeded to Lt Col Chapman as expland in my letter
Major	John Tullekens .... 26th April 1757		In the Succession of Lt Col Chapman as expland in My letter
Captain	William Littler .... 25. Decem^r 1756		By your Royal Highnes's Order Receved from Col Provost in the Room of Capt De Schol who Did not Accept
Surgeon	Arthur Nicholson ...... 25. ditto		From the Hospital
Surg's Mate	Van Hulst .... 24. Feb^{ry} 1757		Had the care of the Recruts brought from Germany by Col Provost
Chaplain	Michael Schlatter ...... 25 March.		Is the leading Clargeman among the Germans in Pensilvania was Recomended to me by Mr Pen and Since by Col Provost and is a good man

---

| Major Brigade | Capt Roger Morris ..... 8th March 1757 | | **To Remain** in that Cappasity with Mr Webb |

| Dep: Q^r Mr Genl | Maj: James Robertson . 8th March 1757 | | To Act in that Cappasity with Me During Sir John St Clairs Illness on 10 Shillings a Day |

| Ast Dep. Q^r Mr Gen. | Capt Gabriel Christie .. 8. March | | To Act in that Cappasity with Mr Webb on 10 Shillings a Day |

Capt: Paul Demeri's Indep^t Company

| Ensign | Lauchlin McIntosh .... 25th Decem^r 1756 | | The Vacance happened a Great while ago and the offcer not returned to Me |

Capt Ezra Richmond's Ind^t Comp^y

| Lieutenant | Archibald McCawlay ... 25th Decr 1756. | | Recomended By Provost, McCawley Caryed Arms five years in Holland |

Rank	Officers Names	Dates of their Comm^s.	

Late Capt Hubert Marshall's Indep^t Comp^y

Captain	Chas Crookshanks ..... 17th April 1757		The Seconed Lt in the Royal Americans in Place of Capt Harbord Mortial Broak by a Court Martial He takes the Company as it is with the Money that may be in the Agents hands and furnishes what is wanting to Compleat it
Lieutenant	John McKane .... 18. ditto		In the Place of Lt Rossaboom McKane was brought from M G Corveys Horse by Mr Webb and in the former List of Commissions was appointed an Ensigne in the 45 Lt Rossaboom bought his Lt from Goveror Clinton Payed the Goveror £466–13–4 and to his Secretary £17–10 was an indean Treader and Bought the Commission to cary on his Tread with the more Advanage has been ill ever since the war began and Sayes his Disease is a Rising in his Throot that is like to Chock him when ever there is any Destoubence in the Canal Ensigne Wallace who has got McKanes Commission in the 45 Payes Rossaboom £156–13–4 for which he Desired to Resigne I thought McKane fitter for the Independent Company

———

Capt Peter Wraxall's Indep^t Comp^y

Lieutenant	John Martin .... 26th April 1757.		Reomended by the Earl of Eglinton & Ld Barrington caryed armes in the Highland Regt

———

Garrison of Annapolis Royal.

Surgeon	John Steel .... 7. Feb^{ry} 1757.		Recomended by Lt Col Lorrance

———

Rank	Officers Names	Dates of their Comms.

Hospital.

Surgs Mate	John Loch	25. Decemr 1756
Apothry Mate	James Ross	25. ditto.

———————

[*Endorsed*] List of *Commissions,* granted by the Earl of *Loudoun;* from *Decemr 1756:* to *April 1757.*

COLONEL JAMES PREVOST [1] TO CUMBERLAND

(L.S.)

Perth Amboy le 12 May 1757.

Monseigneur,

Le Sutherland a bord duquel Je m'etois embarqué à Corke le 21me Octobre dernier arriva le 20e Janvier à la nouvelle York, et des lors j'ai doné tous mes soins à former et discipliner le Battaillon dont il a plu au Roi de me confier le Commandemt.

Persuadé que le Comte de Loudoun rend comte à votre Altesse Royale de tout ce qui se passe d'essentiel dans ce païs, Je ne dirai qu'un mot du Régiment en Général et de mon Battaillon en particulier.

Le Regiment est a environ 800 Effectifs par Battallion, Les hommes en Général sont mauvais et l'ecume de ces Colonies. Ce que nous avons eu d'Irlande ne vaut pas mieux; la plupart des Regimts se sont empressés a composer leurs Compagnies additionelles de ce qu'ils avaient de Viellards, d'Infirmes, d'Yvrognes et de Voleurs. A juger des autres Battons par le quatrième Votre Altesse Royale ne sera pas trompée en les reduisant l'un dans l'autre a 400 passablement bons homes.

Les Quatre Battaillons aiant été levés en commun et la répartition des bas Officiers et des Recrues faites par le Sort. Je pense que le compte que je rens du quatrième convient aux autres, avec cette difference que

---

[1] James Prevost (1725–1778), a Swiss by birth, had served in the Sardinian and perhaps in the French army. He was a major in the Dutch service in 1749, was highly recommended to Cumberland by the Princess of Orange, and proposed the scheme which developed into the Royal American Regiment, in which he became colonel commandant of the fourth battalion. Engaged in recruiting for the regiment in the German states, he did not join the army in America until 1757. Though he possessed an inventive brain and showed those qualities of adaptiveness to various sorts of warfare which had long distinguished the Swiss, he was unfit for high command, being irascible and insubordinate. With the exception of a few malcontents, the entire British army hated and distrusted him, but for political and perhaps diplomatic reasons he was continued in his post until the end of the war. Most of his letters to Cumberland have been calendared in the appendix, as dealing with too insignificant a complaint to present in full.

le premier et le sécond aiant été ensemble tout l'hiver a Philadelphia et New York ils ont eu plus de moyens et de facilités de se discipliner que le troisième et le quatrieme qui ont été l'un et l'autre séparés jusqu'au milieu de Mars en Cinq a Six differens Quartiers.

Le Corps d'officiers du quatrieme Battallion est aussi bon et aussi bien composé qu'on puisse l'esperer dans un Regiment de nouvelle levée, L'experience, le Zêle, et l'application de ces Messieurs me feroient esperer de rendre tel celui des bas Officiers sans la différence des Principes, des Moeurs, et de la Langue qui forment des obstacles que je comence a croire absolument insurmontables.

Je supplie votre Altesse Royale de se rapeller mes craintes sur le succès de ce mélange, L'evenement les justifie; Avec beaucoup de Zêle, d'Activité, et les intentions les plus droites, j'ai eu le malheur de deplaire a My Lord, et ce qui augmente encore le chargrin que j'en ressens, C'est que je l'ai meritté, en manquant de prudence & de menagem^t a son égard. Si Votre Altesse Royale joint a cela le desavantage que me dõne la qualité d'Etranger, l'envie, et la jalousie que ses bontés m'ont suscité, Elle sentira d'abord combien j'occupe inutilement une place dans laquelle sans Authorité on ne peut que nuire au bien du service.

Je laisse à My Lord a rendre compte de ma conduite particuliere, de mon application, des talens que je puis avoir et des progrès qu'a fait le quatrième Battaillon sous ma direction; Mais je croirois manquer a la fidelité que je dois au Roi et a ma respectueuse Reconnoissance pour votre Altesse Royale si je me taisais sur la situation ou je me trouve, et si je ne donnois pas a considerer s'il ne servit pas convenable au bien du service de me Rapeller en Angleterre et de mettre a ma place un Officier plus agréable à My Lord, qui joignit a mes bonnes intentions plus d'Experience et de talens militaires avec plus de prudence et de circonspection.

Au Surplus Monseigneur je declare a Votre Altesse Royale avec la meme sincerité que je me suis devoué au Service de sa Majesté, que je ferai tout ce qui sera en mon pouvoir pour gagner les bonnes graces de My Lord et que je continuerai a force de Zêle, d'activité, d'obeissance et par un travail continuel a suppleer a ce qui me manque de support de sa part et de talens de la mienne.

Je joins ici quelques observations que j'ai cru devoir soumettre aux lumieres de Votre Altesse Royale; je m'estimerai tres heureux si elles peuvent contribuer au bien du service de sa Majesté, si la volonté du Roi ou les ordres de Votre Altesse Royale me rappelloient a Londres après la Campagne je serois a portee de demontrer d'une Maniere sensible l'utilité d'un Plan formé sur ces obversations et de faire voir la possibilité et meme la facilité de l'executer: Rien ne seroit plus propre a diminuer les dépenses de la Nation et a faire prosperer les Armes du Roi; Je conçois tres humblem^t que je me rendrois par la plus utile au service de sa Majesté que je ne puis espérer de le devenir ici dans les circonstances ou je me trouve.

Je Supplie Votre Altesse Royale de me pardonner la hardiesse que j'ai prise de l'entretenir si lontems, j'aurois voulu pouvoir garder le silence ou n'obéir a l'ordre qu'il Lui a plu de me donner de lui ecrire que pour rendre compte de mes obversations et exprimer la parfaite soumission et le profond Respect dont mon coeur est Remplie pour Votre Altesse Royale

JA^e PREVOST

[one enclosure]

MÉMOIRE SUR LA GUERRE D'AMÉRIQUE

(A.D.)

Pour se faire une idée juste de ce qu'on connoit de la Partie Septentrionale de ce Vaste Continent, il est necessaire de se representer une forest immense et continuelle coupée de grandes Rivières d'un nombre de Torrents et de beaucoup de Lacs dont les pais occupès par les Anglois et les françois font une partie infiniment petite qui peuvent être comparès avec beaucoup de vérité aux trouees qu'on trouve dans les forets de la pologne, Pour ne pas s'etendre trop Sur ce Sujet il est à propos de se borner aux Etablissements de ces deux Nations en observant qu'il y a cette difference entre eux que les habitations des Anglois s'etendent au long de la Mer du Nord Sur une ligne courbe sans penetrer dans les terres a plus de 60 lieues et que celles des françois forment en quelque Sorte la perpendiculaire par la tête qu'ils avancent de Montreal au fort du Quesne en prenant la sage precaution d'assurer leurs comunications par des forts qui les rendent Maitres du Comèrce des pelleteries et tiennent les Nations Indiennes dans leurs Dependances.

De Cet exposé il est naturel de penser que les Troupes destinées a servir dans cette partie du Continent doivent être levées habillées Armées, disciplinées, payeés & entretenues sur un pied different des Regiments d'Europe.

Les Recrues doivent être choisies avec soin & Composeés d'hommes, sobres, jeunes, forts, robustes capables de suporter une très grande fatigue, le nature du pais y rend la Guerre extremement rude, La Pensylvanie, les Jerseys, la Nouvelle York, et la Nouvelle Angleterre peuvent aisèment fournir 8 a 10,000 tels hommes san nuire a L'Agriculture & Surcharger ces provinces.

L'Habillement de cette troupe devroit etre Un Manteau d'un bon drap bien refoulé & leger, que le Soldat porteroit roulé et lié comme il fait Sa Couverte de laine, une verte longue les Manches aisées, le Corps large et croisant sur la poitrine la Culote longue et large, les bottines de Cuir joignant la culotte au dessous de la Jointure du genouil ou mieux encore le Jupon Ecossois un peu changé, et la Chaussure Indienne, deux paires de souliers de la meilleure espèce, un bonnet a l'Allemande dont le Casque seroit de Cuir bouilli et battu, et le derrière de veau tourné qui pouvant se baisser sur les Epaules le garantiroit du froid et de la pluye, Une Seconde Chemise feroit tout l'Attirail dont il faudroit embarrasser le soldat.

L'Arme seroit un fusil leger et plus court de quatre pouces que les nôtres pourveu d'une bayonette tranchante longue de deux pieds selon le modele donne a S.A.R. en 1755. Le soldat devroit être pourveu de poudre et de balle en aussi grande quantité qu'il est possible et devroit la porter de la manière la plus propre à la preserver de l'Eau et du feu.

Cette Troupe devroit etre exercée à tirer au blanc dans toutes sortes de Situations, A Marcher en raquettes courir sauter nager; obéir au Siflet etre pourveus d'un nombre de chiens dressès à chasser les Sauvages, Elle devra être instruite aussi à Combattre en Colomnes et à se former en bataille, Chaque Mille homes devroit être pourveu de 6 pieces de Canon depuis 3 jusqu'a 6 ll [lb.] de balles, et de 6 haubits servant à jetter des grenades et des feux d'artifice de toute espèce.

Un Nombre de Soldats dans Chaque Compagnie devroit être capable de construire et conduire les batteaux ou Canaux necessaires pour la Navigation des Lacs.

Les Artisans & Soldats de toute espèce requise dans la composition de cette Troupe devroit être repartie egalement dans chaque Compagnie, en sorte que chacune d'elles peut agir seule comme en Corps.

La paye devroit etre un Shelling Sterling par jour, Celle des Artisans Canoniers, Nageurs, bas Officiers et Officiers a proportion.

On ne fourniroit de provisions à cette Troupe que lors qu'on l'enverroit à la Guerre, Ses Provisions devroient consister en farine, de bled d'Inde, Clams, & porc Salé, En Eté on y pourroit joindre quelques boeufs distribues aux Comp[es]. Et les Commandants de Corps devroient apporter la plus grande attention à mènager cette partie de la nourritures, Les deux premiers articles sont legers et nourrissants, et sont en usage chès les Indiens et Canadiens dans leurs Expéditions.

L'Exposé cy dessus suffit pour donner une Idée generale du projet, il reste à dire que la depense de cette Troupe en tems de Guerre n'excedera pas celle du même nombre de troupes reglées en ce païs, et qu'en tems de paix on pourroit Conserver un fond suffisant pour etre d'abord preparé à la guerre par la seule augmentation des Compagnies, ce qui ne couteroit pas au delà de £60,000 Stg par an au Gouvernem^t ce que Les Colonies sont très en etat de supporter, bien entendu qu'elles n'auroient rien à demeler avec Le Commandement ou le payement de la Troupe.

Un tel Corps seroit en état de ravager le Canada à tout instant feroit respecter les Anglois par les Nations Indiennes, et assuroit par la Crainte leur Amitié et le Commerce lucratif qu'on fait avec elles. En travaillant sur ce plan on donneroit du jeu aux forces des Colonies qui n'ont besoin que de cela pour être infiniment superieurs a toutes celles que la France y a actuellement, ou qu'elle Sera en état d'y envoyer aussi longtems que nous conserverons la superiorité sur Mer.

Dans Cette Troupe qui Seroit en effet le Régiment Royal Americain il conviendroit de donner des Comissions à toutes les jeunes gens de famille du pays qui auroient quelque Inclination de Servir dans le Militaire ce qui faciliteroit infiniment la levée & contribueroit à attacher de plus en plus ces Colonies au Gouvernement.

L'Execution de ce plan evitcroit au Gouvernement la nécessité et la depence d'envoyer de la Grande Bretagne des troupes disciplinées à l'Europeeñe que ne seront jamais propres qu'à garder les Villes et les Provinces exposées ou à executer quelque Entreprise par Mer sur les Isles françoises, Le Cap Breton, la Louisiane ou le Canada par le fleuve S^t laurent, dont le success sera toujours très precaire veu le nombre des Circonstances qui peuvent les faire echouer qu'on ne sauroit ni prevoir ni prevenir.

A la paix ce Corps devroit former une Colonie Militaire qui s'etabliroit dans telle partie du païs que le Gouvernem^t jugeroit la plus convenable ce qui feroit d'abord par la reduction des Compagnies, et ensuite en congédiant chaque Année le nombre d'hommes dont le terme seroit fini, et qui desireroient de s'etablir, On fourniroit à ces soldats Congediés les Instruments propres au labourage, la demie paye la premiére année et dans la suite un Sol Sterling par jour à condition d'exercer de passer revue et de faire le Service Militaire que le Roy ou Ses Generaux leur prescriroient, Il est aisé de sentir combien un pareil Establissement contribueroit à la seureté des frontieres, des Provinces de Caroline, Virginie et de Pensylvanie, En même tems qu'il previendroit qu'aucune Insulte fut faite aux Provinces Situées plus à l'Est par la promptitude avec laquelle Cette Troupe toujours prete pourroit se porter partout ou il seroit besoin.

[*Endorsed*] Memoire du Colonel Prevost, sur la Guerre d'Amerique: May 1757.

COLONEL JAMES PREVOST TO CUMBERLAND
(L.S.)

New York Le 23ᵉ May 1757

Monseigneur,

Ma lettre du 12ᵉ May fut écrite a la fin d'avril, et datée du tems que je prevoiois que le paquet mettroit a la voile. Dès Lors il s'est passé diverses choses, qui me font sentir tous les jours d'avantage combien je Suis inutile au Service du Roi, et m'obligent a me jetter aux pieds de Vôtre Altesse Roiale, pour la Supplier de m'emploier ailleurs ou de permettre que je me retire: Ma Situation est plus malheureuse que je ne puis l'exprimer? Mon Respect en épargne les dètails a Vôtre Altesse Roiale: J'en ai touché un mot au Général Napier qui sans doute lui en rendra compte. Je me rèfére a celui que My Lord Loudoun vous rend, Monseigneur, au Sujet des Commissions quil à donné aux officiers étrangers que Vôtre Altesse Roiale a attirez au Service du Roi: Mʳ de Bonneville l'un des plus distingués, le quel a été élevé a la suite du Marechal de Saxe pendant le derniere guerre et qui apres la mort de ce Général a Servi le Roi de Prusse en qualité de Capitaine Ingenieur de Campagne a la Suite de Sa Majesté, n'a pas jugé a propos de Reçevoir Sa Commission, parce que My Lord n'a pas voulu lui donner le rang d'anciennêté qui lui avoit ètè promis. Je ne saurois cependant vous dissimuler, Monseigneur, que sa veritable raison de ne la pas accepter, êtoit moins la dâte, que les dèsagremens, les humiliations et les dangers aux quels nous sommes continuellement exposez, par la haine, l'envie et la jalousie du reste de l'armée contre nous, L'acceuïl qu'il a reçu en arrivant, la façon dont il a vû que nous étions traitez, qui est la consequence naturelle du peu d'egard et de protection que My Lord nous accorde lui a fait prendre ce parti. J'ai fait tout ce qui a été en mon pouvoir pour l'en dètourner, mais inutilement. La Justice que tout le monde rend a Sa Capacité et aux connoissances qu'il à dans le metier, me donne bien du regret de le perdre: La Conduite qu'il a tenu avec les 170 hommes qu'il a amenez ici apres un voiage de Six mois en mer, le rend bien digne de Louange de tous les Militaires, par la façon dont il les a disciplinez et par la belle dèffense qu'il a fait contre des Corsaires francois, avec un vaisseau qui faisoit eau de tout côté et prêt de couler a font a tout moment. Il Seroit en état d'informer,

Vôtre Altesse Roiale, de bien des particularitez sil peut avoir l'honneur d'être admis aupres d'elle. J'ai tirés parolle de lui, qu'il ne serviroit pas pendant cette guerre en Amerique contre les troupes du Roi. J'ai jugé cette precaution necessaire dans les circonstances ou nous sommes, vis a vis d'un officier aussi clairvoiant.

Les Majors Yo[u]ng et Robertson, Le Chev^{er} de St. Clair lui même a qui j'avois donné ma confiance accause de l'estime que Vôtre altesse Roiale m'avoit parru avoir pour lui, sont les gens qui prennent soin d'aigrir My Lord contre moi, et qui ne trouvant aucune prise sur ma conduite, ont recours aux insinuations et a L'artifice en donnant des fausses Couleurs a toutes mes actions: Ce sont eux qui me procurent dans l'exercise de ma charge, tous les dèsagremens qu'il est au pouvoir d'un Gènéral en chef de donner a un Colonel; de façon que je me trouve sans authorité ni consideration.

J'ai reflechi Serieusement, Sur les Moyens de tirer parti des officieres étrangers, et je n'en apperçois plus d'autre, que Celui de les mettre en un corps, en laissant a celui que Votre Altesse Roiale choisira pour les commander, la nommination de ses officiers sous l'approbation du Général en Chef. L'Article de ne pouvoir servir qu'en Amerique, nous donne un discredit étonant, on nous regarde dans ce paÿs et même a L'armée comme d'un ordre inferieur d'officiers a peu pres comme les Marrines sont regardez en Angleterre. On pourroit tirer parti de ce dèsavantage même pour en faire un corps tel que celui que je propose dans mon memoire. Je Vous Supplie, Monseigneur, de me pardonner les Libertez que je prend dans cette Lettre, elles me sont dictées par l'amour du bien et de la verité. Je ne desire rien plus que d'obtenir l'approbation de vôtre altesse Roiale, pour qui je suis penétré de Reconnoissance, de Soumission et de Respect.

JA^{es} PREVOST

BARRINGTON [1] TO CUMBERLAND [2]

(A.L.S.)

Cavendish Square 3^d June 1757

Sir,

. . . . . .

The same uncertain situation of Office has prevented any thing being done finally with relation to the Enquiry into Mr Shirley's conduct; on which subject I should not have troubled your R.H. just

---

[1] William Wildman Barrington, Viscount Barrington (1717-1793), was secretary at war from 1755 to 1761, and from 1765 to 1778.

[2] Paragraphs in this letter not relating to American affairs have been omitted.

now, if I had not found it mention'd in your Letter to Gen[l] Napier. I could not get the Papers relating to Gen[l] Shirley from the Secretary of State's Office till a day or two before M[r] Pitt was dismiss'd; and tho' on perusal of them I found many charges, I discover'd no Proofs. The Papers I have since received from your R.H. contain nothing more than Charges, or at least no Proofs which can be authenticated; nor do those in the Plantation Office. I apprehend I shall find none in some other Papers which Napier has wrote for. Now Sir, an Enquiry without Evidence can answer no good purpose; and I see no way of geting Evidence but by sending for it to Lord Loudoun, and apprising him of the intended inquiry. I find his Lordship in some of his Letters mentions an intention to appoint Persons who should draw up a charge and collect Evidence in support of it to be sent hither; and I wish he had not afterwards lay'd aside this design. I was very much surprised on reading the Papers to find no better materials for an Enquiry, and Lord Halifax agrees with Gen[l] Napier and me, that so defective an Enquiry must either produce a report that nothing can be done; or what is worse a justification of M[r] Shirley on a partial hearing: The Hopes of the last make him very impatient and urgent for it; but I will not venture to carry any Warrant to the King, till I have your R.H.'s farther Orders; and I conceive that you would have the whole of the Case as it now appears to be, lay'd before the King's Servants, there being a mixture of Consideration of State in it, as well as of Military discipline.

As yet I have not officially mention'd anything of this matter to any of the Minister's; but whenever another Secretary of State shall be named I will not lose a moment in bringing the whole before him, for his own Consideration and that of the rest of the King's Servants. . . .

The gracious Postscript added to the Letter I last received from your R.H. is more than all I can ever do will deserve. It has always been my wish that the whole Kingdom might know as well as I do, how much this Country is served and obliged by the constant Care and Attention, as well as ability with which the Army is superintended by your R.H. It is particularly my duty to declare this truth, at all times and in all places; because I know it better than others. I am greatly obliged to those who have so favourably reported me to your R.H. whose Approbation is justly my greatest pleasure and Pride. I have also a just Sense of your intended Goodness to my brother at a proper time; and as that time cannot well happen till after your return, I am now angry with my self for having presumed unnecessarily to trouble your R.H. about him, which I did intirely without his knowlege or desire. I submit him and myself intirely to your good pleasure and I am with the greatest duty and respect Sir Your Royal Highness's Most humble & Most devoted Servant

BARRINGTON

[*Endorsed*] Cav: Square; June the *3ᵈ 1757* Lord Barrington to *H:R:H:* Recᵈ the *13:* Ansᵈ the *Same Day.*

LOUDOUN TO CUMBERLAND

(A.L.S.)

New York, April 25: 1757.
concluded, June 3: 1757.

Sir

The last Packet bringing nothing but Duplicates of the Letters of Dec[ember] was a very great Disapointment to me, as they contain only a Promise of a Plan which I am to prepare for before it arrives or before I know where I am to meet the Reinforcements, so that I do not see a Possibility of moving till the next Letters arrive and the Season is far advanced.

The Letter I had the Honour to write to your Royal Highness before I set out to Philadelphia would show you the Plan I was preparing for, and my Publick Letter now will show you the General Situation of things.

I have gone no further in that Letter, imagining that it was more proper to reserve the more minute Military part for my Letter to your Royal Highness.

The first thing I shall mention is the Command in the different Places where Troops are to be. In this I am obliged to take my Measures on the People I have on the Spot, for I have not from any Quarter the least Intimation of who or what Corps come out, nor can I form any Guess who the Officers will be.

As Mr Webb is the third in Command here, I can not doubt that his Situation of now acting as a Major General with the Pay by your orders has occurred to you, from whence I imagine there will be no elder Colonel sent out without particular Orders how I am to act.

I have no doubt that my Post is with the greatest Number of the Regular Troops, destined for the most material Service, therefore I go with the Expedition.

And as Colonel Dussaux and next to him Col: Prevost are the Senior Officers in the Troops that go on this Service, I think it absolutely necessary for the Service to have a Second in case of any Accident happening to me, and as the Command is material, I have pitched on M.G. Abercromby to go along with me.

As to Mr Webb, I have given the Account I received when I was absent from him. When I was here, you have had an account of his Health as it realy was. When I returned from Philadelphia, he was very low spirited and could bear no Noise. I was obliged to have him present at several Conversations with Colonel Prevost, whose Memory is short and makes it necessary on many Occasions to have a Witness, or the Colonel forgets what was settled half an hour before; but the Colo[nel's] Voice and Impetuosity overcame him so much, that he could not bear it, and in general was forced to retire, but he is at present much better.

I have been forced to go into this Digression in order to show your Royal Highness the Difficulty I labour under, in appointing one to Command at the Forts, and of giving him proper Assistance.

Mr Webb has the Command, the next to him is Lieut. Colo Monro, an old Officer but never has served. Major Fletcher the next. The other Battalion is a present commanded by Major Prevost, who is very new in such an office, but I shall have Occasion to give my Reasons for this opinion before my Letter is closed.

I have left with Mr Webb a power to grant Warrants for the Pay of the Troops and for carrying on the necessary Works and other Contingencies.

I have likewise given him a power to hold Courts Martial and to confirm or respite in the case of Private Men.

It appeard to me that as I may be absent for Six or Eight Months, perhaps longer, the Service could not go on without it. I shall enclose a Copy of his Instructions and likewise of his Queries and the Answers to them. You will see by them that Diffidence that a Man without Health, especially when the Disease is on his Spirits, naturally has. And that Diffidence made it impossible for me to get him to his Post without giving him positive Orders, which would have sunk him all at once.

The third Command I have given to Colonel Stanwix in Pensilvania, as being the next eldest officer. He has five Companys of his own Battalion, the Remains of the Pensilvania Troops, those of Maryland, Virginia, and the North Carolina People. I have directed for his Outsett, subject to what Alterations he sees necessary, his posting himself with the five Companys in the Neighbourhood of Carlisle as a middle Station, from whence he can distribute his Orders and be in a Situation to support either Fort Cumberland, Fort Augusta at Shemockin, or to support Philadelphia, if it is attacked by Sea.

I have directed that His Bills for the Pay of the five Companys should be answered, he sending a signed Return of his Effectives along with it. And I have given him a Credit for Contingencies not exceeding £1500, as he must provide Carriages. If that Sum is not sufficient he may apply to General Webb, but four hundered Miles I thought was too great to apply at on every Occasion.

I send the other half of the first Battalion to South Carolina under the Command of Lieutenant Colonel Bouquet, where your Royal Highness will see that the Troops of different Sorts will amount to two thousand Men, which is a great Command for a Lieut. Colonel just come into the Service. And here I may meet with Blame, but the Light this appears in to me, and from whence I have taken my Measures, is: after Colonel Stanwix is employed, I have but two Colonels, in my opinion better employed with me than on a separate Command. Therefore I take them along with me, at the Head of their own Battalions. The next Officer is Colonel Monro. That Battalion is in Mr Webb's Division and requires both the Field Officers, tho it is much mended, and Mr Webb thinks himself too weak already, but I hope Your Royal Highness will not be of that Opinion. Either of the Lieut. Colonels of the 44th or 48th Regiments would have done well, but I could not want them from the Regiments, whom I look on as the best Corps I have here. Lieut. Colonel Bouquet is the next, and is pointed out by belonging to the Corp that goes to that Country. I have sent with him Pay for the five Companys compleat to Christmas, in Bills to be negotiated there. The Method of managing them is settled by the Contractor's Agents. I send it compleat altho they are not so at present with Orders to be accountable for the Pay of the noneffectives, as I hope they will soon be compleated in that Country and North Carolina, from whence we have had very few Recruits on account of the great distance.

I have given Orders both to him and Col. Stanwix, who is posted in the best recruiting Country we have, not only to compleat their Battalion, but to enlist as many more as they possibly can, to be ready to recruit the other three Battalions at the end of the Campaign. As I have kept the money matters of the four Battalions in one common Fund, it will make no Confusion.

I have given Lieut. Col. Bouquet Bills to the Amount of £2500 for Contingencies and to assist him in Recruiting if he has Success.

The Reason of entrusting him with so large a Sum is that I can not remit him Money from hence, and the length of the time I shall probably be absent.

Your Royal Highness has the Return of the Troops, but I am not yet able to inform you of the exact Number that will be on each Command, as I shall leave all the Invalids belonging to the Battalions that go with me and join them to the Battalions with Mr Webb, for in my Situation I must keep the Hospital as low as possible, or it will grow unwieldy.

I have been obliged to make several Additions to the Staff. I acquainted Your Royal Highness of Sir John St Clair's Illness. I thought he must have died, but Doctor Huck, since he has employed him, finds that it is an Ulcer in his Kidneys and has recovered him greatly, but will not be able to serve this Campaign. I have appointed Major Robertson to act in his Place, in the mean time he has ten Shillings a Day; he must have an Assistant with five Shillings a Day. I have continued Captain Christie and Mr. Leslie who were Deputys of Sir John's to act under Mr Webb, the Duty there can not be done with fewer.

As Colo Stanwix's Battalion is divided between him and his Lieut. Col., and each of them have a great Number of Men under their Command, I have allowed of an Additional Adjutant and Quartermaster for the time they are so separated, at two Shillings a Day each.

I have been forced to encrease the Hospital from the many parts I am forced to divide the Troops into on this Occasion. I have appointed Mr Napier the Director to act as first Surgeon, as Mr Middleton did in Flanders under your Royal Highness. I mention the Precedent only to justifie the Manner, for it was the want of Numbers made me come into the Measure.

Besides the additional Surgeons Mate to each Battalion, I have for the Campaign added of Mates five for the Expedition, three to the Hospital at Albany, one Mate for the Troops at Number 4 and one for the People at the Forts on the Mohawk River, who has likewise the Charge of the Indians; and I have given one to Lieut. Colo Bouquet's Command, as I could not send those five Companys to that Sickly Country with one Mate, where they could have no supply in case of his being sick.

I have appointed Captain Roger Morris Major of Brigade with Mr Webb, he is in the 48th Regt. With such a Number of People as he has under his Command, he can not be without an Officer in that Station.

I send your Royal Highness a List of Commissions, with Notes, but as some of them require longer Explanations than are proper for such a Paper I shall beg leave to give you them in my Letter.

Before I received Orders to break the two Regts. I had brought Lieut. Nat: Williams of the 51st Regt to a Court Martial who broke him.

On my Return from Philadelphia I found Captain Hubard Martial's [Marshall] Independent Company about half Compleat, no Money or Credit to pay the Men or clear the Quarters, no Camp Equipage provided, tho ordered at the End of the Campaign. I ordered one of my Aid de Camps to advance Money to a Lieutenant of the Company to clear the Quarters, as the Company had orders to march. As soon as they arrived here, I brought the Captain to a Court Martial for Neglect of Duty, Disobedience of Orders, and embezeling the Funds of the Company.

They broke him but with great Difficulty. This is the first Court Martial I have had any Difficulty with. They took a compassionate Turn for the Man's Poverty, tho he has been for twenty Years the worst Capt with the worst Company in the King's Service.

I have given the Company to Lieut. Crookshanks of the Royal Americans, on condition of his taking it as it is, paying all Debts due by the Company, and recruiting it at his own Expence, beyond what Ballance may be in the Agent's Hands. The Expence will be upwards of £400. The former Captain says he has about £300 in the Agent's Hands. This I do not believe, for last Summer he told me he had £500 in his Hands which turned out at June last to be under £40. I shall send the Agent Orders to stop what ever Money is in his Hands till the Debts are paid and the Company compleated. The Debts I mean are Money advanced for the Subsistance of the Company. In case your Royal Highness is [not] in town I have orderd him to apply to M:G: Napier in relation to this Order.

Lieut. Crookshanks was entirely a Stranger to me when I came to this Country, but he has been severely wounded in the Service, is a dilligent Officer, and seems to me a proper Man for an Independent Company.

I should have given this Company to Lieut. Ogilvie, who is the eldest Subaltern in those Companys that is able to do Duty, but he was on the Mohawk River, and I had no Reason to believe he had the Money necessary to set the Company in Motion. He served in Flanders and is a good Officer, but an opportunity immediately offered of promoting him, and as he was an elder Lieut. I have given him the Rank.

Captain Richmond arrived from Boston with his Company not half compleated, tho he had his Choice of his recruiting Quarter. This is the Capt. Lieut. of M. G. Shirley's Regt. to whom he gave the Independent Company, and I had Orders to supersede him if I saw Reason. There appeard no Reason when I arrived for making Use of that power, but when he came down from the German Flatts he brought a very bad Company with him. I then told him his Situation, and what the Consequence would be if he did not make it a good one by the opening of the Campaign. When he returned with the Company in this Condition, I lost all Patience; he was frighted for a Court Martial and proposed to M.G. Abercromby to sell for £300, I accepted of the Offer and a Friend of Lieut. Ogilvie's in this Town offered to pay down the Money.

This made two Lieuts. vacant in the Independent Companys here and an Ensigncy in those in South Carolina, from whom at last I have got a Return. I have given those three Vacancies to Volunteers who had carry'd Arms several Years, who I think fit for them but are People who ought never to go higher than Lieuts. I have sent one of them to South Carolina by whom I expect constant Accounts of the real Situation and Management of those Corps.

Captain David Kennedy, who has been in the 44th since the Regt was raised and who was brought into the Service by the Recommendation of Lt. G: Sir James Campbell, was ill when he came here and has been greatly afflicted by Fluxes and the Rhumatism, has sold his Company to Lt. Harvie [Hervey] Brother to the Earl of Bristol.

These are the Reasons he assigns for selling, but the real State of the Case is that altho he has been in general ill since he came to this Country, he is now very able to serve, but Major Eyre being put over him in the Regiment has made him give over the thoughts of being a Soldier, and applied to me to get out as soon as I arrived, and I have staved it off till now, and as he is of great Use to me in Elections in the Shire of Air, I have now agreed to it, which I hope your Royal Highness will excuse, as I tell you the Case fairly.

The next is Lieut. Col. Chapman. Enclosed your Royal Highness has a Copy of his Letter to me. I do not think him so ill as he does himself, but on the other hand he has done no Duty, and that Battalion has been taken no care of which did not come to my knowledge till lately as they were in Maryland, I obliged to be to the Northward, M. G. Abercromby at Albany, and Mr Webb ill here, who was destined for the Southern Command, and the Field Officers making no Complaints of any thing wrong. But I am told by every body that Major Prevost knows nothing of commanding a Battalion, and I must own that when I followed their Route from Philadelphia I saw nothing to contradict that Report, for I found their Sick and Men ill of the Small Pox left all Scattered over the Country without any Person or any Money to support and take care of them, their Arms and Accoutrements left in the same Manner. As the Major commanded, I thought this too strong a Proof of what I had heard, and altho I had not agreed to Lieut. Col. Chapman's Request when he first made it, I began to think it necessary for the Service that there should be another Field Officer with that Battalion, even when the King should be pleased to appoint a Col. to it, and have agreed to Lieut. Col. Chapman's resigning his Commission, and half the Pay of it, and selling his Company for £1200, the Price that has been given here, and have promoted Major John Young to be Lieut. Col. on Major's Pay, and Capt. Tulikin to be Major on Captain's Pay. The one is the Eldest Major in America, the other the eldest Captain in the Royal Americans. Major Tulikin will make as good a Major as any in the Service, and I think I can answer for Lieut. Col. Young's making that a good Battalion. Besides, as he remains with Mr Webb, he will be an usefull Man for settling Points with the Provincials, as he is a sensible cool Man, and indeed I think will be of great use to him on many Occasions.

Major Tulikin I send with Lieut. Col. Bouquet, in order to prevent the Command falling into the Hands of Provincial Officers, in case of any Accident happening to Lt. Col. Bouquet, for that Command is at too great a Distance to be able to apply Remedys if any Accident happens.

I hesitated much more on agreeing to Lieut. Col. Chapman's going out, altho it was plain he will be of no use to us, than I should otherwise have done, on account of Major Young's being his Successor, as I was afraid it might have the appearance of a Job to your Royal Highness, from the Major's being almost the only Man here connected with me; but I hope it will not appear in this Light to you.

I have agreed to Lieut. Pottinger of the 44th selling out. He bought his Commission, and is entirely a Sot.

So far I had writ of this Letter, when the Ferret Sloop arrived, on the First of May after Dinner, by which I had the Honor of a Letter from your Royal Highness and letters from the Ministers, with the Plan of operations, and Directions to take up Transports &c and an Account of the Succors coming out, with a large Train of Artillery and six Engineers.

On the 11th of May the Packet arrived with Mr Pitt's Letters of Febr. 19th with additional Instructions and Copies of those to the Admirals and Directions about Captures and the List of the Ordnance and warlike Stores. The Packet informs me that the Fleet was not sail'd, that he had met on the 18th of March 11 of the Transports at Sea going to Cork, who put back to Falmouth; from whence I conclude I shall be at Halifax before them, as the three Regiments from Albany are all arrived now, May 14th, but five Companys of the 42d who are on their way and 200 of the Rangers. There are likewise wanting five of the Transports, who I expect this Night with some Provisions that I expect with them. The only thing I can forsee that can stop us is Sailors, which I think we shall be able to get. The Troops are all encamped, ready to embark, except those I mentioned above.

Your Royal Highness with your usual Goodness and that Attention you have for the carrying on the Service everywhere has supply'd us extremly well with Artillery and every thing necessary in that Branch, so far as I can see from the Return.

I should have been glad to have known who the Engineers are that come out, in order to have made the Division here. From private Letters from People of the Ordnance to their Friends here I find that Dugal Campbell comes out, who is older than Mr Montresor, for which Reason and because Mr Webb thinks himself weak in that Article and that I do not think he will be of any great Use to me, I have determined to leave Mr Montresor here.

I had, till I had those Letters, determined to have carryed most of the People belonging to the Train, leaving only a Proportion for the Forts, but since I find there is so large a Proportion coming out, I leave Capt. Ord, and only take with me a small Detachment, almost all of those that were brought from Halifax, to manage the Field Guns and the 4 light 12 Pounders which I carry from hence, thinking they will be necessary for the Defense of our Corps[Camps]. By this Disposition Mr Webb will have Six light 12 Pounders and some old Brass 6 Pounders, besides Mortars &c, in case he finds it proper to proceed, with Captain Ord and most of the remaining People of the Artillery, with Mr. Montresor Gordon and Williamson Engineers, and some of the forreign Engineers and Artilery Men.

I shall make no Observation farther than to say it was well we had got so far in providing before the regular Orders arrived, which had so very long a Passage from England. We shall be late now, but we should have been much later if we had not.

I have chose not to fix the Operations absolutely till we arrive at Halifax and meet with the Admiral. My Letters point out Louisbourg strongly, I don't choose to say more, but the Season I think incline both Sir Charles Hardy and M. G. Abercromby to think that the likely Plan. If that takes Place, I doubt it will be too late for going up the River, so that the Campaign will in that case end in Nova Scotia. I mean nothing definitive in what I say here, but if I may use the Phrase, I would think aloud to your Royal Highness. If the French Fleet are there before us the Sailors tell me we can do nothing except we can first beat them. But this I will assure your Royal Highness, that nothing shall be left undone that I am able to perform.

I shall have the honour to write a short Letter as soon as I get to Sea. I have ordered the 1st Battalion of the Royal Americans to be mustered compleat. In the first place, I think we have enlisted more men than to compleat the whole, and this I shall see in a few days, but what made me muster them so at this time was, part of them going at so great a Distance, I have no chance of being able to muster them again for some time; and I mean this only for clearing their Accounts at the Pay Offices, at the same time being accountable for the Disposal of the Non effective Fund as directed.

The Expence of fitting out the Men before a Campaign in this Country, where all must be provided before they take the Field, everything at such extravagant Prices that you will not believe me when I tell you that the four Battalions of the Royal Americans are near £6000 in Debt to the Officers, and how that will be stopt I do not see. I must beg that I may be allowed to let the Capt[ains] have the four Men for the Companys at 100, as your R. H. allowed them 3 Men at 70. All the Allowance I had was to advance Money out of the Non Effective Money for Recruiting.

This Letter has been begun a great while, and yet I am forced to send it to Your Royal Highness without Correction or being able to copy it.

I have been in the greatest Distress for want of Money, for by the Negligence of the Contractors' Agents I have been reduced to £3000, with many small Demands remaining to satisfy and in Apprehensions of reducing the Publick Credit as low as I found it, besides having nothing in Hand to maintain the Troops the whole Campaign; but at last I have an Account from the Contractors Agents at Boston that by a Letter from the Contractors, which came by the last Packet to this Post, he has the Account of £63000 [£36,000] [1] being shipt in the Fleet. Had any of the Offices wrote me an Account of this, it would have saved me twelve very anxious Days and been no loss to the Service. This total want of Information from all Offices gives me great uneasiness and puts the Government to great Expence, for when they do not inform me that they are to supply me, I dare not trust, and by that means come to be overprovided in many Articles, as I am at present in Working Tools, which will not be lost, but the Money needed not

[1] For words set in brackets in A.L.S. Loudoun to Cumberland letters, see the note on p. 234. The correct figure was £63,000.

have been laid out so early. These were agreed for before I had the Honour of receiving your Royal Highness's long Letter, and till the Ferret Sloop arrived on the 1st of this Month I have not had any Account of any one thing that was to be sent me from any one but your self. I received the Secretary's Letter in Febr. acquainting me in general of a Reinforcement.

Your Royal Highness will see by my Publick Letter the Accounts we have by the Privateers of this part, who dogg'd the French Fleet from Cape St Francis from the 4th to the 12th of this Month, and that of [by] the Prisoners they took in five merchant Ships, part of the Fleet of Merchant Men who took the Opportunity of sailing with them, for the Ships of War took no Charge of them.

By their returning their Pilots, and by their leaving both the Officers and Sailors of the Greenwich whom they had taken, and by the Course they steered which was North and rather a point West, and by their taking no Charge of the Trade, I have no doubt of their being bound for Louisbourg on the River St. Lawrence. The Force of the French is Monsr Beaufromont in a Ship of 80 Guns, two Ships of 74 guns, two of 64 guns, and a Frigate of 26 guns.

Our Situation: the Troops all embarked, most of them got down to the Hook, only waiting the Return of the Pilot to carry them down and a Wind, as tis thirty Miles of Pilot Water; our Convoy, which we have collected from all Places from whence we could draw any assistance, The Sutherland of 50 Guns, two 20 Gun Ships, The Nightingale and Kennington, and two Sloops, The Ferret and Vulture.

In this Situation I had a Meeting with Sir Charles Hardy and M. G. Abercromby to concert what was proper to be done. As we have been able to learn nothing of the Enemy's Motions farther than the Latitude 27, and as their Force must make an End of our Fleet immediately if we meet, there is Danger of the Service being disapointed; and if they have Intelligence of the Preparation for an Embarcation, which probably they may, for neither the Orders from home, nor the Embargo laid on here have been able to prevent the People of those Provinces from supplying the neutral Islands with Provisions, and I have just now an account of three Vessels from Rhode Island going into the Cape with Provisions just before this Fleet sailed, in which case they may hover at Sea for us. And I have no certain Account of the Motions of the King's Fleet, but from the Secretary of State, by which they should now be at Halifax, tho the Account of the Master of the Packet nor the Merchants Letters do not mention their having sail'd so soon.

On the other Hand if we wait for Returns from Halifax which

probably would take a Month, the Campaign is lost and nothing can be done. Therefore we have unanimously determin'd to sail in four or five Days if the Wind will permit, and in the mean time have dispatched Letters to Admiral Holbourne and the Commanding Officer at Halifax acquainting them with our Intelligence and our Motions; one Copy we have sent by Land to Boston, to be dispatched in a Sloop from thence, the other we have sent in a Pilot Boat thro' the Sound. From hence I hope this Measure will appear to your Royal Highness to be a right one, as in that time we shall probably hear some account of the Enemy if they are waiting for us. Of this last, there certainly is a Risk of losing those Troops, but that Risk must be run, altho they are of great Consequence to the Service here, for nothing can be done without it.

Whilst I am writing another Captain of one of the Prizes is arrived, who still confirms the Intelligence we had from the other Prisoners but acknowledges what the others all denied: that they had Instructions from the Admiral, and that he took Charge of the Trade till they were thro' the Crossing [?; Courses], that after that he made them a Signal that they were to throw their Orders overboard and to make the best of their Way, on which he crowded all the Sail in his power and stood North and a point West, that sometime after he traversed and stood east, which he believed was to deceive them and to prevent the Merchant Ships being able, if they were taken, to give an Account of his Course, for next Morning he saw him standing west of the north again. He farther adds that they had heard nothing of any Preparations making here for embarking Troops, but that it was said the French Ships of War at Martinico were to join Monsr Beaufromont, and that they consisted of one Ship of 70 Guns, two of 60, and two Frigates. This Intelligence he had from his Brother, Master of the Tonnant, and that they were to sail for Canada, in which Expression they all include Louisbourg.

If the Fleet is arrived and can meet those parts of Fleets of the Enemy, they will be able to give a good account of them, but if there comes a Fleet from France and those large Ships now in this Country join them, I doubt they will be too strong, from any Account I have been able to pick up of the Strenth of the Fleet coming out. There is one Account from Newry in Ireland of the Fleet being come to Cork, but all the other Ships that are arrived bring an Account of their having left them at Spithead, and of their having met with contrary Winds for a great while after they themselves sailed, from where I am afraid they are not arrived in this Country yet.

I was in hopes of not being under a Necessity of mentioning Col. Prevost any more to you in this Letter, but he has put that out of my Power by his Behaviour. On the 24th of May I met him on the Street as I was returning from Sir Charles Hardy's. The Col. was extreamly out of humour, and was a little indecent, and complain'd that his Battalion was not cleared and were embarked.

I was not willing to have this Conversation in the Street and called M. G. Abercromby to be present, as I have not chose for a considerable time to have any Conversation with the Col. but before Witnesses. He desired I would call Lieut. Cols. Gage and Burton who were standing near, so those three were present at the whole with Col. Prevost, Lieut. Col. Young and me, where Col. Prevost behaved with more Indecency than I ever knew any Officer to his Supperiors, and did indeed behave with all the Insolence that Pride and Folly joined can make any Man guilty of.

I did humble him before we parted, and let him know that such Behaviour was very improper in the Situation we happened at present to be in, and that it was such as in no Situation I would permit any Man to behave to me.

Had I put him in Arrest, any Court Martial would have broke him. But I did not choose to carry Matters to that height, as your Royal Highness had brought him into the Service, for which Reasons only I have taken so much Pains to keep him Decent, if it had been in my Power. I began with him in the openest frankest Manner; that he cured me of presently, for he found every one thing I had done wrong and determin'd to set me right without good Manners. I then tried him by being very civil, hearing all he had to say, which seldom cost less than four Hours of a Day when he was in the Quarters with me, and after all that still every thing was to do again, for he would have his own Way and throw every thing into Confusion and I had an eternal Plague with making up Differences between him, his Battalion, and almost every Officer present; for it was one continual Complaint of his behaving in the strongest Manner to every body; for he took it in his Head that he would pick the four Battalions to make up his own to his Liking, pretended this Officer and t'other Officer were engaged to be in his Battalion and would break their Hearts and die if they were any where else but with him; the same with Sergeants and Private Men. All which I presume he will deny to your Royal Highness, for he denies it to me. I beg leave to give you one Instance in each Case. He desired to have his Brother the Capt. changed into the 4th Battalion in place of Captain Gmeling, who I think will be broke,

that is, that no Officer will ever do Duty with him on account of a Pros-
ecution that is going on against him on things stole in the Transports.
I think him not guilty of the Theft, but he has certainly acted like a
Fool, and there will be a legal Proof. He desired to have Lieut. Rotzen
changed from the 1st Battalion, as he would die if he was not with
him, and was to give Lieut. Gagie of his Battalion in place of him.
These two I agreed to. I was at Philadelphia when Rotzen took leave
of Col. Stanwix, which he did with Tears in his Eyes, and this is one
of those People who would have died if he had been kept from that
Battalion the Col. commanded. He at the same time got Col. Stanwix
to consent to allow him to take Lieut. Elrington from the 1st Battalion,
to make him act as Adjutant to his Battalion, which I likewise consented
to, and as soon as he got back to his Battalion he began a Dispute by
Letters with Col. Stanwix about Lieut. Gagie whom he himself had
given him for Rotzen. The Dispute was like to grow warm between
them, and I, to put an end to it, left Gagie with him, and he now insists
to me that I have never given him the Choice of any Officer, nor showed
him any Indulgence in any thing but in changing his Brother. Things
were in that Situation in the 4th Battalion that Lieut. Elrington, who
I am told was a Sergeant Major in England but makes a very good
Officer and knows his Duty, he has, after showing that he could be of
no Use where he was as Adjutant, as he was not allowed to teach the
Men the Discipline according to your Royal Highness' Orders and he
understood no other Method, he went so far at last as to beg that I
would return him to the 1st Battalion as a Sergeant, rather than remain
a Lieut. in the 4th Battalion.

  As to Sergeants, I shall trouble but with one Instance which was in
the 2d Battalion. They were out at Exercise and he came out to see them,
where he demanded a Sergeant in the Battalion as having been enlisted
in Germany to serve in Col Prevost's Battalion, that he had enlisted
with Col. Prevost, that he should fulfill his Promise to him, and that
the Man would break his Heart and die if he was not permitted to go
along with him. As Col. Dusseaux had drawn this Man at the forming
the four Battalions after their Return here from Saratoga where I
had carried the whole in one Corps after the loss of Oswego, Words
arose, and in the mean time Major Robertson went to the Sergeant,
who was in his Company, who did not find that the Sergeant had any
such Plan, desired the Sergeant might be asked about this. The whole
officers walkt up to the Man and Col. Prevost asked him if he had not a
mind to serve in his Battalion; the Man answered he was very willing
to serve in any Battalion. Being then asked if he had his Choice, which

Battalion he would serve in, O Sir, if I have my Choice I will remain where I am. Those Sorts of Disputes have brought the Col. into great Disrepute among the Officers.

The Dispute about the Private Man was this. Col. Prevost had been here about ten Days, had met with Col. Dusseaux every day without mentioning any Business to him; when he was going away, left a Message by a common Soldier for Col. Dusseaux, that the Soldier should acquaint him that he was enlisted in Germany for Col. Prevost's Battalion, that he should allow him to stay a little while where he was, but that he should very soon order him to his own Battalion. As Col. Dusseaux complained to me of having eternal Trouble with Col. Prevost's claiming of Men from his Battalion after they had fallen to him by a fair Division at forming the four Battalions, and likewise of the Indecency of sending such a Message by a Common Soldier, when he had so many opportunitys of talking to himself, when Col. Prevost returned I talked to him very gently before Mr Webb, showed him that the Men enlisted in Germany were at the common Charge of the four Battalions, that they were fairly divided among them and that he had no distinct Right to any of them, and that sending such Messages tended only to make ill Blood among us, and beged he would not do it any more. When he came back next Day, M. G. Webb likewise present, in the middle of a Conversation he started up to his Feet all at once and says, My Lord, I have examined that Man; he never carried any such Message; Col. Dusseaux lies (I ask Pardon for writing such a Word in a Letter to you, but no Word but the Word itself could have conveyed the Idea that he would have behaved in that manner). M. G. Webb who was as much provoked as I was can witness this.

Mr Webb can likewise acquaint you with the Necessity I am under of having a Witness by, when I have any Business with him, as the Colonel's Head runs so fast that it leaves his Memory behind, for it does not only happen that next Day he denies what past, but that when Business has been finished as Mr Webb and I imagined and I had writ it down in the Col's Presence, in five Minutes after he has forc'd [faced] us down, in contradiction to both our Memorys and my writing, that he has never said one Word of it. That makes unpleasant Dealings, and makes it very necessary to have Witnesses. The real Case of Col. Prevost is what Col. Bouquet says. I give it you in his own Words, That his Prosperity has turned his little Headpiece. As to what he is in the Field I know not, but I will venture to assure Your Royal Highness that he knows nothing of commanding a Battalion in Quarters.

The first thing that made a difference between him and the Officers of his Battalion was his having promised the Adjutancy and Quarter-master's Place to many different People; to get out of this, he proposed to name two for each and leave me to choose out of them. Before this happened I had seen his Disposition and had not the least Doubt that if I made that Choice, he would have represented to Your Royal Highness that those were People of my Choice and that I had left him no Choice in them. Three of the four he named to me were British; I told him, as you had desired, these might be left, one of each of those Ranks, for the Gentlemen that came from foreign Service; he had but to give me their Names and they should have the Commissions. And I have had many different Sets named for it, and when I took down their Names I had a new Set next Day, and when he left me I had a Message for a new Set. At last I pinn'd him down and made my Secretary take Names from his own Mouth and fill them up directly. He went directly out of my Room into the next, and as my Secretary came out desired he would not fill up the Adjutants. However, as he did not talk of it to me, I went on and told the Col. I would give it to whomsoever he would name, but that Man would not make an Adjutant. He assured me again and again that the Man had been an Adjutant in France; that it was the thing in the World he was fondest of and insisted with him to have. During the whole time the Man himself was applying to me, saying it was totally against his Inclination to have that Commission, that he was not capable to execute it, that Col. Prevost was forcing him to accept of it, and that he should make so bad a figure in it that he would be undone by it, and begging to remain a Volunteer till I should think proper to make him an Ensign. And now that the Commission is vacant, begs not to accept, and I shall give him the first Ensigncy that is vacant and since the Col cannot find an Adjutant, I shall find one for him. He has made his Secretary Quarter Master. I have never seen him, but they tell me a little hump back'd Man.

This letter is so long and undigested, which I have not time to amend, that I have only mentioned the Affair of the 24th in general Terms, as I thought it was too long to trouble you with the Particulars. Therefore I have writ it to Mr Calcraft, that your Royal Highness may be able to come at it by Mr Fox, for I beg leave to assure Your Royal Highness that I have not one Secret in the World that you are not welcome to know, if you choose to take the trouble to look into it.

When I began the Paragraph about Col. Prevost, I thought I had acquainted you in the former Part of this Letter that the Col. had entrusted me with the Secret of his having writ to your Royal Highness to beg leave to resign his Commission, and that the Letter was gone a fortnight before by a merchant Ship, and that he had read to me in presence of Sir John St Clair a Paper which he said was a Copy of that Letter. As he mentions in that his having no Command of the Battalion, I asked him what he meant by that. If I had put the Command of that Battalion into any other Person's Hands. He said no, I had not. I then enquired if he meant my giving him Orders about it, if he thought that was interfering with him. He said after the Letter I had writ him about the Men to be discharged and ordering the Surgeons of the Hospital to review Men reported by him unfit for Service, it was impossible he could have any Command after that. I said I was very sorry for that, as I had learned that Method under your Royal Highness, and that in this particular Instance I begged him to remember that whilst I was at Philadelphia he had discharged a great Number of Men, two of which I met; the first had been but thirteen Days in the Regt, and was discharged for having Fitts with his Cloathing on; the next was a Corporal, with his Clothing and Knot; that as he was one of the Drafts and a Soldier that had served, I had writ him a Letter from the next Stage to desire no more might be discharged that were able to do Garrison Duty, as we could find employment for them all, and that I did not choose, when the Campaign was just beginning, to discharge Men if we could have but one Campaign of them.

That your Royal Highness may see the whole of this Affair, I send enclosed Copys of those Letters which he complains of; they contain likewise the Complaints of the Provisions.

I was misinformed in relation to the throwing down the fresh Provisions and trampling on them, for on farther Enquiry it proved to be done by some Men of the first Battalion.

The Paragraph relating to tying Men Neck and Heels was occasioned by Complaints having been brought to me of Col. Prevost's having introduced several new Punishments, one of which was what they call the Book. A Soldier had got drunk, the Col. stood by and saw him tied in this Manner in the Evening and laid on his Face in a Corner of the Guard Room, with a Stick thrust thro' his Legs and Arms to prevent his being able to turn out of that Posture. He kept him in this Way all Night and next Day till the Evening before he gave Orders to untie him, and if the Officer of the Guard had not untied him in the Night he would have been dead before Morning.

I talked to the Colonel of this as a thing done by some of his Officers, tho I knew he was the Person gave the Order and saw it executed; told him it was contrary to the Custom in the British Troops and must be laid aside. As the Col. after this added the Paragraph on that Subject in his Letter to my Aid de Camp, I thought myself under a Necessity of taking some Notice of it in my Answer, and the more so from other Accounts of the Proceedings in that Battalion. Particularly one of the Drafts from Ireland had been confined, and making some Noise they sent in two Corporals who beat him with Sticks so that he died in ten Days after, without taking proper Care of him. The Man complained as I am informed, from that time, that he was a dying of the Bruises; this they huddled up, tried the Corporals by a Regimental Court Martial, broke them and buried the Man. By their Distance from me, this did not come to my knowledge for some time. I believe Col. Prevost was absent when this happened.

Your Royal Highness has now the Paper relating to this Affair before you and you are the proper Judge whether I was entitled in these Circumstances to write such a Letter to an Officer under my Command. At present I think it was my Duty to act as I did. If you think otherwise, I am sure I am wrong.

I see I have neglected above to acquaint your Royal Highness that the next Day after Col. Prevost had complained so loudly of his Battalion not being cleared, he paid back from that Battalion £1346–5–5, which he himself had overdrawn for them.

I have but one thing more to trouble your Royal Highness with, which is the Dating of the Commissions of the foreign Officers, which has puzzled me extremly, as I have had no Information to guide me but from Col. Prevost who has puzzled the Affair so that I do not understand it. He says that your Royal Highness had agreed to four Captains and four Lieutenants in place of those that did not accept. I acquainted your Royal Highness in a former Letter that one of those Captains and a Lieut. were gone back to France in the Zephir Frigate, and that by the Report made to me the Circumstances were not favourable, that as they were Prisoners I had issued no Commissions to them.

In the end of April Capt. Bonneville and Lieut. De Noyailles arrived from Antigua, where the Capt. had brought the Lieut. before a Court of Inquiry, who, tho they could not proceed to sentence they have given an Opinion, and as the Proceedings were transmitted to me the Question arose whether in that Situation it was proper for me to issue his Commission, and I on this refered it to another Court of Inquiry for their Advice how to proceed, and I have transmitted both those to your Royal Highness.

Since those, Blows have past between Captain Bonneville and him, and I have given Mr De Noyailles £50 to carry him home or to dispose of himself here as he may choose. Col. Prevost and he differ very widely in Accounts, but as I have had no Information of what has been ordered to be advanced to them, and as the Col. has settled and paid up all those to this time without either consulting or acquainting me with it till now that the Dispute among them has brought it to light, I have declined meddling in it till I receive Orders, or at least Information from England. And he goes so far as to accuse him of the refusing to account to him for Goods he took the Charge of to the Value of £500. All the Col. will say to him on that Subject is that they must have been in one of those Ships that fell into the Hands of the Enemy, without showing him any Bill of Lading.

On the 1st of May arrived Capts. Williamouz and Dufez in the Ferret Sloop, still without any Directions. And prior to their arrival I received Orders to break the 50th and 51st Regts. and to place such Officers belonging to them as I should judge proper to be employed to vacancies as they happened in the Troops here. Some of the Captains in those Corps had been twelve Years Captains in the Service.

Col. Prevost argued on behalf of the foreign Gentleman that they had received their Pay from Christmas 1755, and that by that they were Captains in the Regiments from that time. On the other hand the others were reduced and ordered to be provided in the first Vacancies, and their Commissions delayed only till I should receive Orders from your Royal Highness and Information what Commissions had been issued by the King; and that Situation, as they were old Captains in the Service, they thought it hard to be made younger in the Regiment, when the Commissions were to be issued at the same time. This Affair I thought too big for me to determine, and as there were Six Companys vacant in the Royal American Regiment, four by the Captains that did not accept of the first nomination and two by the Death of Capts Stanwix and Faesch, I filled up the Commissions of the three former Captains and the three from the Half Pay, all of the 8th of March, which was the Day after those Regiments were broke. The Rank of the Forreigners among themselves is settled by Col. Prevost. The British Rank is settled by their former Commissions, and by giving the Commissions this Date they come directly from their former Regiments into the Royal American Regt. without ever being on Half Pay. And in order to prevent the Seniority being determined between those two Sets of Officers till I have received your Orders upon it, I have divided them in the different Battalions so that they may not meet on Duty this Campaign.

Before I took this Step I consulted with every body from whom I could expect Information. I acquainted Col. Prevost and Lieut. Col. Haldimand with the Difficultys that appeared to me, in order that all partys might be informed, and acquainted them that the Rank was not to be determined till I received your Orders.

When the Commissions were issued, and not till then, Col. Prevost brought me a Letter from Capt. Bonneville to him, declining to accept of his Commission. I should have mentioned that I had not determined absolutely on the Dates of those Commissions till the 19th, and Captain Bonneville's Letter is dated on the 15th. I told the Col. that if the Captain did not choose to accept, he ought to write me a Letter, which he did, and I send the Copies enclosed. I accepted of his Dismission, and at his Desire gave him leave to return to Europe.

The Captain seemed to be very happy when he arrived here first, but from the time he returned from Col. Prevost at Amboy, I was informed that he talked of returning to Europe, except he was made Captain of the Engineers, but this is only Information.

We have the Small Pox raging among the Troops that are embarked, and among the Ranging Companys. Mr Webb has it among the Troops, the Independent Companys, and the New York Provincials; it has not yet begun among the New England Provincials; but the kind is good and very few die, but I expect it will go over the whole Continent. The Terror People have for it in this Country is inexpressable, altho that is a good deal diminished from the Care we have taken, both of the People that are infected with it and to prevent its spreading.

Sir Charles Hardy went on board last Night, June 2d, in order to regulate the affairs there, and has desired me to join him on Sunday, but I shall go on board tomorrow. We have a Report last Night by a Vessel from Georgia that Monsr Beaufromont's Fleet was lying off for us in Latitude 38. It appears to me to be some Ships that have sail'd from Virginia, now that I have examined the Master, but we have sent out to see who it is, and taken all necessary Precautions. I have the Honour to be with the greatest Respect, Sir, Your Royal Highness's most Dutifull and obedient Servant

LOUDOUN

P.S. Since signing my Letter, an Express arrived from Halifax with a Letter from Admiral Holbourn, March 10th, and one from M. G. Hopson, Febr. 25th, which arrived there on the 21st of May in the Speedwell Capt. Bond, with an Extract of Mr. Baker's Letter, which is all the Letters I have received from England. Col. Lawrence mentions a Change in the Ministry. All quiet in Nova Scotia, but a Report of Indians and Canadians assembling on St. Johns River, and that they had sent a Sloop of War to look in there.

New York June 3d 1757

LIST OF COMMISSIONS GRANTED BY HIS EXCELLENCY THE Rᵀ HONᴮᴸᴱ THE EARL OF LOUDOUN [1]

Rank	Officers Names	dates of their Commissions	

22ᵈ Regiment

Rank	Officers Names	dates of their Commissions	
	John Foxen	8. March 1757.	From Half Pay of 51ᵗ
	John Williams	8. ditto.—	Changed from the Royal Americans
	James Sinclair	8. ditto.—	Changed from 35ᵗʰ
	James Campbell	8. ditto.—	Changed from 45ᵗʰ at His owen & Lt Col Rollos Deser
Lieutenants	Henry Alt	8. ditto.—	From Half Pay 51ᵗ Son of Moss: Alt
	Henry Elwes	1. May.—	Ensigne in 48ᵗ
	John West	2. ditto.—	Ensigne in 44ᵗʰ
	John Vickers	3. ditto.—	Ensigne in the 48ᵗʰ
	John German	4. ditto.—	Ensigne 48ᵗʰ
	William Hamilton ...	17. ditto.—	Elest Ensigne 22ᵈ
Ensign.—	James Malcolm	8. ditto.—	Recomended by the Earl of Murray caryed Arms
Quar. Mastʳ	Lᵗ John Rollo	10. January—	Son to the Lt Col:

35ᵗʰ Regiment

Rank	Officers Names	dates of their Commissions	
Lieutenants	Thomas Fortye	8ᵗʰ March 1757.	Half Pay 50ᵗ
	William Fredᵏ Phillips	16ᵗʰ May—	Eldest Ensigne 35ᵗʰ
Ensign.	Robert Bayard	8. March.—	Half Pay 51ᵗ

42ᵈ Regiment.

Rank	Officers Names	dates of their Commissions	
Lieutenant	Archibald Lamont ...	15ᵗʰ May 1757.	Eldest Ensigne 42ᵈ In place of Lt James Campbell who remaind in Irland when the Regᵗ came out and has never Acknowledged the Orders I sent him from London by H R H Orders
Ensigns.—	John Smith	15. ditto.—	Caryed Armes Son of Cornet Smith of M G Cholmondly
	Peter Grant	16. ditto.—	Payed £50 to cary Ensigne McLagon home who had Sufferd himself to ill used the Regᵗ refused to do Duty with him and he Resigned his Commission

[1] The notes are in Loudoun's handwriting.

Rank	Officers Names	dates of their Commissions	

44th Regiment

Ensigns—	Stephen Kemble ..... 3d May 1757.	Of the Jerseys had one of Mr Shirlys Commissions that were Supperseded
	Andrew Brown ...... 9. ditto.—	Recomended by Mr Brown now a Ld of Sesion Caryed Arms
	James Dunbar .... 10. ditto	Caryed armes a Relation of Lord Finlaters
	Achilles Preston ..... 14. ditto.—	Recomended by the D: of Bolton

Those four are in place of the three Eldest Ensignes Promoted and Ensigne Rodes who resigned without any money

45th Regiment

| Lieutenant | Thomas Ervin .... 8th March 1757. | Half Pay 50t in Place of Lt Campbell now in the 22d |

48th Regiment

Ensigns.—	Edmonstone .... 5th May 1757	Caryed armes Recomended by Mr Wattson of Berwick
	Alexander Dowal .... 12. ditto.—	Caryed Armes three years in the Resv
	Robert Freser .... 17. ditto.—	Caryed Armes and was in the Artilery Son to Mr Paxton at Boston
Chaplain	Michael Houdin ..... 29. April—	Is a Missionary at Trenton in the Jerseys and lived several years at Quebeck and is well aquanted with the Place and Country

I bought out the former Chaplin for £300 which I pay out of the Stopages from the Absent Chaplines he doing the Dutty for them in the maintime he would not go with us without a Chaplindry

Royl American Regiment.

| Captain | John Dalrymple ..... 7th March 1757. | As Your Royal Highness made him Capt Lt and as he was so very Particular in all his |

Rank	Officers Names	dates of their Commissions	

Royal American Regiment

Rank	Officers Names	dates of their Commissions	
			behaviour I did not think him fitt to be Promotted therefore took his Resignation at the Same time that I gave him the Commission and made him Exchange on Cap Delancees Half Pay as he was put in by Your Royal Highness I hope you will not Disapprove
Captains.—	Samuel Williamos ...	8. ditto.—	Brought over by Colonel Provost May 1^t
	George Du Fez	8. ditto.—	Brought over by Col Provost May 1^t
	Hyacinth Bonneville .	8th March 1757.	Brought over by Col Provost in the Transport that was at Antegoa Did not accept his Commission
	Thomas Jocelyn	8. ditto.—	Half Pay 50^t
	John Bradstreet	8. ditto.—	Half Pay 51^t
	James DeLancey	8. ditto.—	Half Pay 51^t
	Stephen Gaulley	21st May—	Capt Lt in the Royal Americans in Place of Capt Bonneville that Did not Accept
	William Stewart	25. ditto.—	Purtches Lt Col Chapmans Company was the Eldest Lt would Purtches
Capt Lieuts	Gilbert McAdam	8. March 1757	Eldest Lt in Place of Capt Lt John Dalrymple Promotted
	Samuel Holland	21st May.—	Eldest Lt in Place of Capt Lt Gaulley Promoted
Lieutenants—	Beamsley Glazier	8. March	Half Pay Lt of Sir William Pepperels first Reg^t an Active uesfull officer
	John Rodolph Rhan ..	8. ditto.—	Brought over by Colonel Provost he came in the Transport which was at Antego one of Col Provosts last list came out a Sergant
	Peter Penier	8. ditto.—	
	John Billings	8. ditto.—	Half Pay 50^t as Ensigne had a Commission of Lt which I supperseeded
	John Polson	5. May.—	Ensigne in 44th
	James Calder	6. ditto.—	Ensigne in 44th

Rank	Officers Names	dates of their Commissions	

Royal American Regiment

Rank	Officers Names	dates of their Commissions	
Lieutenants	Stair Campbell Carre .	7. ditto.—	Eldest Ensignes in the Royal American Reg^t
	Walter Kennedy	8. ditto.—	
	Michael Davis	9. ditto.—	
	William Potts	10. ditto.—	
	William Jones	11. ditto.—	
	John Bell	12. ditto.—	
	Nicholas Sutherland .	13. ditto.—	
	William Ryder	14. ditto.—	
	Thomas Vinter	25. ditto.—	Purchesed in Lt Wisenfelts Succession, the officers have refused to Do Duty with him and I have allowed him to Sell for £150 to Pay his Debts and cary him Back to Holland Lt Vinter Payed £100
	James Ralfe	25. ditto.—	Purtchesed in Lt Col Chapmans Succession
Ensigns—	Ranslaer Schuyler	8. March	Half Pay 51^t
	Peter de Witt	1st May—	Had a Commission in the 51^t from Mr Shirly Supperseeded by me
	John Dow	4. ditto.—	Recomended by Lt Col Holden caryed Armes
	John Rodolph Fæsch .	6. ditto.—	Son of Capt Rodolph Fæsh who Died at Philadelphia
	Francis Gordon	7. ditto.—	Caryed armes has lived in South Carolina and Brother to a Gentleman in the Shire of Air
	William McClure	11. ditto.—	Enlisted for the Reg^t 42 Recruts
	Arthur St Clair	13. ditto.—	Caryed Armes Recomended by Sutherland of Gower and the M^{c}kays
	Alexan. McIntosh	18. May 1757	Caryed Armes in the 42^d
	Henry Peyton	25. ditto.—	Purtchesed in Lt Wisentelts Succession Payed £50
		26th ditto.—	To Purtches in Lt Col Chapmans Succession
Adjutant	Charles Rhoir	24. February	Recomended by Col Provost will not Accept
Qu^r Master ..	James Saml Engel ...	24. ditto.—	Recomended by Col Provost
Surgeons Mates	James Diemer	25. April—	
	Peter Welsh	3. May—	

Royal Regiment of Artillery.

Rank	Officers Names	dates of their Commissions
Comm^{ry} of Stores—	James Hockett.—	25th April 1757

Rank	Officers Names	dates of their Commissions	
	Late Capt Richmonds Ind^t Comp^y		
Captain	William Ogilvie	16th April 1757	Explaned in my letter Payed £300 to Capt Richmond
Comm^{ry} of Stores.	John Knox	24. Feb^{ry} 1757.	
	The Hospital.		
Chief Surgeon.—	James Napier	24th Feb^{ry} 1757.	

[*Endorsed*] Dates of Commissions from Lord Loudoun June 5 Rec^d July 6. 1757.

LOUDOUN TO ROBERT NAPIER

(A.L.S.)

From on board Kelbes [Kilby's] Sloope going doon to the Hook to go aboard the Sutherland along with Sir Charles Hardy June 5^t 1757

My Dear General

I had not time to fill up the two Inclosed Pappers for H R H till I got on board. The List of the Half Pay Officers I doubt will not be ready to go to the offices till the nixt Packet. You will observe that I have Provided for all those that are fitt to serve but Major Grovor [Craven] and Lt Elrington who go to England to settle the Accounts of the Reg^t. The Coppy the Major has given to me is a very irregular one, and altho he charges many things there ought not to be in that Account, such as Spatterdoshes Blankets &c, he makes but a Small Ballance to himself and at the same time takes Credit for the whole £1252 advanced to the 50^t Reg^t, and does not give them Credit for the £500 they have repayed of that Sum.

Lt Goldthwait insisted on Going to Boston to settle his accounts; I told him I intended to Provid for him but if he could not attend his dutty this Campain I should delay giving him a Commission till he could attend and as he is gon I have delayed it till he can serve.

You will likewais observe that the Regts were brook March 7^t and those I have Provided are on March 8^t so that they will have no Clame for half Pay.

I have been greatly distrest for want of Information both of what you have done in Commissions In England and what you expected me to do, and delayed filling up here till I Expected no furder Information from England before the Campain as the duplects of the letters with the Fleet are Arived. My Dear Sir be so good as to lett me know where in H R H Disaproves of the management that I may change it.

I think Sir Charles will sail in two or three Days but he must have a Report from his Crusers that the French Fleet under Moss Bofremony is not lieing of for us.

The Ireland letter was put into my hands since I com on board. I ever am with sincer Regard My Dear Sir Your most Obedient humble Servant

LOUDOUN

[*Endorsed*] E. of Loudon.—June 5 Rec^d July 6, 1757 with Return of officers promoted or provided for.[1]

CUMBERLAND TO BARRINGTON
(A.L.)

H:Q^r at Bielefelt 13: June 1757

. . . . . .

I have observed the Same difficulties concerning Mr *Shirley's* Examination, that they do not amount to Proofs tho' they are very grievous accusations: & therefore, tho' it ought not upon any account to be neglected; yet, one can not be too Cautious, in appointing the Enquiry. for which reason the measure you propose to take & are concerting with Lord Halifax & G^l Napier, are I think the most proper. I am extremely pleased with the Reports you have Sent me of the Highland Batt^s, & very glad my *Pcs:* in my own Hand answered my Intention So well in convincing you how well pleased I was with your Behaviour, both in *Parl^t* & in your Station.

THOMAS PENN [1] TO CUMBERLAND
(A.L.S.)

Sir

Your Royal Highness having been pleased to allow me to send any american intelligence, I thought necessary to be communicated to you, I should before this time have wrote, had I received any accounts from Pensilvania, but there has not a Packet arrived, or other Vessel, with a

---

[1] The list of commissions, granted from December, 1756, to May, enclosed in this letter is a composite of the two lists above, without the comments.

[1] Thomas Penn (1702–1775), son of William Penn, was one of the proprietors of Pennsylvania. He had appointed William Denny governor on Cumberland's recommendation.

short passage, and I now presume to trouble your Royal Highness with accounts, which I received before, but as they related to Mr Denny, I had great reluctance to mention them, tho on further consideration, as not only my Character, and the interest of my family may suffer, but his Majestys interest, and that of his people Committed to our Care, if he does not apply himself to the Dutys of his station, or act worthy of the Confidence placed in him, which I fear is the Case, from several Letters I have lately received, I cannot longer defer laying extracts of them before your Royal Highness; they were wrote by persons of great honour, and on whom I can firmly depend; to this your Royal Highness will allow me to add, that I do not know what he means by being deceived, as I told him, exactly, on what he was to depend, but had there been any mistake, I humbly submit to your Royal Highness, whether it would not have been more propper to have represented it to me, than to have laid such a charge upon me before the people there, which he has never done, or indeed sent me such accounts of business, as a deputy Governer ought, and as former Governers were were always accustomed to do.

I must now beg your Royal Highnesses pardon for the length of this, and am with the greatest respect

Sir Your Royal Highness's most humble, Most obedient and most faithfull servant

THO PENN

Spring Garden
June 18th: 1757.

[*Endorsed*] Mr *Penn*, to *H:R:H:* Rec^d July 3. Ans^d the 5. inclosing one Paper.

EXTRACTS OF SEVERAL LETTERS FROM PHILADELPHIA [1]

I cannot help saying that the Governor treats every body with neglect but the Commissioners, and Assembly, and they do with him what they please, he raves against them in conversation, but is obsequious to them in Business, and they treat him with contempt, which he bears, they have suffered his Speech to them, tho' it contains so many necessary Matters to be yet unanswered, and have done nothing since the 14th of October, [this was Dated the 11th of December] [2] but heard the merits of a controverted Election.

[1] Enclosed in the preceding letter.
[2] The notes in brackets are Penn's.

Extract of Another Letter

I know not what to say about the Governor, he is peevish & averse to Business, I know him not enough to pronounce positively about him, but I see so little Judgement, such difficulty of access, such a dread of visits, tho' from Men of influence, & character, so little enquiry into the nature of the matters before him, and such a fear of disobliging the Assembly, that it does not appear to me, that your Affairs will be put on a good Issue in his Administration, he affects not to know you, says he is appointed by the Crown, and will leave you to justify your Instructions without giving himself any trouble about them.

Extract of Another Letter

Mr Franklin behaved with great rudeness, & insolence, to the Governor, in the Conference on quartering Soldiers, declaring he was no Governor as he did not protect the People, calling him in express Terms a Bashaw, or worse than a Bashaw, which the Governor tamely put up with, in the presence of his Council, without any apparent resentment or reply, nay continued to confer after this unprovoked attack on his Character.

Extract of Another Letter

The Governor expressed himself before Mr Chew [the Attorney General] in a very indecent manner of the Proprietors, as having deceived him in many things, asked him in a peevish Strain, what they allowed him for Council Business, said he deserved a great deal and hoped he was paid by the Proprietors to his satisfaction, as to himself he could not fight the Proprietors Battles, nor assign any reasons but the Proprietors Instructions (which they were to defend not he) for his refusal, tho' every body would see it wrong in the Proprietors neither to be here themselves, in such time of imminent Danger, nor suffer him to relax a single point. this was a shocking situation and what the Proprietors could not justify, and he believed they would be flung. in short, he says so much and so often of this sort that I am quite unhinged—he cares not to write a single line, nor to let others write for him, he blames with justice the Commissioners and Assembly, but exerts no Authority, nor regulates any thing where they make objections. I grow extreamly uneasy for the Proprietors, and see clearly that this Gentleman will not answer the difficultys of his Station, nor do any thing for the Publick Service, if in the least controverted, but grows sour & peevish, likes nobody, seems to have no affections, his polite taste for Men and Books will not suffer him to find any satisfaction in his Station.

Extract of Another Letter

The Commissioners Orders are to be paid by the Trustees of the Loan Office, and whether the Business done has had the Governor's previous approbation, cannot appear to them; to remedy this the Governor, in his Message, in which he assigns reasons for refusing the Bill, proposes that no Orders of the Commissioners shall be paid, by the Trustees of the Loan Office, unless countersigned by him; even to this necessary amendment, he for a long time would not consent, on account of encreasing Business, and giving him too much trouble, tho' it be absolutely necessary for the preservation of the little Authority left him.

Extract of a Letter from a Principal Quaker in Philadelphia

As to our present Governor his time has been so short, as yet, among us, that it is not quite fair, to pass any Judgement on him, but I may venture to say this that I much doubt his Abilitys, being equal to his Station, and I think in case of any difference with the Assembly, or any matter of Debate shou'd arise, he will not have either Talents or steadiness of Temper to manage it.

[*Endorsed*] Extracts of Several Letters from *Philadelphia*, written to Mr *Penn*. *1757*.

LOUDOUN TO DANIEL WEBB

(COPY)

on board His Majestys Ship Sutherland, the
20th June 1757.

My Dear Sir,

It is now ten o'Clock, and we are under Sail with the Fleet, which must make our Correspondence come Slow to one another, for the remainder of this Campaign; And for that reason I could not depart, without giving You my Opinion of the Situation of things on your side of the Country.

I am this morning informed, that there is a Serjeant of Captain Rogers Company, returned from Montreal with Eight Men, who brings an Account, that the Enemy have Changed their first disposition, of sending their Forces up to the Forts, and that they are now drawing their whole Force to Quebec, for the Defence of their Capital; by which means, You will have nothing to oppose You at Tienderoga & Crown Point, but the Garrisons, and, I imagine, very few more for Scouting. This Intelligence only confirms me in my former Opinion, that they would keep their whole Force, to defend their Capital, as their whole depends upon it; for when once that is taken, there is an end of all their Forts to the Northward, and of Course, of their Influence and Command over the Indians.

Now, My Dear Sir, if you find this Intelligence proves true, which you can easily be certain of by your Rangers & Scouts, who, in this Situation, I imagine can bring you certain Intelligence; and still to make you the more sure of it, I think you ought to send with them an Officer, on whose Accounts you can depend, to reconnoitre the place and Avenues to it, and to bring You an Account of the Numbers they have; then You will Act on a certainty; And in case You find things as I expect, and as this Serjeant informs Us, The method I would advise, is to make as little appearance of Your Intentions as possible, till You can fix an En-trenched Post, at the Landing place at the lower end of Lake George; If you had 800. or 1000. Men posted there, and Entrenched, I think if you have nothing but the Garrisons to deal with, Your business is done; for with that head, you can support yourselves against all they can do, till You can reinforce your Troops, to whatever number You please.

As soon as you are sufficiently strong, I would Invest the place, and then bring up my Artillery; for till the place is invested, I would carry no Artillery, but a few of the light Field pieces to secure the Entrenched Camp, in case they have any Indians with them, as those will keep them in Awe.

I am aware of the Objection that may be made, of getting possession of the Landing places at the lower or North end of Lake George, from the want of Boats, arising from those burnt last Winter by the Enemy; but you have still remaining, one Sloop unhurt, and another that wanted little repair, with the Bay boats and Gondolas; And I should hope, that one or two of your Galleys might be finished by this time; with those, to carry Regular Troops with your Rangers, and what you can pick out of the Provincials to Act in that Shape, to be first carried down the Lake so far, and then to go by Land, I should think it not difficult, to get the necessary Force there.

The greatest difficulty that occurs to me, is the supplying Your People with Provisions; to obviate this is [as] far as possible, it will be necessary to throw in a large Quantity into Fort William Henry, and likewise into Fort Edward, to Supply that as it is drawn away; and to secure the

Communication with Albany, it will likewise be necessary, to leave a strong Post at Fort Edward, in case the Enemy should make an Attack on that, by South Bay.

Your Brass Guns and Your large Mortar, are I presume still at Albany; the Guns are easily moved, and two Ox Carts brought down the Mortar: the moment You move that, the Enemy will be informed of your Intentions, therefore I would leave that, to be among the last things I did.

I would likewise keep out large Scouting parties from Number 4, to Alarm their St Francis Indians, and prevent their being able, to employ them against You.

I am the more eager in my Wishes that this should not be delayd, if You find it practicable, and that the Enemy have kept their Force below, because I am very Apprehensive, from the Fleet & Succours from Europe coming so very late, it will not be in my Power to get to Quebec; and if it should happen, that we are forced, from the Season being so far advanced, to sit down before Louisbourg, the Enemy will then see the impossibility of our getting to Quebec, and will be at liberty to turn their whole force against You, and make the end of the Campaign a very troublesome one to You, which will be entirely prevented, if you are able to take both or either of those Forts.

I have here given you my thoughts in general, on your Situation, and what appears necessary for you to do in it; leaving it to You to Act, as Circumstances and your own Prudence directs You; And wishing You all Success and honor in the Campaign, both on Account of the Publick and for your own Sake, I am, with Sincere Regard and Affection, Dear Sir, &c.

[*Endorsed*] Copy of a Letter from Lord *Loudoun* to Major General *Webb*. 20th *June 1757.*

LOUDOUN TO CUMBERLAND

(A.L.S.)

From on board the Sutherland at Sea
June 22d 1757

Sir

Since I had the Honour to write to your Royal Highness from New York the Incidents that have happened are: Sir Charles Hardy fell down to the Hook on the 3^d; I went on board with him on the 5th; on the 6th he sent out The Kennington of 20 Guns and the Ferret Sloop on a

Cruise to sail South South East 50 or 60 Leagues, and from thence to range Eastwards off the Nantuket Shoals, in order to discover whether there was any Truth in the Report we had on Mons[r] Beaufromont's lying up to wait for us. They met with Calms and did not return till the 17th. We then called a Council of Sir Charles Hardy and M. G. Abercromby to consider what was proper to be done.

Here it will be proper for me to give you a short Account of our Situation. As to our Knowledge of the Sailing of the Fleet and Succors from Europe, I am informed by the Secretary of State that they were to be at Halifax the latter end of March or beginning of April. And those Letters arrived on the 1st of May, the Duplicates came May 11; since which I have no Letters from the Ministry. May 21 Capt. Bond arrived at Halifax in the Speedwell Ketch after a Passage of five Weeks from Falmouth; he brings me no Letters of any kind, but one from Admiral Holbourn of March 10, and another from M. G. Hopson, nothing but Letters of Compliment such as pass between People employed in the same Service. Capt. Bond acquaints Mr Lawrence, who wrote it to me, that the Fleet was not sail'd from Portsmouth before he left Falmouth, but imagined he would sail with the same Wind. We have since then a Report by a Merchant Ship that the Fleet was seen off of Kingsale April 20, that they were to wait there till the Transports join'd them from Cork; but this is all I know from Europe or of the Fleets and Succor expected.

On the other hand we have certain Accounts of the Enemy having taken the Advantage of making Use of their Squadron at the Cape against us here, and of their having sailed from the Cape May 4th, and of their having steered a Northerly Course till the 12th, when the Privateers left them with the Prizes they had taken. On the 4th I had an Account from Boston of such a Fleet as Mon[r] Beaufromont's having been seen on the 28th of May off Halifax by a Ship from Cadiz and a Fishing Vessel. This is but Sea Intelligence, but in my own Mind I have no doubt it was that Fleet. So stood our Information when we met to consider what was proper to be done. As to Sailing, Sir Charles Hardy and I were clear it was right to sail; M. G. Abercromby did not oppose it but plainly wished to have a little more Information of the Motions both of our own and the Enemy's Fleets; as in case we met them, our Convoy of one 50 Gun Ship, two of 20 Guns and two Frigates, all which but one 20 Gun Ship on the Station we have got by our own Industry and I am not sure but I shall be found fault with for it by Admiralty, are not able as they tell me to deal with Mons[r]. Beaufromont's Ship alone.

However we immediately unmoor'd to be ready to sail on the 18th.

However as the General, tho he did not oppose, seemed anxious, I thought it right to have a Second Meeting in the Evening; and the General still wishing for more Intelligence I proposed, as the Post from Boston arrived at New York next night, to send a Pilot Boat up for the Letters, as this would delay our Sailing only one Day, which we accordingly did.

What determined my opinion for Sailing was that I must give Credit to the Fleet's being to sail early as the King's Ministers have informed me; that altho all my Information from them has come very late, and indeed not full, and altho I know by other Means it has not sailed as they expected when they writ to me, yet taking it on Capt Bond's Information that they probably had sail'd with the same Wind he did, in that Case Mr Holbourn had the five Weeks he was on the Passage, the four Weeks that are elapsed since, which makes nine Weeks, and as our Voyage will naturally take ten Days or a Fortnight, that will give the Admiral about eleven Weeks for embarking the Troops and making his Voyage, which is surely enough, altho he has a bad Passage; from whence I conclude he must be on the Coast before us.

We have taken every Precaution we could think of as soon as we had the Accounts of the Enemy having sent their Fleet from the West Indies Northward. We dispatched a Vessel from New York thro' the Sound between the Main and Long Island with an Account of it and our Intentions as to Sailing, with Letters to the Admiral and Commanding Officer, that he might give us such Protection as he saw necessary. We sent Duplicates by Land to Boston, which were dispatched from thence immediately. We then sent our Cruizers from the Hook to beat the Seas as wide as we could without losing too much time.

And further, as nothing can be done whilst we lie still and the Season so very far advanced, I can see nothing to justify our delaying to sail in these Circumstances. Besides, it appears to me that were we to wait till Mr Holbourn could send a Fleet to meet us, that there is danger of the Enemys Fleet growing too strong for him, in case the Intelligence should be true that the Fleet from Martinico is to join them with the Ships from the Coast of Guinea. That I own I do not believe, because the Martinico Fleet is very weak and the Ships from Guinea must be very sickly and I cannot think they will leave their Islands without any Ships of War, but they certainly expected to find Monsr Salvert with a Fleet from France in Canada, and as his being forced to look after us may give those Fleets an opportunity of joining, I think it my Duty to Sail. And if I should have the Misfortune to lose the Six Battalions, which I do not expect, I hope those Reasons will justify me to my Master and Your Royal Highness.

The Pilot Boat did not return with the Letters till the 19th in the Morning. By then [her] I had Letters from Governor Lawrence of June 1, with an account of those large Ships being seen on their Coast on the 29th of May. A Copy of that Information I have sent to the Secretary of State. No account of Mr Holbourn. Capt Rous writ to Sir Charles Hardy with the same account, and the Station he had given to his Ships and Sloops, which are three lying off for Mr Holbourn and one sent to look into Louisbourg. As there is no Account of those Ships having seen either an Enemy or that Number of Ships, I do not apprehend that they were lying off for us, but only on their Passage.

Mr Lawrence, altho our Intelligence of the French was not arrived when those Letters were writ, very judiciously judges them to be come from the West Indies.

On the 19th the Wind was foul; on the 20th we sailed; it blew fresh soon after we were out, and one Ordnance Ship, one Hospital Ship, and a Transport lost each a Topmast, but as Sir Charles has carry'd an easey Sail they are all repaired and got up with us, and indeed tis impossible for any Man to take more anxious Care of a Fleet than he has done of every Ship in it.

I have been very tedious in my Narrative of this Affair, but I hope your Royal Highness will make some allowance for my being at Sea, where I am never well, and my Head always muddy, and not able to write one Sentence to an End, and get through a Letter only by Perseverance, and that the Packet must go this Night or tomorrow Morning or we shall take her out of her way, which we do not intend, so that I have not time to correct what may be amiss in it. And that as this is a material Point, it was necessary for me to explain it farther to your Royal Highness than to the Ministers, because if an Accident do happen I hope to have your Protection, if you see there is Room for it.

From the Season being so far advanced before the Fleet arrives, and the Enemy having so many Capital Ships in those Seas as we know to be come from the Cape, I doubt we dare not leave them and Louisbourg behind us; so that I am afraid my next Letters will tell you that we are going to Louisbourg and that the Campaign will end with that Siege and that if I find it possible afterwards an attempt on St Johns River, for I do not see that the Season will permit our going to Quebeck after. But Quebeck must be taken, and that will finish every thing of consequence to the Northward, for all the others will fall easily afterwards.

The Navigation of the River is long, and tho not so dangerous as the French have represented it, still tis hazardous.

By my Publick Letter your Royal Highness will see the Accounts I have got of the French drawing all their Force to defend their Capital. Enclosed I send you a Copy of my Letter to Mr Webb before I sailed. He has been much better in Health and Spirits since he went up to take the Command. As Lord Howe's Battalion is with him, I shall dispatch him to him when ever I meet him. I suppose he is with the Fleet. I think he will be of great use to him.

As the Merchants will probably complain of the Embargo I was forced to apply to the Governors to lay, pardon me to mention that Affair. As the Smuggling Trade to the West Indies and Holland are so very beneficial, without it I could have had no Transports, and after I had got the Ships I could have had no Men to sail them. Privateering is so much in fashion and so beneficial to the Sailors New York alone has above 3000 Men employed in it. Their Situation is: the Owner of the Vessel fits her out in every Article and furnishes the Provisions, for which he has but one third of the Prizes, the other two thirds go to the Crews; and as they have been extreamly successful they all make Fortunes. And when I had got the Men I was not able to keep them, so that we have been obliged to the last Day to press out of all the inward bound Ships, and we have none to spare. Mon[r] Beaufromont's coming into these Seas made us think it necessary to keep it on till we sail'd, to prevent the Enemy getting Intelligence, as much as possible, of our Motions. But the Truth is no Rule or Law has any force in this Country, and all of them, but particularly the People of Rhode Island, have carry'd on a Trade with the Enemy the whole time. They take Clearances to the British Islands and give Security; they trade notwithstanding with the Dutch and Spaniards at Hispaniola; they go to St. Cristo, make a sham Sale of their Ships and Cargo to the Spaniards, put Spanish Crews on board who carry the Ship to St Francis, at the Cape sells the Cargo to the French, loads with Sugar and Molasses, brings her back to the Owners who come directly home with her again. Others clear for St Christophers, from there run down to St Eustatia, sell their Provisions, and return with Clearances from Anguilla which they can buy at very reasonable Prices; so that in reality they have not been hurt, and now that the Embargo is off, the French will be supplied with everything they want in spite of all the Regulations. By my Publick Letters your Royal Highness will see the Complaints I have made against the Southern Provinces; if there is not an effectual Stop put to that Precedent now begun in Maryland, the King will at once lose the Command of all Troops raised by the Provinces. This seems to me a very bold Attack on the Prerogative, and as the Disposition every where is to levelling [encreases], it will be followed universally. Had I been able to have been there, I would have stopt at nothing that could have crushed this Attempt.

I have likewise mentioned in my Publick Letter Lieut. Govr Dinwiddie's Conduct, which is in my Opinion very strong. As he is a Man of Sense, I can account for it no other way but that, as he has desired leave to resign, he has done this for Money, and is determined to get all he can in any Shape before he goes.

I shall not be able to write to my Lord Halifax by this Packet, but will begin to write to him on the State of the Colonies as soon as this is gone, that it may be ready for the next opportunity. In my last I recommended Lt. Col. John Young to him, for a Successor to Mr Dinwiddie, in case his Lordship had no better Man in his View. He is one I am sure Money will have no Influence on, or he must change strangely before it has. If Mr Dinwiddie's Behaviour appears in the same light it does to me, I should think superseding him, in place of giving him leave to retire, would have a good Effect.

I have the Honour to transmit herewith a List of the Commissions I have given since my last, by which you will see I have consented to Capt. Mulloy of the 44th and Capt. William Morris of the 48th retiring on their Pay. They are both entirely incapable of serving; and so many of the Captains of those two Regiments are employed in Publick Offices that it would have been very hard for them to have served in the Field. Their Successors go in Course. The Quarter Master of the 2d Battalion has been so ill he desired to resign. The Adjutant of the 4th that resigns is the one that Col. Prevost named. In my last Letter I acquainted your Royal Highness that the Man was miserable, begged not to accept of the Adjutancy, that I had insisted on his trying it, that it should not hurt him if he was not able to execute it, and that I would give him an Ensigncy when I took the Adjutancy from him. But he was so miserable and in so much Terror for Col. Prevost that he got the better of me, and I gave him liberty to go in the Ordnance Ship with the Engineers. This gave the Col. so much offence that he came to me at the Hook, in the Cabin with Sir Charles Hardy, accused me of Breach of Promise that I had not given him the Naming of an Adjutant. I asked him if I had not, when he varied so often as who he would have, at last made my Secretary take down the Names from him, and if I had not given the Commissions to those he named. He owned I had, but says he, You don't call giving a Commission and taking it away in twenty four Hours keeping your Promise to me. I then told him, I do not know what you mean; you know when I gave that Commission and I have not yet taken it away. On which he told me he had a right to appoint another. Sir, said I, if tis a Point of Right, I shall show you how that stands, and I shall name whom I please and shall do that when I please, and pray let us not trouble the Admiral in his Cabin with this Sort of Discourse. I heard no more of the Col. for three Days, and I then made my Aid De Camp write to him for a List of the three Officers in the 4th Battalion whom he thought the most proper to be made Adjutants. He answered that Letter and sent the List, and strongly recommended one of them, and I immediately ordered a Commission to be made out to the Officer he recommended, but after I had signed it I found the Col. had from the time he had had that last Dispute with me never sent any Officer to receive Orders when the Signals were made for the Adjutants. On which I locked up the Commission, and made my Aid De Camp write the enclosed Letter to him. He made no Answer to it that Night, which I suppose was to get time to go to Lieut. Col. Haldimand, for he knows, so far as I have been able to see, nothing of Duty or Service himself. Next morning he came and was very submissive, but would have put it on my having told him I would appoint one to do the Duty of Adjutant in the mean time, and that he thought it would be wrong to employ any officer to receive Orders till I did. I showed him no such thing either had, or could naturally have happened in that Conversation. He then insinuated that I was his Enemy. Sir, I think I can to your own Conviction show you that I am not, for you have given me three different opportunitys within this Month to have brought you before a Court Martial, and I have not done it.

The first I mentioned to Your Royal Highness in my last Letter: his Behaviour to me in presence of M. G. Abercromby and Lieut. Col. Gage and Burton. The Second was a false Return he made me when the Regiment was to embark. The Battalion was encamped in Nutten Island and the Col. was in New York; the Major made a Return of the Strenth of the Battalion in order to fix the Transports. When the Col: joind them he made a new Return of about 300 [100] Men more, by which he had a Ship of 150 Tons added to his Transports. When I came to the Hook I had a Return of the Officers and Men on board in each Transport, which Return agreed with the Major's Return, and discovered the Error of the Colonels. The third was his obstinately determining to receive no Orders, for it comes out that he gave Orders that the Officers who had for two Months done the Duty of Adjutant should not go for Orders when the Signal was made. I think those three Instances ought to convince you that I have treated you with great Lenity. But now, Col., you have wore out all my Patience and I will go on in this Stile with you no longer, for endeavouring to keep you right takes up one half of my time and gives me more trouble than all my other Business, so you must change your Method, and act like other Officers; and if you will condescend to look on your self only as a Colonel in this Army, and act accordingly, you may still live with me as easily as with any Man alive, but if you will still imagine that you have a Right to command this Army and me, I do assure you I will from this hour treat you as your Actions deserve; and I shall forget all that is past, except you bring them back to my Memory by some new Act of yours, in which Case I do assure you I will bring the whole upon you at once.

The Col. is addicted to Passions that at times he has not the least Government of himself, and in them he goes Lengths that are very improper for me to suffer, and that are indeed very improper that I should, for if my own Temper would submit I must immediately lose all Command over others, if I permit him to behave as he very often attempts, and then he represents every thing so very different from what it was at the time it happened that I have told him I never will have any Dealings with him but in Writing, that the Words may remain.

Tis now June 23ᵈ, the Wind is fair and we are near the Nantucket Shoals, but the Sea runs so high that I can do no more, but am with the greatest Duty and Regard, Sir, Your Royal Highness's most Dutefull and Obedient Servant

                                                       LOUDOUN

CUMBERLAND TO THOMAS PENN

(A.L.)

                                          Dankerren, July 5: 1757

Mʳ: Penn. I received yours of the *18:* June, concerning your Dissatisfaction of Lᵗ Govʳ *Denny's* Behaviour and conduct. I must confess the extracts you have Sent me are very Little in his favour I recommended him to you as you desired me to look out for an officer that might be fit for that employment, & further, I have nothing to do with him. But you will give me leave to say he has had a very short Tryal, & as he has always been reckoned a man of Sense, I should hope that proper Directions & Reproofs would set him right. But, this affair regards you so particularly, besides the Public, that I must entirely leave it to your own judgment I hope we shall soon hear good news from that part of the world; at least we have a right to expect it, considering what a Force we have sent there both by Sea & Land. I remain

BARRINGTON TO CUMBERLAND

(A.L.S.)

Cavendish Square 8th July 1757

Sir,

I thought it right some time since, to apprize the King that your Royal Highness had order'd me to recommend Colonel Whitmore in your name to the first old Regiment *at home;* and that he should be succeeded in the 53^d Regiment by Lieu^t Colonel Whitmore of Manners's. This is the first day that I have attended his Majesty since the Death of Major General O'Farrel, when he was pleas'd to give the 22^d Regiment to Lieutenant Colonel Whitmore, with direction that he should immediately repair to it. This was the first order the King gave me, and I am perswaded it came intirely from himself. I presumed in my Letter of the 24th June to mention Maj^r General Lambton to your R.H. for the 22^d Regiment, in order to make a Vacancy for Col. Stanwix in Ireland; but having had no Orders from you on that subject, I would not propose Lambton to the King tho it might have forwarded one of the Points on which I am honour'd by your R.H.'s instructions, as it would have interfered with another part of them, & might have postponed the preferment of a good officer. In all these things my object is to do what I think your R.H. would have directed; and I humbly hope that I have not erred in this particular.

After Colonel Whitmore was disposed of, I acquainted the King that your R. Highness recommended Lieutenant Colonel Wilkinson to succeed him when there should be a Vacancy in Manners's, to which his Majesty immediately consented; and order'd me to propose a Lieutenant Colonel for the 57th. I beg'd leave first to know your R.H.'s pleasure on that subject, and was order'd by the King to do so immediately.

I was also commanded to ask your R.H.'s Opinion on a subject of more importance. You were pleased to direct just before your departure that at a proper time I should ask the King's servants whether any augmentation was intended, & to inform them that you thought some more additional Battalions to the few old single Regiments remaining in England was the best methode for that purpose. I was in Berkshire when the new Administration kiss'd the King's hand; but at my return four days afterwards I acquainted the Duke of Newcastle with what I had received in charge from your R.H. and he say'd he would talk with the rest of the King's Servants upon it. The next day I saw Mr Pitt by appointment, and found Sir John Ligonier with him. I was told that a large number of recruits would be wanting in America before the next Campain; that as it was of importance that they should be on the spot *early* (which recent experience has shewn to be very uncertain if sent from hence in the spring), it was thought best to send them, so as to arrive before the American Ports were shut up by the bad Weather: That two means were proposed for raising these recruits; one that each Batt^n of Highlanders in America (including Lord J. Murray's Regiment) sh^d have three additional Companies to recruit or augment those Corps. I remember'd the objections made by your R.H. to a proposal of that kind, & I stated them; on which it was agreed that both officers and men should go to America as fast as the Companies were raised, and none of either remain in the Highlands.

The next means proposed were that 40 men and an officer should be draughted from every Battalion in Great Britain and Ireland (the Guards excepted) to be disposed of as Lord Loudoun shall think fit, and the officers to return home. This Sir John Ligonier say'd he had already proposed to the King and that his Majesty had consented thereto, with directions (as he afterwards told me in private) that the worst men should be draughted.

I observed to them that a great number of Recruits had been raised this year in America, and that probably as many at least would be raised the next: but it was answer'd that as the force under Lord Loudoun's Command was at the beginning of the Campain near 1300 Men short of Complement, before the End of it, 5000 might in all probability be wanted, a number much to large to be got in America. The King's consent made it unnecessary & improper for a Secretary at War to urge any farther his opinion against a measure already determind. It was say'd farther that 40 Men p. Regiment would soon be recruited by officers who might be immediately spared for that purpose from each Regiment.

I then mention'd what I had before say'd to the Duke of Newcastle about an augmentation at home, which I found had also been consider'd by Sir John Ligonier & Mr Pitt; who thought that an Additional company of 100 Men & four Com^d officers to each marching Battalion, would be the most agreeable methode to the King and that those Companies might be afterwards turn'd into any shape which your R.H. should approve: That to make this change the more easy those Companies might at first be cloth'd in plain red, to which any facings or lace &c might be cheaply and easily added afterwards.

I immediately consulted Gen[1] Napier on these points, and advised with him what would be most agreable to your R.H. He thought you w[d] like that the Duke of Argyll should recommend the Highland officers and take upon him to raise the Companies as he had raised the Battalions. I find to day by M[r] Pitt that his Grace has no objection to give his assistance as before, and does not doubt the success. The only business which I shall have with these Companies is to see that they be well accoutred &c and sent out of Scotland as soon as possible.

M[r] Pitt to day proposed to the King this project of raising an Add[l] Company to each Battalion, to which immediately afterwards his Majesty was pleased to acquaint me that he had agreed. I beg'd that I might be allow'd to ask your R.H.'s Opinion concerning the best methode of making this augmentation before any thing was finally determin'd, to which the King most readily consented, and order'd me to write this Evening. I am to meet Gen[1] Napier to morrow and we shall endeavour to find out some proper methode of appointing the officers which we shall submit to your R.H..'s consideration by the first opportunity.[1]

. . . . . .

Your Royal Highness's most humble & most devoted servant

BARRINGTON

BARRINGTON TO CUMBERLAND

(A.L.S.)

Cavendish Square 12. July 1757

Sir,

Two Letters, one dated the 28. June the other the 5th July with which your Royal Highness has been pleased to honour me, I have received since I presum'd to write my last Letter to you dated the 8th instant. As I have your R.H.'s consent to propose Major General Lambton for an older Regiment, I shall propose him without loss of time, whenever a vacancy happens which can bring Col. Stanwix here, without interfering with your prior Instructions in favour of Col. Whitmore of the 53[d] Regiment. . . .

The three Lieutenants of Shirley's and Peperels (turn'd over to the

---

[1] The rest of the letter deals with the promotion of officers in England.

Royals and remaining here being Prisoners on Parole) are now exchanged; & I have got a passage for them to America. I hope we have French Soldiers enough here to exchange all our's taken by them, & I have written on their subject to the Admiralty. . . .

It is said that Col. Prevôt will quit at the End of the Campain: Lieutenant Col. Gage has written to desire I will recommend him to your R. H. for the Battⁿ.

Sir John Ligonier is to write to your R.H. on a Subject which he can explain much better than I can, & which may occasion my being honour'd by some Commands from your R.H. which shall (like all others) be punctually obey'd. Every day shews more and more how much you are wanted here.

P.S. Mr Shirley's affair is under the consideration of the Secretary of State for the Southern department.

SIR JOHN LIGONIER [1] TO CUMBERLAND

(A.L.S.)

Sir,

Since the Last I Had the Honour of writting to your Royall Highness, his Majesty has been Pleased to Signifie his Pleasure that 2000 Recruits taken equaly from every Battaillon In Brittain and Ireland, should Be Ready as Soon as transports Can be Gott, to Embark for america, this detachments Comes to 40 men Pr Battaillon to be Comanded By a Subaltern from Every Corps, and the whole By a field officer, who is to Return with the Subalterns, as Soon as they have deliver'd the men to Lord Loudon, the additionall Companys design'd to Be Raised I suppose your R H has heard from Lord Barrington, I fear officers Such as your R H would Like will be difficult to be found, His Majesty has been Pleased to give O'ffarells Regiment to Lieu^t Coll^o Whitmore, and to make Major Wilkinson Lt Coll^o to Ld Robert Manners,

All the troops are In their Respective Camps, and hard at work, I Hope to see them soon and Be able to Give your Royall Highness a Good acount of their Performances; those Reg^{ts} that want men Have had orders to Compleat themselves as Soon as Possible

I Return your R H my most Humble thanks for your Goodness to my nephew, I Hope he will Endeavour to make Himself worthy of it,

We are very happy here that your R H Has been able to keep Mr Destrées at Bay so very Long, In my own mind sir I Cant Help Being

<hr>

[1] Sir John Ligonier, at this time lieutenant general of the Ordnance, was made commander in chief upon Cumberland's retirement in October, 1757.

in Pain for you, when I Consider His Great Superiority and the Space you are to deffend, and the Long fatiguing summer you Have Before, you, tho I think I Reason as a Soldier, yett I Hope my fears are ill Grounded, and I ardently wish your Royall Highness all the success Imaginable

I am with the most dutyfull Respect Sir Your Royall Highness's Most Humble and Most dutyfull servant

July ye 12: 1757

J. L. LIGONIER

[*Endorsed*] London, July the *12. 1757*. Sir John Ligonier to *H:R.H.* Rec^d *20:* Ans^d *22.*

THOMAS PENN TO CUMBERLAND

(L.S.)

Sir

I beg leave to return your Royal Highness my most humble thanks for your Letter, and having since I wrote received Letters from Pensilvania, thought it necessary to inform you what is doing there.

Mr. Denny having recommended to the Assembly to provide for the debts of the last, and the services of the ensuing year, they (after a long delay) presented a Bill for raising one hundred thousand pounds, by a Land Tax, clogged with the same unjust, and unconstitutional, clauses, which he objected to in all the former, but exempted mine and my Familys estate; he was advised to make several amendments, but being informed if he did not pass it, as it was, they would immeadiately adjourn, as they were resolved not to admit the most minute alteration, and as the Provincial Forces wanted pay, and the Treasury was exhausted, my Lord Loudoun advised him to pass it, which he did.

I beg your Royal Highness will believe, the not subjecting my estate to the Tax, does not by any means reconcile me to.it, I desire to contribute my share to all publick services, in such manner as is just, and consistent with the rights of Government, which I cannot consent should be trampled upon, to the subversion of his Majestys prerogative, and the security of his people, and that I will not take any advantage of this exemption, but whenever a just method of taxing shal be setled, I will most chearfully pay any sum, that shal be wanting, to make upp what I have already given, my proportion of this, and the former Tax.

The Assembly also presented a Militia Bill, in which they provided, that the private Men should [elect?] their Officers to a Major, and these their field Officers; all these republican schemes are cheifly insisted on by Mr. Franklin, who is coming to England for redress of their Grievances, and I am told the application is intended to be made to the House of Commons.

They write that two hundred Men are ordered as the Quota of Pensilvania to the assistance of Carolina, and that Collonel Stanwix with half a Batalion was to march to the western Frontiers, when Mr. Denny was gone to a Treaty with a large body of Indians.

I beg your Royal Highnesses indulgence to add that I have further accounts of Mr. Dennys conduct, which not only confirm what I wrote before, but add several other things much stronger in his disfavour, and this at the desire of several of the principal people of the place; I have told the purport of these Letters to General Napier, and got from him Letters, that may in some sort be a check upon him, and for the present prevent his exposing himself further. I should with the greatest satisfaction make further tryal, if his behaviour was not of such a nature, as in my opinion makes it almost impossible for him here after to act a propper part, and indeed it is in the greatest degree disagreeable, to trust a Man that has taken so many opportunitys to render me, and my Family contemptible in the Eyes of the people there, of which I could send further accounts, but it would be taking upp too much of your Royal Highnesses time; they shal be sent, or I will shew them on your return here, as I recieve your commands to do; I have wrote to him on the subject, and to some of other Gentlemen to certifye the truth of these charges, which I thought propper to do, as I would act by this Gentleman the most favourable part, considering your Royal Highness was so good to name him to me, being desirous ever to approve my self Sir Your Royal Highnesses most humble, most obedient, and most faithful Servant

Spring Garden   THO PENN
 July 18. 1757

[*Endorsed*] Spring Garden; July *18. 1757* Mr. Penn, to *H:R:H.* Rec^d Augt 4: ans^d 22.

CUMBERLAND TO BARRINGTON

(A.L.)

Afferde, july 22^d 1757. N^o *1.*

My Lord Barrington,
 I have received your two Letters of june *26;* & july *12.* . . .

I shall be very glad if you can get the soldiers exchanged as well as the three officers of Shirleys & Pepperel's in which you have succeeded. & I should be glad if you coud get Lt *Fuzer* & a L^t whose name I have forgot likewise exchanged. It will be time enough to settle who shall have *Prevosts'* commission When he resigns. . . .

I am glad they have once began the Enquiry about Mr *Shirley.*

As to what concerns the Draughts for N. *America,* I find it is fixed; & therefore I have nothing to say about it

As to what relates to this Augmentation, I inclose herewith a *Scheme* for it which you will shew to Sir John *Ligonier,* as coming from me

CUMBERLAND TO SIR JOHN LIGONIER
(A.L.)

[July 22, 1757]

. . . . . .

I understand by your Letter that H: M. has been pleased & has settled, that *2000.* Recruits taken equaly from every *Batt^n* in Britain & Ireland should go to *N: America* I hope care will be taken that they are Recruits tho' serviceable men, as we can not spare a number of Disciplined men, out of the few we have left.

. . . . . .

SIR JOHN LIGONIER TO CUMBERLAND
(A.L.S.)

Sir

. . . . . .

Intimation was given by the Kings Commands to me tho not In orders, not to Send the Best men for the American draughts; it has been added according to your R H orders that they must be Recruits,
12 Battaillons Give none [1] viz

1st Batt	Buffs	1st Batt	Cornwallis
	Bentinck		Home
1st Batt	Kings own		Louden
	Amhursts		Hudysons
1st Batt	Kingsleys		Brudnell

The above ten Battaillons named By the King are now Encamped In the Isle of Wight, under the Comand of Sr John Mordaunt Majors

---

[1] These were the troops designed by Pitt for the expedition against Rochefort.

Gen[ll] Conway and Cornwalis, Stewarts and Effinghams second Batt[ns] are on Board the fleet. . . .

London y[e] 3[d] of august 1757

REASONS AND OPPINION DRAWN BY SIR CHARLES HARDY AGAINST GOING TO LOUISBOURG AUG[T] 1757 [1]

(COPY)

For the following Reasons

1st   That the Troop's Stores and Artillery in all probability cannot be Landed in less than ten or twelve days after their arrival at Chapeau-rouge Bay, even if it was attended with more favourable Weather and Circumstances then we have reason to expect near that Coast from this time forward, to Which may be added the Enemy having built a Battery on Black Rock or Cape Noir which annoyce the best and nearest Landing place

2   That if the Troops Should Land Successfully it will require more time to draw the Artillery and other Stores thro' the Swamps and bad Ground from the place of Landing. From this Circumstance alone it must be about the beginning of September before the first Battery can be raised

3   That it also appeared by the examination of Pilots and others that the middle or latter end of September is the latest time their ships can preserve any station off the Port of Louisbourg, or on the Coast of the Island of Cape Breton, and even then with the greatest uncertainly[ty], We do therefore Humbley Conceive should the Fleet be forceed off the Coast by Gales of Wind and stress of Weather, To Which its Subject, they may not be able to return in due time To give any assistance that may be wanted from them

Upon the whole for these Reasons with many others that might be drawn from the minutes of The Council and that under such apparent difficulties and disadvantages as result from a due consideration of the Enemys strength and the forces that can be employed against them, and that the Season will be so far advanced before any progress can be made in the Seige, We cannot advise that the Attempting The Reduction of the Fortress of Louisbourg this Year is for his Majesty's Service but we can not avoid expressing our Concern in finding ourselves und[er] the disagreeable Necessity of giving this advice as the Fleet and Army for this Service did not arrive in due time and the

[1] Enclosure in Loudoun to Cumberland, August 6, 1757.

French Fleet having got into Louisbourg before the arrival of Our Squadron.

VICE ADMIRAL FRANCIS HOLBURNE TO HOLDERNESSE
(COPY)

Newark, in Halifax Harbour 4th Augt 1757

My Lord,

I have the Honor to inclose to your Lordship a Duplicate of what I wrote at Sea in my Passage; Afterwards I found, by examining the Prisoners, that Monsr Beaufremont's Squadron was sailed from Cape Francois for North America, which I imagine to be the Third of the Enemy's come this way, so that to my arrival upon this Coast, I thought it not Advisable to divide the Squadron, & send Part to Cruize to stop up the Port of Louisburgh, as left to my Discretion in my Instructions, & which was too late, as the Enemy's Ships must have been in, long before I came near the Coast; Nor were Our's in a Condition so to do at that Time, being very sickley, & in want of Water: We were Five Days off the Harbour within hearing of the Guns, attended by Twelve or Thirteen Vessels, sent to look out for Us, with Pilots on Board, & could not get in till the 9th of last Month, being in a thick Fog all the Time: The rest of the Squadron & Transports got in that Day, or the next, except what had arrived before Us: The Fogs We met with for a long Time had greatly distressed the Ships, & separated many of them; from being as Healthy as most that ever sailed from England, We had between Nine Hundred & a Thousand Men put ashore to the Hospital, Five Hundred of which will be left behind Sick, besides Two Hundred Dead, since We first Sailed. I found The Earl of Loudoun, & Sir Charles Hardy, arrived here Eight Days before Us, with the Forces from New York; immediately ordered the Squadron to be refitted, & got ready for Sea: One of the Men of War having lost Her Main Mast, & every Thing belonging to it, took up some Time: The Second Day after my Arrival I dispatched away Three Frigates, one Sloop, & Two other Vessels for Intelligence, as one of Our Frigates had been chased off Louisbourgh before: An Officer of Governor Lawrence's, who had been sent by Sir Charles Hardy on the same Errand, returned the 13th, with an Account of seeing Ten or Twelve tall Ships in the Harbour; He took them to be large Men of War, but being chased off there could not inspect more narrowly: This was in a small Shalloop formerly taken from the French, which was thought most proper; & would pass unsuspected.

Captn Rous, who commanded the Frigates, I sent out, took a few Leagues from Louisburgh, one of their Shalloops, &, by a very intelligent Fisherman, confirmed several Men of War being in that Port: (The Weather was so Thick Capt Rous told me that He could not look into the Harbour the whole Time He was out.) So that with the Intelligence We had received before of the Squadron from the West Indies, That from the Mediterranean, and those from Brest, which I gave an Account of in the Duplicate, and which were seen by some of Our Fishermen on the Bank Vert afterwards, the Bank that the French Ships usually come on in their way to Louisburgh, who assured us they were Men of War, & I am certain it could not possibly be any part of our Squadron, convinces us of their having great Strength in these Seas: Lord Loudoun upon this Information thought proper to call a Council of War to inquire into the State of Louisburgh, the Country about, the Strength of the Harbour with regard to the possibility of the Squadrons forcing it, the Place of Landing the Troops, in Gabareuse Bay the nearest to Louisburgh, & every other Thing relating to the Attack of that Fortress, and asked our Opinion which of the Two, Quebec or Louisburgh was the most proper to attack: There was no difficulty in answering, That, as we could not possibly think of leaving such a Strength behind us in the Isle of Breton: Upon this the Council was dissolved and His Lordship gave Orders for embarking the Troops immediately, & I intend proceeding with them to Gabareuse Bay when the Wind & Weather will permit, and give them all the Aid & Assistance in my Power, but there is not the least prospect of being able to force the Harbour, if I had double the Number of Ships. It would have been very happy if we had been off there in the Month of May, as we should have had a Chance of intercepting the different Squadrons of the Enemy: I carry with me every Ship & Vessel here, which are Sixteen of the Line, Four Frigates, & Four Sloops, and have taken into the Men of War, Seven Hundred of the Troops, which are to be landed with the rest: This goes by the Packet that came from New York, and has been detained ever since, expecting daily to be able to send more satisfactory Accounts, and indeed the hearing the different People in Council has taken up some of our Time lately, but not a Moment has been lost with that, as we could not possibly have got out ever since I arrived, except one Day soon after we came in. I should have endeavoured to have been at Sea some time ago with the Squadron off Louisburgh, and left the Frigates & Sloops to bring down the Transports, but Lord Loudoun and the other General Officers, seemed to think our joyning them when they came off Gabareuse Bay, very precarious. Major General Hopson, who had commanded there, particularly mentioned it, as he is a very good Judge of the Weather off that Port, which made me determine to keep all ready here for their Escort.

The Earl of Loudoun thinking it necessary to send two Engineers to look out for the most proper Place for landing the Troops, I ordered two of our best Sailing Sloops with them for that purpose, and directed the Captains to inspect the S:W: Corner of the Bay, the Place proposed to lay the Transports in, after the Troops are landed, and in their Return to look out for us: We are all laying ready, but the Winds are from the Sea every Day, and very thick with Fogs, till there is an Alteration of Weather, there is no possibility of moving with the Fleet. This was our Situation yesterday, when an Express Schooner arrived from Capt Edwards at St John's in Newfoundland, a Copy of his Letter is enclosed, with the List of the French Squadron said to be in Louisburgh, which the Second Captain who is here, agrees in. This too well confirmed me of those Ships being there, as all the former Intelligence agrees with the Number, and many of the Names of the Ships: I immediately acquainted my Lord Loudoun therewith, who I believe is convinced of the Certainty of that Force being there: with additional Regiments, & has, in consequence of that asked my Opinion, as Your Lordship will see by the Enclosed Letter, as likewise my Answer, which is to the best of my Judgement as a Sea Officer: My Lord Loudoun has taken his Resolutions accordingly, and as soon as I have settled with his Lordship the proper Ships to escort the Troops where he proposes (as I find his Lordship has no other Intention of attempting any other Enterprize this year, where the Ships can act jointly with the Army) the Frigates and Sloops being sufficient for that, I shall not loose a Moment afterwards in proceeding with all the Line of Battle Ships off the Port of Louisburg.

The Windsor, & Granada Bomb are just arrived here after a Passage of Nine Weeks.

Another Express will soon follow this, when your Lordship shall be informed of our further Proceedings.

I have the honor to be &c^a

FRA: HOLBURNE

Halifax
Augt 6. 1757

[*Endorsed*] Halifax Augt 4th & 6th 1757 Vice Adm^l *Holburne* R 30th by Capt Loring *N° 6*. the Papers inclosed in this Letter are the same as those in Ld Loudoun's
[*Endorsed again*] Lord Holdernesse G. Sept^r *5:1757*

LOUDOUN TO CUMBERLAND
(COPY)

Halifax 6th August 1757.

SIR,

Enclosed, I have the honor to transmit to Your Royal Highness, a Copy of my Publick Letter, as I thought it might not have come to Your hands otherwise; By it You will see, that the Fleet and Transports from Ireland, did not arrive till the 9th of July, at which time I had the honor to receive, from Major General Hopson, Your Royal Highness's Letter of March 22d, and likewise a Message, to direct and Assist me in my Trade, for both which, I lie under the greatest Obligations to Your Royal Highness: but Alass, Sir, that Transaction was finished in January, on the Intelligence I then had of the Weakness of the Place, and the Wants they had of every thing, and in the hopes, that Our Fleet would arrive before that of the Enemy, Whereas the Enemy had thrown in three Fleets, from different places, with a Garrison and every thing necessary for the defence of the Place, before my Masters Fleet arriv'd in this Country; And Your Royal Highness's Message did not arrive till the 9th of July, by which I was bereft of the benefits of it.

As the Admiral is sending off a Sloop; in order to inform the Kings Ministers, of the Situation of Affairs in this Country, that they may take their measures, before the general Accounts arrive of the Enemys Strength, I have only time, in this Letter, to shew Your Royal Highness some particulars, from whence You will see the difficulties I labour under.

By my last Letter, Your Royal Highness will see, the Necessity I was under at New York of making delays, on Account of Mor Beaufremont's Squadron, and from want of Intelligence of the Motions of the Fleet from England, and the risk the Troops run in bringing them here.

As soon as the Fleet arrived, and brought the Account (tho' not then a certain One) of Ten more french Ships of War being come to this Country, and found that the Fleet could give me very little Assistance in reducing the Place, by which means, all the Men belonging to the Enemys Ships, would be at liberty to be employed in the defence of the Place, I did, in Conjunction with the Admiral, call a Councill of War, which shall come by next Opportunity, as it is realy not yet Copied; The Enquiries are long, and in the very beginning of it, Lord Charles Hay took a very odd turn, and behaved very indecently to almost every Member in the Councill; Seldom sett at the Table but got to the Window, laid up his legs in it and looked out, except in the course of Examining People any thing happened to hit his Fancy, then he Asked odd Questions, grinning and Laughing, and using all the Gestures of a Man out of His Senses: In the Mornings he was Gallopping along the Fronts of the Camp, and every now & then Stopping and Collecting Crouds of People about him, and Haranguing them: And as I had order'd the Engineers to mark out an Angle of a Fort, and Trace out an Attack on it, in order to Shew the Troops their duty at a Siege, in which I employed the Picquets, without any Expence to the Government, whilst the Fleet was repairing the damage they had received in their Masts, and Watering; At this Exercise, where Crowds were always attending, and in the Neighbourhood of which the Troops were Clearing a Piece of Ground, in order to Sew Turnips and other Greens for themselves, the only thing that either prevents or recovers them, out of those inveterate Scurveys we are Infested with in this Country from the Salt Provisions, therefore I provided a Garden here on the Common, as I do in all Places, to be ready at my return.

With those Picquets, Lord Charles held his principal Harangues, not only tending to expose and lessen every Man in Command, by telling the Men, that, that was the only Attack that would be undertaken this Year; that the Admiral was to carry the Fleet up to the Bason, and there have a Mock Sea fight, and then we were to go into Winter Quarters: That it was another Mediteranean Affair; And that altho' We did not Fight, there should be Blood.—These things, I believe Your Royal Highness will think, must have very bad tendencies in Army.— But My Lord went even further, and represented the Hardships of the Mens being Employed in such Works.—As those things happened towards the Close of the Councill of War, and as they arose from his Misfortunes, I did not chuse to Confine him, as I must in that Case have called a New Council of War, which would have occasioned a delay.

In this Situation, as People were Shy of talking before Lord Charles, as he carried every thing to the Line, it became necessary to have private Meetings, to consider the proper methods of proceeding; the first of which was on board the Admirals Ship, where were present, Sir Charles Hardy and Commodore Holmes, Major General Abercromby, Major General Hopson & Captain Fowke; there were two more Meetings afterwards in my room, at both which, all the Members but Lord Charles Hay were present; where, after I Stated to them the Question I should put to them for their advice, they Agreed on the Advice they would give, against undertaking the Siege at this Season of the Year,

The Gentlemen of the Fleet insisted on the Season, as that was what they were Judges of, and did not chuse to enter into the Strength of the Garrison.

In the Council I put my Question, and after talking upon it, it was adjourned to next Morning, in order to prevent Lord Charles from discovering, that the business was carried on without him.

Next morning, before the Councill mett, Major General Hopson started a difficulty on the words of Mr Secretary Pitts last Letter to me, of the 17^t of March, which arrived with the Fleet on the 9^t of July, where he Acquaints me, that he has the Kings Commands, to Explain some part of my Instructions; and goes on,

"By my Letter of the 4^t past, Your Lordship is directed, to begin "with an Attack upon Louisbourg, and to proceed in the next "place to Quebeck: The King still thinks those two places, the "great Object of Offensive Operations for the ensueing Campaign "in America, and Judges the taking of Louisbourg, to be the more "practicable Enterprize: His Majesty Nevertheless, is pleased to "leave to Your Lordship, to use your discretion, with regard to "which of the two abovementioned Attempts, You shall Judge it "most adviseable first to proceed."

The doubt arising from those words, made them Shy of giving any Explanation, on a doubt of the meaning of Instructions; on which it was Judged necessary to wave my first Question, and put the short one Your Royal Highness will see in the Council of War, which put an end to it.

On a further Consideration of the Strength of the Enemy, I could not reconcile myself to acting in that way, of following on Instructions; if that is the meaning of the Words, which I do not see now so strong as when Major General Hopson first Started it, and which occur'd to none of Us at the first reading, and by Quibbling on Words to Shelter myself from Blame, without a prospect of Success, to endanger the entire loss of my Masters Army, which might probably have been attended, with the loss of part of his Dominions in this part of the World, before he could have remedied such a Misfortune.

The last Intelligence, from Captain Edwards, put an end to any doubts on this Subject, and I immediately took the resolution, You will see in my Publick Letter. I send Lord Blakeneys, Major General Kennedys & Major General Murrays Regiments, directly to Fort Cumberland: As Major General Hopson is not able for such an undertaking,

I put them under the Command of Lieutenant Colonel Laurence, who is Acquainted with that part of the Country, and in the Train of getting Intelligence.

I think those three Regiments, Entrenched under the Fort, with the present Garrison, will secure that Post for the Winter.—I put Major General Murrays Regiment entire into that Fort, which is all it can contain: Major General Kennedys Regiment, I put into Annapolis Royal and Pissiguid, which is as much as they can hold: when the Campaign is over, I send Lieutenant General Lord Blakeneys Regiment to Boston; and bring back here, the present Garrison of those Forts; which at once, brings the duty in this Province to be done by Battalion, as Your Royal Highness directed it should.

Here, I leave the remains of the three Regiments that were here, with the Royals and Lieutenant General Braggs, and Lieutenant Colonel Frazers, when they arrive.—The Royal I leave here all Winter, as I apprehend I should lose most of the Oswego Men, were I to carry them into New England: But the other two Battalions, I propose sending to Boston in the Winter, as they cannot be put under Cover here. With those Troops I carry to New York, if the circumstances will permit, I will make a push; but till I arrive there, it is impossible to foresee, what the Situation may be: however, I have sent to have every thing in readiness for what may happen. As the Admiral is impatient, I must here make an end. I am with all Duty and Respect Sir Your Royal Highnesss Most humble and Most Obedient Servant

LOUDOUN

[*Endorsed*] Halifax, August 6th 1757. Lord Loudoun, to *H:R:H:* Rec^d October the 1^t Ans^d Novr 26: inclosing 5: Papers.

BARRINGTON TO CUMBERLAND

(A.L.S.)

War Office 16th August 1757

Sir,

Lieutenant Colonel Frazers Battalion has but one Major with it; Mr Campbell being at Spa in hopes to recover his Limbs, of which he has almost lost the Use. Captain Sutherland of Warburton's has been proposed by the Duke of Argyll and others as Major *en Seconde* to that Battalion, which is certainly in great Want of another field officer; but I have refused recommending any thing of this sort to Lord Loudoun, till I know your R.H.'s pleasure therein.

Lord Loudoun has allow'd Lieutenant Colonel Chapman of the Royal Americans and Captain Mulloy of the 44th Regiment to go out on their pay. This I conceive was not within his Lordship's power; and that he should not have done it without permission. He has apply'd for Warrants confirming this transaction, which I suspend till I re-ceive your R.H.'s Instructions: I believe a Caution to my Lord for the future would prevent a repetition of the same thing; and perhaps in-conveniences might arise if what is done already were set aside. I am Sir with the greatest duty & Respect

Your Royal Highness's most humble & most devoted Servant

BARRINGTON

P.S.

What your R.H. was pleased to mention concerning the Highlanders at the End of your Plan of Augmentation, I have shown to his Majesty and to the Ministers: I have no doubt but that the additional High-land Company's will be sent to America as soon as they are raised; & that none will be suffer'd to remain in the Country, on any pretence.

[*Endorsed*] Cav: Square, August *16. 1757*. Lord Barrington to *H:R:H*. Recᵈ *25*. ansᵈ *28*.

CUMBERLAND TO THOMAS PENN

(A.L.)

Verden, August *22: 1757*.

Mʳ *Penn*, I have received your Letter of July *18:* & am obliged to you for the Several Particulars you inform me of relating to affairs of *America*. But, I am sorry to see the former complaints against Mʳ *Denny* recur again, & indeed, supported from more than one Quarter. I must own, it gives me the more concern that you should have reason to make complaints, & those not groundless against him, as my having recom-mended him for this employment was owing to the Character he bore in the world, & to my own opinion that he would answer the Purpose of that Service he was sent upon to *Pensilvania*. I can not but thank you for the Regard you have shewn me throughout, in this Dispute between Yourself & Mʳ Denny as my Intention & Disposition in his behalf all along, were Solely grounded upon the Persuasion that He was a proper Person, well qualified in every Respect, for discharging that Trust; if His Behaviour proves unjustifiable, I am far from supporting him in it; but, must give way to what is reasonable and just; & what may be most conducive to *H:M:* Service in those Parts.

SIR CHARLES HARDY TO LOUDOUN
(COPY)

Invincible, Halifax Augt 24th 1757

My dear Lord—

We Returned to this Harbour with the Squadron Yesterday, after having look'd into Louisbourg early in the morning of the 20th and there saw the whole of the French ships of Warr amounting to seventeen ships of the Line, besides Frigates Commanded by one, Vice Admiral, one Rear and Two Chef D'Escadres I take for Granted that Fleet are Composed of the Ships assembled from the Cape, Brest and Toulon, a List of them you saw before we saild, and by the Number & the Four Commanding officers having their Flags flying, I should judge they have sent none up the River of St Lawrence, there Appearance was very fine indeed and seem'd to be all in Mottion, Many signals made, and repeated by all the Commanding ships, Boats appeared to be going from the shore full of men to the ships, & some think, they were Unmooring, the wind was fair for them to have slipt, & come out to us and they had Time for it, as we were a long time running in under an easy sail, & brought too Close in. I believe you will join with me in thinking we should have had warm work, if they had come out, a very thick Fog came on soon after we brought too, & obliged us To stand off the Land, so we saw no more of them, In running down to the Harbour, from Cape Gabarouse I saw several Encampments, one of which appeared very large upon a Hill that seem'd to have had the wood Cleared Very lately, Some think, they saw Batteries and Intrenchments in Gabarouse Bay when of the Harboure I saw either the old repaired or a new Battery erected on the light House Ground, & to the Eastward of the light house, Some very large Tents which I Imagine were raised with ships Sails, Numbers of Men appear'd upon the shore & the works of the Toun I look'd for the Black Rock, but being un acquaint'd with the shore, could not find it, but one of our Captains tells me he saw it plain, with a work erected upon it. In short there appears to be every preparation Necessary for Y^r Reception and such a one that in my opinion Must have ended with the Ruin of your Army, if a Landing had been Attempted, I could see but little of Gabarouse Bay, the Knock appears to be only sheltered by some Rocks & by no means a safe Place to Harbour ships.

I confess I felt extremely happy that you were not with us, & I trust when this Account gets home, Admiral Holburne Sent the Speedwell

immediately off with it, peoples minds will Cool upon the disappointment in the Expeditions not going on I am sure whoever will give themselves Time to think must Bless themselves that the Army has been preserved by it and they may take into it, the Fleet too.

The Loss of Fort William Henry, I fear may be followed by Fort
Edwards being abandon'd for want of Sufficient Reinforcements getting
to General Webb in due Time, should this happen I take for Granted
the Settlements on the Mohawks River will be all deserted, and we
must content our selves with Albany for a Frontear, if the Progress of
the Enemy can be stoped there, Your Lordship's presence with the
Troops has been much wanted to raise the drooping Spirits of the
People, who I find are much Alarmed, and Indeed with Great Reason.

What the French will do with their Forces in Louisbourg is not easy,
I am afraid to come at, tho Necessary for our own Conduct, and they
must be Attended, by small Vessells and the best Sailing ships in our
squadron at all Risks there Circumstanced Your Lordship has a hard
Task & a difficult Card to play, and Mr Holburns Situation is not better.

Surely Peoples Eyes in England will be open'd and I trust they will
be Convinced, if our advices get safe home that Conquest on our side
was Impracticable. My Good Lord God Bless you, & may you Land in
Time to stop Mr Montcalms Career, Success & Honour attend you in
this Cause my Respects Attends General Abercromby, Forbes & Friends
with You and believe me

My Dear Lord—Your most faithfull humble Servant

(Sign'd)

CHS HARDY

P:S: Some of the Transports with Frasers arrived this afternoon they
parted with the man of warr and the rest off the Island of Sable three
days ago, that we may expect them every hour Montgomerys parted
with thise about 150 Leagues to the westward of Ireland & stood to the
Southward in their way to Carolina.

[Endorsed] Copy of Sir Chas Hardy's Letter to Lord Loudon Dated. Halifax
24th August 1757.—Receved Septr 6t 1757.

CUMBERLAND TO BARRINGTON

(A.L.)

Head Qurs at Rothenburg, August 28: 1757

My Lord Barrington, I have received your Letter of the 16: If Major
Campbell, of Fraser's Battalion, quits, I have no Objection to Captain

Sutherland, of *Warburton's;* who is a very proper Man. But, I can not allow of *three* Majors to a Highland Battalion.

As to what Lord *Loudoun* has done, about Lieuten^t Colonel *Chapman,* & Captain *Mulloy:* tho' I don't approve of it in general, yet, I think it was necessary upon that occasion; & therefore, hope it will be confirmed.

I am glad that you have Settled the additional Highland Companies upon Such a Foot, that you have no doubt that they will be Suffered to remain in the Country, on any Pretence.

I must desire that you will acquaint Sir John *Ligonier,* for the Army in general; & to all General officers commanding Corps, Sir John *Mordaunt* not excepted, that I am Surprised to hear that my orders as to the *Fireing* and *Posting* of the officers, approved & confirmed by His Majesty, are changed according to the Whim & Supposed Improvements of every fertile Genius; and that therefore, it is my *positive order,* that in the *Forming* & *Telling off* of Battalions, they conform *exactly* to those *Standing orders,* which they have *all* received; and that no one presume to introduce new Schemes, without their having been approved of by His Majesty, or by my orders.

CUMBERLAND TO HOLDERNESSE

(A.L.)

Stade, Septr 15: 1757

My Lord Holderness, I have now by me three Letters of yours, un-answered. . . . I am heartily sorry to see by them the small Hopes there now remains of any thing considerable being done in *N. America* this Year; & I am the more sorry for it, as I am convinced both by my personal knowledge of Lord *Loudoun* & by His Letters, that all we can hope for would have been done, had our Forces been able to assemble earlier this year; & Lord *Loudoun* seems to have taken the most prudent Part in making what Haste he can to support the Force under Co^l *Webb,* who seemed to run some Risk, if Lord *Loudoun* can't get back in time. . . .

CUMBERLAND TO BARRINGTON

(A.L.)

Stade, Sept^r *15: 1757*

My Lord Barrington, I have received your two Letters of the 30: of last month & 2^d of this; by the first of which I am heartily sorry to see that after the immense Expence we have been at in our *Am*ⁿ Expedition, there is so little likelyhood of any thing being done this year; and what is still more unfortunate for England, by Lord *Loudoun's* state of the Case to me, he does not seem blamable for it.

As you mention Co¹ Perry's vacancy, I humbly am of opinion that the Regt: ought to be given to some of the Lt. Co¹ˢ that have been upon Service there; & Lᵗ Co¹ *Lawrence,* appears to me to be the properest; if H.M. aproves of Lt. Co¹ *Lawrence,* I should humbly be of opinion that some of the Colonels of the 62. should succeed Colonel *Perry,* & Colonel *Lawrence* succeed to that Battalion become vacant in the *Royal American,* that by that means he may continue with his own Corps in *nova Scotia.* And this may easily be settled from the Return & State of H:M: Forces in N: *America,* which was transmitted by Lord *Loudoun* in his last Dispatches; and wherein he mentions the manner in which he proposes to dispose of them.

What you mention of Lord *Charles Hay* being in arrest proves but two true; & as I fear he is out of his senses, I should think it great goodness in *H.M.* if he would give him the Governᵗ of *Sterling Castle* which is vacant, in lieu of his Regiment; which *H.M.* might give to Co¹ Whitmore, of the 53. In this Case, Co¹ *Ross* whose Health will not allow him to remain at *Antigua* might have Co¹ *Whitmore's* & Lᵗ Co¹ *Talbot* of the 38. might succeed Co¹ *Ross* in the Regiment. you will be so good to mention these Proposals of mine to nobody, till *H.M.'s* Pleasure is known whether they shall succeed or no.

As to Co¹ *Haldane's* Request I see no Reason why he should be struck off of the List of *Lᵗ Colonels. . . .*

LOUDOUN TO CUMBERLAND

(A.L.S.)

New York October 17: 1757

Sir

As Major Horgraff is going home, who will take Care to deliver my Letters safe, I take the Opportunity of writing to Your Royal Highness a Private Letter.

You will be surprised I have said so little of the Affairs in the Back Country. The real Case is I know very little with any Certainty of what past there, more than what I have received from Mr Webb, who sent off the Packet two Days before I arrived with his Account of it.

The Country make great Complaints of his Conduct and of his Treatment of their People. As to the first, I am told by Mr Delancy that on an Information of the Enemy's advancing he went to Fort William Henry, where he received certain Accounts of it, which he concealed and returned to Fort Edward from whence he writ to acquaint Lieut. Col. Monro.

As to the Complaints of his ill Usage of the Militia, it rather appears to me that the Militia came very slow up, and when they were arrived to about the Number of 2000 the Desertion from that time was equal to their Acquisition by the Arrival of new Reinforcements. And this, Lieut. Govr. Delancy, who was then at Albany, took many of them Prisoners, and killed one of them who would not be stopt, told me.

As soon as I arrive at Albany I will inform my self of every Particular. If I see Cause, which I hope will not be the Case, I will order a Number of the Principal Officers to examine and report.

I have given your Royal Highness, in my Letter, several Reasons for not chalking out a Plan for the Operations of next Campaign. There is one more which remains.

When I arived here I was in great hopes with the Force I brought with me that I should have been able to have pushed forward to Tienderoga, but when I made a Computation of the time each part of the Operation would take, without Opposition, and the Difficultys I had to overcome, I found it impracticable.

I likewise found that the Season would not permit my building a Fort at Fort William Henry that might protect Vessels I might build to enable me to attack Tienderoga in the Spring.

On which it occurred to me that if the Winter proved to be hard Frost, with a good deal of Snow, I could take it much easier in the Winter than I could do in the Summer, and that then I should be free of the Bush Fight, in which they have so great an advantage by their Indians and Canadians.

If I succeed in this, I am then Master to go into their Country by that Road and can save the Government that intolerable Expence of Transport. Besides the Preparations for what ever Operations are to be carried on will depend on ourselves, and of course will be ready at the proper time, and will not subject us to the Arrival of Fleets, which I never expect to see in those Seas in time.

I have been the more encouraged to enter into this Plan from the Information I have got from several Prisoners who have made their Escape from the Enemy, particularly one who was taken in the Spring, 1755, at the Great Meadows, and has been a Servant to a French Officer ever since.

By those I find that the People who attacked Fort William Henry last Winter did not suffer as I expected; and by Lieut: Cols: Gage and Burton, who both marcht out on that Occasion and lay among the Snow for many Nights without Tents, that it is not so terrible a thing as they expected, and I find we had no Men disabled by it.

The method of lying on those Occasions is: as soon as you take up your Ground, they make Bush Tents of Pine Boughs, two opposite to each other, leaving a Space between them in which they make great Fires, and the men in each of the Tents lie with their Feet to the Fires in which Situation they are tolerably comfortable.

My Plan is, after I have settled all my Business above and fixed the Winter Quarters, to return here to give no Suspicion, and as soon as the Frost is hard enough with a good deal of Snow to carry me over every thing, to set out in Slayes as if for Boston, but to go directly to Albany, where I will have every thing in readyness to set out the next Day.

For this Service I propose to carry three thousand of the Regular Troops and one thousand Rangers, both to enable me to send back such as I find not able to bear the Cold and Fatigue, but to be strong enough to oppose any Force they may be able to send to the Relief of the Place in case I am discovered.

As I dare give no previous Notice to equip those Men for such an Expedition, I must find other Pretences to provide the things necessary for it, such as Shoes, those I have got, warm Stockings, Socks, Mittens and woolen Caps, those are ordered for different Regts. and will be ready in a Fortnight. Flannel waistcoats I have; those first ordered for the Royal Americans were taken at Sea; the second set is just arrived. I say the Men are already provided, and I will not put them to the Expence of new ones till those they have are wore out. And every Soldier in this Country carrys a Blanket, and I will have some ready in case of Accidents. Snow Shoes I can supply by my Rangers, as I will take care they shall have a large Provision for themselves, and a few Men going with them in the Front beat a Path for the others to follow without them. Clamps for walking on the Ice is the most difficult to provide without giving Suspicion, but I think I shall accomplish that.

The next Article is Provisions. I shall supply my self at the different Posts till I leave Fort Edward, for which purpose I will take care that they shall be properly supplied. From Fort Edward I will carry Bisquit, Pork, some live Cattle, and a little Butter, with some Rum and Ginger, which last we find of great use, as it prevents the bad water from throwing the Men into Fluxes.

For the Transportation of those things I would provide Hand Slays which the Men could draw, but they would discover me at once. Therefore I must press Slayes with Horses, which at that Season of the Year I think I can do in one Day sufficient to serve me, as each Slay carrys the double of what a Waggon does with the same number of Horses.

For the Maintainance of them I shall lay in Forage at Fort Edward, which I can do without Suspicion as tis only taking care to have a sufficient Stock to leave when I bring down the Troops at the End of the Season; besides, I can carry Forage from Albany to Fort Edward with those Slays that are to carry Provisions from thence.

The Articles [Artillery] I propose to carry are principally Mortars and a few light Cannon and some Scaling Ladders, all which are ready above.

The Road I at present propose is from Fort Edward to Fort William Henry, and from thence down Lake George; my People are now employed and before that time I shall know every practicable Path.

If the Frost proves hard, with Snow, I think I can hardly fail to take a Garrison of three or four hundered Men in it. If tis open rainy Weather tis impossible to go to it, besides I should lose the whole Troop in attempting it.

On this Expedition I must go myself, for neither M.G. Abercromby nor Mr Webb's Constitutions are able to bear either the Fatigue or the Cold.

I do not expect to find any Reluctance in the Men to going on this Service, but still further to prevent it I shall go without a Tent and live as they do.

If I succeed in this Attempt, I think it will open a Door to get into Canada this Way. Then nothing more will be wanted, with the Fleet you must have in this Country, for the Defence of it, but to stop early their throwing in Provisions and Supplys of any kind, and to make a Feint as if Quebec was the Point in order to divide their Force.

Your Royal Highness will observe I have said nothing of this Plan in my Publick Letter.

In the first Place the Execution must depend on the Season, and I do not choose to raise their Expectations when I am not sure of gratifying them, and I can have no Aid from home in the Execution of it.

In the second Place, so many People must see my Publick Letter that it can be no Secret, and I do assure you that I have often accounts from Montreal of what is doing in London in relation to the Service here.

As your Royal Highness has been so good as to allow me to think aloud to you, I have made use of that Permission and laid before you my first Thoughts on a Plan I have still time to make many Amendments to, and I do promise you I shall not be idle.

By next Packet I shall send an Account of the Winter Quarters, which at first Sight may surprize you, but I hope the above Plan will explain and justify it.

My general Plan is to have as many Regts. above as I can quarter. I hope on the Mohawk and Hudsons River to have Six or Seven Regts. And as the Regts. that have been in the Back Settlements are greatly infected with the Scurvey, I propose to keep the Regts that came last over, there, and what more men are necessary for that Service I propose drawing from the other Corps, keeping above so many Companys as I can form of men in perfect Health, and forming all those into a Detachment that are any way infected with the Scurvey and sending them down to the Low Country for the Benefit of Vegetables and to recruit for their Corps. The 44th and 48th Regts. I think will particularly be in this Situation, as both their Commanding Officers and their Men are necessary for my Plan.

Of the Troops that go into Pensilvania, I propose to put as many as I can into Reading, Lancaster, and York, as these are good Quarters, cover the Frontier, and are the best Places for recruiting.

When I have settled the Quarters in the Back Country I will dispose of the others in the great Towns, so as to be able to collect them.

This brings me to mention Sir John St Clair. He recovered so as to desire to go with the 55th Regt who I had ordered to clear the Road thro' the Highlands in their way to Albany. There are very few Inhabitants in that part of the Country, so that I could not get it done by them, and by opening this Road I shall have a Communication the whole Winter between New York and Albany for Troops and Carriages, which, while we had only a Communication by Water, was commonly shut up for four Months every Winter.

This has brought back Sir John's former Disease, and his other Kidney is now supperating. If he recovers, Dr Huck thinks it will be necessary for him to go to Bath, but there are many bad Symptoms attend his Case.

I acquainted Your Royal Highness with the Account M: G: Hopson gave me of what he understood to be your Intention as to Captain Scott, and that I had made him Major of Brigade. Capt Scott seemes to be a very good Man, but for the Duty of Deputy Quarter Master General he is in no Shape equal to Major Robertson. Besides, that Department in this Country is so extensive that I must have a great deal of Labour to instruct every new Man that comes into it, for which Reason I propose to leave things on the present footing till I have the Honour to receive your Commands.

There is one thing more I must beg leave to trouble you to read in my Bad hand, which is in Relation to my Friend Governor Pownal, who is the greatest Man I have yet met and from whom I forsee more trouble to whoever Commands in this Country than from all the People on the Continent, except he quarrels with the People of his own Government, which I think he is likly to do. As to his own Government, he has hitherto managed there with a very high Hand. But they have found out that if they Disput [are resolute] he will compound, and it appears to me as if they would not submit much longer.

His Vanity and Pride are beyond all I ever saw before. I err every Day in those Points from not understanding Forms and the Honours due to him, without Intention.

His knowledge of this Country is extreamly superficial and in many Cases erroneous.

He has no knowledge of Men. All merit consists in joining implicitly in his Opinions and in Adulation of his Perfections.

As to his Notions of what is necessary for an Army, and the Powers that must be in the Person that commands them at the time that War is actually in the Country, he has formed them from a superficial Reading of Law at School without any Practice. Every Act of a General is an Infringement on the Liberty of the People, and if the Civil Magistrate does not furnish Carriages every thing must stand still, and if he does not give Quarters the Troops must perish in the Streets. But where his own Power is concerned, there he has no Bounds.

Altho we are great Friends, he has conceived an immense Jealousy of me; and it will be necessary for me to give Your Royal Highness some few Instances to show you that I do not speak without Book. In this last Case I wrote to the Governor from Sea, all which went open thro' Mr Pownal's Hands to forward, and to enable him to cooperate with me. I applied to Governor Belsher of the Jerseys to have a Body of Militia ready, in case I found them necessary on my Arrival. The Governor fell ill and died just as I arrived here, and the Council acquainted me of his Death and that the eldest Councilor on whom the Government devolved in the Absence of the Lieut. Governor declined acting, from whence no Act of Government could be done in that Province. This gave Mr Pownal very great Offence, in so much that he could not conceal it from me. I showed him that in Consequence of my Instructions and of the Instructions to each Governor on the Continent I had called for Aid, and as at that time the Government of the Jerseys happened to be in a Situation in which it could not act, it was the Duty of the Council to inform me of their Incapacity of furnishing that Aid at that time; notwithstanding when he went from me to the Jerseys he rated them for writing any Letter to me; what Business had I to meddle with any Civil affairs where he was Lieut. Governor.

He has acquainted the People there that he has taken Care of them, that he has found a very proper Person for their Governor, and he was ready to set out as soon as Mr Belsher's Death should be known; and many such things, as he has chose to have the Apperance of having the Direction of every thing in America.

The State of the Affair above was: Mr Morris who was formerly Governor of Pensilvania is the Second Councilor in the Jerseys. The eldest Councilor is an old weak infirm Man, and Mr Morris wanted to have the Management of that Province, and had endeavered underhand to prevent the eldest Councilor from acting, and writ me a very artfull Letter from the Council to throw it into my Way to advise him, in the present Situation of Affairs, to act. This I saw, and as I thought him a very improper Person for that Trust, as he is one of the great Claimers in that Province upon the Proprietory Right, has great Causes depending, and by getting the Seales into his Hands could have aided himself and his Party in these Causes, therefore I writ him a very civil Letter containing nothing, and immediately acquainted Mr Pownal at Boston of Governor Belcher's Death, all which I showed him on his Arrival here.

I must beg leave to give your Royal Highness one Instance of his Notions of Military Power.

On my Arrival in this Country I found at Albany the Governor, Sir Charles Hardy, and the Lieut. Governor, who is likewise Chief Justice. As there were no Carriages provided for the Army, I applied for Warrants to press twenty Waggons to carry Stores to Schenectady, which were to go with Mr Webb to Oswego. They immediately issued these Warrants and sent out these officers, but by those I could get only five, and as the Service was urgent, I immediately pressed what I wanted.

Mr Pownal represented to me the terrible Infringement this was on the Liberty of the Subject and that I should be undone by it immediately; but not being able either to convince me of that or to let the Business stand still till the People should be in the Humour to do it, he gave me over and I did not see him for ten Days, altho he was my Secretary with a very good Sallary.

This he did from a Notion that as I was a Stranger I could not go on without his Assistance, but finding that the Business went on without him and that I did not send for him, he returned.

The next thing he undertook was to prove to me that Sir Charles Hardy must certainly command the Troops that were quartered in the Town of New York, the Capital of the Province, where he resided himself. When he was beat out of that, then he was clear there could be no Dispute between Sir Charles Hardy's Command and any Officer under me. I showed him the Command was totally Military, that in no shape the Governor could have any Command over them, and that if I had the Command, it must descend in my Absence to the next Officer in Rank, and so on to the End. His next Point was whether in case the Governor should call out the Militia to defend any part of the Country whilst I was at a distance with the Army, if I would take the Command of them. I showed him that by the King's Commission I was to have the Command of every Man in Arms; but that he could not imagine that I was so fond of Command as to be riding all over the Country to command Militia, but that where ever I was I must command all Men in Arms.

He remained with me long enough after this to see that except in time of War the Military Power came in to support the Civil; where it could not execute its own Orders all Business must stand still and the Country be undone. But since he returned from England he is back where he was. At Halifax he begun with insisting that he, as Governor, should have the Command of what ever Troops were quartered in the Barracks of Castle William. I again showed him that he could have no Command of the Troops, and that I command that and every other Castle in America.

I am afraid he has not stopt there (but this I cannot say with absolute Certainty). But I have a strong Suspicion that he has been endeavouring to debauch Lieut. Gov: Delancy, and will try others to resist what he calls Military Power. But a little time will show, and when I have an opportunity your Royal Highness shall know what happens, as I mean this Intelligence at present only for your self.

At the same time he professes the greatest Personal Friendship for me, altho I am forced to set him right very often.

He has told me that he is still to continue my Secretary as he is on the Establishment, and for that purpose that he has a Liberty to be absent from his Government.

I have paid him his Sallary up to the 24th of June and shall continue till I am told that tis wrong, as it will be a Handle to keep him right. Tis necessary your Royal Highness should know that from the Beginning he thought it an Afront to be my Secretary. That appeared early, by his insisting to have some other title. Many were proposed to me, which I have forgot, as I said he might take any he pleased. But by Accident this came out stronger, for when he went to England he desired I might open all Letters that came directed for him, particularly those from his Brother, as they would probably contain News of the Affairs in Europe.

The first that arrived from his Brother I opened, by which it appeared that Mr Pownal had represented to him the Disgrace it was to him to be on the Footing of my Secretary, and that he could not submit to it. The main of his Brother's Letter was to show him that it was both honourable and very profitable to him. This put an entire Stop to my opening of his Letters. But that Letter I have kept, as I was ashamed to give it him, as it showed so much Weakness.

I ask Pardon for troubling your Royal Highness with so long a Narrative, but as I think Disputes will arise and I am far from being sure what Representations he will make, I thought it right you should be apprised of it, and see the Reasons for my Suspicion.

In my other Letter I have showed your Royal Highness the great Number of Troops that are employed at present in Nova Scotia and South Carolina, and how that robs the Main Body and weakens them.

I hope to receive Orders as to Nova Scotia, both as to changing the Corps and the Number to be left there.

As to South Carolina, I think there is more Force there than necessary and the Highlanders do not appear to me so proper for that Service as for being with the Army. And if I were to bring back Lieut. Col. Bouquet, Lieut. Col. Montgomery seems to me too young for that Command among such a Sett of People as he must have to deal with there, and at such a Distance that if any Dispute or Accident happen, it takes a long time before I can be informed or have it in my power to apply a Remedy.

The Sending that Battalion there seems to me to be a Measure taken on the Application of the People of that Colony. And if those Sorts of Applications are to take place, the Army will be posted in such a Situation that they will neither be able to support one another in a Defensive War or to make any Attack on the Enemy in an Offensive one.

I have acquainted your Royal Highness that Mr Campbell the Engineer is dead. The Service has not suffered much by it. If you should approve of it, I am of Opinion that Mr McKellar would be of more use here than any other Man, as he knows so much of the Country and has been in the two principal Places in Canada. If he is sent out, there will be no occasion for Mr Montresor's removing.

The Accounts I have just received by the Packet of the Supperiority the Enemy have in Numbers against your Royal Highness gives me that Concern which a Man feels who is thoroughly attached to his Master's Interest, and who has his General's Success and Satisfaction sincerly at heart. I am so little informed of your Situation that I do not know where to look for Troops to put you on an Equality with the Enemy in Numbers. Could I see that, I should be much easier in my Mind than I feel at present.

As I can see no Certainty from any Information I have got of your Royal Highness's returning to London this Winter, I have allowed Mr Fox to see my Letters to you, as I can depend on his Secrecy; and it appears to me necessary that some one there should know the Contents. This I hope will not appear wrong to Your Royal Highness.

I am with all Duty, Sir, Your Royal Highness's most Humble and most Obedient Servant

LOUDOUN

WILLIAM SHIRLEY TO CUMBERLAND

(L.S.)

MAY IT PLEASE YOUR ROYAL HIGHNESS.

As I could not have the honour of an Audience at your Royal Highness's last Levée, I beg leave, Sir, to lay before your Royal Highness the purport of what I intended to have say'd.

Some time before your Royal Highness left England, an Inquiry was order'd to be made into my late Conduct, as Commander in chief of his Maj^y's Forces in North America, by a Board of General Officers.

As I had not the least Doubt, Sir, that in such case I could clear up my Behaviour in every branch of his Maj^y's Service, to the intire satisfaction of your Royal Highness, and to the whole Nation, against any Imputations of what kind soever, I sollicited, several Months, to have the benefit of that Inquiry; But some Circumstances prevented my having the Effect of it.

As I could have no Opportunity to make Application to your Royal Highness upon that Occasion, when abroad, I had Thoughts of reporting to his Maj^y for his Royal Consideration of my Case; But as I had it at heart to clear up my behaviour to your Royal Highness against all Imputations, I chose to wait your Royal Highness's return, in hopes that your Royal Highness would then permit me to have the honour of doing it.

I hope your Royal Highness will not disapprove of my mentioning upon this Occasion, that thro' the whole Course of the last Warr with France; which I had the Chief Conduct, and Direction of in North America, everything then succeeded there for his Maj^y's Service: The Events of that Warr, and the National Advantages gain'd in it are so perfectly known to your Royal Highness, that I need not mention them here.

As to the present War, Sir, I have been principally instrumental in every part of his Maj^y's Service in it, which has been attended with Success, particularly the Expedition against Beau Sejour, and the other French Incroachm^ts in Nova Scotia; of my Conduct in which I had the honour to have his Maj^y's Royal Approbation signify'd to me; And I have not been in the least accessary to any Misfortune, which has befallen his Maj^y's Service in the whole Course of it: For neither the loss of Oswego, which happen'd seven Weeks after the Expiration of my Command, nor the failure to prosecute the Expedition ag^t Crown point can justly be imputed to me, as I can fully evince by incontestable facts.

Upon transmitting the Account of my Conduct from Oswego and New York in 1755 to be lay'd before his Maj^ty (the Justness of which I can verify) his Maj^ty was pleased to order it to be signify'd to me; "that "his Removal of me from the Command of his Forces in North America "was not owing to his Dissatisfaction with my Services; that on the con- "trary it was his Intention, as a Mark of his Royal Favour, to Appoint "me to be Governour of Jamaica."

But since my Return to England, Sir, I have had the Mortification to find that Injurious Representations, from America, of some parts of my Conduct, have so far operated to my prejudice, that I am deprived of every Mark of his Maj^y's Royal favour, to which a long series of faithful services had before advanced me, without having acquir'd any private Fortune in his Maj^y's Service to support me out of it.

I hope therefore your Royal Highness will pardon my being so Anxious, and Importunate to obtain a favourable Access to your Royal Highness; which I shall ever esteem the highest honour.

I have the Honour to be, Sir, Your Royal Highness's most Dutiful, and most Obedient Servant,

W. SHIRLEY

Conduit Street Novr 19. 1757.

Cumberland to Loudoun

(A.L.)

Cranbourn Lodge Novr 26: *1757.*

My Lord Loudoun, I have not improved the opportunity of writing to you by the Packet-boat which has sailed for *N: America,* since my arrival in England, because I could not inform you of Particulars relating to myself, which had not yet taken place then tho' resolved upon by me, at that time. The unfortunate circumstances of the Campaign in Germany & *some other particular* Reasons, have induced me to determine to lay down entirely all military command. I was willing to give you the earliest Information that I COULD, WITH PROPRIETY, of the Step I have taken; and therefore, I make use of the first Conveyance that I can write to you, to acquaint you of it.

The Multiplicity of affairs during this campaign in *Germany,* has been the only cause which has prevented my acknowledging & answering the Several Letters I have received from you, during that time. I can assure you I have read them all with that Satisfaction, your Dispatches have always given me, as these latter ones have afforded me fresh Proof of that Diligence, Care & Prudence & Zeal with which you have all along exerted yourself in His Majesty's Service, since you have been in N: *America.*

As I am always inclined to promote every Thing in my Power, which may be conducive to your advantage, I must own to you I am sorry that the Step I have thought proper to take, and which you easily conceive must have been the Result of mature consideration with myself, deprives me of the Pleasure I should have to assist you, as heretofore, in the arduous & important Task you are engaged in, & which I make no doubt, but what you will continue to use the same constant & active Endeavours to fullfill, as you have done hitherto. But you may always depend upon my sincere good wishes & be assured I remain your very affectionate—tho' useless Friend.

A Description of the Town of Quebeck
Its Strength and Situation [1]
(COPY)

1757

General
Description

This Place consists of what they call the upper and lower Town, which are parted from one another by a high Cliff or Precipice of Rock, runing in the form of a Horse Shoe, and is a natural Fortification to above three fourths of the upper Town.

Cliff or
Precipice

This Cliff begins up the River, a good way above the Town, its greatest Height (about 200 feet) is at the south End if it; it runs from thence with a Curve outwards to the North End, where it may be about 80 or 90 feet high. In this part near the North End, is a Break which forms one of the two principal Communications between the upper and lower Towns. From the north End, it runs with a Curve likewise outwards to the southwest, and loses itself some little way in the Country; this part runs from 80 to 50 feet high, with a Break near the southwest End, which forms the other principal Communication between the two Towns.

Upper
Town

The upper Town, from these differences of Heights in the Precipice, has a Declination from the south and southeast, to the north and northwest; the surface of it has several Waves and risings, and there being a pretty many Churches, religious Houses and Gardens, there is a great deal of vacant Ground. The Buildings are retired from the Edge of the Precipice on the east side, a few excepted, such as the Governor's House and about ten or a dozen more to the Northward of it.

Lower
Town

The lower Town is a flat slip that runs along the foot of the Precipice and follows its turnings, a great part of it seems to be made Ground. Upon the southeast, East and northeast sides, it is bounded by the main Trough or Channel of the River, which is the anchoring place for the Shipping; and upon the north, northwest, and west

[1] "Major's Mackellar's Description of Quebec," printed in A. Doughty and G. W. Parmelee, *The Siege of Quebec and the Battle of the Plains of Abraham*, II, 271–280, seems to be an amplification of this original draft. It has references to a map drawn by Mackellar, which was probably based upon the plan in Charlevoix.

sides, it is bounded by a large Bay, which runs in to the Country where the Land is low; at the Bottom of this Bay, which is dry at low water, there runs in a small River called St Charles fordable at a pathway which leads across the Bay when the Tide is out; The Bay then has the appearance of a spacious strand, but the Bottom of it is a flat Rock which looks as if it had been trimmed with a Tool.

East Side

The lower Town upon the east Side, consists of the Dock Yard (which has only one Slip where they build 70 Gun ships) and an anchor Wharf; from the Dock to the north end, it consists of the principal Merchants Houses and Magazines; this is much the richest part, the most spacious and where the Buildings are most crowded, there is a Church and a Market Place.

North and West Sides

At the north End and a little to the westward of it, the Town is very Narrow, there being only single Houses, inhabited by poor people, and with small passages from one to another; from thence it widens gradualy as far as the Intendant's house, which is one of the last Buildings upon that side. Within the Intendants there are some of the King's Magazines and a Slip for building of small Vessels.

Principal Communications

There are two principal Communications where Carriages can pass between the upper and lower Towns, one upon the East side near the north End, and the other upon the west side near the west End.

East Communication

The east side Communication, leads from the rich part of the Town above mention'd, with three Windings or turnings in to the upper Town, the middle turning goes along the front of the Bishop's Palace leaving it upon the Right; at the foot of this turning, there is a passage to the right, which leads to a Battery upon the top of the Precipice behind the Bishop's Palace.

West Communication

The west side Communication leads from the lower Town, a little way within the Intendants, through a Gateway into the upper Town; the first turning to the Left within the Gateway, leads to the top of the Precipice behind the Nunnery. Between these two Communications, there are several others smaller, but they are so narrow and steep, that they scarce deserve the name of Communications.

Defences to the River or Anchoring Ground

The upper Town has the following Defences towards the River or Anchoring Ground.

Nᵒ of Guns

A Battery halfway up the Cliff, over the principal Dock, in a Line with the back Front of the Governor's House . . . . " " 14

A Battery of 57 Guns upon the top of the Precipice behind the Bishop's Palace and Gardens, of which there are about 36 that bear upon the River . . . . " " 36

The lower Town has the following Defences to the Anchoring Ground.

A Battery above the Dock which I am informed consisted of . . . . " " 16

A Battery between the Dock and the Beach or landing place . . . . " " 8

A Battery below the landing place . . . . . " " 12

Total Guns that bear upon the River or anchoring Ground . . . . " " 86

Upper Town secure from Fire of Shipping

The upper Town I think cannot be hurt much by the Fire of Shipping, it stands too high and is too much retired from the edge of the Precipice, to be within reach of Canon, and there is so much vacant Ground, that I think there may be a great number of Shells thrown, before they can do it any considerable Dammage.

Lower Town exposed to the Fire of Shipping

The lower Town upon the east side is very much exposed to the fire of Shipping, and the only part worth firing at, being the richest, it is a fair object for Canon, and the Buildings are so much crouded, that a shell can scarce fail to do Execution.

Attack from the lower upon the upper Town

In case of making an attack from the lower upon the upper Town, the communications above mentioned are the only places where it can be done, and they are easily defended and communicate one, with another only at low Water.

Places to be first secured

If an attack upon the upper Town should succeed, I think the properest place to be first secured, is the great Square and all the Buildings round it, especially the Hospital, Jesuits Convent and Church opposite to them. It will be proper to secure the 57 Gun Battery at the same time. These places can have no Fire of Canon to defend them.

Citadel

There is what they call a Citadel in the front of the Governor's House, but it seems designed for the Defence of that House only, and serves as a Court yard to it; it has very little Command of the streets, and none in the places above mentioned.

Defences
towards
the Land

The Defences of the Place to the Land, I can give but an imperfect Account of, but as far as I cou'd see or learn, they consist of a Fort and a Tower which stand upon the highest Ground at a small Distance from one another at the south End of the Town; without them there are Lines, which upon the highest Ground over the River, are doubled one without the other; the Inner Line runs quite accross the Neck, to the Bay on the north west side, they are built of Masonry and have some Bastions which are very irregular; the little I saw of them are thin and without Ramparts, and seem to have been designed only against small Arms. I saw Embrazures in some places viz. opposite to the Intendants, and upon the highest Ground at the south End of the Town, from the narrowness of the Embrazures, I concluded the Walls must be thin. I believe in general, the place to the Land must be weak, both from the difficulty they made of our seeing it, and from what I had learned of servants who had strolled out that way.

Charlesvoix's Plan shews most of the Particulars above mentioned.

Navigation down the River St Laurence from Quebeck.

I observed only two difficulties in the Navigation of this River, which are pointed out in the Cart lately published by Mr Jefferies, I shall however mention them that they may be the less lyable to escape observation.

The first Difficulty I observed was in making the Traverse or Crossing at the lower End of the Isle of Orleans, where the Channel is very narrow and somewhat crooked. The Directions and Soundings in the Draught seem sufficient to shape the Course; it must be attempted only with a fair Wind and enough of Day-light; for these reasons we came to an Anchor a little above it, and had full two hours Daylight and a tolerable Wind.

The next difficulty was at the Island of Coudres, where there is a Whirlpool that forms two different Currents according as it happens to be Tide of Flood or Ebb, and the passage of it is not to be attempted, without a fair Gale sufficient to stem the Current, otherwise the Vessels infallibly run ashore.

Charlesvoix I remember mentions several other Difficulties in the Acount of his Voyage up the River, which ought to be perused, he particularly mentions some danger round the red Island; He says there is no Harbour in the Island of Anticosti, contrary to the received opinion.

There are probably several other difficulties and the Voyage seems to require the assistance of a good Pilot, who knows the anchoring places and Headlands.

Fire Rafts

The Baron Diesko and his Aid de Camp talked of an Invention, the french had discovered for infallibly destroying Ships going up the River; At Quebeck we found this Invention to be, what they call fire Rafts, of which there is a store provided. They are Logs of Timber tyed together at one End, and coated over with a strong Composition; they are to be set on Fire and floated off from some of the Islands down the stream, and to Cling round the Ships Bows and set them on fire.

Tho this Invention does not seem to threaten much danger, especialy if the Boats are out, it will be right to be prepared against its taking Effect.

Landing the Troops

It will be advantageous to land the Troops on the Town side which is the North. Below Cape Torment, the Mountains are impassable; the Landing must therefore be on Cape Torment Meadows, in the north Channel, or above the Isle of Orleans, and I am very doubtfull, whether their landing can be cover'd by the shipping in any of these places.

Their landing on the south side, will be attended with Crossing the River and a second landing.

[*Endorsed*] Description of *Quebec,* from Charlevoix &c: by .... *1757.*

Cumberland to Loudoun

(A.L.)

Cranburn Lodge, Dec^r *10: 1757.*

My Lord Loudoun, I had wrote my other Letter to be Sent to you by
the first conveyance, when I received your ample Dispatches of August
the *16.* continued till october *17:* with the Inclosures, Duplicates &c &
in particular, your *Private* Letter, in your own Hand, of this last Date
from *New York.* I very sincerely return you thanks for your attention
in transmitting to me all those Papers, which contain full & convincing Proofs of your indefatigable activity for the good of *H: M:* Service
& Possessions in North *America.* I most heartily wish your *future Endeavours,* may meet with better Success; and you will readily persuade
yourself that notwithstanding my present circumstances, tho' I am an
unactive, I never can be an unconcerned Looker-on with regard to what
is transacting in your Parts, & wherein you have yourself so ample a
Share in the managem^t of affairs in N: America. I remain &

Extract of a Journal of the Proceedings of the Fleet and Army Sent against Louisbourg [1]

(copy)

May 28th 1758	Admiral Boscawen embarked on board the Namur, met the Dublin off the Harbour of Halifax with General Amherst on board coming from Europe. The same day arrived Bragg's Regim^t.
29th. . . .	Fine weather, fair wind, all well, the Ships a hundred and fifty six in Number.
30th. . . .	Wind and Weather fair, made the Island of Cape Breton by 4 o'clock in the Afternoon.
31st. . . .	The Island appears very plain; Signal made by the Admiral to chase two Ships.
June 1st. . . .	Wind not fair for getting into Gabarous Bay. The Quarter Master General sent on board a Frigate to make discoveries; reported he saw Six Line of Battle Ships and five Frigates in the Harbour.

[1] Prevost's covering letter of July 9, 1758, does not identify the author of this
Journal. He wrote, "Je transmets à Votre Altesse Royale le Journal de leure Operations depuis le depart d'Hallifax, tel qu'il a eté envoié au General Abercrombie par
le Colonel Moncton." The author was probably the deputy quartermaster general
himself, James Robertson of the Royal Americans. According to Amherst's journal
Robertson was sent on June 1 to examine Gabareuse Bay (J. C. Webster, ed., *The
Journal of Jeffery Amherst* [1931], p. 47).

2ᵈ. . . .　Came to an Anchor in the Bay at 1 o'Clock. Saw 13 Ships in the harbour. Genˡ Amherst Brigadier Laurence with the Quarter Master General went to reconnoitre the Shore. Twelve Rockets were order'd that night to be fired at different places out of boats to alarm the Enemy.

3ᵈ. . . .　The weather too bad for the Troops to Land. The Kennington order'd to silence a Battery of two Guns at freshWater Cove.

4ᵗʰ. . . .　Violent rain and blowing weather with fogs. the Sutherland and Trent in distress, being too 'near the Shore when the wind increased.

June 5ᵗʰ. . . .　The weather foggy, the surff too great to land, Brigadiers Laurence & Wolfe sent to reconnoitre the Shore.

6ᵗʰ. . . .　The same Weather, an attempt to land that Morning but without Success.

7ᵗʰ. . . .　A fine day but the Surff too great to Land.

8ᵗʰ. . . .　At two o Clock in the Morn Signal made to Land at four, the boats proceeded to the Cove, the Enemy let them come within half Musket shot, and gave them a warm Reception from their Entrenchment, with great Guns and small Arms, but they were soon silenced by the sudden attack of Major Scott at the head of a body of Highlanders and Rangers on their Flank, by which, they thought it was impracticable to come to them, being in their Opinion no Landing there, on account of the Rocks with which the Beach is coverd; they retired to the Town leaving their Cannon, warlike Stores, Provisions and some money, and 100 Men killed on the Spot. The same day some parties of the Enemy were made prisoners.

9ᵗʰ. . . .　The Quarter Master General busy in marking out the ground for the Encampment.

10ᵗʰ. . . .　Brigadier Wolfe march'd with 2000 Men to take possession of the Lighthouse battery, which the Enemy had abandoned. A small party from the Garrison was attacked by our Rangers and obliged to retire with the loss of three Men; This day and the following to the 15ᵗʰ were employed in getting Provisions ashore, and nothing extraordinary happened during that time, ex-

cept our Picket being attack'd by a party from the
Woods, which was repulsed with the Loss of Seven
Men killed and one taken prisoner: On our side we had
two Men killed, & One Officer wounded.

[Enclosed in Prevost to Cumberland, July 9, 1758.]

WILLIAM EYRE TO ROBERT NAPIER
(A.L.)

Lake George
10th July 1758

Dear Sir.

I cannot help taking the most early opportunity of acquainting you
of an unhappy affair we have very lately been engaged in. this is the
Attack of the french Intrenchm^t before Tyunderoga the 8th Inst: We
embark'd from hence the 5th And the next morning arrived in sight
of the Enemys advanced Post, where they had about 3 or 4 hundred
men; We were in Number about Sixteen Thousand Men, five thousand
Regulars, & the rest Provinciels, light Armed Troops, Ranger, & Battoe
Men; we landed without oppossition the Enemy retire'd a Cross the
Carrying Place to the Saw Mill: & in two or three hours after we got
Ashore We proceeded on our March towards the Fort. We were about
four Mile & a half to go close to the falls leaving it on ye R^t Hand, &
about Six Miles if we kept further from the falls, which was the Way
We intended to go, & only three Miles to go by the Carrying Place: this
last, would be difficult if the Enemy Opposed the Passage of the River
at the Saw Mill, on Acc^t of the adventage of the Ground. We proceeded
the Other Way, (that of Six Miles) being the most Secure but before
we got much more than A Mile our advanced Partys were Attacked,
or fell in with near 300 of the Enemy, which were almost kill'd And
taken Prisoners, all Regulars: in this first Skirmage the Gellant and
good Ld Howe fell, kill'd Upon the Spot, greatly lamented (And that
with great Justice) by the Army. I observed this little firing threw our
Regulars in to some kind of a Consternation, which, tho' ended Soon,
And luckily, Struck me, and gave me some uneasyness. I observed the
fire round them, tho' at some distance, seem'd to Alarm them; in the
Wood, where nothing can be Seen, but what is near, the men fancy is
worse, or the Enemy more Numerous than they Are; our own fire they
Are Apt some times to think is the Enemy's Our Irregulers Yelling is
believed by those who Are not engaged, to be the Enemy; in short Sir,

I am more than ever convinced that numbers of our People cannot hear a great deal of firing round them coolly. I mean when they hear & do not See: these Are A few Observations I made during this little Scramble. however we continued our March on towards the Fort; this Affair I think happen'd about 3 or 4 O'Clock in the Afternoon, & about Sun set or a little after, as the Heads of the Columns were descending a low ground, A fire Was heard in the front; We Marched, I think in three Columns, I mean the Regulers the Other Troops were Upon Our flanks and Front, as it was intended they should; the firing grew quicker, & it was followed by a loud heidious Yell those in the front gave Way immediately in the greatest Disorder, and it ran down for two or three hundred Yards along each Column, as it appeared to me; no intreaty could prevail with the men for some time, but in about an hour's time after this, we found out, the fire that began this Confusion in the front was from Our Selves, & by all I could learn Since not a Single shot was fir'd against us by the Enemy; by this time it was almost Dark, we were seperated & had som difficulty to Join Afterwards; but in a very irregular Way, the Reg^{ts} intermix'd with each Other, And as it appeared to me in a most wretched situation: I must confess to you, that it's my opinion, two or three hundred Indians surrounding us that night, with the Apprehensions that some of Our people Shew'd, must have Ended fatally; believe me Dr Sir, I do not Exagerate this affair, I cannot describe as it appeared to me, without making you think I carry it further than it reely was. however, time will inform you better of it. We remained there All Night, I must observe to You, all the Army was not at this Place, part of ye 55th & the 42^d had returned to the Landing place before night, having lost the rest of the Army, during the Skirmish, with a great Number of the Provincials. I must confess the Colony Troops behaved extremely Well, were in great Spirits & was Willing to do Any thing they Were desired. however next Morning we got some Guides to shew us the Way back to the Landing Place, & there the Army Joined in one Body. not long after this, the 49th, Six Companies of the Royal Americans, & four Reg^{ts} of Provincials marched to take pesession of the Saw Mill, this As I observed to You before was the nearest Way to the Fort; Upon Our Arrival there we found it Abandoned, & the Enemy fled likewise from the Other Side of the River, And retreated to their Breast Works before the Fort. Our Rangers And light Armed Troops with some of the Provincials pursued them to that place, where they continud all night the Enemy not daring to selly out: Upon this the whole Army follow'd And cross'd the River And Encamp'ed opposite the Saw mill, this Place is one Mile And A half from ye Enemys Fort, the Carrying Place is also one Mile a half A Cross. the next Morning it was resolved to Attack the Intrenchm^t, & in conesquence of it all the Commanding officers of Reg^t were call'd together; as I had the honour to be at the heed of the 44th Was one of the Number: I remember it was asked whether We should Attack three or four deep, it was carry'd for three, the next question if the Granadiers & Pickets of the Regulers should attack at the Same time or support each Other, it was agree'd to support each Other. there was a Plan of the Ground, & the Intrenchm^t given in by Mr Clerk Who had the Direction of the Brigade: This Departm^t devolved Upon Me by Col. Montresor being ill & not Able to Act, but, I was told if I did not give Up the Command of ye Reg^t I must have nothing to do with it; to this, I answer'd, I could not do Voluntarilly, As there was no field Officer to the Reg^t but myself, but was very Willing if the General was pleesed to order me, or allow me to Act as Majer And I would do my utmost in directing & Superintending the Brigade, and carrying on that Service; this, I was Sensible I could do in the most Important Parts of it, but it was not comply'd with, & from that time, I was never Asked or spoke to, in relation to that Branch, Until I arrived at this Place after our Retreat. I beg pardon for dwelling Upon this Article, but I fancy'd you might Ask how it come about I was not employ'd or conselted before the Attack of the intrenchm^t was made, as you know I have been Generally in time of Service employ'd in that Branch of the Service. however the Attack was made, I am Sorry to Say not in the most Regular Manner, some of the Reg^t beginning before the Others were form'd, particularly the Brigade—I think to the R^t which consisted of the 27th Regt & two Batallions of the Royal Americans,—that of the left was the 42^d & 46th the Center the 49th & 55th Col Holiman, commended the Granadiers which Supported the Pickets, that were under Majer Proby who began the Attack. Unhappy for us we presently found it a most Formidable Intrenchm^t & not to be forc'd by the Method we were Upon. for upwards of one hundred Yards in front of it, Trees were fell down in Such Manner that it Broke our Batallions before we got near the Breastwork, as we march'd a Batallion in Front three Deep; I was of opinion we should attack it in Column, each Reg^t picking one, or two to Support each Other, As we could more easily force Our Way thro' the fell Trees than by making so large A Front, but it was said this would cause confusion; in short, it was said, we must Attack Any Way, and not be losing time in talking or consulting how. Attack we did, but it's hard to describe which way, The Pickets and Granediers With the Reg^t to the R^t, began the Attack before the Center Brigade had formed: we Marched from ye R^t, the Center Brigade followed, the Left brought Up ye Reer, We form'd to the left when we came Upon Our Ground; this I know, the Reg^t upon My R^t & left did, so, Apprehend the Others did the Same. I found the Attack had been began some time before I could form Our Reg^t this beeng done, all was left for each Commanding Officer of A Reg^t to do, was to support & march up as quick as they could get Upon their Ground And so on to the Intrenchm^t. after it was found that this Scheme would not do, we remained some time before We had any order to do Any thing; I cannot tell how Matters were going on in the whole, but it was plain, some thing should be undertaken; We had at last orders to draw off the Regulers, & some Provincial Reg^{ts} were order'd Up; we retreated to two Breesworks that were made between this Place & the Saw Mills, And After that, (towards Evening) All the Troops filed off by the Saw mill A Cross the River, & so continued their March to the Landing Place that night Where we embarked next Morning in Our Battou, & the Same Evening arrived at this Place.

Great faults are found with the Method of the attack the little knowledge we had of the Strength of the Enemys Works, & the Sudden Retreat to this Ground. Col. Donalson Col: Bever, Majer Proby Majer Campbell & Majer Rutherford, kill'd; Majer Browning, Majer Tuliken & myself Wounded, Mine is only A flesh Wound thro' the Side of My face, the Jaw-Bone I hope has escaped. I believe we may have lost near Two thousend Men kill'd And Wounded, I fancy about fifteen or Sixteen hundred of them Regulers.

I hope Sir, You will excuse the rough Manner I send this Acc^t to You, I Am pretty Sure the facts I have related are exact, tho not properly digested And put in order, but this, I presume you will be so good As to pardon On Acc^t of the hurry I Am in to Send you the most early Notice by the first Messenger that goes from hence.

I have done my Endeavour to get a Strong Fort built this Campaign at the Onida Carrying Place at the head of the Mohawk River, this is almost one hundred Miles from Albany; A Place I think has been long neglected, & yet I fear there will be nothing very respectable built there; I offer'd to undertake to build one in three Months with two thousand Men & finish it so far before the Winter as to be out of Danger of Any Insult, there are near five thousand Men going Up there, what they will do is more than I can say; some Diversion may be made On lake Ontario If whale Boats are carried there.

there is some talk of re building Fort Wm Henry, but this I Apprehend will not be carried into Execution; what we shall do now, or how we are to proceed, heaven knows; surely we are the most unfortunate People that ever met together. A few Days Ago every thing looked cheerful, now the Contrary.

I understand Col: Gage's light Arm'd Troops is approved of; I hope I shall be Appointed to Succeed him in the Reg^t, there is but three Majors in America Older than Me; there Are Several Lieu^t Colonelcy's Vacant. this I hope will give me a better title to Succeed in our Reg^t, for should I be removed into a New Reg^t & it reduced, by being An Eng^r I am not entitled to half Pay. We hear the Siege of Louisbourg is going on successfully, may heaven grant them More Success in the End, than us, tho' it's impossible that they could have a better Appeerance upon Landing on ye Island of Cape Breton than we had on that at ye Advanced Guard.

I hope His Royal Highness the Duke is in health and Spirits, long may He live, be happy, & Prosperous, is, and always are my Constant Wishes.

My best Comp^{ts} to Mrs Napier. I am Dear Sir, Your Much Obliged And Most Obe^t hum^l Servt

P.S:—I send you inclosed a Sketch of the Ground round Tyconderoga

You Rember, Sir, I mention'd to You my Proposiel of Purchassing if Co^l Gage sold, last Winter if it's to be sold I am still Willing (tho' things are very different now from what they were then) rather than have Any one to buy over my head or to be fixed in a Young Reg^t.

I forgot to inform You that we had part of Our Artillery not far from the Rear of the Attack, but no use was made of them either before or after.

COLONELS PREVOST AND GAGE TO JAMES ABERCROMBY
(COPY)

Camp Lake George Jul. 20th 1758.

Monsieur

Vous nous ordonnez de vous communiquer librement nos avis sur les moiens les plus propres a établir la discipline, l'harmonie & la confiance dans l'armée nous allons donc vous soumettre nos sentimens, avec tout le zèle & la verité dont nous sommes capables,

La malheureuse affaire du huit nous réduit certainement a la défensive il faut donc prendre toutes les mesures qui peuvent la rendre bonne, & nous mettre a portée de la tourner en offensive, en cas que le succes des expeditions au Sud et a l'Est, ou de l'une des deux ou encore la diversion sur le Lac Ontario nous en fournisse une occasion favorable.

Il nous paroit d'abord d'une nécessité absolue de donner a votre autorité toute l'étendue qu'elle doit avoir, ce qui ne se peut qu'en suivant la metode de la faire passer par les canaux qui lui sont naturels.

De remplir sans délai les vacances de l'armée Chaque personne chargée d'un département public doit immediatement se camper au Quartier Gen¹ & ne s'en absenter pour aucune cause sans y laisser quelqu'un qui sache ou le trouver. Chaqu'un d'eux doit être muni d'instructions & de pouvoirs par ecrit & répondre de l'èxécution des ordres qu'il recevra; Il devra mème repondre de la conduite des personnes qu'il emploiera sous lui.

Ils devront tous etre soutenus dans l'exercice de leurs charges & dans les affaires de leur département qui que ce soit ne pourra etre admis a s'addresser au Gen¹ que par leur canal En cas d'incapacité, de négligence ou de quelqu'apparence de malversation, ils devront etre privez sur le champ de leurs emplois

Ce petit nombre de mesures qui n'admettent point de délai introduiront dans peu l'ordre d'ou naissent les succes. étoit signé Prevost Gage

Au Camp du Lac George le 29ᵉ Juillet 1758

Monsieur

Le silence que vous gardez avec nous sur les mesures que nous vous avons proposé par vos ordres, nous fait craindre que la façon dont nous l'avons fait ne vous ait déplu Ces mesures étoient si simples qu'elles n'ont peut etre pas fixé votre attention, nous vous supplions d'observer qu'elles en feront naitre nécessairement d'autres qui améneront l'ordre qui seul peut produire le succes

Il n'est pas necessaire de vous faire sentir la nécessité d'un plan fixe & déterminé Cependant permettez nous Monsʳ d'entrer dans une discussion plus particulière des avantages qui en résulteront & des facheuses conséquences qu'on peut prévoir qui procèderont de la manière dont les affaires sont actuellement conduites

Au moment que vous aurez formé un plan vous serez a mème de juger comment & jusques ou chaque département de votre armée peut contribuer au succes

Si vous trouvez que les particuliers qui en sont chargez ne sont pas égaux a la besogne & que vous craignez leur indolence leur mauvaise volonté ou leur incapacité, vous pourrez sans préjugé chercher a les remplacer, il faut emploier de bons yeux dans cette recherche, & ne vous en rapporter qu'a vous meme pour l'éxamen des sujets qu'on vous proposera

La metode la plus simple & la plus claire de conduire les affaires doit etre établie dans chaque département, un livre doit etre tenu ou l'on entrera les ordres ou instructions qui seront données au chef qui sera *responsable* dans toute l'étendue de ce terme de leur exécution

Chacun d'eux rendra compte a jour aux Officiers Genéraux sous vous de toutes les occurrences quelque triviales qu'elles puissent étre, vous pouvez compter que comme par leur silence ils se rendroient responsables de l'évênement aucun des deux ne vous taira rien de ce qui doît venir jusques a vous

Cela posé chacun dans votre armée saura ce qu'il aura a faire & jusques ou il peut aller, insensiblement l'ordre s'introduira & ce ne sera plus la confusion actuelle ou chacun négligeant ses fonctions empiète sur celles qui lui devroient etre absolument étrangéres

Les avantages personels que vous en recevrez seront une tranquillité desprit qui vous permettra de tourner toute votre attention a procurer la sureté de votre armée & la réputation des armes du Roi

Si l'instabilité du Ministère en Angleterre ou quelqu'autre cause que ce soit occasionne votre rappel, vous laisserez autant d'ordre dans les affaires que votre prédecesseur y a laissé de confusion & cela seul vous sera personellement aussi honorable, qu'avantageux au service du Roi & de la Nation

Tous vos ordres seront obéis ou bien vous serez informé sur le champ de leur inéxécution rien de plus aisé alors que de remonter a la source dans l'instant & bientot une rigueur utile salutaire & indispensable vous épargnera les occasions de l'emploier

Les inconveniens qui résulteront de la maniére dont les affaires sont actuellement menées sont sans nombre & si sensibles qu'il ne faut citer que ce que nous avons éprouvé depuis le six du Courant pour convaincre tout homme raisonnable qu'il procède de ce que nous n'avons agi sur un plan déterminé

En effet M^r nos idées semblent concentrées a nous défendre contre un ennemi inférieur en nombre & qui de vrai vaut moins que nous, cependant telle est notre situation que ce n'est qu'a mesure qu'il frappe quelque coup que nous pensons a y remedier, jusques ici aucune peine n'a été prise pour le prevénir

Nous ne voions pas comment vous pouvez répondre a la Nation de laisser votre armée dépourvue d'un Ajudant Genl d'un Quar^{tr} Maitre

Gen¹ d'un plus grand nombre d'emploiez dans les vivres dans les charois & dans les Hopitaux. Une économie qui va a la ruine des affaires du Roi cesse de l'etre & sera blamée par tous les gens de bon sens qui seuls feront votre réputation Le secret & la diligence sont l'ame de toutes les entreprises vous ne pouvez vous assurer de l'un et l'autre qu'en ne rendant votre acces moins facile & en ne consultant pas les personnes dont l'emploi n'est pas de vous conseiller mais d'éxecuter vos ordres

Nous savons Mʳ qu'on vous fournira une quantité de pretextes spécieux pour justifier l'inactivité de l'armée & nos mauvais succes, le peu de discipline des troupes réglées c'est a dire leur peu d'usage de la guerre dans les bois, l'espèce de gens que sont les Provinciaux combien peu l'on doit compter sur eux a tous égards et enfin le peu de secours que vous recevez des Officiers commis aux départemens publics de l'armée qui en font l'ame; Croiez nous Mʳ Cela ne fera impression que sur peu de gens & nous sommes obligez de vous dire que nous pensons que ce sera avec raison parceque nous estimons les pouvoirs que vous avez receu de la Couronne, suffisans pour corriger ou remédier aux inconvéniens qui nous conduisent a notre ruine certaine, nous vous supplions d'y refléchir sérieusement & de ne vous en rapporter qu'a vous meme

Soiez convaincu Mʳ que le bien du service & notre sincère attachement pour vous nous ont dicté ces avis que si vous les suivez, en rétablissant l'ordre vous gagnerez l'estime & la confiance de l'armée & que quoi qu'il en soit nous vous demeurerons inviolablement soumis & attachez sans reserve /

Fort Edward Aug. 20ᵗʰ 1758

Sir

I wish your Excʸ joy of the surrender of LouisBourg and am in hopes that it will afford you still an opportunity to end this Campaign with honour

I beg leave to submit my opinion in that respect to your judgement, and I shall take it as a favour if I am mistaken that you will set my notions right in regard to the practicability of my Plan I have strong reasons to think that most part of the Indians and Canadians have left *Moncalm* to go home to their harvest and strong presumptions that Admiral Boscawen is sailed up the River St Lawrence (which I suppose you will be acquainted with by your letters,) in that case Canada being kept by him in play, will not be able to afford any assistance to the Forts at this end of *Lake Champlain*

This point being granted I wou'd propose another attempt according to the following disposition vizt /that two thousand men of the Militia of New York be order'd to come up immediately in the communication there to take post and remain during the expedition

Whilst you are getting yourself in readiness at Lake George (which might be executed in two Days: Major Rogers with all the light troops /except those you may want for pilots/ to be sent by night opposite to *Sabbath Day* point, from thence to proceed carrying his Boats to Wood Creek as he did before: where I can meet him with about two thousand five hundred men, in which number is included all that can be spared from Halfway Brook

When joined to detach Maj^r Munster and five hundred men to the East of Wood Creek with directions to shew themselves on the shore opposite to Tiondoroga, the rest to proceed partly by water under Maj^r Rogers or any other and partly by Baron Dieskau's Road under myself to take post between the Fort and the Saw Mill

This part of the plan being well conducted wou'd prevent any thing considerable to come from the Forts to obstruct your landing, wou'd probably make you once more Master of the Post at the Saw Mill and with a little time of both forts

I humbly conceive that no bad consequences can arise from this undertaking the more so as our victorious Army at LouisBourg wou'd certainly prevent the ennemy to think of making any impression on your Colonies in case you shou'd meet with a repulse

On the other side the least advantage you can reap from such an attempt, will be a useful diversion in behalf of our Fleet and Army by preventing *Moncalm* sending any assistance to Canada and if he shou'd your task wou'd be the easier

The shortness of time and the bounds of a letter will not allow me to be more explicit, but if your Exc^y shou'd approve of the above plan or form any other to that purpose in the execution of which you shou'd think proper to employ me, I can easily attend your Commands at the Lake this Evening Forgive me Sir for taking the freedom of giving an unasked advice but it flows from an unfeigned zeal for the honour of his Majesty's Arms and the welfare of this Country

I am with great respect—

P.S. If the Returns sent me from the Agent Victuallers and the Commissary of Artillery are true, your Ex^y may depend of being supply'd plentifully in both these branches for sixty thousand men for three Mounths and more

[*Endorsed*] Copy of Colonels *Prevost* & *Gage's* Letters to General *Abercrombie:*
Lake *George* July 20: & Fort *Edward* August *20: 1758 No 2.*
[Enclosed in Prevost to Cumberland, Aug. 21, 1758.]

COLONEL JAMES PREVOST TO CUMBERLAND

(A.L.S.)

H.R.H. ye Duke

Fort Edward le 21st Aoust 1758
Monseigneur

Jarrivai au Lac le 17e Juillet et J'y trouvai larmée dans la defiance le descouragement et la consternation qui suivent d'ordinaire une defaite; Un tiers des Troupes reglées, hors de Combat, laissoit le reste sans Action, a cause de la quantité dofficiers tuez ou hors detat dagir; La mort de Myld How y avoit eteint le peu d'activité quily avoit introduit, La discorde y regnoit avec Empire, Enfin tout annoncoit des malheurs prochains et loeuil le plus perçant n'y Appercevoit pas de remede.

Telle a été notre Situation jusques au 1er du Courant, un de nos convois attaqué & taillé en Pièces sans resistance, & un de nos postes a sept miles du Camp attaqué en plein jour huit jours auparavant nous tira de lengourdissement ou nous etions; Quelques Mesures prises pour Assurer Notre Communication du Lac George a Albany dont on me donna le Commandemt le 4, ont depuis trois Semaines fait parvenir nos Convois en Sureté, et des lors si nous avons vû lennemi, c'est a moitié chemin entre lui et nous.

Sensiblement touché de la honte detre battu avec des forces aussi superieures que les notres, Jai medité depuis mon retour sur les Moiens davoir notre revanche; Je communiquai mes idées au Genl hier par le meme Exprès qui lui porta la nouvelle de la prise de Louisburg, Je prens la liberté de les soumettre A V.A.R., Je ny ai pas eu de reponse quoi que le poste *venant du Lac* ait passé ici ce matin, portant a ce que je soubconne ordre au Paquet de mettre a la voile

Contre lordinaire le Courrier ne sest pas Arreté, un jeune Officier sans experience laiant laissé passer a sa Garde, sans en faire rapport; Je crains que ma lettre nait deplu & quon nait en dessein de prevenir que je n'ecrivisse en Angleterre par cette Occasion.

J'y joins aussi Copie dun papier que nous avons signé le Brigadier Gage et moi contenant la Substance dune Conference que nous eumes avec le Genl deux jours Apres mon Arrivée au Camp & quil nous pria de lui donner en ecrit; Dixjours Apres voiant quil ne prenoit Aucune resolution; Je proposai a Monsr Gage de renouveller nos instances et je lui communiquai ce que javois preparé sur ce sujet, il convint du fond des choses mais persuadé de linutilité de cette demarche et craignant de lui faire de la peine nous supprimames cette demarche; Je n'envoie donc cette copie A V.A R. que pour lui donner une idée des Maux sous lesquels nous gemissons & qui Malheureusem^t sont sans remede pour cette Campagne Nous nous determinames donc a vivre du jour a le journée & Malgré la necessité dun Plan fixe nous nous bornâmes a faire de notre mieux chacun dans notre place; cest dans cette disposition que jai été detache avec 3000 hommes dont 500 de Troupes Reglées pour garder une Communication de soixante miles dans les Bois, les garnisons de huit postes y comprises.

Je doute quil yait de remede a des maux que lon ne connoitra en Angleterre quen faisant venir quelque Officier qui par ses lumieres et son zele soit en etat den faire connoitre les causes, Elles sont telles Monseigneur quil ny aura pas trop de toute lauthorité du Gouvernement pour les detruire et y substituer les seuls Principes qui puissent operer la conservation de ce Paisci. J'ecrivis par le dernier Paquet au Gen^{le} Napier a ce sujet en lui envoiant une lettre pour MyL^d Barrington Aqui jinsinuois la Necessité que ces causes fussent prombement devoilees, Mais a lavenir, a Moins dun ordre je suis resolu de ne plus en ecrire a personne, Je gemirai en secret, Je ferai de mon mieux partout ou je serai emploié, et jattendrai avec patience la fin de la guerre qui sera toujours bien desagreable a cause du desavantage avec lequel nous la ferons Aussi longtems que nous ne changerons pas de Mesures et de principes. V A R daignera pardonner a mon zéle la liberté que je prens de lui soumettre Mes Observations et mes idées, Je le fais avec dautant plus de Confiance que comme je ne cherche a Nuire a personne en particulier Je puis aussi en sureté prendre *Dieu a temoin,* que loin de me croire les Talens necessaires pour remedier aux maux que j expose a ses yeux, il n'est rien au monde que Je redoute plus quun commandement tant je me trouve denué des qualitez Necessaires pour men aquiter convenablement.

          Jai lhonneur detre avec le plus profond respect.
   Monseigneur De Votre altesse Royale Le tres humble & tres Soumis Serviteur

                                   J PREVOST

Major James Robertson to the Earl of Morton [1]
(COPY)

New York, Dec[r] 19th 1758.

My Lord,

To give your Lordship Information, is I think the most agreable Method one who has been much obliged to you can take, to show his Gratitude, especialy as the Subject is perhaps the only important one upon which you are not already well informed.

I mean to lay before you a true State of the War in America this last year, but in place of a Detail of Actions, where an attentive Officer, would learn better what to shun than what to imitate. I will lay before you the Plans that we formed for the Campaign, and show what we have lost by laying aside Lord Loudoun's, which was calculated to improve every Advantage, that Climate, Situation and Numbers could give us over the Enemy, And by adopting another, made without any knowledge of these Advantages, which by a Misapplication of our Force, made even Numbers and Expence destructive to our Scheme.

By both Plans Ticonderoga, Louisbourg & Fort Duquesn were to be attacked, but very different were the Means proposed for the Execution of these Designs.

Let us begin with what was reckon'd the most considerable. His Lo[p] intended to penetrate to Montreal by Ticonderoga and destined for this Service Twelve Battalions of Foot. By the Plan sent from England, Six Battalions and Ten Companys of Foot and 17,000 Provincials were ordered to be employed. Very different Consequences flowed naturally from these Dispositions.

The Rivers and Lakes that lead to Ticonderoga from hence, open a fortnight earlier than those that lead from that Place to Quebec. Lord Loudoun, who would have watched the Seasons with Troops he could move on an Hour's Notice, for whose Transportation across the Lake and Maintainance, half the Preparation necessary for the other Plan would have suffis'd, Could have been at Ticonderoga by the End of May, and before the Enemy could have brought together a Thousand Men to oppose him.

Whereas by the other Plan, General Abercromby, who could not get the Provincial Troops in motion till late in the Season, and who had double the Number of Battoes to build and Provisions to carry, could not arrive at Ticonderoga till the 8th of July, and there found the

---

[1] James Douglas, 14th Earl of Morton (1702–1768), one of the representative peers of Scotland, who for some reason was considered as an authority upon America.

Enemy's whole Force entrench'd, the greatest part of which had only been able to get there a few Days before General Abercrombie.

It is therefore Plain, that Lord Loudoun must as necessarily have taken the Place with small resistance in the beginning of June as Gen[l] Abercromby was defeated before it on the 8th of July. But had General Abercrombie been victorious, he could not have penetrated to Montreal. His Army was too large, and too little accustomed to the Field, to move fast. The difficulty of supplying them with Provisions at 200 Miles distance from our Frontier, was extreamly encreas'd by both these Circumstances.

Lord Loudoun well apprised of this, was to have taken few Troops well accustomed to the Field whose goodness supplied the want of Numbers and formed a greater Force than what Gen[l] Abercromby had.

His Lordship's first Battle would have been for Montreal, to secure the Success of this, he had plann'd the Attack of Cataraqui, which was to have been made by Bradstreet with 800 Battoe Men and the Jersy and New York Provincials, about the time his Lo[p] propos'd to penetrate into the Enemys Country. This Project was adopted and executed in August, the Enemy on the Report of its being attack'd, detach'd 3000 Men, but as we had then no other Project the Enemy lost nothing by the detaching, which in the other Case would have cost them Montreal.

Your Lo[p] will think that the Missapplications of our Force and Advantages could not have been greater, but you will find them exceeded when we consider the two Plans for the Attack of Louisbourg and their natural Consequences.

It was well known that the Garrison of Louisbourg, in the Winter, did not exceed 2,000 Men, and that it could not contain above four, That the greatest Difficulty would be in forcing a Landing, That however great the Force that went against this place was, we could upon this Occasion employ no more than the Boats of the Fleet could hold. But as the Ground about the Town is the most Rocky and Morassy in the Universe, that after the Landing there would be little fighting and an immense deal of Labour.

Lord Loudoun destin'd Six Regiments of Foot who were actually in Nova Scotia, any Troops that might come from England, and all the Provincial Troops of the four eastern Colonys for this Service. These last, in complyance with the Requisition made from England were to be 17,000 Men, but his Lo[p] better apprised of the Number of Servicable Men these Colonys can raise, demanded but half as many, but as these were to have been embarked at the Ports near to which they were rais'd, all of them would have arrived at Louisbourg, Whereas being mostly

press'd Men and having 300 Miles to march half of them never join'd
General Abercrombie.

By the other Plan Fourteen Regiments & Four Score Workmen were
ordered to besiege Louisbourg. What happen'd The Men, the Boats of
the Fleet and Transports could contain forced a Landing. Afterwards
we had no fighting, The Roads, the Transportation of the Train &c.
employe'd us from the 8th of June to the 20th July when our first Battery opened, after which the Siege lasted but Six Days.

What would have happened had the other Plan been followed. The
Provincials being better Labourers, and all employed in carrying on
the Works, as they would have been double the Number of the Troops
we employed to work, Louisbourg would have been in our Possession
by the 1st of July. Here every labouring Man was worth two Soldiers,
here any Number could be easiely supply'd with Provisions. With General Abercrombie's Army, every Man but a good Soldier was an unsup-
portable Burthen.

Now the Advantage of being early possessed of Louisbourg, will
appear from what the French themselves acknowledge. Monsr Drucour
was pressed to suffer the Commodore to escape, with all the Men of War
then lying in the Harbour, he would not suffer this, because, said he,
tho these Ships cannot save the Place, they will retard the Siege and
save Quebec.

Lord Loudoun intended to send two Regiments against Fort Duquesne, and these he had quartered in the nearest habitable Places to
that Fort. His Lo^p had formed a Friendship with a Gentleman of Honour and Fortune,[2] who by good Offices and Generosity had acquired
an Interest among the Indians. This Gentleman actualy brought 600
Cheroquees to march with our Forces against Fort Duquesne. These
would have scoured the Woods and have enabled our Army to make
such Marches, as would have brought them before Duquesne, by the
Middle of June. But the Substitution of the English Plan as effectually
ruin'd this as it did the other Services.

The two Regiments that were ready and at hand to march against
Duquesne, were sent to Louisbourg, and Troops at 1,000 Miles distance were ordered in their Room. The Indians weary of Inactivity
would not wait the Arrival of this distant Force and dispersed and
carry'd their Resentment and the Opinion of our being Trifflers, among
their Nations, and are weavering whether they should treat with us or
the French.

Mr. Forbes, in a State of Body that would confine any other Man to

2 William Byrd of Virginia.

his Room, has undergone the Rigours of a severe Season and has forced the Enemy on the 26th of November to abandon and blow up that Fort. Mr. Forbes has infinite Merit, but the Victory brings little Advantage. The Expedition has cost half a Million, and the French will make another Fort near the former for £1,000, but had this Place been attacked at the time Lord Loudoun proposed Presquile, Venango and Niagara would soon have shared it's fate, or the Enemy would have been obliged to detatch Troops from their Grand Army, which would have facilitated the Invasion that would have been made upon Quebec and Montreal.

Had Lord Loudoun's Plans been pursued, you see all the Outworks of new France would have been in our Possession, at a Season when it would have been proper & easey to proceed into the heart of the Enemys Country, whereas by the other, Mr. Amherst tho victorious & eager to proceed to farther Conquests, was obliged by the Season to rest satisfied with that of Louisbourg.

His Lordship's Recal has evidently saved Quebec, or postponed its Fall to another Year. His Plan would have succeeded in any Hands but could have been put into none better than his own. The faults of the other were so gross, that little more could have been done than what has been.

That the Raveings of a Madman like Lord Charles Hay, The Fustian, Lyes and Missrepresentations of the most abandon'd Imposter that ever gull'd a Nation, Prevost, who, without a single Quality of a Soldier, and even without having ever seen or learned Service, has lyed himself into a Rank of a General, should be listen'd to by the Mob and the Ignorant, is matter of no wonder to me, nor Concern to his Lo^p.

However indistinct this Narrative may be, it contains Facts, from which your Penetration will trace Conscequences, more clearly than I have been able to lay them down. I shall be happy in being the mean Instrument of conveying Truth to the wise & the Discerning. You will not think the worse of his Lo^p, perhaps you will love him more, because he has been prevented from reaping a Glorious and allmost certain Conquest. And because he who would cordially have ended the War in America this Year, has been traduced as the Author of Delays and Disgrace. With Gratitude & Esteem I have the Honour to be

My Lord &c.

EXTRACT OF A LETTER FROM AN OFFICER IN MAJOR
GEN^L WOLFE'S ARMY. ISLAND OF ORLEANS
10TH AUGST 1759
(COPY)

April 30th. Col¹ Carleton Embarqued with 4 C^{os} of Grenadiers under
his Command on board of Adm¹ Durell's Squadron, We Sailed the 5th
May for the River of St. Laurence, & came to an Anchor at Isle Dubik
the 22ᵈ.

The Design of the Admiral Sailing before the rest of the Fleet, was,
to intercept Succours from getting into Quebeck; & Col¹ Carleton had
Orders to Land or take Post wherever he thought it most convenient or
necessary. At Isle Dubik we had intelligence that two Frigates & 14
Transports, with Provisions stores & Troops, had got up to Quebeck;
this you may imagine was Mortifying News to Us; We soon left Dubik
& got to Isle Aux Couders; Col¹ Carleton landed some Men there, &
soon after came to the Isle of Orleans, where we came to an Anchor the
14th June. The French Account of the Navigation of the River of St.
Laurence We found to be a Mere Bugbear; we remained off the North
point of Orleans till the 25th, when we were joined by the Fleet &
Army; we all proceeded immediately & landed the 27th at St. Laurence,
a Village about 4 Miles from the South Point of the Island, from whence
Brigadier Monckton was Detached with 4 Battalions to Point Levy,
Opposite the Town, & has Bombarded & Cannonaded it very effectually; The rest of the Army marched to the South point of Orleans, where
Major General Wolfe established his Magazine & Hospital & fortified a
Post to protect them; when this was finished he determined to Cross the
water & take Post upon what is called the North Shore, before the Falls
of Montmorency. This was effected without Opposition the 8th of July
at Night, with three Battalions, the Grenadiers, & light Infantry of the
Army. The next Night we were joined by two More Battalions.

From the Point of Orleans We observed several Encamptments on
the opposite Side, betwixt the Town & Falls, & that the Shore was
strongly fortified; The Beach was commanded by a very high Steep
Bank, on the Top of which was a Strong Intrenchment, with Traverses
& Redouts; The Beach was likewise defended at different places by
Redouts & Batterys, particularly just above the Falls.

Mr. Wolfe's Camp was now divided from the Advanced Posts of the
Army of the Enemy, by the Montmorency River only, (Narrow but

Deep with high & steep woody Banks) & the Falls, the Foot of which is fordable at Low Water: The General resolved to Attack the Enemys Entrenchments just above the Falls.

The Grenadiers of the Army Commanded by Col¹ Burton were to Attack in Front, supported by two Battalions.

Brigadier Townshend's Brigade, consisting of three Battalions, with all the light Infantry of the Army, under the Command of Col¹ How, were to Cross at the Falls; The General Landed 50 Peices of Cannon to Enfilade the French Trenches & frighten the Canadians & Indians.

On the 31st of July all was ready, ships run aground to silence the Batterys, & the Centurion Man of War went Close in.

We were all in our Flat Bottom Boats at Noon, rowing backwards & forwards, in sight of the Enemy, & exposed to their shells for six hours, waiting I believe till the Batterys were silenced, (which the ships could not Effect) & till the Water was low enough to Cross at the Falls a little past Six we had orders to follow Col¹ Burton & row ashore; the Grenadiers showed uncommon Bravery in this Affair; We got out of our Boats & formed as well as we could in the Water, which came up to our Waistbelts.

The General Ordered the Grenadiers March to Beat, which Animated our Men so much that we could scarce restrain them, we moved on thro a very bad Muddy Beach & Attacked the Redout & Battery which we carried.

The French in their Lines upon the Hill kept their Fire till we reached the Redout, which they intirely Commanded; They then gave us an incessant & extraordinary heavy Fire: The Redout could not be Maintained under their Musketry; & the Bank proving inaccessable, we were ordered to retire which we did very regularly; There were Indians concealed in the Brush Wood on the Front of the Bank so that we had Fire upon us from all Quarters. There were near 400 Grenadiers killed & wounded on this Attack, One officer killed & 23 wounded, in which Number I am included, having a Shot thro' my Leg.

A Heavy Storm of Thunder & Rain came on, as we had orders to retreat, which Occasioned the whole to retire. The two ships that run aground were burnt, to prevent their falling into the hands of the Enemy.

This is the Most Memorable Event that has as yet happened in this Army; the next Attempt will, I hope, be more practicable & more successfull; if we cant beat them we shall ruin their Country, for this years harvest is lost to them; &, as there is a scarcity of Provisions already amongst them, they must be in the Utmost Distress before the Winter is over.

It is thought the French have 15 or 16000 Men in the Field, Encamped in Posts under the Command of Messrs De Montcalm & Vaudreuil

The Town is almost Destroyed by our Shells & Carcasses, which have been very well thrown & the Artillery has been extreemly well served.

COPY OF A LETTER FROM ON BOARD THE LIZARD SEP^{TR} 5TH 1759 AT COUDRE 17 LEAGUES FROM QUEBEC

I don't doubt but you think me negligent as you have not heard from me but I can assure you that I have not had an opportunity, as to News I can send you but very little not having been a Spectator of the Siege as yet. What Particulars are come to my knowledge I will here inform you of. The Fleet sail'd from Louisbourg the 5th of June and landed the Troops on the Island of Orleans which is a few Leagues from Quebec, the 27th, four thousand Men immediately went over to the South Shore & began to erect Batteries at Point Levey which is opposite Quebec at about a Mile's Distance, the 6th of July they began to cannonade & bombard the Town from thence—On the 9th Genl. Wolfe with the remainder of the Forces landed on the North Shore—I believe without any Loss—On the 31st there was an Attempt made for Genl. Wolfe to cross the Falls of Momorossa—Genl. Monckton went at the same time from the shipping with Amherst's Regiment, the Highlanders & Grenadiers of the whole Army, they went in three divisions consisting of 40 Boats each & Cover'd by two Catts arm'd on Purpose, the Boats lay a considerable time exposed to a heavy Fire from the Enemy—the reason why I can't inform you, but I have been told it was to wait for low Water that Genl. Wolfe might cross the Falls at the same time they landed—at last they did land and behaved with the greatest Courage imaginable—took two Pieces of Cannon from the Enemy, but there were such Lanes made thro' them by the small Shot & Grape from the Enemy that they were obliged to retreat wth the Loss of 51 kill'd & 350 wounded the Cats that cover'd the landing had grounded so that they were obliged to set them on fire to prevent their falling into the Enemys hands—The French are deeply intrench'd between our Forces & the Town and all the Inhabitants live in the Trenches, for the Town is entirely destroy'd having been set on fire three times & burn'd for several times together, a Magazine blow'd up &c:—His Majesty's Ships Sutherland and Squirrel with 2 Catts and 14 flat bottom'd Boats were above the Town & carried with them Genl. Murray & 12 or 1300 Men. I have the pleasure to acquaint you that he executed the Service he was sent upon, that is destroy'd several Villages & the Country for many Leagues up the River but particularly a Magazine with the Cloathing in it for four complete Regiments, Stores for the Indians & some Gunpowder & the Prisoners say the Military Chest was there, he has taken some Prisoners.

On the Arrival of the Fleet off the upper end of the Island Orleans, the French sent down 6 Fireships but by the vigilance of the Boats was prevented from doing Execution—they afterwards sent down Rafts of Yards & Topmasts chain'd together with an Intent to force our Ships from their Anchors but their Scheme was so far from succeeding that it proved of infinite service to our Transports they being in want of such things. After this they sent down 120 Fire Stages all fasten'd together brought them down within 500 Yards of the nighest Ship then set them on fire but they were prevented in the same manner as before. We have a number of Boats lie on guard every night under the Walls of the Town ready to receive any fire Machines that may be sent down—the French being sensible of this contrived a Machine with an Intent to destroy the Guard Boats—the Description of it is as follows, it is 15 Foot Square & 4 or 5 Foot deep about 2 foot above the Surface of the Water, there are holes bored, thro' which Holes, there are Muskets pointed & underneath these Muskets there is loose Powder & Hand Granades and Springs that go across from one Triger to the other fasten'd very securely over all there is a false Platform which by the least weight falls in & letts off the Works—this Machine was sent down one night & the Dublin's Boat being nigher and brisker than the rest got to it first, the Midshipman was the first Person that jump'd into it, as soon as he was in, the Works went off & blew him into the water, wounded three of the Crew & damaged the Boat a good deal it was very fortunate there were no more Boats near, whatever honours are due to the Army or Navy from this Siege we are noways entitled to for we have been cruising at the Mouth of the River, the whole time the Siege has been.— Various are the Opinions concerning Quebec some think it will fall others it will not, so I must leave you to your own Opinion. The Town is entirely demolish'd the produce of the Year spoil'd & it's thought the Siege will continue six weeks longer if the place don't surrender. Mr. Durell sail'd for the River some time before Admiral Saunders but not time enough to hinder a Fleet of French Store Ships under Convoy of five Frigates arriving at Quebec the 16th May, we have taken a Ship bound out with a Pacquet for Quebec—but the Pacquet was destroy'd.

Septr 7th. P.S. General Wolfe has evacuated his first Post embark'd and landed above the Town without the French knowing anything of the Matter there is a Corporal & 4 Mohawk Indians arrived from Genl. Amherst, by whom we learn that the first Dispatches from General Amherst was intercepted by the French—the Corporal was 16 days on his Passage from Mr. Amherst to Mr. Wolfe & the reason Mr. Wolfe has shifted his Post is to intercept any supplies that may be sent from Montreal to the French—here is a Detachment of a thousand Men come down to destroy the French Settlements all down to the River. Mr. Amherst is expected every day & there are great hopes of the Place surrendring.

An Account of the Action Which Happened Near Quebec, 13th September 1759

(copy)

An Account of the Action which happen'd on the 13th Septr 1759 between the English commanded by General Wolfe, and the French commanded by the Marquis de Montcalm, on the 12th Septr at 9 at night the light Infantry of the Army under the command of Colonel How, with Braggs, Kennedys, Lascelle's, and Anstruthers Regiments with part of the Highlanders and Moncton's Grenadiers amounting in the whole to 1800, embarqued near Cape Rouge from on board the men of War and Transports, and proceeded in the flat bottom'd boats down the River, the men of War, Transports, and Arm'd Sloops follow'd with the rest of the Troops, the two floating Batteries accompanied the first embarkation, about half an hour after four on the 13th in the morning the Boats arrived at Sellery Bay, being seven or eight miles from Cape Rouge, the Troops landed immediately at which time four pieces of Canon were instantly fired from a battery, to the left of the landing place, and a number of Musquetry from the top of the hill, but this did not hinder the light Infantry from advancing briskly up a small path which lead by several turnings to the Top, whilst two Regiments scrambled up an almost perpendicular Ascent on the right of the road, in short the Troops gained the summitt with little loss, the defence of which was committed to the care of a Captain with one hundred men, and might have been defended by a Serjeant and twelve men, as soon as this part of the army had got footing on the top of the hill, the boats returned to the men of War and Transports, who had by this time fallen down the river to the landing place, and brought on shore Amhersts Lawrences, Otways, another detachment from the Highlanders, and the Grenadiers from Louisbourgh, Webbs and Monckton's from the other side of the River, who had been drawn from Isle of Orleans, and Point Levi and were ready to come over before day break, the whole being landed amounted to 4,500, soon after our gaining the heights some light Infantry were sent to take possession of the four Gun Battery, which was effected with small loss, Lawrences battallion took post there, and in the two houses near it, as soon as it was broad day, we perceived the french in motion betwixt the Town and our little army, they appear'd to be very numerous, and we observ'd they had some Canon, the Genl. immediately disposed the Troops in order of battle, his right occupying the brow of the small eminence, and the left being cover'd by two small houses, into which we threw a Company of Grenadiers, a Battallion & some light Infantry, were extended from those two houses to another house surrounded with Pallisadoes, in the rear of our left from whence the light Infantry occupied the whole space to the battery which was on the rear of our Right, which disposition seemed doubly necessary as we had observed a large detachm^t of the ennemy filing off from their main body towards our left Flank, and as we knew there was a body of Troops that had been sent up the River, & might be expected at our backs, upon the news of our landing the ennemy soon began to canonade us, and their Irregulars & Indians advancing among some bushes in our front annoy'd us much, as our light Infantry were otherwise disposed of, we were obliged from time to time to advance plattoons from the Battallions to keep these at a distance we had now got 2 short six pounders with which we play'd upon the enemy, who were formed in three Columns in our front, all their Irregulars being disposed of upon our left Flank and Rear, and along the face of the hill below our right, where the bushes afforded them all the advantages they could hope for, the two Armies remained sometime in this situation, our General having delay'd attacking the ennemy in hopes of his bringing up the rest of his field Artillery, but the French either willing to deprive us of this advantage, or fearing we might be reinforced; or perhaps from a contempt of our numbers, advanced upon us in three columns in front, & harrass'd our flanks at the same time with their Irregulars; when they were within 50 paces of our line, they began their fire, which our people received with great firmness for about two minutes, when they three [threw] in their whole fire upon them, which putting them into disorder our people immediately advanced upon them with their Bayonets, and in a few minutes put the whole to flight, which was very precipitate towards the Town and the River St. Charles, our Troops pursuing them with great slaughter, and making many Officers & men prisoners the Irregulars seeing the main body give way, soon follow'd them, and thus ended the Action, in which the French lost their General Montcalm, the 2^d in command Monsr de Sansargues with about 30 Officers, and 1500, men killed, wounded and taken, we lost Genl. Wolfe, Brigadier Monckton wounded with 30 Officers killed and wounded, the Ennemy left one field piece, and a great deal of Ammunition on the field, in consequence of this victory, Quebec by capitulation surrender'd the 18th when our Troops took possession of it.

JOURNAL OF HAPPENINGS AT QUEBEC BY AN OFFICER OF ROYAL AMERICANS [1]

(COPY)

Monsieur.

La Situation où l'armée Britanique s'est trouvé cêt hyver, merite, à cc que je crois l'attention de tous les militaires; Quand aux Curieux qui fouïllent l'antiquité pour y trouver des prodiges, ils ne seront pas peu surpris de voir, que si nous n'avons pas surpassé les anciens, nous les avons au moins égalé en beaucoup de choses: Cela paroitra peutêtre un paradoxe bien fort à soutenir, mais si l'on veut donner un peu d'attention & se rappeller les differens tems, l'on verra que les hommes ont été à peuprès toujours les mêmes, & que la Superiorité des uns sur les autres n'a eté occasioñée que par la discipline, l'habileté & l'harmonie des Chefs.

Avant que d'entrer en matiére, il est necessaire de faire voir l'etat de notre armée, celui de la ville & fortifications de Quebeck, tel qu'il etoit au dèpart de notre flotte, de même que l'etat de l'armée françoise, avec le nombre de Canadiens et Sauvages qu'ils avoient sur pied, & enfin les avantages qu'ils avoient sur nous.

Dix Bataillons, deux Compagnies d'Artillerie, une Compagnie de Chasseurs de bois, tous gens harrassez par une Campagne des plus

---

[1] The author of this journal would seem to have been Lieutenant L. F. Fuser [Fuzer], commissioned in the Royal American Regiment January 27, 1756. Hollandt, des Barres, and Fuser were the only foreign officers acting as engineers at the siege of Quebec.

rudes & des plus fatiguantes, et dont la plus grande partie etoit attaquée du Scorbut, faisant en tout 7,000 hommes, formoient nôtre Armée.

La Ville de Quebec, qui devoit être nôtre Quartier d'hyver & enfin nôtre tout, n'etoit pas à l'abry d'un coup de main; Six Bastions avec leurs courtines formant une Chaîne depuis l'escarpement du Cap au diamant, jusques à celui de Ste Rose, etoit alors toute nôtre deffense: point de banquettes aux Courtines ni aux Merlons, point d'embrasures aux faces, point de chemin Couvert, ni aucun ouvrage extérieur & enfin le Canon qui etoit aux flancs, etoit Si mauvais qu'il ne pouvoit être d'aucune utilité.

Il ne Seroit pas possible au juste de dècrire l'etat pitoyable de la ville: Près du tiers des maisons etoit reduit en cendres & celles qui restoient etoient si abîmées du Canon, que tres peu etoient logeables.

L'Armée Françoise etoit composée de cinq bataillons de vieilles troupes, de trente compagnies de Marines, de deux Compagnies de Chevaux legers, de 1200. Sauvages, & aux environs de 8,000 Canadiens, faisant à peu près 13,000 homes, tous gens qui se portoient bien, qui n'avoient Souffert ni essuyé la 10me partie des peines & fatigues que nos troupes avoient essuyé.

Cette armée avoit sans doute, beaucoup d'avantages sur nous; 1° Elle se portoit bien. 2° Elle connoissoit parfaitement le païs. 3° Elle avoit des provisions fraîches en abondance; ayant toute la Côte du Sud, depuis Quebec en bas, sous leur domination. Et, enfin, aucune de nos Manoeuvres, ni le moindre de nos mouvements ne leur etoit inconnu, par la Situation Singuliére de la Ville.

Voila l'Armée qui nous etoit opposée. On S'imaginera peut-être que nous avons eté blocquez, pendant tout l'hiver: Point du tout; Nous ne sommes restés dans nos murs, qu'autant de tems qu'il en faloit pour rétablir nos maisons & les rendre logeables, & mettre notre rempart à l'abry d'un coup de main.

Rétablir prés de 300. Maisons; construire huit redoutes de bois, au dèhors de la place; faire des banquettes le long des remparts, couper des embrasures; placer du Canon; fermer les avenues des fauxbourgs avec des pieux, et transporter pour onze mois de provisions dans la haute ville, faire un Magazin de 4,000 fascines, furent les prémices de nos peines & de nos travaux.

Dans le même tems les Patrouîlles ennemies venoient nous enlever nos bestiaux sous le Canon de la Place. Ils ne le firent pas impunément. Dès que les circonstances le permirent & que nous eûmes fait ce que la Prudence exigeoit de nous pour nôtre Conservation, nous nous mimes

Pris poste à Ste Foi le 11 *Nov^bre* en Campagne: Six cents hommes partirent d'icy sur deux Colomnes; L'une de 200. hommes alla a Ste Foix, & l'autre de 400, alla à Lorette; L'on prît poste à ces deux endroits, & dès qu'ils furent établis, un Corps de 700. hommes alla à St Augustin, enleva l'avantgarde ennemie, quantité de bestiaux & dèsarmérent les habitans.

à Lorette, le 12e *dètachem^t à St Augustin le* 15e.

Ces deux postes furent de la derniére consequence; 1° parce-qu'ils nous mettoient à même d'être informés des mouvements de l'ennemi, & qu'ils couvroient d'une certaine façon les nôtres; 2° Ils mettoient onze paroisses sous nôtre obéïssance, les quelles ont contribué beaucoup aux besoins de la vie animale, par la quantité de provisions fraîches qu'elles ont apporté icy pendant l'hyver; de même les Corvées qu'elles ont fait, ont été d'un grand secours à la Garnison, & enfin, le Bois, objet des plus critiques & des plus intéressants, mérite d'être dètaillé.

Au dèpart de la flotte, nous n'avions que pour 15. ou 20, jours de bois, tout au plus. L'hyver s'avançoit à grands pas; la Forêt la plus proche de la Ville etoit celle de Ste Foix; Il nous faloit près de 16,000, Cordes de bois, pour les besoins des hôpitaux, des Gardes et des Quartiers, & nous n'avions alors que tres peu de bois de coupé à l'isle d'Orléans, & le transport etoit tres lent et tres difficile, vû que la riviére etoit pleine de glaces mouvantes.

Ce fut quelques jours après l'établissement des postes de Lorette & de Ste Foix, que l'on mit 200. Coupeurs de bois dans la ditte forêt, & que l'on construisit des traineaux à main. Presqu'a la fin de novembre, l'on commença à distribuer le bois: Les Regiments envoyoient tout ce qui n'etoit pas de Service avec les traineaux & ils amenoient autant de bois dans la garnison, qu'ils en pouvoient traîner. Il est a remarquer qu'on a cherché le bois, pendant près de 3. mois, pendant des tems presqu'inconnus en Europe, & que cêt article seul peut être mis en paralelle avec les Campagnes les plus rudes & les plus fatiguantes qui se sont faites au Nord.

Nos affaires etant en bon train, & nous voyant à l'abry d'un Coup de main, on envoya un dètachement de 2,000. hoṁes au delà du fleuve St Laurent, qui dèsarma les habitants & leur fit prêter serment de fidèlité: Cette Manœuvre mit la Côte du Sud sous notre obéïssance, & nous procura quantité de provisions fraiches.

Détachement au delà du fleuve. 30e *Nov^re.*

Il y avoit dejà quelque tems que l'armée Françoise avoit pris ses quartiers d'hyver. Leurs gardes avancées etoient à la pointe aux Trembles, St Augustin, et le Calvaire; Le reste de leur armée etoit entre les trois riviéres et Jaques quartier.

Les Generaux François etant informés, que nôtre Garnison s'affoiblissoit de jour en jour, par les fatigues continuelles & inévitables auxquelles nous etions assujettis, formérent le dessein de nous attaquer de vive force au cœur de l'hyver: Ils firent en consequence tous les préparatifs nécessaires; Des raquettes furent distribuées à toute l'armée, et quantité d'échelles furent construites; L'on exerça même les Soldats à poser les echelles et à y monter.

L'attaque devoit se faire dans le milieu de fevrier, et malgré les précautions que les ennemis prirent pour nous cacher leurs desseins, en coupant la communication de Jaques Quartier, qui avoit eté ouverte jusques alors aux Canadiens, nous en fumes avertis.

Les François pren- L'ennemi qui ne perdoit pas son projet de vuë, en-
nent poste à la P. voya un dètachement à la pointe de Levi, pour y
de Lévi. 5e fev^r. prendre poste, rassembler les habitans de la Côte du
Sud, pour les joindre à l'armée, & y faire un magazin de bouche. Les postes de Calvaire & de St Augustin furent aussi renforcés par quelques Compagnies de Grenadiers.

Il y avoit près de 8. jours que les ennemis etoient à la pointe de Lévi, où ils avoient fait un amas considérable de farines, & fait tuer 400, bœufs pour la Subsistance de leur Armée pendant l'expédition, quand
Nous les chassons nôtre Infanterie légére avec un détachement de 200.
de la pointe Lévi. homes les alla dèloger. (nous ne pûmes le faire plûtôt,
13. fev^r. parce que la riviére n'etoit pas prise). Ils perdirent peu de monde, parceque leur retraite etoit précipitée; Nous fimes un Officier & onze hommes prisonniers. Nous primes poste dans l'Eglise de St Joseph, jusques à ce que deux redoutes de bois, dont l'une avoit du Canon, fussent construites, & nous nous enpârames de la plus grande partie de leurs provisions.

Quelques jours après, les ennemis vinrent en forces pour nous enlever le dit poste; mais en ayant êté avertis à tems,
ils viennent nous y l'on fit marcher quelques bataillons sur la glace, pour
attaquer le 24. fev^r, les couper, & quelques autres avec l'Infanterie légére
et ils sont repoussés. pour les attaquer, pendant qu'ils etoient occupés a faire l'attaque de l'église. Les Ennemis se voyant pris de tous côtez, songérent à se retirer; ils le firent si précipitamment, que malgré la diligence de nos troupes, on ne pût atteindre qu'une partie de leur arriére garde. Après leur retraite nous fimes nos redoutes, abatimes quantité d'arbres, et mîmes nôtre poste à l'abry de toute insulte.

Quelques jours après, ce même dètachement qui nous avoit voulû forcer, alla prendre poste à St Michel, au dessous de la pointe de Lévi: Nous ne jugeames pas à propos de les aller dèloger, vû la distance.

Il Sembloit alors, que les François avoient changé de Sentiments, & qu'ils vouloient remettre l'affaire au Printems & nous assiéger dans les régles; au moins, tous leurs préparatifs nous l'annonçoient. Ils armérent leurs galéres, faisoient des boulets & des bombes & une quantité prodigieuse de fascines & de gabions, & en un mot tout ce qui peut etre nécessaire pour un siége. Nous fimes de nôtre côté, quantité de fascines, palissades & piquets, pour nous retrancher sur les hauteurs d'Abraham, dès que le tems nous le permettroit.

Ce fût pendant que ces préparatifs se faisoient de part & d'autre, qu'une partie de nôtre infanterie légére avec un dè-

Nous leur enlevons 3 postes avancés le 20e Mars. tachement de l'armée, alla surprendre les postes avancés des ennemis à St Augustin, la Maison-brulée, & le Calvaire; Malgré leur promptitude à se retirer, nous fimes 90, prisonniers. Quelque tems après, ils voulurent avoir leur revanche, ils tentérent d'enlever nos Coupeurs &

ils veulent surprendre nos Chasseurs. 10e Avril. nos Chasseurs qui couvroient Lorette et Ste Foix, mais ils furent repoussés.

Le tems venoit de jour en jour plus critique, et il y avoit apparence que les vaisseaux & l'armée françoise descendroit avec les derniéres glaces & que la terre etant encore gelée nous n'aurions pas le tems de faire nos lignes. Les circonstances obligérent d'envoyer l'infanterie légére au Cap-rouge, afin de s'y fortifier,

Nous voulons nous établir au Cap-rouge le 18e Avril. tant pour empêcher les ennemis d'y débarquer, que pour les observer de plus près. A peine avoit on commencé les ouvrages, que la riviére s'ouvrit & que les Vaisseaux ennemis descendirent; L'Armée debarqua à St Augustin, et se mit tout de suite en marche, dirigeant leur route du côté de Lorette, afin de surprendre ce poste, & ensuite nous couper ceux du Cap-rouge et de St Foix; On les prévint: Le poste de Lorette se

Poste de Lorette retiré, le 26e Avril. replia sur St Foix, & une partie de la garnison sortit et protégea la retraite des deux postes; nous ne perdimes que deux hommes.

La nuit du 27. au 28. Avril, toute l'armée Françoise se trouvoit à St Foix, et leur avant garde etoit à la portée de fusil de la ville.

Le 28e au matin, nôtre infanterie légére & nos Volontaires chassérent l'avant-garde ennemie & lui firent prendre le large.

A neuf heures du matin toute nôtre armée sortit de la ville, avec 20. piéces d'artillerie & des outils propres à remüer la terre, dans l'intention de nous retrancher sur les hauteurs d'Abraham: A peine y fumes nous, que nous vimes l'avantgarde des ennemis sur des petites hauteurs, à l'entrée du bois de Sillery, & le gros de l'armée ennemie en marche le long du chemin de St Foix; à mesure qu'ils avançoient, ils se jettoient dans le bois & s'y formoient: C'est dans ce moment qu'il fût dècidé de leur donner bataille, afin de profiter de tout l'avantage qu'on peut avoir sur un ennemi qui n'est pas formé.

Ce fût en conséquence que nôtre armée s'ébranla; Nous avions 8. bataillons, en prémiére ligne & 2. en Seconde: L'infanterie légére & deux Compagnies de Grenadiers couvroient nôtre flanc droit: Nos Volontaires, les Chasseurs de bois & un dètachement de 100. hommes, couvroient nôtre flanc gauche. Dès que nous fûmes à la portée du mousquet, l'infanterie légére attaqua les grenadiers de la gauche des ennemis & les repoussa vivement; Dans le même instant, les Volontaires & les Chasseurs attaquérent leur droite qui plia aussi, & s'emparérent d'une redoute que les ennemis avoient en possession: Leur Centre plia sans etre attaqué.

Pendant que nous chassions ainsi l'avantgarde, Le gros de l'armée ennemie avançoit à grands pas, & se formoit en Colomnes; A peine furent-ils formés, qu'une Colomne vint soutenir les Grenadiers que nôtre infanterie légére poursuivoit; elle se glissa tout de suite le long de l'escarpement & prît notre aile droite en flanc. Dans le même instant, une Colomne conduite par le Chevalier de Levi se glissa le long de nôtre flanc gauche; Les Bataillons en seconde ligne se portérent à droite & à gauche, pour protéger nos flancs. Le moment etoit Critique; nous etions sur le point d'avoir toutes les forces du Canada sur les bras, & d'être Coupez. Cêt événement nous mit dans la nécessité de nous retirer, etant trop foibles pour leur résister, n'ayant pû les empêcher de se former. Nous fumes obligés de laisser notre Canon, vû la difficulté de l'emmener, à cause de la neige & de la bouë qui se trouvoit par intervalles.

Nous eumes 300, hommes de tuez ou prisonniers & 700, de blessés. Les ennemis ont perdu 2,500. de leur propre aveu.

L'Armée Françoise etoit composée de 10. bataillons complets, (ayant completté leurs bataillons avec l'élite des Canadiens;) de 400. Sauvages, & de 7,600. Canadiens, faisant en tout 13,000. hommes. Nôtre armée etoit de 3,111. hommes avant l'action.

L'ordre de Bataille des François etoit; 10. Compag^{es} de Grenadiers, 2, de Volontaires & 400, Sauvages formoient l'avantgarde; 8. Bataillons, formant 4, Colomnes, avec des Corps de Canadiens entre les intervalles formoient le Corps de bataille; 2, bataillons & quelques Corps de

Canadiens, sur leur flanc, formoient l'arriére, & enfin, 2000, Canadiens formoient un Corps de réserve; telle etoit leur intention, si nous leur avions donné le tems de se former.

La nuit du 28. au 29., les François ouvrirent la tranchée & leurs Vaisseaux vinrent mouïller au foulon, au dessous de leur Camp. Ils furent occupés, pendant plusieurs jours à dèbarquer leurs Canons, Mortiers & autres Munitions: Ils travaillérent constamment à perfectionner la tranchée & à construire des batteries.

Le 11. May, ils ouvrirent trois batteries de Canon & une de bombes.

Nous fimes tout ce qui etoit necessaire pour la deffense de la Place: Nous plaçames du Canon dans toutes les faces, & même dans les Courtines: Nous élevames deux Cavaliers, & fimes des Ouvrages extérieurs. Ils nous Canonnérent vivement le prémier jour, mais nôtre Artillerie (qui leur avoit dèja fait changer leur attaque) les fit bientôt taire, de façon que leur feu se rallentissoit tous les jours. Nous avions avant l'ouverture de leurs batteries 132, piéces de Canon sur nôtre rempart, dont la plus grande partie y fût menée par les soldats.

Malgré cette formidable artillerie, les Circonstances etoient critiques: Si une flotte Françoise etoit arrivée la prémiére, il y a apparence que (malgré la résistance opiniâtre que nous nous etions proposés de faire, & que nous aurions sûrement fait) nous avions infailliblement succombé.

Le 9e May, une de nos Fregates vint mouiller dans le bassin, & nous annonça que nous avions des Vaisseaux dans la Riviére. Le 15e au Soir, un Vaisseau de Ligne & une Fregate vinrent mouiller dans le Bassin & le 16e au matin nos deux Fregates mirent à la Voile, passérent la Ville & allérent attaquer l'Escadre Françoise; Elle leva l'ancre tout de suite, mais elle fut suivie de si près & canonnée si vivement, qu'elle echoua entiérement en trois differents endroits. (Leur Chef d'Escadre fut pris & enfin l'on y mit le feu.) Leur flotte etoit composée de Six Fregates de Roi.

Ce fût un Coup de foudre, pour l'Armée Françoise. Ils dècampérent le même soir & levérent le siege si precipitamment, qu'ils abandonnérent 34. piéces de Canon, 6. mortiers, tous leurs equipages, leurs vivres, & enfin un attirail immense de toutes sortes de Choses pour faire un Siége.

Notre infanterie légére & nos Grenadiers les poursuivirent jusques au Cap rouge & firent plusieurs prisonniers. L'Ennemi est à Jaques Quartier; nous ignorons leurs desseins.

Si l'on fait une récapitulation de ce qui vient d'etre mentionné & qu'on y ajoute 1000. homes qui sont morts pendant l'hyver, & près de

2000. qui ont été alternativement dans les hôpitaux, L'on Verra que 4000 hommes seulement ont fait tous les travaux & essuyé des peines & des fatigues incroyables, pendant 8. Mois consecutifs, dans un tems destiné dans d'autres païs au retablissement des troupes. Qu'on remarque aussi que l'Armée n'a pas reçû un sol de paye, pendant tout l'hyver & que personne ne s'est plaint; (chose extraordinaire dans le Soldat) Alors l'on verra que nous avons égalé & même surpassé les Anciens en plusieurs choses.

Le Capitaine Holland, Desbarres & moy avons deffendu la place, en qualité d'Ingénieurs. Le Capit^ne Wettestrom & les deux von Ingen ont eté avec l'Artillerie. Le 4e Bataillon est à Oswego, Ils sont tous attaquez du Scorbut.

[*Endorsed*] Journal of what occurr'd last Winter at *Quebec,* & in its Neighbourhood, in a Letter from an Officer of the Royal Americans. Quebec, May the 24. *1760.*

Description Militaire des Pays entre Albany, Montréal et Quebec [1] [1760]
(copy)

La distance d'Albany au Fort Edward est denviron 56 Miles la nature du terrein est telle que les chemins qu'on a fait de l'un a lautre et qu'on y fera dans la suite, seront passablement bons & faciles a entretenir.

On trouve 4 Postes entre l'un et l'autre, le premier qui est Half Moon es a 12 Miles d'Albany, il etoit sans Fortifications au Mois de Janvier 1759.

Still Water est a 14 Miles de la sur la riviere, il y a un Magasin, au Mois d'Octobre 1757 on y traça un Fort quarre flanqué de 4 demi bastions, on y peut loger 100 hommes.

Saratogaw, sur la même riviere, est un asses bon poste à 16 Miles de la; on y a construit un petit fort avec des casernes. pour 100 hōmes cest un Magazin asses considerable; les environs en sont agreables; Le païs est ouvert, il etoit habité il y a qúelques années, mais les habitans furent obligés de l'abandonner pendant la derniere guerre ainsi que Schorticock.

A 7 Miles de la est le Fort Miller qui est un quarré formé par des pieux fichez en terre, vis a vis de Great Falls ou My Lord How a campé

[1] This document is a slightly expanded copy of an "Itineraire des Pais entre Albany et Montreal" enclosed by Prevost in a letter to Cumberland of July 6, 1758.

partie des Mois de May et de Juin 1758 pour favorïser le transport des Magazins de l'Armée; Ce petit Fort dont la Construction est tres bonne, est capable de contenir 100 hommes pendant l'hiver; Il y a un Magazin assez bon mais mal situé.

Le Fort Edward en est eloigné de 7 Miles, au Confluent de deux rivieres qui ne sont navigables que pour de petits bateaux, il est capable de loger 600 hommes dans un besoin: Il ne peut être bien deffendu quautant qu'on aura une Armée aux environs, Il est commandé de trois cotés et peut être tourné avec Facilité.

Lemplacement du Fort Willm Henry est a 16 Miles du Fort Edward, le Chemin entre deux est tres bon, lórsque le Fort fut pris en 1757 il y avoît tout au pres un retranchement, deffendu par 2000 Hommes qui ne furent point attaqués, le poste est bon il est a l'extremité du lac George au Sud.

Carillon est a l'autre extremité du Lac a la distance de 33 Miles par eau et de 36 parterre; La place de debarquement dou lon fait le portage pour y arriver en venant du Sud est a la distance de 4 Miles du Fort, dans un chemin extremen^t coupé de Colines; ce fut en gagnant la premiere de ces hauteurs le 6me Juillet 1758 que My Lord How fut tué par un parti ennemi qui s'etoit egaré dans le bois, en cherchant a se retirer sous le Fort.

Ce portage est occasioné par la chute du Lac George dans le Wood Creek qui comunique avec le lac champlain, tout pres de cette chute est le moulin a Scie au dessous duqúel lon se rembarque; Le Col¹ Bradstreet avec ses nageurs sempara de ce poste le 7me Juillet et l'Armée campa tout au pres la nuit avant l'attaque des retranchements, que les Francois assurent q'uils ne commencerent que le matin du même Jour.

Ce retranchement a été perfectioné, l'etendue de son front peut être de Mille Verges dans l'interieur, a environ 1000 pas du Fort, qui est situé ainsi que son nom le designe au Confluent de deux eaux, et qui forme en qu'elque façon la Citadelle, comandant egalem^t tout le revers du retranchement; dont la droite est appuiee au Wood Creek et la Gauche au Lac George; Sa hauteur est en qu'elques endroits de 10 a 12 Pieds mais en general de 7 a 8—. En avant de ce retranchement l'Ennemi avoit un abbatis assés bien fait qu'il a poussé depuis jusques a la chute. Le Fort Carillon ou Ticonderoga n'est pas achevé et ne sauroit contenir plus de 400 Hommes.

Le Fort Frederic ou de la Couronne 15 Miles au dessus de Carillon est situé sur le Wood Creek qui entre dans le Lac Champlain, c'est un Poligone regulier bien muni dArtillerie, capable de contenir 600 Hommes au plus, Le Gouverneur habite un corps de logis detaché des casernes, que les François appellent a Citadelle, le tout bien attaqué ne sauroit tenir 3 Jours.

Unpeu au dessous de ce Fort on entre dans le Lac Champlain dont la traverse jusques au Fort St Jean est denviron 80 Miles, la Navigation en est aisée, on y trouve quelques Isles que les Francois nomment des quatre vents.

A L'extremité du Lac Champlain au Nord est situé le Fort St Jean, qui n'est qu'un mauvais quarré flanqué par quatre Tours de bois; cest sous ce Fort que les François tiennent les Barques, Bateaux, & Canots dont ils se servent pour la comunication, il paroit même qu'il n'a été construit que pour cet usage; Ils ont trois Barques armées sur ce Lac.

Du Fort St Jean au Fort de la Prairie on compte 24 Miles par terre, depuis l'arrivée des troupes de France on a fait un grand chemin entre ces deux Forts coupé par un ruisseau sur leqúel on a jetté un pont de bois, les chemins quoique faits ne sont praticables qu'en Eté ou dans les gelées, les terres entre le Lac Champlain et le Fleuve etant Basses et Marecajeuses.

Le Fort de la Prairie est situé sur le Fleuve St Laurent, vis a vis Montreal, il est sans artillerie et n'est proprement qu'un corps de Garde.

La largeur du Fleuve dans cet endroit est denviron 9 Miles; Quoique le passage soit facile elle exige quelque connoissance des Brisans qui sont pres de Montreal au dela du Canal du Fleuve au dessous des quels il faut descendre pour aborder, il y a avance fort avant dans leau et qui conduit a la Ville.

Montreal ou Ville Marie, est bien située les environs en sont tres beaux & tres fertiles, elle na pour deffence du cote du Fleuve qu'une mauvaise muraille, & du cote de la terre qu'un fossé et deux Bastions mal entretenus; C'est la principale Etape du comerce des Peleteries et le rendezvous des Nations Indiennes lorsqu'elles ont a traiter avec le Gouverneur General, & c'est de ces environs que Quebec tire la plus grande partie des provisions que le pais fournit.

L'Isle de Montreal est par 44 degrés 30 Minutes d'elevation du Pole a 75 Miles de Trois rivieres.

La Ville de Trois rivieres est encore moins fortifiée que Montreal; Il y a cependant un etat Major; Toutes les autres habitations le Long du Fleuve de Montreal a Quebec sont des Vilages ouverts et sans deffense; Les marées sont sensibles jusques a cette Ville qui est a plus de 400 Miles de la mer la distance de Trois-rivieres a Quebec est d'environ 80 Miles, les deux cotés du Fleuve sont passablement cultivez.

Quebec est par 47 Degrés 56 Minutes la ville est asses grande, et contient environ 12000 Ames, elle est passablement fortifiée du Coté du Fleuve mais assés mal du coté de terre.

Recapitulation=

D'Albany au Fort Edward ....56 Miles—du F.E.

au Fort William Henry ....16..... du F.W.H.

a Carillon ....36..... de Carillon.

au Fort Frederic ....15..... du F.F—c

a St Jean ....80..... de St Jean

a la Prairie ....24..... de la Prairie

a Montreal qui fait la largeur

du Fleuve 9

236 Miles

——

La route ordinaire de St Jean a Quebec, est par Ste Therese et Chamblit, sur la riviere Sorel, qui se jette dans le fleuve unpeu au dessus du Lac St Pierre; Si le General Amherst prend cette route, il sera obligé vraisemblablement, de faire un portage depuis St Jean, jusques au dessous du Fort de Chamblit, parce quentre ces deux Forts la riviere est si pleine de Roches et en quelques endroits si basse, qu'elle n'est navigable que pour de tres petits Bateaux.

Chamblit est meilleur que St Jean, c'est un Fort de Pierre quarré et flanqué de quatre Bastions, il est situé a 18 Miles de St Jean, sur le bord d'une rapide, vis a vis d'un petit lac formé par la riviere, on peut aisement le tourner.

De St Jean a Chamblit...18 miles de Chamblit

a Trois rivieres..........63......de Trois rivieres

a Quebec...............80

——

161

Dalbany a St Jean......203

——

Total....364 Miles

——

JOURNAL OF THE OPERATIONS OF THE ARMY IN THE
ISLAND OF MARTINICO FROM THE 16TH JAN^{RY} TO
5TH FEB^{RY} INCLUSIVE [1] [1762]

(COPY)

Janry

16th   Weighed & sailed for Fort Royal Bay, ten Ships most of
the Line brought 100 opposite the Enemies Batteries, along
the Shore, from Point Negro to Case la Haye, which they soon
silenced. The Disembarkation of the Light Infantry. Grend^{rs}
and part of the Troops made at Case la Haye that Evening.
The Rest compleated next Morning of the

17th   The Light Infantry push'd towards the Left where they
occupied a good Post three Miles up the Country close to the
Mountains, about 10 o'clock Welsh's Brigade, who had likewise filed off to the left were joined by the Light Infantry,
(except 150 Men who still occupied their Post,) had Orders to
cross the River of Case Navire, & take Possession of an intermediate Hill, which came between the Enemies Retrenchments, on the Grounds of the Tortueson, and the High
Grounds of Case la Haye. While they were under Orders to
march, the Enemy made a Push at the light Infantry Post, but
were repulsed with Loss before Morgans came up to support
them. Brigadier Welsh covered by two Field Pieces on our
Side the rising-Ground crossed a very bad Gully and the
River, and the Enemy retired to their Works on the other
Side— At 11 o'clock the first Brigade march'd to the Left and
possessed themselves of the light Infantry Post. As from the
Appearance of the Country, the General had Reason to think
the Army could cross the great Gully of Case Navire, near the
Mountains, and take the Enemies Works of Tortueson in the
Rear. Had this been practicable a Passage might have pre-
sented itself likewise to the Morne Grenier

18th   Reconoitred towards the left, found the Country impracticable and the Enemy in Possession of every Part that commanded the great Ascents.

19th   The General being desirous of crossing the Gullys that
separated the Enemies Works, proposed it to the Consideration of the Brigadiers of the Army and laid before them the

---

[1] An account by Gordon of the siege of Martinique is in Add. MSS. 21, 648, f. 176,
and was printed in the *Aberdeen Free Press*, Aug. 8, 1905.

Reports of the Engineers who had been sent out to view the Roads, which were rather favourable. The Brigadiers being averse (as it seemed to us by the Consequence) to the Troops crossing till Batteries were raised to cover the Ascent. The Batteries were accordingly ordered, one for 5 Guns on the intermediate Hill which Brigadier Welsh had possessed, and another on the Right for four Howbitzers and 1 Gun on the right Point of the same Ground of that continued Ridge. In the Night of the

21st   The Batteries were begun and altho' the Earth was scarce and to be brought some Distance they were ready on the Morning of the

23rd   The Batteries fired with Success and a Situation marked out in the Center for the Royals within Distance of the Enemy, where a Place being made for them under the Direction of Capt Lewis of the Artillery, they were removed there that Night. When the General having determined to pass the Troops the next Morning at Day Break, gave the Brigadiers his Scheme of the Attack which was as follows

Brigadier Rufane supported by the Marines, and the Appearance of the Flatt bottomed Boats off Point Negro, to march along the great Road near the Sea Side conducted by Lieut Mulcaster Engineer. The Grenadiers conducted by Capt Williams Engineer to march along the Path in Front of the Howbitzer Battery, to attack the Redans on the Edge of the rising Ground, the Redoute to the Right of the Village, and support & join Brigadier Welsh's Brigade, who conducted by Capt Williamson Engineer were to cross the Gully by their Right, and to march directly up to the Enemies Retrenchment & attack it, the Village or House of D'Arché, The Light Infantry of Col. Scot on their Left to endeavour to get behind the Village and Retrenchment, & take the the Redoute behind it in Flank. From a Report of the Practicability of Brigadier Havilands Brigade crossing the Gully, he was ordered to cross and check the Enemy if they should attempt the supporting the lower Retrenchments by marching from the Heights on the left. Lord Rollo's Brigade had Orders to march partly in the Rear of the Grenadiers, and towards Brigadier Rufanes Left with which they were to communicate & likewise support the Attack of the Grenadiers commanded by Brigdr Grant.

24th   The Grenadiers and Welsh[s] Brigade marched briskly to their Attacks, & after some firing from the Enemy from the Redans, without receiving a Shot from the Retrenchment to the left of the Village, as they had been a good deal disheartned by the Fire of the five Gun Battery Howbitzer Royals, and some twelve p[drs] that were ordered up to the left of the Howbitzer Battery, all which kept an incessant Fire from Day Light and while the Troops were mounting. They ascended with great Impetuosity, carried the Redans, Retrenchment, Village, & Redoute to the Right of the Village —afterwards advancing still in Front towards the Retrenchments on the further Eminence of Tortueson, were checkt a little in Front from the Redoutes and Retrenchments, and the Point of the Wood on their Left. The General formed Lord Rollo's Brigade behind the Village, sent repeated Orders to Brigadier Rufane to advance on the Right, whose Brigade seemed to get on slowly. He likewise sent Orders to the light Infantry to push into the Wood and take the Enemy in Flank—Who only waited till the Appearance of Rufane's Brigade and the Sound of the light Infantry—and those ordered into the Wood—to evacuate all their Works and quit the Wood— They were pursued to the Town & received a considerable Loss in their Retreat along the great Road. We likewise lost a Lieu[t] of Montgomerys and several Men at the End of the Bridge.

As soon as they had given Way The Marines formed a Front to the Left & the light Infantry and some Companies of Grenadiers marched towards the higher Village and House of D'Arché on the Left— The Light Infantry push'd forward and possessed themselves of a very advantageous Ground opposite to Morne Grenier, which being viewed by the Engineers and reported to the General as a convenient Ground to cover the Passage to the Morne Grenier Brigadier Havilands Brigade who had pass'd the Gully late in the Day— occasioned by the Difficulty of the Grounds, were ordered to take Possession of. The Light Infantry were posted on their Left— The same Night— The same Night a Battery for ten Cannon, was mark'd on the nearest Point of the Tortueson, and work'd upon, some Epaulements which communicated with the Enemys Redoutes on the same were made to cover the Troops from the Fire of Morne Grenier.

25 & 26   Two Batteries were work'd on, one a good deal towards the left to enfilade the Citadel & one of Six Guns to the right of the ten Gun Battery. The two eldest Engineers ordered to view the Roads from the advanced Posts on the Left to ascend the Morne Grenier. They made a favourable Report of them at the same Time added the placing of Guns necessary to cover the Ascent—

27   About half after 3 o'clock in the Afternoon the Enemy made an Attack in three Columns on Brigad^r Havilands Post. They advanced briskly with 3000 Men but were well received, and upon the light Infantry, who were nigh the Left Attack, having taken them in Flank they gave Way— The Troops on all sides pursued them, crossed the River and Gully which separated them from the Morne Grenier, continued the Pursuit up the different Roads, and having been supported by the Generals Orders by the Grenadiers and nearest Brigades, were in Possession of the Enemies, Redoutes Batteries, and Works by nine o'clock at Night Major Leland with the second Division of Light Infantry pushing on in the Front— We were amazed at day Light at the Advantages of Ground, Works & Artillery the Enemy abandoned to us, even with such Precipitation that the left one of their Mortars, and eight Pieces of large Artillery not spik'd

29th   The Battery of ten Guns and that on the left of four Guns and three Mortars received their Pieces. The Enemies Guns on Morne Grenier were turned against them— The

30th   The Batteries begun firing—their Distance being considerable and their Powder bad, The Shot from the ten Gun Battery which was not twelve Hundred Yards and commanded the Citadel at 15 Degrees fell short— The four Gun Battery being 3 or 400 Yards further, altho' in a good Position to infilade the Cittadels Works—was still at that Dissadvantage

31st   The Powder being better and the Guns more elevated the Shot went Home but the Enemy increasing their Fire dismounted 3 Guns on the ten Gun Battery—when the bringing up of Ship 32 pdrs was proposed—

1st Febry.   opened another Battery of Six Guns on the Right which with some iron Guns brought on the 10 Gun Battery gave us a Superior Fire, and the Guns on Morne Grenier being pointed ag^t the Cavalier to infilade it. The Enemy found it very inconvenient to stay in their Upper Works. This Day the

Engineers were ordered to view the Grounds to the S.E. as Lelands light Infantry had been ordered to take Possession of the Mouth of the River Monsieur and the Enemies Batteries on that Side— They viewed the Morne Capucin, and another rising Ground under Grenier, The Entrance of the River Monsieur for landing Artillery, and the Passage from thence to the Morne Capucin, which last commands extremely at a small Distance the Fort

2   Dispositions were made for Batteries on the Morne Capucin, and at Night an Engineer was sent into the Town to cover 7 Royal Mortars the General ordered there— A Cover was markt out for them in the Range of the Length of the Fort at 600 Yards Distance not being able to get a View of the Fort in any Place nigher without going on the Glacis or into the Morass— That Night the Parapet was not compleated

3rd   The Chief Engineer went & mark'd the Place for the Batteries on Morne Capucin In the Evening a Party was sent to finish the Royal Mortar Battery, and the Guard of 300 Men advancing towards the Streets of the Town next to the Cittadel a deserter going over to the Enemy with an Opinion this Party was designed for an Escalade, which he told them. They beat the Chamade at 7 o'clock in the Evening— An officer was dispatchd to the General, with Proposals, and a Desire for a Cessation of Hostilities— Orders were sent to the Batteries and working Parties to desist. The Officer was to return next morning with further Articles— The

4th   The Officer returned and the Capitulation was signed the Grenadiers took Possessn of ye Citad[1] at 5 o'clock in the Afternoon. 5th The Garrison march'd out with the Honours of War two Pieces of Cannon, Colours &ca they consisted of betwn 6 & 700 Men, Grenadrs Troupes de Colonie Flibustiers Canoniers &ca— The Fort had been great plunged by our Battries some of the Merlons shattered, and the Guns dismounted. Their Loss was about 150 Men killed and wounded. But the Garrison might have safely waited the Effects of the Batteries on Morne Capucin, which would no Doubt have made a Breach in the East Side of the Fort, which is the weakest, and that in a short Time. These Batteries were only traced. The Enemy were much harrassed as but a few went in the Casemates, and no Place in the Fort was safe from the cross Infilades of our Cannon— The Batteries on the Morne

Grenier altho at the greatest Distance were the severest upon them, as they plunged the Length and Breadth of the Fort & Entrance into their Casemates.

HARRY GORDON   ENGINEER

COLONEL WILLIAM EYRE TO SIR WILLIAM JOHNSON
(COPY)

New York 7th Jany 1764.

Dr Sir William

The Route I took from Niagara prevented me from seeing you on my Return, which I intended if that had not taken Place: Indeed I should have been glad particularly at this troublesome Time, to have the Satisfaction of your Thoughts upon Indian Matters; my Politicks in Regard to these Gentry being somewhat different from most others, so much so, as I have Scarcely met with one to think as I do in particular Situations relative to these Savages. However I am persuaded we must alter our Way of thinking, and act differently from our present Plan, or there will be no End to the Insults we must at all Times be subject to, whenever the Indians are pleas'd with or without Cause to be angry with us; Give me Leave to tell you the Ideas I have conceiv'd of these troublesome Neighbours of ours, and the Method we should take according to my opinion in our present State of Affairs; In the first Place, our taking Posts, and so many of them far advanc'd amongst the Indians, must for some Centuries put ourselves in their Power, when they are pleas'd to take up the Hatchet; Therefore our withdrawing our Posts is the only Safety left us; by acting from this, we give less Cause of Umbrage to the Indians to quarrel with us, if they do, we can better Support these Posts, and the Enemy will have the further to come to attack them, consequently be less formidable than if they were in their own Country, as they could not in this Case lay any Time before them with any Number for Want of Subsistance: As to taking our Posts by Force, its plain they cannot, however they can, and always will, be able to cut off more or less the Communication to them, which is taking them in Fact, or rendering them useless; its true our late Commander imagin'd that the Indians could not cut off so easily our Communications between these distant Posts, nor did he think they would dare attempt it: This last Summer makes this Affair very plain, he, at first, after they were Surpris'd, seem'd determin'd to have them all reinstated, and gave Orders accordingly to Major Gladwin; This Proceeding I must confess to you astonish'd me, and the more so, it being very unlike his usual just Way of thinking, however I was within myself convinc'd it was not in our Power, and tho' it was possible to effect it by Dint of Numbers, and that at a great Expence, as well as the Number of Lives which must be lost upon Such an Undertaking, how could we after this go between these Posts whilst at War with the Indians? As for Example, for a Party to go between Miamis and St Josephs or Onatenau upon the Wabash River; to Support such a Communication would require an Army in them Woods, and tho' it was possible to maintain one there, and repulse the Indians at every Attack they would make, we should even in these Victories lose ten Men for one, nay twenty if we consider Sickness and Accidents: In short to pretend to keep Posts in these distant Places without the Consent of the Indians, or without having them by their own Desire, and under their Protection, I consider as vain and delusive; Therefore I hope such a Thing will never be undertaken more. You will perhaps want to know what I mean by withdrawing our Posts, it is this, Niagara at most should be my furthest Post in that Quarter, and I think Littleton far enough for the present on the Ohio Side, untill that Country is thicker inhabited: The Query then is whether we shall not lose a great Deal of the Indian Trade by this Method, its granted we may, tho' not probable we shall, for by taking such Measures, the Indians in this Case would request of us in the strongest Manner, that we would Send our People to trade with them into their Country; this might be agreed to, but not upon our present Plan, by Way of Posts. If any went they should be chosen People, Officers we shall Suppose, with four or six Men, the Officer by Way of Magistrate to see Justice done between the Indians and the Traders, and the Men only to assist the Officer in executing this Trust, and to go Expresses when Occasion required: By this Means we may keep up a Trade with the most distant Nations, retain their good Opinion, and totally prevent any Jealousy of our intending them any Ill. These small Small Settlements / : as I may call them: / of our People amongst them by their own Request, would retain a Possession of these Countries and that under their Protection, would most certainly prevent the Indians from hurting any of them, as they must be convinc'd it could only tend to their own Disadvantage, as in the first Place, it would put a Stop to any Trade in that Way for the future, so that the killing of a few Men cannot effect their Cause, and can only create themselves Enemies, without any Prospect to themselves of Good. I have for near Years past hinted partly what I now communicate to you, to our General, and

indeed have Sent Home my Thoughts to Some Friends there on this
Head. Of late I have wrote to England more fully my Thoughts on
these Matters, and I must confess to you, that I am so prepossess'd in
Favor of this Scheme, that I believe none but this, or something of this
Kind will keep us on good Terms with the Indians. How is it possible
to pretend to take Possession in any other Way of the Ilinois Settlement, which is twelve or thirteen hundred Miles up the Missisipi River,
Surrounded with endless Tribes of Indians. As we encrease in Numbers
on this Continent, its easy and Safe to advance our Settlements in
Townships, tho' this I would do, only by Cession or by Purchase of the
Lands to prevent the Shadow of an Excuse for the Indians to quarrel
with us, and if they should by Settling in this Manner, we could always
defend ourselves, and in a little Time convince them of the Vainess
of their Attempts. Should the French presume to Settle any Posts in
any of these Places, it would be easy to revenge the Perfidy by attacking
New Orleans, or any other Part of their Dominions, that was most
convenient. However I would remove every Canadian from all our
Posts to the inhabited Parts of Canada, as also the Priests, to prevent
their doing Mischief: I wish the same could be done with Respect to
those at the Ilinois, but these the Indians, I am afraid would not allow
to be sent from thence—No Doubt but it will be found necessary to
erect a Fort at the upper End of the River Iberville, or somewhere in
that Neighbourhood in order to have a respectable Post to command
the Entrance of that River, as also the Missisipi River in that Part,
being the lowest Place on the Eastern Side which is ceded us by Treaty:
Somewhere thereabouts, I do presume, the Government will think, as
I before mentioned, to fix a Post at, and perhaps at other Places in that
Quarter. These Places of Arms may hereafter be fixt upon at Leisure,
which require to be strong, but as to our Frontier Forts or Block
Houses towards the Indians, they need not be very much so, as Indians
from the Nature of their Attacks, can never be very formidable in these
Respects, so they can easily be guarded against; all that will be necessary in erecting these Posts are to make them of such Materials as will
be durable, and that they cannot set Fire to by Fire Arrows or any
other Means. I am very apprehensive for the Fate of Pittsburgh, should
there be a high Flood there this Winter, in the Situation it now is in.
However there is one Consolation the Government has if they should
withdraw our Frontier on that Side, is, that tho' Fort Pitt has cost so
much Money, it is now of no Value, therefore if one was was necessary
to be kept up there, it must be began in another Place, therefore no
Loss to remove it nearer: What a most unhappy and expensive Under-

taking the attacking that Part of this Country has been to the Crown: The Works alone have cost more Money than all the other Forts put together in this Department, but this Expence is a mere Trifle to the Article of the Transportation of Provisions and warlike Stores over the Mountains to that unlucky Fort. But what need I mention these Things to you, who must have had various Accounts of them from many Hands. I shall conclude in requesting you will do me the Favor to let me know your Sentiments upon the present Posture of Indian Affairs, as they seem now to wholly engross all our Attention, and most certainly its of the greatest Consequence what Measures we now pursue for the future Repose and Peace of all the People living on the Frontier of our several Colonies. Your Compliance will much oblige me, and should I be lucky enough to think as you do upon these Points, will doubtless give me much Satisfaction, however be this as it may, I shall be very happy to have your opinion to correct mine; and be assured no one pays greater Deference to you than I do, not only in Respect to these Matters, but in many Things else, wherein you chuse to offer your Sentiments. Believe me to be Dear Sir William your very sincere, and affectionate Friend, and most obed[t] humble Serv[t]

Sign'd WILL: EYRE

SIR WILLIAM JOHNSON TO WILLIAM EYRE
(COPY)

Johnson Hall Jan[y] 19th 1764.

Dear Sir

I thank you for . . . .

I cannot but coincide in Opinion with you on the greatest Part of what you have mention'd on Indian Affairs, and I could wish for the Good of the publick, that every Person had been of the same Way of thinking, which might have proved a Means of preventing the many Losses we have lately felt.

The Causes to which the Defection of the Indians may be attributed are, *First* their Jealousy of our growing Power and Occupancy of the Out Posts, where they neither met with the same Treatment, nor reap'd any of Advantages which they enjoy'd in Time of the French. *Secondly* the Reports industriously propogated by many of the French, tending to set our Designs in the most odious Light, and to represent the Indians as on the Brink of being enslav'd.

It will not appear extraordinary that the French who had purchas'd the Indians Favor at a high Price, should obtain Credit from such Representations, especially when there were but too many concurring Circumstances to strengthen the Belief of a People naturally credulous and jealous of their Liberties. The Indians began with Remonstrances, represented many Grievances, and demanded Redress, these Complaints I communicated from Time to Time with my Sentiments and apprehensions thereon, but the inconsiderable Opinion too universally entertain'd of their small Power and Abilities occasion'd it to be treated with Neglect, To particularise all their Complaints would exceed the Bounds of a Letter, it will be sufficient to observe, that I declar'd it as my Opinion that the Indians should not be totally neglected, but that /: after Redress of their Grievances:/ we should cultivate to the utmost of our Power a good Understanding with them, at least until we became more formidable and our Frontiers better established, and this I thought we could effect at an Expence infinitely less than any other Method, and on Principles the best adapted for securing Peace, promoting Trade, and encreasing our Frontiers.

The Expence, Difficulty and Dangers attending other Expedients, the Stagnation of Trade, Destruction of our Posts and Frontiers, and the small Advantages to be gain'd by a War with Indians, are now obvious to most People, and are so well represented in your Letter that they need not to be enlarg'd upon.

The Difficulty and even Impossibility of securing our Communications, or maintaining our Out Posts contrary to the Indians Inclinations is very clear to me, but I am pretty certain we can purchase all these Advantages, and Secure their Inclinations by a proper Treatment, which will gain us a Sufficient Credit with them, and a Use of their Country, as it will remove all their Prejudices, and which no other Steps can effect.

The Inland Small Posts don't appear to me very necessary, they are too great a Temptation to the Indians, whenever they are induc'd to quarrel, and from their Distance and Difficulty of obtaining Succours must always fall into their Hands, the same Reasons induce me to think, that the Persons and Properties of Traders would not be safe amongst them, for whilst there are any French there, they will certainly thro' Jealousy, promote a Quarrell, and even were there none there, the Expence of transporting Goods is so great that they must Sell at a Price which would not be agreeable to the Indians, as well as be guilty of many Frauds, not in the Power of an Officer to discover or prevent; Whereas the Indians /: who think little of going a good Way to purchase Necessaries:/ would find them cheaper at our large Posts And the Traders would be less expos'd to Risques.

Whenever we can have a good Communication by Water we might tolerably well maintain Posts, and if some small Vessells are kept up on Lake Erie, Detroit, or even Michilimakina might be kept up, the latter being well calculated for drawing down the northern Furr^s.— After all that can be said we shall be liable to many Broils, till the french Inhabitants and Jesuits are removed, the latter being no longer a Society in France, we might very well appropriate their Lands to His Majesties Use—I dare say they would endow a Bishoprick in Canada, and provide for good Missionaries, and I imagine an Episcopal Foundation in that Country would greatly contribute to bring over the French, and make good Subjects of them in Time.

The late Offers of Peace made by some of the Nations has been greatly promoted by the Attachment *the 5 Nations, Indians of Canada* &^{ca} have manifested during the Course of the War, which makes our Enemies dread they will accompany our Troops against them in the Spring, for they have much more Reason to fear Indians than the best Troops in the World.

Indeed the aforemention'd Nations of Indians have made me so many Offers of Service, that I have no Doubt of their Sincerity, and I am now sending out a considerable Party of Oneydas, Tuscarora's and Mohawks, who I hope will greatly distress our Enemies, as well as convince them that we are not without Allies of their own Sort, this will likewise contribute to disunite them, a Circumstance too important to be neglected.

Whenever the present unhappy Troubles shall be ended by an Accommodation, I trust such Measures will be taken at Home, as may ensure a lasting Peace to the northern Colonies, on which Subject I have lately receiv'd some Letters from the Lords of Trade, expressing His Majesties favorable Sentiments, and those of their Lordships concerning my late Representations.

I heartily wish you well and am Dear Sir Your most sincere Friend and Humble Servt

Signd/
Wm JOHNSON

Colonel William Eyre to General Robert Napier

(A.L.S.)

New York
12th April 1764.

Dear Sir

I have been in hopes at different times Since the Reduction of Canada to be allowed to go to England to Settle My Private Affairs, but One Incident or Other still Interven'd which Prevented that Design from taking Place, however Upon the Definitive Treaty being Signed, I thought then I could not fail, but in this I have been also Equally disappointed; I only asked for a few Months, And that during the Winter Season, but Such was My fate it was not Granted to Me, upwards of Nine Years Close Duty in this Country was not sufficient Plea to Entitle me to that Indulgence, Such it Seems is my Destiny, so I shall Endeavour to be Satisfied with My Lot; it's what we Are Sub-· ject to as Soldiers, it's our Duty to Obey, therefore I shall wait with Patience Until the Lucky time comes. Indeed Sir, it was these Pleasing Expectations of Returning to England which prevented me from troubling You of Late with More Epistles; however as I have (not long ago) received Some Draughts from the East And West Florida's, I here with Inclose two or three of Them to You, thinking it might be agreeable to You to Communicate Them to His Royal Highness the Duke of Cumberland.

As Indian Measures for Some time Past have Engross'd all our Attentions in this Part of the World, And the Means that should be used to reduce these Savages to Reason And keep Them hereafter in Awe, is Matter of much dispute, few Joining in Opinion about the most Effectual Way, which have Induced Me to trouble You with the Inclosed Copys of Two Letters wrote Upon this Subject, One of Them from Me to Sr William Johnson, And the Other His Answer to it; These Will in Part give You Some Idea how He And I consider this Matter. As to Occupy All the Posts that the French And Spaniards have had, Seems to me to be by no Means requisite; on the Contrary it makes us More liable to be Insulted, besides the Immense Expense it must draw the Crown into Annually. Whilst this Country was divided between the English, French, And Spaniards, it was in Some Part necessary for Each Nation to have Posts Amongst the Indians for two very good Reasons, the first, as it prevented the Others from Engrossing all the Fur Trade between Them, the Second Equally necessary, to keep Up a Connection And Acquaintance with as Many Tribes of Indians as Possible, in order to have Them As Auxiliarys in Case of a War: These Posts I say were to Each of the Three Powers very Essential when the Country was divided between Them, but that being not the Case now, The Causes for these Places being Removed, the Effects of Course do Cease; Therefore it follows, what was good Politicks then for us to Pursue, may be now the Contrary; And I am further of Opinion that besides withdrawing our Posts in the Manner I have hinted in My Letter to Sr William Johnson, The most Certain And Effectual Method to distress And Punish the Indiens now, or at Any Other time hereafter should the[y] Attack us, Will be, to Cut off all Supplys of Every kind, or have Any Intercourse with Them; it's now in Our Power by being wholly Master of the Country which we never could Effect before that happened: This, And This only, Seem to Me to be the most Safe And Certain Way, And that without Putting the Crown to Expence, for Indians having been So long used to Blankets, Arms, Ammunition, &c that the Want of These Articles would Infaliably reduce them to great Miseries: I am realy convinced within my Self should it be found Necessary not to make Peace with Them, that if Penal Laws were made in Each of the Colonies for this Purpose, it would very Sensibly hurt the Indians And Moreover Oblige Them to Sue for Peace And our Protection, in the most Abject And Supplicating Terms; They Cannot Scarcely kill Sufficient Food without fire Arms being so much accustomed to Them; This I am pretty Certain of from the knowledge I have acquired of the Nature of their living, at the different Times I have been Stationed at.

Colonel Bradstreet is going this Summer to the Detroit with Some Regulars, 300 Canadians formed into a Battalion, And A Body of Indians of the five Nations: These Indians have of late Exerted themselves very remarkably in Our Interest, much beyond most Peoples Expectations, & I make no doubt but thro' their Means the Enemy Indians will be brought to A Proper Sense of their Misconduct. If You should Apprehend Any Information of this kind would be Agreeable to His Royal Highness the Duke, I flatter MySelf You will take An Opportunity to Communicate it.

I have An Immense Deal of Publick Acc^{ts} that were Incurred in Carrying on Works in this Department, Lodged With Me, by the Several Engineers Employed, which I presume Will Call me home to have Them Pass'd. I have Many Draughts And Sketches of Different Parts of this Country, which I hope when I have the good fortune to See You, may be A means to Amuse You for A few hours. I must

Confess I cannot help thinking if I had been Allowed to go to England last Winter but I might have been of Some little Use, As I am informed the Government has or Soon will fix upon Places for Posts that Are to remain hereafter; My Residence in this Country for Upwards of Nine Years, And being Continually Employ'd As An Engineer, And the most Part of Them as Chief could not fail of Giving me frequent Opportunitys of being thoroughly acquainted with All the Posts in the Department of New York: As to Those in the East And West Florida's, And the Carolina's, I know nothing About Only by Draught or Discription, for These Places, I Presume there Will be A Chief Eng^r Appointed for that District; And Also it's probable there will be An Other Sent to the Northward to Direct Any Works that may be order'd to be Carried on at Newfound Land, Louisburg, Halifax &c, As it's Impossible for the Person Who is Chief at this Division of the Continent can Superintend to the Northward & Southward. This Department here call'd by the Name of New York, Comprehends All Canada, The Posts Upon the Communication between Albany And that Country, As Also All Them between Albany to the Westward, Namely, Fort Stanwix, Fort Onterio (Oswego) and Niagara, Without Mentioning Detroit, & Other Posts that were formerly Upon the Lakes more remote, which were distroyed by the Indiens.

I am Sir, with Great Esteem, Your Much Obliged, And most Obed^t humble Servant

WILL: EYRE

Since I wrote My Letter, there Are Accounts come from Sr William Johnson, that the Senecas and Chinesacs Indians have Several Deputies at His House from their Castles, Supplicating for Peace; by Other Accounts they Are very much Alarmed at the late Spirited behaviour of the rest of the five Nations, So that it's Imagined They Will thro' fear make An Ample Restitution for their perfidious behavior last Summer; it was Them that were chiefly if not Wholly Concerned in Cutting off Lt Campbell's Party Upon the Niagara Carrying Place. The Cognewagoes being Part of the five Nations residing in Canada, have made the strongest Offers of their Service of Any of the Others, by declaring they will go along with our Troops or by themselves against Any Indians whatsoever (tho' they were of their own Tribes) if in War against us: These Menaces of theirs, Joined to the Body of Canadians who are preparing to go against Them, Added to the Spirit which These Indians have Shewn who have been lately Employ'd by Sr William Johnson, must have the Wish'd for Effects, And I make no doubt but We shall Soon have these Gentry brought to acknowledge, & be Obliged to make proper Restitutions for the many Crueltys they have Committed during the Course of last Summer.

Memorial Concerning the Back Forts in North America

(A.D.S.)

1st Their Usefulness with Regard to Trade is, when properly situated and constructed, they ought to afford Cover & Protection to the Traders and their Goods during the Time of Trade, and during the Winter; as those Traders who intend for the far Lakes must get up at least as high as Niagara, to be ready to push on to these Lakes for the furr Trade, that opens in April & continues till the middle of June. That they are necessary for the Traders, in case of Indian Discords or Discontents, to be at no vast Distance, & where they may remain in or retire to, 'till Matters are cleared up and setled— If the Indian Trade is to be carried on in Vessels, which I think it ought for a few Years, as there are now several on the Lakes, & untill the Natives are more setled in their Dispositions: Then Forts properly situated are necessary to protect the Loading, and unloading of them, to lay them up at in Winter &ca. I am much of Opinion, if proper Regulations are made and observed, That the Freights of Trade, will goe nigh to defray the Expence of such Vessels as are wanted to carry Necessaries for the Garrisons. Lastly that the present Disposition of the Indians with Regard to the English is still such, as makes it adviseable, & prudent to carry on Trade among them in as much Safety as the proper Value of it will warrant & defray. That it can be only carried on to the best Advantage, by advancing into the upper Lakes is deducible from the following Reasons. First that it has been customary, when the French had Possession of the whole upper Trade, (which they have had near a century) for their Traders to carry their Goods among the Nations bordering on, or nigh those Lakes, and never for the Indians to bring their Furs, to any great Distance, to the Traders. Secondly that the Neighbourhood of the French along the West Side of the Mississipi, makes it absolutely necessary, if we chuse to have even but a Share in the Trade, to send Traders among the Nations near the Lakes, otherwise the French will, and carry it wholly down that River. Thirdly that the only Part of this Commerce worth being possest of is the Furs got from the Upper Nations. Lastly Were the whole Forts abandoned and the Vessels laid up immediately, I really imagine that this Branch of our Comerce would be so exposed and unsupported, as to render it impracticable for the Traders to advance into the Places where the most valuable Commodities are only to be had—neither would it be attempted I suppose by Brittish Merchants of any Character, but entirely fall into the Hands of the French of Canada, and mostly into those of the French Kings Subjects; by these Means the greatest Part (as has been the Case for two Years past) would certainly be sent to France.

2^{ndly} That altho scattered Forts in an Indian Country without large Garrisons, could never be made formidable to them, or check their Incursions when they had a Mind to make any against our Frontiers— Yet in Point of good Policy, it seems very improper to leave those numerous Nations to be practised on by Emissaries sent among them by our European Rivals, without our Knowledge, and who might bring them to such Attempts, in Case of a Rupture at Home, against our Colonies, as might oblige us to employ a far greater Number of Troops, and at a higher Expence, than would have been wanted to keep a few Posts, and take Methods to prevent Interlopers of other Nations coming among the Natives, and endeavour to get Intelligence of their Dispositions for publick Purposes.

3^{rdly} That from such Dispositions it becomes prudent to preserve an Inlet amongst them, and Places whereto, from the Nature of the Country we can always have Access, and from whence we can, in Cases of Need, enter among their principal Places of Residence— That their Dispositions are very sensible of the Advantage such Posts gives us, over whose Communication or Deffence their Attempts will not be able to prevail, and by their Cover always have Necessaries at Hand to act against them.

4^{thly} That to favour the Extension of our Frontiers which is in several Respects (too plain to be all mentioned) the Interest of Great Brittain to incourage; it will be absolutely necessary to have advanced Posts, and take other Measures to influence the Indians to Peace; which is surest done by courting of them, and at the same Time convincing them that a contrary Conduct will return Vengeance on themselves.

5^{thly} The above considered and balanced with the Advantage and Expence of having any Posts, will very readily ascertain their Number and Situation. The Purposes of Trade, as it is now under Regulation, would demand a great Many— Its being only to be carried on at Forts, is as improper in my Opinion as to have none at all to cover or support it—nor should the Respect to Trade ever ingage us to an unmilitary Position of Forts, neither does it demand it; For could the Position of them at first have had a military Regard, we should probably have saved a Number of Soldiers, and an Expence of £150,000 which the last Indian War cost Us. The grand Avenue by which Trade must be carried on, is by the Comunication of the Western Lakes, such an Inland Comunication as cannot be equalled by any other on this Globe that is yet discovered— If this grand Avenue is properly attended to and secured, Trade may safely branch out from it in all the different Chanels by which it is necessarily to be carried on, and it may doe so, with more Safety, without Posts on *all* these Chanels than with them or at them— For what Security can any Posts be to Trade, when it can in so many Places be interrupted or cut off, in going to or coming from them? But that Forts should not be presented at all, for the Purposes of Trade mentioned in the first Article, does by no Means follow— The first shews too much Distrust of the Indians, but the other is necessary to influence their general Conduct and Behaviour to the Traders among them and in their Power.

To determine therefore, the Situation of these Forts for such necessary Purposes of Trade &ca As the most valuable Part of it lays at a great Distance, it would require one Post to be considerably advanced, I think as far as the Bottom of La Baye, if the Vessel now in Lake Huron can comunicate directly with it. At that Place the most valuable Furs are to be had in great Quantities, where our Traders ought to go to, and from whence, for Want of English Traders, The French have carried the best Furs, to a large Amount, for Years past, down the Mississipi. The Intrusion of French Traders, into these Parts, will not be known nor prevented without a Look out at La Baye— If the Vessel can comunicate with it, and lay up at it during Winter, she will bring back Intelligence, and a very valuable Cargoe, early in the Spring— Should these Circumstances be of Weight enough to establish a Post at La Baye and send a small Garrison there, one at Michilimackinack is no more necessary— The French Houses will cover the Goods, and a proper Person to watch over Trade will be sufficient there; The Vessel may just call in passing or repassing to or from La Baye, and serve to carry the Trade from and to Michilimackinack or Parts adjacent.

The next Garrison will be conveniently posted at Detroit, nearly the Center of the Grand Comunication, pleasantly and properly situated on the navigable River that is 30 Miles long, & joins the upper Lakes, Michigan, La Baye, Huron, & St Clair, to Lake Erie. As the Situation of Detroit is so centrical, a proper Garrison at it, will enforce Respect among all the western Nations. Its being a convenient Place and Deposit for the Trade designed for the uper Lakes to winter at or retire to, and as the Country near it is already considerably improved; with smal Encouragement given to the Inhabitants to raise Provisions, would soon be able to supply 2 or 300 Men, who may be supported here at no very great Expence. The Commandant ought to have Powers of civil Magistracy, and proper Persons pick'd out among the Inhabitants and Traders to execute the Functions of Justice and Government, which are absolutely necessary in Trade, & to incourage & ascertain the Inhabitants in Property, and Cultivation— Smal Atention and Expence will put this Colony in such a prosperous Way as will make it of great Benefit to Great Brittain.

Lake Erie being and ought to be navigated by deck'd Vessels, it will be proper to keep up the Post now established at the East End of it, just above the swift Water of Niagara River, the Vessels should never descend lower than this Post, and a Warf should be built to lay them up by during Winter— The Fort is small and with a very little Addition of Expence may be defended by 30 Men. From Fort Erie the Water runs very rapid for about 16 Miles to another Fort called Fort Schlosser at the upper End of the carrying Place round the Falls of Niagara—at the lower End of this carrying Place is a small Fort likewise, in either of which there seems but little Occasion for Garrisons— The Battoes, that are to carry Goods or Provisions from Fort Schlosser to Fort Erie, between which the Water is too rapid to use Vessels, ought to be laid up at Fort Erie, and only three Men with a small Canoe or advice Boat left at the other for the sake of communication— The Garrison of Fort Erie will be sufficient for Battoeing, but if they should not a Detachment from that of Niagara can easily be sent to assist them, nor is any other Number of Men needfull or the Expence of any Forts necessary on the carrying Place except at Niagara.^{wch} from its Situation is the second best Position for a considerable Garrison on this whole Communication. It presents a fine Harbour for the Vessels on Lake Ontario, and will always be found convenient to protect and shelter the Traders who can get no higher before Winter. Its Garrison may influence the conduct of the Seneca Nation, one of the most turbulent among the Indians; and who look upon themselves Umpires of all the others. This carrying Place is one of the greatest Bars on this long Communication—gives the Indians the principal Means of interrupting our Trade, that suffers here by several other Inconveniencies, one is the Land Carriage which is very high— It would be of the greatest Assistance to the Traders were there a few

Setlers near the carrying Place by whose Means Carriage would be more moderate, and other Refreshments and Advantages could be procured— On these Accounts it appears necessary to have a Garrison and Fort at Niagara— The present one is large, but as it cuts across a Point of Land, does not demand so great a Number to defend it—during Winter is the most dangerous, yet an officer who is attentive, and who can give a few Presents, may always know what passes among the Nations round him from one or other.

It will be necessary likewise to Garrison the Post of Ontario, in order to protect that Entrance into the Lake from the Province of New York. And to have a few Men at Fort Stanwix, which is on the carrying Place between the Mohock River and Wood Creek the eastern and western Course of the Waters; on this last there are Sluices that save the Water to carry down Battoes in the Summer, & without this Precaution they could not pass in that Season. A small Garrison must be kept at Oswegatchie or at Cataraqui as the Vessels must goe to either of these Places to load the Goods & Provisions that come from Canada, & that are designed for the Garrisons & Trade on the Lakes.

The whole Number of Posts therefore that seem indispensibly necessary, on this grand Avenue to Trade and Intercourse with the Western Indians, may be reduced to six, or at most seven; That at La Baye should it be established, included. The Number of Men need not be great; except Detroit & Niagara, either of the Rest may be garrisoned by 30 or 40 Men, and some will not require half that Number. The Posts proposed are LA BAYE, *DETROIT,* FORT ERIE, *NIAGARA,* ONTARIO, OSWEGATCHIE or CATARACUI & FORT STANWIX. Those seem proper Situations to be occupied for the Purposes mentioned at the beginning of this Memorial. The Accomodations made last Summer and Works carried on at Detroit and Niagara will make the Expence of these Posts very inconsiderable, with Regard to that of Works at them. It may with proper Regulations be otherwise much diminished, and will be found considerably less even next Year— The greatest attending them has been the Article of Provision, and indeed the Quantity that has been condemned and destroyed is prodigious. But there is now good Cover for it at the Posts, & much Attention payed to the Condition it is sent & received from Canada. The Diminution of the Posts and Garrisons, will make it easy for the Vessels to Suply those that are to be kept up, & carry Trade also, before the Weather gets bad on the Lakes, so as they need but run little Risque— These Matters once fixed and proper Attention given to what passes among the Natives, A Vein of Commerce will be opened, and will yield very considerable Advantage. The other Purposes answered, and a Peace established, and continue so long till those Indians may change their Disgust to us into Respect, and we be as much esteemed by them, as the French, who have taken so much successfull Pains to work themselves into their Affection, Love & Regard—

With Respect to the other inland Comunication into this Country which is by the Rivers, & the Forts necessary to be upon them, It may be said, in short, that to make it safe & open, a very considerable number of Men will be required, Or great Attention given to the Politicks, and considerable Presents made to the Indians. As I look upon the whole Troops on the Mississipi Frontier to be Prisoners at large or otherwise, according to the Opinion & Humour of the Indian Nations that surround them.

The Usefulness of Crown Point and the Posts on that Communication never appeared, since the Accession of Canada, worthy the Expence attending them, in Charge of Provisions, Works or any other Kind. QUEBEC is by far the best, surest, & now a sufficient Check on Canada—while that Door of the Country is barred against the Intercourse of the Canadians & old French, the former will not think of making any Disturbance, nor the later find an Opportunity or think it worth their while to promote such— But the Works of Quebec merit more Regard than has been hitherto given to them, without it, they will soon be in complete Ruins—

If the Forts on the Mississipi are to be garrisoned I cannot help reflecting on the unnatural Choice of the Way of communicating with, and sending Troops to them— They enter by PENSACOLA or MOBILE, unhealthy Places at that Season, at which they take Provisions sent from here— Then they strugle against the Stream of the Mississipi for 12 or 1300 Miles, and as it is only to be ascended when there is a Flood in the River, that by spreading over its Banks diminishes the Strength of the Current, which is prodigious when confin'd within them; therefore the Passage up this River is long, fatiguing, incertain, expensive, and thence becomes dangerous— Whereas were the Troops to be landed from England in any of the Northern Colonies or Provinces, Provisions bought near and sent up the Potowmack along with them to Fort Cumberland, from thence transported, & the Troops marched, along the Passage opened by order of General Braddock across the Alegheny Mountains, to the Monongehela— They then would pass thro' a healthy Country, be plentifully supplyed with all Kinds of Necessaries, and goe down Stream to within 100 Miles of their Quarters, by the finest River, that runs thro' the finest of Countries, in large Craft, without any Risque, (provided any Measures are kept or any Attention pay'd to the only two Nations of the Delawares & Shawnese) and be able to perform their Route in two Months from their Landing, whereas the other cannot be well done in less than Six, & perhaps take two Floods, which seldom happen above once a Year—

Before I finish the last Subject I must observe the extraordinary Infatuation that has attended likewise the Choice we have made of our Route, in all our Operations this Way, subsequent to the first Year. We then took the natural Advantages of the Country, navigated the Potowmack, with large Vessels to Alexandria, & with smal ones most Part of the Rest of the River to Fort Cumberland. By these Advantages we brought a Train of Artillery with its Ammunition, & Provisions for five Months for 3000 Men, to that Post by the 7th of May. From thence we viewed, discovered, & opened a Passage thro' the Mountains in a very short Time after, and had the Pensylvania Carriages arrived soon enough instead of being with a sufficient Body of Troops Artillery &c within 7 Miles of Fort du Quesne the 9th of July; we certainly should the 9th of June, before the Canada & Indian Reinforcements got there, & by that Means have probably prevented a War— In the Year '58 altho in the Ordnance Distribution for the Siege of Louisbourg, I was with Lieut. Clerk countermanded from that Distribution by the Commander in Chief, and both sent on different Services. My Orders were to attend Brigadier Forbes who commanded a Body destined to act against the Enemy on the Ohio. I waited on the Brigadier at Philadelphia, who told me his Intention was to march to Rays Town, from whence I was ordered to view the Country, and see if a Route could not be made practicable directly to the Ohio, as he had Objections to the crossing so many Rivers on Braddocks Road— I expressed my Opinion, from the former View I had taken, of the Difficulty of the Country for that Purpose, and assured Him the Rivers never were above a few Hours unfordable, so high up, during the Summer Season. However I marched with Colonel Bouquet to Rays Town, but his Determination being also to penetrate the Mountains directly, and no where to fall into the former made Road, I could not prevail on that Officer to order me or allow me to view or give my Opinion of the Country, thro' which he intended to cut his Road, untill a considerable Progress was made in the Work— As soon as I had an Opportunity of observing the Difficulty of this, and great Difference there was in the Nature of the Mountains & Country, compared with that over which the old Road was carried, I thought myself obliged to remonstrate in the strongest Terms, to the Brigadier then ill & behind in Pensylvania these Difficulties, and this Difference—earnestly beging the Virginia Troops might not be ordered from Fort Cumberland; but that we might be sent there to join them, and pursue our March along the old Road— That much Labour Time and Expence would be thereby saved— The Troops be able to arrive on the Ohio, two Months sooner, join the Enemy, and make a decissive & glorious Affair— Norwithstanding of this just Report, I had no Answer, we proceeded, and by the immensest Labour & as great Expence we got, by the 11th of Novr. 15 Days Provision, but Not above half the Artillery and Ammunition we had with Mr. Braddock, to Loyal Hanning, just to the westward of the Mountains & still 50 Miles distant from the Ohio. We were only able to arrive at Fort du Quesne to look at it leisurely deserted, and in Flames, the 24th of the same Month, and very soon after obliged to march back or Starve— I beg'd leave of the Brigad^r to view the Monongehela River as high as above Redstone Creek, and as we should pass over Part of the old Road, should be glad to have Major Shippen, one of the best Officers of the Pennsylvania Troops, who could have no Partiality in Favour of that Road, along with me; The General was pleased to order this: When we were on the highest Part of the Laurel Mountain, I askt that Officer (who was very intelligent & is now Secretary to the Province of Pensylv^a) whether he thought we really were so—he would hardly believe it, nor the same concerning the Allegheny, 'till the Distance we travelled to the Eastward convinc'd him. From that Time the Politicks of some, and the lateness of the Arrival of other Officers, who have had the Command of Troops in that Part of the Country, have caused the same Route to be taken, to the great Charge and Disappointment of the Kings Service. The only Excuse for this Digression is the Reflexion naturally arising, & strongly pointing out the Loss the Nation will always sustain when it has not some great Cheif, of a military Genius, in the Command of Its Army, who would impartially attend to the Progress of its Arms and to Representations concerning them, and not suffer the Vain Inventions of particular Commanders to begin prevail or go on to the great Prejudice of the Nation, and which these last will be bent to preserve and continue, in order to screen their Blunders and support their foolish Proceedings.

HARRY GORDON.

[*Endorsed*] A Memorial concerning the back Forts in N America Dec:17. 1765.

APPENDIX I

[The documents calendared below are of insufficient importance to justify printing in full. They have been selected either because they are unique, or because they furnish information on some particular point. From the correspondence between Cumberland and officials in London, only those parts which relate to American affairs—in some cases no more than a sentence or two—have been abstracted.]

July 2, 1751. London. William Bradley to Cumberland (A.L.S.). He has been long resident in America. He offers to communicate a plan to give Cumberland "such a Power over all the Disaffected in those Parts as will secure all their Interest to His Majesty" forever.

April 14, 1755. Boston. Charles Brome to the Board of Ordnance (L.S.). He has inspected artillery and stores purchased for the Chignecto expedition. Expects to sail in ten days. The artillery officers are badly provided for; he bought a tent at an extravagant price.

April 22, 1755. Instructions for the Lords Justices, from His Majesty (Copy). The sections relating to North America authorize the Lords Justices to send orders to the fleet, to Braddock, and to the governors of American colonies.

June 19, 1755. Whitehall. Sir Thomas Robinson to Braddock (Copy). He awaits news of Braddock's meeting at Alexandria. Encloses copy of a letter to governors directing them to apply only to Braddock for monies required for military operations.

July 16, 1755. Philadelphia. Extract of a letter from Thomas Pownall to his brother. Colonel Johnson says that his conference with the Indians ended Saturday, that they unanimously declare they will support the English, that the confederacy is better disposed than for forty years past, and that he thinks more will join him than provided for by the several legislatures.

July 30, 1755. Whitehall. Sir Thomas Robinson to Braddock (Copy). Though no general fund is yet raised in the colonies, the Lords Justices order Braddock to meet Governor Lawrence's demands, if reasonable and necessary, either from the general fund or by drawing bills. Acknowledges letters of April 19 and June 2. His Majesty approves Braddock's conduct.

Aug. 13, 1755. Whitehall. Sir Thomas Robinson to Lt. Governor Charles Lawrence (Copy). The Lords Justices have ordered £10,000 in specie sent to Lawrence for repairing forts taken from the French. He is to do nothing more to Beauséjour than the construction of a fossé and a covered way, and to transmit frequent accounts of the expenses and progress, both to Robinson and to Braddock. Bedding for the Nova Scotia regiments has been ordered in accordance with Lawrence's representations to the Board of Trade.

Aug. 13, 1755. Whitehall. Sir Thomas Robinson to Braddock (Copy). £10,000 has been sent Lawrence to repair Fort Beauséjour and other captured French forts.

Aug. 23, 1755. London. Admiral Augustus Keppel to Lord Albemarle (A.L.S.). He has just arrived after a twenty-seven days' passage from Virginia. Braddock is killed, his army routed.

Sept. 6, 1755. State of Small Arms in Great Britain for Land Service. 52,707 muskets; 8,528 carbines; 7,878 pairs of pistols; 445 wall pieces.

1755. Extract and Observations upon the Act of Settlement and Naturalization with Regard to the American Colonies. Though 12 & 13 William III, c. 2, and 1 Geo. I, c. 4, incapacitate naturalized foreigners from accepting military commissions in America, 13 Geo. II, c. 7, prohibits them only from enjoying such places in Great Britain and Ireland. An act to naturalize a certain number of protestants to enable them to accept commissions in America only will put them on the same footing as foreigners who, having resided seven years in the colonies, can accept posts.

Feb. 8, 1756. London. Colonel James Prevost to Cumberland (A.L.S.) [in French]. He acknowledges receipt of the bill to naturalize a certain number of foreign protestants, pledges faithful service from his colleagues, and hopes soon to deserve a rank without the limitations imposed by the bill.

[Feb., 1756]. Oath to be Administered to All Such Persons as Enter into the King's Service in the Pay of the Government of Pennsylvania. To serve King George within the province of Pennsylvania and neighboring provinces, and to obey the orders of the Governor and the officers set over him by the King's authority. [There is appended a form of attestation by a Justice of the Peace that the recruit has heard read the 2d and 6th sections of the Articles of War.]

[March, 1756]. Sketch of Regulations and Measures Proposed by . . . with Regard to 1) Recruits for the Established Regiments; 2) Irregulars; 3) Indians; 4) Vessels on the Lakes; 5) Exportation of Provisions, in North America. [Henry Fox's letter of March 13, 1756, to North American governors follows almost verbatim the proposals herein contained.]

March 23, 1756. Troops in Great Britain fit and ready to take the field. There were 14 cavalry regiments, 4,452 officers and men; 11 infantry regiments, 10,918 officers and men.

July 23, 1756. New York. General Dieskau to Cumberland (A.L.S.) [in French]. Asking permission for his aide-de-camp, Sieur Bernier, to pass into France on Dieskau's personal affairs.

Aug. 30, 1756. Boston. William Shirley to Lt. Col. John Bradstreet (Copy). Aware that he will be blamed for the loss of Oswego, he asks for an account of the works and troops there, the causes of its surrender, and whether the arrival of the 44th regiment and 1,000 batteaumen would have made any difference. He will support Bradstreet at home. [Enclosed in Loudoun to Cumberland, Oct. 3, 1756.]

Sept. 7, 1756. Boston. William Shirley to Colonel John Bradstreet (Copy). He asks for information about the failure of the 44th regiment to march to Oswego in July. He will support Bradstreet in England, "particularly with Regard to the Indian Affairs." [Enclosed in Loudoun to Cumberland, Oct. 3, 1756.]

Sept. 9, 1756. Extract of a letter from Benjamin Franklin to Thomas Pownell (Copy). In the Act of Assembly passed yesterday was a paragraph appropriating £10,000 towards a general fund, subject to Loudoun's orders.

Nov. 23, 1756. St. James's Place. Governor William Shirley to Cumberland (A.L.S.). Enclosing a representation of the state of the 50th and 51st regiments, from the time they were raised to the surrender at Oswego, which he hopes will clear them and him of any misrepresentations.

Jan. 26, 1757. Minute: Granville, Devonshire, Holdernesse, Halifax, Temple, Legge, and Pitt. Six Irish battalions, augmented to 1,000 each, to be ready for embarkation by February 20. Orders to be sent Loudoun and American governors to raise same numbers of troops as last year. Instructions to be sent Loudoun for the campaign. Orders to be sent Loudoun to dispatch one battalion to the Capes of Virginia for the defense of the Southern colonies.

April 22, 1757. War Office. Barrington to Cumberland (A.L.S.). It is reported that Colonel Webb is dead. Vacancies in regiments will be filled as they occur from among the half-pay officers of the 50th and 51st.

April 26, 1757. Hanover. Cumberland to Barrington (A.L.). "I flater myself that Things carry a tolerable good appearance in North America." He has no further suggestions to make.

April 26, 1757. Hanover. Cumberland to Robert Napier (A.L.). Asking him to see Barrington, explain the state of the foreign officers of the Royal American regiment, and send the information to Loudoun.

April 26, 1757. Hanover. Cumberland to Barrington (A.L.). Send Loudoun a fresh list of the new commissions in the 22d regiment, and with Napier explain the state of the foreign officers of the Royal American Regiment, in order to send it to Loudoun.

April 28, 1757. Arlington Street. Minute: Granville, Devonshire, Bedford, Winchelsea, Holdernesse. On advice that four French ships have passed Gibraltar and are headed for North America, to reinforce Holbourne's squadron with three ships of the line.

May 2, 1757. Hanover. Cumberland to Barrington (A.L.). He approves Barrington's scheme of filling vacancies from the officers of the Oswego garrison.

May 4, 1757. Newark, in Corke Harbour. Vice-Admiral Francis Holburne to William Pitt (Copy). He has received orders from the Admiralty to take three more ships of the line under his command. All baggage was loaded yesterday and one regiment embarked; today three more regiments; tomorrow all the rest, so that, provided General Hopson is ready, he should sail the 6th.

May 12, 1757. War Office. Barrington to Holdernesse (Copy). With reference to Loudoun's proposal, Cumberland is of opinion that as Loudoun is empowered to grant warrants on the deputy paymaster general in America for recruiting, such money to be issued out of the subsistence of the corps remaining in the deputy paymaster general's hands, no further powers are in any respect necessary.

June 5, 1757. New York. Colonel James Prevost to Robert Napier (L.S.). Introducing Captain Bonneville, formerly aide-de-camp to Marshal Saxe and a captain engineer under the king of Prussia, to whose service he is returning. As he is "of no use here," Prevost begs either to be permitted to resign or to be employed elsewhere than under Loudoun.

July 11, 1757. Portsmouth in Piscataqua. Extract of a letter from Robert Traill to John Perks, merchant in Bristol. News of the safe arrival at Halifax of the fleet from England. Loudoun arrived safely some days before them. [*Endorsed.* No 1. Lord Holdernesse B. August 9:1757.]

July 15, 1757. London. Sir Everard Fawkener to Cumberland (L.S.). News from America that Loudoun embarked for Halifax, with 13,000 men and a wretched convoy. A French fleet is off Cape Breton, "about which I doubt if We are so well informed as might be wished." The Italian and Turkey fleets, under convoy of a 60- and a 20-gun ship, are safely arrived, worth £1,200,000. The four French ships which sailed from Toulon should have waited to intercept them. It is the opinion that Boscawen has gone to reinforce Holburne.

July 22, 1757. Affrede. No. 2. Cumberland to Barrington (A.L.). "I shall say nothing upon the Point relating to the Draught to be sent to *N: America,* as it is a Point resolved upon, & which H:M: has approved of."

Aug. 7, 1757. Halifax. Loudoun to Cumberland (L.S.). He gave leave to Lord Charles Hay to return to England, then withdrew it on the ground that only the king could give such leave. Hay refused to comply, is under arrest. "It was impossible to keep any Discipline in the Army, if I had overlooked this." [Correspondence dealing with the arrest is enclosed.]

Aug. 6, 1757. Drakenburg. Cumberland to Holdernesse (A.L.). Acknowledging letters of July 26 and 29. Anxiety for Loudoun seems ungrounded, as he seems to have taken precautions against Beaufremont's intercepting him.

Aug. 8, 1757. War Office. Barrington to Cumberland (A.L.S.). "The Draughts for America are not yet made; and I shall keep them back as long as I am able."

Aug. 16, 1757. Verden. Cumberland to Barrington (A.L.). "I hope, but can hardly flater myself, that the Draughts for *America* will be no longer thought necessary. But I am so used to see Popularity take Place in lieu of *Essentials,* that I suppose they will be made at last."

Sept. 2, 1757. Cavendish Square. Barrington to Cumberland (A.L.S.). The King has ordered that Hay return to England. "By all accounts his head is turn'd, and it is now said this is not the first time." Lieutenant Colonel Haldane, probably going to Jamaica as governor, desires a colonel's brevet, or at least to be continued on the list as a lieutenant colonel.

Sept. 15, 1757. Halifax. Lord Charles Hay to Cumberland (A.L.S.). He cannot understand why he is in arrest, and encloses copies of correspondence. He can easily demonstrate his innocence and his concern for the honor, success, and reputation of His Majesties' forces in this part of the world, "which is sunk to that degree, as no age can parallel."

March 1, 15, 16, 1758. New York. Colonel James Prevost to General James Abercromby (Copy). Four letters dealing with the promotion of colonels younger than he to be brigadier-generals; his resignation, which Abercromby did not accept; his willingness to serve according to his rank under any senior colonel; and [written to Captain James Abercrombie, the general's aide-de-camp] an intimation that Abercromby's refusal to let him return will be interpreted at home as done in Loudoun's interests.

March 17, 1758. New York. Colonel James Prevost to Cumberland (A.L.S.) [in French]. Asking that if the good of the service demands his withdrawal, he receive some mark of favor and Cumberland's continued support.

[March, 1758] Mémoire: Les raisons qui ont fait que Le Colonel Prevost s'est addressé a S.A.R. pour etre employé ailleurs ou pour avoir la liberté de se retirer sont de deux espèces, les unes personelles dont il peut fournir des preuves par ecrit & par témoins, les autres qui luy étoient communes avec le reste de l'Armée pour lesquelles il n'a d'autres preuves que les Ordres publics & le Succes des Armes du Roy en Amerique. [Enclosed in Prevost to Cumberland, March 17, 1758.]

June 4, 1758. On board *Ludlow Castle,* Sandy Hook. Captain James Cuningham to Lord ? (Copy). He had been sent by Abercromby to report on the proceedings at Halifax. Boscawen arrived there May 9, sailed May 28 with 170 sail. Sir Charles Hardy saw seven ships in Louisbourg harbor, imagines three are men-of-war. Since the store-ship with artillery and arms for the provincials is not yet arrived, Abercromby will be delayed.

July 6, 1758. New York. Colonel James Prevost to Cumberland (L.S.) [in French]. Information which has reached him on the progress of the campaigns in Pennsylvania, New York, and Louisbourg. Gratitude for his promotion to be brigadier. He is awaiting Abercromby's commands.

July 9, 1758. New York. Colonel James Prevost to Cumberland (Copy) [in French]. Additional information on the campaigns.

July 12, 1758. New York. Colonel James Prevost to Cumberland (A.L.S.) [in French]. News of Abercromby's defeat, without detail, from Stanwix at Albany and Captain Delancey. He is leaving at once for the army, in hopes that Abercromby will employ him according to his rank, even though his new commission has not arrived.

July 19, 1758. Petition to the King of Major Charles Craven (Copy). He was appointed major to the late 51st regiment because of his capture of Dr. Cameron, an attainted rebel in Scotland. He asks for an enquiry into his case, the payment of the £300 due him, and rank as lieutenant colonel which Loudoun denied him.

July 20, 1758. London. Major Charles Craven to Cumberland (A.L.S.). He has petitioned the King again, lest the enquiry into his case be indefinitely postponed, Webb having gone abroad and Loudoun about to leave for Scotland. He would not have had to wait so long, were Cumberland still at the head of the army.

Oct. 24, 1758. Fort Edward. Colonel James Prevost to Cumberland (Copy) [in French]. Abercromby prevented him from writing by the last packet. He has nothing to add to his previous letters on the causes of the army's disgrace. Few officers supported him in his suggestions for saving the campaign, which are justified by the confusion now reigning in the conduct of affairs. He encloses a plan of Fort Edward, a fort so badly placed that a Vauban could not make it tenable against four mortars.

Dec. 17, 1758. New York. Colonel James Prevost to Cumberland (A.L.S.) [in French]. He relates the arrangements he made with Amherst before he knew he was recalled to England. In private conversation, he told Amherst that while the law did not exclude him from the supreme command, he had never been so foolish as to aspire to it; that if he received the assurance that his foreign status would not prevent his advance in rank, and the least hint that his service as a brigadier according to his seniority as colonel would be favorably regarded, he was ready to serve. Amherst replied that he had been recalled. He expects to leave next month.

March 2, 1761. George Street, Hanover Square. James Prevost to John Calcraft

(Copy). Asking for the method taken in April, 1756, to repay the King the £2,500 Prevost received for engaging officers for the Royal American Regiment; the means by which he was paid the balance of £1,773 due him on that account; copies of Loudoun's order of 1756 to pay off-reckonings in the regiment to the colonels-commandant, and of Loudoun's subsequent order that off-reckonings should not be paid to him.

July 2, 1763. W[indsor] G[reat] L[odge]. Cumberland's answer to the contents of a letter from Charles Gould, Judge Advocate to Mr. Mason, dated June 30, 1763(A.L.). With reference to the off-reckonings of the Royal American Regiment, he remembers that the King preferred the colonels-commandant to have the same emoluments as colonels of other regiments; that he left it to Loudoun to choose between having the fourteenth day's pay for himself, or the clothing and other emoluments, in which latter case Loudoun would allow the colonels-commandant an annual sum equivalent to their usual profits. Loudoun chose the former.

APPENDIX II

A Proportion
of Brass Ordnance, Howitzers and Stores for the intended Expedition to North America, By Order of the Board dated the 12th October 1754
(D.S.)

				No
Light Brass Ordnance mounted on Traveling Carriages compleat with Limbers, Ammunit^n Boxes and Elevating Screws	12 Pounders ....4.			
	6 Po^{rs} ....6.			
Brass Howitzers with Carriages and Limbers compleat	8 Inch ....4.			
Forge Cart compleat with Anvil &ca ....1.				
Sling Cart compleat ....1.				
Ammunition Carts ....8.				
Tumbrils ....2.				
Money Tumbril ....1.				
Cover'd Waggons compleat ....16.				
Woulding Sticks for D^o ....48.				
Tryangle Gyn compleat ....1.				

Spare Carriages with Limbers	12 Pounder ....1.		
	6 Po^r ....1.		

Spare Wheels, Shod for	12 Po^r	Fore ....1.	
		Hind ....1.	
	6 Po^r	Hind ....1.	
	Howitzer	Fore ....1.	
		Hind ....1.	
	Waggon	Fore ....1.	
		Hind ....1.	
	Ammunition Cart ....1.		

Spare Axletrees bound for	12 Po^r	Fore ....1.	
		Hind ....1.	
	6 Po^r	Hind ....1.	
	Howitzer	Hind ....1.	
	Waggon	Fore ....1.	
		Hind ....1.	
	Ammunition Cart ....1.		

Drag Ropes with Pins	12 Pounders ....10.	
	6 Pound^{rs} ....14.	
	Howitzers ....8.	
Draught Chains for Howitzers ....Pairs....4.		

479

N⁰

Ladles with Staves ....
- 12 Pounders ....4.
- 6 Po^{rs} ....6.

Spunges with Rammers ....
- 12 Pounders ....4.
- 6 Po^{rs} ....6.
- Howitzers ....4.

Spunge Bags Painted ....
- 12 Pounders ....4.
- 6 Po^{rs} ....6.
- Howitzers ....4.

Wadhooks with Rammers ....
- 12 Pounders ....4.
- 6 Po^{rs} ....6.

Field Tampeons with Collars ....
- 12 Pounders ....4.
- 6 Po^{rs} ....6.
- Howitzers ....4.

Tarpaulins ....
- 12 Po^{rs}.
  - For the Guns ....4.
  - Spare ....1.
- 6 Po^{rs}.
  - For the Guns ....6.
  - Spare ....1.
- For the Money Tumb^l: ....1.
- Large Spare ....6.

Spare Spunge & Rammer Heads ....
- 12 Pounders .... each { 4.
- 6 Po^{rs} .... { 6.

Handspikes ....
- 12 Po^{rs}.
  - For the Guns ....8.
  - Spare ....2.
- 6 Po^{rs}.
  - For the Guns ....12.
  - Spare ....2.
- For the Howitzers ....8.
- Spare ....20.

Aprons of Lead .... for ....
- 12 Pounders ....4.
- 6 Po^{rs} ....6.
- Howitzers ....4.

Round Shot with Wooden bottoms ....
- 12 Pounders ....100.
- 6 Po^{rs} ....450.

Flannel Cartridges ....
- 12 Pounders ....1700.
- 6 Po^{rs} ....2850.
- Howitzers ....100.

Tin Cases filled with Iron Shot and fix'd with Wooden bottoms ....
- 12 Pounders ....400.
- 6 Po^{rs} ....1200.

Grape Shot compleat with wooden Tampeons and Pins .... for ....
- Howitzers ....100.

Empty Shells for Howitzers ....7¾ Inch ....400.

Spare Flannel Cartridges ....
- 12 Pounders ....170.
- 6 Po^{rs} ....285.
- Howitzers ....10.

No

Spare Round Shot	12 Pounders	1200.
	6 Pors	1200.
Grates compleat for heating Shot		2.
Tin Tubes	12 Pounders	2040.
	6 Pors	3408.
	Howitzers	220.
Boxes for Tin Tubes wth Straps	12 Pounders	8.
	6 Pors	12.
	Howitzers	4.
Iron Crows		6.
Corn'd Powder, Copper hoop'd for the Guns, Howitzers & Small Arms	Whole Barrels	560.
Hand Screws	Large	1.
	Small	1.
Budge Barrels Copper hoop'd		7.
Copper Powder Measures	to contain 3 lb.	2.
	Do ...... 2 lb.	2.
	Do .....1½ lb.	2.
	Do ..... 1¼ lb.	2.
	Do ...... 1 lb.	2.
Funnels of Plate		4.
Match	Cwt	5.
Linstocks with Cocks		7.
Tann'd Hides		24.
Wadmill Tilts		8.
Powder Horns		14.
Priming Irons		42.
Sheep Skins		24.
Spunge Tacks		6000.
Hammers	Claw	2.
	Small	2.
Lanthorns	Muscovy	6.
	Tin	12.
	Dark	6.
Hair Cloths		8.
Candles Tallow	lb.	40.
Links	Dozens	5.
Leather Buckets		7.
Mens Harness ...... 12 to a Sett	Setts	30.
Horse Harness	Thill wth Cart Sadles	45.
	Trace	87.
	Bitt Halters	132.
	Wantys	45.
Cart Whips		45.
Swingletrees		8.
Spare Ladle Staves		14.

N°

			N°
Iron	Flat Bar	Cw^t	5.
	Square D°	Cw^t	5.
	Rod D°	Cw^t	3.
Steel		Cw^t	2.
Couples for Chain Traces			100.
Spare Streak Nails			200.

	Clouts	Body	216.
		Linch	216.
Spare	Linch Pins		20.
	Washers		20.
	Tug Pins		20.

Forelockkings ....48.
Forelock Keys ....Pairs ....100.
Spring Keys ....Pairs ....12.
Steel Spikes for Nailing Guns ....100.
Punches or Drifts & Hammers for the Vents ....each ....14.
Spare Punches ....10.
Camp Colours ....12.
Sea Coals ....Chaldrons .....5.
Copper Canhooks ....Pairs ....2.
Splinter Padlocks ....48.
Hambro' Line ....lb. ....172.
Packthread ....lb. .....30.
Twine ....lb. .....10.
Tarr'd Marline ....Skains ...20.
Grease, in Iron hoop'd Firkins ....Firkins ...12.
Hemp Rubbish ....Cw^t ....2.
Marline Spikes ....2.
Ballast Baskets ....20.
Melting Ladles ....2.

Intrenching Tools	Pickaxes helved	300.
	Spare helves for d°	50.
	Spades	400.
	Shovels	200.
	Felling Axes	100.
	Hand hatchets	300.
	Hand Bills	250.
	Cross cut Saws	6.

Sand Bags	Bushel	2000.
	Half Bushel	0000.

Wheelbarrows ....200.
Handbarrows ....50.
Park pickets ....40.
Wood Mauls ....4.
Pane Mauls ....4.
Whole Deals ....12 Feet ......50.
Mantlets ....25.

                                                                N°

Nails	40 Penny	5000.	
	30	5000.	
	20	10000.	
	10	15000.	
	6	10000.	
	4	4000.	
	Clout	7000.	
	Dog	2000.	
	Copper	200.	

Spikes .... 6 Inch ...... 600.
Gimblets of Sorts .... Dozens. .... 8.

Tarr'd Rope	Picket line 2½ Inch		1.
	2 Inch	Coils..	1.
	1 Inch		1.

White Rope	5 Inch		1.
	4		1.
	3	Coils..	1.
	2		1.
	1		1.

Tallow .... Cwt .... ½.
Wall Pieces .... 10.
Carbines Rifled Barrel'd .... 12.
Molds for D° .... 12.
Lead .... Cwt .... ½.

FOR SMALL ARMS

Spare Ramrods	Musquet	Steel	50.
		Wood	400.
	Carbine	60.	

Flints .... for	Musquet	142,000.
	Carbine	1,800.
	Wallpiece	200.

                                                        Tons C Q^rs

Lead Shot .... for	Musquet	44 :0: 0
	Carbine	0 :8: 0
	Wallpiece	0 :1: 2

Fine Paper .... Rheams ..... 187.

LABORATORY STORES

Hand Granadoes Fix'd .... 1000.
Spare Fuzes for D° .... 50.
Port Fires, Small long .... Dozens. ...... 30.
Composition for Port Fires .... lb. .... 100.
Empty Cases for D° .... 500.
Mould for D° .... 1.
Drifts, Formers, Mallets and Ladles for d° .... Set .... 1.

No

Worsted	lb.	6.
Green Soap	Firkin	1.
Needles	Dozens	6.
Knives		6.
Scissars	Pairs	4.
Mealed Powder	lb.	200.
White Wine Vinegar	Gallons	2.
Spirits of Wine	Gallons	2.
Quick Match for Tin Tubes	lb.	12.
Tin Plates	Sheets	50.

Paper
- Cartridges, Rheams .... 1.
- Blue . . . Quires .... 4.
- Brown . . . Rheams .... 6.

Cartouches of Leather
- 12 Pounders .... 8.
- 6 Pors .... 12.
- Howitzers .... 4.

Barras .... Fine	Yards	10.
Kitt	lb.	28.
Iron Kitt Kettle and Trevit	each	1.
Flax	lb.	8.
Rasps		10.
Pinchers for Drawing Fuzes	Pair	1.
Machine for Do ... Small		1.
Brass Scales .... Small	Pair	1.
Brass Weights	8 lb. Pile	1.
Fix'd Fuzes for Howitzers	7¾ Inch	440.
Port-fire Sticks		16.
Copper Salting Boxes		6.
Copper Funnels for Filling Shells		2.

Seives with Tops & Bottoms
- Lawn .... 1.
- Hair .... 2.

Drawing Knives for Paring Fuzes		2.
Forms and Staples for Do		2.
Tennant Saw for Fuzes		1.
Three Square Files		3.
Twine	lb.	2.
Cat Gut	Knots	40.
Mallets for	7¾ Inch Fuzes	4.
Setters for	7¾ Inch Fuzes	8.
Rockets for Signals	Dozens	6.
Laboratory Chests		4.

FOR SERVICE OF THE ENGINEERS

Theodolite compleat with Tellescope Sights		1.
Plain Tables compleat with Indexes		2.

Surveying Chains .... of
- 100 Feet .... 2.
- 50 Feet .... 1.

Cases of Pocket Instruments compleat .... 4.

No

Parrallel Rules from 12 to 18 Inches ....4.
Drawing Pens ....6.
Pocket Compasses with a Spare Needle to each ....4.
Camp Colours White without Cyphers & Staves ....12.
Officers Tents compleat with Poles, Pins & Mallets ....5.
Armour ....⎧ Backs ....3.
............................⎨ Breasts ....3.
............................⎩ Head pieces ....3.
Field Beds compleat with Bedding ....2.

FOR THE ARTILLERY & CIVIL OFFICERS AND ARTIFICERS

Brass Quadrant ....1.
Brass Callipers ....Pair ....1.
Small Case of Instruments ....1.
Gauges .... for⎰ Shot .... Set ....1.
⎱ Musqᵗ Shot .... Set ....1.
Camp Kettles with Frying Pan Covers ....40.
Canteens for holding Water ....100.

Tents Compleat ....⎧ Officers ....8.
⎪ Horsemen ....8.
⎪ Foot ....20.
⎨ Army ⎰ Officer ......1.
⎪ Guard ⎱ Horsemens ..4.
⎪ Bell ....1.
⎩ Laboratory ....1.
Field Bed compleat with Bedding ....1.

Hammock Bedding compleat ....⎧ For Cradles ⎫ ....39.
⎨ and Cabbins ⎬
⎩ Single ....65.
Hammocks Single ....65.

Setts of Tools & Materials ....⎧ Carpenters ....3.
⎪ Wheelers ....2.
⎪ Smiths ....3.
⎨ Cooper ....1.
⎪ Collar Maker ....1.
⎩ Armourers ....2.

FOR THE SURGEON

Chest of Medicines ....1.
Chest of Instruments ....1.

FOR THE PAY MASTER

Iron Chest ....1.
Scales and Weights to Weigh 1 lb. ....Set ....1.
Dᵒ to Weigh Single Pieces of Money ....Set ....1.

Nº

Musquets of the Kings Pattern without Nosebands with Steel Rammers .... 1400.

Cartouch Boxes with Straps .... 12 Holes ... 1400.

Swords with Scabbards and Brass hilts for ....
- Serjeants 20
- Grenadiers 82
- Private Men 738
- Drummers 20
860.

Halberts .... 60.

Drums .... 20.

Tents compleat for ....
- Officers .... 40.
- Foot .... 400.

Musquets with Bayonets.
- With Single bridle Locks Nosebands & Woodrammers — 1000.
- Dutch with Nosebands and Woodrammers — 1000.

Cartouch Boxes with Straps .... 12 Holes ... 2000.

Swords wᵗʰ Scabbards

Brass hilts
- Serjeants 80
- Grenadiers 200
- Drummers 40

Iron hilts
- Private Men 1800

2120.

Halberts .... 80.

Drums .... 40.

Tents Compleat for ....
- Officers .... 56.
- Foot .... 570.

ADDITIONAL PROPORTION TO BE SENT BY HIS MAJESTY'S SHIP THE CENTURION, PER ORDER OF THE BOARD NOVEMBER THE 16ᵗʰ 1754

Brass Coehorn Mortars mounted on their Beds with Lashing Ropes compleat — 4⅔ Inches .... 15.

Spare Beds for Dº .... 2.

Muzzle Caps .... 18.

Aprons of Lead .... 18.

Spunges .... 20.

Spunge Bags Painted .... 20.

Tarr'd Marline .... Skains .... 4.

Linstocks with Cocks .... 5.

Hambro' Line .... lb. .... 20.

Powder horns .... 8.

Priming Irons .... 16.

Sheep Skins .... 6.

Spunge Tacks .... 200.

No

Small hammers . . . . .2.
Corn Powder Copper hoop'd . . . . .Whole Barrels 12.
Budge Barrels Copper hoop'd . . . . .2.
Tann'd Hides . . . . .2.
Match . . . . .Cwᵗ . . . . .½.
Hair Cloth . . . . .1.
Hand Barrows . . . . .20.
Leather Buckets . . . . .4.

LABORATORY STORES

Shells Empty . . . . .4⅖ Inches . .1500.
Fix'd Fuzes for Dᵒ . . . . .1650.
Portfires . . . . .Dozens . . . . . . .6.
Meal'd Powder . . . . .lb. . . . . .50.
Quick Match . . . . .lb. . . . . .4.
Flax . . . . .lb. . . . . .6.
Tow . . . . .lb. . . . . .2.
White Wine Vinegar . . . . .Gallon . . . . . . .1.
Canvas fine . . . . .Yards . . . . . . .10.
Cotton Wick . . . . .lb. . . . . .1.
Copper powder Measures from 40 Oz to ¼ Oz . . . . .Setts . . . . . . .2.
Rasps fine . . . . {Flat . . . . .12.
                                                                    {Half round . . . . .6.
Files three Square . . . . .6.
Pincers . . . . .Pairs Pincers . . . .4.
Hand Saws . . . . .Small . . . . .3.
Small Scales . . . . .Pair . . . . .1.
Brass Weights 2lb pile to ¼ of an Oz . . . . .Set . . . . .1.
Copper Salting Boxes . . . . .3.
Small Copper Funnels for shells . . . . .4.
Setters of Wood for Coehorns . . . . .8.
Mallets for Dᵒ . . . . .6.
Quadrants . . . . .3.
Twine . . . . .lb. . . . . .1.
Shaving Knives for Fuzes . . . . .2.
Whetstones . . . . .6.
Laboratory Chest with Padlock and Key . . . . .1.
Leather Haversacks . . . . .3.
Common Corks for Stopping the
Fuze holes of the Coehorn Shells } . . . . .1550.
Scrapers . . . . for{8 Inch Shells . . . . .3.
                                                              {Coehorns . . . . .6.
Copper hoop'd Barrels for packing the Fuzes . . . . .3.
Boxes for Packing the Shells . . . . .107.

CHARLES FREDERICK Survʳ Genˡ

INDEX

Abercrombie, James, captain in 42d regiment, 476

Abercromby, James, ensign in 44th regiment, 332

Abercromby, James, major general, letters to, from Prevost and Gage, 422; from Prevost, 476; hampered by campaign plans, xix; orders from, at Oswego, 208; Loudoun on, 235; Cumberland on, 253; orders of, on exchange rates, 271; uncle of Watson, 282; brings over Lt. Gullen, 285; recommends Fraser, 285; goes to Halifax, 317, 344; prefers Louisbourg attack, 350; Loudoun consults with, 352, 373-374; at Council of War, 392; mentioned by Hardy, 397; poor health of, 402; difficulties of, in 1758, 429-430; uncertainty of, 424-425, 428; sends Cunningham to Halifax, 477

Acadians, in 1749, 8; need of removing, 25, 29, 155, 222; removal of, 148; with Abenakis, 182-183; return of, 305-306

Accoutrements, 83, 320

Acts of Parliament, proposed for Massachusetts, 75; on indented servants, 185; opposition to, in America, 273

Adjutant general, in South Britain, x; in America, 324

Adjutants, regimental, 286, 357, 377-378

Adlam, John, lieutenant in 40th regiment, adjutant, 331

Administration, British, inefficiency of, 259, 298, 351

Admiralty, Board of, instructions of, to Keppel, 48; Loudoun on, 373

Afferde, letter from, 385

Agriculture, in Nova Scotia, 28

Albany, letters written from, 128, 223, 230, 239, 263; roads to, 33, 38, 446; general headquarters at, 134, 228-229, 253; center of illegal trade, 141; quartering at, 231, 273; troops at, 264

Albany Conference, Colden on, 20-21; Shirley on, 25

Albemarle, George Keppel, earl of, letter to, from Augustus Keppel, 474

Alexander, William, Shirley's secretary, 202, 229, 243, 268, 289

Alexandria, Virginia, communications of, 32; troops quartered at, 64; meeting of governors at, 81, 137, 473

Alleman, village de, 12, 14

Allen, James, lieutenant in 60th regiment, 283, 286, 293

Alt, Henry, lieutenant in 22d regiment, 362

Americans, character of, Colden on, 19; St. Clair on, 64; Loudoun on, 233, 241; Bouquet on, 329. *See also* New Englanders, Virginia

Amherst, Jeffery, major general, xviii, 416, 417, 432, 437, 477

Ammunition, kinds of, 480-481. *See* Artillery Stores

Anguilla, colonial trade to, 376

Annapolis River, 25

Annapolis Royal, 8, 28, 293, 394

Anonymous letter on Braddock's campaign, 112

Antigua, troops in, 9

d'Anville, N. de la Rochefoucauld, duke, 310

Appy, John, Loudoun's secretary, 234n

Apthorp, Charles, agent to money contractors, 275

Archbold, George, lieutenant in 60th regiment, 283

Argyll, Archibald Campbell, duke of, 382, 394

Arkansas, French fort at, 12

Armor, 485

Arms, *see* Small arms

Armstrong, J., engineer, in New York, 19

Army, in Great Britain, 380, 474. *See* Regiments, Provincial troops

Army Lists, note on, 281n, 331n

489

(1)

INDEX

illegal colonial, with France, 52, 74, 144, 231, 352, 376; convoy of, 476. *See also* Indian trade, Fur trade

Traill, Robert, letter of, to John Perks, 475

Transportation, on Braddock's expedition, 58-65, 82, 85, 93, 94 (cost of), 110, 120 (cost of); inadequacy of, on Lake George expedition, xvii, 142, 150; in 1756 campaign plans, 135; in winter, 144, 401-402; in New York, 239-240; impressment of, 405; in 1758, 429-430

Transports, for Braddock's forces, 34, 48-49, 50-51, 58, 77; number of men apportioned to, 48n; commissary of, 230; chartering of, 260; on 1711 expedition, 297-298; from colonial ports, 323; distribution of troops on, 378

Treasury Board, on exchange rates in America, 244-248, 256

Trent, H. M. S., 417

Trenton, New Jersey, 33, 363

Trexler, captain of Pennsylvania troops, 167

Trois Rivières, 448

Troops, *see* Regiments, Provincial troops

Tullikens, John, lieutenant colonel of 60th regiment, 333, 349, 421

Turnips, 392

Tuscaroras, 460

Tyrell, Thomas, *see* Pichon, Thomas

Uplinger's House, 167

Upper Marlbro', 64

Van Etten, John, captain in Pennsylvania troops, 167

Van Hulst, Abraham, surgeon's mate in the 60th regiment, 333

Vaudreuil, marquis de, letter to, from Contrecœur, 129; mentioned, 435

Venango, fort at, 32, 432

Verden, letter written from, 395

Vickers (Vicars), John, captain in 50th regiment, report of, on Oswego, xvii, 286-290; mentioned, 294

Vickers, John, lieutenant in 22d regiment, 362

Vinter, Thomas, lieutenant in 60th regiment, 284, 365

Virgin Islands, 169

Virginia, exchange in, 5-6, 42-43; Washington's force in, 25; roads in, 31-33,

61, 93, 470; recruiting in, 34, 62, 65, 78, 88-89, 314, 319, 344; in campaign plans, 39, 144, 177, 255; Keppel to proceed to, 48; St. Clair in, 58-66; produce of, 68; inhabitants of, 84-85, 93; request of, for supplies, 168; transports from, 324; governor of, 377

Volunteers, 270, 274, 281, 284, 357

Von Ingen, Peter and Ja., captain lieutenant and lieutenant in 60th regiment, 446

Vulture, H. M. S., 352

Wabash River, 456

Waggoner, Thomas, captain of Virginia rangers, 88

Wagoners, with Braddock, 96n

Wagons, *see* Transportation

Waldo, Samuel, 304

Walker, Hovenden, expedition of, 297-298

Wall pieces, 300

Wallace, Hans, ensign in 45th regiment, 332

Walpole, Horace, on Cumberland, x

Walsh, Hunt, brigadier general, 450, 451

Warrant men, 290, 351

Warren, Peter, admiral, 305

Washington, George, 28, 82

Watson, Andrew, ensign in 44th regiment, 282

Watts, John, letter of, to Cotterell, 148; notice of, 148n

Wattson, of Berwick, recommends Edmonstone, 363

Wayne, Isaac, captain of Pennsylvania troops, 167

Webb, Daniel, colonel of 48th regiment, major general in America, letter to, from Loudoun, 370; command of, on Mohawk River, 228, 232, 234; Loudoun on, 235; Cumberland on, 253; at Philadelphia, 273; recommends McKane, 282; illness of, 293-294, 317-318, 344, 402; paid as major general, 343; present with Prevost, 356; in command in New York, 344, 346, 350, 370, 399, 400

Weiser, Conrad, 330

Welsh, Hunt, *see* Walsh

Welsh, Peter, surgeon's mate, 365

Wender, Joseph, lieutenant in 50th regiment, 231